THE WILKES CO. HOMESTEAD OF COL. LODOWICK MERIWETHER HILL (1804-1883)
From a Photograph Taken in 1898 While Owned by His Son, Duncan Chatfield Hill (1857-1908)

Col. Lodowick Meriwether Hill
1804-1883
Wilkes County, Georgia

THE HILLS

OF

WILKES COUNTY, GEORGIA

AND

ALLIED FAMILIES

JOHNSON-DALLIS COMPANY
Atlanta, Georgia

ALLIED FAMILIES

Anthony	Lumpkin
Barrow	McGehee
Billups	McIntosh
Calhoun	McKinley
Callaway	McKinnie
Clark	Pope
Colquitt	Quakers
DuBose	Ransom
Exum	Richardson
Grigsby	Shepherd
Harvie	Spalding
Henderson	Walton
Jordan	Webster
Lane	Wellborn
Lewis	Willis
Lipscomb	Wootten

EXPLANATION

The different generations will be indicated as follows:
  1st by Capital letter O.
  2nd by Capital letter P.
  3rd by Capital letters A, B, C, D, E, F, etc.
  4th by Roman numerals I, II, III, IV, V, VI, etc.
  5th by Arabic numerals 1, 2, 3, 4, 5, 6, etc.
  6th by Arabic numerals, followed by letter a.
  7th by Arabic numerals, followed by letter b.
  8th by Arabic numerals, followed by letter c.
  9th by Arabic numerals, followed by letter d.
  10th by Arabic numerals, followed by letter f.
  11th by Arabic numerals, followed by letter g.
  12th by Arabic numerals, followed by letter h.

Letters or numerals, or both, in parentheses immediately following a name, denote the parent, gr. parent, etc.

To get the meaning clearly in mind, turn to p. 130. Here we have 3b.—Janie May Hill[7]. The Arabic numeral followed by "b" indicates 7th generation and the figure 3 the 3rd child of her parent (in parenthesis), 10a.—James DuB. Hill[6] (p. 129), 6th generation and 10th child of his father, 2.—Col. L. M. Hill[5] (p. 120), 5th generation and 2nd child of his father, X.—Wylie Hill[4] (p. 103), 4th generation and 10th child of his father, B.—Abraham Hill[3] (p. 63), 3rd generation and 2nd child of his father, P.—Abraham Hill[2] (p. 16), 2nd generation and only child of his father, O.—Henry Hill[1] (p. 7), 1st generation.

ABBREVIATIONS:
  a., ante; b., born; c. or circa, about; d., died; d. s. p., decessit sine prole—died without issue; d. y., died young; d. in inf., died in infancy; ink., issue unknown; m., married; N. R., no further record; p., after; pro., probably; q. v., quod vide—which see; unm., unmarried.

CHARTS
OF
THE HILLS OF
WILKES COUNTY, GEORGIA
AND
ALLIED FAMILIES

Note:—In the Charts, men are placed on the left and women on the right of the page. Where daughters are in direct line of descent, it is indicated by an asterisk.

CHART No. 1.

HILL.

HENRY HILL[1] of Nansemond Co., Va., b. 1660-'75; d. 1719-'20.
m. c. 1697
MARY ...., d. p. 1720.

ABRAHAM HILL, SR.[2] (c. 1698-1760), of Chowan Co., N. C.
a. Oct. 29, 1729
m.
JUDITH ...., d. p. 1760.

ABRAHAM HILL, JR.[3] (c. 1730-1792), of Chowan and Wake Cos., N. C., and Wilkes Co., Ga.
m. Jany. 7, 1756
CHRISTIAN WALTON, d. 6 July, 1808, dau. of Thomas Walton, Jr. (c. 1713-1759).

WYLIE HILL[1] (1775-1844), b. in Wake Co., N. C.; d. in Wilkes Co., Ga.
m. March 29, 1799
MARTHA (PATSY) POPE, b. April 18, 1782; d. July 15, 1853, dau. of Burwell and Priscilla (Wootten) Pope.

LODOWICK MERIWETHER HILL[5] (1804-1883), of Wilkes Co., Ga.
m. Dec. 16, 1824
(I) NANCY HILL JOHNSON, b. July 11, 1808; d. Oct. 21, 1846, dau. of Col. William and Nancy (Hill) Johnson.
m. July 8, 1847
(II) MARTHA STROTHER WELLBORN (1816-1884), dau. of Abner Wellborn and his wife, Martha Render.

LODOWICK JOHNSON HILL, SR.[6], b. Jany. 16, 1846, and had:
ANNIE LAURA HILL[7], b. Aug. 16, 1875;
m. Sept. 28, 1871
MARY RUTH HENDERSON, b. Jany. 12, 1849; d. May 21, 1918, dau. of Brig. Genl. Robert J. Henderson and Laura Elizabeth Wood, the gr. gr. dau. of Genl. Richard Richardson, Sr., of Va. & S. C.

LODOWICK JOHNSON HILL, JR.[7], b. 12 Dec. 1877.
m. 1896
(I) SARAH JAMES WILLINGHAM, d. in 1897.
m. Nov. 28, 1917
(II) ANNA REBECCA, called REBIE, HARWELL, dau. of W. D. and Anna (Dunlap) Harwell.

CHART No. 2.

POPE.

WILLIAM POPE¹   m.   MARIE ....
c. 1634-c. 1700, and had: c. 1660

HENRY POPE²   m.   SARAH WATTS, dau. of John Watts and
1663-1728, and had: c. 1684   his wife, Alice English, dau. of John English, d. 1678.

JOHN POPE³   m.   MOURNING MCKENNIE, dau. of Col. Barnabie McKennie, Sr.
c. 1700-1745, and had: c. 1722

HENRY POPE⁴   m.   TABITHA .... She m. (II)
c. 1725-1764, and had: c. 1749   Col. Thomas Wootten.

BURWELL POPE⁵   m.   PRISCILLI WOOTTEN, 1756-1806, sister of
1751-1800, and had dau:*   8 Sept., 1772   Col. Thos. Wootten, above.

    m.   *MARTHA ("PATSY") POPE, 1782-1853.
    29 March, 1799

WYLIE HILL⁴   m.   (I) NANCY HILL JOHNSON, 1808-1846.
1775-1844, and had: 16 Dec., 1824

COL. LODOWICK MERIWETHER HILL   m.   MARY RUTH HENDERSON, 1849-1918,
1804-1883, and had: 28 Sept., 1871   dau. of Gen. Robert J. Henderson, of C. S. A.

LODOWICK JOHNSON HILL
b. 1846, and had:

(1) ANNIE LAURIE HILL   m.   (I) SARAH JAMES WILLINGHAM, d. 1897.
(2) LODOWICK JOHNSON HILL, JR.   1896 (I)   (II) ANNA REBECCA ("REBIE") HARWELL.
    1917 (II)

CHART NO. 3.

LEWIS.

(Part 1st, Tentative)

SIR EDWARD LEWIS[1] of Van and Edginton, Wiltshire, and had:
m. ANN............, dau. of Earl of Talbot

ROBERT LEWIS[2] of Brecon, Wales, b. 1579, and had:
m. ....

GEN. ROBERT LEWIS[3] who came to Virginia, 1635, settled in Gloucester Co., and probably,
m. ANN WASHINGTON.

JOHN LEWIS[3] came from Wales to Virginia, c. 1640, and pro. had:
m. ELIZABETH ....

(Part 2nd, Positive)

EDWARD LEWIS, SR.[4(1)] Pat'd Land in 1663 on Totusky Creek, Va., and had:
m. c. 1652
MARY ...., pro. dau. of Thos. Holman, of York Co., Va.

EDWARD LEWIS, JR.[5(2)] and had dau.:*
m.
MARY .... (a dau. Elizabeth, b. 8 March, 1674).

WILLIAM LYNTON (LINTON)[6] 1st Wife, Will 1733, and had dau.:*
m.
*JOHANNA (or JOANNA) LEWIS[6(3)], b. 8 Sept., 1676.

HILLIARE ROUSSEAU[7] 1st Husband, d. 30 June, 1720, and had dau.:*
m.
*ELIZABETH LYNTON[7(4)] (Will 1750; pr. 1751).

BENJAMIN WOOTTEN[8] Will 26 June, 1764, and had dau.:*
m. after 10 Jan. 1736
*ELIZABETH ROUSSEAU[8(5)], b. after 1720.

BURWELL POPE[5] 1751-1800, and had dau.:*
m. 8 Sept., 1772
*PRISCILLA WOOTTEN[9(6)], 1756-1806.

WYLIE HILL[4] 1775-1844, and had:
m. 29 March, 1799
*MARTHA ("PATSY") POPE[10(7)], 1782-1853.

COL. LODOWICK MERIWETHER HILL[5] 1804-1883, and had:
m. 16 Dec., 1824
(I) NANCY HILL JOHNSON, 1808-1846.

LODOWICK JOHNSON HILL[6] b. 1846.
m. 28 Sept., 1871
MARY RUTH HENDERSON, 1849-1918.

CHART No. 4.

WALTON.

THOMAS WALTON, SR.
c. 1690-1750-'51, and had pro.:
        m.
SARAH ....

THOMAS WALTON, JR.
c. 1713-1759, and had dau.:*
        m.
        c. 1735
SARAH ...., pro. dau. of Francis Rountree, his will 30 Sept., 1730; pr. 27 June, 1734; d. 1761.

ABRAHAM HILL[3]
c. 1732-1792, and had:
        m.
        7 Jan'y, 1756
*CHRISTIAN WALTON, b. c. 1739; d. 6 July, 1808.

WYLIE HILL[4]
1775-1844, and had:
        m.
        29 March, 1799
MARTHA ("PATSEY") POPE, 1782-1853.

COL. LODOWICK MERIWETHER HILL[5]
1804-1883, and had:
        m.
        16 Dec., 1824
(I) NANCY HILL JOHNSON, 1808-1846.

LODOWICK JOHNSON HILL[6]
b. 1846.
        m.
        28 Sept., 1871
MARY RUTH HENDERSON.

CHART No. 5.

McKENNIE.

MICHAEL MACKQUENNEY
Will, Isle of Wight Co., Va., April 15, 1686; pr. Aug. 9, 1686, and had:
        m.
        c. 1665
ELIZABETH ...., 1st Husband.

COL. BARNABY MCKENNIE, SR.
c. 1673-c. 1740, and had dau.:*
        m.
        1703
MARY (EXUM) RICKS. She m. (I) 14 Oct., 1699, Jacob Ricks.
*MOURNING MCKENNIE.

JOHN POPE[3]
c. 1700-1745, and had:
        m.
        c. 1722
TABITHA ...., d. 1808; 1st Husband.

HENRY POPE[4]
c. 1725-1764, and had:
        m.
        c. 1749
PRISCILLA WOOTTEN, 1756-1806.

BURWELL POPE[5]
1751-1800, and had dau.:*
        m.
        8 Sept., 1772
*MARTHA ("PATSY") POPE, 1782-1853.

WYLIE HILL[4]
1775-1844.
        m.
        29 March, 1799

CHART No. 6.

EXUM.

RICHARD EXUM
c. 162..-c. 1668, and had:

m. ....

JEREMIAH EXUM
Will 1712; pr. March 28, 1720, and had dau.:*

m. ANN LAWRENCE, dau. of John Lawrence, pro. son of Robert and Eliza Lawrence.

COL. BARNABY McKENNIE, SR.
c. 1673-c. 1740, and had dau.:*

m. 1703 *MARY (EXUM) RICKS; 1st Husband Jacob Ricks.

JOHN POPE³
c. 1700-1745.

m. c. 1722 *MOURNING McKENNIE.

CHART No. 7.

HENDERSON.

....
and had:

m. EDITH (........?) HENDERSON.

LEMUEL HENDERSON
and had:

m. SUSAN ANN HENDERSON.

ISAAC PURNELL HENDERSON
1789-1864, and had:

m.
9 Dec., 1821
(II) MRS. RUTH (SHEPHERD) JOHNSON, 1791-1872.

GEN. ROBERT J. HENDERSON
1822-1891, and had dau.:*

m.
2 April, 1846
LAURA ELIZABETH WOOD, 1829-1899.

LODOWICK JOHNSON HILL⁶
b. 1846.

m.
28 Sept., 1871
*MARY RUTH HENDERSON, 1849-1918.

CHART No. 8.

RICHARDSON.

CHARLES RICHARDSON
of Virginia, and had: m. .... BURCHELL.

GEN. RICHARD RICHARDSON, SR.
1704-1781, and had: m.
                         11 Oct., 1736   MARY CANTEY, d. 1767. ..

COL. RICHARD RICHARDSON, JR.
1741-1818, and had dau.:*   m.
                            1761   DORCAS NELSON, 1741-1834.

WILLIAM BILLUPS
1763-1817, and had dau.:*   m.
                            9 Oct., 1787   *MARY RICHARDSON, 1763-1803.

CARY WOOD
1794-1857, and had dau.:*   m.
                            16 Oct., 1823   *MARY RICHARDSON BILLUPS, 1803-1874.

GEN. ROBT. J. HENDERSON
1822-1891, and had dau.:*   m.
                            2 April, 1846   *LAURA ELIZABETH WOOD, 1829-1899.

LODOWICK JOHNSON HILL[6]
b. 1846.   m.
                            28 Sept., 1871   *MARY RUTH HENDERSON, 1849-1918.

CHART No. 9.

BILLUPS.

JOSEPH BILLUPS, SR.
Probably son of John, 1685, and had:

ROBERT BILLUPS
and had: m.
                            14 June, 1755   ANN RANSONE (Pro. gr. dau. of James Ransone[2]).

WILLIAM BILLUPS
1763-1817, and had dau.:*   m.
                            9 Oct., 1787   MARY RICHARDSON, 1763-1803.

CARY WOOD
1794-1857.   m.
                            16 Oct., 1823   *MARY RICHARDSON BILLUPS, 1803-1874.

CHART No. 10. RANSONE, RANSOM
(Tentative)

PETER RANSONE[1] m. ....
b. before 1628; d. before 1652; and
had:

JAMES RANSONE[2] m. .... (Probably
b. before 1649; d. after 1704; and a daughter of Capt. Ambrose Dudley).
had:

ROBERT RANSONE[3], and m. ....

PETER RANSONE[3] m. ....
and one of these two had dau.:*

ROBERT BILLUPS m. *ANN RANSONE.
and had: 14 June, 1755

WILLIAM BILLUPS m. MARY RICHARDSON, 1763-1803.
1763-1817.

CHART No. 11. LANE.

THOMAS LANE[1] m. ....
in Isle of Wight Co., Va., before
1687, and had:

JOSEPH LANE[2] m. JULIAN ....
c. 165..-after 1727, and had:

JOSEPH LANE[3] m. PATIENCE McKENNIE, dau. of Col. Bar-
c. 1705-1773, and had: 1730 naby McKennie, Sr.

JESSE LANE[4] m. WINNIFRED AWECK (AYCOCK), 1741-
1733-1800, and had: 1766 1774.

JOSEPH LANE, JR. m. ELIZABETH HILL, dau. of Isaac and
1775-...... 1806 Nancy (Crain) Hill.

PREFACE

In searching for and collecting the data for this work I have received valuable and most generous aid from Mrs. Annie Noble Sims, decd., of Savannah, Ga., Mrs. Ella Barrow Spalding, of Savannah, Ga., Mrs. Annie Hill Snyder, of Austin, Tex., Mrs. Joel Kendall Mathis, of Mooresville, Ala., and Memphis, Tenn., Mrs. Jesse Mercer Callaway, decd., of LaGrange, Ga., and, in lesser degree, from many others, too numerous to mention. To one and all of these I extend my most sincere thanks. Without their kindly co-operation the task would have been well nigh impossible. As it is, the work is not as complete as I would have it. The descendants of many families have not been traced, from inability to get in touch with them, others only partly traced, because of indifference, or lack of interest on the part of those applied to for information. Nevertheless, I hope and believe it will prove both of interest and value to the descendants of every family treated, especially so to those who feel any interest in their ancestry or have any affection for their kin.

I have labored earnestly and diligently to ascertain the real truth, the actual facts, as to the lineage and history of each family, and have given the result in plain and unvarnished language in these pages. That there are shortcomings, deficiencies and probably errors, I fully realize. But I trust and believe, credit will be given for whatever of real value has been presented, and errors will be viewed with indulgence. If appreciated by those for whom compiled, and prove helpful to such as may wish to make further research, I shall be amply rewarded.

As a prelude to a genealogical work the following article is so apposite, and expresses so perfectly my own views, that I (by consent) reproduce it here.

THE COUNTY COURT NOTE-BOOK.

Vol. 1.   December, 1921.   No. 2.

[Mrs.] Milnor Ljungstedt, Editor and Publisher, Bethesda, Route 1, Maryland.

THE EDITOR'S LETTER.

"Now, what I want is, Facts. . . . You can only form the minds of reasoning animals upon Facts. Stick to Facts, Sir!"—(Dickens, Hard Times, p. 7).

The Editor "admires" facts—to drop into a dear New England colloquialism. The Editor even loves facts. The beautiful consecutiveness of the alphabet—the fact that two and two make four and don't and can't make anything else—these are so restfully definite. It is strange to the Editor that anything doubtful about figures or ancestors can hold any charm. Our ancestors were our ancestors, for good or ill, and for all eternity. Kings and princes; peasants and pirates; they are with us forever.

The Editor does think that if a person's ancestor had to be a king, he might at least be a respectable one. But so many of the kings who pose as ancestors aren't so very respectable. The Editor bears a personal grudge against one of hers—he was one of the very worst of them all. And the shocking thought comes ocasionally—how much of that detestable person am I? The Editor is merely aiming at this—take your ancestors philosophically. They didn't know anything about you—and they didn't know you were going to know anything about them, dig them out of their royal tombs and lowly graves, and exhibit them to the eyes of the modern world in their unveiled skin and bones, so to speak. Treat them kindly, but exactly. If I were an ancestor, I would hate to have my dates mixed up, and my wives made into my daughters, or even my granddaughters. The best we can now do for them is to be frank when we can, and respectfully reticent when we can't.

It gives this compiler especial pleasure to add that Mrs. Ljungstedt, the Editor of the County Note-Book—*an unique bulletin*—is "a painful, conscientious and faithful" searcher. She has given her attention, in a large measure, to reading the old unpublished records at the various county seats in Virginia and Maryland, and is publishing in the "County Court Note-Book" brief abstracts of these old records, and I know of no source from which one can obtain so much and so varied genealogical information.

Respectfully,

LODOWICK JOHNSON HILL, SR.

Atlanta, Ga., 1922.

"He only deserves to be remembered by posterity who treasures up and preserves the history of his ancestors" (Edmund Burke).

The Hills of Wilkes County Georgia And Allied Families

According to family tradition, positive, persistent and unvarying, the ancestors of Henry Hill[1], of Nansemond County, Va.,—the branch of the family of which I treat—were Scotch-Irish, from County Down, Ireland. I therefore note a few of the Hills of Ireland.

Moses Hill, with a number of other prominent persons, were invited to Ulster, Ireland, to populate and develop it, 1605-1618.

Moses Hill had wood land given him, which being thereafter demolished, left a fair and beautiful country, when a later heir of the Hills built Hillsborough (Foote's Sketches of N. C., pp. 88-89—taken from "A short account of the Church of Christ as it was amongst the Irish at first; among and after the English entered; and after the entry of the Scotts", by Rev. Andrew Stewart).

Sir Moses Hill, of Hillsboro, d. Feby. 1629, ae. 76, had sons:

Peter and Arthur, d. 1632, who afterwards succeeded; two sons, Francis and Randall. Francis died without male issue and the estate devolved upon his uncle, Arthur Hill, of Hillsboro, who during the period of the Irish rebellion built a fortress at Hillsboro, in recognition of his devotion; this was in 1660 erected into a Royal Garrison and he and his heirs made Constable of the Castle; died 1663. Some of his sons died young and none were of the names of those that came to America. (Collins' Peerage—Edition of 1768—Vol. VII).

Moses Hill went to Ireland 1573.

Seats.—Hillsborough Castle and Merlough House, Dumdrum, County Down; and East Hampstead Park, Wakingham, Berks. The Marquis of Devonshire. Motto: "Per Deum et Fermen Ostium".

Samuel Hill, an ancestor of the Hill family in Ireland, was Treasurer for the County of Buckingham during the time of Oliver Cromwell, 1642.

Sir Hugh Hill, son of Rowley[3], son of John[2], son of Samuel[1], was created baronet in 1779, and represented the city of Derry in Parliament 1768 to 1795, when he died.

The arms as here presented are taken from Crozier's General Armory, as brought to Virginia by Col. Humphrey Hill, of King and Queen County, d. 1775, and are described as:

"Arms.—Azure, on a chevron between three owls argent, three mullets, sable, a bordure ermine."

The arms as given *Sir Hugh Hill*, bore:

"The chevrons, with erminois points instead of mullets, and were placed between three leopards' heads instead of owls; but the differences between the two are easily attributable to the intermarriages with other families bearing arms of that distinction."

Sir Henry Blyth Hill, 6th Baronet, of St. Columbs, County Londonderry, Captain and Brevet Major late Royal Irish Fusiliers, sometime Governor of Bohrel el Gazol, attached to the Egyptian Army 1898-1908, etc., etc.

Lineage.—Samuel Hill, first ancestor of the family in Ireland, went from Buckinghamshire to Ireland as Treasurer of that Kingdom under Oliver Cromwell in 1642. John, Samuel, Hugh, etc., etc.

Motto.—"Ne tentes aut perfice"—"Complete what you attempt," or "Attempt not, or accomplish." (Burks' Peerage, Baronetage and Knightage, under head of "Hill".)

Samuel Hill in Warwick County, Va., in 1693, but no further record of him. (N. C. H. & G. R. 1-1-52.)

The Viscount Hill (*Sir Rowland* Richard Clegg-Hill) of Hawkstone and Hardwicke, Salop, Baron Hill, of Almares and Hardwicke, in the same County, etc., etc.

Lineage.—The residence in the County of Salop, of this distinguished family, can be traced to a period antecedent to the reign of Edward I, but the name, instead of Hill, was formerly spelled Hull, or de la Hull—*Humphrey Hill*, of Buntingale, living tempo Henry V; Ralph, Thomas, Rowland, etc.

Motto.—"Avancez". (Burk's Peerage, Baronetage and Knightage, head "Hill").

The coat of arms of Col. Humphrey Hill are identical with those of Isaac Hill, of King and Queen County, Va. (Old King William Homes and Fams., pp. 64-'5, by Clarke.)

Edward Hill[1] in Virginia, 1622; d. 15 May, 1624. His son and grandson bore the same name. All were Burgesses, Members of Council, and held other prominent offices. The tomb of the third Col. Edward Hill, of "Shirley", bears the arms: A lion passant. Crest: a demi-lion. The tinctures are not designated.

The arms of Hill, of the County of *Wexford, Ireland,* contain a lion passant, with a demi-lion passant for a crest. ("Va. Heraldica", Vol. V, p. 46; E. S. of Ala., p. 383, footnote).

From a copy of the Raleigh News and Observer, of some years ago, is taken the following:

The Hill Family, of Elizabeth and Charles City Counties, Va.: Arms: Gules, two bars, ermine; in chief, a lion passant, argent. Crest: A boar's head, sa.; in the mouth a trefoil slipped, ppr. Motto: *"Spe labor levis".*

Nathaniel Hill, great-grandfather of the late Nathaniel P. Hill, U. S. Senator from Colorado, was born 1705 in the North of *Ireland,* and about 1730 emigrated to New York and settled on the western frontier of the Scotch-Irish settlements then already established west of the Hudson River. (Frances Cowles). The late Governor David Hill, of New York, descended from Adam Hill, of *County Derry, Ireland,* who emigrated to Schenectady, N. Y., where he died 1764.

There are some fourscore possible coats of arms for the Hill family, one being as follows:

Arms: Gules, two bars ermine, in chief a lion passant, per pale or and argent. The crest is a fleur de lys argent.

The Motto—which is always an optional matter, is "Esse quam videri", literally "to be rather than to seem", or freely, "Better to be than to seem to be".

"In 1661, the Marquis of Worcester obtained letters patent for a breech-loading gun or pistol. In *1664 Abraham* Hill obtained *letters patent* for a similar invention, viz., a new way of making a gun or pistol, the breach whereof rises upon a *hindge* by a contrivance of a motion from under it, by which it is also let downe againe and bolted fast by one and the same motion". (N. E. H. & G. Reg., Vol. 33, p. 351).

In "Dic. of Natl. Biography", Vol. XXVI, p. 389, we find:

"Abraham Hill, b. 1635; d. 1721, came of an old family seated at Shilstone in Devonshire; father, Richard Hill, a merchant and alderman of London, was appointed by the Long Parliament treasurer of sequestrations in the summer of 1642 till 1649. At the accession of William and Mary, Abraham Hill became a Commissioner of trade, and Bishop Tillotsen appointed him Comptroller of Canterbury. He is buried in the Chancel of Sutton Church. He married Anne, daughter of Sir Bulstrode Whitelocke, Knight, had son Richard and daughter Frances."

In the Colonial Records of North Carolina are numerous records of the transactions and communications of the "Lords of Trade". In Vol. I, p. 540, Lords of Trade to Gov. Nicholson July 22, 1701, Whitehall. (Signed) Stamford, Ph. Meadows, *Abraham Hill*, Matt. Prier, *Lords of Trade*.

In C. R. N. C., Vol. I, p. 464, is a petition, September 7, 1696, to remove the Attorney General, signed by Abraham Hill et al., Lords of Trade, and on page 524 to Governor Nicholson relative to the boundaries between North Carolina and Virginia, signed January 14, 1699-1700, Whitehall, by Abraham Hill et al., Lords of Trade.

The name Henry occurs, probably, more frequently than any other in the Hill family, not only in one, but in all of its branches and in every generation. The names Abraham and Moses quite often in Chowan County, N. C., and that of Hugh once. The loss of all the records of Nansemond County, Va., has made it impossible, not only to connect Henry[1] with his overseas ancestors, but also to learn who were his parents or grandparents. There were several Henry Hills in Norfolk County in the 17th Century, one in 1646, and later, who was a man of substance and influence. In 1644 a John Hill, Gent., obtained a patent in Nansemond County, in the section where we later find Henry Hill[1], for his own adventure and importation of three others, but there is no later record of him preserved. There were also numerous Henry Hills in the middle of the 17th century in Maryland, and a Henry Hill, Commander of

Horse, 1630, Accomack County, Va. In the 17th century there was a very decided movement, to and fro, of the inhabitants of Norfolk, Nansemond and Isle of Wight Counties and it is not impossible that Henry's[1] parents came from the County of Norfolk. Green Hill, Sr., born in Isle of Wight in 1714, removed to Bute County, N. C., and named his eldest son Henry. Benjamin Hill, born 1697, in Nansemond, removed to Bertie County, N. C., and died 1758; named a son Henry. Isaac Hill, d. 1708, Bertie County, N. C., had a grand son, son of John, named Henry. All suggestive of a common origin. Considering all the records and facts above referred to, it seems not unreasonable to believe the tradition as to origin of Henry Hill's[1] ancestors is based on fact.

No claim is made to a royal lineage, to noble blood, or right to bear a coat of arms.

If, as a matter of fact, they have such an heritage, their right is dormant and barred by inability to connect these early Virginians with their overseas ascendants.

They, however, take pardonable pride in having an ancestry of unblemished characters, who were blessed with hearts and minds which commanded esteem, made them the peers, and won for them the friendship and confidence of those of the highest standing in their sections; who were peace-loving, law-abiding and God-fearing, industrious, progressive and constructive; who achieved signal successes in every field of endeavor and were potent factors in promoting the general well-being of their fellowmen, the liberty, stability, civilization and welfare of their country. Many have attained to great eminence in the professions, filled the highest public stations with credit to themselves and to the honor and glory of country.

O.—Henry Hill[1], of the Upper Parish of Nansemond County, Virginia, whether native or immigrant not yet definitely ascertained, was the first and earliest of our Hill ancestors, in America, of whom we have definite and certain knowledge.

"John Odom to Nicholas Stallings, Assignment of a patent, *Oct. 19, 1700.* Test., Will Hunter, *Henry Hill*, Robt. Rountree". (N. C. H. & G. Reg., 1-1-89).

"To all &c., Whereas, &c., Now know ye that I, the sd. Francis Nicholson, Esq., Governor, &c., Doe with the advice and consent of the Councill of State accordingly give & grant unto *Henry Hill* five hundred acres of land situate lying and being in the *upper parish* of *Nansemond County near Bennett's Creek;* Beginning at a white oake, a corner tree of *John Rice* and *Edward Holms* their land, and a line Easterly fifty nine degrees one hundred and eight poles to a pine, thence North Easterly fifty-four degrees one hundred and thirty six poles to a pine, thence North Easterly forty degrees one hundred and sixteen poles to a pine, thence North Westerly five degrees forty poles to a pine, thence North Easterly 17° 74 poles to a pine, thence North Westerly fifty eight degrees eighty poles to a pine, thence South Westerly seventy three degrees one hundred and four poles to a pine, thence South Westerly forty six degrees seventy four poles to a pine, thence Due West one hundred and four poles to a white oak in Speight's line, thence bounding on ye sd. line to the first station, the said land being due unto ye sd *Henry Hill* by and for the transportation of ten persons into this Colony *whose names are to be in the records mentioned under this patent.* To have and to hold &c. To be held &c., Yielding and paying &c., Provided &c. Given under my hand and ye seal of the Colony this *25th day of Aprill Anno Domini 1701.* Fr. Nicholson."

Names of persons transported were:
"William Casey, Mary Cucke, Charles Westonnon, Thomas Clarke, Robert Deaver, Robert Nelson, Benjamin Hentschell, John Yates, Bryon Skerring, John Wallington". (Office of Land Patents at the Capitol, Book 9, p. 304, Richmond, Va.). As the names of himself and family are not among the headrights, he was evidently a resident of the County previous to that date. He removed with his wife, Mary, and son Abraham Hill[2], to Chowan, now Gates County, N. C., about 1702 or 1703, as shown by the following records, viz.:

"*Henry Hill* proved his rights for the importation of Henry, Mary and Abraham Hill, John, William and Elizabeth Hinton, John Maulby and Joh Webb, Oct. 29th .... (prior to 1710)". (N. C. H. & G. Reg., Vol. 2, No. 2, p. 305).

". . . Abraham Hill, Jr.[3], son of Abraham[2], son of Henry[1], who first settled in Chowan (now Gates) County, about 1700" (N. C. H. & G. Reg., 2-2-310).

Mary Hill's maiden name not yet ascertained.

These Hintons, who were imported by Henry Hill[1], are the ancestors of all of this name that are so prominently featured in the subsequent annals of North Carolina and other Southern States. The very intimate and close association of the Hills and Hintons during this early period and the succeeding generation, as evidenced by numerous records, suggests the probability of a matrimonial relationship between them, either that Mary Hill was a Hinton, or that Elizabeth Hinton was a Hill, or that Mary Hill and Elizabeth Hinton were sisters. This, however, is purely speculative, no records, so far discovered, showing intermarriage. We must not overlook, however, the fact that all the "Nansemond County records were destroyed in 1865. It was a great public calamity as they contained some of the richest and most valuable historic information of old Virginia". ("The Winbornes of Old", p. 37).

The records given are the oldest so far discovered that relate definitely to this Henry Hill[1]. He was born, probably, circa 1670; died intestate between July 11, 1719, and April 18, 1720. (Book "F", No. 1, pp. 8, 14; Book "H", No. 1, p. 101). In most of the records made in North Carolina, prior and up to 1730, Henry[1] and Abraham Hill[2] are described as of Nansemond County.

Jno. Watson to Hen. Hill—Deed 8th May, 1716.

To all those people to whom these presents shall come, greeting &c, Know ye that I, Jno. Watson, of Chowan Precinct in North Carolina, Planter, for & in consideration of the sum of .... pounds in good lawful money of Carolina afsd to me in hand before the ensealing hereof paid by *Hen- Hill, in ye County of Nansemond in Virginia, also Planter*, the receipt whereof .... hereby acknowledges and myself therewith fully satisfied & contented & thereof & of every part and parcel thereof Do Exonerate & discharge the sd. Henry Hill his heirs & assigns forever by these presents have given, Granted, bargained, sold aliened conveyed & confirmed and by these presents do fully freely & absolutely Give Grant bargain sell Alien Confirm Convey unto him the said Henry Hill his heirs & assigns forever a tract of land containing one hundred & fifty acres lying on the Northeast shore of Chowan on deep run beginning at a white oak Dan'll Halsey's corner tree then S. 30 wt 40 pole to a pine then S. 70 Et. 154 pole to pine N. 15 Et. 94 Pole to a red Oak, then N. 50 Wt. 332 Pole to the centre of five pines & two Oaks then along Jam.s Farlow's lines S. 10 Wt. 139 Pole to a Poplar on deep run then along the said line to the first station.

To have & to hold the sd. granted Bargained Premises with all the appurtenances privileges & commodities to the same belonging or in any ways appertaining to him the sd Henry Hill his heirs & assigns forever to his & their only proper use benefit & behoof forever and I the Sd. John Watson & Mary my wife for us our heirs Exrs. do covenant promise & Grant to & with the Sd. Henry Hill, his heirs & assigns that before the Ensealing hereof I am the true Sole and lawfull owner of the above bargained Premises and am lawfully seized and possessed of the same in mine own proper Right as a good perfect & absolute estate of inheritance in fee simple and have in myself good right full power and lawfull authority to grant bargain sell convey & confirm the sd. bargained Premises in manner above said and that the Sd. Hen-ry Hill & assigns shall & may from time to time & at all times forever hereafter by force & virtue of these presents Lawfully Peaceable & Quietly have hold use occupy possess & enjoy the Sd. Demised & bargained premises with the appurtenances free & Clear acquitted exonerated & discharged of & from all & all manner of former & other Gifts Grants bargains Sales Leases Mortgages Wills Entails Joyntures dowers judgments executions Incumbrances &c Extents furthermore I the Sd. Jno. Watson for myself my heirs exrs. admrs. do convenant and engage the above demised premises to him the Sd. Henry Hill his heirs and assigns against the Lawfull Claim or demand of any person or persons whatsoever forever hereafter to warrant secure & defend and Mary Watson the wife of me the Sd. Jno. Watson doth by these presents freely willingly give yield up & surrender all her right of dower & power of thirds in & unto the above Demised premises unto him the Sd. Henry Hill His heirs & assigns. In witness whereof I have hereunto set my hand & seall the 14th day of April 1716.

         Jno. T. Watson ( )
         Mary R. Watson ( )

Signed sealed & Deld. in the Presence of
      Nick Stallings,
      Jam,s I. Farlow,
      Jno. T. Honton (Hinton)

(Reg. Vol. 1, No. 2, p. 292; also Vol. 2, No. 3, p. 473).

Jno. W. Watson to Henry Hill, Assignment of Patent for 140 acres of Land, Dated 1 April, 1713. } Know all men by these presents that I, Jno. Watson, of Chowan Precinct, doth by virtue of these presents assign and make over all my whole right and title of this within patent to *Mr. Henry Hill*, of Nansemond County. Witnesseth my hand this 16th day of April, 1716.

              Jno. Watson.

Test: Christopher Dudley.
  Jno. Gordon. Nov. 5, 1729.
      The above assignment was proved by the oath of Christopher Dudley, one of the evidences thereto before me.

Regd. 5 Nov. 1729.   C. Gale, C. J.

It will be noted that the above assignment was made in 1716, but not proved and registered until 1729, ten years after the death of the assignee, Henry Hill. (Reg. Vol. 2, No. 3, p. 447).

Henry Hill[1] prosecutes his suit against James Fleming. Continued to next Court. Court adjourned to next court in course. (Court held at house of William Branch, 1716). (N. C. H. & G. Reg. 1-1-150).

Henry Hill[1] purchased a tract of land represented as containing ninety acres. Later, when he had it surveyed, it was found to be 220 acres. To perfect his title to the tract he took out a patent, as here shown:

"Henry Hill 220 acres of Land in the Upper Parish of Nansemond County, near Bennett's Creek. Granted by Alex. Spotswood July 11, 1719". (Land Book, at Richmond, No. 10, p. 444). This tract was sold Dec. 8, 1756, by Abraham Hill[2] and wife, Judith, to Josiah Granberry and registered April 15, 1757. The above stated facts are recited in this conveyance. (Book H, No. 1, p. 101).

O.—Henry Hill[1] and Mary ......, his wife, had an only son:

P.—Abraham Hill[2], born in 1697 or '8, in Nansemond County, Virginia; died in Chowan, now Gates, County, N. C. Will dated April 18, 1760; married prior to October 20, 1729, Judith ......, maiden name not learned. (N. C. H. & G. Reg. 1-1-105; 1-4-553; 2-3-474).

Showing Henry Hill's[1] death are the following:

"Mary Hill to Thomas Harmon; Power of Attorney: Know all men by these presents That I *Mary Hill, Widow of Henry Hill late of the Upper Parrish of Nansemond County*, hereby have assigned and ordained and made and in my stead and place by these presents put and constitute my trusty and well beloved friend Mr. Thomas Harmon, Gentleman of the County of Albemarle and Precinct of Chowan in North Carolina, as my true and Lawful Attorney General in my name & to my use and behalf to ask recover or to receive of any person or persons that stands justly indebted to me in the County of Albemarle and Precinct aforesaid giving and by these presents granting unto my said Attorney full power and lawful authority in the premises to do as aforesaid, all & such act & acts, thing & things, devise and devises, in Law whatsoever for the recovery of all of Debts aforesaid as fully largely and amply in every respect as I myself might or could do, if I were personally present, and upon which thereof acquittances or other discharges for & in my name to make ratifying and allowing whatsoever my said Attorney shall lawfully to be done or cause to be done in and about the premises by virtue of these presents be good. In Witness whereof the said Mary Hill hath hereunto set her hand & seal *the 18th of April, 1720.*

MARY HILL. (SEAL).

Signed, sealed & delivered in the presence of us

Richard R. (his mark) Brothers.
Thos. Rountree.

At a Court held for Chowan Precinct on the 3rd Tuesday in April 1720 at the Court House in *Queen Anns Town* the within power of attorney was proved by the oath of Richard Brothers & Thomas Rountree, the evidences thereto are on motion ordered to be recorded and is recorded.

Test. Thos. Henmon, Clk." (Book F, No. 1, p. 8).

"*Abraham Hill*[2] To Thomas Rountree: Power of Attorney: North Carolina SS *April 20/1720.*

Mr. Thomas Rountree, I do hereby authorize and empower you to appear for me and prosecute or defend any cause in North Carolina against or at the suit of *John Watson* and this shall be your warranty.

Abraham Hill.

At a Court mentioned and held for Chowan Precinct at the Court House at *Queen Ann's Town* on the 2nd day of April, 1720, the within named Abraham Hill acknowledged the within Power of Attorney to the within named Thomas Rountree, and on motion is ordered to be recorded and is recorded.

Thos. Henman, Clk &c."

(Book F, No. 1, p. 14).

Abraham Hill[2] attained his majority by July 1719.

To Abraham Hill[2] of Nansemond Co., Va., from *Richard Skinner*, July 13, 1719, 200 acres of land near the Punch Bowl (now Centre Hill). (N. C. H. & G. Reg. 2-3-473; Book "W", No. 1, p. 189 —at Edenton).

Richard Skinner, Sr., of Perquimons, to Abraham Hill[2], Upper Parish, Nansemond Co., Va., Said Abraham, son of Henry Hill, 200 A. beginning at a pine near Punch Bowl, in the Meadow, Wm. Woodley's corner line, to Bear Swamp, etc. July 13, 1719. Test.: John Geisa, William Watson, Thos. Rountree. (N. C. H. & G. Reg. 1-1-105; Book "W" at Edenton).

To Abraham Hill, of Nansemond Co., Va., from Richard Benfield, Aug. 5, 1720, 500 acres land in Perquimon's Precinct. (Book "W", No. 1, p. 597; N. C. H. & G. Reg. 2-3-473).

Abraham Hill, of Nansemond Co., Va., to *William Hinton, of same place,* Jany. 30, 1720, 75 A. at the head of Horse Pool Swamp. (Book C, No. 1, p. 111; N. C. H. & G. REG. 2-3-474).

Abraham Hill, of Nansemond Co., Va., to Edward Bass, of Norfolk Co., Va., 100 A. lying at the head of the Horse pool Swamp—patented by said Hill's father, March 1, 1718. Deed dated Jany. 30, 1720. Test.: Wm. Hinton, Thos. Rountree. (Book C, No. 2, p. 113; N. C. H. & G. Reg. 2-3-474; 2-4-616).

Abraham Hill, of Nansemond Co., Va., to John Bass, of Albemarle Co., N. C., Jany. 30, 1720, 200 A. adjoining above tract. Test. Wm. Hinton, Thos. Rountree. (Book C. No. 1, p. 115; N. C. H. & G. Reg. 2-3-475).

William Jones, of Perquimons, to Abraham Hill, of Nansemond Co., Va., 640 acres in Bear Swamp. Assignment of Patent dated Nov. 27, 1727. Deed dated Dec. 15, 1727. Test.: Richard Bond, Thomas Walton, Wm. Havield. (N. C. H. & G. Reg. 2-3-445).

Abraham Hill was here (in Chowan County) over twenty-one years old in 1721; he and his father came from Nansemond County, Va. (Extract from letter of J. R. B. Hathaway, of Edenton, Editor of the Register, to L. J. Hill, of Atlanta, Ga., 13 Feby. 1902).

Abraham Hill dealt largely in real estate. The above records are but a few of the many at Edenton and are given here to establish his age and nativity. The following record shows that he married prior to October 20, 1729.

. . . . Spivey a Deed, the 20th Oct. 1729. Regd. 7th Feby. 1732. Between Abrm. Hill of the ...... & Precinct of Chowan in No. Carolina & Judah ...... one part & Jacob Spivey of the same County of the ...... Witnesseth that th. Sd. Abrm. Hill for the consideration of ...... pounds current money of No. Carolina to him in hand pd. ...... Spivey the rect whereof he the sd. Abrm. Hill doth ...... acknowledge & for himself his heirs Exrs., Admrs. ...... acquit exonerate & discharge him the sd. ...... his heirs & assigns forever have given bargained & sold & by these presents doth fully clearly & absolutely give, grant, bargain alien, sell & forever make over & confirm unto the said Jacob Spivey his heirs

& assigns one hundred acres of land Situate lying & being in *Perquimons Precinct in North Carolina* afsd. at a place commonly known by the name of *Bear Swamp* near the *Punch Bowl* & joining on the line of a parcel of land belonging to Sam Pagette being part of a Patent granted to *Wm. Jones* of Chowan Precinct for 640 acres bearing date the 27th Nov. 1727 doth & may appear & was by the Sd. Wm. Jones sold & conveyed to the Sd. Abrm. Hill. To Have & to Hold unto the said Jacob Spivey his heirs & assigns with all the rights members and apurt thereof & all other liberties & privileges therein & thereon contained and the said Hill & Judah his wife for them & each of them their & each of their heirs Exrs. & Admrs. do by these presents promise & warrant at the ensealing & delivery hereof that they have a good right title & estate in the premises in fee simple, & hath full right & lawful authority to bargain & sell the same unto the said Jacob Spivey his heirs & assigns forever & that the said land & premises with all & singular the apurts. now are & so shall & may forever hereafter remain continue & be unto the said Jacob Spivey his heirs & assigns free & freely clear & clearly acquitted exonerated & discharged of & from all manner of gifts grants leases sales, mortgages, deeds, Bonds, Judgments, Forfeitures ...... and arrearages of rents & all their incumbrances ...... nature & kind so ever but that the said Jam.s ...... & assigns shall & lawfully may from time ...... times peaceably & quietly have ...... enjoy the afs. land & premises with all ...... without any the lawfull set suit trouble ...... molestation interruption execution of ...... heirs or assigns or any other person from by or under him or them or any ...... person or persons whatsoever. In Witness ...... Abraham Hill & Judah his wife have ...... & affixed their seals the day and year first ....

            Abra ....
            Judah ....

Signed, sealed and delivered in presence of
  Thos. Rountree
  Wm. Rice.

The above deed, bearing date 20th Oct. 1729 shows that Abraham Hill and his wife, in this deed *called Judah*, were married prior to that date, and the many blank spaces attest the age, effaced and illegible state of these old records. "All the Blank Spaces above were blank in the Deed Book. R. M. Boyle".—The Register who made copy.

On 26th Sept. 1749, Abraham Hill[2] and *Judith*, his wife—so named throughout the deed—make a conveyance to Moses Hambletion of 100 acres lying near the head of *Gum pocosin* in Chowan, part of a patent Granted to Henry Hill[1], *father* to the said Abraham Hill, &c &c., Reg. May 4, 1750. Pr. James Craven, Reg. C. Co.

"*This Indenture* made this eighth day of december in the year of our Lord Christ one thousand seven hundred and *fifty six* Between *Abraham Hill* and *Judith Hill* his wife of the one part and *Josiah Granbury* of the other part all of them of the County of Chowan in the Province of North Carolina, Witnesseth: That the said Abraham Hill & *Judith* his wife for and in consideration of the sum of ninety five pounds good and Lawfull money of the colony of Virginia already in hand paid them by the said Josiah Granbury the receipt of which said sum they the said *Abraham & Judith* doth hereby acknowledge & themselves thereof fully and entirely satisfied have bargained sold aliened enfeofed & confirmed & by these presents doth bargain, sell alien & enfeof & forever confirm unto the said Josiah Granbury his heirs & assigns forever all those two tracts dividendends & parcels of land hereinafter mentioned that is to say that parcel of land, which the said *Abram* purchased from one John Perry of the County of Bertie containing by estimation one hundred acres and is bounded as follows: towit: Beginning at a marked pine standing in or near a certain branch thence running by a line of marked trees till it meets the old dividing line made between Edward Homes and John Perry so along the said dividing line till it comes to the said branch, thence down the said branch and bounded thereon to the first station and is part of a patent granted to Edward Homes & John Rice in the year Anno Domini 1695. *Also one other tract or parcel of land which was sold by John Rice to Henry Hill farther of the said Abraham for ninety one acres, but the same being surveyed there appeared to be two hundred and twenty acres for which said two hundred and twenty acres the said Henry Hill obtained a patent dated the 11th day of July Anno Domini 1719 is bounded* as follows; viz:

Beginning at a stake by the side of a branch called the Merry branch & runs thence So. 130 poles to a stake thence South 81—W. 304 poles to a poplar standing at the mouth of the Meherrin Swamp thence up Bennett's Creek according to the various courses thereof to the mouth of the aforesaid Merry branch thence up the same according to the various courses thereof & bounding thereon to the first station which said two parcels of land lies situated in the County of Chowan in the Province of North Carolina adjoining each other and containing in the whole quantity of three hundred and twenty acres be the same more or less according to the most known and reputed bounds thereof together with all houses orchards, gardens, marshes waters woods ways mines & minerals & all other the profits & commodities thereto belonging or in any wise appurtaining with the reversion & reversions remainder & remainders, rents issues & profits thereof & of every part & parcel thereof to have and to Hold the said bargained premises unto the said Josiah Granbury his heirs & assigns forever to his & their only benefit & behoof forever and the said *Abraham Hill* and *Judith* his wife for themselves their heirs, executors & administrators doth covenant promise Grant and agree to & with Josiah Granbury his heirs & assigns forever in manner following, That is to say, that

they the said *Abraham Hill* and *Judith* his wife at the time of ensealing & delivering of these presents is and stands lawfully seized & possessed of a good free estate in fee simple of and in the premises and that they have good right & lawful authority to sell and pass away the fee simple estate of the said land unto the said Josiah Granbury his heirs and assigns forever that the said land is fully freely & clearly discharged & acquitted of all bargains, sales, Jointures, dowers, rents & arrearages of rents & of & from all manner of incumbrances whatsoever, and the said *Abraham Hill* and *Judith* his wife doth for themselves their heirs executors administrators further promise covenant and agree to and with the said Josiah Granbury his heirs & assigns forever that the said Abraham & Judith their heirs & Exrs. will at any time hereafter when reasonably thereto required by the said Josiah Granbury his heirs & assigns do or cause to be done any other or further act thing or things for the more & better securing unto the said Josiah his heirs & assigns a good & sure title to the bargained premises & lastly the said bargained premises unto the said Josiah Granbury his heirs & assigns forever that the said Abraham Hill and Judith his wife their heirs executors administrators will warrant & forever defend against the lawful claims of all manner of persons whatsoever. In Witness Whereof the said Abraham Hill & Judith his wife hath hereunto set their hands & seals the day & date first above written.   Abraham Hill   (S)
The mark of
Judith Hill   (S)

Sealed & delivered ...... acknowledged & recorded in presence of us

Edwd. Riddick } Received the eighth day of December Anno
Henry Hill   } Domini 1756 From Josiah Granbury Ninety
Abram Hill   } five pounds current money of Virginia in full
               } consideration of the within deed from Abraham Hill.

Judith mark Hill.

F. 95 Witness Abraham Hill, Edwd. Riddick, Henry Hill.

The above deed was proved & acknowledged in due form of law Judith Hill having been first privately examined this 13th day of April 1757 before me. Let it be registered.

Peter Henly C. J.

Registered 15th day of April 1757 by

G. Disbrowe Reg.

In the Field Book of the Surveyors of the boundary line between Virginia and North Carolina on March 30, 1727/8 is the following entry:

"At 365 chains from the beginning (Viz.: the Burnt pine and George House) is the *road from Abraham Hill to Meads* . . At 390 chains from do. burnt pine & they crossed a Branch of Bennett's Creek". (C. R. N. C., Vol. 2, p. 805).

Abraham Hill[2] was added to the list of jurymen for Chowan County, Feby. 25, 1739-'40 (C. R. N. C., Vol. 4, p. 517); was a member of Capt. James Farlie's Company, of Col. Robert Burden's Regiment of North Carolina Militia, as reported Nov. 25, 1754 (Time of French & Indian War). (S. R. N. C., Vol. XXII, p. 357).

His Will: "In the name of God Amen. I Abraham Hill of North Carolina of the County of Chowan, being in good health and of sound and perfect memory and calling to mind the uncertainty of this life do make and ordain this to be my last will and testament. *Principally and fiirst* I recommend my soul to Almight God that gave it me and my body to the earth to be decently buried at the discretion of my executors hereinafter mentioned.

Item. I give and bequeath to my well beloved wife the use of the plantation whereon I now live during her life time, the use of my negroes, stock of cattle and hogs, household goods and all the rest of my movable estate during her widowhood and at the time of her marriage or death, then I give the estate in the manner and form following.

Item. I give and bequeath unto my son Henry Hill the plantation whereon I now live and Two hundred acres of land joining to the said plantation, a large *silver Baker*, a large brass kettle and all *my carpenters tools* after the death or marriage of his mother to him the said Henry Hill and his heirs forever, also a negro called Millie.

Item. I give and bequesth unto my son Abraham Hill the plantation whereon he now lives, containing about two hundred acres, to him and his heirs forever, also a negro fellow called David and a *Silver Baker* and all *my coopers tools* and a copper kettle, after the marriage or death of his mother.

Item. I give and bequeath unto my son Isaac Hill a negro woman called Bett, a feather bed and furniture, one *silver cup* and one large Iron kettle after the marriage or death of his mother, to him and his heirs forever.

Item. I give and bequeath unto my son Theophilus Hill the land and plantation I bought of Daniel Pugh containing two hundred acres to him and his heirs forever, also a negro man called Demsa, a negro boy called Peter, a negro boy called Charles, one feather bed and furniture, one *silver cup*, two *silver spoons*, one large Iron pott, Twenty five pounds of the best Peuter, one small Iron pott, one Iron Grey mare, after my wife's marriage or death, to him and his heirs forever. Also I give him all my land at the point to him and his heirs forever. I give and bequeath to *my two sons Henry* and *Abraham* all my land in the piney woods to be equally divided, to them and their heirs forever.

I give my spoon moulds to my four sons to be equally divided between them.

I give and bequeath to my grand-daughter Leah Hunter one small gilt trunk and one three year old heifer after the marriage of her grand-mother or death.

I give and bequeath to *my daughter* Sarah Hunter a negro girl called Hannah, to her and her heirs forever.

I give and bequeath to my daughter Mary Easton a negro girl called Nanny, to her and her heirs forever.

If any of my children should quarrel or differ about this my last will and testament then it is my desire that they shall be cut out of any part of my estate, only what the law allows.

Lastly. I nominate and appoint my well beloved wife Judith Hill and my son Henry Hill my whole and sole executors of this my last will and testament and my well beloved friend Marmaduke Norfleet to be my trustee to this my will fulfilled in Witness Whereof I have hereunto set my hand and seal, this 17th day of April 1760.

his
Abraham X Hill
mark

Signed, sealed and acknowledged as his last will and testament in presence of
    Shergriss Ederingame
    William Hinton
       his
    Clary X Blanchard.
       mark

North Carolina, Chowan County, I, F. W. Hobbs, Clerk Superior Court for and in above named State and County, hereby certify the foregoing sheet to contain a full, true and correct copy of the will of Abraham Hill, as same appears of record in this office, in Will Book "A" at pages 53 and 54. In testimony whereof, I hereunto put my hand and affix the seal of this office, at Edenton, N. C., this April 24th, 1913.

F. W. Hobbs,
Clerk Superior Court".

Query.—May not Judith Hill have been *Judah Hinton*, daughter of John and Mary Hinton, of Chowan County, named in John Hinton's will, June 27, 1730; Oct. , 1732?

1716. Nicholas Stallings to *John Hinton*, 126 A. south side Bennett's Creek; April 17, 1716. Test.: *Henry Hill*, John Gordon. (Reg. Vol. 1, No. 2, p. 292).

1717. Richard Berryman to John Rus (Bass?), 100 A. bought of Thos. Garrett, Sr., July 16, 1717. Test: Daniel Halsey, *Henry Hill*.

1720. To *Abraham Hill*, of Nansemond County, Va., from Richard Benfield, *Aug. 5, 1720*, 500 A. in Perquimons Precinct. (Book W, No. 1, p. 597; Reg. 2-3-473).

1726. Edward Bass and wife, Love, of Bertie County, to Jos. Riddick, of Nansemond County, Va., 100 A. on Horse Pen Swamp, adjoining land of *Abraham Hill*, March 28, 1726. Test: John Rice, Joseph Petilloe. (Reg. 2-3-446).

1728. Wm. Jones, of Perquimons, to Sarah Bond, 100 A. part of 550 A., bounded (bonded) by said Jones to *Abraham Hill*, Nov. 8, 1728. Test.: Robt. Hicks, Ellinor Jackson. (Reg. 2-3-444).

1728. Wm. Jones, of Perquimons, to *Orlando Champion*, 50 A. adjg. land of *Widow Bond* and Chas. Jordan, Dec. 15, 1728.

1728. Wm. Jones to *Thos. Walton*, 50 A. adjg. *Orlando Champion's land*. (Reg. 2-3-447; Reg. 2-3-444).

1740. *Abraham Hill* to Samuel Harrell, *Feby. 7, 1740-'1*, 100 A. of land taken up and *in the possession of his father, Henry Hill*. (Book C, No. 2, p. 120; Reg. 2-3-475). It does not mean that his father Henry was alive in 1740-'1, but simply that during his life time he was in possession of the land.

1740. *Abraham Hill*, of Chowan, from *Jno. Perry*, of Bertie, July 26, 1740, 100 A. of land patented by *Edward Homes* and *John Rice*, of Nansemond County, Va., 1695. (Book C, No. 2, p. 122; Reg. 2-3-473).

1743. *Abraham Hill*, of Chowan County, N. C., to Richard Briggs, July 19, 1743, 150 A. lying on *Bass' Marsh*, being part of a tract granted by (to?) *my father Henry Hill*. (Book A, No. 1, p. 251; Reg. 2-3-475).

1743. *Abraham Hill* to John Rice, July 18, 1743, 100 A. lying near the *Great Marsh* part of *above patent*. (Book A, No. 1, p. 262; Reg. 2-3-475).

1745. *Abraham Hill* to John Jones, Jany. 12, 1745-6, 200 A. on the *Horse Pool Pocosin*. (Book B, No. 1, p. 64; Reg. 2-3-475).

1745. *Abraham Hill* to James Phelps, Jany. 14, 1745, 100 A. lying in Hickory Neck, bought by said *Hill's father, Henry Hill*. (Book E, No. 1, p. 66; Reg. 2-3-475).

1757. *Abraham Hill*, Sr., from Daniel Pugh, March 25, 1757. Part of a tract of land patented by his grandfather, April 26, 1698, 50 A. on *Cypress Swamp*, in Chowan County. (Book H, No. 1, p. 106; Reg. 2-3-473).

The *Henry Hill* named in the following records *may possibly* have been *the son of Henry Hill* and born after his removal to North Carolina, possibly 1708 or 1710, but I *don't think he was.*

1733. Thos. Hoyter King of the Chowan Indians, Jemiah Pushing, Charles Beaseley, James Bennett, Chief men of the tribe, to *Henry Hill*, 50 A. on Bennett's Creek, *Aug. 4, 1733*. Test: John Freemax, Michael Word, Wm. Flemmons. (Gates) (Reg. 1-1-106).

1733. To *Henry Hill*, of North Carolina, from Chowan Indians, Aug. 4, 1733, 50 A. on *Bennett's Creek Swamp*. (Book W, No. 1, p. 216; Reg. 2-3-473).

1734. *Same* (as above) to James Brown, 100 A. adjoining *Rountree* and *Hill's* land, Jany. 27, 1734. Test.: Richd. Minchew, Michael Ward, *Benjamin Blanchard*. (Reg. 1-1-114).

1734. *Same* (as above) to *James Hinton*, 100 A. adjg. land of Lasseter and Wm. Hill; Nov. 22, 1734. Test.: *Henry Hill*, Thomas Morris. (Reg. 1-1-114).

1734. *Same* (as above) to *Jacob Hinton*, 50 A. head of Juniper *Swamp*, and up Mirey Branch; Nov. 22, 1734. Test.: *Henry Hill, Wm.* Hill, Wm. Trevathon. (Reg. 1-1-114).

1742. *Henry Hill*, 640 A., Chowan County, 7th May, 1742. (C. R. N. C., Vol. IV, p. 619).

1742. *Henry Hill*, of Chowan County, from Chowan Indians, Mar. 22, 1742, 300 A. on Bennett's Creek Swamp. (Book A, No. 1, p. 173; Reg. 2-3-473).

1744. *Henry Hill* from Chowan Indians, June 19, 1744, 640 A. beginning at the lower end of the old Indian town, thence to Bennett's Creek Swamp. (Book E, No. 1, p. 62; Reg. 2-3-473).

1747. *Henry Hill* to *Thomas Walton*, Feby. 20, 1747, 142 A. with the *Islands on Catharine Creek*. (Book E, No. 1, p. 293; Reg. 2-3-475).

1747. *Wm. Hill* from *Henry Hill* and Chowan Indians, Sept. 19, 1747, 150 A. on Mirey and Gabriel branches. (Book F, No. 1, p. 224; Reg. 2-3-475).

1743. Henry Hill, James Hinton, Gabriel Lassiter. Petition as to having purchased land from Chowan Indians, *25 March, 1743* (date of petition). (C. R. N. C., Vol. IV, pp. 630-1).

1744. The Indians acknowledged to the Assembly, Dec. 4, 1744, that they had received from *Henry Hill* purchase money in full for 640 A. and it was ordered that deed be made to said *Henry Hill* accordingly. (C. R. N. C., Vol. IV, p. 417).

1746. Petition by James Bennett, a Chowan Indian, against *Henry Hill* as to land, March 14, 1746. (C. R. N. C., Vol. IV, p. 802).

Henry Hill, it appears, had several deals with the Indians.

Juda Hill married in Chowan, Feby. 14, 1765, Nehemiah Bunch, Surety, Micajah Bunch. (N. C. H. & G. Reg., Vol. 1, p. 241). Whether she was maid or widow, not indicated as here published. She could hardly have been the widow of Abraham Hill[2], deceased. Moses Hill, of Bertie, in 1762 names his youngest daughter, Judith Hill, as one of his executors, (therefore of marriageable age). (N. C. H. & G. Reg., 2-3-339).

P.—ABRAHAM HILL[2] and his wife, Judith, had issue:

A.—Henry Hill,[3] born, circa, 1730; died in Wilkes County, Ga., in 1804; B.—Abraham Hill,[3] born, circa 1732; died in Wilkes County, Ga., 4 Feby. 1792; C.—Isaac Hill[3] born, pro. circa 1734; D.—Theophilus Hill[3]; E.—Sarah Hill[3], married Jacob Hunter and had daughter, Leah Hunter, who married Seth Riddick; F.—Mary Hill[3] married ...... Easton, N. R.

A.—*Henry Hill³* (Abraham², Henry¹), 1730-1804; married Sarah Cotten—date not learned—her will dated 13 Nov., 1812; probated 3 May, 1814, in Wilkes County, Ga.

He was a member of Capt. John Summer's Company of Col. Robert Burden's Regiment of North Carolina Militia, so reported Nov. 25, 1754, time of French and Indian War (S. R. N. C., Vol. XXII, p. 355); removed, circa 1769, to that part of Johnston, now Wake County, N. C., thence in 1787 to Wilkes County, Ga., where he received a grant for 200 acres of land on Dec. 31, 1787.

State of Georgia. By the Hon. Geo. Mathews, Esq., Capt. Gen¹, Govr and Commander in Chief &c. Know ye That in pursuance of the Act for opening the Land Office &c., In the Name and Behalf of the said State Do give and grant unto HENRY HILL, SR., his heirs and assigns &c Two hundred acres situate lying and being in the County of Wilkes butting and bounding on all sides by vacant property as appears by a plat of the same hereto annexed, 31 Dec. 1787.

Signed by the Govr in Council.
Registered 3 Jany. 1788 ⎰ J. Meriwether C. C.
(Land Grant Book P. P. P., p. 117, at State Capitol.)

In Johnston County, N. C., we find the following records, viz.:

Aug. 28, 1764, Timothy Rich of Johnston Co., N. C., sells to Henry Hill of sd. Co. 540 A. lying on both sides of Neuse river for 200 £ Proc. money,—land touching John Hinton's line. Wit: Theophilus Hunter, Josiah Hunter. (Deed Book E. 1, p.—omitted in copy).

Aug. 12, 1669, Richard Weatherdon to Henry Hill, both of Johnston County, 200 A. on North side Neuse river for 60 £, Book L. 1, p. (old No. 4, new No. 177). It is not certain that this Henry Hill was the Henry Hill³ of Chowan County, but it is probable as Abraham Hill³ bought lands here about this time, as will be shown later.

Wilkes County, March 15, 1804. Theophilus Hill gave bond in the sum of $2000.00 as *administrator of the Estate of Henry Hill, Senior.* Securities were: Augustine Edwards and Frances McLendon. Recorded Aug. 21, 1805, at Washington, Ga. Attest: Davied Terrell, C. C. O. (Book YY, 1800-1819, p. 55).

Will of SARAH (COTTEN) HILL. In the name of God, Amen. I *Sarah Hill* of the State of Georgia and County of Wilkes well knowing it is once appointed all to die, being weak in body but sound in memory hath constituted this my last Will and Testament as touching my worldly matters, as to my Soul I recommend & give it unto him that created me, hoping for his loving mercy, as to my burial I leave to the discretion of Sons John and Abram Hill, which I hope will be plain and decent without pomp or state.

Item.—It is my will and positive desire that all my just debts be justly paid.

Item.—It is my desire for my Negro Girl Eliza to be sold and give twelve months credit, out of the said money arising from said sale to be paid unto my dearly beloved son John Hill two hundred and twenty dollars, also one large Bay Mare called Locket, one blue chest, also one young bay mare to his son James Henry Hill.

Item.—I give and bequeath to my dearly beloved son Abram Hill one negro woman called Dinah, two bay horses, also all my stock of every kind and my plantation also *one still* with all the appurtenances thereto also all the present crop of every kind, also one yoke of steers, also two new blankets and five sheets too.

Item.—I give and bequeath unto my son Theophilus Hill deceased   children the balance of the money arising from the sale of Eliza be it what it may, to be equally divided to them & given as they may come of age or marries, one feather bed, one new blanket, two sheets, a bolster & two pillows to his daughter Elizabeth Hill one bay filly to his son Granberry Hill.

Item. I give and bequeath unto my dearly beloved daughter *Nancy*, one safe and an arm chair. I give unto her daughter Sarah one good trunk.

Item. I give and bequeath unto my dearly beloved daughter Mary Jossey an equal part of all my clothes as hereinafter nominated, also I give unto her son Henry Jossey beaufolt (?), also one new bed quilt to Keddy Jossey.

Item. I give and bequeath to my dearly beloved son Henry Hill twenty shillings cash.

Item. I give and bequeath to Sarah Wood, John Hill, Abram Hill, Keddy Pope, Mary Jossey, Nancy Johnson equally all the residue of my bedding of every description & my wearing apparel also all the crockery and the balance of my household furniture I give unto my son Abram Hill.

Item. I give unto my son Abram Hill all the debts due me of every description, out of which he is to pay all my debts.

Item. I do constitute and appoint my two sons John and Abram Hill my lawful Executors of this my last Will & Testament, revoking all others that I have heretofore made, as witness my hand and seal this thirteenth day of November one thousand eight hundred and twelve and in the thirty seventh year of the Independence of the United States of America.

Sarah Hill (L. S.)

Signed, sealed and acknowledged in the presence of us
Jacob G. Matthews
Nathaniel Bailey
A. Edwards

Georgia
Wilkes County.

Personally in open Court Nathaniel Bailey and Augustine Edwards two of the subscribing witnesses to the within will, and being duly sworn deposeth and saith that they saw the within named Sarah Hill, sign, seal, publish, & declare the within instrument of writing to be her last will & testament and that at the time of her so doing she was of sound mind and memory and that Jacob Matthews subscribed his name as a concurring evidence to the same, in the presence of the Testator and in the presence of each other.

Sworn to in open court this 3rd May, 1814.
Nathaniel Bailey.
A. Edwards.

D. Terrell Clk.

Recorded the 11th of July, 1822.

A.—Henry Hill[3] and wife, Sarah Cotten, had (order of births not known):
  I.—John Hill[4], born in North Carolina; died in Meriwether County, Ga.
  II. Abram Hill[4], born in North Carolina, 4 Sept. 1778; died 4 Oct. 1852.
  III. Theophilus Hill[4], born in North Carolina, circa 1765; died between 1805 and 1812.
  IV. Nancy Hill[4], born pro. circa 1770; died in 1739.
  V. Mary Hill[4], born 17 Sept. 1758; died 17 Feby. 1831, in Tennessee.
  VI. Henry Hill[4], born pro. circa 1780.
  VII. Sarah Hill[4].
  VIII. Catharine, called "Keddy" Hill.

I.—JOHN HILL[4] (Henry[3], Abraham[2], Henry[1]), born, pro. circa 1776, or earlier; married Bettie Edwards. (See E. S. of Ala., p. 417), and had:
  1. James Henry[5], called "Jim", Hill, who married Carrie (?) . . . . . . , and died s. p. in the 70's in Albany, Ga.
  2. Caroline Hill[5], married William Hudspeth, 2nd wife, born, in 1802, in Wilkes County, Ga., and had a daughter, Julia T. Hudspeth, who married Columbus Brooks, of Albany, Ga. (Memoirs of Ga., Vol. 1, pp. 253-4).

II. Abram Hill[4] (Henry[3], Abraham[2], Henry[1]), 1778-1852; married, 4 Dec., 1806, in Wilkes County, Ga., Clarissa Calloway, born 5 Jany. 1790; died 26 Dec., 1855; daughter of Joseph Calloway (son of Job and Mary Calloway) and his wife, Nancy Ragan, daughter of Jonathan Ragan, Sr.

Georgia, Wilkes County. Will of Job Calloway. In the name of God Amen: I Job Calloway of the County and State aforesaid being in sound mind and memory do hereby make this my last Will and Testament, revoking and disannulling all others made by me heretofore.

First: I give my beloved wife May Calloway, during her natural life my negro man named Will, and his wife Lucy; my negro man

Sam and his wife Dinah; my negro man Gabe; my negro man Solomon, my negro woman named Crease, my negro woman Big Doll, my negro woman Abby, my negro boy Fed, my boy Herson and my negro boy Bill, one third of my sheep cattle and Hogs and one third of my household and Kitchen Furniture, and one third of my plantation tools and her choice of one of my Horses or Mares I may die possessed of. Likewise my dwelling house and all other houses on the Plantation I live on with one third of the Plantation and orchard.

Secondly: I give and bequeath to my son Jacob Calloway the Plantation and Tract of Land whereon he now liveth containing five hundred and fifty eight acres agreeable to a plat and survey made by Sanders Walker and which is annexed to this my Will with the negroes Jack, Talbot, Carot and her child Henry to him his heirs and assigns. Likewise my negro man named Solomon after my wife's death to him his heirs and assigns.

Thirdly: I give and bequeath to my son *Joseph Calloway* all that tract or parcel of land whereon he now liveth containing five hundred and forty five acres agreeable to a plat and survey made by Sanders Walker and annexed to this my Will the negros Mack, Darr, Spencer and Rachel. Likewise my negro man Gabriel after my wife's death to him and his heirs and assigns for life.

Fourthly: I give and bequeath to my son Job Calloway all that tract or parcel of land on which he now liveth containing six hundred and fourteen acres agreeable to a plat and survey made by Sanders Walker and annexed with this my Will, with the negros Sam, Charity, Lilly and her child Mintah and after my wife's death my negro boy Bill, to him his heirs and assigns forever.

Fifthly: I give and bequeath to my son Joshua Calloway all that tract or parcel of land on which he now liveth containing six hundred and sixty six acres agreeable to a plat and survey made by Sanders Walker and annexed to this my Will with the negros Maks, Nelson, Beck and Tom and after my wife's death my negro boy Fred to him his heirs and assigns.

Sixthly: I give and bequeath to my son Isaac Calloway two thirds of the tract or parcel of land on which I now live and on the death of *my wife Mary Calloway* the remaining third, the whole tract containing five hundred and ninety four acres agreeable to a plat and survey made by Sanders Walker and annexed to this my will. Also two hundred acres of land granted to John White and purchased him by Sanders Walker and purchased by me of Sanders Walker adjoining my home tract with my *two bigest stills* and the corks and implements thereunto belonging with the negros Mike, Sealy, Harvey and Ms (?) and after my wife's death my negro man named Sam to him his heirs and assigns.

Seventhly: My will is that if *my wife Mary Calloway* and my son Isaac Calloway cannot agree to a division of the land agreeable to the intent of this my will that my executors my *son Joseph Calloway* and Job Calloway shall make such division which shall be binding on the parties.

Eighthly: I give and bequeath to my daughter Eunice Griffin five negroes, a negro woman named Luce and her child named Lewis, Stephen, Patience and Milly, and after the death of my wife my negro woman known by the name of Big Doll to her heirs and assigns.

Ninthly: I do make over and bequeath in Trust to my son *Joseph* and *Job* Calloway all that tract or parcel of land containing two hundred acres which I purchased of Isaac Miligan and on which Wm. Parks now liveth to be by them disposed of in the following manner, vis.: The use, profits and emoluments thereof to be applied towards and for the maintenance of my *daughter Mary Parks* and her children during her natural life and at their option to live on and keep possession of said land during her natural lifetime. But she is by no means, nor shall any person claiming said land sell or lease in virtue of her life estate thereto but by the consent and advice of said trustees above named first have under their hands in writing with the negro woman called Little-Doll, Joseph and Nancy Crete and Cato and after the death of my wife my negro woman named Luce and at the decease of my daughter Mary Parks I do bequeath the above named land and negros which I give to the lawful heirs of my said daughter Mary Parks that is her children born of her body and come to lawful age and if she should leave no children that may arrive to lawful age, then said land and negroes to be sold and the amount of such sale to be equally divided amongst my remaining children and descendants.

Tenthly: To the residue and remainder of all and every kind of my estate, it is my will that after my debts are paid, my executors call on three or more reasonable house holders of their neighborhood who shall according to their skill and judgment appraise and value all such remaining property not divided which property so appraised and valued shall be divided in seven lots. If such division can be made anywise practicable after which the lots to by Seniority by my children and the lots that fall to the heirs of my daughter Mary Parks is to be put into the hands of my executors in trust to be managed to the best advantage to be disposed of in the same manner as the land and negroes for the support of my said Daughter Mary Parks during her life and at her decease to go to her heirs coming to lawful age.

Eleventhly: This my Will, is that all that property divided to my wife during her life, be at her death be appraised in the same manner as that property ordered to be appraised at my death and that it be divided and disposed of in the same manner. This is one seventh to my son *Joseph*, one seventh to my son Job, one seventh to my son Joshua, one seventh to my son Isaac, one seventh to my daughter Mary Parks to be managed as above mentioned.

Twelfthly: And it is my further will desire that if any doubts or misunderstandings arise in the construction or intention of this my will, that the parties doubting or disagreeing shall choose two men of judgment which two men shall choose a third, a majority which three shall divide on the premises, which division so made and subscribed under their hands and seals of said arbitrators, shall be as binding as if done in any court of justice and for the carrying into effect of this my last will and testament I do appoint my beloved wife Mary Calloway executor and my sons Joseph Calloway and Job Calloway executors. In witness whereof I have hereunto set my hand and affixed my seal this 10th day of Feby. 1803.

          Job Calloway (Seal).

Signed and sealed in presence of:

              his
Thos. McLaughlin, Johnson Wellborn, Adam X Lovin.
              mark

Personally appeared in open court Thos. McLaughlin, Johnson Wellborn and Adam Lovin the subscribing witnesses to the within will and being duly sworn, saith that they saw Job Calloway sign, seal, publish and declare the within testament of writing, to be his last will and testament and at the time of his so doing he was of sound and disposing mind and memory and that *Wm. Wilborn* and *John Lovin* heard him acknowledge same to be his last will.
Sworn in open Court this Mar. 5th, 1804.
    Da. Terrell, C. C. Ord.

          Thos. McLaughlin.
          Johnson Wellborn.
          his
         Adam X Lovin.
          mark

Georgia, Wilkes County. This is to certify that the above and foregoing is a true & correct copy from the records of Ordinary's Office, Will Book G.G., pp. 81-'2-'3-'4-'5-'6-'7-'8. Copied by Mrs. J. F. Lindsey.

Will of Jonathan Ragan, Sr.

Georgia, Oglethorpe County. In the Name of God Amen: I, Jonathan Ragan, of the State of Georgia and County of Oglethorpe, being of sound and disposing mind and memory and knowing that I must shortly depart this life, do make and ordain this my last will and testament in manner and form following, (viz.).

Item 1st. I give to my daughter, Polly Phillips, five dollars also I lend her my negro girl, Creasey, now in her possession during her natural life and at her death I give the aforesaid negro girl and her increase to my two granddaughters, say Nany & Cynthia Phillips to them and their heirs forever.

Item 2nd. I give to my son, Nathaniel Ragan, Ten Dollars.

Item 3rd. I give to my son, John Ragan, one feather bed and furniture.

Item 4th. I give to my daughter, Nany Calloway, one negro girl, Zenah, now in her possession also Ten Dollars which she is to receive at my death.

Item 5th. I give to my daughter, Rebecca Calloway, one negro girl, now in her possession also Ten Dollars which she is to receive at my death.

Item 6th. I give to my daughter, *Winney Calloway*, one negro girl, Hannah, now in her possession also Ten dollars which she is to receive at my death.

Item 7th. I give to my daughter, Abi Haynes, two negroes now in her possession named Patience and Celea to her and her heirs forever.

Item 8th. I give to my daughter, *Elizabeth Lumpkin*, one negro girl, Cheney, now in her possession, also Ten dollars which she is to receive at my death.

Item 9th. I give to my son, Asa Ragan, Seven Hundred and Fifty Dollars, which he has received as a part of his coto of my estate.

Item 10th. I give to my son, Jonathan Ragan, Six Hundred dollars, which he has received as a part of his coto of my estate.

Item 11th. I give to my son, David Ragan, Two Hundred dollars which he has received in a negro boy as a part of his coto of my estate.

Item 12th. I give to my son, Jehu Ragan, my negro man, Jack, which is to be appraised to him at my death as a part of his coto of my estate.

Item 13th. I give to my six youngest sons, namely, Asa, Jonathan, David, Jeremiah, Marcus B. and John Ragan, all the balance of my personal estate, including my nineteen negros Tobe, Cupit, Hal, Lewis, Lotte, Melle, Jordan, Delpha, Mosses, Mary, Silvah, Rhoda, Jared, Sinah, Judah, Hartwell, Sopha, Greenville, Vinah and their increases, together with my stock, household furniture and plantation tools, all of the above named property to be sold and after paying all demands against said estate, be so divided as to form an equal division between my six last named children, including the several sums before mentioned that they have received and are to receive to them and their heirs forever.

Item 14th. I give to my two sons, Marcus B. and John Ragan, all that tract of land whereon I now live (containing five hundred and fourteen acres) to be enjoyed in union, or sold and the amount of the sale equally divided between them as they or my executors think proper also the crop that has been last made or is making on the plantation at my death, to them and their heirs forever.

Item 15th. Lastly do make and ordain and appoint Jonathan Ragan and Thomas Rhodes my true and lawful executors to execute this my last will and testament made.

In testimony whereof I have hereunto set my hand and affixed my seal, April 6th, 1813.

his
Jonathan X Ragan, Sen. (Seal)
mark

Attest. Jas Rhodes
   Wm. Adams
   Ruth Rhodes

Probate of Will.

You, Richard Rhodes and William Adams, do solemnly swear that you saw the within named Jonathan Ragan, deceased, sign, seal, publish and declare the within instrument of writing to be his last will and testament and at the time of his so doing he was of sound mind and memory to the best of your knowledge and belief. So help you God.

      Wm. Adams
      Rich'd Rhodes, Sen.
      Jas. Rhodes by interrogatories.

Sworn to and subscribed before me in open Court by two of the witnesses and the other by interrogatories and ordered to be recorded. March Term, 1814.

      Mathew Ramey, C. C. O.

The following is an extract from letter written by Mrs. Eliza (Calloway, Wootten-Maxwell) Arnold, of Wilkes County, Ga., Sept. 11, 1870, to her nephew, Dr. Henry Willis Hill, of Mooresville, Ala.: "My father had 5 brothers and 2 sisters. The brothers were: Jacob, James (?), Joshua, Job, Isaac, Joseph. The sisters were Eunice Griffin and Polly Parks. . . . .

    (Signed) Your affectionate Aunt,
          Eliza Arnold."

II.—*Abram Hill*[4] and wife, *Clarissa Calloway*, had:
1. Josiah Woods Hill[5], born 2 Jany., 1808; died 12 Jany. 1863 in Mississippi (q. v.).
2. John Middleton Hill[5], born 4 May, 1810; died 25 May, 1875 (q. v.).
3. Sarah Ann Hill[5], born 18 Nov., 1812; died 26 Nov., 1862 (q. v.).
4. Albert Gallatin Hill[5], born 11 Sept., 1815; died 7 Sept. 1848 (q. v.).
5. William Granville Hill[5], born 20 Feby. 1818; died 17 Oct. 1892 (q. v.).
6. Abraham Marshall Hill[5], born 29 Nov., 1820; died 11 Dec. 1853 (q. v.).
7. Eli Hill[5], born 3 July, 1821; died 28 Nov. 1852 (q. v.).
8. Henry Willis Hill, born 9 Jany., 1827; died 2 Feby., 1904 (q. v.).

1. Josiah Woods Hill[5], 1808-1863, married 22 Sept., 1831, Sarah McGehee, 1st husband, daughter of Samuel (brother of Micajah McGehee) and Nancy (Tate) McGehee, of Meriwether County, Ga. Removed in 1843 to Mississippi. Issue:

1a. Madison Hill[6], died in infancy; 2a. Eliza Hill[6], born in Meriwether County, died at 8 years of age; 3a. Martha Hill[6], born in Georgia, died in her 13th year; 4a. William Hill[6], born in Georgia, married a Miss Moore and moved to Paris, Tenn.; 5a. Woods Hill[6], died at age of 6 or 7 years.

Mrs. Sarah (McGehee) Hill married (II) a Mr. Sheets, no issue; married (III) Myron Ellis, of Meriwether County, Ga., third wife, no issue. She was living in 1882, died later in Newnan, Ga., where she is buried.

2. John Middleton Hill[5] (Abram[4], Henry[3], Abraham[2], Henry[1]), 1810-1875, married (I) 10 July, 1834, Elizabeth Holland; married (II) 14 Nov. 1848, Mary E. Teasley. Issue, first marriage:

1a. Emily Hill[6], married Thomas Bussey, who served in Confederate States Army (q. v.); 2a: Abram Hill[6], never married, was mentally weak, and in 1882 was living with his brother-in-law, Tom Bussey, near Vaiden, Miss.

Issue by second marriage:
3a. Clara Hill[6], was still living in 1882; 4a: William Hill[6], married Miss Downer; 5a: Henry Willis Hill[6], married Miss McEachern; 6a: Ada Hill[6], and 7a, Ida Hill[6], twins. The last was very slim and six feet two inches tall, living in 1882, single.

1a. Thomas Bussey and wife, Emily Hill[6], lived at Vaiden, Miss., and had:

1b. Charlie Bussey[7], married ......; 2b: Ben Bussey[7], married ......; 3b: Tom Bussey, Jr.[7], single; 4b: Mattie Bussey[7], married Walter McBride; 5b: Bettie Bussey[7], married George Downer, cousin of the wife of her uncle, William Hill.

3. Sarah Ann Hill[5] (Abram[4]), 1812-1862, married 24 Sept. 1829, Judge Abner Reeves, born Feby., 1805; died 14 Oct., 1857. Issue:

1a. Andrew Jackson Reeves[6], served in Company A, 30th Miss. Regiment, C. S. A.; lived near Blackhawk, Carroll County, Miss.; married ......, and had several children.

2a. Lizzie Reeves[6], married Cal. J. Coleman, first wife, who served in C. S. A.

3a. Amelia Reeves[6], called "Mitt", married Cal. J. Coleman, second wife, and had: 1b: Hattie Coleman[7], married John Downer, brother of William Hill's wife; 2b: Ab Coleman[7]; 3b: Lizzie Coleman[7].

4a. Abner T. Reeves[6], married ......, and had several children. He interfered in a fight between a man and his wife and was killed by the former.

5a. Albert Gallatin Reeves[6], called "Gee", married ......, and lived at Vaiden. Had several children.

6a. Martha Reeves[6], called "Mattie", lives near Blackhawk; married ..... Vandiver; had several children, of whom two were living in 1882.

4. Albert Gallatin Hill[5] (Abram[4]), 1815-1848; married 9 July, 1835, Martha E. Render, died 4 April, 1880. Issue:

1a. Sarah Frances Hill[6], born 7 Oct., 1836; died 4 July, 1858.

2a. Nancy Victoria Hill[6], born 8 June, 1838; died in 1920 in LaGrange, Ga. (q. v.).

3a. Mary Agnes Hill[6], born 4 April, 1840.

4a. Carolyn Eugenia[6], called "Tallie", Hill, born 6 Jany., 1842, unmarried, living in LaGrange, Ga., in 1916.

5a. Martha Wellborn Hill[6], born 14 Dec., 1844; was living in LaGrange, Ga., in 1880. (Letter to her uncle, Dr. H. W. Hill, 6 July, 1880).

6a. Abram Christopher Hill[6], born 16 Nov., 1846. N. R.

7a. Albert Gallatin Hill, Jr.[6], born 30 March, 1849; living in 1880.

2a. Nancy Victoria Hill[6] (Albert Gallatin[5]; Abram[4]), 1838-1920; married 21 May, 1857, Jesse Mercer Calloway (his second wife), son of Rev. William A. Calloway (son of Isaac Calloway and his wife, Polly Barrett—Mrs. Mary Toombs ?) and his wife Martha Pope, daughter of John and Elizabeth (Smith) Pope; died in 1907. (Jesse Mercer Calloway married (1) 26 Feby. 1852, Elizabeth S. Huling, and had: Elvira Pope Calloway, died in infancy; Andrew W. Calloway, who reared a large family). Issue:

1b. Sarah Frances Hill Calloway[7], lived, in 1916, in Atlanta, Ga.; married Nov., 1879, W. E. Oslin, of Atlanta, Ga.

2b. Martha Elizabeth Hill Calloway[7], married T. J. Stovall, of Atlanta, Ga.

3b. George Wiley Hill Calloway[7], married Bessie Harris, of Tuskeegee, Ala.

4b. Ella Pope Hill Calloway[7].

5b. Thomas Merrill Hill Calloway[7], a preacher, living, 1916, at Dawson, Ga.

6b. Albert Gallatin Hill Calloway[7].

7b. Jesse Mercer Hill Calloway[7].

8b. Julia W. Hill Calloway[7], married C. D. Brady, of Newark, N. J.; living in 1916.

9b. Mary Joe Hill Calloway[7], died at four years of age, the first death in the family. Then followed, in order, Ella Pope, Jesse Mercer, Albert G., George, and then Martha—Mrs. Stovall—then the father, Jesse Mercer Calloway, in 1907. The above records supplied by Mrs. Jesse Mercer Calloway. The lines have not been traced.

5. William Granville Hill[5] (Abram[4]), 1818-1892, married, 25 Nov., 1847, Hepzibah E. Wellborn, daughter of Col. Abner Well-

born and his wife, Martha Render, and sister of Martha Strother Wellborn, second wife of Col. Lodowick Meriwether Hill, and Susan Wellborn, who married Dr. Andrew B. Calhoun, of Newnan, Ga. Issue:

1a. Mattie Hill[6], graduate of College Temple, Newnan, Ga., married Montgomery, called "Doc", Thomas, of Newnan, and has a daughter who married and lives at Union Springs, Ala.

2a. Susie Hill[6], educated at College Temple, married W. Ben Orr, of Newnan, Ga., a widower. She died there.

3a. Abner Wellborn Hill[6], known among the kin as "Aunt Heppie's Wellborn". Died in middle age, unmarried.

4a. Lizzie Hill[6], married W. Ben Orr, deceased, third wife. No issue.

5a. Willie Hill[6], married ...... McClasham, of Meriwether County, Ga.

6. Abram Marshall Hill[5] (Abram[4]), 1820-1853, married 31 Oct. 1849, Lucinda Ann Lipscomb, 1st husband, born 28 Jany., 1826 (died in Arkansas after 1882). Issue:

1a. Emma Hill[6], married Mr. Matthews, of Arkansas, and had:

1b. Willie Matthews[7]; 2b. Clyde Matthews[7]; 3b. Bennie Matthews[7].

2a. Willie Hill[6] died at age of eight years with typhoid fever.

Mrs. L. A. (Lipscomb) Hill married (II) Mr. Hilliary Talbert, a widower with son Tom Talbert, and had:

3a. Abram Talbert[6], married ...... (?); 4a: Mattie Talbert[6], married William Hayden, and in 1882 they had one child; 5a. Hattie Talbert[6], married ...... Neeley, in Feby., 1882.

Mrs. L. A. (Lipscomb Hill) Talbert was the daughter of Baker Lipscomb and Almeda (Calloway) Pope, widow of Josiah Woods Pope[5].

7. Eli Hill[5] (Abram[4]), 1821-1852, married 28 Sept., 1852, or 1851, Miss Mary Ann Jones, removed to Mississippi, and d. s. p.

8. *Henry Willis Hill*[5], M.D., (Abram[4], Henry[3]), 1827-1904,"was a prominent physician of Mooresville, Limestone County, Ala., was reared in Georgia and received a good education at Brownwood School. at LaGrange, and when he had passed through this school his father removed to Mississippi. In 1846 he began the study of medicine with Dr. A. B. Calhoun, of Newnan, Ga., as preceptor, and in the same year entered the South Carolina Medical College at Charleston, remaining through 1846-'47, and in the spring of 1847 entered the University of the City of New York and graduated in medicine in 1848. He first located for practice at Blackhawk, Miss., and remained in Mississippi, but at diffierent points, until the outbreak of the Civil War. In 1862 he enlisted, was with General Chalmers, and served on his staff about six months, when he was taken sick and returned home, where he remained eight months, and then returned to the Army as a Surgeon of Col. Fish-

er's Regiment, with which he served until the close of the war. He was a member of the Masonic order, of the Council degree, Royal and Select Master (?)." While his home was at Mooresville, Ala., he died at the home of his son, then living at Rome, Ga., and was buried at Newnan, Ga.

He married (I), 12 July, 1849, Mary E. Lipscomb, born in Georgia, 10 Jany., 1833, daughter of Baker Lipscomb and his wife, Almeda (Calloway) Pope, widow of Josiah Woods Pope and sister of Dr. Hill's mother, Clarissa (Calloway) Hill. No issue. Married (II), 22 March, 1855, Ann Temperance Hall, born in Mississippi, 16 June, 1835; died 25 Oct., 1857, daughter of Dr. James Gattling Hall and his wife, Elizabeth S. Wood (both died 1878); granddaughter of Spencer Hall, Jr., and his wife, Polly Gatling, and of William Wood and his wife, Ann Granberry; great-granddaughter of Spencer Hall, Sr., and his wife, Director Hall, of James Wood, of James Gatling and his wife, Mary Riddick, and of Josiah Granberry and his wife, Ann Gregory, daughter of James Gregory and his wife, *Patience Godwin*, daughter of Thomas Godwin[3] (and wife Mary), son of *Col. Thomas Godwin*[2] and his wife, *Hester Bridger*, who was the daughter of *Col. Joseph Bridger* and his wife, *Hester Pitt*, daughter of *Col. Robert Pitt*, of the Isle of Wight County, Va. Married (III), 10 Feby., 1859, Mrs. Mary E. (Girault) Poitevant, a native of Mississippi, born in Feby., 1827; died 14 Nov., 1885, daughter of James A. and Susan Girault. All three wives and the Doctor were members of the Baptist Church. Issue by second marriage, none by last: two sons, the younger d. y.; the elder:

1a. James Abram Hill[6], born 8 Feby., 1856, d. 28 Jany., 1822; educated in medicine, first in New Orleans, and later graduated at Vanderbilt University, at Nashville, Tenn., in 1884. (See Memorial History of Ala.—Historical and Biographical—1893).

Dr. James Abram Hill is one of those sterling characters that makes life worth while and yet causes no excitement in the outside world, acting upon the principle that virtues self-extolled are rendered obscure. He was a partner of his father in the practice of medicine before the latter's death, a member of the Baptist Church, and of the Knights of Pythias. He married, 7 Oct., 1885, Sarah Elizabeth Woodroof, born 26 Nov., 1856, daughter of James William Woodroof and his wife, Harriet Atwood Wright; granddaughter of William Woodrooff and his wife, Elizabeth Avent, and of Williams Wright and his wife, Sallie Mitchell; great-granddaughter of John Avent, of Richard Woodroof and his wife, Susannah Hobbs, daughter of James Hobbs; great-great-great-granddaughter of Col. Thomas Avent, the emigrant. Issue:

1b. James Woodroof Hill[7], born 13 Aug., 1887; died 28 June, 1888.

2b. Annie Atwood Hill[7], born 29 Nov., 1888; graduated at Shorter College, Rome, Ga., in 1907; President Polymnian Society,

1906-'7; married 17 June, 1914, Joel Kendall Mathis, born 19 Aug., 1886, son of Joel Fletcher Mathis and his wife, Susie May, of Memphis, Tenn. No children.

3b. Henry Willis Hill, II[7], born 23 Dec., 1892. In 1908, completed course at Columbia Military Academy, Columbia, Tenn.; in 1912, graduated at University of Alabama, with degree of B.A.; member of D. K. E., Skulls, Black Friars; 1912-14, clerked for D. J. Taylor & Son, Hardware Co., Decatur, Ala.; 1914-'17, farmer at Mooresville, Ala.; Dec. 14, 1917, enlisted in U. S. Army, assigned to 501 Laundry Co., Q. M. C.; 28 March, 1918, sailed from Philadelphia Navy Yard, arriving at Brest, France, assigned to American Salvage Depot, Intermediate No. 8, Laundry Dept., St. Pierre des Corps, France; March, 1919, transferred to American Expeditionary Forces University at Beanne, Cote d'Or, France; 13 June, 1919, shipped from Marseilles, France, arrived at New York 1st of July; 12 July, 1919, honorably discharged at Camp Gordon.

4b. Elizabeth Hill[7], called by the family "B. B.", born 30 Oct., 1894; member class of 1915, Brenau College-Conservatory, Gainesville, Ga., B. Z. O. Sorority.

5b. James Gatling Hill[7], born Oct. 20, 1896; for two years in Gulf Coast Military Academy, Gulfport, Miss., graduating in 1914 with rank of First Lieutenant; enlisted May, 1918, in Fourth Officers' Training School, Camp Pike, Ark.; later transferred to Inf. Rep. (?) Training troops, Camp Grant, Ill., where, after six months, he was discharged.

III.—Theophilus Hill[4] (Henry[3], Abraham[2], Henry[1]), c. 1765—c. 1810, married, 16 Jany., 1787, Patsy Pope, of Wake County, N. C.; removed in the 90's to Wilkes County, Ga., where, as previously shown, he, in 1804 and 1805, administered his father's estate, and was named in the will of his mother, Sarah Hill, 13 Nov. 1812, as deceased. He was head of a family in Wake County, N. C., in 1790, having a wife, son and two daughters (U. S. Census). His mother, in her will, directs certain property to be divided equally between his children when they come of age or marry, and then makes specific bequests to his daughter, Elizabeth, and his son, Greenberry Hill. No further records relating to him have come to my knowledge; but in 1902, Mr. J. W. Billings, then in Atlanta, gave to me from memory the following:

"Harriet Hill, born in Wilkes County, Ga., 14 Feby., 1808; married, in 1824, Bardwell Billings, who moved to Jasper County, Ga., and died in 1843. He left a son, John D. Billings, of Columbus, Ga., who is my father. Harriet Hill's father was Theophilus Hill, brother of John and Abraham Hill. She had a brother, Green Hill, who died, circa 1895, in Florida, and sisters, Bettie and Winnie, both older than Harriet, and Martha Hill, who married Redding, of Cuthbert, Ga., and died circa 1894 or '5."

Theophilus[1] and Patsy (Pope) Hill, accepting the above as correct, had:

1. Elizabeth Hill[5]; 2. Greenberry Hill[5]; 3. Winnie Hill[5]; 4. Harriet[5], married Bardwell Billings, and had: John D. Billings[6], who had J. W. Billings[7]; 5. Martha Hill[5], married Redding. These lines not traced.

IV.—Nancy Hill[4] (Henry[3], Abraham[2], Henry[1]), c. 1770-1839, married pro. 1785-'90, Col. William Johnson, born pro. 1755-'60, in Wilkes County, Ga. He was for many years High Sheriff of the County; was a *Captain* in the Revolutionary War (D. A. R. 3rd Report, 1898-1900, p. 355); received Bounty Warrant, etc.

"*William Johnson* granted, Oct. 12, *1785*, Two hundred eighty-seven and one-half acres, in Washington Co., bounded Easterly by North fork of Oconee River, on all other sides by vacant land. (*On Bounty*). S. Elbert. Geo. Handley, C. C." (Land Book I. I. I., p. 129, Office Sec. of State.)

"*William Johnson* granted, April 25, *1786*, Two hundred eighty-seven and one-half acres in Washington Co. bounded East by Ohoopee river, South by Samuel Underwood's land, on all other sides by vacant lands. (*On Bounty*). Reg. May 3, 1786.
(Land Book I.I.I, p. 759, Sec. of State's
 Office). Edward Telfair
 G. Handley, C. C."

"*William Johnson* granted, Sept. 23, 1786, Two hundred eighty-seven and one-half acres in Washington Co. bounded West by William Bishop's land, on all other sides by vacant lands. (*On Bounty*). Reg. Sept. 27, 1786.
 (Land Book L.L.L., p. 76). I. M. Stewart pro C. C."
 Edward Telfair

"*William Johnson* granted March 3, 1785, Two hundred acres in *Wilkes Co.*, bounded Southerly by Smith's land and by Young's land, Northwesterly and Northerly by Young's land, Easterly by unknown lands.
 (Land Book GGG, p. 256). S. Elbert."

"*William Johnson*, granted March 17, 1786, Two hundred acres in *Wilkes Co.*, bounded Southwardly by Humphrey Tomkin's land, on all other sides by vacant land.
 (Land Book I.I.I., p. 578). G. Handley, C. C."
 Edward Telfair

"*William Johnson* granted, March 17, 1786, One hundred and fifty acres in Wilkes Co., bounded on all sides by vacant lands. Reg. March 26, 1786.
 (Land Book I.I.I., p. 603). Samuel Elbert
 G. Handley, C. C."

"*William Johnson* granted, March 2, 1791,, Three hundred and eighty acres in Wilkes Co., bounded Southwest by Black's and un-

known land, Northeast by vacant and Elduff's land, all other sides vacant lands. Edwd. Telfair.
Reg. March 5, 1791". (Land Book U.U.U., p. 348.)

"*William Johnson* granted, Dec. 21, 1791, One hundred in *Wilkes Co.*, bounded Southeast by land laid for Edward Welborn, on all other sides by vacant lands. Reg. Dec. 22, 1791.
(Ld. Book V.V.V., p. 201). Edwd. Telfair".

"*William Johnson* granted, 19 Dec., 1798, Two hundred and fifty acres in Wilkes Co., bounded Northwardly by B. Smith's, Welborn's and James Mathew's, Northeasterly by Esau Smith's land, Southeasterly by William Simmon's and Southwesterly by Daniel Wagner's land.
(Land Book A5, p. 757). James Jackson
Thos. Johnson, S. E. D."
Reg. 19 Dec. 1798.

"*William Johnson,* granted, Feby. 25, 1801, Two hundred acres in Wilkes Co., bounded Southeast by Richardson's land, on all other sides by vacant lands.
(L'd Bk. D5, p. 94). James Jackson
Thos. Johnson, S. E. D."
Reg. 25 Feby., 1801.

"William Johnson granted, Oct. 25, 1793, One thousand acres in Franklin Co., bounded Southeast by Micajah Williamson's land, Southwest by James Edmond's land, Northwest by vacant land, Northeast by Jo. Wilson's (bounds given by measurement). Reg. 26 Oct. 1793. (Ld. Bk. B4, p. 232).
E. Telfair
N. Urquhart, S. E. D."

"William Johnson granted, Feby. 4, 1787, 150 acres in Greene Co. (Ld. Bk. M.M.M., p. 424); April 17, 1789, 58 acres in Greene Co. (Ld. Bk. S.S.S., p. 32); 13 Oct., 1817, 164 acres in Warren Co. (Ld. Bk. L5, p. 217); Nov. 13, 1807, 10½ acres in Elbert Co. (Ld. Bk. G5, p. 198).

There are quite a number of other grants in various Counties to a *William Johnson,* and candor constrains me to say that as there were contemporaneously, apparently, three William Johnsons, it is not possible to say, *positively, to which one* any particular grant was made. Evidently, however, all three were thus favored.

Mrs. Nancy (Hill) Johnson, in 1839, was on a visit to her brother, Abram Hill, in Meriwether County, Ga., when she was thrown from her carriage, sustaining injuries resulting in her death. She was buried there in her brother's cemetery. In middle age she had an eye pierced, by some accident, and thereafter wore an artificial one, so perfectly imitating in its coloring, etc., the natural eye that the defect, it was told me, was hardly noticeable, and unknown save only by intimate associates.

Will of Col. William Johnson:

Georgia, } In the name of God Amen.
Wilkes County. } I William Johnson being unwell at present, but of sound and disposing mind and memory, do this day make my last Will and Testament.

1st. My will and desire is that all my just debts be paid by my Executors whom I shall hereafter constitute, nominate and appoint, as soon as convenient after my decease.

2nd. I loan to my daughter Elizabeth Cunningham & her lawful increase which she now has or may have hereafter the tract or parcel of land whereon her husband Drury Cunningham & she now lives in the County and State aforesaid on the waters of Clark's Creek containing by estimation one hundred and seventy eight acres, be the same more or less, adjoining Richard Hudspeth, Dabney A. Martin, Joel Appling and others, also the following negroes Lucy Cate, Edmund, and Dennis, also two beds & furniture, one red work steer, a quantity of household & kitchen furniture which she has now in her possession, all the said property is for the use and benefit of her and her children and said property is not to be taken from her by any person, or persons whatsoever nor be liable to pay any debts that are already or may hereafter be contracted by her husband Drury Cunningham, and at her decease said property together with its increase and that which she may hereafter receive in the same way of my estate to be divided equally the lawful heirs of her body.

3rd. I give to my daughter Mary Spratling the following negroes Fannie and her two children, Nice and Mariah and Dick, also two beds and furniture & other household & kitchen furniture which she has in her possession at present.

4th. I give to my daughter Susan M. Johnson the following negroes Celia, Emella, Grandson & George.

5th. I give to my son William Johnson the following negroes, Big George, Suckey, America, John and Haulker, and Sixty dollars.

6th: I give to my son John P. Johnson the following negroes, Big Thomas, Caty, Lucy and Eveline and Pollard and Sixty dollars.

7th. I give to my daughter *Nancy H. Johnson* the following negroes, *Mariah, Nelson, Eliza* and *Henry.*

8th. I give to my three youngest children Stephen W. Johnson, Martha Johnson and Catharine A. Johnson the following negroes, Little Thomas, Solomon, Aaron, Meeley, Charles, Randolph, Sana, Miles, Nero, Ned, Burwell, James and July to be equally divided among my three youngest children as above named as they become of age or marry.

9th. I give to William Norman who has married . . . ., the following negroes, Annola, Milley, Peter and Matilda also one bed & furniture which they have now in their possession and no more or hereafter.

10th. I give to *my wife Nancy Johnson* during her lifetime that tract of land called and known by the name of *McLendon place* also the tract of land whereon I now live adjoining C. Orr and others all the plantation tools, all my stock of every kind and all the household and kitchen furniture and the following negroes, Fibby Johnson, Fibby Hill, *Little Fibby*, Charity, Vinen, Marietta, *Hester*, Aaron, Joseph, Sam, Mike, Jeffery, Billey, Daniel, Peter and Nat & Clary, with this property she is to be under obligation to keep and decently support and maintain my daughter *Sarah* Johnson as long as she shall live, but if my wife should die before my daughter should, she is to have the following negroes for her maintenance Little Phoeby, Peter, Marietta & Mike to be put in the hands of Henry Spratling and he is to be under strict obligations to maintain and support her, and at her death said property together with its increase and any other that she may receive of my estate hereafter to be equally divided between her living, lawful Brothers and Sisters, but if my daughter Sarah Johnson should depart this life before my wife Nancy Johnson should, all the property I have left to her (my wife) is to equally divided between my lawful children except the lands which I have loaned her (during her lifetime) which is to be at her death equally divided between my (a little confusion in this clause in the copy) three sons William Johnson, John P. Johnson and Stephen W. Johnson.

The lands which I have not loaned my wife (viz.) the tract on Clark's Creek & Long Creek and what *I own out of Wilkes County* I wish to be sold together with any other property which I have not left to my wife Nancy Johnson, at the discretion of my Executors to the payment of my just debts.

11th. My will and desire further is that the negroes which I have willed away to my three youngest children should be hired out, and the whole amount of hire to be equally divided amongst them annually for their education.

12th. My will further is that as my children becomes of lawful age or marries that my wife Nancy Johnson should give to each of them as much household and kitchen furniture and other property as the others have had given to them who have left us, or if my wife should die before they arrive at Lawful age or marry then it is my will that my Executors give to each of my children that, are under age or unmarried as much household and kitchen furniture and other property as the others have had given them who have married and left us, or the worth thereof in money as they arrive at lawful age or marry.

13th. I constitute, nominate and appoint Sylvanus Gibson, Henry Spratling and Richard J. Willis Executors of this my last

Will and Testament in Witness Whereof I have hereunto set my hand and seal this 11th day of July, 1821.

Daniel Carrington ⎫   Wm. Johnson   (L.S.)
Robert H. Moore   ⎬   N. B. It is my further will and desire that
Martin Andrews   ⎭   my wife Nancy Johnson shall have my *riding carriage* and new wagon and gear during her life time, which I intended to of given to her in this my foregoing will but forgot to have it mentioned when it was written. Witness my hand and seal this 30th day of July, 1821.

                                    Wm. Johnson   (L.S.)

    Stephen Johnson
    George Willis
    Henry Pope

Georgia   ⎫ Personally appeared in open Court Daniel Car-
Wilkes County.   ⎬ rington & Martin Andrews two of the subscribing witnesses to the annexed will and being duly sworn saith that they saw the Testator William Johnson, sign, seal, publish & declare the annexed instrument of writing to be his last Will & Testament and at the time of his so doing he was of sound disposing mind and memory, that they subscribed their names as witnesses in the presence of the Testator and at his request & that they also saw Robert H. Moore subscribe his name for the same purpose at the same time.

                                            Daniel Carrington
                                            Martin Andrews

    Sworn to in open Court this
    3rd day of September, 1821.

                                    John Dyson, C. C. O.

Georgia   ⎫ Personally appeared in open Court Stephen
Wilkes County.   ⎬ Johnson, George Willis and Henry Pope the subscribing witnesses to the Codicil to the annexed will & being duly sworn saith that they saw the Testator William Johnson sign, seal, publish and declare the said codicil to be a part of his last Will and Testament and at the time of his so doing he was of sound disposing mind and memory that they subscribed their names as witnesses to said codicil in the presence of the Testator and at his request.

    Sworn to in open Court this 3rd day of September, 1821.
John Dyson C. C. O.

Recorded this 26th day of Sept. 1821.

                                            George Willis
                                            Stephen Johnson
                                            Henry Pope

    In a letter by Wylie Hill, of Wilkes, 6 Jany. 1822, to his cousin Lodowick Hill, Richardson's Tavern, Edgefield District, S. C., he says: Col. Johnson left us some time last fall with the consumption—he is all the connection that has dy'd since you left us. Josiah Jordan interlined.

Will of William Johnson, Jr.

"State of Georgia, } In the name of God Amen.
Wilkes County. } I William Johnson being unwell, but of sound and disposing mind and memory, do this day make my last will and Testament in manner & form following, viz.:

1st. My will and desire is that all my just debts be paid by my Executor who I shall hereinafter name & appoint as soon as convenient after my decease.

2*ondly*. I give and bequeath to my mother Nancy Johnson all my estate both Real and personal during her lifetime consisting of the following land and negroes, viz.; the one half of an undivided Tract of land which belongs to myself and John P. Johnson jointly and one other tract in Dooly which I drew in the late land lottery & the six following negroes to wit: Dann, George, Suckey, Anaka, John & Halker, one Iron Gray Horse and four head of cattle and at her death to be equally divided between each of my Brothers and Sisters and

3*rdly*, and lastly, I constitute and appoint my friend Richd. J. Willis Executor of this my last Will and Testament.

In Witness Whereof I have hereunto set my hand & seal this 3rd day of May, 1823.

William Johnson (L.S.)

In presence of
Henry Spratlen
Wm. Norman
Drury Cunningham

Georgia { Personally appeared in open court Drury Cunningham one of the subscribing witnesses to the within will who being duly sworn deposeth and saith that he saw the Testator William Johnson sign, seal and publish and declare the same to be his last Will and Testament and that he also see Henry Spratlin and William Norman sign their names as witnesses to the same in his presence and at his request, and that he was of sound disposing mind and memory. Sworn to in open court this 7th day of July, 1823.

Attest. John Dyson C. C. C.   Drury Cunningham.
Recorded the 16th of September, 1823."

Col. William and *Nancy*[4] (*Hill*) *Johnson* had:
1. Elizabeth Johnson[5], married Drury Cunningham. Had children, but not traced.
2. Mary Johnson[5], married 15 Sept., 1813, Henry Spratlin (q. v.).
3. Susan M. Johnson[5], married 15 April, 1822, Judge James Dabney Willis, born Oct. 21, 1793, 1st wife. (q. v.).

4. William Johnson, Jr.[5], born circa 1800; died in 1823, unmarried. (See his will above).

5. John Pope Johnson[5], died after 1823; married Prudence Irvine (q. v.).

6. Nancy Hill Johnson[5], born 11 July, 1808; died 21 Oct., 1846; married 16 Dec., 1824, Col. Lodowick Meriwether Hill[5], 1804-1883, her second cousin, his first wife. (See p. 120, 2, Wylie[4], Abr.[3], Abr.[2], Henry[1]).

7. Stephen W.(ebster) Johnson[5], born circa 1810, died when circa 16 years of age, was on the eve of leaving for Franklin College, at Athens, when taken with measles and died.

8. Martha Pope Johnson[5], born 10 May, 1814; died 19 June, 1893, in Meriwether County; married (I), 18 Nov., 1829, Burwell Pope Hill[5], 1800-1833, second wife, in Wilkes County, Ga., her second cousin. (See p. 103, 1, Wylie Hill[4], Abr.[3], Abr.[2], Henry[1]).

9. Catharine A. Johnson[5], called "Kitty", born 16 Oct., 1816; died in July, 1872. (q. v.).

10. Sarah Johnson[5], living in 1821; probably afflicted in some way. No further record.

2. Mary Johnson[5] and her husband, Henry Spratlin, who was the son of James and Martha (Calloway) Spratlin (vide Cya. of Ga., Vol. 3, p. 587—Wilkinson) had—order of births not known:—

1a. William Spratlin[6]; 2a. James Spratlin[6]; 3a. Nancy Spratlin[6]; 4a. Martha Spratlin[6]; 5a. Mary Ann Spratlin[6]; 6a. Rowena Spratlin[6]; 7a. John Pope Spratlin[6]; and 8a. *Amelia T. Spratlin, called "Emily"*, born 17 April, 1829; died 13 Dec., 1894; married 23 Jany., 1845. *Major Uriah Baylis Wilkinson,* of Newnan, Ga. (the brother of John, James, Emily, Joel, Fanny and Kitty Wilkinson), and had:

1b. Edward Black Wilkinson[7], born 22 Nov., 1847; married Missouri Gorham.

2b. John R. Wilkinson[7], born 20 June, 1856; died 7 April, 1915; married, 26 Nov., 1878, Annie Wade Wood, born in 1860; died, 14 Feby., 1921; daughter of Capt. Winston B. and Mariah L. (Dent) Wood. (q. v.).

3b. Mattie C. Wilkinson[7], born 10 Dec., 1845; married, 26 May, 1864, Rev. Francis M. Daniel, died 22 Dec., 1892. Issue: one son.

4b. William Henry Wilkinson[7], born April, 1854; died, Dec., 1855.

5b. Mary Emma Wilkinson[7], born 1852; died Dec., 1855.

6b. Lucy Pope Wilkinson[7], born June, 1850; died Dec., 1855.

7b. Joel Wilkinson[7], born June 18—; died Nov., 1853.

8b. Lillian Gertrude Wilkinson[7], born Jany., 1862; died Oct., 1867.

9b. Thomas J. Wilkinson[7], born Jany., 1864; married Lilly Parks.

AND ALLIED FAMILIES 37

10b. Mell R. Wilkinson[7], born 1 Jany., 1865; married Annie Van Winkle. (q. v.).

2b. John R. Wilkinson[7] and wife, Annie Wade Wood, had:

1c. Harry Eugene Wilkinson[8], of Atlanta; 2c. William Barrett Wilkinson[8], of Jacksonville, Fla.

John R. Wilkinson was for many years Judge of the Court of Ordinary of Fulton County, a most popular and efficient official, whose memory will long live in the hearts of hundreds of Atlantians. He was also a most prominent Mason, holding the highest station of the order in the State.

10b. Mell R. Wilkinson and wife, Annie Van Winkle, have one daughter, Miss Margaret Wilkinson. He has occupied many positions of honor and trust, having been President of the Chamber of Commerce of Atlanta, and is the honorary President for Life of the Presidents' Club of Atlanta.

2. Susan M. Johnson[5] and her husband, Judge James Dabney Willis, had:

1a. William J. Willis[6], born 25 Jany., 1823; died 13 June, 1823.

James Dabney Willis married (II), 17 Aug., 1824, Nancy Tate Anderson, and had:

2a. George Willis[6], born 23 May, 1825; died 27 May, 1825.

3a. Susan Johnson Willis[6], born 6 Aug., 1826; died in Nov., 1827.

4a. Thomas Richard Willis[6], born 17 Dec., 1827; married Elizabeth Marshall. He was Colonel of a Regiment of State troops, C. S. A. (?)

5a. William Anderson Willis[6], born 2 Feby., 1830; died 17 Sept., 1831.

6a. Sarah Elizabeth Willis[6], married *Thomas Calloway*.

7a. Willis Lumpkin Willis[6], born 7 Oct., 1833; died March, 1858.

8a. Lucy B. A. Willis[6], born 28 Dec., 1836. (q. v.).

9a. James Anderson Willis[6], born 4 April, 1838; died Sept. 9, 1858.

10a. John Baker Willis[6], born 23 Sept., 1842; died 8 July, 1843.

11a. George Willis[6], born 11 May, 1844; died 2 May, 1845.

8a. Lucy B. A. Willis[6] married (I) Wylie Hill DuBose[6], died 29 June, 1862, in C. S. A., son of James Rembert and Martha Pope (Hill) DuBose; married (II), Col. W. W. Simpson, of Hancock and Wilkes Counties, second wife. Issue by first marriage, none; by second marriage:

1b. Sallie Toombs DuBose[7], born 1859; died May, 1908 (q. v.).

2b. Betty Vance DuBose[7], born ......; died 28 June, 1918 (q. v.).

3b. Wylie Hill DuBose II[7], born 1862; died 7 June, 1920. (q. v.).

1b. Sallie Toombs DuBose[7], 1859-1908, married (I), Samuel Sims; married (II), James Wylie Arnold, Jr. Issue by first marriage, none by second marriage:

1c. Samuel Wylie Sims[8], died in young manhood.

2c: Lucy Mary Sims[8], changed name later to Mary Rembert Sims.

3c. Elizabeth Sims[8], married Raymond R. Smith, of Washington, Ga., who died 26 Feby., 1919. Issue: 1d.—R. R. Smith, Jr.[9], died young; 2d.—Elizabeth Raymond Smith[9].

4c. Anson Pope Sims[8], died young.

5c. Sadie Sims[8], married A. Loyd Johnson, son of William T. Johnson. Issue: 1d.—Sarah DuBose Johnson[9].

2b. Betty Vance DuBose[7], died 28 June, 1918, in Atlanta, Ga., married William Mays Sims, attorney-at-law, of Washington, Ga., died 11 July, 1904. Issue:

1c. Lucy DuBose Sims[8], married Howell Eugene Dodd. Issue:
1d. Howell E. Dodd, Jr.[9]; 2d.—William Sims Dodd[9].

2c. William Edward Sims[8], married Maryhill Jolley.

3c. Lelia Alexander Sims[8], married Harold Huntington White. Issue: 1d.—Clifton Huntington White[9]; 2d.—Elizabeth DuBose White[9].

4c. Marion DuBose Sims[8], married Juliette Smith, daughter of Robert Motte Smith. Issue: 1d.—Marion DuBose Sims, Jr.[9]; 2d.—Juliette Smith Sims[9].

5c. Rembert Mays Sims[8], married Jo. Mary Spruell.

6c. Edith Sims[8], married Paul Newsom. Issue: 1d.—Bettie DuBose Newsom[9]; 2d.—Edith Sims Newsom[9].

7c. Mildred Sims[8].

3b. Wylie DuBose[7] married Julia Anthony. Issue: 1c.—Lucy Willis DuBose[8], and, 2c.—Julia Toombs DuBose[8], twins.

5. John Pope Johnson[5] (Col. William[4]), who married Prudence Irvine, died, after 1823, a month before the birth of his son and only child, John Pope Johnson, Jr.[6], who married a daughter of Welcome Fanning, of Wilkes County, Ga., and moved to Blackhawk, Carroll County, Miss., where their children were reared and lived. Mrs. Prudence (Irvine) Johnson married (II) Mr. ...... Brooks. Record not traced.

9. Catharine A. Johnson[5], called "Kitty", (Col. William), 1816-1872, married, 18 March, 1834, George W. Chatfield, born 7 June, 1807, in Wilkes County (probably son of George and Margaret (Coats) Chatfield, early settlers of Wilkes. Their record not traced. See: Also Mem'rs of Ga., Vol. 2, p. 519). Moved first to Meriwether County, Ga., then to Auburn, Ala., and later to Newton, Miss., where both died. Issue:

1a. J. Bonnell Chatfield[6]; married ......, lived for a time at Meridian, Miss., but his widow living, in 1913, in Montgomery, Ala. They had several children but can't recall their names.

2a. Hallie Chatfield[6]; married ......, and left a daughter, Mrs. Steele, living in Texas in 1917, and possibly other children.

3a. Mary[6], called "Sissie", Chatfield; born 1 Dec., 1845, died 5 Sept., 1914, at Corpus Christi, Texas; married Albert (?) Watts, died circa 1909. Issue: four sons and a daughter, all married, and each of the sons (1914) had two children. The daughter married (I) ......, and had a son, died young; married (II) Oscar M. Suttle, of the law firm of Suttle & Todd, of Corpus Christi.

4a. Frank Chatfield[7]; married ......; not traced. There were probably other children. Order of births not known.

V.—Mary Hill[4] (A. P. O.—Henry[3], Abraham[2], Henry[1]), born Sept. 17, 1758; died Feb. 17, 1831; married (I), circa 1781, Henry Jossey, Sr.; married (II), in Maury County, Tenn., John Macon. Issue by first marriage (none by second):

1. Sarah Jossey[5], born Sept. 18, 1783; died July 22, 1830; married May 9, 1805, or '6, Jonathan Webster III (?), his second wife, born Nov. 17, 1767; died April 25, 1845; removed about 1807 to Maury County, Tenn. (q. v.).

2. James Jossey[5], born 20 Nov., 1786; died 12 Feb., 1831; married Nancy Coleman. Their descendants live in Williamson County, Tenn.

3. Henry Jossey, Jr.[5], born ......; married (I), 10 Jany., 1812, Huldah Pope, daughter of John and Elizabeth (Smith) Pope; married (II) the widow, Sarah Twining. (q. v.).

4. Christiana[5], called "Keddey" and "Kittie", Jossey, born 27 Nov., 1793; died 18 Feby., 1847; married 3 Dec., 1812, Col. Richard Jefferson Willis, his first wife, born Nov. 12, 1789; died Oct. 18, 1866. He married (II) Sarah Foster, born 1801; died Jany. 18, 1884. No issue by second marriage. (q. v.).

5. Rowena Caroline Jossey[5], born 1797; died 1827 (?), aged thirty years; married Dr. J. W. P. McJemsey, of Manry County, Tenn., his first wife. He married (II) before 10 Feby., 1830, a Miss Gillespie.

1. Jonathan Webster III and his wife, Sarah Jossey[5], 1783-1830, (Mary[4], Henry[3], Abraham[2], Henry[1]), had issue:

1a. Mary Jossey Webster[6], born Jan. 7, 1807; died 1881. (q. v.).

2a. James Henry Webster[6], born June 30, 1808; died Oct. 8, 1873. (q. v.).

3a. George Pope Webster[6], born Oct. 26, 1809; died .... (q. v.).

4a. William Johnson Webster[6], born April 19, 1811; died Feby. 3, 1859. (q. v.).

5a. Caroline Webster[6], born June 18, 1813; died April, 1852. (q. v.).

6a. Felix Webster[6], born 1810.

7a. Albert Webster[6], born June 18, 1818.

8a. Rowena Christiana Webster⁶, born April 26, 1821; died 1907, aged 86, unmarried.

1a. Mary Jossey Webster⁶, 1807-1881, married (I) Col. Tate, of North Carolina, who lived only six months; married (II), Col. J. C. Camp, of Huntsville, Ala.; married (III), Col. Andrew Erwin, who was a brother-in-law of both John Bell and Henry Clay. No issue.

2a. James Henry Webster⁶, 1808-1873, married Sarah Jane Weakley, of Huntsville, Ala., and had:

1b. Sallie Weakley Webster⁷, born 11 Jany., 1807; died 6 May, 1872. (q. v.).

2b. Fannie Pattison Webster⁷, born Aug. 21, 1838; died 2 May, 1920. (q. v.).

3b. William Henry Webster⁷, born April 27, 1840; died Sept. 22, 1862. Killed in battle of Chickamauga.

4b. Rowena Caroline Webster⁷, born 11 April, 1842; married Austin Powell.

5b. James Jonathan Webster⁷, born Aug. 9, 1843; died Oct., 1918; married Fannie Robertson.

6b. Martha Jane Webster⁷, born 11 Feby., 1847. (q. v.).

7b. Elizabeth Dougan Webster⁷, born 21 Jany., 1849; died 5 Aug., 1902; married William Porter.

8b. Nancy Weakley Webster⁷, born April 26, 1850; died Aug. 2, 1855.

9b. Juliet Pauline Webster⁷, born Nov. 15, 1852; died 11 Aug., 1854.

10b. Katherine Willis Webster⁷, born 25 July, 1854; married Charles H. Sanders.

11b. Frank Weakley Webster⁷, born 3 April, 1859; married Alice Crocket. (q. v.).

1b. Sallie Weakley Webster⁷, 1837-1872, married Jesse Sherwood Harris, and had:

1c. Sherwood Harris⁸, born 17 Jany., 1860. Bachelor.

2c. Jennie Weakley Harris⁸, born 23 March, 1861; died 14 Jany., 1920. (q. v.).

3c. Webster Harris⁸, born 22 Jany., 1864. Bachelor.

4c. Walter Hayes Harris⁸, born 9 Aug., 1865; married 14 Dec., 1892, Elizabeth B. *Wilemans* (?).

5c. Jessie May Harris⁸, born 17 Feby., 1868; married 31 March, 1904, Frank Masten, of Huntsville, Ala.

6c. Sallie Willis Harris⁸, born 31 Aug., 1870. Single.

2c. Jennie Weakley Harris⁸, 1861-1920, married 15 June, 1892, Patrick H. Southall, and had:

1d.—Sarah Elizabeth Southall⁹, born 25 March, 1893.

2d.—Pattie Harris Southall⁹, born 18 Jany., 1895; married 12 April, 1920, Charles Deere Wiman, of Moline, Ill.

2b. Fannie Pattison Webster⁷, 1838-1920, married Thomas L. Porter, and had:

1c. Janie Porter[8], born 18 Feby., 1861.
2c. Willie Porter[8], born 11 June, 1862.
3c. William W. Porter[8], born 20 Jany., 1864. (q. v.).
4c. James Porter[8], born 15 March, 1866.
5c. Thomas Leroy Porter[8], born 11 Feby., 1868; married 7 Nov., 1900, Bessie Moore.
6c. Fannie Porter[8], born Sept., 1869; married 11 June, 1893, Will Moore, and had daughter, Frances Moore[9], born 13 Jany., 1894.
7c. Bessie Porter[8], born 19 Sept., 1871. (q. v.).
8c. Nimrod Hammon Porter[8], born 16 Sept., 1873.
9c. Frank Porter[8], born 27 May, 1875.
10c. Martha Porter[8], born 27 Aug., 1877; died 22 Oct., 1909; married, 2 March, 1904, Van Hendricks, and had:
1d.—Martha Porter Hendricks[9], born 16 Oct., 1909; died Oct., 1919; 2d.—Van Hendricks, Jr.[9], born 16 Oct., 1909; twins.
3c. William W. Porter[8], born 20 Jany., 1864; married, 1 June, 1899, Mollie (or Mallie) Beadle, and had: 1d.—Ami Webster Porter[9], born 9 May, 1907; died 1 Jany., 1920; 2d.—William W. Porter, Jr.[9], born 13 May, 1909.
7c. Bessie Porter[8], born 19 Sept., 1871; married 26 Feby., 1902, John W. Black, and had:
1d. Fanny Porter Black[9], born 3 Oct., 1904; died 1904.
2d. Frances Black[9], born 26 June, 1906; died 22 Jany., 1908.
3d. John W. Black, Jr.[9], born 8 Aug., 1909.
4d. Bessie Porter Black[9].
6b. Martha Jane Webster[7], born 11 Feby., 1847; married 15 Dec., 1870, Shade Murray, and had:
1c. Janie Murray[8], born 21 Sept., 1871.
2c. James Webster Murray[8], born 26 June, 1873; died 23 Sept., 1879.
3c. Edwin Murray[8], born 6 Feby., 1876. (q. v.).
4c. Martha White Murray[8], born 7 Feby., 1878; married, 19 April, 1898, Frederick Sandusky, and had:
1d. Murray Sandusky[9], born 24 Nov., 1899.
5c. Mabel Murray[8], born 25 Aug., 1882; married Herbert B. Keith.
6c. Elizabeth Murray[8], born 20 Jany., 1886; married Frederick C. Lindsley, and had:
1d. Frederick Cleeland Lindsley[9].
2d. Elizabeth Murray Lindsley[9].
3d. Martha Lindsley[9].
3c. Edwin Murray[8], born 6 Feby., 1876; married Cornelia Morgan, and had:
1d. Cornelia Murray[9].
2d. Sara Murray[9].
3d. Shade Murray, Jr.[9]

11b. Frank Weakley Webster[7] (born 30 April, 1859,) and wife, Alice Crockett, had: 1c.—Frank Webster[8]; 2c.—Robert Crockett Webster[8]; 3c.—William Penn Webster[8]; 4c.—James Henry Webster[8]; 5c.—Macon Plumm (?) Webster[8]; and 6c.—Sarah Weakley Webster[8].

1c. Frank Webster[8] (son of Frank Weakley Webster), married Cora ......, and had: 1d.—Frank Webster, Jr.[9]

2c. Robert Crockett Webster[8] (son of Frank W. Webster), married Corinne White, and had: 1d.—Robert Crockett Webster, Jr.[9]

3a: George Pope Webster[6] (son of Jonathan), born 26 Oct., 1809, married Harriet Blair. Issue:

1b. Henry Webster[7], Capt., C. S. A.; died during the war, in the service at LaFayette, Ala.

2b. Mary Camp Webster[7], born Nov., 1841; married, 20 Aug., 1863, Richard Cross Gordon, born 28 Feb., 1837; died 8 April, 1903. He was an officer in one of the first regiments to volunteer for Confederate service, was soon after made Captain on General Rain's staff, later discharged on account of inflammatory rheumatism. He was the only son of Major Bolling Gordon, directly descended from Pocahontas, and whose father was the first Postmaster of Nashville, Tenn. (q. v.).

3b. George Pope Webster, Jr.[7], born 1848; died ......; married Effie Laurie Webster, and had: 1c.—George Webster, Jr.[8]; 2c.—Annie Laurie Webster[8].

4b. Harriet Blair Webster[7], born 1850; married Clark T. Jones, and had: 1c.—Cornelia Jones[8], married Bruce Cochran; 2c.—Clark Jones[8], married Kate Gordon, died 1920, leaving two children.

5b. Blair Webster[7], born Aug., 1851.
6b. Caroline Turner Webster[7], born Aug., 1852.
7b. Ella Webster[7], born 1854.

2b. Richard Cross and Mary Camp (Webster) Gordon[7] had:

1c. Caroline Gordon[8], married Hunter McDonald, and had: 1d.—Hunter McDonald, Jr.[9]

2c. Lucile Gordon[8], married Hinton Frierson. They have an adopted child, Addie Armstrong[9].

3c. Camille Gordon[8], single.

4c. Bessie Gordon[8], married Carter Cox, and they have an adopted son.

4a. William Johnson Webster I[6] (son of Jonathan III), 1811-1859, married Oct. 23, 1844, Mary Ann (Porter) Booker, born Nov. 15, 1818; died Oct. 27, 1867, daughter of Nimrod and Della (Hanman or Hammon) Porter, and widow of Henry Booker. Issue:

1b. Florence Webster[7], born Sept. 8, 1845; died 2 Jan., 1847.
2b. William Johnson Webster II[7], born 17 Oct., 1847. (q. v.).

3b. Hammon Porter Webster⁷, born 22 April, 1849; died 24 Jany., 1914, unmarried.

4b. Elizabeth Webster⁷, born 1850; died, 1852, of diphtheria.

5b. Mary Porter Webster⁷, born 20 Jany., 1853; died 27 Jany., 1914, unmarried.

6b. Mattie Rowe Webster⁷, born 12 Dec., 1855; living in 1920, unmarried.

7b. Carrie Delene Webster⁷, born 22 Aug., 1857; died 6 Aug., 1862.

2b. *William Johnson Webster II*⁷ born Oct. 17, 1847; married Oct. 23, 1872, Mary Catherine Allison, born 17 April, 1853; died 15 May, 1913, only child of Dr. Jacob Hylemon and Octavia (Hill) Allison, and granddaughter of Col. William K. Hill and his wife, Rebecca Harris. Dr. Jacob Hyleman Allison was the son of Dr. Hugh Lee Allison (and Mary Catherine Beakman or Buchman, his wife), son of Jacob, or Simeon (?) Allison (and Margaret Lockwood, his wife), son of Rev. Hugh Allison and Dorothy Simson (?), his wife. Issue:

1c. William Johnson Webster III⁸, born 21 Feby., 1874. (q. v.).

2c. Hylemon Alison Webster⁸, born 8 Sept., 1875. (q. v.).

3c. Virginia Morgan Webster⁸, born 19 Aug., 1877; married 28 Dec., 1899, Eugene Webster Long⁹, and they have one child: 1d.—Octavine Alison Long⁹.

4c. Hugh Lee Webster⁸, born 19 Sept., 1888; married 30 Sept., 1913, Delia Arnold, born 25 Jany., 1893, and they have: 1d.—Hugh Lee Webster II⁹, born 25 Sept., 1918.

5c. Joseph Dobbins Webster⁸, born 6 Aug., 1890, unmarried.

1c. William Johnson Webster III⁸, born 21 Feby., 1874; married, 17 June, 1914, Mary Buchman, born 6 Dec., 1895, and they have:

1d.—William Jonathan Webster⁹, born 31 Aug., 1916.

2d.—Robert Wright Webster⁹, born 1 Dec., 1920.

2c. Hylemon Alison Webster⁸, born 8 Sept., 1875; married, 5 Nov., 1903, Olivia Barrow, born 15 Dec., 1880, and they have:

1d.—Hylemon Alison Webster II⁹, born 7 Sept., 1904.

2d.—Marian Webster⁹, born 30 Jany., 1909.

5a. *Caroline Webster*⁶ (*daughter of Jonathan* and Sarah (Jossey) Webster), 1813-1852, married, in 1833, William Henry Turner, born in Albemarle County, Va., in 1809; died in July, 1867. Issue:

1b. James Sugars Turner⁷, born 1834; married Fannie Williams, of Arkansas, and had several children, among them being: 1c.—James Sugars Turner, Jr.⁸; 2c.—Anna Price Turner.

2b. Sarah Webster Turner⁷, born 5 July, 1836. (q. v.).

3b. William Henry Turner⁷, born 1838; married Eleanor Finley, of Arkansas, and six children were born to them.

4b. John Acklen Turner⁷, born March, 1840. Served through the Civil War; became a Captain, and died April, 1909. (q. v.).

5b. Caroline Webster Turner[7], born Jany. 30, 1842; died unmarried, at the age of 22 years.

6b. Mary Rebecca Turner[7], born 24 March, 1843. (q. v.).

7b. Edward Deloney Turner[7], born Sept., 1845; died in camp, 1864, during Civil War, of dysentery.

8b. Rowena Turner[7], born Oct. 1, 1847; died May, 1872; married, 1871, or '2, Judge James R. Dowdell, of Opelika, Ala., who became Chief Justice of the Supreme Court of Alabama, serving for sixteen years in that office. Judge Dowdell married (II), in 1878, Ella Ware, daughter of Jonathan Ware, and by her had two daughters, Annie Love and Sarah. (See Ala. Memoirs).

9b. Robert Webster Turner[7], born Sept., 1849.

10b. Thomas Isaac Turner[7], born April, 1851.

2b. Sarah Webster Turner[7] (daughter of William Henry Turner), born 5 July, 1836; died March 15, 1915; married (I), May, 1856, John A. McEwen, lawyer of Nashville, Tenn., his third wife, and had one son: 1c.—John Alex. McEwen, Jr.; married (II), March, 1870, Henry Childress Shepard, and had:

2c. Mary Erwin Shepard[8], born March, 1871.

3c. Rosa Turner Shepard[8], born Nov., 1872.

4c: Norman Smith Shepard[8], born Sept., 1874.

4b. John Acklen Turner[7] (son of William Henry Turner), 1840-1909; married in 1861, Miss Mary Elliott, of Athens, Ala. Issue:

1c.—Caroline Webster Turner[8], born in March, 1864, m. . . . . . Drake and had one daughter.

2c. Edward Pearson Turner[8], born . . . . . , 1866; married Willis Lipscomb, and had: Edward P. Turner, Jr.[9], and Harris Turner[9].

3c. Fannie Turner Turner[8], born 1870.

4c. William Henry Turner[8], born 1874.

5c. Margaret Elliott Turner[8], born 1878. Single.

6c. James Webster Turner[8], born 1880; married (I) Mabel Wilkes, and had: 1d.—Webster Turner, Jr.[9]; married (II) . . . . . .

6b. Mary Rebecca Turner[7] (daughter of William Henry Turner), born 24 March, 1843; married 18 Jany., 1876, George Searight, of Nashville, Tenn. Issue:

1c. George Turner Searight, born 19 Nov., 1876; married, Dec., 1898, Mary Jean Myers. Issue: Five children.

2c. Henry Brown Searight[8], born Aug. 27, 1878. Presbyterian minister. Married (I), in January, 1904, Ebben Barker Armistead, died Dec., 1904, no issue. Married (II), in March, 1911, Mary Kathleen Bogart, of Washington, N. C. Issue: Three children.

3c. Fauntleroy Searight[8], born Nov. 1, 1883; died at 21 years of age, unmarried.

4c. Carrie Louise Searight[8], of 655 North Boulevard, Atlanta, Ga., born 26 Aug., 1886; married in Feby., 1905, Rogers McMillan Lemon. Issue: Two children, living.

5c. Paul Searight[8], born 16 Feby., 1888; died, aged 10½ years.

6a. Felix Webster[6] (son of Jonathan), born 1810; married Margaret Crosby, and had:
1b. Sarah (or Sadie) Webster[7], married Miles Mayes. No issue.
2b. Felix Webster, Jr.[7], married Mattie Fouchéé, and had: 1c.—Sallie Webster[8], died in infancy; 2c.—Laurence Webster[8], single; 3c.—Fannie Thomas Webster[8], died when about grown; 4c.—Lucy Webster[8], married Dr. Bledsoe Brown; 5c.—Felicia Webster[8], married Ross Burns.
3b. Albert Webster[7], married Mary Andrews. Issue: 1c.—Felix Webster[8]; 2c.—Andrew Webster[8]; 3c.—Mary Webster[8], married .... Clawson, and had two daughters; 4c.—Samuel Webster[8].
4b. Maggie Webster[7], married Nat. Yeatman, and had: 1c.—Sallie Yeatman[8], married .... Graham; 2c.—Penelope Yeatman[8], married .... Murray.
5b. Thomas Crosby Webster[7], married Mary Porter Black, and had: 1c.—Thomas Webster[8]; 2c.—Mary Webster[8].
6b. Fannie Knox Webster[7], married Judd Loyd.

7a. Albert Webster[6] (son of Jonathan), born 18 June, 1818; married Mary Fisher. Issue: 1b.—Sallie Webster[7]; 2b.—Rowena Webster[7]; 3b.—Eva Webster.

In removing from Wilkes County, Ga., to Maury County, Tenn., Jonathan Webster III and his wife were accompanied by his three children by his first marriage; by Mrs. Mary (Hill) Jossey (his mother-in-law) and two of her children, viz.: Janes Jossey and Rowena Caroline Jossey. The other two children, Henry and Kitty, remained in Wilkes County, Ga. Both married there in 1812. (See Webster).

EXCURSUS: *WEBSTER.*

"Joan Pope, of Bristol, England, widow of Thomas Pope[2], on 20 Dec., 1700, revoked and annulled a Power of Attorney recently given to Lewis Markham and *Alexander Webster* of Va. to manage her plantation called "The Cliffs" and negroes and things thereon and appoints in their stead John Herman, merchant, of Va. and her son John Pope, of Bristol, England". (Va. Library, York records, Book 1694-1702, p. 470).

In Burke's Peerage, we find record of marriage of Capt. Webster and Elizabeth Webster, daughter of Sir Thomas Webster. Circumstances indicate that this Capt. Webster was the Jonathan Webster I with wife Elizabeth, who had son Jonathan Webster born ye 11 D. Nov. 1740 as recorded in Bristol Parish Reg. p. 390. Their mottoes were the same, "fides et justitia". This son Jonathan Webster II, by tradition, married Miss Johnson, supposedly sister of Col. William Johnson of Wilkes County, Ga., and had: Abner, Pherobea, Samuel, Benjamin, Thomas, Jonathan III, born 17 May, 1767; died 20 April, 1845, and *Mary Johnson,* who married Thomas

Miller, who owned Cumberland Island, just across from St. Mary's, Ga. They are buried there at a fort called St. Peters. Their children lived in Augusta, Ga.

Pherobea Webster married Absalom Jackson, of Augusta, Ga.

Abner's will in Wilkes County, circa 1807. He was a Revolutionary soldier (Ga. Roster, p. 324).

Benjamin and Thomas Webster were killed while serving in the Revolutionary Army at Augusta, Ga.

Jonathan Webster III, 1767-1845, married (I) Miss Williams; married (II), May 9, 1805 or '6, Sarah Jossey. He served as a private in the Revolutionary War as evidenced by a Certificate for "a Bounty of 250 A. of good land", signed on the 8th day of Sept., 1784, by Col. Elijah Clarke. By his first marriage, he had: 1. *John Green Webster*, born 4 March, 1800; died 8 Dec., 1825; married Emily L. Gant and had a daughter, Emily Green Webster, married Felix Compton. 2. *Robert P. Webster*, born 1801; married, 17 Dec., 1828, Sarah Henry Anderson (a sister of Nancy Tate Anderson, second wife of James Dabney Willis), of Wilkes County, Ga., and had: Mary, Carrie, John, Lee, Lucian, William, Robert, Ada, Bettie, and Walton Webster. 3. *Mary Eliza Webster*, married Col. James Dobbins, and had: Addeline, Mary Eliza, and Major Joseph J. Dobbins, who married, in 1864, Catharine Heard, of Augusta, Ga., daughter of Stephen D. and Mary Jossey (Willis) Heard.

In a book entitled "Mount Pleasant, Especially Western Part of Maury County, Tenn.", by Nat. Willis Jones, on pp. 17, 18 and 19, we find: "Jonathan Webster was one of the first settlers; he came here, I think, from Georgia. He built one of the first gristmills in Bigby, about one hundred yards above the present one. This mill has always belonged to some of the Webster family. It is at present the property of Jonathan Webster's grandson, G. P. Webster. Jonathan Webster was the wealthiest man in the neighborhood. He was one of the first men to bring jacks and jennets to this section. Up to this time we had no mules; oxen were used on every farm. He also kept some of the fastest race horses in the county, racing being great sport at this time, though he abandoned everything of the sort long before his death. His children by his first wife were Jack, Robert and Mrs. Compton". (Note. There is one error in it. Mr. Jones alludes to my cousin Emily Green Compton as a daughter of Jonathan Webster. She was a grand daughter, being a daughter of John Green Webster". Wm. J. Webster in letter dated March 14, 1921).

"His second wife was a Miss Jossey, who was noted and beloved far and near for her charity and kindness to her friends in sickness and in distress. She was always to be found at their bedsides. Well do I remember seeing her riding on her horse (there were no buggies or carriages in those days) and a negro on a horse beside her, with a bushel basket on his arm containing delicacies for the sick and poor in her neighborhood; and well is she represented at this day by some of her descendants. Her children were, Mary, James, George, Caroline, William, Felix, Albert and Rowena, all of whom have passed away except Miss Rowena, the youngest child. I think she now lives in Nashville.

Jonathan Webster's neighbors were Joe and John McMurray, Edward English, George Lipscomb, Sam and Joe Majors, Dr. Frierson, Dr. McGimsey, Henry Kirk, *Nat. Willis*, John L. Macon, David Thompson, Monson Hart, the Strayhorns, Mixons and others.

Mrs. Webster ministered to the sick, Dr. Frierson practiced medicine and Scott Mays wielded the lancet—all free of charge".

The following is a copy of a slip of paper handed to H. Alison Webster, son of William Johnson Webster II, of Columbia, Tenn., who found it in a letter of his Aunt Rowe to his son W. J. Webster, Jr., who had it and kept it with the letter to him and also the inventory of Jonathan Webster II.

"Given by Aunt Rowe Webster   1882
        To
Alison Webster

The head of a cane used by his great great grandmother on his father's side. Her mother was a Miss Cotton of Ga. & she was a Miss Hill who married Henry Jossey of Clarke (?) Co., Ga., removed to Tenn. and married a Mr. John Macon."

3. Henry Jossey, Jr.[5], son of Henry and Mary (Hill) Jossey, married (I), 10 Jany., 1812, Huldah Pope, daughter of John and Elizabeth (Smith) Pope; married (II), the widow, Sarah Twining. Issue by 1st, none by second, marriage: 1a.—John Jossey[6]; 2a.—Mary Elizabeth Jossey[6] (q. v.); 3a.—Harriet Jossey[6] (q. v.); 4a.—Kitty Jossey[6], who m. John Simonton. These 3 sisters all died in Greenville, Ga.; 5a.—Sarah M. Jossey[6], who m. 10 Dec., 1829, William Reeves, of Wilkes Co. There may have been other children.

2a. Mary Eliz[h] Jossey[6] (Henry, Jr.[5]), m. Myron Ellis, of Greenville, Ga., his 1st wife. Issue: 1b.—Robert N. Ellis[7]; 2b.—Miss Avilla Ellis[7]; 3b.—Rev. Henry Jossey Ellis[7] (q. v.); 4b.—Willie Ellis[7], m. H. W. Adair (parents of Miss Irene Adair, et al., of Greenville, Ga.).

The Rev. Henry Jossey Ellis, d. Nov. 16, 1921, Methodist minister, the blind Chaplain of the Ga. State Senate, has a dau. Ethel Star Ellis, who m. Rev. Benj. Oglevie Hill (Methodist minister) of Bastrop, Tex., a gr. gr. son of Thomas and Sallie (McGehee) Hill. Other daus. are Mrs. H. M. Veasey and Mrs. Eugene Ragland, of Atlanta, Ga.

3a. Harriet Jossey[6] (Henry, Jr.[5]), m. Dr. Clark Taylor Williams, son of John and Lilly (Taylor) Williams, among early settlers of Clarke Co., the former from Va., the latter from Wilkes Co., Ga. They had, among others: 1b.—John H. Williams[7], of Meriwether

Co., b. 9 Jany., 1834; m. in 1862, Martha S. Robertson, b. in 1844, in Luthersville, Ga. Issue:

1c. Mary L. Williams[8], m. William Taylor, of Griffin, Ga.; 2c.—Howard R. Williams[8]; 3c.—Albert C. Williams[8]; 4c.—Gustavus Williams[8]; 5c.—James H. Williams[8]; 6c.—Harriet J. Williams[8]; 7c.—Mattie L. Williams[8]; 8c.—Minnie C. Williams[8]; 9c.—Eliza K. Williams[8]; 10c.—Henry C. Williams[8]; decd.; 11c.—Sallie P. Williams[8], decd. (Memoirs of Ga., Vol. 2, p. 525).

4. *Christiana, called "Keddy"* & *"Kittie", Jossey* (dau. of *Henry & Mary (Hill) Jossey*), 1793-1847, m. 3 Dec., 1812, *Col. Richard Jefferson Willis*, his 1st wife. He was born 12 Nov. 1789, and died Oct. 18, 1866. He was the representative from Wilkes, 1828-1831, and state senator 1832-'36. Issue:

1a. George Washington Willis[6], b. Oct. 23, 1813; d. Sept. 16, 1838; m. Margaret Lane.

2a. *Mary Jossey Willis*[6], b. 5 June, 1815; d. 5 Dec. 1886; m. April 5, 1836, *Stephen D. Heard* (q. v.).

3a. Rowena Jossey Willis[6], b. Feby. 10, 1817; d. 29 Jany., 1829.

4a. James Henry Willis[6], b. 20 Feby., 1819; m. 6 May, 1840, Sarah Ann Barksdale, and d. in 1904 or '5.

5a. Stephen Harris Willis[6], b. 5 Feby., 1821; m. Elizabeth Wells Truitt.

6a. John Thomas Willis[6], b. May 2, 1823.

7a. William Willis[6], b. June 9, 1825.

8a. Richard *Webster* Willis[6], b. Aug. 11, 1826.

9a. *William Johnson* Willis[6], b. Oct. 19, 1828.

10a. Dabney Willis[6], b. Nov. 1, 1829.

11a. Josiah Willis[6], b. Feby. 17, 1831.

12a. Lewis (Brown) Willis, b. Apr. 28, 1832.

2a. *Mary Jossey Willis*[6] (dau. of Rich J. Willis), 1815-1886, and her husband, *Stephen D. Heard,* had:

1b. Catharine Heard[7], m. in 1864, Major Joseph J. Dobbins, a gr. son of Jonathan Webster III.

2b. Mary Louisa Colquitt Heard[7] (q. v.).

3b. *Anna Heard*[7], m. June 2, 1868, *Hon. James C. C. Black*, lawyer, orator, statesman and ex-Member of Congress. Issue: 1c.—Catharine Black[8]; 2c.—James C. C. Black, Jr.[8], m. in 1913, Miss Lilly Rountree; 3c.—Merial Black, m. 1 Oct., 1921, Thos. D. Cary, broker in stocks and bonds.

4b. Richard Willis Heard[7], b. April 19, 1845; d. June 12, 1880 (q. v.).

5b. Stephen Heard[7], d. in infancy.

6b. Emmie Dampiere Heard[7], b. Oct. 22, 1853; d. July 10, 1919; m. Isaac Thomas Heard, b. Feby., 1850. Issue: 1c.—Thomas Heard[8], b. May, 1886; d. Oct., 1891; 2c.—Dampiere Heard[8], b. July 12, 1889; 3c.—Catharine Heard[8], b. April 14, 1892; m. Feby. 5, 1921, Dr. Righton Robertson.

2b. Mary Louisa Colquitt Heard[7] (dau. of Stephen D. Heard), m. June 10, 1859, E. J. Walton. Issue:
  1c. Virginia Walton[8]; 2c.—Kitty Willis Walton[8], m. April, 1889, James Bayard Walker, and had:
    1d. Mary D'Antignac Walker[9], who m. John Harper, and had Walker Harper[10].
    2d. Louisa Walker[9].
  3c. Martha Whitfield Walton[8], m. George W. Warren, and had:
    1d.—Julia Warren[9]; 2d.—Louise Warren[9], who m. Roger Gamble and has 2 children.
  4c. Richard Walton[8].
  5c. Anna Walton[8], m. Dave Jacks and has one child, Lucy Jacks[9], m. latter part Sept., 1921, James Frazier, of Atlanta, Ga.
  6c. Mary Jossey Walton[8].
4b. Richard Willis Heard, 1845-1880 (son of Stephen D. Heard), m. June 3, 1868, Anna Platt: Issue: 1c.—Charles Stephen Heard[8], b. April, 1869; m. Fancha Eaton and had: 1b.—Stephen Heard[9]; 2d.—Hamilton Heard[9].
  2c. Richard Willis Heard, Jr.[8], b. 1871; m. Virginia Lord Nesbit and had: 1d.—Virginia Heard[9]; 2d.—Richard Willis Heard III[9]; and, 3d.—Alexander Heard[9].
  3c. Frank Muir Heard[8], dead.

Myron Ellis (2a, p. 47), m. (II) Mrs. Mary Allen Jackson, of Oak Bowery, Ala.; m. (III) c. 1868, Mrs. Sarah (McGehee-Hill) Sheets, her 3rd husband. Her first husband was Josiah Woods Hill[5], 1808-1863 (V. A. P. O.). No issue by last two wives.

EXCURSUS: *WILLIS*.

Stephen Willis, who lived in Gloucester, New Kent or King William Co., Va., was closely related to the Byrds and Burwells. He married circa 1728, *Susana Dabney* & had: Rebecca, Joel *George* and Susannah Willis, who m. Sampson Harris.

George Willis (he was a Rev'y soldier—Ga. Roster of Rev'y Soldiers, p. 324), b. Oct. 16, 1754; d. April 19, 1827; m. Oct. 16, 1777, Susanna Baker, and came from King William Co., Va., in 1784, to Wilkes Co., Ga. Susanna (Baker) Willis, b. Aug. 24, 1757; d. April 30, 1843. Their children were:
  1. Stephen Willis, b. Aug. 23, 1778; d. Nov. 21, 1801.
  2. George Dabney Willis, b. Nov. 11, 1780; m. 26 Nov., 1807, Susannah Barkwell, Jesse Mercer, M. G., officiated.
  3. William Willis, b. March 26, 1784; d. Jany. 16, 1793.
  4. John Cruthchfield Willis, b. Nov. 28, 1787.
  5. *Richard Jefferson Willis*, b. *Nov. 12, 1789*; d. *Oct. 18, 1866*.
  6. James Dabney Willis, b. Oct. 21, 1793.

7. Elizabeth Dabney Willis, b. Oct. 13, 1796; m. 14 April, 1814, John H. Milner. Issue:
1. Susan Willis Milner, m. J. M. Putnam.
2. George Willis Milner, m. Mary Bouland.
3. Richard Willis Milner, m. Sallie E. Raven.
4. *Pitt* Milner, m. ...... Wright.
5. Attilla Ann Milner, m. S. G. Beckman.
6. Elizabeth Sims Milner, m. (I) John Epinger; m. (II), J. F. McLeod.
7. Eliza Penelope Milner, m. J. M. Wood.
8. Martha Rowena Milner, m. Richard Raven.
9. Jonathan James Milner, m. Nancy T. Bouland.
10. Mary Jane Milner, m. .... Reid.
11. Rebecca Amoretta Milner, m. Austin Harris.

VI.—*Henry Hill*[4] (Henry[3], Abr.[2], Henry[1]), b. pro. circa 1780; pro. m. 10 Dec., 1802, Redy Walker, of Warren Co. I say probably married, since a Henry Hill married as stated, but it is not certain that he was Henry[4], but I feel quite sure he was, though without proof of identity. No record of him later than 1812, when named in his mother's will, but one H. A. Hill is mentioned as being in Clarksville, Ga., in 1820-'30, and he probably is the same. (L. M. & L., by Knight, Vol. 2).

VII.—SARAH HILL[4] (Henry[3], Abr.[2], Henry[1]), m. before 1812, Josiah Woods, said to have been of Va., but of whom we have found, so far, no positive record. It is highly probable that he was a Rev'y soldier, a member of Capt. Swinfield Hill's Co., of Henry Co., Va. A General Order by Col. Abram Penn commanding Militia of Henry Co., preparatory for battle of Guilford C. H. 1 March, 1781, ordered to march to Hillsboro, N. C., or any post where Genl. Stevens may be with his Command. Josiah Woods was a member of Capt. Swinfield's Co. in this movement. (Va. Mag. of His. & B., Vol. 17, p. 192).

VIII.—*Catharine*, called "Keddy", Hill[4] (Henry[3], Abr.[2], Henry[1]), m. in the '90's, John Pope, d. in 1818, son of Willis Pope (son of Henry and Tabitha Pope) and his wife, Mary ...., maiden name not learned. (See Popes). Issue:
1. Henry Pope[5], b. 1796-1800; d. 1838, or '40. (q. v.).
2. Tabitha Pope[5] (q. v.); 3.—Nancy Pope[5] (q. v.); 4.—Elizabeth Pope[5], who pro. d. in 1829. In a letter of that year she is mentioned as being very ill. No further record. There may have been other children.

1. HENRY POPE[5], (Catharine[4], Henry[3], Abr.[2], Henry[1]), 1796-1840. In July, 1821, was a witness to the codicil to his grandfather's (Col. Wm. Johnson) will; representative from Wilkes in the State Legislature in 1833; removed in 1836, or '8, to Athens, Ga., and in 1838, or '40, while visiting his plantation called "Chehaw", in Lee Co., was taken ill and died, & was buried in the

cemetery lot of Judge D. A. Vason, of Albany, Ga. He m. c. 1818, Urania Calloway, b. 1800; d. 1872, dau. of Isaac Calloway and his wife, *Winnefred* Ragan, dau. of Jonathan Ragan, Sr., of Oglethorpe. (See above his will.)

WINNEFRED CALLOWAY, ABSOLOM JANES and *Henry Pope administrators* Estate of Isaac Calloway, Aug. 3, 1820. (Book ZZ, Admrs. Bonds, Wilkes Co., p. 31.)

HENRY POPE was this 12 Jany. 1824, appointed Guardian to *Mary Anne Calloway*, orphan of Isaac Calloway, decd. Surety Henry Terrell. Wit.: Thomas Wootten, one of the Judges Court of Ordinary. Recorded 6 April, 1824. (Guardians' Letters, Book L.L., p. 43).

Henry Pope, also guardian of *Martha Henrietta Calloway*, orphan of Isaac Calloway, decd. Surety, Terrell. Witness: Thomas Wootten. Recorded April 6, 1824. (Guardians' Letters, Book L.L., p. 44). Issue—order of births not known:

1a. John Pope[6], m. Miss Gilbert, called "Mitt", and had a son, Henry Pope[7], who was living about 1895.

2a. William Pope[6], said by one, "d. after maturity, unm.", by another, "m. (I) in Augusta, Ga. . . . . ; m. (II), near Albany, Ga."

3a. Chandler Mercer Pope[6], b. 1834; m. Anne Haseltine Brown, and had: 1b.—Lottie Pope[7], m. W. J. McLeod, of Sylacauga, Ala.; 2b.—Mrs. E. G. Crowell[7]; et al.

4a. Fannie Pope[6], d. c. 1890; m. (I), James Bartlett, of Monticello, Ga., son of George and uncle of Hon. Charles T. Bartlett, ex-Congressman, of Macon, Ga.; m. (II), William Malcom Janes, nephew of Col. Absolom Janes, and had: 1b.—Willie Janes[7], who m. Charles H. Swift, decd., of Atlanta, Ga.

5a. Cordelia A. Pope[6], eldest dau., m. 6 Nov., 1837, Judge D. A. Vason, of Albany, Ga., 2nd wife.

6a. Marie Indiana Pope[6], pro. youngest dau., m. Judge D. A. Vason, 3rd wife.

7a. Sallie Pope[6], m. Dr. Hendley Varner Calloway, son of Rev. William A. and Martha (Pope) Calloway, her second counsin.

8a. Celeste Pope[6], m. . . . . Davis, of Atlanta, Ga., and d. s. p. Said to have been an unhappy marriage.

2. Tabitha Pope[5] (Catharine[4] (called "Keddy"), m. William Thurmond. Both d. circa 1836-'38, near Mallorysville, Wilkes Co., Ga. They had:

1a. Nancy Pope Thurmond[6], b. April 3, 1832; d. 27 July, 1916, 85 years of age; m. in 1849, Major Robert Ligon McWhorter, of Greene Co., Ga., 2nd wife, and had: 1b.—Judge Hamilton McWhorter[7], of Athens, Ga.; 2b.—Joe V. McWhorter[7], of Woodville, Ga.

Her uncle, Henry Pope, was her guardian and carried her, when quite a child—about 6 years old—to Athens, Ga. Maj. Robt. L. McWhorter's (son of Hugh and Helen (Ligon) McWhorter) first wife was a dau. of Col. Absolom Janes and his wife, Cordelia Calloway, and by her had a son, Col. Robert Ligon McWhorter, Jr., who was 2½ years old, b. in 1846, or '7, at time of his second marriage.

3. Nancy Pope³ (Catharine⁴, called "Keddy"), m. Guilford Cade, 1st wife, son of James Cade and his wife, Mary Ann Wootten, dau. of Col. Thomas Wootten and his 2nd wife, Tabitha (. . . .) Pope. Issue: 1a.—Ben A. Cade⁶; 2a.—Wylie Pope Cade⁶; 3a.—Guilford M. Cade⁶; all decd. before 1898. Guilford Cade m. (II) Jane Turner, niece of William Trion. Issue: 4a.—James C. Cade⁶; 5a.—John R. Cade⁶; 6a.—Thomas Wootten Cade⁶. These last three were reared by William Trion and his wife, Amelia Cade, a sister of Guilford, their father, who d. when his son James C. Cade was 4 years old and his wife, Jane (Turner) Cade, 6 years later.

B.—ABRAHAM HILL³ (Abraham², Henry¹), c. 1732-1792, b. in Chowan, now Gates, County, N. C., was a member of Capt. John Summer's Co., Col. Robert Burden's Reg. of N. C. Militia, 25 Nov., 1754, at the time of the French and Indian War (S. R. N. C., Vol. XXII, p. 355; N. C. H. & G. Reg., 1-3-463; 2-1-159; 2-2-310; 2-3-472-'3-'4); removed circa 1768 to what was later Wake Co., N. C.; on June 4, 1771, was Justice of the Peace and member of the *first* Court of Pleas and Quarter Sessions for Wake Co. ("N. C. Booklet", Vol. 5, July, 1905, No. 1, pp. 3-17,—Article entitled "Genesis of Wake Co." by Marshall DeLancy Haywood); was continuously in said office to 1776, and probably later ("Minutes of Wake Co.", Book A, pp. 1, 6, 13, 14, 15, 19, 21, 29, 128 and 129, and until 1776); re-elected 23 Dec., 1778, by the Provincial Congress of N. C., at Halifax, to serve for the ensuing year. (S. R. N. C., Vol. XXIII, p. 995). "The *chief* legal tribunal of a County in N. C. was called the "Inferior Court of Pleas and Quarter Sessions". It was composed of all (or a quorum) of the Justices of the Peace meeting in joint session four times yearly. There were also Judicial Districts in the Colony, composed of several counties, over all of which the "Superior Court"—the highest tribunal in the Colony—and their sessions presided over by the Chief Justice and two "Assistant Judges", had higher jurisdiction than the above County courts. Wake County was in the Hillsborough District. The lawyers of that day often came down from Hillsborough and from other localities, even Virginia, to appear in the Wake Court of Pleas and Quarter Sessions". This Court on June 4, 1771, was held at Bloomsbury—present site of Raleigh. "Present: The worshipful Theophilus Hunter, Presiding Justice and the following Justices: Joel Lane, Joseph Lane, Benjamin Hardy, James Martin, Hardy Sanders, ABRAHAM HILL, THOMAS WOOTTEN, James Jones, Thomas Crawford and Tignall Jones". Here is shown the kind and character of men who composed this court. "This Court was abolished in N. C. by the Canby Constitution 1868. It existed in England and was the principal Court of the people in Colonial times".

AND ALLIED FAMILIES 53½

The following should come between the 18th and 19th lines from bottom of page 53. Its omission was not discovered until after the book came from the press:

Candor constrains this compiler to say:

I doubt seriously the right to credit the military service here shown to our Abraham Hill[3]. There were three other Abraham Hills in N. C. contemporaneous with him. The War Dept. at Washington fails to show place of residence, either at time of enlistment or of discharge, or to give the age of this Revolutionary soldier. It is therefore manifestly impossible, without other evidence, to say positively which of the four Abraham Hills rendered this service. Furthermore, we know that the Provincial Congress at Halifax, on 23rd Dec., 1778, named Abraham Hill[3] as one of the Justices of the Peace for Wake County, to serve for the ensuing year, viz., 1779. If he discharged the duties of a Justice during 1779, he could not at the same time have rendered uninterrupted military service. That he rendered some military service I am well assured, but when, where, and in what capacity, I am not prepared to say. An examination of the Wake County Minutes for 1779, if in existence, and of the Ms. Rolls—never published—of the 26,822 Revolutionary Soldiers, in the custody of the Historical Commission at Raleigh might enlighten us and settle the question definitely.

LODOWICK J. HILL.

The military record of ABRAHAM HILL is as follows: "Abraham Hill, Private in Capt. Grime's Co. 15th Va. Regt., commanded successively by Lt. John Innes and Major Gustavus Wallace. He enlisted Jany. 8, 1777, to serve three years; transferred June, 1778, to Lt. John Cropper's Co., 11th and 15th Va. Regt., commanded by Lieut. John Cropper and Col. Dan Morgan; about Dec., 1778, to Capt. David Mason's Co., 11th Va. Regt. commanded by Col. Abram Buford, and about May, 1779, to Capt. Mayo Carrington's Co., 5th and 11th Va. consolidated, commanded by Col. William Russell. Name last appears on muster roll for Nov. 1779. (W. R. T. Saffell Rec. of Rev. War, p. 268; part from War Dept. at Washington, and part from Va. State Library; also D. A. R. papers of Mrs. Annie Hill Snyder, of Tex.).

The Report of the Library Board and State Librarian, 1911-1912, by H. J. Eckenrode, Archivist (Va.) gives the following references as to record of Abraham Hill: (II V. R.) W. D. 231, 1; (15 V. R.) W. D. 275, 1; (5 & 11 V. R.) W. D. 335, 1; (11 & 15 V. R.) W. D. 337, 1. The letters "W. D." for War Dept. Folders.

ABRAHAM HILL'S Bounty Warrant now, in manuscript, in State Library, Richmond, Va., as follows:

"I do certify that Abraham Hill enlisted in 15th Va. Regt., 8th Jany., 1777, and that he served in the said Regt. as a good and faithful soldier until the 8th of Jany. 1780, when he was discharged. Given under my hand Nov. 10, 1784. John Cropper, Jr., formerly Lt. Col. Command 7th Va. Regt.

Passed—Cha. Jones, Com. Nov. 30, '84.

A Copy—John White P. A."

ABRAHAM HILL, 100 acres, pt. Va. Continental Line, 3 years, Dec. 19, 1785. ("Year Book 1913 of Ky. So. Sons of the Rev. and Catalogue of Va. Military Land Warrants", p. 226).

There is of record in the Ordinary's Office, at Lexington, Oglethorpe Co., Ga., a "Register of Land Grants, for Services rendered as Soldiers of the Revolution, or as *heirs* of such soldiers". Among those receiving such grants were Noah, Miles, Wylie, and Thomas Hill, all of whom were born after 1770, not themselves Rev'y soldiers, but sons and heirs of Abraham Hill, who was.

HENRY HILL and ABRAHAM HILL to WILLIAM HINTON, March 3, *1763*, 401 acres of land formerly belonging to HENRY HILL, *adjoining Isaac Harrell's* line. (N. C. H. & G. Reg. 2-3-475; Book L, No. 1, p. 135, at Edenton).

ABRAHAM HILL to Moses Speight, Feby. 21, *1763*, 174 A. of land patented by *said Hill* in 1759, lands at head of *Loosing Swamp*. (N. C. H. & G. Reg. 2-3-476; Book N, No. 1, p. 97, at Edenton).

Henry, Abraham and Theophilus Hill—3 brothers—all sold lands in Chowan in 1763, after the death of their father.

Theophilus Hill, of Dobbs Co., N. C., to Elisha Hunter, Nov. 5, 1763, *640* acres land in Bear Swamp granted *Wm. Jones* by a patent dated March 20, 1730, which he *sold to Abraham Hill, father of said Theophilus.* (Book M, No. 1, p. 73; N. C. H. & G. Reg. 2-3-475).

THEOPHILUS HILL, of Dobbs Co., N. C., to Wm. Speight, Nov. 7, 1763, 150 A. in *Cypress Swamp*, land purchased from Daniel Pugh by Abraham Hill. (Bk. M, No. 1, p. 86).

Henry Hill to William Hinton, Dec. 21, 1763, 250 acres on Mirey Brook, issuing out of Bennett's Creek. (Book M, No. 1, p. 90; N. C. H. & G. Reg. 2-3-475,-'6).

THEOPHILUS HILL, of Edgecombe Co., N. C., Nov. 8, 1763, to Samuel Hicks, 200 A. of land in Chowan Co., known as the *Punch Bowl* (*now Centre Hill*), part of a relapsed patent bearing date 1718. (Book M, No. 1, p. 130; N. C. H. & G. Reg. 2-3-476).

1767—*Henry Hill* to *Timothy Walton*, July 15, 1767, 150 A. on Crooked Branch issuing out of Bennett's Creek, formerly part of the grant to the Chowan Indians. (Book W, No. 1, p. 56; Reg. 2-3-476).

1767—HENRY HILL to *Robert Taylor*, July 10, 1767, 160 A. part of grant to Chowan Indians on Bennett's Creek. (Book N, No. 1, p. 141; Reg. 2-3-476).

1769—HENRY HILL to Wm. Coffield, Nov. 19, 1769, 100 A. on Bennett's Creek Swamp. (Book O, No. 1, p. 176; Reg. 2-3-476).

1771—HENRY HILL to Edward Briscoe, Oct. 25, 1771, 25 A. on Bennett's Creek Pocosin. (Book P, No. 1, p. 91; Reg. 2-3-476).

These last four records (above) are by the *Henry Hill*, who in 1733 and '42, bought lands of the *Chowan Indians* and who *may not have* been *a son* of *Henry Hill*[1]. It will be noted that in none of his records is there reference to, or the name of, his father.

Johnston Co., N. C., Deed Book L, p. old No. 11, new 184. This Indenture made this first day of April, 1769, between *Robert Nutt* to *Abram Hill*, both of Johnston Co., 100 acres land on Walnut Creek in Johnston Co. patented by Nutt 1761, for 22 £ 10 shillings.

(Signed) Robert Nutt.

Wit.: Theophilus Hunter
      Wm. Walton
      Joshua Suggs

Book L, p. 20 (old No.), new No. 193. Deed May 22, 1769, from Joshua Sugg to *Abraham Hill*, both of Johnston Co., N. C. 60 A. land, granted Theophilus Hunter by Earl Granville Oct. 8, 1752, for 20 £.   (Signed) Joshua Sugg.

    Henry Hill
    John Orr.

"Methodism in N. C.", by W. L. Grissom, Vol. 1, p. 98.

"When Mr. Asbury visited N. C. in 1780, to quiet the excitement among the preachers concerning the administration of the Sacraments, he traveled through *Wake*, Orange and Cumberland; showing that Methodism had already been planted in these Counties. Among those *who entertained the preachers at this early date, and who opened their homes for the preaching of the Word, are Kimbrough* and *Abraham Hill*; Tignall Jones and *James Hinton*; Merritt Crump and Taylor; R. Kennon White, and Harris; West, Trice, and Roades. Most of the preaching was done in private houses, though Mr. Asbury mentioned several chapels & school houses where he preached, & two meeting houses, those of Neuse and Taylors."

"The Conference was held at a meeting-house near Deer Creek in Md. The Circuit in 1777 appears on the minutes as North Carolina, with John King, John Dickens, Lee Roy Cole, and *Edward Pride*. This was evidently one of the most promising fields in the connection—great in possibilities and great in territorial extent." ("Methodism in N. C.", Vol. 1, 57).

"EDWARD PRIDE, the 4th man on the N. C. Circuit for 1777, appears on the minutes this year; and in 1778, he was second man on the Brunswick Circuit with John Dickens as principal. After this there is no record of him in the minutes". (Ibid, p. 63).

"The first Methodist College in the world was Cokesbury College at Abington, Md., which was begun in 1784, and named in honor of the first two bishops—Coke and Asbury". (Ibid, p. 137).

To the fund for the founding of this college *Abraham Hill*[3] *was a contributor.*

B. ABRAHAM HILL[3], c. 1732-1792, removed from Wake Co., N. C., to that part of Wilkes Co. that is now Oglethorpe Co., Ga., in 1785.

Wake Co. Deed Book H, p. 26. Deed from *Abraham Hill, Sr.*, of *Wake Co., N. C.*, to *Edward Pride* of *same Co.* and State, 143 A. land in Wake Co. on Richland Creek. Consideration 300 £ Specie. *Jany. 1, 1785.*   (Signed) Abraham Hill.
Wit.: William Walton } Regd. April 4, 1788.
      M. Brown

Wake Co., N. C., Deed Book "G", p. 202.

State of North Carolina } Know all men by these presents
Wake County.   } that I *Abraham Hill* of the
County of Wilkes in the State of Georgia from the certain assurances I have of the Honor, Integrity and Assiduity and many other good reasons to Abraham Hill, *Junior* of the County of *Wake* in the State of N. C. aforesaid have constituted and appointed and by these presents do for myself, my Heirs Executors and Administrators absolutely constitute and appoint the said Abraham Hill, Junior my whole and sole attorney to do and act for me and in my name to sign any Conveyance or Instrument of Writing whatsoever that may be Consistent with the Office and duty of an attorney as aforesaid and further I do hereby promise and agree that all and everything that the said Abraham Hill, Junior, may do and perform for and in my name as my Attorney aforesaid shall be good

and valid in law. In Witness Whereof I have Hereunto set my Hand and Seal the *22nd Day of December, 1785.*
(Signed) Abraham Hill.
Signed, sealed and delivered in the presence of us
William Walton
James Penny

Recorded Wake Co. March Term 1786.
Henry Lane Clerk Ct.
James Hinton Register.

Wake Co. Book G, p. 232.

Abraham Hill, *Jr.*, of Wake Co. N. C., makes deed, 7th March, 1786, to Halsey Dupry of same Co. to *640* A. on both sides Mill Branch in Wake Co. beginning at a Red Oak at John Ring's corner, etc. The land was granted *Abraham Hill, Sr.*, by the State of N. C. March 29th, 1780. Consideration paid to Abraham Hill, Jr. was 80 £ Specie.

Wit.: William Walton   (Signed) Abraham Hill, Jr.
      Richard King.

Wake Co. Book H, p. 421. Deed from Abraham Hill of the Co. of *Wilkes* and State of Ga., Dec. 19th, 1788, to Theophilus Hunter of Wake Co., N. C. 150 A. granted said *Abraham Hill* by Richard Carswell. Land on Steep Hill Creek. Consideration 100 £.
(Signed) Abraham Hill.

Wit.: William Walton, Josiah Akins, Theophilus Hunter, Jr. Recorded Oct. 31, 1789.

Abraham Hill granted Two hundred acres in Wilkes County bounded southwardly by Long Creek, Eastwardly by Henry McLeroy's land, *West by said Hill's land,* and on the other sides by vacant lands. Aug. 17, *1785.*

(Signed by) S. Elbert, Gov'r.
Recorded 22 Aug. 1785.   G. Handley, C. C.
(Head Right Book H.H.H., p. 318—in Sec. of State's Office).

It would seem from above grant that he already *owned* lands here prior to this grant.

12 July, 1787. Granted to Abraham Hill his heirs, &c., 1000 A. in County of Franklin bounded on East by *Henry Pope's* land South by *John Taylor's* land and on all other sides by vacant land. By Govr George Mathews in Council.
12 July, 1787.   J. Meriwether C. C.
(Land Book O.O.O., p. 97).

31 Dec., 1787.—Granted by George Mathews Govr to *Abraham Hill,* his heirs &c a tract containing 206 A. in County of Wilkes, bounded North by vacant lands, East by *Drury Cade's* land and vacant land South by Richard Wood, James Patton and vacant land, and West by Zachariah Lamar's land. 31 Dec., 1787, by his Honor the Govr in Council,   J. Meriwether C. C.
(Land Book P.P.P., p. 112).

Jany. 1, 1788.—Granted to *Abraham Hill* 460 A. in County of Greene bounded Westwardly by south fork of Oconee river, Southwardly by Wm. Daniel's and vacant land and all other sides by Vacant lands. Jany. 1, 1778, by the Govr in Council.

J. Meriwether C. C.

Reg. 6 Jany, 1788 (Land Book P. P. P., p. 120).

Abraham Hill[3] acquired by grants and purchase lands lying on both north and south sides of Long Creek, about three miles above its confluence with Dry Fork Creek, and about twenty miles northwest of Washington, Ga. Here south of the Creek, and a quarter of a mile north of the main road from Petersburgh to Lexington, he erected a large, commodious frame two story homestead, with brick chimneys and foundations, esteemed in those days as truly palatial. It was probably about the first plastered house in that part of Georgia. Completed circa 1790, it remained practically unchanged for a hundred years. But in the latter part of the 19th Century it passed into alien hands, and though still standing in almost its original integrity, is dilapidated, ramshackle, virtually a ruin and the abode of negroes, markedly symbolizing the instability and impermanence of the cherished plans and works of man and the mutability of all mundane things. His homestead must have been very near the Indian line, for in 1790 the Cherokee border was only 20 miles west of Washington. During this year it was removed 20 miles further west, but there was little security either to life or property, in this exposed neighborhood. "Two of Georgia's most distinguished and honored families were planted in Wilkes at the close of the Revolution, the Hills and the Popes". ("L. M. & L.", Vol. 2, p. 1046-'50, by Dr. L. L. Knight). Besides four daus. Abraham and Christian (Walton) Hill had 8 sons, only one of whom failed to reach adult years. Burwell (one of 5 brothers) and Priscilla (Wootten) Pope had three sons and four daus. Two of Burwell Pope's brothers married daus. of Abraham Hill and three of the latter's sons married daus, of Burwell Pope—to quote the late Judge Pope Barrow—"the Hills and the Popes intermarried backwards and forwards, right and left".

B.—ABRAHAM HILL[3], c. 1732-1792 (Abraham[2], Henry[1]), m. 7 Jany., 1756, CHRISTIAN WALTON, b. c. 1736; d. 6 July, 1808, dau. of Thomas Walton, Jr.(b. c. 1713; d. 1759) and his wife Sarah......, maiden name not learned, d. 1761 (N. C. H. & G. Reg. 1-2-239; 1-3-456; 2-1-33 and 159; 2-2-272; 2-3-472-'4; Book H, No. 1, p. 189—at Edenton, N. C.). The marriage bond in the body says Katharine but is briefed Christian, which is correct (Reg. 2-3-472).

"Know all men by these presents that I Thos. Walton of Chowan County province of No. Carolina Esq. for & in consideration of the sum of one shilling current money already in hand paid me by my son-in-law Abrah-m Hill & *Christian* his wife & also for & in consideration of the natural love & affection which I have & do bear towards them do bargain, sell, give, grant, set over and deliver unto them the sd. *Abrm Hill the younger & my daughter Christian his wife* one negro man named Duke & twelve head of meat cattle one sorrel mare named Bonney, two sheep, ten hogs, & one case of bottles, which sd. cattle hogs & sheep are under my proper mark, To Have & to Hold the sd. negro goods & chattels unto my sd. *son in law Abrm Hill & my daughter his wife* & their heirs & assigns forever to their own proper use benefit & behoof forever & I th sd. Thos. Walton doth hereby quit possession of the same unto them the sd. Abrm and Christian their heirs & assigns forever & will warrant & forever defend a good sure title to the same unto the said Abrm. & Christian their heirs & assigns forever against the lawful claims of all & every person or persons whatsoever. In Witness of which I have hereunto set my hand this 3rd day of Aug. 1757. Thos Walton (†)

Signed sealed & delivered in the presence of Chas. Rountree, Hardy Hunter, Thos. Rountree—North Carolina Chowan County: Aug. 5, 1757. The execution of the above deed was proved in due form of law by the oath of Thos. Rountree one of the subscribing witnesses. Let it be registered.

Peter Henly C. J.

Reg. 18th Aug. 1757.

Geo. Disbrowe Reg."
(Recorded in Book H, No. 1, p. 189; Reg. 2-1-159).

Thomas Walton, Jr., of Chowan, Nov. 9, 1736, to Thos. Hansford, of Bertie 270 A. land in Bertie—lately conveyed, 24 Mar. 1736, by John Glover & May Glover his wife to the sd. Walton—for 400 £ current money of N. C.   (signed) Thomas Walton

Wit: J. Pratt
     Jno. Wynns } Sarah Walton, *wife* of Thomas Walton relinquishes dower.
     Thos. Crew

(Book E. p. 45—Windsor, Bertie Co. N. C.)

"Sarah Walton, *widow* and guardian of John Walton, *orphan* of *Thomas Walton, decd., 1759.*" (N. C. H. & G. Reg. Vol. 1, No. 3, p. 456).

Will of Sarah Walton, wid. of Thos. Walton, Jr.

"In the name of God Amen on the Twenty third day of June in the year of our Lord one thousand seven hundred and sixty-one I Sarah Walton being very sick and weak of body but of perfect mine do make and ordain this my last will and testament. As to what worldly it has pleased God to bless me with I give and desire and dispose of the same in manner and form following.

In the first place I give and bequeath to my well beloved son Richard Walton three pounds proc¹ money that is due from him to me, and one ox bell and one oxe yoke and ring and stapel that he has now in his possession and that to be his full share of my estate.

I give and bequeath to *my well beloved daughter Christian Hill* my riding *mare called Boney*, one wooling wheel, and all my cards, and all my cloth that is wove with all my thread, flax, wool and cotton and one tin callender and one stone butter plate.

I give and bequeath to my well beloved daughter Sarah Walton one new feather bed, one blanket, two sheets, one good rugg to be purchased by my executors out of the money arising by the sale of my goods not given, and one large trunk, one walnut spinning wheel.

My will and desire is that my son Thomas Walton have one third part of my crop that is ready growing, and I likewise bequeath to my well beloved son Thomas Walton my negro woman called *Dinah*, and further it is my will and desire that all the rest of my estate not before given be sold by my executors, and after paying my debts and necessary charges, I give one half of it to my well beloved *son William* Walton and the other half to be divided equally between my two sons *Thomas* Walton and *John Walton*. I likewise constitute my *friend Timothy Walton* and *my son-in-law Abraham Hill* my executors of this my last will and testament. In Witness Whereof I have hereunto set my hand and seal the day and year above written.

her
Sarah X Walton
mark

Signed sealed and delivered in the presence of us
    her
Kissiah X Taylor
    mark
Richard Garrett, Jnr

Thos. Walton, Jr., *was the son(?) of Thos. Walton, Sr.*, b. pro. in Va., c. 1690; removed c. 1727 to N. C.; d. 1750-51. Thos. Walton, Sr., was elected Vesteryman for Parish of Chowan, April 7, 1740 (Reg. 1-4-603); was elected Feby. 27, 1740, as a member of the Assembly (House of Burgesses) of N. C. for Chowan Co., and again in 1746. (C. R. N. C., Vol. IV, pp. 493, 499, 506, 1180). He was appointed Justice of the Peace July 10, 1750 (C. R. N. C., Vol. IV, p. 1046; Reg. 2-2-296), d. between Nov. 13, 1750, and July 5, 1751 (Reg. 1-4-512).

Thomas Walton, Jr., b. pro. in Va. c. 1713; removed to N. C. c. 1727 (S. R. N. C., Vol. XXII, p. 241 et seq. & 258; Reg. 2-3-444-'5; 1-1-108; 3-1-128; Book D, p. 280 and Book E, pp. 45 and 285 in Bertie Co.); on May 19, 1757, took his seat as a Member of House (of Burgesses) from Chowan Co., Assembly held at Newberne (C. R. N. C., Vol. V, p. 847); "27 May, 1757, *allowance due and payable to Thomas Walton*", and other Members of Assembly, "this 4th session held at Newberne (which seemingly implies that he was a member before 1757), (C. R. N. C., Vol. V, p. 868); was a member also Nov. 29, 1758 and Dec. 14 and 23, 1758 (C. R. N. C. Vol. V, pp. 1046, 1071).

See Excursus: Walton, Jr.

Will of ABRAHAM HILL, Senr.

In the name of God, Amen. I Abraham Hill, Senr., of the County of Wilkes and State of Georgia, being weak in bodily health but of sound and perfect mind and memory (blessed be God) do make and ordain this to be my last Will and Testament in manner following, that is to say:

First: I lend unto my wife Christian, for, and during the term of her natural life my negro fellows Ben and Dick, and my negro wenches, Jude, Jean and Sall, all my stock of horses, cattle (except six young heifers which are to be disposed of hereafter) Hogs, Sheep and Poultry, likewise one of the best feather beds and furniture (her choice) and all the remainder of my household and kitchen furniture (my other beds and furniture excepted).

It is my will and desire that my wife have the use of my land lying on Long Creek on the south side including my Mannor plantation except two hundred acres, and including the plantation whereon my son Henry now lives—for and during the term of her natural life, likewise four acres of my land lying on the north side of said creek, opposite to the upper end of my Mannor plantation, including my old plant beds, during the term of her natural life.

I give and bequeath to my son Abraham my land lying on the north side of Long Creek, the said Creek to be the dividing line between said land and my Mannor plantation land—to him, his heirs and assigns forever, the four acres above mentioned excepted.

I GIVE and bequeath unto my sons *Theophilus* and *Noah*, my tract of land lying on the South side of Broad River, on said River in Wilkes County containing Two Hundred acres—as also my tract of land lying on the Apalachee River, North side in Greene County, containing four hundred and sixty acres, to them, their heirs and assigns forever.

I GIVE and bequeath unto my son *Wylie*, two hundred acres of my land lying on the South side of Long Creek (it being part of the tract I now live on) including the plantation whereon my son Henry, now lives, and also one half of the low grounds belonging to the tract I now live on, to him, his heirs and assigns forever.

I GIVE and bequeath unto my son *Thomas*, all the remainder of my land lying on the south side of Long Creek including the plantation whereon I now live, after the death of my wife, then to be his, his heirs and assigns forever, as also the four acres above mentioned including my plant beds.

I LIKEWISE GIVE unto my son *Theophilus*, my negro fellow Bob and my wench Phillis, and all her future increase, to him, his heirs and assigns forever.

I GIVE unto my son *Myles*, my negro fellow Jacob, my boy Lee, and my negro wenches Rose and Cynthia and all their future increase, and also one feather bed and furniture *when he comes of age*, to him, his heirs and assigns forever.

I GIVE and bequeath unto my son Noah, my negro fellow Jupiter and my wench China and all her future increase, to him, his heirs and assigns forever, and also one feather bed and furniture *when he comes of age.*

I GIVE and bequeath unto my son Wylie, my negro boy Ned and my girl Dinah and after my wife's decease my negro fellow Ben and my wench Jean and all of the future increase of Jean and Dinah, likewise one feather bed and furniture *when he comes of age*, to him, his heirs, and assigns forever.

I GIVE and bequeath to my son *Thomas*, my negro boy Isaac and my negro wench Kate and all their future increase *when he comes of age* and after the death of my wife, my negro fellow Dick, to him, his heirs and assigns forever, and likewise one feather bed and furniture (lent to his mother) after her decease, to him, his heirs and assigns forever.

I GIVE and bequeath to my daughter *Mary*, my negro wench Peg and her children Sue and Nancy, and all their future increase, likewise one feather bed and furniture to her, her heirs and assigns forever, *when she comes of age.*

My will and desire is, that after the death of *my wife Christian*, my executors hereinafter named, do sell my negro wenches Jude and Sall, to which ever of my children will give the most for them, and the money arising from the sale to be equally divided amongst all my children, to be for the use of them, their heirs and assigns forever.

I GIVE and bequeath unto my Grand son Henry *Blake* one young heifer and the increase to him, his heirs and assigns forever.

I GIVE and bequeath to my Grand Daughter *Mary Blake* one young heifer and all the future increase of said heifer to said Mary her heirs and assigns forever.

I GIVE and bequeath to my Grandson JOHN POPE, one young heifer and all the future increase of said heifer to him and his assigns forever.

I GIVE and bequeath to my Grand Daughter SARAH POPE one young heifer and all the future increase of said heifer, to said *Sarah* her heirs and assigns forever.

I GIVE and bequeath to my Grand Daughter *Betsy Jordan* one young heifer and all the future increase of said heifer, to said *Betsy* her heirs and assigns forever.

I GIVE and bequeath unto my grandson, Whitman Cocke Hill, one young heifer and all the future increase to him his heirs and assigns forever.

Out of the money due me from Edward Pride, it is my will and desire that my Executrix and Executors hereafter named, do purchase one young wench (likely negro) which said negro wench and all the future increase she may have, it is my will and desire that my *son-in-law, Josiah Jordan* and likewise five shillings to be the sole use and benefit of him, his heirs and assigns forever.

It is my will and desire that my Executrix and Executors hereafter named, as soon as they can collect in the balance of the money and etc., due to me by sundry persons, that they discharge all of the just debts owing by me, and if there should be any money remaining after my just debts &c. are discharged, *and the cost of finishing my house*—it is my will and desire that my Executrix and Executors hereafter named, do purchase a horse for my *son Noah*, and to be his use his heirs and assigns forever, but in case there should not be money enough, my Executors, after the death of my wife, must sell enough of the stock to purchase my *son Noah* a horse.

It is my will and desire that after the death of my wife, all my stock of cattle be equally divided amongst my children, Theophilus, Noah, Miles, Thomas, Wylie and Mary, and that all the stock of horses, hogs, sheep and poultry that may be left at my wife's decease, be equally divided amongst my children, Noah, Miles, Wylie, Thomas and Mary, to be to the sole use and profit of them, their heirs and assigns forever, likewise all the increase after my wife's death.

It is my will and desire that the negroes that I have given to my children, Noah, Miles, Wylie, Thomas and Mary, all work on the plantation where I now live, under the *direction of my wife* and *my son Abraham,* until my said children, Noah, Miles, Wylie, Thomas and Mary come of age or marry, and the use and profit of said negros be for the support and maintenance of my wife and said children and schooling said children.

I constitute and appoint my wife, Christian Executrix, and my sons Abraham and Henry Executors of this my last will and testament. In witness whereof I have hereunto set my hand and seal, this 23rd day of Nov., A. D. 1790.

      ABRAHAM HILL, SENR.   (Seal)

Signed, sealed and acknowledged in presence of
 J. Abernathie
    his
 Joshua J. Johnston
    mark

Whereas, I Abraham Hill, Senr. of Wilkes County, State of Georgia, having in my last will and testament dated this 23rd day of Nov., 1790, omitted leaving part of my property to my son Henry, and my sons in law, Benjamin Blake and Henry Pope of the County and State aforesaid, it is my will and desire that my Executrix and Executors as soon as they possibly can, give or pay unto my son Henry Hill, the sum of five shillings to be for the sole use of him, his heirs and assigns forever, and likewise the sum of five Shillings to each of my sons-in-law Benjamin Blake and Henry Pope, to be to the use of them, their heirs and assigns forever.

These presents I the said Abraham Hill, Senr. do acknowledge to be a codicile to my last will and testament, date aforesaid. In

Witness Whereof I have hereunto set my hand and seal, this 23rd day of Nov. 1790.

Abraham Hill, Senr. (Seal)

Signed sealed and acknowledged in presence of
J. Abernathie
    his
Joshua X Johnston
    mark

This Will was proven before David Terrell Registrar P. C. Feby. 29th 1792. It was recorded Feby. 29th, A. D. 1792 and letters testamentary granted to Henry and Abraham Hill Executors.

"This is a correct copy of the will of Abraham Hill found in the registry of Wills, in the Ordinary's Office of Wilkes Co. *I* copied it Dec. 13th 1894 and affirm it is a perfectly correct copy.

(Signed) Eliza A. Bowen."

B.—*Abraham*³ and *Christian (Walton) Hill* had:
  I—John Hill⁴, b. pro. circa 1757. N. R.
  II—Abraham Hill⁴, b. 14 Jany., 1759; d. 24 April, 1818. (q. v.).
  III.—Judie (Judith) Hill⁴, b. c. 1761; d. 20 June, 1794. (q. v.).
  IV—Clara Hill⁴, b. 9 Aug., 1763; d. 16 Nov. 1798. (q. v.).
  V—Sarah Hill⁴, b c. 1765; d. 26 Jany., 1816. (q. v.).
  VI—Henry Hill⁴, b. 1767; d. 5 Aug., 1829. (q. v.).
  VII—Theophilus Hill⁴, b. 1769; d. 19 Aug., 1829. (q. v.).
  VIII—Noah Hill⁴, b. c. 1771; d. 13 March, 1805. (q. v.).
  IX—Miles Hill⁴, b. 13 March, 1774; d. 4 Nov., 1844. (q. v.).
  X—Wylie Hill⁴, b. 26 Dec., 1775; d. 3 April, 1844. (q. v.).
  XI—Mary (Polly) Pope⁴, b. c. 1777; d. 2 June, 1849. (q. v.).
  XII—Thomas Hill⁴, b. 12 July, 1780; d. 9 Feby., 1816. (q. v.).

11—Abraham Hill⁴ (Abraham³, Abr.², Henry¹), 1759-1818, removed from N. C. to Wilkes Co., Ga., soon after 7 March, 1786; was a private in Capt. John Reid's troop of Light Dragoons, Lt. Col. Wade Hampton's Reg., and Genl. Sumpter's Brigade of the Rev'y Army. ("Documents relating to the His. of S. C. during Rev'y War, p. 63, by Salley).

"Abraham Hill⁴, Oct. 1, 1784, late private in Reid's Troop, W. Hampton's Reg., Sumpter's Brigade, for 94 £ Sterling—amount pay and bounty for service from April 1, 1782, to date hereof.

P¹ 94 £ O. O.

Int,—6 11, 7". (Stub Entries to Indents for Rev'y Claims", Book L—N, p. 129, by Salley).

II.—ABRAHAM HILL⁴ was waylaid, robbed and murdered while going from his home in Oglethorpe Co. to Lexington, Ga., by one James Carter, a young man whom he had taken into his home, while childless, and treated as a son, and who expected to be the heir. But when the rightful heir came, this boy, now a man, grew restive and selfishness overruled gratitude and led him to rob and murder his benefactor. He fled and was never apprehended, or heard of until long years thereafter an old and broken man wandered back from the West to the old homestead, lingered awhile, and asked to be buried in the family burying ground beside his benefactor whom he had robbed and murdered. ("Francis Morgan an Early Va. Burgess &c", p. 130, by Annie Noble Sims; Article in Athens Banner by Mrs. Augusta Hill Noble.)

He m., 5 May, 1791, Elizabeth McGehee, b. 21 Oct., 1773; d. 5 Aug., 1816, dau. of Micajah McGehee, b. c. 1745; d. 31 July, 1811, son of Edward and Elizabeth (DeJarnette) McGehee, of Cumberland Co., Va., and his wife, Ann Scott, b. c. 1753; d. 23 Feby., 1816, dau. of Capt. James Scott, b. c. 1725 (son of Thos. Scott and Ann Baytop, his wife) and his wife Frances Collier, b. c. 1731, dau. of John Collier and his wife, Nancy Eyres, or Epps. (See "Francis Morgan an Early Va. Burgess &c., p. 54).

Issue—two children—the first born 16 years after their marriage:

1—Abram Scott Hill[5], M. D., b. 24 Aug., 1807; d. 12 July, 1866, graduated at the University of Ga. in 1827 with degree of A.B. and at University of Penn. in 1832 with degree of M.D.; was Surgeon of 1st Ga. Regt., Mexican War, 1846-'47, under Genl. Henry R. Jackson; m., 25 Nov., 1835, Susan F. Holsey, b. 15 April, 1807; d. 12 Jany., 1840, dau. of James and Susannah Holsey. Issue: 1a.—Holsey Hill[6], b. 20 Aug., 1836; d. 22 Aug., 1837.

2. Elizabeth Ann Hill[5], b. 12 Jany., 1810; d. 2 Mar., 1894; m., 19 May, 1825, her cousin, Blanton Meade Hill[5], b. 5 May, 1802; d. 3 Feby., 1857, son of Miles[4] (1774-1844) and Tabitha (Pope) Hill. (See W. & M. Qly., Vol. XXVII, No. 1, July 1918, p. 57; No. 2, Oct. 1918, pp. 106-'7; E. S. of Ala., p. 450). Issue, 7 children:

1a. Alonzo Alexander Franklin Hill[6], b. 4 Dec., 1826; d. 9 Jany., 1872. (q. v.).

2a. Elizabeth McGehee Hill[6], b. 3 April, 1828; d. 19 Sept., 1834.

3a. Georgia Anna America Hill[6], b. 9 May, 1830; d. 17 Sept., 1889. (q. v.).

4a. Clara Eletheura Hill[6], b. 11 Dec., 1831; d. 7 Dec., 1855; m. 11 Sept., 1855, William R. Cunningham, banker and planter, of Aberdeen, Miss.

5a. Felixina Augusta Hill[6], b. 28 Feby., 1834; d. 17 Nov., 1908, in Phila., Penn. (q. v.).

6a. Blanton Abraham Hill[6], b. 5 Oct., 1836; d. 2 Sept., 1864, unm. (q. v.).

7a. Susan Tabitha Hill[6], b. 11 Oct., 1848; m. 20 April, 1871, Robert Huger Johnston, d. Sept., 1898, of Griffin, Ga. Issue:

1b.—Susan Tabitha Hill Johnston[7], living in Phila.; 2b.—Helen Love Johnston[7], living with her mother in Atlanta and College Park, Ga.

Mrs. Susie (Hill) Johnston was the idol of her family, reared in luxury and ease, with brothers and sisters who humored her, and servants to minister to all her needs. By the death of her husband was left dependent with the responsibility of rearing, maintaining and educating her two daughters. She faced the situation with courage; obtained immediately employment in Atlanta as a typist and by her indefatigable energy, efficiency, intelligence and fidelity, advanced from station to station, until she now occupies an important and remunerative position in one of the largest insurance companies in the city, and is honored, esteemed and appreciated by both associates and employers.

1a. Alonzo Alexander Franklin Hill[6], M. D., 1826-1872, son of Blanton Meade[5] and Elizabeth Ann Hill[5], graduated at the University of Ga. with 3rd honor and degree of A.M. in 1845; in 1848 received degree of M.D. from Jefferson Medical College, Phila., Pa., and soon thereafter was appointed Assistant Surgeon on one of the Flag Ships of the U. S. Navy, on the Pacific, serving seven years from 14 March, 1848, to 6 April, 1854. ("Hammersley's General Navy Register", p. 256); then studied law and graduated from the University Law School, at Athens, Ga., in 1860. He entered C. S. A., was Capt. 10 April, 1861, Co. A, in 1st Reg. Ga. Regulars, promoted Major, Sept. 3, 1864, and was later made Lieut. Col. (Ga. Soldier Roster Commission; "History of Ga.", p. 661, by Col. I. W. Avary; Article by Mrs. Noble in Athens Banner. Framed Roster of the 2 Regt. of Regulars in C. S. A. in possession of the Ga. Hisl. So'y, at Savannah, Ga.).

In the "Annals of Athens", by A. L. Hull, on p. 246, he says: "that Frank Hill—with others—became a Colonel during the War", and on p. 214 we find: "Col. Hill was interested in everything going on. He was Capt. of the Fire Co., belonged to the Guards, organized the Artillery, chaperoned Picnics, led the dances and filled a large place in the social life of the town. He wore his hair long and parted in the middle, and his beard long and pointed; in fact was distinguished by having the longest beard of any man in town. He was a great beau in Society and a very general favorite". While on a visit to his kinsman, Col. L. M. Hill, of Wilkes, he laughingly told him of a visit to a lady in Miss., from which he had just returned, said he discovered that the Pater-familias" was keenly anxious to learn his financial status and ability to support a family, whereupon he had casually remarked in his hearing that he gave little thought to the matter of finances, save only to make sure, by self denial and sane expenditure, that on returning from his wanderings, he should have a quarter in his pocket to pay bus fare from the railroad to his home. It was then made evident that though his society was agreeable, as a suitor for the daughter's hand he would be persona non grata. "Yet in him God's richest gifts were sweetly blended". He m. 16 June, 1869, Gazalena Williams, of Barbour Co., Ala., and had only one child—a dau.: 1b.—Frankie Williams Hill[7], b. 5 Jany., 1872.

3a. Georgia Anna America Hill[6], 1830-1889 or 1899, dau. of Blanton Meade[5] and Elizabeth Ann Hill[5], m. 14 Oct., 1852, Martin Luther Strong, called "Doc", of Aberdeen, Miss., d. 13 Aug., 1877, a Major in C. S. A., son of Genl. Elisha Strong, b. in Hanover Co., Va.; d. 21 Nov., 1879, in Ga., and his wife, Ann Scott Hill[5], 1804-1878, dau. of Thomas Hill[4], 1780-1816, and his wife, Sallie McGehee. Issue, 4 children:

1b. Annie Hill Strong[7], b. 3 Oct., 1854; m. 22 Feby., 1876, Henry Clopton.

2b. Blanton Hill Strong[7], b. 6 March, 1857.

3b. Abraham Hill Strong[7], b. 28 June, 1859.

4b. Sallie Hill Strong[7], b. 6 Aug., 1861; d. 17 April, 1875.

5a. Felixina Augusta Hill[6] (dau. of Blanton Meade & Eliz'h Ann Hill), 1834-1898, graduated with degree of A.B. from Wesleyan Female College, at Macon (Catalog 1915-'16, p. 101) ; m. 23 June, 1859, William Giles Noble, of Nottaway Co., Va., b. 15 Aug., 1810; d. 29 March, 1881, son of Josiah and Ione (Beadle) Noble, and gr. son of Joseph Noble, Ensign in the Rev'y War, and of Lieut. John Beadle, of the Revolution; was six feet three inches, proportionately broad; an Episcopalian, and for some years Vestryman of Emmanuel Church, Athens, Ga.; when married was engaged in the wholesale business of importing silks and laces in N. Y. City. (Vide Francis Morgan an Early Burgess of Va., &c., &c.", pp. 179-180, by Annie Noble Sims; "Va. Militia in the Rev'y War", pp. 177-179, by J. T. McAllister). Issue:

1b. Blanton Hill Noble[7], b. 13 April, 1860; d. 9 Sept., 1914, unm., in Phila., Pa. He graduated from the U. of Ga. in 1880, taking the degrees of A.B and B.Ph.; afterwards studied and practiced law in Athens and later in Phila.

2b. Annie Frank Noble[7], b. 8 May, 1862; d. 3 June, 1921, in Rochester, Minn., at Mayo Bros. Hospital; buried 6 June in Atlanta, Ga. (q. v.).

3b. Mary Ella Noble[7], called "Pidgeon", b. in Louisburg, N. C., 3 Jany., 1865; m. 11 Oct., 1893, Arthur Holley Allen, of Phila. Issue, five children, of whom were: Isabel Noble[8]; Augusta Hill Noble[8]; and Arthur Hartman Allen[8].

4b. Augusta Hill Noble[7], b. 31 Jany., 1868; d. 21 Oct., 1896, in Norfolk, Va.; m. 5 June, 1889, Eugene Lawrence Mayer, of Norfolk, Va. Issue, 4 children: Claudia (?) Augusta; Eugene Noble; Charles Leonard and Augustine.

2b. *Annie Frank Noble[7]* (dau. of Wm. Giles and Augusta (Hill) Noble), 1862-1921, member of Ga. Society of C. D.s., and of the D. A. R.; m. 21 Aug., 1884, in Athens, Ga., William Irvin Sims, of Fulton Co., Ga., b. 26 Nov., 1852; d. 25 Jany., 1911, in St. Louis, Mo., son of William Edward Sims, Lieut. in Co. B, 7th Ga. Reg., C. S. A., and his wife, Virginia Elizabeth Doneho, and gr. son of

Edward Sims, of Kershaw Dist., S. C., and his wife Jane Oliver. Issue, 3 children:

1c. Irvin Augustus Sims[8], b. 13 Jany., 1887. (q. v.).

2c. Alice May Sims[8], b. 30 April, 1889; d. 10 Sept., 1890.

3c. Annabel Noble Sims[8], b. 16 Jany., 1892; graduated from Mary Institute, St. Louis, Mo., in 1910; m. 28 May, 1913, Charles Blackburn Sims, who graduated from the U. of Ill. and received degree of L.L.B. from the Chicago Law School, was son of William Blackburn Sims, M. D., and his wife, Sarah Jane Medley, gr. son of William Gray Sims, a soldier of the War of 1812, and gr. gr. son of James Sims, a Rev'y soldier. Issue:

1d.—Kathleen Blackburn Sims[9], b. 30 Oct., 1914.

2d. Charles Gray Sims[9], b. 15 April, 1919.

1c. *Irvin Augustus Sims*[8], b. 13 Jany., 1887 (son of Wm. Irvin and Annie (Noble) Sims), graduated in 1909 from Washington University, St. Louis, Mo., taking the degree of B.S. in E.E., is a Son of the American Revolution, a Thirty-Second Degree Mason, a Knight Templar and a Shriner. He m. 26 Oct., 1914, Dorothy Hubbard (A.B., Wells College, 1912), dau. of Henry Fitch and Sarah (Rowe) Hubbard, gr. dau. of Robert Morris and Sarah (Ross) Hubbard. She is a descendant of Jonathan Hubbard, a Rev'y soldier, also of Mayflower descent, three of her ancestors, Richard Warren, John Tilley and John Howard, were passengers on that historic vessel. ("Francis Morgan an Early Va. Burgess &c.", pp. 190-'1, by Annie Noble Sims). Issue:

1d. Henry Fitch Hubbard Sims[9], b. 25 Nov., 1915.

2d. Dorothy Sims[9], b. 6 Jany., 1917.

6a. *Blanton Abraham Hill*[6] (son of Blanton Meade and Elizabeth Ann Hill), 1836-1864, attended the U. of Ga. from 1854 to 1857, then engaged in planting in Barbour Co., Ala.; Elected First Lieut. of Co. D, 15th Ala. Infantry, at age of 24 years, later promoted Captain, was mortally wounded at Fursell's Mills, on the Darbytown Road, near Richmond, Va., 16 Aug., 1864, was breveted a Colonel. He d. on 1st Sept. following. ("War between the Union and the Confederacy", p. 620, by Col. *Oates*, Comr. of this Reg.; "Francis Morgan", p. 165). The names of the brothers A. A. F. Hill and Blanton Abram Hill are engraved on the Confederate Monument at Athens, Ga.

III.—JUDIE (Judith) HILL[4] (Abr.[3], Abr.[2], Henry[1]), 1761-1794, m. Josiah Jordan, d. 1821, 1st wife. He m. (II), 17 March, 1795, Milly Parks, of Oglethorpe Co., Ga.; was representative from Oglethorpe Co. 1801-'2. Issue by 1st mar., no record as to second:

1. Martha (Patsy) Jordan[5], m. 21 Aug., 1806, Hartwell Mitchell, in Oglethorpe Co. N. R.

2. Temperance Jordan[5], m. 6 Oct., 1806, in Oglethorpe Co., Nathaniel Raines Mitchell, son of Thos. and Ann (Raines) Mitchell.

They had, among others, a dau. Anna Greene Mitchell, who m. John B. Tison and their dau. Annie Lee Tison m. James Silas Wright, of Brunswick, Ga. Mrs. Wright's No. in Georgia Society of Colonial Dames is 362.

IV—CLARA HILL[4] (Abraham[3], Abr.[2], Henry[1]), 1763-1798, m. in Wake Co., N. C., between 1778 and 1783, *Henry Augustine Pope* (son of Henry and Tabitha Pope), b. Aug. 6, 1760, in Halifax Co., N. C.; d. Dec. 9, 1807, in Oglethorpe Co., Ga., his 1st wife. He m. (II), May 27, 1799. *Mary Davis*, d. Feb. 28, 1840. (See Wills of Henry A. and of Mary (Davis) Pope in Pope record). Issue by 1st marriage (issue by 2nd mar., p. 88):

1. John Pope[5], b. before 1790; d. before 1807; named in will of his gr. father, Abraham Hill[3], but not mentioned in that of his father. His name, however, is inscribed on his father's monument.

2. *Sarah Pope*[5], b. before 1790 (q. v.).

3. Hillsman Pope[5], b. prob. circa 1792; d. before 1807; name not mentioned in father's will, but inscribed on his monument.

4. Middleton Pope[5], b. May 2, 1794; d. Nov. 21, 1850. (q. v.).

5. Burwell Pope[5], b. prob. c. 1796; d. before 1807. Name omitted in father's will, but inscribed on his monument.

2. *Sarah Pope*[5] (Henry A.[4]), m. c. 1810, Rev. George Lumpkin, 1st wife (vide his will in Lumpkin record), brother of Gov. Wilson Lumpkin, and son of John and Lucy (Hopson) Lumpkin. He m. (II) Lucy Davis. Issue by 1st marriage:

1a. John Henry Lumpkin[6], b. 12 June, 1812; d. June 6, 1860. (q. v.).

2a. Sarah Lumpkin[6], m. Wm. Davis (q. v.).

3a. Matilda Lumpkin[6], m. . . . . Milner.

4a. Angelina Lumpkin[6], m. . . . . Davis.

Issue by 2nd mar.:

5a. Martha Lumpkin[6], m. Burnett Moore, had children.

6a. Dr. George Lumpkin[6], of Antioch, Ga., m. Janie Bowdre, cousin of Mrs. Ferdinand Phinizy, who was Harriet Bowdre. Was a fine physician and lovable man. Issue: 1b.—George Lumpkin[7]; 2b.— Bowdre Lumpkin[7]; and a daughter. Records not traced.

1a. *John Henry Lumpkin*[6] (Rev. George, John), 1812-1860, was graduated from U. of Ga. and from Yale; admitted to the bar in 1834; practiced in Rome, Ga.; representative in Legislature in 1835; Solicitor General, 1838; Member of Congress, 1843-'5-'7-'9, and 1855-'57; Judge of Superior Court 1849; Delegate to Charleston Convention, 1860; and came near being elected Governor in 1857. (Nat. Cy'a of Amer. Bio., Vol. 1, p. 225; Knight's Ga. Vol. 2, p. 546). He m. (I) Miss McCombs, of Milledgeville, Ga., and had:

1b. Anthony (Tony) Lumpkin[7], d. s. p.

2b. Madeline Lumpkin[7], m. her cousin, Joseph Gerdine, (brother of Dr. John Gerdine, of Athens, Ga.), son of William

Gerdine and his wife, Lucy Lumpkin, dau. of Chief Justice Joseph Henry Lumpkin. No issue.

2a. Sarah Lumpkin[6] (Rev. George Lumpkin), m. William Davis and had a large family; one son, Middleton Pope Davis[7], m. ...... Aycock and lived with his uncle, Middleton Pope[5], 1794-1850.

4. MIDDLETON POPE[5] (son of Henry A. and Clara (Hill) Pope, 1794-1850—said by his dau. to have been very much like his cousin, Ludowick Meriwether Hill,—m. 27 Nov., 1820, *Lucy Hopson Lumpkin*, b. 28 Feby., 1803; d. 24 Aug., 1888, dau. of Gov. Wilson Lumpkin and his 1st wife, Elizabeth Walker (who were married 26 Nov., 1820, when he was 18 and she 14 years of age), dau. of Rev. Sanders Walker, a Baptist minister, and his wife, Sarah Lamar, widow Cincequefield. (See Lumpkin.)

Oglethorpe Co., Ga., Will Book D, p. 260—Will of Middleton Pope as follows:

"Georgia, Hall County. I Middleton Pope of the County of Oglethorpe and said State being of advanced age and knowing that it is appointed unto man once to die, deem it right and proper both as respects my family and myself that I should make a disposition of the property with which a kind providence has blessed me, do therefore make this my last will and testament hereby revoking all others heretofore made by me.

Item 1st: I desire and direct that my body be buried in a decent and Christianlike manner suitable to my condition and circumstances in life. My soul I trust shall return to God who gave it.

Item 2nd: I give and bequeath unto my beloved wife Lucy Pope four negroes towit, Reuben, Monroe, Dulcy and Milly, to her sole and separate use during her natural life, and at her death the said negroes to go to the children of my dau. Sarah P. Barrow, the said boy Reuben to select to which of the children he will belong.

I also give my wife a decent carriage to be furnished by my executor, worth six hundred dollars together with a good pair of carriage horses or mules as she may select.

Item 3rd: I give and bequeath unto my beloved wife in addition to the above bequest the sum of one thousand dollars annually to be paid her by my Executor hereinafter named, the first thousand to be paid at my death and a thousand dollars annually thereafter so long as she may live. Provided however that if at any time my wife shall prefer it, I direct that my Executor pay her in land and negroes Fifteen thousand dollars in lieu of the said Thousand dollars annually.

At the death of my wife the said land and negroes if taken and preferred as aforesaid to revert to and become part of my estate and be divided among the children of my daughter, Sarah P. Barrow as my executor may direct.

Item 4th: I give and bequeath unto the children of my Daughter which she now has or may hereafter have thirty negroes of average value with the balance of my negroes to be divided between them as my Executor may direct.

Item 5th: I give and bequeath all the rest and residue of my estate real and personal, consisting of lands, negroes, horses, mules, money, bonds, notes, household furniture, etc., etc., to my daughter Sarah P. Barrow, to her sole and separate use during her natural life, and if my son-in-law David C. Barrow should outlive my said daughter, then my desire is that he have the use of my said property during his natural life, then the said property to be divided between the children of my said Daughter as my said son-in-law may think best, and in the event that my Daughter shall outlive her said Husband, then at his death the said property in this Item mentioned to be equally divided between the children of my daughter.

Item 6th: My will and desire is that my Executor may at any time sell any or all of the real estate mentioned in this will, and invest the money arising from said sale in lands or other property, when or where or as he pleases for the interest of himself and family.

Item 7th: I hereby appoint my son-in-law David C. Barrow Executor of this my last will and testament.

(Signed) Middleton Pope.

Signed, sealed, published and declared by Middleton Pope as his last will and testament in the presence of us the subscribers, who subscribed our names hereto in the presence of said testator (at his special instance and request) and of each other, this September the 21st, 1850.

Wit.: George Dent, Wm. H. Hull, P. H. Hanson, I. H. Taylor, L. A. McAfee.

Ordinary's Office January Term 1851. Georgia Oglethorpe County. The within last will and testament of Middleton Pope deceased, having been exhibited and duly proven at this Regular Term of the Court in open Court upon the oaths of George Dent, Wm. H. Hull, Phillip H. Hanson and J. H. Taylor all subscribing witnesses to the same.

Ordered that the same be admitted to Record and that letters Testamentary issue on the premises.

Henry Britain C. C. O.

Recorded the 17th day of January, 1851".

In Court Minutes 1845-1851, p. 309, we find: "Minutes of the Court of Ordinary January Term 1851 Oglethorpe County, Georgia. David C. Barrow having been appointed but now the qualified Executor of the last will and testament of Middleton Pope, deceased, prays the Court to appoint Commissioners to appraise said Estate. Wherefore, It is ordered that William Edwards, William J. Davis, Richard R. Winfrey, James Jewell and John Holmes be and they are hereby appointed Commissioners to appraise said estate according to Law."

In Annual Return Book in Ordinary's Office, p. 212, Oglethorpe Co. Ordinary Office May Term 1851, Inventory and appraisement by Commissioners above named, made the 30th April, 1851, is recorded showing a very large estate.

1a. SARAH ELIZA POPE[6], b. 17 Oct., 1821; d. 13 Sept., 1855 (6th in descent from Col. Barnaby McKinnie, Sr., 5th from John Pope, 6th from Thos. Walton, Sr., 5th from Thos. Walton, Jr., and 4th from Abraham Hill, Jr.).

"Her chief characteristics were courage and devotion to duty in which she was firm and persevering. Her teachers testified that at school she was affectionate, dutiful and studious; with intense maternal devotion inculcated in her children and those entrusted to her care, those precepts of right living, which were stamped indelibly on their minds, formed their characters and guided their lives. She joined the Methodist Episcopal Church at the age of 19 and continued a consistent and devout member till her death. Her life was that of a Christian, her death that of the righteous." (Extract, not literal, from obituary by Rev. Habersham Adams).

The second Mrs. David C. Barrow, Jr., said of her: "She could have more irons in the fire and keep all hot than anyone she ever knew" and "to do a thing as Grandma did it" was all she desired. Her efficiency was demonstrated by her successful management of a large plantation.

SARAH ELIZA POPE[6] m. 23 Oct., 1838, DAVID CRENSHAW BARROW—1st wife—of Milledgeville, Ga., b. in Baldwin County on his father's plantation, "Beulah", 26 July, 1815, and who had arranged for the purchase of a plantation within a few miles of the "Home Place" to which to take his bride, but she being an only daughter, and supported by her parents, prevailed upon him to forego the purchase and live with them. He removed to Athens, Ga., in 1861 and d. March 18, 1899, was the son of James Barrow[3] b. Jan. 31, 1757, in Edgecombe Co., N. C.; d. Jan. 20, 1828, in Baldwin Co., Ga., and his 3rd wife, Patience Crenshaw, b. May 15, 1779; d. Oct. 26, 1817 (they were married Oct. 13, 1814) dau. of Jesse Crenshaw, b. Sept. 11, 1755, and his wife Precious Cain, b. Feb. 6, 1758.

JAMES BARROW[3] was the son of Thomas Barrow[2], b. c. 1690, on Nottaway River, Southampton Co., Va. (and Elizabeth Atkinson, his 2nd wife, b. Jan. 31, 1757) son of Thomas Barrow[1], b. 1640 in Lancashire, England, who emigrated, before he was of age, to Virginia, and d. in 1730, aged 90 years, in Southampton Co.

James Barrow[3] left a diary in which he tells of his service in the Rev'y War: "That he enlisted when 18 years of age, April 1776, in the N. C. Continental Line as a private in the Regt. of Col. Jethro Sumner; says they were at Charleston, S. C., when Independence was declared and published; from there were ordered to Savannah, Ga., under Gen. Lee, were marched thence northward and at Georgetown on the Potomac, I had small pox by inoculation, and in June 1777 joined the army in Penn." Says: "I was this year (1777) in the noted battles of Brandywine and Germantown, still being preserved by the same Providence. We encamped this winter (1777-78) at the Valley Forge on the Schoolkill River" . . . "saw service in New York, discharged Nov. 10, 1778 in N. C.; called to service again under Col. Jonas Johnson and served until the close of the War. November 1789 removed to Georgia and in 1792 purchased 1500 Acres in Burke Co. which I yet hold (1819)". Removed to Baldwin Co. 1802 where he "purchased a large plantation and made his home" until his death 1827.

An entry in his dairy when his son David was 9 years old says: "David reads latin", and on 27th April, 1821: "I have for a few days been much delighted with reading Doctor Chalmer's Sermons on Astronomy in connection with Christianity; surely he was a heavenly minded man". He had a home in Milledgeville also, and here he erected a building in his yard to house his valuable library, which has been dissipated, only a few valuable and choice volumes that were in the hands of his children having been preserved. These properties he left to his children. (Mem. of Ga., Vol. 2, pp. 534-'5).

David Crenshaw Barrow[4], 1815-1899, after his father's death, when only 12 years of age, was sent to Dr. Carlisle Beaman's School for Boys, Mt. Zion, near Sparta, Ga.; when 15 years old was sent by his guardian, Dr. Benj. White, of Milledgeville, Ga., a two weeks' trip by stage to Phillips' Academy, Andover, Mass., under Mr. John Adams. Later he matriculated at Harvard, but did not graduate, returning to Ga. in the early 30's. He joined the Macon Volunteers, Capt. Seymour's Co., Cooper's Battalion, for the Indian War, 1836, against the Seminoles in Fla. He was a "Son of the American Revolution" by right of his father, and while he had no political aspirations, nor desire for public office, served as State Senator and as a member of various conventions—the National Democratic in 1860, and the deferred convention in Baltimore, and the Secession Convention in 1861. That he was an ardent and devoted supporter of the Confederacy, it is needless to say—giving three sons to the cause, and of his substance without stint. With great liberality he supplied the needs of the refugees in Athens, and his family hold letters from many of the home people to whom he extended a helping hand, expressing their gratitude.

I give herewith a copy of one of these letters written Oct. 5, 1865, by Rev. Nathan Hoyt, D. D., beloved pastor, for many years, of the Presbyterian Church, in Athens, Ga., addressed to Col. David Barrow, Athens, Ga.

"My Dear Friend. Permit me to return you my most sincere & heartfelt thanks for your great, *very great* kindness to me & my family. How very kind in you to go & pay that $10. pew rent at such a time as this, when a large proportion of my own congregation as yet, are not, as I suppose, able to pay me anything. That $10. will buy me ten loads of wood, which I *greatly* need. And now the wheat is a long way over measure & better in quality than I expected. "Blessed is he that considereth the poor—the Lord will deliver him in time of trouble". That blessing is surely yours.

The Lord reward you, my dear friend, for all your kind favours to me and others in distress.

Your grateful devoted friend,
(Signed) N. Hoyt."

NOTE: Dr. Hoyt's daughter m. Dr. Axson, pastor Independence Presbyterian Church, Savannah, Ga., and their daughter was the first wife of Prest. Woodrow Wilson.

Mr. Barrow, being a large land owner, realized the necessity of restoring the agricultural interests of Ga., which were prostrate where not destroyed by the invader. "A few patriotic men, viz., Benj. Yancey, David C. Barrow, Dr. John S. Hamilton, Richard Peters, Mark A. Cooper, David W. Lewis, et al., organized the Ga. State Agricultural Society, and sent out circulars and premium lists for a Fair to be held in Macon, Ga., 1868. . . . . The exhibition at this Fair of the varied products of Georgia was a matter of wonder not only to those outside the State but to our own people also. Then began the true, honorable reconstruction of our grand old State". He was for years a Vice-president of the Society and an enthusiastic supporter of the work it was doing to rehabilitate the State he loved. He was a whole-hearted supporter of all educational institutions and movements, for years a trustee of the U. of Ga. and, until his death, of the Lucy Cobb Institute. He lived to be 83 years old, never lost interest in life or public affairs, nor weakened mentally, nor in the firm force of character which so distinguished him. He was a man of clear vision, sound judgment and strict integrity, who had the confidence and friendship of Toombs, Stephens and other leading men of his day. His love for children was a marked characteristic, and he was greatly beloved by them. In control and guidance of his children was kind and wise, indulgent, but firm in correcting faults and derelictions of duty. Insisted on right principles, faithful discharge of duty and living up to the standards of life to which it had pleased God to call them. "To thine own self be true, and "Noblesse oblige" were frequent admonitions. His eye would pierce to the very soul of the wrongdoer. One of his sons, after his death, said: "The only man in the world I feared is gone". A grandson, speaking of his reproof by his eyes, said: "I would rather both my father and mother whip me than have grandpa look at me".

DAVID C. BARROW[4] and his WIFE were devoted members of the Methodist Church. The ministers of that circuit were ever welcome guests and some of the young unmarried ones found a home in "brother Barrow's" house. They were blessed with nine children, and the mother dying when the eldest was only 16, the task of mothering the nine fell to their grandmother, Mrs. Middleton Pope, nee Lucy Hopson Lumpkin, which she fulfilled lovingly and with absolute unselfishness. She was one to whom "none could cry for help and find her hand withdrawn". With parentage and ancestors of unblemished records for generations back of them, it is not surprising that those nine Barrow children grew up to be men and women of the highest type of Southern civilization in mind and character. David Crenshaw Barrow in the early 50's secured as a teacher for his children Mr. Ripley Perkins Adams, son of his "old preceptor" at Andover, Mr. Wm. Adams. His neighbors asked him to build a schoolhouse that their children also might receive instruction from Mr. Adams. He accordingly built one on an eminence almost in sight of his home at the junction of three roads. Here the three older boys were prepared for college, and the three girls and younger brothers were also attendants. Children in those days started to climb the "Hill of Knowledge" by the time they were four. Clara, the 2nd daughter, it is said, could read a chapter in the Bible when she was four years of age. When the Lucy Cobb Institute opened Jan. 1, 1859, the three girls, with Miss Sawyer, their governess, were sent there as boarders. They had a sitting room and bed room on the top floor of the building, their own piano and furniture and their own servant. The youngest of the girls, E. P. B., had her 10th birthday after entering the school. Their youthfulness made it necessary for their governess to be with them though she had no duties connected with the school—was a boarder only. When, in 1861, Mr. Barrow moved to Athens from the country, his three youngest sons were sent to the University High School (where the Normal School now is), Mr. Carroll, Principal, and Col. L. H. Charbonier, later Professor for many years at the U. of Ga., instructors. Here they were prepared for college.

David Crenshaw Barrow[4] m. (II), 3 Jany., 1872, *Priscilla Flint Sawyer*, who d. 25 Dec., 1910. She was a true, devoted wife, with strong mind, unselfish character and great efficiency. She was devoted to her husband's children by his first wife, and said they were the finest family of children she ever knew. No issue. Issue by 1st marriage to Sarah Eliza Pope[6].

    1b.   Middleton Pope Barrow[7], b. 1 Aug., 1839, at the home place of his maternal gr. parents in Oglethorpe Co.; d. 23 Dec., 1903, at Savannah, Ga.; buried at Home Place, the 4th generation there interred. (q. v.).

    2b.   James Barrow, b. 26 March, 1841; d. 20 Feby., 1864. (q. v.).

    3b.   Thos. Augustine Barrow[7], b. 25 March, 1843; d. 11 Jany., 1897. (q. v.).

    4b.   Lucy Pope Barrow[7], b. 7 Feby., 1845; d. 2 June, 1885. (q. v.).

    5b.   *Clara Elizabeth Barrow*[7], b. 24 Dec., 1846; d. 24 May, 1880, unm., a cultured and highly accomplished woman, impetuous and high strung, but learned rigid control as she grew out of childhood. Upon graduation took charge of her father's household, her grandmother then being too old for the cares—to which she gave unselfish devotion to the end of her life. Was Secretary for years to the Ladies' Memorial Association. She gave service to her home, her friends, her city and her church with unstinted generosity, loving and beloved, making friends in every walk of life. She was the highest type of Southern womanhood.

6b. *Ella Patience Barrow*[7], b. 8 Feby., 1849. (q. v.).

7b. Benjamin White Barrow[7], b. 11 March, 1851; d. 22 March, 1876, unm. (q. v.).

8b. *David Crenshaw Barrow, Jr.*[7], b. 18 Oct., 1852. (q. v.).

9b. Henry Walker Barrow[7], b. in Oglethorpe Co., July 18,1854; d. June 21, 1876, unm. Alumnus U. of Ga. 1873, A.B.; 1874, B.S.; memeber Chi Phi Frat. and Demosthenian Lit. Soc. A classmate wrote of him: "Both in the U. and Law School he was acknowledged by every one to be the 1st and best man in his class, beloved and honored by professors and associates, a soul above all that was little, mean or selfish". (See p. 86.)

1b. *Middleton Pope Barrow*[7] (Sarah Eliza[6], Henry Augustine[5], Henry[4], John[3], Henry[2], William Pope[1]), 1839-1903, known only, even by his most intimate friends, as "Pope Barrow", prepared for college at the home school by Mr. Ripley Perkins Adams, graduated at U. of Ga. (then known as Franklin College) in class of 1859, sharing 1st honor, with A.B. degree, and in Lumpkin Law School (now a branch of U. of Ga.), degree of B.L., in 1860; member of Demosthenean Society—no Greek letter chapters until after the Civil War; was practicing law in Athens when Georgia seceded; volunteered in April, 1861, made 2nd Lieut. of Troop Artillery, C. S. A., which served in Va.; later appointed Capt. & A. D. C. on staff of Major General Howell Cobb, C. S. A., and was captured in battle of Columbus, Ga., April 16, 1865, one of the last of the war. After the war resumed practice of law at Athens, removed in 1892 to Savannah, where he was a leading and successful lawyer, and in both private and public life was beloved beyond the fortune of most. He was a member of the Constitutional Convention in 1877; State Senator in 1880; U. S. Senator 1882-'3—elected by the Legislature to succeed the Hon. Benjamin H. Hill, decd.; delegate to the State Convention and to the National Democratic Convention at St. Louis in 1888. It is of interest to note that his gr.gr.gr. father,John Lumpkin, was delegate from Oglethorpe Co. to the famous Constitutional Convention of Ga., 1798. He was appointed in 1900 Judge of Superior Court of the Eastern Circuit, Savannah, Chatham Co., which position he occupied at the time of his death, 23 Dec., 1903. (Special) Savannah, Ga. "Judge Pope Barrow of the Superior Court, was stricken today in his court room, and tonight at 8:30 o'clock, he died at his home. The stroke was caused by uraemia, and the physicians say that there was probably a hemorrhage at the base of the brain. There may, too, have been apoplexy. Judge Barrow had just finished a charge to the jury in a civil suit. He arose from the bench and was seized with a weakness of the legs. Those near him noticed this but thought that his limbs were weak or asleep from long sitting. When he attempted to move he faltered and almost fainted. He caught upon the shoulder of Edwin A. Cohen, and A. Pratt Adams, a young attorney, hurried to his assistance. He was supported into his private office. This was at 2 o'clock. Physicians were summoned and also a carriage. He was driven to his home, where he remained unconscious until 4 o'clock, and from then until the hour of his death he was in a state of coma. He met the final summons, a jurist without a blemish, a "gentleman unafraid". Judge Barrow had been on the bench since Jan., 1900, when he was appointed to succeed the late Judge Robert Falligant. His long legal training rendered him well qualified to fill the position with signal ability and that he did so is the unanimous opinion of the Savannah bar. He was very popular, had an ease and grace of manner that won him friends readily and ever retained them." He declined, for family reasons, before his removal from Athens, appointment to the State Supreme Court Bench. He was Second Vice-President General, Sons of the Revolution, by right of James Barrow[3], his grandfather, and was an active member of the Confederate Veterans' Assn. of Savannah.

1b. *Middleton Pope Barrow*[7], 1839-1903, m. (I), 5 Mar., 1867, Sarah Church Craig, b. at Fort Jessup, La., 18 Sept., 1844; d. 28 Dec., 1881, dau. of Lt. Col. Lewis Stevenson Craig, U. S. A., and his wife, Elizabeth Whipplehunt Church, dau. of Rev. Alonzo Church, L. L. D., President of Franklin College and later of U. of Ga. for 30 years, and his wife, Sarah Trippe, of Putnam Co., Ga.; m. (II), June 24, 1884, in Marietta, Ga., Cornelia Augusta Jackson, b. at Savannah, 23 April, 1852; d. 26 Sept., 1899, dau of General Henry Rootes Jackson, U. S. A., of Savannah, Ga., a member of the Aztec Club, and his 1st wife, Cornelia Davenport. Issue by 1st marriage:

1c. Middleton Pope Barrow, Jr.[8], b. 24 March, 1868, attended U. of Ga.—withdrew before graduation—and Gordon Military Institute. He is a member of the Aztec Club, Officers of the Mexican War, by right of his gr. father, Lt. Col. Lewis Stevenson Craig's, U. S. A., service in Mexican War., 1845. He m. 5 Sept., 1906, Alma L. Jones, decd., of Norcross, Ga., and had: 1d.—Pope Barrow[9], b. 2 Sept., 1907; 2d.—David Craig Barrow[9], b. 24 June, 1909; 3d.—James Barrow[9], b. 30 Sept., 1912.

2c. Elizabeth Church Barrow[8], b. 13 Nov., 1869; d. 6 June, 1919, unm. She was a member of Christ Episcopal Church; member of Board of the Episcopal Orphans' Home, Christ Church Parish; member Froebel Circle King's Daughters and Red Cross during World War. In all of these she gave efficient, untiring service, discharged all the duties of life with faithfulness and loyalty to family and friends.

3c. James Barrow[8], b. 5 July, 1872, at the "Home Place", graduated Eastman's Business College, N. Y., Treasurer of City of Athens, Vestryman Emanuel Episcopal Church; m. 23 June, 1915, *Clara Elizabeth Barrow*, dau. of Thomas A. and Jennie (Turner) Barrow, and had: 1b.—James Barrow[9], b. 26 July, 1917; 2d.—Thomas Augustine Barrow III[9], b. 7 Oct., 1920. (See p. 80.)

4c. David Crenshaw Barrow III[8], b. 6 June, 1874, at the "Home Place"; alumnus U. of Ga., class 1894, degree of A.B.; Frat. S. A. E., Demosthenean Society; course in law at U. of Va.; prominent lawyer in Savannah, member of firm of Stephens, Barrow and Heyward; served in Cuba in Spanish-American War, 1898-'99; afterwards Captain, Oglethorpe Light Infantry, and Major of National Guard, retiring in 1908; member of Legislature, 1907-'08; Collector of Customs during both administrations of President Wilson; member of Sons of the Revolution by right of James Barrow[3], and of St. Andrew's Society by right of Adam Craig. He m., 10 Dec., 1907, in Savannah, Ga., Emma Middleton Huger, dau. of Joseph A. and Mary (Elliott) Huger. Issue:

1b.—Pope[9], b. 13 Dec., 1909; 2d.—Mary Elliott[9], b. 7 Dec., 1911; 3d.—David Crenshaw Barrow IV[9], b. 2 May, 1913; 4d.—Arthur Elliott Barrow[9], b. 24 Dec., 1917.

5c. Craig Barrow[8], b. 12 May, 1876, alumnus U. of Ga., class 1896, A.B. degree, Frat. S. A. E., Demosthenean Society; medical course U. of Md., Baltimore, degree M.D., 1899; attended U. of Bresslau, Germany, 1900; in 1902 opened office in Savannah, Ga.; volunteered in Medical Dept., World War, rank Capt., 1918; in 1921 made Chief Surgeon, Central of Ga. R. R. Residing in Savannah, confines private practice to surgery; member Sons of Colonial Wars, ancestor Barnaby McKinnie; Sons of the Revolution, ancestor James Barrow. He m. (I) Oct., 1902, Alice Barker, of Atlanta, Ga., who d. 8 May, 1903. No issue; m. (II), 6 June, 1906, Elfrida DeRenne, dau. of Wymberly Jones and Laura Camblos DeRenne, of Wormsloe, Savannah, Ga. Issue by 2nd mar.; 1d.—Craig, Jr.[9]; 2d.—Wymberly Jones DeRenne[9], d. in inf.; 3d.—Elfrida[9], b. 13 Oct., 1909; 4d.—Muriel Barrow[9], b. 23 Dec., 1913.

Issue of 2nd mar. (Middleton Pope and Cornelia Augusta (Jackson) Barrow:

6c. Florence Barclay Barrow[8], b. 27 April, 1885; d. 27 July, 1901.

7c. *Lucy Hopson Lumpkin Barrow*[8], b. 11 July, 1886, member Christ Episcopal Church, m. 24 Nov., 1909, Frank Percival McIntire, son of James William McIntire and Catherine Foley, his wife, of Savannah, Ga. He served as Capt. of Ga. Huzzars in Texas throughout the Mexican Border trouble, promoted Judge Advocate; retired as Major. Issue: 1d.—James William[9], b. 1910; 2d.—Cornelia Jackson[9], b. 1911; 3d.—Lucy[9], b. 1912; 4d.—Ella Patience

Barrow[9], b. 1919; 5d.—Francis Percival McIntire, Jr.[9], b. 17 July, 1921. Mrs. McIntire was educated at Hartridge School, Sav'h, Ga., and at St. Timothy's, Balt., Md.; Predt. Chatham Co. Equal Suffrage Ass'n from 1915 to 1917; Prest. Ga. Equal Suffrage Ass'n, 1918-19; 1st Vice-Prest. Savannah Women's Federation, 1919-'20-'21; Prest. Chidren's Free Clinic & Tuberculosis Assn., 1919-'20-'21; Chairman Baby Welfare Work for Federation of same; first National Democratic Committeewoman from Georgia; member of "Prosodists"—an organization, or association, for writing and criticising poems—has had several poems accepted. Prest. Margaret Bottome Circle King's Daughters, which maintains the Free Clinic. With all of these outside activities, it must be said, meets home and family duties and obligations.

8c. Davenport Jackson Barrow[8], b. 8 July, 1888; d. 30 Aug. 1888.

9c. ELLA PATIENCE CRENSHAW BARROW[8], b. at Athens, Ga., 5 Aug. 1889, educated at Pope's School, "Old Fields", Md.; member Christ Episcopal Church, Elizabeth Butler Circle King's Daughters, of the Ga. Soc. of the Colonial Dames of Ama., and Lachlan McIntosh Chapter D. A. R.; prominent in King's Daughters Chap. Red Cross, World War; m. 2 June, 1915, Lionel Edward Drew, son of Mr. & Mrs. Edward Bangs Drew, Cambridge, Harvard College, Lieut. Aviation Corps, A. E. F. Issue: 1d.—Edward B. Drew[9], b. 1919, d. an infant; 2d.—Lionel Edward Drew, Jr.[9], b. Sept., 1920.

10c. Cornelia Barrow[8], b. at Athens, Dec., 1890; d. an infant.

11c. Basil Prince Barrow[8], b. at Savh., Ga., 25 March, 1893; d. 6 Feby., 1894.

12c. Sarah Pope Barrow, b. 28 March, 1895, educated at Pope School, "Old Fields", Md.; member Christ Episcopal Church, Elizabeth Butler Circle King's Daughters; of Union Society—a Colonial Benevolent Society,—has charge of Bethesda Orphanage; member Ga. Soc. Col. Dames of Ama.; m. 25 Feby., 1915, Gustav Ludwig Karow, d. June, 1920, son of Mr. and Mrs. Edward Williams and Annie (Wilson) Karow, dau. of Gen. Stewart Wilson, C. S. A., Capt. U. S. Marines—Regular Establishment—rank of Major in World War; Mason and Shriner; mem. Amn. Legion Officers, Grt. War; on list of distinguished alumni V. M. I. Issue: 1d.—Gustav Karow, Jr.[9], b. 7 Dec., 1918; 2d.—Davenport Jackson Karow[9], b. 5 Jany., 1921—posthumous child.

2b. *James Barrow*[7], 1841-1864, son of David C. and Sarah Eliza (Pope) Barrow, b. 26 Mar. 1841, at home of his maternal gr. parents in Oglethorpe Co.; killed at the battle of Olustee, Fla.— "pierced through the heart by a minie ball"—Feb. 20, 1864; Lieut. Col., C. S. A. Unmarried. He was a cadet at Ga. Military Institute when appointed to West Point Military Academy by Senator Alex. H. Stephens in 1858. When Georgia seceded he resigned and came home; commissioned Lieut. of Ga. State troops by Gov. Joseph E. Brown 1861, assigned to duty drilling and instructing Volunteer Troops. Commissioned as Adjutant 16th Reg. Ga. Vol., July 1861, applied for by Col. Howell Cobb commanding. Commissioned A. Adjutant Genl. of Gen. Howell Cobb's Brigade—applied for by Gen. Cobb. Wounded in the battle of Dam No. 1, Va., April 16, 1862. On return to service, resumed his duties on Gen. Cobb's Staff. Accompanied the command to Fla. when Major General Cobb was put in command of the Middle District of that State, with headquarters near Quincy. Commissioned Lieutenant Colonel 64th Regt. Ga. Vols., C. S. A., 1863. In an obituary notice of Col. Barrow written by Gen. Cobb, he writes, when the 64th Regt. was sent to his headquarters near Quincy, Fla., there being no field officer appointed to instruct the officers and drill the regiment, "General Cobb knowing the high qualifications of the young officer for the duty, requested him to undertake it, he responded with his usual promptness and cheerfulness". "No better evidence can be given of the manner in which he discharged that duty than the simple statement that the regiment, to whom he was an entire stranger, both officers and men, earnestly and unanimously asked that he be appointed Lieutenant Colonel. That request was granted". He continues: "In the bloody battle of Ocean Ponds (Olustee), it fell to the lot of our noble young friend with colors of his regiment in his hands, rallying and leading his troops to victory, to fall and fill a soldier's grave. He fell with the flag of his country in his hands, his Bible in his bosom. A Soldier's death with a Christian's hope". A hero and man of lofty character. That the 64th Regiment retained the high opinion of him is shown by the following from an account of the battle written by a veteran in 1903: "here was where the 64th Georgia lost the best commanding officer she ever had, James Barrow". His name is inscribed in the roll of heroes on the Confederate Monument in Athens, Ga.

3b. THOMAS AUGUSTINE BARROW[7], 1843-1897, son of David C. and Sarah Eliza (Pope) Barrow, was a student in Junior Class, half advanced, U. of Ga.; member Demosthenean Society, when the State seceded. In his Sophomore year bore off the medal. In April, 1861, he resigned from college and joined the Troop Artillery as a private, when just turned 18 years, served with it at Savannah until July, 1861, when it was ordered to Virginia. In the Western Virginia, and in the Pennsylvania campaigns, and in the seven days battle around Richmond, he displayed a high order of courage and coolness which distinguished him throughout the war. At Crampton's Gap in Md., he, with exceptional and conspicuous gallantry, rescued two of his comrades, John O. Waddell and Robt. M. Thomas, who had been wounded and had fallen almost within the enemy's lines, and manifested the like courage at the battle of Fredericksburg. Later he was attached first to the Staff of Gen. Thos. R. R. Cobb, until his death, and then made Adjutant of

Hood's Battalion of Cavalry, in which he served until the surrender.

From a letter by his brother, Pope Barrow, to his father, dated Camp Tom, seven miles northeast of Winchester, Sept. 30, 1862, I take the following: "Tom Barrow says it is a wonder the General was not killed, and the General says that Tom rode into a fire that he never would have allowed him if he could have stopped him, waving a sword over his head to rally the men". In 1865 he removed from Athens to the "Blowing Cave" plantation in Decatur Co., which he inherited from his father, and later to Pelham, where he lived till his death in 1897. On 8 Feby., 1872, he m. (I), Miss Jennie Turner, dau. of a Presbyterian minister, d. 17 June, 1880; m. (II), 25 Sept., 1882, Miss Alice Josephine Hand, sister of Judson L. Hand, of Pelham, who survived him. In 1889 he was ordained a Baptist minister, made pastor of the Baptist Church at Pelham, and as such was a useful, zealous and indefatigable laborer; was beloved and revered by his congregation and the entire community. He was a friend to man, a helper of the helpless, put Christianity into his every day life, and was both an examplar and a blessing. Issue by 1st marriage:

1c.—Sarah Pope Barrow[8], b. 17 Feby., 1873; d. 16 July, 1876.
2c.—David Crenshaw Barrow IV.[8], b. 10 Feby., 1875. alumnus U. of Ga., Frat. S. A. E., Demosthenean Society, m. Emily Hand and had: 1d.—David Crenshaw Barrow V[9]; 2d.—Thos. Lee Barrow[9]; 3d.—Jean Turner Barrow[9]; 4d.—Emily Hand Barrow[9].

3c. *Clara Elizabeth Barrow*[8], b. 11 Jany., 1877; m. 23 June, 1915, her cousin, James Barrow, son of Pope, and had: 1d.—James Barrow[9], b. 26 July, 1917; 2d.—Thos. Augustine Barrow III[9], b. 10 Oct., 1920. She graduated at Lucy Cobb Institute 1895, later taught Mathematics there and then was principal of one of the public school of Athens. (See p. 77.) Issue by 2nd mar.:

4c. Thos. Augustine Barrow, Jr.[8], b. 21 June, 1883 (q. v.).

5c. Francis Cuthbert Barrow[8], b. 26 Aug., 1890, attended U. of Ga., served in World War, m. Marie McDonald and has: 1d.—Frances Marie Barrow[9].

The three brothers are in the Long Loan Co. at Pelham.

4c. *Thos. Augustine Barrow, Jr.*[8], son of Thos. A. and Alice (Hand) Barrow, alumnus U. of Ga., class 1903, Frat., K. A.; volunteered spring of 1917, trained at Ft. McPherson, commissioned 1st Lieut. of Artillery, ordered to France in fall of 1917. In March, 1918, was decorated by the French with Croix de Guerre for bravery under fire while taking observations in captive balloon over German lines. His balloon was struck eighty times by shots from two German airplanes. He and his French companion jumped for their lives in parachutes when a strong wind landed them safely within their own lines. He was figuring Artillery data for the Allied Artillery when attacked. He m. 25 Sept., 1921,

Joyce (or Loyce) Smith, and is Cashier of the Farmers Bank at Pelham.

4b. *Lucy Pope Barrow*[7], 1845-1880, dau. of David C. and Eliza (Pope) Barrow, was cultured and had a high sense of the duties and obligations of life; in all the fine, sweet qualities of self-forgetful womanhood was the examplar; fulfilled all of life's requirements as a dutiful daughter, affectionate sister, devoted wife and mother, and as a devout Christian "Given to good works" her life was a blessing. She m., 29 July, 1863, *John Addison Cobb,* of Americus, Ga., b. 20 Oct., 1838, eldest son of Maj. Gen. Howell Cobb and his wife, Mary Ann Lamar, Capt. in C. S. A., Senior Warden Episcopal Church of Americus, Ordinary Sumter Co. and ex-President Ga. Agricultural Society, oldest in point of age in the State: Issue:

1c. Wilson Lumpkin Cobb[8], b. 12 Dec., 1865; d. 30 May, 1871, —named for his gr. father Lumpkin, who was still living.

2c. Howell Cobb[8], b. 29 May, 1868; d. 5 Sept., 1892; m. 14 Feby., 1892, Amoret Gray, b. 17 March, 1871; d. 22 March, 1914, dau. of Wm. C. and Amoret (Dawson) Gray, of Columbus, Ga., and had: 1d.—Sarah Pope Cobb, b. 13 Sept., 1892; m. 17 April, 1912, Benjamin M. Cowan, b. in State of Maine, Constructing Engineer, Stone and Webster Co.; 2d.—Amoret Dawson Cobb[9], b. 25 April, 1895, m. 19 Aug., 1916, Clifton H. Green, of Nashville, Tenn.; 3d.—John Addison Cobb III[9], b. 29 Dec., 1896, d. in inf.; 4d.—Howell Cobb[9], b. 12 March, 1898, unm.

3c. Sarah Pope Cobb[8], b. 31 Oct., 1870, at Athens, Ga.; unm. Educated at Public Schools of Americus, Ga., and the Lucy Cobb Institute; Principal Furlow Grammar School, Americus Public Schools. In her chosen profession has few superiors, is a devout member of the Episcopal Church, active in Church work and for the good of the City.

4c. John Addison Cobb, Jr.[8], b. 11 Feby., 1873; d. 9 April, 1907; attended U. S. Naval Academy, but resigned; m. 5 April, 1899, Bessie DuBerry. No issue.

5c. Lucy Middleton Cobb[8], b. 8 Aug., 1875, at Athens; member U. D. C., D. A. R., and the Ga. Soc. of Colonial Dames of Ama.; m. (I), 10 Nov., 1897, James Taylor, b. in Americus, Ga., 8 May, 1873; d. 21 March, 1910, alumnus U. of Ga., lawyer, son of Mr. and Mrs. Elazor Taylor. Issue: 1d.—Lucy Barrow Taylor[9], b. in Americus, Ga., 28 Sept., 1898, unm.; m. (II), 25 Oct., 1911, Nathaniel Bacon Stewart, Consul General of the United States of America, b. 4 Jany., 1871, Taylor County, Georgia.

6c. Mary Ann Lamar Cobb[8], b. 10 May, 1877; d. 26 Oct., 1880.

6b. ELLA PATIENCE BARROW[7], dau. of David C. and Sarah Eliza (Pope) Barrow, b. 8 Feby., 1849, in Oglethorpe Co., Ga., is a woman of culture and refinement, possessing those qualities of heart and mind which command esteem, win and hold the confidence, friendship and affection of all who know her. She was educated at Lucy Cobb Institute, is a member of Christ Episcopal Church, Savannah, Ga., of the Woman's Auxiliary of that Church; member Charter Chapter of U. D. C. at Savannah by right of father and brothers; Lachlan McIntosh Chapter D. A. R. by right of James Barrow[3], of N. C. and Ga., Abraham Hill, Jr., of N. C. and Ga., and Capt. Henry Hopson, of Va. Offices held: Registrar, Historian and Vice-Regent; member of the Ga. Soc. of the Coll. Dames of America by right of Abraham Hill, Jr., Col. Barnaby McKennie, Sr., John Pope, Thos. Walton, Sr. and Jr.—all of N. C. Member Board of Managers, 1918-'20-'21, Ex-Treasurer, Necrology Committee, 1919-'20-'21; of Savannah Assn. for Education of Ga. Mountaineers—Managers 1920—in which work she has taken a deep interest; of the Ga. Historical Society; Secretary of the Board of The Savannah Widows' Society since 1912, and now revising its Constitution and By-Laws—a benevolent soc. founded 1822 for care of aged, indigent women and widows with young children; member of Red Cross during the World War and now. She takes a deep interest in current world events, and is a registered voter. In charitable work is ever ready to extend the helping hand, and to speak words of sympathy and kindness to the needy and distressed, and while fully discharging the obligations of her various memberships, she leads a quiet homekeeping life of devotion to family, relatives and friends.

Ella Patience Barrow[7] m. 3 Nov., 1874, Bourke Spalding, of Sapelo Island, Ga., b. 23 Feby., 1851; d. 5 Sept., 1884, son of Col. Randolph Spalding, C. S. A. (and Mary Dorothea Bass, his wife), son of Hon. Thos. Spalding, of Sapelo Island, b. 1774 on St. Simons Island, Ga.; d. 1851,—in whose honor Spalding Co. in this State was named in 1851 (see White's Statistics)—(and Sarah Leake, his wife (m. 1795), only child of Richard and Jean (Martin) Leake (m. 1778), dau. of Clement Martin, King's Council, 1761), only child of James Spalding, (b. 1735; m. 1772; d. 10 Nov., 1794, only son of Thomas and Anna (Lermouth) Spalding, who were m. in 1734, in Edinburgh, Scotland (heir to the estate and Barony of Ashantilly, County Perth, Scotland, who emigrated to Ga. in 1760, was a signer of the protest against the Stamp Act, member of the Royal Council of Fla.—where he resided during the Revolution, a Commissioner from Glynn Co., Ga., in 1792, and member of the Ga. State Senate in 1794) and his wife, Margery McIntosh, dau. of Major William McIntosh (and Mary McKay, his wife) of the Continental Line and an original member of the Society of the Cincinnatti in Ga., and son of John Mohr McIntosh and his wife, Marjory Fraser. Issue:

1c. *Randolph Spalding*[8], b. on Sapelo Island, 30 Sept., 1879, unm. Real Estate, Savannah, Ga., member of the Ga. Soc. of the Cincinnatti by right of paternal ancestor in 6th degree, Maj. William McIntosh, and has "Cross of Honor", U. D. C., by right of his gr. father Randolph Spalding, Col. C. S. A.; member of the

Hibernian Soc., Savannah, Ga. He is a man of fine qualities of mind and sterling character, of strength and determination. He is the present representative of the Ashantilly Spalding family, County Perth, Scotland.

2c. Clara Lucy Spalding[5], b. on Sapelo Island, 27 May, 1881; d. in Athens, Ga., 3 Sept., 1881.

7b. *Benjamin White Barrow*[7] (named for his father's guardian, Dr. Benj. White), son of David C. and Sarah Eliza (Pope) Barrow, b. in Oglethorpe Co., Mar. 11, 1851; d. with hemorrhage March 22, 1876. Alumnus U. of Ga., class 1869, degree of A.B.; 1870, B.L.; Frat. S.A.E.; Demosthenean Society. Had a quick and brilliant mind and a memory of extraordinary powers of retention and graduated with high marks of distinction. He removed to Milledgeville and practiced law with his relative, Col. Wm. McKinley, who m. 23 Feby., 1836, Precious Patience Barrow, the only sister of his father. He was an exemplary Christian, studious, a fine writer, a clever, forcible and earnest speaker, with powers of discrimination of no ordinary sort, and scrupulously honorable; combined many of the numerous attributes essential to the successful lawyer, and his intellectual qualities, great as they were, were not more remarkable than those of the heart which made him the idol of his family and the object of his friends' affection. So amiable, so considerate, so unselfish, so kindly spoken was he, that it was well nigh impossible to know and not to love him. Well may it be said, "He died without an enemy in the world". The Milledgeville bar appointed Capt. C. P. Crawford, Judge T. W. White and F. G. DuBignon to draft resolutions expressive of their respect and appreciation of the dec'd.

8b. DAVID CRENSHAW BARROW, JR.[7], son of David C. and Eliza (Pope) Barrow, b. Oct. 18, 1852, is an alumnus of the U. of Ga., class 1874, degrees B.S. and C.E. & M.E.; member Chi Phi Frat. and Demosthenean Society. He received the degree of L.L.D. from Emory University. After graduation was admitted to the bar and practiced a short while with his brother, Pope Barrow, in Athens, Ga. But destiny called him and he entered upon his life work as a member of the faculty of the U. of Ga. in 1878. He continuously served on the faculty as Ass. Prof. of Mathematics, Prof. of Civil and Mining Engineering, Prof. of Mathematics and Dean of Franklin College. In 1906, while filling the chair of Mathematics, was called to the Chancellorship of the U. of Ga., which office he still fills. Under his wise administration the University has grown and enlarged in all branches—evidencing his devotion to its interests. Chancellor Barrow's life and character fully exemplify Georgia's Motto—"Wisdom, Justice, Moderation". He is a devout member of the Methodist Church and in its Sunday School has always taught a class of students, and there, as in all relations of life, he has met every obligation, fully, completely and unselfishly. At a banquet by the alumni in his honor, in Atlanta, Ga., the last of

May, 1921, the Hon. John D. Little, in introducing the Chancellor, said: "For fifteen years this grand old man has occupied the highest educational position in the gift of the State. He is the only man I ever heard of in such a position for such a length of time who conducted himself in such a manner that nothing but words of love and praise were uttered in reference to his work". "He is one of the most highly esteemed men in the State; his popularity with the students is unbounded, nor is he less securely entrenched in the confidence of the Alumni and Board of Trustees. He is admittedly one of the most successful heads of educational institutions in America; is at once both firm and gentle, characteristics most powerful when united. On July 7, 1914, the State named Barrow County in honor of Pope Barrow and David C. Barrow. (L. M. & L., Vol. 1, pp. 277, 433-'4; Vol. 2, p. 577, by L. L. Knight). He is a member of the Society of the Sons of the Revolution by right of his gr. father, James Barrow[3]. "He is one of Georgia's purest and most honored citizens, is a brilliant and forcible speaker, and when he essays a subject it is thoroughly analyzed. The South has produced few such men as Col. Barrow. He would grace any position within the gift of our Republic".

As Chancellor of the University of Georgia, one of the highest dignitaries in the State, he meets the honor with dignity and credit to himself and the State, and is perhaps the best loved man in Georgia. He is also a public spirited citizen and aside from his duties on the Faculty has served the City of Athens for years on the Board of Education and as Alderman.

(Atlanta Journal:) Athens, Ga., June 13, 1921.—"David C. Barrow, Chancellor of the University of Georgia since 1905, succeeding the late Walter B. Hill, who died in December 1904, as the head of the institution, tendered his resignation, effective Sept. 1, 1922, to the Board of Trustees meeting here Saturday.

This was the most surprising development of the pre-Commencement period, and while it came out in the Chancellor's letter to the board that he had made his intention known to at least one of its members, the chairman, a year ago, it had not been anticipated by the other trustees and caused deep regret among the members.

In his letter of resignation, Chancellor Barrow told the Board that he "told the Chairman of the board one year ago that at this time he expected to resign, and now did so, effective Sept. 1, 1922, or at any earlier date the Trustees might desire."

Effective that date it would give the board time to select his successor, said the Chancellor, and added: "It will also give me opportunity to participate in the War Memorial Fund drive, in which I feel a great interest". The Chancellor stated that he took this action on account of "my advancing years". He added that it had been a great pleasure for him to serve "this board all the way from an instructor to Chancellor, and I deeply appreciate the friendship of all the trustees".

"The resignation was referred to a special committee from the board, and it is not believed that it will be accepted. Possibly no other living Georgian has been and is still so close to so many of the native sons of the commonwealth as is the chancellor. An instructor in the college since his graduation and at the head of the University for seventeen years, Dr. Barrow has grown to be loved and esteemed not only by the student body with which during those years he has been associated, but with the alumni of former years as well. His connection with the institution and with educational affairs in the State has thrown him into touch with the people and one could hardly mention a name more familiar or a man more admired in any section of Georgia.

He is the State's only living citizen who has had the honor of having a county named for him—Barrow—formed a few years ago from Jackson, Gwinnett and Walton, with Winder as its county seat.

Chancellor Barrow says in his letter to the board that his resignation was predicated upon "his advancing years"—but he is a man who has grown old gracefully, and while great responsibilities have been his, he has kept young in heart with the wisdom of age, and has a most kindly and gentle outlook upon life, yet with a wonderful insight and realization to and of its potentialities.

He is sixty-eight years of age, a graduate of the University, a member of the Chi Phi fraternity, and a member of the Methodist Church".

Atlanta Journal, June 14, 1921: "Rejection of the resignation of Chancellor David C. Barrow was urged on the trustees of the University of Georgia at meetings of the faculty and members of the class of 1921. Memorials were sent to the Board."

Atlanta Journal, June 14, 1921: "Yielding to the earnest solicitations of the student body, faculty and hundreds of alumni gathered here for reunion, Chancellor David C. Barrow, Tuesday withdrew his resignation as head of the university system of the State of Georgia."

David C. Barrow, m. Feb. 5, 1879, Fances Ingle Childs, of Athens, Ga., b. Oct. 18, 1857, dau. of Asaph King Childs, of Mass. (mem. of Home Guards of Athens, 1861-'65), and Susan Ingle, his wife, of Washington, D. C., descendants of well known Colonial families of Mass. and Md. Issue:

1c. Susan Childs Barrow[8], b. Nov. 27, 1879, m. June 30, 19 . ., Samuel James Crowe, M. D., b. 16 April, 1882, son of Dr. Walter A. and Mrs. W. A. Crowe, alumnus of U. of Ga. 1904, A.B. degree, studied in Germany; of Johns Hopkins, degree of M.D., and on Surgical Staff of Johns Hopkins Hospital since graduation. Issue:

1d.—Samuel James Crowe, Jr.[9], b. 1909; 2d.—David Francis Crowe,[9] b. 1913.

2c. Benjamin Henry Barrow⁸, b. Jan. 17, 1883, attended U. of Ga., left before graduation; member Chi Phi Frat., Demosthenean Society; is a realtor at Athens and County Surveyor for Clarke Co., Ga.; m. Aug. 14, 1907, Henry Lucas, dau. of Frederick W. and Susan Holmes (Taylor) Lucas. Issue: 1d.—Susan Frances Barrow⁹, b. Nov. 23, 1908.

3c. Eleanor Priscilla Barrow⁸, b. April 17, 1886; m. June 24, 1914, Rev. H. L. Jewett Williams, of the Protestant Episcopal Church, son of Dr. Howard J. and Mrs. Kittie (Jewett) Williams, of Macon, Ga., an alumnus of U. of Ga. 1907, degree A.B.; Rhodes Scholarship, Christ Church, Oxford, England, degrees B.A. and B. Litt., Prof. Greek Testament, University of the South; volunteered World War, trained at Ft. McPherson, Capt. Inf., A. E. F.; ordered to France April, 1918. Killed in action June 9, 1918, at Albert, France. Issue: 1d.—H. L. Jewett Williams, Jr.⁹, b. Aug. 8, 1915; 2d.—Eleanor Barrow Jewett Williams⁹, b. Jan. 2, 1917.

4c. David Francis Barrow⁸, b. Nov. 14, 1888, alumnus U. of Ga., class 1910, degrees A.B. and B.S.; Chi Phi Frat.; Demosthenean Lit. Soc.; Scholarship U. Ga. to Harvard; scholarship Harvard to Harvard; scholarship Harvard to Universities of Europe (Higher Mathematics). Additional degrees M.A. and Ph.D. Was Instructor at Yale when he resigned and volunteered in World War, and was retained in Washington, D. C., in Aviation Dept.; was Prof. of Mathematics in U. of Texas, and now in U. of Ga. He m. July 29, 1914, Mary Augusta Arnold, dau. of Walter and Ida (Daniel) Arnold. Issue: 1d.—Ida Frances Barrow⁹; 2d.—David Barrow⁹, and, 3d.—Walter Henry Arnold Barrow⁹, d. in inf., twins, b. Oct., 1918.

9b. Henry Walker Barrow⁷, 1854-76, son of David C. and Sarah Eliza (Pope) Barrow, alumnus U. of Ga., class 1872, of the Lumpkin Law School, class 1873. In 1874 he entered upon the practice of his profession in Milledgeville, Ga., with his brother, Benjamin White Barrow. His health soon failed him and he sought to repair it by a visit to Sapelo Island, but in a short while realized his tenure on life was brief. Accompanied by his sister and brother-in-law, he left for his home in Oglethorpe Co., and on reaching Brunswick was found to be so weak that he was taken to a hotel in the city where in a few moments he died. "In him all that was noble and all that was reputable were most happily combined. A manly and intellectual face, an eye that bespoke the heart, a soul that lifted itself above all that was mean, little or selfish, a mind highly cultivated and trained, a ripe and reliable judgment, a purpose always honorable and commendable, an integrity as pure and undefiled as the ether he breathed, a firm and unflinching friend through every turn and fortune. In short, every element that makes up one of "nature's noblemen" was united in Henry W. Barrow".

All of the Barrows who attended the U. of Ga. were members of the Demosthenean Literary Society.

The Barrow family is probably eligible to membership in the Maryland Society of "The Ark and the Dove" by right of John Neville, ancestor in the Lumpkin line who came to America in "The Ark" or "The Dove" in 1633-'34. The fourth and fifth generations of Barrows in Georgia, both men and women, are prominent citizens in their various communities, socially and otherwise, and maintain the highest standards of life, and equal in public spirit, patriotism, civil and military services and professional distinction and achievement, their honored progenitors.

"Through the marriage of Clara Hill and Henry Augustine Pope, this Barrow family is doubly related to Lodowick Johnson Hill, Esq., of Atlanta, Ga., and to Mrs. Annie Noble Sims (d. June 3, 1921), of Savannah, Ga., whose articles in W. & M. Q'ly, Vol. XXVII, July, 1918, p. 57, and Oct. 1918, p. 104, give much valuable information relating to the early histories of these families in Virginia".

The "home place" of Henry Augustine Pope in Oglethorpe Co. is at present owned in part by four sons of the late Hon. Pope Barrow, and the balance by Chancellor Barrow. The latter has added, besides other contiguous properties, what is known as "Remembrance Field", the place whereon Burwell Pope lived, and where he and his wife are buried. No vestige remains of the residence, nor does slab or tomb mark their graves, but their locations are known to the family.

PRECIOUS PATIENCE BARROW, only sister of David C. Barrow, Sr., and dau. of James and Patience (Crenshaw) Barrow, b. Sept. 2, 1817; m. Feb. 23, 1836, William McKinley, of Lexington, Ga. He met her while a member of the Ga. Legislature, at Milledgeville. She lived in Lexington, Ga. She was educated at Dr. Andrews' School or Institute for Young Ladies at New Haven, Conn., to which she was sent by her guardians, Mr. and Mrs. Stubbs, of Milledgeville. They had:

1. Katherine McKinley, m. Jan. 7, 1863, Richard DeLoney Bolling Taylor and had one child, Kate McKinley Taylor, who m. Edward D. Treanor.

2. Archibald Carlisle McKinley, m. Nov. 19, 1866, Sarah Elizabeth Spalding, dau. of Randolph Spalding, of Sapelo Island. No living child.

3. Caroline McKinley, died young.

4. Mary McKinley, m. May 22, 1865, Howell Cobb, son of Hon. Howell Cobb, of Athens, Ga., and had a large family. She lives in Athens.

5. Sarah Barrow McKinley, m. Jan. 3, 18.., Thomas Spalding, son of Randolph Spalding, of Sapelo Island. (Two McKinleys and one Barrow married Spaldings, children of Randolph Spalding, of Sapelo Island, Ga. See Spalding).

HENRY AUGUSTINE POPE, 1760-1907, and his second wife, Mary Davis (vide ante p. 68), had:

6. Clara A. Pope[5], b. 29 Sept., 1801; d. 25 Nov., 1850; m. Samuel Baldwin and had son, Augustus Baldwin[6], who lived in S. West Ga.

7. Benjamin Pope[5] (Rev), b. 26 Nov., 1804; d. 18 Dec., 1855; m. Eliza S. Rountree, b. 27 Sept., 1807; d. 23 March, 1866. Issue: 1a.—Mary Susan Benjamin Pope[6], b. 14 Dec., 1833; d. 13 Aug., 1844; 2a.—Clara Nancy Eliza Pope[6], b. 30 May, 1835; d. 25 May, 1840. These are all buried in the family burying ground of Henry Augustine Pope, Home Place plantation, Oglethorpe Co., Ga.

8. *Henry Jefferson Pope*[5], b. 1806; d. 1854. Note: Both Benjamin and Henry Jefferson Pope were members of the class of 1825 of Franklin College which was so highly complimented by its President. (E. S. of Ala., p. 8).

He m. (I) Sarah Toombs, the only sister of the late Hon. Robert Toombs, m. (II) in 1842, Abigail Davis, dau. of Abner Davis from Phila., Pa., and his 2nd wife Elizabeth Parrish from Va., who m. in Greensboro, Ga. Issue by 1st mar.:

1a. Clara Julia Pope[6], m. Edwin M. Anthony, of Washington, Ga., and had 13 children, of whom:

1b. Mary Lou Anthony[7] m. Wiliam Burdett, of Valdosta, Ga.

2b. Gabriel Toombs Anthony[7], merchant, Washington, Ga., the 6th child, b. 9 June, 1868, m. Janet Paddison, of Fla. No issue.

3b. Henry Anthony[7]; 4b. Roberta Anthony[7], m. John Burdette; 5b. Pope Anthony[7]; 6b. Ernest Anthony[7]; 7b. John Vance Anthony[7]; 8b. Julia Anthony[7], m. Wylie Hill DuBose II; 9b. Jean Anthony[7]; 10b. Katherine Anthony[7], m. Kimbrel Aubrey Wilheit; 11b. Sarah Anthony[7]; 12b. Ouida Anthony[7]; 13b. Willie Belle Anthony[7].

2a. *Henry Abner Pope*[6], b. 1843; d. 1884; m. Lucy Howe, of Macon, Ga., and left one son: 1b.—Paul Marvin Pope[7], b. 1881.

3a. Benjamin Middleton Pope[6], b. 1845; d. 1864.

4a. Mary Elizabeth Pope, b. 1847; d. 1851, and

5a. Sarah Katherine Pope, b. 1847, twins; d. 1912, m. Henry Allen Pope, her 4th cousin, and left one son: 1b.—William Pope[7], b. 1882.

6a. *Abbie Davis Pope*, b. 1849. (q. v.).

7a. Augusta Pope, b. 1851; d. 1871.

8a. Robert Toombs Pope, b. 1853; d. 1864.

6a. *Abbie Davis Pope*[6] (dau. of Henry Jefferson and Abigail (Davis) Pope, b. 1849, m. 1869, *James Rembert Anthony*, son of Micajah and Mary Rembert (DuBose) Anthony, Capt. 1st Ga. Regulars, C. S. A., d. 1918, at West Palm Beach, Fla. Issue:

1b. James Rembert Anthony, Jr.[7], b. 1870; m. 1907, Rose May Seaward, of Petersburg, Va., has one son and two daus.

2b. Henry Jefferson Anthony[7], b. 1872; d. 1900.

3b. *Augustus Pope Anthony*[7], b. 1874; m. 12 Sept., 1900, *Lucy*

Jordan Hill[7], dau. of Duncan C. and Ophelia (Holliday) Hill. For issue, see p. 128.

 4b. Leila Davis Anthony[7], b. 1875; d. 1909; m., 1907, George Glen Strohm and had: 1c.—Anthony Strohm[8].

 5b. Emile DuBose Anthony[7], b. 1881; m. 1906, Gertrude Holden, of Crawfordville, Ga., and has three sons and one dau.

 6b. *Roscoe Tate Anthony*[7], b. 1891; m. 1919, Winifred Clark, of Philadelphia, Pa. He served in World War.

 V.—*Sarah Hill*[4] (Abraham[3], Abr.[2], Henry[1]), b. c. 1765-1816, m. *Benjamin Blake*, d. 4 Jany., 1797. Issue:
 1. Polly Blake[5], m. James Jordan (q. v.).
 2. Henry Blake[5], m. Betsy Mitchell. Not traced.
 3. Benjamin Blake, Jr.[5], m. Lucy Mitchell. Not traced.
 4. Elizabeth Blake[5], m. . . . McGehee. Not traced.

 Polly, Henry and Benjamin Blake, Jr., received grants of land in 1804 as orphans and heirs of a Rev'y Soldier (Records at Lexington, Ga.).

 1. Polly Blake[5], d. 6 Aug., 1829, (dau. of Benj[n] and Sarah (Hill) Blake) and her husband James Jordan, who was State Senator from Oglethorpe Co. 1819-'20, removed to Lexington, Ga., in 1821, or '22. Among their children was a dau.:

 1a. *Maria Louisa Jordan*[6], who m. Col. Alexander Sidney Reid, of Edenton, Ga., and they had: 1b.—Mary Elizabeth Reid[7], b. 6 Aug. 1841; d. 13 Nov., 1885; m. 4 Feby., 1864, *Mathew Henry Talbot*, of Wilkes Co., Ga., b. 3 April, 1836; d. 27 Sept., 1876, a Capt. commanding a troop of Cavalry, C. S. A., and had a dau.:

 1c. *Rosa Talbot*, who m. (I) . . . Reid; m. (II), in 1919, or '20, *Dr. Lucian Lamar Knight*, 2nd wife, L. L. D., Prest. Ga. His[l] Society, Author, Orator, and Compiler of Georgia State Records, and member of the Royal Society of Arts.

 James and Polly (Blake) Jordan had other children, and from them are derived Mrs. DeLoney Evans, of Warrenton, Va., and Mrs. M. G. Chambers, of Tompkins Cove, N. Y.

 Mrs. Lawson Brown, lately decd., nee Mamie Wiley, and her mother, Mrs. Col. C. M. Wiley, of Macon, descend from Benjamin and Sarah (Hill) Blake.

 VI.—*Henry Hill*[4] (Abraham[3], Abr.[2], Henry[1]), 1767-1829, m. *Bettie Andrew*, d. 11 June, 1830, dau. of *Benjamin Andrew*, patriot and president of the Rebel Council, Member of the Committee of Safety, of the Assembly in 1774 to protest against British Tyranny, of the Continental Congress in 1780, was an uncle of Bishop Andrew, refugeed to Columbia Co., then St. Paul's Parish, and d. in the up country.

 Abstract of Will of *Henry Hill*[4], of Oglethorpe Co., 29 April, 1829; R[d] 16 Sept., 1829. (Will Book C, p. 75). My loving Wife Elizabeth Hill; my son Whitman Coke Hill; my dau. Sophia Wesley Lucas; my dau. Susannah Hampton Williams; my son Henry

Philbin Hill; my dau. Elizabeth Walton Hardeman; to the Missionary Society of the Methodist Episcopal Church $100.; speaks of land lying in Wilkerson; Exx: my loving Wife Elizabeth Hill; Exr.: my son Whitman Coke Hill; Exr.: my son Henry Philbin Hill. April 29, 1829. (Signed) Henry Hill. Wit.: William McElroy, James Tippen, Jacob Jones. Recorded Sept. 16, 1829. W. D. Smith, C. C. O.

He disposed of very large estate.

Henry[4] and Bettie (Andrew) Hill had:

1. Whitman Coke Hill[5], Methodist minister, m. Jane Smith. N. R.
2. Sophia Wesley Lucas[5]. N. R.
3. Susannah Hampton Williams[5]. N. R.
4. Henry Philbin Hill[5], b. in 1807; d. in the '90's. (q. v.).
5. Elizabeth Walton Hardeman[5]. N. R.

4. *Henry Philbin Hill[5]*, 1807-189 . . , m. Augusta Prichard, dau. of William Hurst Prichard and his wife, Elizabeth Cotton, removed to Griffin, Ga. Issue, an only dau.:

1a. *Elizabeth Andrew Hill*, b. 1861, m. Hon. Fleming G. Bailey, of Griffin, Ga. No children.

VII.—THEOPHILUS HILL[4] (Abraham[3], Abr.[2], Henry[1]), 1769-1829, was a Lieut. in the Indian Wars succeeding the Revolution ("Ga.'s Roster of the Revolution", p. 403; D. A. R. Mag., Vol. 16, p. 352; Records of Executive Council, 1790-'9, pp. 112-113). Received Bounty Warrant (Ga. Roster of Rev. Soldiers, p. 398; D. A. R. Mag., 1898-1900, p. 365; "Story of Ga.", by Smith), and in Oglethorpe Co., Ga., 1794-1800, received grants for self and 14 persons (J. H. Coll., Vol. III). He became an early settler of Walton Co., and at his death in 1829, had 42 negroes, 22 sheep, 350 bbls. of corn, 12 beds and bedsteads, 100 dollars worth of hogs, 2 cotton gins, etc. ("Story of Ga.", pp. 326-'7). He d. intestate, and, unexpectedly, while on a visit in Auburn, Ala.

He m. Polly Jordan (and, possibly, married a second time, in his old age, as there is in Wilkes Co. record of marriage of Theophilus Hill, Oct. 9, 1823, to Nancy Poss). Issue by 1st mar.:

1. Martha (Patsy) Hill[5], m. 22 Nov., 1808, William ("Billy") Mitchell. N. R.
2. Abraham Hill[5], m. Martha Harden, lived near Social Circle, Ga., and d. s. p.
3. Elizabeth Hill[5], m. 5 Jany., 1814, Augustus George C. Mitchell. N. R.
4. Harriet A. Hill[5], m. 27 June, 1817, Abraham McGehee, in Oglethorpe Co., Ga., son of Micajah and Ann (Scott) McGehee, his 1st wife (q. v.).
5. Theophilus Jordan Hill[5], b. c. 1793; d. 1868, in Walton Co., Ga., aged 75 years. (q. v.).
6. Warren Jordan Hill[5]. (q. v.).
7. Benjamin Hill[5], blessed with an attractive personality, was

exceedingly popular, but resisted the "wiles of women" and d. unm., after middle life.

8. Mary Ann Hill[5], b. 6 June, 1815; d. Oct. 6, 1891. (q. v.).

9. Adeline Hill[5], m. . . . . Wellborn and their dau.[6] m. Dr. W. A. Dunn, of Columbia Co., Ga. N. R.

4. Harriet A. Hill[5] (dau. of Theophilus and Polly (Jordan) Hill) and her husband, Abraham McGehee, had:

1a. James McGehee[6], m. . . . . ; d. s. p.

2a. Harriet Sophia McGehee[6], m. Lawson Porter, of Miss., and had:

1b. Martha Harriet Porter[3], m. J. H. Jarnagan.

Abraham McGehee m. (II) Catherine Peniston; m. (III) Miss . . . . Smith, of Ala. (Vide E. S. of Ala., p. 452).

Note: It is possible that this Harriet A. Hill, above, may have been dau. of Henry Hill[4] instead of Theophilus Hill[4]. In a chart of the family made prior to 1890, both Theophilus and Henry are credited with a dau. Harriet. It says of Harriet, dau. of Theophilus simply that she died; of Harriet, dau. of Henry, no further information is given. Henry[4], in will 1829, makes no mention of dau. Harriet; however, this omission may have been because of her pre-decease. Henry named a dau. Sophia, and Harriet (Hill) McGehee named a dau. *Harriet Sophia* McGehee. The records so far discovered and examined do not definitely identify this Harriet. Further research would probably do so.

5. *Theophilus Jordan Hill*[5], 1793-1868, son of Theophilus and Polly Jordan Hill, was a member from Walton Co., Ga., of the Anti-Tariff Convention in Nov., 1832; m. Salina Huntington Wellborn, d. after 1878, dau. of Elias Wellborn (brother of Abner) and his wife, Miss . . . . Marshall, dau. of the eminent divine, Abram Marshall. (It is possible, he m. (I), 9 Oct., 1823, Nancy Poss, of Wilkes Co.). Issue:

1a. Martha Hill[6], m. John F. Kinsey, of Warrenton, Ga. N. R.

2a. Mary Anna Hill[6], m. Rev. J. Benjamin Bussey. (q. v.).

3a. Emma Hill[6], living 1916, m. Phocian Ramsey, of Columbia Co., Ga., son of Isaac Ramsey, d. 1869, and his wife, d. 1861, who was a dau. of Johnson Wellborn, bro. of Elias and Abner, of Wilkes Co., Ga. N. R.

4a. Eugenia Victoria Hill[6], called "Jennie", m. Dr. George Coleman Kramer, decd., of N. Y. She was living in 1917 at Edenton, Ga. No issue.

5a. Edwin Hill[6], N. R.; 6a. James Hill[6], N. R.

2a. *Mary Ann Hill*[6] and her husband, Dr. J. B. Bussey, had dau.:

1b. Anna Augusta Bussey[7], who m. William H. R. Stone and had:

1c. Annie Laurie Stone[8], who m. Dr. Floyd Clark Timmons, of Monroe, Ga., and they have:

1d. Lamar Hill Timmons[9], their youngest son, and others.

8. Mary Ann Hill[5], 1815-1891, dau. of Theophilus[4] and Polly (Jordan) Hill, m. *Dick Halliday*, formerly spelt Holliday, of Auburn, Ala. Issue:
 1a. Abraham Halliday[6], m. . . . . Mitchell. (q. v.).
 2a. Mack Halliday[6], d. N. R.
 3a. Gus Halliday[6], d. N. R.
 4a. *Ophelia Jordan Halliday*[6], b. 26 Feby., 1839; d. 30 Aug., 1898; m. 12 Feby., 1861, Duncan Chatfield Hill, 1837-1908. (Vide post p. 128.)
 5a. Mary Halliday[6], m. Dr. . . . . Foreman and had: 1b.—Ophelia Foreman[7], who m. . . . . Adams and had two children; 2b.—Mary Mac Foreman[7], N. R.
 6a. Warren Halliday[6], m. . . . . Mitchell and d. s. p.
 7a. Lou Halliday, m. . . . . Walsh, and had: 1b.—Eddie Walsh[7]; 2b.—Willie Walsh. N. R.
 1a. Abraham Halliday[6] and his wife, Miss Mitchell, had:
 1b. Georgia V. Halliday[7], m. Harvey DuBose Hill[7]. (Vide post p. 130.)
 2b. Iuka Halliday[7], d. when about 18 years of age, unm.
 3b. Alice Halliday[7], m. Henry Casey Hill[7]. (Vide post p. 130.)

VIII.—*Noah Hill*[4], 1771-1805 (Abraham[3], Abr.[2], Henry[1]), received a land grant 1794-1800, as son of Rev'y Soldier (Records at Lexington, Ga.), m. 28 April, 1796, *Ann (Nancy) Pope*, b. 28 April, 1780; d. 6 June, 1805, dau. of Burwell, 1751-1800, and Priscilla (Wootten) Pope.
 Abstract of Will of NOAH HILL, of Oglethorpe Co., 25 Feby., 1805; R[d] 20 June, 1805. (Will Book A, p. 152). My three children Alexander Franklin Hill, Walton Pope Hill and Paulina Hill. Exrs.: Abraham Hill, Wiley Pope, Miles Hill and Robert Pope.
 (Signed) Noah Hill.
Wit.: Thomas Wootten
 Benjamin Taylor
 Wiley Pope.
 Evidently *not a complete abstract*.
 Abstract of Will of WALTON POPE HILL, of Oglethorpe Co., 17 Dec., 1826; R[d] 27 Sept., 1827. (Will Book C, p. 27).
 My sister, *Paulina*, and my bro.-in-law John Hardeman. Exr., Burwell Pope. (Signed) Walton P. Hill.
 Charles V. Collier, D. C. C. O.
Wit.: Miller Grieve
 Hopson M. Hubbard
 James Gillespie
 Noah[4] *and Ann (Pope) Hill* had:
 1. ALEXANDER FRANKLIN HILL[5], M.D., b. c. 1798; d. 10 Oct., 1824, unm. He was on volunteer duty in a hospital in Phila., in which were many cases of smallpox. Inoculation was beginning to be practiced in England, and to test its efficacy before resorting

to its use in the hospital, had himself inoculated and died from the effect. His life was the price paid for his zeal and ambition to spare his fellow man a loathsome affliction and untimely death. He possessed unusual endowments, had the promise of a brilliant professional career, was beloved and esteemed by all. All other Hills bearing his christian name have received it in his honor,— among these were Maj. A. A. F. Hill, of Athens, Capt. A. F. Hill, of Meriwether Co., Ga., Alexander Franklin Pope, of Oglethorpe Co., Ga., &c. The latter wrote this compiler in the 90's that his father, Gen. Burwell Pope, had named two sons in his honor, the first having d. as an infant.

2. Walton Pope Hill^5, d. 21 March, 1827 (vide Will above).

3. Paulina Hill^5, m. John Hardeman and d. 10 Dec., 1827. N. R.

IX.—MILES HILL^4, 1774-1844, (Abraham^3, Abr.^{2}, Henry^1), received land grant as son of a Rev'y Soldier in 1794-1800 (Records at Lexington, Ga.); m. 26 Jany., 1795, *Tabitha Pope*, b. 11 Feby., 1778; d. 25 April, 1852, dau. of Burwell, 1751-1800, and Priscilla (Wootten) Pope.

Will of MILES HILL, of Oglethorpe Co., 16 April, 1842; R^d 23 Jany., 1845. (Will Book D, p. 147).

"In the name of God, Amen. I Miles Hill of said State and County being of sound mind and disposing memory, but being advanced in life, and knowing the uncertainty of human life, do make and ordain this to be my last Will and testament.

1st Item. I give my body to the earth whence it came, and my soul I commit into the hands of a Merciful God in Christ Jesus.

2nd Item. It is my will that at my death all my just debts be paid.

3rd Item. I give and bequeath unto my beloved wife Tabitha Hill all my estate both real and personal, or so much thereof as she may desire to keep, for and during her natural life, and after her death to be equally divided between my five children, or in case of any of them be dead, then the child or children of him or her so deceased shall inherit equally with any living child.

4th Item. If my wife shall choose not to keep any portion of my estate, herein devised, it is my will that she divide and give off such portion equally among my children or their heirs as aforesaid.

5th Item. I do hereby appoint Hampton W. Hill, Nicholas Taliaferro and Blanton M. Hill my Executors to this my last will and testament, hereby revoking any will I have heretofore made, and I do hereby desire to exempt my Executors from the necessity or obligation to make inventories, appraisement and returns of my estate, unless they should choose to do so.

Given under my hand and seal this sixteenth day of April, 1842.

(Signed) Miles Hill.

Signed and sealed in presence of

David C. Barrow, Middleton Pope, John G. Hammock. Recorded Jany. 23, 1845.   Henry Brittain, C. C. O.

"Miles Hill and his wife Tabitha (Pope) Hill were Methodists and noted for their piety and philanthropy. There are three graves which are still well preserved, because there is no opening in the wall surrounding them, on the plantation of Miles Hill in Oglethorpe Co. The wall is high and solid, and over each grave is an old fashioned box tombstone of heavy, white marble. These are handsome but much discolored by age. On one is the following inscription:

In Memory of
Tabitha Hill
Who was born
February 11, 1778
and died
April 25th, 1852.

"Yea though I walk through the valley of the shadow of death, I will fear no evil, for thou art with me, thy rod and thy staff they comfort me".

On another is the following:

In Memory of
Miles Hill
Born March 13th, 1774
Died November 4th, 1844.

"Blessed are the dead who die in the Lord from henceforth, Yea saith the Spirit that they may rest from their labors and their works do follow them".

(Article by Annie Noble Sims, W. & M. Q., Vol. 27, Oct. 1918, pp. 106-'7).

IX. MILES[4] *and* TABITHA (Pope) Hill had:
1. Malinda Hill[5], b. 3 July, 1796; d. (q. v.).
2. James Alford Hill[5], b. 2 Dec., 1797; d. 2 Feby., 1831. (q. v.).
3. Hampton Wootten Hill[5], b. 9 March, 1800; d. 12 Sept., 1851. (q. v.).
4. Blanton Meade Hill[5], b. 5 May, 1802; d. 3 Feby., 1857. (q. v.).
5. Ann Hill[5], b. 18 Dec., 1804; d. 31 Jany., 1868. (q. v.).

1. Malinda Hill[5] (Miles[4], Abraham[3], Abr.[2], Henry[1]), b. 3 July, 1796; m. John Scott McGehee, son of Micajah and Ann (Scott) McGehee. (Vide E. S. of Ala., pp. 451-'3). Issue:
1a. Miles Hill McGehee[6], b. 26 Nov., 1813; d. 15 Jany., 1860. (q. v.).
2a. Edward F. McGehee[6], b. 6 April, 1816; d. 10 Nov., 1879. (q. v.).
3a. Tabitha Ann McGehee[6], b. 10 April, 1818; d. 21 Jany., 1888. (q. v.).
4a. Sarah E. McGehee[6], b. 12 Feby., 1820; d. 17 Sept., 1895. (q. v.).
5a. Mary Pope McGehee[6], b. 6 Feby., 1822; d. 29 Aug., 1880. (q. v.).

6a. John Hampton McGehee⁶, b. 20 Aug., 1824; d. 17 Aug., 1827.
7a. James Blanton McGehee⁶, b. 18 March, 1826; d. 27 Sept., 1866. (q. v.).
8a. Lucinda Scott McGehee⁶, b. 3 Feby., 1828; d. 10 March, 1847. (q. v.).
9a. Nicholas Abner McGehee⁶, b. 6 April, 1830; d. 11 Aug., 1834.
10a. Martha Malinda McGehee⁶, b. 7 Nov., 1832; d. 13 Aug., 1872. (q. v.).
11a. William Thomas McGehee⁶, b. 16 Dec., 1835; m. (I) Linda Malone; m. (II) Pattie Hardman. No issue by either marriage.
12a. Louisa Terrell McGehee⁶, b. 17 Nov., 1837. (q. v.).
13a. Ella Hill McGehee⁶, b. 19 April, 1839; m. Thomas H. Hunton, of N. O. Issue:
1b. Annie Hunton⁷, m. Gilbert Green, merchant, of N. O.
2b. McGehee Dandridge Hunton⁷, of N. Y., m. Mary Moss, of Columbia, Mo.

1a. MILES HILL MCGEHEE⁶ (son of John Scott and Malinda (Hill) McGehee), 1813-1865, was a planter of great wealth (Vide "Georgians", by Geo. R. Gilmer); m. Miss ...... Travis and had:
1b. Ida Blanche McGehee⁷, b. 6 Oct., 1849; d. 12 Aug., 1889,—fell from second story window of her home; m. James F. Stokes and had several children, all d. y. except:
1c. Harry S. Stokes⁸, atty.-at-law, who was killed on 26 April, 1916, by Charles G. Trabue, an atty.-at-law, at Nashville, Tenn.
M. (II), Mrs. Mary (Crouse) Porter and had a dau.: 2b.—Kate Crouse McGehee⁷, born in 1852 and d. y.

2a. Edward F. McGehee⁶ (son of John Scott and Malinda (Hill) McGehee), 1816-1879, m. Mrs. Pattie (Williamson) Penn. Issue: 1b.—Pattie McGehee⁷, m. Philip Pointer, of Como, Miss.; 2b.—Edward F. McGehee, Jr., m. Niegra Crabtree, of Trenton, Ga.

3a. Tabitha Ann McGehee⁶ (dau. of John Scott and Malinda (Hill) McGehee), 1818-1888, m. Charles F. Dabdridge and had: 1b.—McGehee Dandridge⁷, killed 7 April, 1862, in battle of Shiloh.

4a. Sarah E. McGehee⁶ (dau. of John Scott and Malinda (Hill) McGehee), 1820-1895, m. her cousin, Edmund McGehee, and had:
1b. Emma McGehee⁷, b. 23 Feby., 1842; d. May, 1877; m. A. S. Yarbrough, of Como, Miss.
2b. William E. McGehee⁷, merchant, of Memphis, Tenn., b. Aug., 1858; m. Kate E. Poston.
3b. John Scott McGehee⁷, b. 21 Aug., 1861; m. Rosa Taylor, of Como, Miss.
There were three other children, who d. in inf.

5a. Mary Pope McGehee⁶ (dau. of John Scott and Malinda (Hill) McGehee), 1822-1880, m. (I), Jacob F. Farrington, of Memphis, and had:

1b. John McGehee Farrington[7], b. 7 June, 1850, who m. Milly White and had:
 1c. Dr. Pope McGehee Farrington[8], of Memphis. (See "White" and "Oliver" in "E. S. of Ala.").

7a. James Blanton McGehee[6] (son of John Scott and Malinda (Hill) McGehee), 1826-1866, m. Eugenia Willick. Issue:
 1b. John Lucius McGehee[7], b. 22 July, 1850; m. Ada Hartridge, of Savannah, Ga.
 2b. Julia Hill McGehee[7], b. 27 Nov., 1854; d. 19 Dec., 1870.
 3b. James Blanton McGehee, Jr.[7], m. Jennie Dalton, of Memphis, Tenn.

8a. Lucinda Scott McGehee[6] (dau. of John S. and Malinda (Hill) McGehee), 1829-1847, m. William M. White and had: 1b.—Ann Scott McGehee White[7], b. 1 April 1846; d. in inf.

10a. Martha Malinda McGehee[6], (dau. of John Scott and Malinda (Hill) McGehee), 1832-1872, m. Simeon Oliver, of Hernando, Miss., and had:
 1b. Linda Hill Oliver[7], b. 16 Feby., 1854; d. Sept., 1884; m. W. P. Martin.
 2b. Charles Dandridge Oliver[7], b. 16 March, 1856.
 3b. Sallie McGehee Oliver[7], b. 19 Dec., 1858; m. G. S. Postom.
 4b. Simeon Shelton Oliver[7], b. 20 Dec., 1867.
 5b. Edward Oliver[7]. See ("E. S. of Ala."—"Oliver").

12a. Louisa Terrell McGehee[6] (dau. of John Scott and Malinda (Hill) McGehee), 1837-   , m. Malcom F. Gilchrist, of Miss., and had:
 1b.—Lula Gilchrist[7], b. Oct., 1858; m. Elzey Meacham, of Memphis; 2b.—Annie Gilchrist[7], d. in inf.; 3b.—William A. Gilchrist[7], b. 31 Dec., 1861; m. Mrs. Laura Shields, of Nashville, Tenn.; 4b.—Malcom Gilchrist, Jr.[7], b. 22 July, 1885; m. Julia Kerr, of Memphis, Tenn.

2. JAMES ALFORD HILL[5] (Miles[4], Abraham[3], Abr.[2], Henry[1]), 1797-1831, m. 29 Oct., 1818, Amelia Walton Hill, his first cousin, b. 12 Aug., 1800, dau. of Thomas (1780-1816) and Sallie (McGehee) Hill ("E. S. of Ala.", p. 529; and post (1, XII, B. P. O.). Issue:
 1a. Bettie Hill[6], m. William Seay, and had: 1b.—Katie Seay[7].
 2a. *Lucinda Malinda Hill*[6], m. (I) Ben Blanton, of Griffin, Ga., son of Rev. Benjamin Blanton (b. in N. C.; d. 5 Sept., 1845, in Oglethorpe Co., Ga.) and his wife, Susannah Davis, b. in Dublin, Ireland; d. 19 Feby., 1844, dau. of John Davis, a Welshman and an officer in the British Army; m. (II) Henry E. Williamson, eldest son of Isaac and Sarah (Freeman) Wilkinson. (q. v.).
 3a. Thomas Hill[6], m. Miss Stratton, of Miss., and moved to Texas. N. R.
 4a. Cordelia Ann Hill[6], m. her first cousin, Peter Oliver, son of Dionysius Oliver and his 1st wife, Lucinda McGehee, dau. of Micajah and Ann (Scott) McGehee, and sister of Sallie (McGehee)

Hill, who became the second wife of Dionysius Oliver. ("E. S. of Ala.", pp. 528-'9).

2a. Lucinda Malinda Hill[6] (2, XII, B. P. O.) had by 1st mar.:

1b. SUSAN AMELIA BLANTON[7], b. Sept. 4, 1844; m. 1 Oct., 1870, *Levi Ezell* Veal, b. 16 Nov., 1836; d. 14 Aug., 1912, and had:

1c. Lizzielee Veal[8], b. 8 July, 1872; d. 19 Feby., 1888, unm., aged 16 years.

2c. Willie Ben Veal[8], b. 4 May, 1876; m. 29 July, 1914, Miss Estelle Johnson, of San Marcus, Tex., and had: 1d.—Dean Johnson Veal, b. 4 April, 1916.

3c. Mary Belle Powell Veal[8], b. 4 March, 1878; m. 27 April, 1911, William Jordan.

Mrs. Susan Amelia (Blanton) Veal, living 1921, in Barnesville, Ga.

3. HAMPTON WOOTTEN HILL[5] (Miles[4], Abraham[3]), 1800-1851, m. EUDOCIA LANE, her 1st husband, dau. of Joseph Lane, Jr., and his wife Elizabeth Hill, dau. of Isaac (1761-1833) and Nancy (Crain) Hill and sister of Nancy Lane, who m. Judge Walter Terry Colquitt. She m. (II) Joseph Winship, of Atlanta, his 2nd wife, father of George (d. 11 April, 1916) and Robert Winship, decd. Issue by 1st mar., none by 2nd:

1a. Tabitha[6], called "Pug" Hill, m. Col. Chesley Howard, of Atlanta, Ga., having children who are prominent both socially and in business.

2a. Miles H. Hill[6], who was Capt. of Co. "B", 4th Ga. Regt., C. S. A. Not traced.

3a. Blanton Hill[6], N. R.; 4a.—Joe Hill[6], N. R.

5a. Nannie Hill[6], m. Major Brow Morgan, of LaGrange and Atlanta, Ga., both decd. Issue:

1b. Lizzie Hill Morgan[7], m. in 1888, Charles T. Hopkins, b. 29 May, 1862; d. 10 Dec., 1921, son of the late Judge John L. Hopkins, prominent attorney-at-law, of Atlanta, Ga., and has several children: Chas. T., Jr.[8]; John L. II[8]; Alex. S.[8], Nancy Hill Hopkins[8].

2b. Gussie Morgan[7], m. Jefferson Pearce.

3b. Charlie Morgan. N. R.

6a. AUGUSTA HILL[6], who m. JOSEPH THOMPSON (d. 3 Dec., 1921, aged 79 years), 1st wife, of Atlanta, Ga. No issue. She was one of the most lovable and adorable women of her day. Nature endowed her with a personality and character so replete with charm and beauty as to win for her unusual admiration and love. A sincere admirer and devoted kinsman always spoke of her as "Sweet Beautiful"—an appellation so appropriate and well merited that many others used it. In the Atlanta Journal, July 13, 1916, appeared the following: "Fire Headquarters Bell soon will be removed and placed in City Park. The bell is named "Augusta Hill" after the decd. wife of Col. Joseph Thompson. In 1866, just before the bell was bought, a fair was held where the James Bank block now stands by the Firemen's Fair Association to raise the funds needed to purchase the bell. A contest was held for the most popular young lady at the fair, and Miss Augusta Hill was accorded the honor and the bell named after her. When later, as the wife of Col. Thompson, the belle of the 60's, for whom the big tocsin was named, passed away, the bell tolled during the funeral."

Joseph Thompson m. (II) Miss Emma Mims, only dau. of Major Livingston Mims, decd., and his wife, Miss Sue Harper, who bore him an only son:

1b. Livingston Mims Thompson[7], of Louisville, Ky., d. 20 Oct. 1920, in Asheville, N. C.; m. Miss Helen Nicholson, dau. of G. A. Nicholson, decd., of Atlanta, Ga. They have two children: Mary[8] and Emma[8] Thompson.

4. BLANTON MEADE HILL[5] (Miles[4], Abraham[3], Abr.[2], Henry[1]), 1802-1857, m. 9 May, 1825, ELIZABETH ANN HILL[5], his 1st cousin, dau. of Abraham[4], 1759-1818, and Elizabeth (McGehee) Hill (vide ante 2, II, B. P. O., p. 64).

5. ANN HILL[5] (Miles[4], Abraham[3], Abr.[2], Henry[1]), 1804-1868, m. 24 Feby., 1824, NICHOLAS MERIWETHER TALIAFERRO, b. 29 Dec., 1801; d. 23 June, 1871, in Ark., son of Genl. Benjamin Teliaferro and his 1st wife, Martha Meriwether, dau. of David Meriwether, Member of 7th, 8th and 9th Congresses—1801-1807—and representative of Presidents Jefferson and Jackson in negotiations with the Creeks and Cherokees. (See "E. S. of Ala.", p. 513; "Va. Alumni Bulletin", Oct., 1913, Vol. 6, No. 3, p. 638; "Georgian", by Gov. Geo. R. Gilmer).

Benjamin Taliaferro was a Capt. and rendered 7 years service in the Continental line (Va. Co. Rec., Vol. 6, pp. 33 and 52), removed soon after the war, in 1784, to Ga., was often a member of the Legislature, served as President of the State Senate, and though he had never even read law, was elected by the Legislature a Judge of the Superior Court, became a Member of Congress, and *declined* to accept a nomination as Governor. (See "Ga. Land and People", pp. 150-'1-'2, by Frances Lutcher Mitchell). Issue:

1a. Benjamin Blanton Taliaferro[6], b. 1 Feby., 1830; d. 8 Nov., 1862, unm.

2a. Malinda Margaret Taliaferro[6], b. 30 May, 1832; d. 1868. (q. v.).

3a. John Nicholas Taliaferro[6], b. 10 May., 1835; d. 9 Oct., 1904. (q. v.).

4a. Miles Hill Taliaferro[6], b. 23 Jany., 1837; d. 12 Oct., 1860, unm.

5a. James Hampton Taliaferro[6], b. 20 Aug., 1842; d. 20 Jany., 1890. (q. v.).

6a. Ann Amelia Taliaferro[6], b. 13 Aug., 1845; d.

7a. *Martha Malinda Taliaferro*[6], b. 1 March, 1847. (q. v.).

2a. Malinda Margaret Taliaferro⁶ (Ann⁵, Miles⁴, Abraham³), 1832-1868, m. Thomas Brewer, of Wilkes Co., Ga. Issue:
  1b. Rosa Brewer⁷, m. John H. Breathwaite.
  2b. Benjamin Taliaferro Brewer⁷, d.
  3b. Nicholas Taliaferro Brewer⁷, d.
  4b. Lucy Carter Brewer⁷, m. Jesse DeLoney and had: 1c.—Antoinette DeLoney⁸; 2c.—Thomas DeLoney⁸; 3c.—Lucy Clive DeLoney⁸.

3a. John Nicholas Taliaferro⁶ (Ann⁵, Miles⁴, Abraham³), 1835-1904, m. in 1858, Ann Barbara Cosby McGehee, b. 10 March, 1838; d. 3 July, 1889. Issue:
  1b. Lucy Hill Taliaferro⁷, b. July, 1860, m. John H. Breathwaite, d. Jany., 1920.
  2b. Mary Edward Taliaferro⁷, b. March, 1862.
  3b. LINDA MARTHA TALIAFERRO⁷, b. 2 March, 1875; d. Jany., 1920; m. 28 Dec., 1898, JOHN HERNDON HOLLIS, of Little Rock, Ark., 1st wife, b. 5 Feby., 1870. Issue:
    1c. Barbara Herndon Hollis⁸, b. 24 Sept., 1899.
    2c. Nicholas Taliaferro Hollis⁸, b. 15 Nov., 1900.
    3c. Mildred Hollis⁸, b. 19 May, 1902.
    4c. Linda Taliaferro Hollis⁸, b. 13 May, 1904.
    5c. John Herndon Hollis, Jr.⁸, b. 3 July, 1906.
    6c. Wiliam Taliaferro Hollis⁸, b. 5 July, 1908.
  4b. Barbara McGehee Taliaferro⁷ (John Nicholas⁶, Ann⁵, Miles⁴), b. 1877; m. Oct., 1904, Eugene Perry Aldredge, b. 30 May, 1875, and had: 1c.—Eugene Perry Aldredge, Jr., b. 5 Jany., 1905.

5a. James Hampton Taliaferro⁶ (Ann⁵, Miles⁴, Abraham³), 1842-1890, m. Rebecca McGehee. Issue:
  1b. John Nicholas Taliaferro⁷, b. 6 Oct., 1871; d. 11 Dec., 1890.
  2b. Miles Hill Taliaferro⁷, b. 13 March, 1873; d. 9 Feby., 1881.
  3b. Edward McGehee Taliaferro⁷, b. 31 Jany., 1875; m. 1 March, 1913, Nora Quinn.
  4b. Julia McGehee Taliaferro⁷, b. 31 Dec., 1876; m. 8 Sept., 1901, S. J. T. Wynne, b. 3 Aug., 1876, and had: 1c.—Clara Taliaferro Wynne⁸, b. 14 Oct., 1902; 2c.—Rebecca McGehee Wynne⁸, b. 6 June, 1904; 3c.—James Taliaferro Wynne⁸, b. 30 Aug., 1909.

7a. MARTHA MALINDA TALIAFERRO⁶ (Ann⁵, Miles⁴, Abraham³), b. 1847; m. (I), 30 Jany., 1873, JAMES MERIWETHER DUNCAN, b. 3 June, 1842; d. 22 March, 1873. (See post 4a, 5, X, B. P. O.), son of Perry Emory Duncan (1800-1869) and his wife, Mary Ann Tabitha Hill; m. (II) in 1877 Horace Jewell, a Methodist minister, b. 3 Dec., 1832, killed in 1917 by train while crossing track. Issue by 1st mar.: a dau., Jimmie Duncan⁷, b. 5 Nov., 1873; m. 7 Nov., 1894, John H. Arnold.

Issue by 2nd mar.
  2b. Albert Taliaferro Jewell⁷, b. 13 Dec., 1878.
  3b. Linda Taliaferro Jewell⁷, b. 23 Aug., 1880.
  4b. Ann Taliaferro Jewell⁷, b. 7 June, 1883; m. (I), 18 June,

1913, Walter Roy Purcell; m. (II), Sept., 1921, John Hollis Herndon, 2nd wife.

    5b.   Horace Hughes Jewell[7], b. 2 Aug., 1885.

    6b.   Nicholas Taliaferro Jewell[7], b. 27 May, 1887; m. 7 March, 1911, Grace Briant.

    X.—WYLIE HILL[4] (Abraham[3], Abraham[2], Henry[1]), 1775-1844, b. in Wake Co., N. C.; d. in Wilkes Co., Ga., eleven miles northwest of Washington, on the south side of the road to Danielsville, where stood the old home of Genl., later Governor, John Clark, who was one of the most commanding and outstanding characters of the early history of the State, and where two of his sons are buried. On one tomb is this inscription: "George Walton Clark, son of John and Nancy Clark, born 11 Jany., 1797; died October 27, 1798". The slab marking the grave of the other son has disappeared. Here on the night preceding the battle of Kettle Creek, the Revolutionary troops bivouacked. Col. Wylie Hill purchased the property in 1799 or 1800, and Mrs. Nancy Clark, because of the graves of her little sons, was so loath to leave the place that she pleaded and prevailed with Col. and Mrs. Hill for permission to remain with them several months after their taking possession. The original building was a large, commodious frame structure, of the best type then prevalent, but in the fifties, after the death of both Col. and Mrs. Hill, it passed into the hands of their youngest daughter, Mrs. Dr. William M. Jordan. She razed the old building and erected in its stead what was probably the handsomest Colonial home in the County. Alas! within a year after its completion, this magnificent mansion was completely destroyed by fire. It was replaced by a roomy cottage—designed to accommodate all comers, but this too has disappeared, leaving naught but the burial ground with its tombs to mark the site.

    WILL OF WYLIE HILL. In the name of God, Amen: I Wylie Hill of the County of Wilkes and State of Georgia, being of sound mind and perfect memory, blessed be God, do make and ordain this to be my last will and testament, in manner following, that is to say:

    First as to my body I wish it to be decently buried in the garden where my two little granddaughters are buried.

    I wish for all my just debts to be paid first and then the balance to be divided as I shall state in this my last will *February Thirteenth, Eighteen Hundred and thirty seven.*

    I wish for my wife and my three sons to have the management of my property at my death, as the boys come of age they will see to it.

    I wish to have a house built over my grave large enough to cover my dear wife also, let the sils be out of old post oak 14 inches square set on rocks one foot from the ground. Have the frame about five feet high covered with good heart shingles fully one inch thick after they are drawn, and good heart weather boarding painted black.

My will and desire is that my dear wife shall have those slaves during her life or widowhood for to support her and my two youngest sons Wylie P. Hill and A. T. W. Hill and school them. These are the negroes I leave to my dear wife: Edward and his wife Sarah and their two youngest children, one leg Grace and their two sons Tony and Frank and one set of the blacksmith Tools, Amanda and Vilo Jacob and his wife Grace and their youngest children Cato and Sandy Squire and Gideon Jeffrey and the use of the upper mill to grind for her during her natural life or widowhood. As to the children, my son Burwell P. Hill had by Martha his last wife, I will them one dollar a piece, and as to the part that would fall to my son Burwell P. Hill's heirs, my will and desire is that his daughter by his first wife should have it, Sarah Ann Eliza Render Hill if she should live to have heir and if she should die it's all to fall back to my children that's living at that time.

My house and plantation where I now live for the use of my dear wife during her life or widowhood, and at her death to go to my son Abraham T. W. Hill making the Crews Creek the line down the meanders of said creek to be the line until it goes to the fork below Clark road, thence to take a due East line to the back line towards *James Render's* old place, all to the south of that line I give to my son Wylie P. Hill, to him, his heirs and assigns forever, as far as my land goes toward Washington, the Newton and Lacky place, and Parks place and Wylie Burks place also, and all on the North of that line, the Clark place, John Hill place and the King place and Barnes Place and the John McGehee place and the saw and grist mills I give to my son Abraham T. W. Hill his heirs and assigns forever:

The Abraham Hill place and the 212 acres up by Sardus and the 100 acres the Thomas Johnston place I give to my son Lodowick M. Hill in lieu of the Dodson place to him his heirs and assigns forever. Now should my son Lodowick M. Hill be pleased with the swap, my son Wylie P. Hill falls heir to the Abraham Hill place and the Sardus lands and the Thomas Johnston lands also. The balance of my landed property to be sold and to be divided between my four daughters, and as to my household furniture I wish at my wife's death to be flung into as many lots as I have living children at that time and to be equally divided among them. I don't wish anything sold out of the house, and as to my Buncombe lands, and stock thats there, I wish to be kept together if it suits for a retreat to any of the children thats amind to go.

My wife is to have *Carpenter James* and his wife Hester and Hannah and one of the small girls also, for which I had left out above.

I leave to my dear wife her carriage and her two choice mules and one road wagon and the best team of mules, one ox wagon and two yoke of oxen, and two of her choice in the horses, and as much of the stock of cattle and hogs as my executors may think will do her and all the balance of the stock and property to be sold and equally divided between my living children at my death, and all the property that I leave to my wife and all the proceeds after supporting her and my two youngest sons to be divided at her death equally between all her living children.

Now these that are married and had of some property I have valued all that I gave them. Burwell P. Had Three thousand and twenty eight Dollars, Lodowick M. Hill Thirty one hundred and seventy three dollars, Sarah C. W. Jordan had three thousand and ninety eight dollars, Martha P. DuBose had Twenty eight hundred and ninety three dollars, Tabitha W. Duncan had twenty eight hundred and ninety five dollars. Now as to the landed property I left to my sons has nothing to do with any other property and also the landed property I left to be sold for my four daughters, has nothing to do with other property. I divided that myself those children that has those amounts of property are so much ahead of the other children which must all be made equal at the division: you will see my valuation on the back part of this book. Now all the money that is due me at my death is to be divided between my wife and my dear children to make them all equal, and as to the ready money thats in hand at my death, I wish to finish my two youngest son's education. As to the boy Joel *I loaned to Sally Holmes*, at her death, he is to be divided as my other property was (?). If my wife wants my gig and harness, let her have it, also now my dear children and wife I never want any of you to have any coldness nor any hard thoughts among any of you about what I leave behind, for my property I worked for, it wasn't given to me. I have left you all a plenty: and took as good care of it as I could, and I wish to dispose of it as I see proper.

x x x x x _ x x x x x

Now my dear wife I have left old man Edward to you during your natural life. I want him treated well and never to be put out under an overseer. I wish for him to do any thing he can for you, but not to be treated ill by anybody, and let him have time to make him a little crop, and land convenient for him to tend, he has been a faithful slave to me, and I want him favored in his old age. I should have left him to have served nobody but I have seen the evil of it they have come to suffer, and when it is the will of God to take you, I wish for him and his wife to go and live with any one of my children that they wish to, that will treat them well, let them have their choice, he has helped me to get what I have got.

I constitute nominate and appoint my wife Martha executrix and my sons Lodowick M. Hill and Wylie P. Hill and Abraham T. W. Hill as they become of age my executors of this my last will and

testament and in Witness Whereof I have hereunto set my hand and seal this 13th day of February 1837.
(Signed) Wylie Hill.
Signed sealed and acknowledged in presence of
Test.: T. J. Walton
Thomas O. Christian
Thomas B. J. Hill

X. WYLIE HILL[4] (Abraham[3]), m., 29 March, 1799, MARTHA ("PATSY") POPE, b. 18 April, 1782; d. 15 July, 1853, dau. of Burwell (1751-1800) and Priscilla (Wootten) Pope. Burwell Pope was a Justice of the Peace and member of the Inferior Court of Pleas and Quarter Sessions, of Wake Co., N. C., during the Revolution; was a member from Wake Co. of the N. C. Provincial Congress, at Halifax, N. C., in 1781-'2; removed to Ga. prior to 8 Feby., 1785 (Wake Co. Deed Book G, p. 38), and obtained grants to 1300 acres of land in Wilkes Co., in July, 1787; member of the Ga. State Senate from Oglethorpe Co., 1794-'5 and 1799; member of the Ga. State Constitutional Convention in 1798; voted against the Yazoo Fraud ("N. C. Booklet", Vol. 5, No. 1, pp. 3-14; Wheeler's His. of N. C.", pp. 421-'2; "Story of Ga.", pp. 173-179, by G. G. Smith; see also *Popes* in this Book). Issue:

1. Burwell Pope Hill[5], b. 19 Feby., 1800; d. 10 Jany., 1833. (q. v.).

2. LODOWICK MERIWETHER HILL[5], b. 27 Nov., 1804; d. 13 Oct., 1883. (q. v.).

3. Sarah Christian Walton Hill[5], b. 5 Dec., 1807; d. 28 June, 1842. (q. v.).

4. Martha Pope Hill[5], b. 30 July, 1810; d. 5 Nov., 1848. (q. v.).

5. Mary Ann Tabitha Hill[5], b. 26 Aug., 1814; d. 22 Jany., 1868, in Panola Co., Miss. (q. v.).

6. Amelia Thomas Hill[5], b. 10 Feby., 1817; d. 9 Jany., 1882. (q. v.).

7. Wylie Pope Hill[5], b. 10 Aug., 1820; d. 10 Sept., 1864. (q. v.).

8. Abraham Thomas Walton Hill[5], b. 25 Jany., 1822; d. 5 July, 1845. (q. v.).

9. Nancy Hill, d. in inf.

1. BURWELL POPE HILL[5] (Wylie[4], Abraham[3], Abraham[2], Henry[1]), 1800-1833. m. (I) 15 April, 1824, Elizabeth C. Render, dau. of James and Elizabeth (Hamilton) Render, James Armstrong, Minister of the Gospel officiating; m. (II), 18 Nov., 1829, Martha Pope Johnson, her 1st husband, b. 10 May, 1814; d. 19 June, 1893, Sylvanus Gibson, M. G., officiating, dau. of Col. William and Nancy (Hill) Johnson, his 2nd cousin. (Vide ante p. 36, 8, IV, A. P. O.). Issue by 1st mar.:

1a. Sarah Ann Eliza Render Hill[6], b. 21 Nov., 1828; d. June, 1885. (q. v.).

Issue by 2nd mar.:

2a. Alexander Franklin Hill, b. in Wilkes Co., 20 Feby., 1831; d. in Meriwether Co., in 1888. (q .v.).

3a. Martha Catharine, called "Kitty", Hill[6]. (q. v.).

1a. SARAH ANN ELIZA RENDER HILL[6] (Burwell[5], Wylie[4]), 1828-1885, m. 7 July, 1853, Dr. WILLIAM FLEMING WALKER, of Okolona, Miss., b. 24 Jany., 1828; d. 18 March, 1910. Issue:

1b. Mary Amelia Walker[7], b. 3 June, 1854. (q. v.).

2b. Martha Hill Walker[7], b. 23 Sept., 1855; d. 9 Dec., 1893; m. (I), May, 1882, William Dukeminier, d. Jany., 1884; m. (II), March, 1897, Dr. James Cook, decd.

3b. Cora May Walker[7], b. 4 Oct., 1857; d. May, 1903; m. c. 1881, Dr. John Wesley Edwards, d. 3 Dec., 1914, and had:

1c. Dr. William Blount Edwards[8], d. 1918, at Albuquerque, N. M.; m. . . . . , and had two sons.

2c. Annie Mae Edwards[8], b. . . . . ; m. 15 Oct., 1917, George Eugene Chambers, 1. in Atlanta, 1920.

3c. John Wylie Edwards[8], single, 1. 1920, at Bartlesville, Okla.

4b. William Burwell Walker[7], b. 24 Jany., 1859; d. 19 Feby., 1904; m. 7 June, 1888, Mary Dudley Sykes, b. 1868. (q. v.).

5b. Lena Clifford Walker[7], b. 28 Jany., 1861; m. 31 Jany., 1882, William J. Burt, d. 9 April, 1907. She lives in Columbus, Miss.

6b. James Meriwether Walker[7], b. 26 April, 1862; m. 4 Sept., 1893, Orpha Roberts—living in Idaho.

7b. Maggie Eloise Walker[7], b. 16 Dec., 1863; d. 23 Jany., 1907; m. 22 July, 1890, Perry Lauderdale, d. 15 Nov., 1913.

8b. Lulu Eliza Walker[7], b. 27 Aug., 1867; m. 29 Oct., 1897, Giddeon C. Ray, d. 23 Jany., 1907. She lives at Carbon Hill, Ala.

1b. Mary Amelia Walker[7] (dau. of Dr. William F.), b. 23 June, 1854; m. 3 Jany., 1878, Thomas J. Dukeminier, b. 18 July, 1854; d. 10 Dec., 1917. Issue:

1c. William Emmette Dukeminier[8], b. 25 Dec., 1878; m. 2 Dec., 1907, Mrs. Jessie Benn.

2c. Algernon Sydney Dukeminier[8], b. 21 Oct., 1880; m. 18 Feby., 1904, Miss Lelia Gillespie.

3c. Mamie Pearl Dukeminier[8], b. 2 Feby., 1883; m. 20 Nov., 1907, Ralph A. Bryan.

4c. Annie Render Dukeminier[8], b. 13 Jany., 1885; m. 21 Jany., 1909, Henry Sudduth.

5c. Mattie Lou Dukeminier[8], b. 5 Feby., 1887; m. 11 Oct., 1908, Raymond Coltram.

6c. Thos. Jefferson Dukeminier[8], b. 6 Dec., 1888; m. May, 1910, Miss Alice Ames.

7c. James Walker Dukeminier[8], b. 3 Oct., 1891; m. 15 Dec., 1912, Mattie Rose Tuberville.

8c. Jesse Julius Dukeminier[8], b. 3 Jany., 1894. Single.

4b. William Burwell Walker[7] (Dr. William F.), 1859-1904,

and his wife, Mary Dudley Sykes, dau. of Capt. Thos. Sykes (son of Dr. William A. Sykes) and his wife, Maria H. Jones, had:

1c. Corinne Sykes Walker, b. 31 July, 1893; m. 29 March, 1918, Dr. James M. Acker, Jr., of Aberdeen, Miss., and has one dau.; 1d.—Corinne Hortense Acker[9], b. c. Jany., 1919, aged 19 mos., Aug. 13, 1920.

2c. Mary Dudley Walker[8], b. 1 Oct., 1899.

3c. William Burwell Walker, Jr.[8], b. 31 Aug., 1903.

2a. ALEXANDER FRANKLIN HILL[6] (Burwell[5], Wylie[4], Abraham[3]), 1831-1888, was a Captain in First Ga. Regulars, C. S. A.. m. c. 1855, Mrs. MARY JANE (WARNER) THOMAS, of Meriwether Co., b. in Knoxville, Crawford Co., Ga., 4 March, 1832, *dau.* of CHIEF JUSTICE HIRAM WARNER, decd., of the Supreme Court of Ga. (b. in 1802 in Mass., son of Obadiah (son of Joshua) Warner and his wife, Jane Coffin, dau. of Capt. Coffin, of Martha's Vineyard) and his wife, Sarah Abercrombie. Mrs. Hill 1. 1921, in Greenville, Meriwether Co., Ga. Issue:

1b. Burwell Obadiah Hill[7], b. 17 Aug., 1856; d. 4 Aug., 1918. (q. v.).

2b. Hiram Warner Hill[7], b. 18 July, 1858. (q. v.).

3b. Sarah Hill[7], b. 1 May, 1860. (q. v.).

4b. Martha Hill[7], b. 1 April, 1865. (q. v.).

5b. Mary Hill[7], b. 20 May, 1867. (q. v.).

6b. Alexander Franklin Hill, Jr.[7], b. 21 Oct., 1867. Single.

7b. Catharine, called "Pip", Hill[7], b. 27 Aug., 1871. (q. v.).

8b. Albert Meriwether Hill[7], b. 12 July, 1874; m. Susie Parks Walker.

9b. Robert Johnson Hill[7], b. 15 Aug., 1876; m. Ethel Dallas and has: 1c.—Mary Jane Hill[8].

1b. *Burwell Obadiah Hill*[7] (Capt. Frank[6], Burwell[5], Wylie[4]), 1856-1918, m. 22 Feb., 1882, Ellen Pinson, of Coweta Co., Ga. Issue: 1c.—Frank Hill[8], d.; 2c.—Martha Hill[8], m. Howard Arnold, of Columbia, S. C., no issue; 3c.—William P. Hill[8], single; 4c.—Jane Warner Hill[8], m. J. D. Hudson, of LaGrange, Ga., and has: 1d.—Ellen Pinson Hudson[9]; 5c.—Obadiah W. Hill[8], m. Mary Render, no children, 1. 1921, in Greenville, Meriwether Co., Ga.; 6c.—George T. Hill, of Greenville, Ga., single.

2b. HIRAM WARNER HILL[7] (Capt. Frank[6], Burwell[5], Wylie[4]), b. 18 July, 1858, educated in the schools of Greenville, Ga., and at Emory College, Oxford, Ga.; later law course at Harvard U., taking his degree in 1881; for eight years member of State Legislature—four years of the time served as Chairman of the General Judiciary Committee of the House; appointed in 1903 for six years on State Railroad Commission and re-elected in 1909 for second term; then appointed Associate Justice of the State Supreme Court, and re-elected to this office which he still fills. He m. Sept. 24, 1884, LENA HARRIS, dau. of *Hon. Henry R. Harris*, decd., and his wife Eliza A. Gresham. Hon. Henry R. Harris was a Member of

Congress from 1872 to 1878, both inclusive, and again in 1884, and later for three years was 3rd Asst. Postmaster General during Presdt. Cleveland's administration. ("Memoirs of Ga.", Vol. 2, p. 510; "Men of Mark in Ga.", Vol. 5, pp. 318-321). Issue: 1c.—Hiram Warner Hill, Jr.⁸, of Greenville, Ga., (q. v.); 2c.—Eliza Pope Hill⁸ (q. v.); 3c.—Frank Hill⁸, single; 4c.—Mary Hill⁸, m. Edmund Walker, of Madison, Ga.; 5c.—Sarah Hill⁸, single; 6c.—Pope Hill⁸, single.

1c. Hiram Warner Hill, Jr.⁸, m. Georgia Kendrick. Issue: 1d.—Virginia Hill⁹; 2d.—Jane Warner Hill⁹.

2c. Eliza Pope Hill⁸ (Hiram Warner, Sr.⁷) m. Edwin Martin, of Fort Valley, Ga., and has: 1d.—Charles Mann Martin⁹; 2d.—Sarah Martin⁹.

3b. SARAH HILL⁷ (Capt. Frank⁶, Burwell⁵), b. 1 May, 1860; m. EDMUND WELLBORN MARTIN, of Atlanta, Ga., a prominent atty.-at-law, ex-representative in the State Legislature from Fulton Co., and for many years President Board of Trustees of the Grady Hospital. He is the son of Col. John Marshall Martin, of Pensacola, Fla., b. in S. C. in 1832; d. Aug. 10, 1921, who was Colonel of the 9th Fla. Reg. in the C. S. A., and was with Genl. Lee at Appomattox at the surrender, and who was also the last surviving member of the Confederate Congress. (Atlanta Journal, May 24 and Aug. 11, 1921). Issue:

1c. WILLIE WELLBORN MARTIN⁸, m. GEORGE FLETCHER HURT and has: 1d.—Edmund Woodruff Hurt⁹, student at U. of Ga.; 2d.—Sarah Bright Hurt⁹; 3d.—Joel Hurt III⁹.

2c. HIRAM WARNER MARTIN⁸, Presdt. and Director of the Lowry Natl. Bank of Atlanta; formerly Presdt. Ga. Bankers Assn.; ex-Vice Presdt. for Ga. of Amn. Bankers Assn.; a former director of the Assn. of Rural-City Banks and ex-Presdt. of the Atlanta Chapter of the American Banking Institute; and member of the Bond Sinking Fund Commission; m. SALLIE BROWN CONNALLY, dau. of Dr. *E. L. Connally* and his wife, *Mary Brown*, dau. of ex-Gov. *Joseph E. Brown*, decd., and sister of ex-Gov. Joseph M. Brown.

3c. Frank Hill Martin⁸, Major U. S. A., in World War. Single.

4c. Edmund Martin, Jr.⁸, d. at age of 9 years.

4b. Martha Hill⁷ (Capt. Frank⁶, Burwell⁵), b. 1 April, 1865; m. James Ogletree Tigner, of Greenville, Ga. Issue.

1c. Mary Jane Tigner⁸. Single.

2c. Leander Hope Tigner⁸, d. unm.

3c. Catherine Tigner⁸, m. Mr. Battle Boddie. Issue: 1d.—James Boddie⁹.

4c. Alexander Franklin Tigner⁸. Single.

5c. Sarah Martin Tigner⁸. Single.

6c. Warner Stinson Tigner⁸; 7c.—James Tigner⁸, d. 1919.

8c. Mattie Ellen Tigner⁸, d. unm.

5b. Mary Hill⁷ (Capt. Frank⁶, Burwell⁵), b. 20 May, 1867; m.

(I), Charles Gates Eckford, of Atlanta; m. (II), John Wesley Milligan, of Pittsburgh, Pa., 2nd wife. Issue by 1st, none by 2nd, mar.:

    1c. Charles Gates Eckford, Jr., m. Nellie P. Hunnicutt, of Athens, Ga., and has: 1d.—Mary DuPree Eckford^9; 2d.—Sarah Elinor Eckford^9.

    2c. William Eckford^8, single.

    7b. Catherine, called "Pip", Hill^7 (Capt. Frank^6, Burwell^5), 1871-1 . . , m. Dr. E. B. Terrell and had: 1c.—Catherine Terrell, m. . . . ., 1921, Thomas Willingham Tift.

    3a. Martha Catharine, called "Kitty", Hill^6 (Burwell^5, Wylie^4), m. Aquilla Chaney, of Chalybeate Springs, Ga. They later removed to East Point, Ga., where both died. Mr. Chaney m. (II) a lady from Texas, who survived him and later returned to Texas. No issue by either marriage.

MARTHA POPE (JOHNSON) HILL^5 (dau. of Col. WILLIAM and NANCY (HILL) JOHNSON and widow of BURWELL POPE HILL, 1800-1833), m. (II). 18 March, 1834, Rev. William D. Martin, of Meriwether Co., Ga., b. in Wilkes Co., in 1806; d. Jan., 1864. Issue:

    4a. Nancy Jane, called "Bouge", Martin^6, b. c. 1835; d. 3 Oct., 1901. (q. v.).

    5a. William Marshall Martin^6, d. in young manhood, unm.

    6a. John Oliver Martin^6, d. y.

    7a. Susan Martin^6, d. y.

    8a. Anna Harriette Martin^6, decd., m. Alonzo Freeman and had: 1b.—Ninda Freeman^7, decd., m. . . . . , and left one child.

    9a. Peter W. Martin^6, d. in middle life, unm. He represented Meriwether Co. in the Legislature, was talented and universally beloved.

    10a. George Johnson Martin^6, decd., represented Meriwether Co. in the Legislature; m. Martha Pinson, of Newnan, Ga. Issue: 1b.—William Martin^7, single; 2b.—George Martin, Jr.^{7}, m. . . . . ; 3b.—Evelyn Martin^7, single; 4b.—Susie Martin, single; 5b.—Peter Martin^7, single; 6b.—Frank Martin^7, m. . . . .

    4a. Nancy Jane, called "Bouge", Martin^6 (Rev. William^5), c. 1835-1901, m. 6 Dec., 1853, Major William F. Slaton, b. 6 March, 1831; d. 29 Nov., 1916, son of John Slaton, of Autauga, Ala., and his wife, Nancy Harris, sister of the late Congressman, Hon. Henry R. Harris, of the 4th Dist. of Ga. He graduated at Emory College, Oxford, Ga., with degree of M.A., later the U. of Ga. conferred upon him the same degree; entered C. S. A. as Lieut.; promoted to Major for conspicuous bravery; was made prisoner at battle of Lookout Mountain Pass, sent to Johnson's Island, and while a prisoner there was made Lieut. Col. In 1874, he was made principal of the Boys' High School in Atlanta, and in 1879 made Superintendent of the Atlanta City Schools, from which he retired in 1907, after serving 28 years in that capacity. At one time he was both President of the Southern Educational Association and director of the National Educational Assn. (Atlanta Journal, Nov. 29, 1916). Issue:

1b. William M. Slaton[7]. (q. v.).
2b. Kate Slaton[7], m. Wade Hill Blanchard, decd. No issue.
3b. Mattie Lee Slaton[7], single. Head of Dept. of French in Girls' High School of Atlanta.
4b. Annie May Slaton[7]. (q. v.).
5b. Lilly Slaton[7], m. Samuel C. Atkinson, Associate Justice of the State Supreme Court, his 2nd wife. No issue.
6b. John Marshall Slaton[7], atty. at law; for several terms president Ga. State Senate, and ex-Governor of the State; m. Sallie Fannie (Grant) Jackson, widow of Thos. Cobb Jackson, and dau. of Capt. William Daniel Grant, decd., and his wife Sallie Fannie Reid, decd. No issue.
7b. *Lula Slaton*[7], m. William A. MacGregor, of N. Y. City and has one child.

1b. *William M. Slaton*[7] (son of Wm. F.), for circa 10 years, from 1907 was Superintendent of the Atlanta City Schools, succeeding his father on his retirement; m. Mattie Jackson, dau. of the late Chief Justice James Jackson. Issue:

1c. William F. Slaton, Jr.[8], Major U. S. A., A. E. F. Single.
2c. Waldo M. Slaton[8], First Lieut., U. S. A., A. E. F., d. in service.
3c. John Marshall Slaton, Jr.[8], 1st Lieut. U. S. A., A. E. F.
4c. James Jackson Slaton[8].
5c. Lamar (a dau.) Slaton[8], m. 1918, Edward N. Hitt.

4b. Annie May Slaton[7] (dau. Wm. F.) m. Albigenes Lamar Waldo, of Atlanta, Ga. Issue:

1c. Sarah Waldo[8], m. A. McD. Wilson, Jr.
2c. Nancy Waldo[8], d. unm.
3c. Kate Waldo[8], m. Robt. H. Jones, Jr.
4c. Nell Waldo[8], m. Capt. William Stockton, U. S. A.
5c. Albigenes Lamar Waldo, Jr.[8], d.
6c. Slaton Waldo[8].

2. LODOWICK MERIWETHER HILL[5] (X, B, P, O), 1804-1883.

He was named for his cousin Lodowick Hill, son of *Theophilus*[3] (PO) and *Theresa* (Thomas) Hill, who died in Edgefield Dist., S. C., 27 July, *1822*, and Hon. David Meriwether, his father's friend, and member of Congress from Ga. from 1801 to 1807, who also represented Presidents Jefferson and Jackson in negotiations with the Creeks and Cherokees. When 14 years of age was placed in the grammar school at Athens and in July, 1821, entered Franklin College and was a member of the class of 1825, which was so highly commended by the venerable president Moses Waddell, and admittedly first in scholarship in the college. Though his father wanted him to complete his college course and to be a lawyer, he was so impatient to marry and begin active life as a merchant and planter that despite urgent protests by friends and faculty and family, he withdrew from college in 1824 when he had just risen to the Senior class, and immediately he engaged in planting and merchandising. On Feb. 29, 1832, he was commissioned as Colonel of the 18th Regt. of Militia, which with the 19th constituted the First Brigade of the Fourth Division. The Washington Guards belonged to his Regt. and Robert A. Toombs (later U. S. Sr.) was commissioned as 1st Lieut. of this Co. on 7 March, 1832. On 21 May, 1835, he surrendered his commission by reason of removal from the Dist.

STATE OF GEORGIA.

By His Excellency Wilson Lumpkin, Governor and Commander in Chief of the Army and Navy of this State and of the Militia thereof

To
LODOWICK M. HILL Greeting:

We, reposing especial trust and confidence in your patriotism, valor, conduct and fidelity, do by these presents constitute and appoint you

COLONEL of the 18th Regiment

of Militia formed for the defence of the State, and for repelling every hostile invasion thereof. You are therefore carefully and diligently to discharge the duty of COLONEL by doing and performing all manner of things thereunto belonging. And we do strictly charge and require all Officers and Privates under your command, to be obedient to your orders as COLONEL. And you are to observe and follow such orders and directions from time to time, as you shall receive from me or a future Governor and Commander in Chief of this State, for the time being, or any other of your superior officers in pursuance of the trust reposed in you. This Commission to continue in force during your usual residence with the Regiment to which you belong, unless removed by sentence of a Court Martial, or by the Governor on the address of two thirds of each branch of the General Assembly.

Given under my hand and the Seal of the Executive Department at the Capitol at Milledgeville this *twenty ninth* day of February in the year of Our Lord, one thousand eight hundred and thirty two and of the Independence of America the fifty sixth.

By the Governor Wilson Lumpkin
E. Hamilton, Secretary of State.

A true copy:
J. Ed. Eubanks, Lt. Col., A. D. C., Apr. 10, 1913.

In 1842 and 1843, he with *Robert A. Toombs* and *William Q. Anderson* were the representatives from Wilkes in the Legislature; in 1844-'5, he and Joseph W. Robinson were the representatives; in 1859 and '60 he was a member of the State Senate from Wilkes, and was Senator from the 29th Senatorial District (embracing

Wilkes, Columbia, McDuffie and Lincoln Cos.) in 1861 and 1862, and the called session of the Senate in March, 1863.

Early in the Civil War he equipped and outfitted out of his own purse about the largest company that went from Wilkes to the war. In his honor it was named the "Hill Wilkes Guards". Its first Capt. was Henry F. Colley, father of Hon. Frank H. Colley; the second was Capt. John T. Erwin. Nine of his sons served in the Civil War. He made to the Confederate Government, in response to a call, a loan of 300 bales of cotton and while in Augusta, Ga., to make delivery he learned that the Government would immediately sell the cotton to supply their pressing need for cash. He, thereupon, proposed to let the Government have its cash equivalent and keep his cotton, which was gladly accepted. For many years he was the largest individual shareholder of the Ga. R. R. & Banking Co., his holdings being exceeded only when, in the 70's, speculators and manipulators began their struggle for control of the road; was made a director in 1868 and continued as such until his death. He was also a large shareholder and director of the A. & W. P. R. R. to the end of his life, and while owning a large interest in the Ga. Central R. R. declined an invitation to accept a directorship as he could not afford the time to attend the board meetings.

Notwithstanding his manifold and exacting business requirements, often, of evenings at home, he would, until the suppleness and sensitiveness of the fingers of his left hand were somewhat impaired by a rising, bring out his violin for the entertainment and dances of his children and their friends. He established and maintained on the homestead for the instruction of his own children until they were prepared for college, and those of his neighbors, one of the best country schools to be found in the State, supplying it with the most efficient, eminent and experienced teachers that could be had. As testimony to their qualifications and reputation many families in Washington sent their sons to this school in preference to those in the town.

Copy of Pardon Papers.

ANDREW JOHNSON

President of the United States of America.

To All To Whom these presents shall come, greeting:

Whereas   L. M. HILL

of Wilkes County, Georgia, by taking part in the late rebellion against the Government of the United States has made himself liable to heavy pains and penalties;

And whereas the circumstances of his case recommend him a proper object of Executive clemency;

Now, therefore, be it known, that I, Andrew Johnson, President of the United States of America, in consideration of the premises, divers other good and sufficient reasons me thereunto moving, do hereby grant to the said

L. M. HILL

a free pardon and amnesty for all offenses by him committed, arising from participation, direct or implied, in the said rebellion, conditioned as follows:

1st. This pardon to be of no effect until the said L. M. HILL shall take the oath prescribed in the Proclamation of the President, dated May 29th, 1865.

2nd. To be void and of no effect if the said L. M. HILL shall hereafter at any time acquire any property whatever in slaves or make use of slave labor.

3rd. That the said L. M. HILL first pay all costs which may have accrued in any proceedings instituted or pending against his person or property, before the date of the acceptance of this warrant.

4th. That the said L. M. HILL shall not by virtue of this warrant claim any property or the proceeds of any property that has been sold by the order, judgment, or decree of a court under the confiscation laws of the United States.

5th. That the said L. M. HILL shall notify the Secretary of State, in writing, that he has received and accepted the foregoing pardon.

In testimony whereof I have hereunto signed my name and caused the Seal of the United States to be affixed.

SEAL
Done at the City of Washington this second day of October, A. D. 1865, and of the Independence of the United States the Ninetieth.

ANDREW JOHNSON.

By the President:

William H. Seward, Secretary of State.

Sent on my acceptane this the 10th day of Sept., 1866.

L. M. HILL.

UNITED STATES OF AMERICA,
DEPARTMENT OF STATE.

To all to whom these presents shall come, Greeting:

I certify that the document hereto annexed is a true copy of the original on file in this Department.

In testimony whereof I, William H. Seward, Secretary of State of the United States, have hereunto subscribed my name and caused the seal of the Department of State to be affixed.

Done at the City of Washington this Seventeenth day of September, A. D. 1866, and of the Independence of the United States of America the Ninety first.

WILLIAM H. SEWARD.

SEAL

Enclosed paper:

September 10th, 1866.

Honorable WILLIAM H. SEWARD,
Secretary of State, Sir:

I have the honor to acknowledge the receipt of the President's Warrant of Pardon bearing date the second day of October, 1865, and hereby signify my acceptance of the same, with all the conditions therein specified.

I am, Sir,

Your obedient servant,

LODOWICK M. HILL.

Will of L. M. HILL,

Georgia, Wilkes County,

I, LODOWICK M. HILL of said County, being of sound & disposing mind and memory, do make this my last Will and Testament hereby revoking all of Wills heretofore made by me.

Item 1st. I desire that my body shall be decently buried.

" 2nd. I desire that all my just debts shall be paid.

" 3rd. I bequeath to my beloved Wife MARTHA S. HILL Forty Thousand dollars; and I direct my Executors hereinafter named to turn over to my wife said Amount either in Money or in Securities to be Selected by her.

4th. I desire that my children or legal heirs be made equal in Advancements, Some having had more than others. The advancements Made to each one of the Children are entered & Charged against them in My large Ledger; the Slaves given before they were set free I have erased as these items are not to be Counted as Advancements. The valuation that I have put upon Said Advancements in Said Ledger is fixed by me & is a part of this my will.

5th. My Taylor plantation in Oglethorpe County, Ga., Containing 2700 Acres More or Less, on the West Side of Long Creek, I will to my Sons Walton P. Hill and Burwell P. Hill to be divided equally between them: valued to them at $5,000 each which will be charged to them in my Ledger with their other advancements, as so much advanced.

6th. I will to my Son Duncan C. Hill my home place & plantation Containing about 4000 acres of Land, on the East Side of Long Creek, mostly in Wilkes County, Ga., & partly in Oglethorpe County, Ga., which tract of land I deeded to Said Duncan C. Hill to be his at my death: Said tract of land being given as an advancement and charged to him in My Ledger at the sum of $13000 (Thirteen thousand dollars).

7th. I desire & Will that all my property not already advanced to my children be collected and divided according to law between my legal heirs (except my wife whom I have already provided for in Item 3rd of this my will) believing that the law makes the best division of An Estate between the heirs at law.

I appoint William W. Hill, Duncan C. Hill, and Abner Welborn Hill my Executors to execute this my last Will.

Witness my hand & Seal this 13th day of Feb. 1882.

L. M. HILL (SEAL)

Signed, Sealed and Published by Lodowick M. Hill as his last Will in our Presence as Witnesses thereto by his request this 13th day of Feb. 1882 We Signing as witnesses in his presence.

Thos. C. Hogue
T. M. Green
B. S. Irwin

CODICIL.

Georgia } Whereas I, L. M. Hill did on the 13th day
Wilkes County, } of February 1882 Sign, Seal and publish my last will in the presence of Thos. C. Hogue, T. M. Green and B. S. Irwin who Signed said Will as Witnesses—And whereas I am desirous of altering and changing Items 4th, 5th & 7th of Said Will in So far as they relate to my son B. P. Hill I therefore make and publish this codicil to Said Will.

1st. I revoke and annul the bequest in My Said Will to my Son B. P. Hill as One of my heirs at law—and I will & devise Said portion that I intended for Said B. P. Hill to my Grandson L. Harry Hill. That is to say, I bequeath to L. Harry Hill that portion (which is a child's part) of my Estate that I intended at one time to leave my Son B. P. Hill. And I will and direct that L. Harry Hill shall stand in the place of his father B. P. Hill both as to receiving a child's portion as aforesaid and as to all advancements made or to be made to B. P. Hill:—Said L. Harry Hill Accounting for all said advancements in the place of B. P. Hill.

And to have it appear more certain in my will as to my wishes & intentions regarding my grandson L. M. Hill I insert in this my Codicil that I will and bequeath to L. M. Hill a child's portion of my Estate he accounting for all advancements made to his father or to himself.

Witness my hand & Seal March 17th 1882.

L. M. HILL (SEAL)

Signed & published as a codicil to his last will in our presence as witnesses thereto by his request Mch. 17, 1882, We signing in his presence.

Thomas C. Hogue
Theo. M. Green
B. S. Irwin

Note.—Substitution of L. Harry Hill for B. P. Hill made by request of B. P. Hill.

STATE OF GEORGIA } By the Court of Ordinary For Said County.
WILKES COUNTY.   } To All Whom these presents shall come—
Greetings:

Know ye, That on the Fifth day of November in the year of our Lord one thousand eight hundred and Eighty-three the last Will & Testament of LODOWICK M. HILL late of Wilkes County, deceased, was exhibited in open Court and in solemn form of law, proved and admitted to record, a copy of which is hereunto annexed, and administration of all and singular, the goods, chattels and credits of said deceased was granted to William W. Hill, Duncan C. Hill and Abner Wellborn Hill, the executors in and by said Will named and appointed, they having first taken the oath., and performed all other requisites required by law, they by order of said Court, and by virtue of these presents, legally authorized to administer the goods, chattels and credits of said deceased according to the tenor and effect of said Will and Testament, and according to law; and they hereby required to render a true and perfect inventory of all and singular the goods, chattels and credits of the said deceased, and appraised and returned to the Court according to law, and to render a true and correct account to the said Court of their actings and doings yearly, and every year, until administration is fully completed.

Witness my hand, as Ordinary, and the seal of the said Court this 5th day of November eighteen hundred and Eighty three.

(Signed) Geo. Dyson, Ordinary.

(Seal, Court of Ordinary,
Wilkes Co., Ga.)

His prominence, the large number of his descendants and connections, warrant the incorporation into his record of the three following tributes to his memory; his portrait is given in "Cyclopoedia Ga.", Vol. II, pp. 271-'2, by Allen D. Candler & Clement A. Evans.

On *Oct. 22, 1883*, the BOARD of DIRECTORS of the Gate City Natl. Bank of Atlanta paid the following tribute to his memory:

"It is with deep grief that we bow to the will of the Almighty in removing from our midst our late associate and friend, Col. L. M. Hill. In paying this tribute to his memory we can truly say, that as a business man he had no superior, his dealings were always fair, upright and honest. The magnificent fortune that he left to his family attests his superb business talents and qualifications. As a public citizen he did all that he could to promote the general welfare. He served his country in her legislative halls with distinction and honor to himself and his constituents. To appreciate him, one should have known him at home in the family circle. He was never happier than when surrounded by his family of twelve children and numerous grandchildren. He was, indeed, like one of the Patriarchs of old. He often had the family gathered at the old family homestead and always delighted in these family reunions. As a friend he was true as steel. A kind Providence permitted him to live to a ripe old age, to see his sons grown up around him to enjoy the fulfillment of his business enterprises, and then quietly and gently as the setting sun to pass away from earth's busy scenes. His memory will ever be cherished by the Directors of this Bank.

Resolved: first, That a page of the minutes of this Board shall be devoted to the inscription of the name, office, birthday and day of the death of our honored associate.

Resolved: second, That a copy of this tribute be sent to the family of the deceased associate and friend and published in the Atlanta Constitution."

(Signed) William A. Hemphill,
Walker P. Inman,
Charles Beerman.

At the regular quarterly meeting of the Georgia Railroad Directors held on Tuesday, the 12th instant, the Committee appointed at the meeting Nov. 13, 1883, to draft resolutions on the death of Hon. L. M. Hill, one of the oldest directors of the Company, reported the following resolutions, which were unanimously adopted:

To the President and Directors of the Georgia Railroad and Banking Company:

Our late associate and friend, COL. L. M. HILL, was born on the 27th day of Nov., 1804, and died on the 13th of Oct., 1883. He very nearly completed his eighty years. He was born in the County of Wilkes in this State, where he lived and died. He was sent by his father when 14 years of age to the grammar school at Athens, Ga., and from thence to Franklin College in which institution he remained until his nineteenth year. While he did not graduate, he remained in college until his Senior year, having surpassed all competitors in scholarship. His devotion to study and the power of acquiring knowledge, his unqestionable industry and energy, so conspicuous in college life, were sure precursors of the success which he was destined to achieve in after life. Upon leaving College he at once married and commenced business as a planter and merchant. By his first wife Col. Hill had ten sons and one daughter; by his second wife two sons, in all thirteen children, of whom all survive him but one. The splendid fortune which he accumulated by planting and merchandising in course of time was invested in railroad enterprises and banking.

After the war, finding it impossible to conduct the business of farming with the punctuality, vigor and fidelity to which he had been accustomed and to which he had disciplined himself, he quietly resigned to his sons his entire farming interests. When chosen as a Director of the Georgia Railroad and Banking Company in the year 1868 he brought to the service of the Company, in addition to a ripe experience in business, the same patience, caution, attention, industry, intelligence and fidelity which he had always shown in regard to his private interests. He believed in the old fashioned idea of rigid economy, faithful service and sound judgment, and thought they were just as useful and just as necessary to the interest of a large corporation as to individuals. His devotion to the welfare and honor of the old Georgia Railroad and Banking Company was unflagging. No matter what might be the impediment, a summons to be present at a meeting of the board or the regular return of the day of meeting, was responded to by his presence. About the time Col. Hill was elected a member of this Board he was elected a director of the Atlanta and West Point Railroad Company and remained a director of each company through life. Whatever might be the changes of time and administrations, when once chosen to fill a public trust, he was continued in it so long as he lived or chose to serve. Desiring to start his sons in life he invested largely in banks at Washington and Atlanta in this State. The Gate City National Bank of Atlanta was founded by him, an institution in which he took much interest, and which promises to be known for a long time as the "HILL BANK". It was only natural and probable that a man of Col. Hill's immense energy and industry, his intelligence and solid integrity should be selected by the people of his native county to represent them in the State Legislature. For several terms he served as a representative and Senator, and only ceased to fill those honorable positions because of his intense love of home and home pursuits. Yet he never ceased to feel a deep interest in the prosperity and glory of his state and County. Whenever it was possible for him to be present he was at the polls and an influential worker. His impartial judgment, hard sense, caution and integrity were often and successfully invoked by his neighbors and friends to adjust differences. While fortunate in life, he was no less fortunate in death. A very brief and sudden sickness terminated his earthly career, and on a pleasant Sabbath morning, in the month of Oct. last, he was borne by his own sons to the place of burial, a short distance from his home. A large assemblage of strangers from distant places, from adjoining counties, from his own county, and of connections by blood and marriage, attended to perform the last duties of friendship and respect. Long may we cherish the memory of this faithful associate.

Resolved by the Board of Directors of the Georgia Railroad and Banking Company, That the above report be and is hereby accepted and approved, and ordered to be spread on the minutes of the Board; that a copy of the same be forwarded to MRS. L. M. HILL and a copy be furnished the city papers for publication.

Augusta, Ga., Feb. 12, 1884.

(Signed)
- W. M. Reese (Judge William M. Reese, of Washington, Ga.)
- J. H. Alexander (of Augusta, Ga.)
- F. Phinizy (Mr. Ferdinand Phinizy of Athens, Ga.)

At a meeting of the BOARD of DIRECTORS of the ATLANTA and WEST POINT RAILROAD Company held Jany. 3, 1884, the President appointed a Committee consisting of Messrs. Bigby, Speer and Berry, to draft suitable resolutions on the death of Col. L. M. Hill. On April 8, 1884, Judge Bigby for the Committee submitted resolutions which were read and unanimously adopted and ordered spread upon the minutes of the Company and a copy sent to the family of the deceased.

L. M. HILL
MEMORIAL to HIS MEMORY.

After a long and remarkable life L. M. Hill, for many years a member of the Board of Directors, has been gathered to his fathers. In the ripeness of an honored old age, and when the measure of his usefulness was full and complete, he has been taken from us. Always sound in judgment, in counsel wise, in action conservative, his loss will be keenly felt. He possessed in an eminent degree, not only a liberal education and varied learning, but he was pre-eminently a man of business affairs. Upon financial questions his judgment was unerring and a large and magnificent fortune was the fruit of his effort and industry. In the friendly walks of life the fascination of his companionship will be missed, and at the accustomed meetings of our Board the wisdom of his counsels will be sorely felt.

Therefore:

Resolved: That in the death of Col. L. M. Hill, the Atlanta and West Point Railroad Company has lost a devoted friend, and our Board of Directors a safe, useful and invaluable member.

Resolved: That his social virtues and manly bearing, not less conspicuous in private than official life, will always command our admiration and respect.

Resolved: That we offer to the stokholders of the Company our sympathy in the loss they have sustained and to the afflicted family our condolence in their great bereavement.

Resolved: That these proceedings be spread upon the minutes of the Board of Directors.

Resolved: That a copy of these proceedings be sent by the Secretary to the family of the deceased.

[William Bird Berry, of Newnan, Ga.]
[Daniel N. Speer, of LaGrange, Ga.]

(Signed) John S. Bigby
W. B. Berry
D. N. Speer
Committee.

The homestead of Col. Lodowick Meriwether Hill, one of the most stately, imposing and beautiful in the County, is situated fifteen miles northwest of Washington, on the road to Danielsville, and one and a half miles from the line of Oglethorpe.

It was originally a large two-story frame building, erected during the first quarter of the last century, with eleven rooms, and a wide veranda. In the eighteen-fifties it was remodeled on the Colonial style, with fourteen rooms—four of which were 20'x20' each. There were wide halls running through from east to west opening upon wide porches, and still wider halls running north and south from the front to the center of the building; besides a wide, long colonnade with massive fluted columns three feet in diameter supporting the parapet roof. The upper front hall opened upon a balcony. This handsome old home is still in a perfect state of preservation and, save an addition of two rooms in the rear, is just as it was in the fifties. The various buildings on the place, such as barns and stables—for horses, mules and cattle, store, gin houses, etc., were large and imposing. All were substantially built and kept in splendid repair. There were so many that the place appeared more like a town or industrial center, than a country seat. (Ga. L. M. & L., Vol. II, pp. 1049, 1050). See frontispiece.

The estate, appertaining to the homestead, in amplitude, was baronial, containing something upwards of 4500 acres lying on the east side of Long Creek, and intersected by the main public roads from Washington to Danielsville, and from Petersburg to Lexington. These, prior to the building of the railroads, were the principal lines of travel between Athens, all North Georgia, and Augusta, and the central and northern parts of South Carolina. Lying on the west side of Long Creek, and opposite the southern part of above, was another plantation of 2700 acres, making above 7000 acres in one body. Four miles east on Clarke's Creek was the King place, and 8 miles northeast on Broad River and Chickasaw Creek was the Wilkerson place, the two containing about 4000 acres. The soil was fertile and productive, the water supply abundant, with innumerable springs of cold and delicious freestone water, branches and creeks. The agricultural products were varied and numerous, consisting of cotton, corn, wheat, oats, barley, rye, peas, potatoes, etc., etc.; with fruits, melons and berries of every kind—40 to 50 acres being devoted to peaches, and some 10 acres or more to apples. All were for domestic, none for commercial purposes. Both peaches and apples were often fed by the four-horse wagon load to the hogs, and watermelons in like quantity distributed among the negroes. Fowls of every kind—turkeys, chickens, geese, ducks, guineas, peafowls, pigeons, etc., were raised in quantities.

Stock, embracing horses, mules, cattle, sheep, hogs, goats, jacks and jennetts, were given especial attention; had its own stallion and jacks. There were usually 20 to 30 colts under 3 years of age, and 20 to 40 milch cows on the place. The horses and mules raised were generally superior both in size, power and endurance, to any that were offered in the market. Hogs killed annually—including those on the outlying plantations—averaged from three to four hundred head, and such a thing as having to buy meat for the plantations was never heard of. The sheep supplied the wool for the winter clothing of the negroes—the spinning, weaving and making all done on the premises. Three or four looms were operated the year round. All meal, grits and flour required for the homestead and other plantations were ground at its own corn and wheat mill located on Amason's branch, just above its confluence with Clarke's Creek, about four miles from the homestead, on the plantation known as the "King Place". It was driven by an overshot water wheel, and besides supplying home needs did custom work—serving the community generally.

For building, carpentry and wheelright work in all their branches there were usually four skilled carpenters and two expert wheelrights. The carpenters erected all buildings, made all repairs, etc., and when not needed at home, did such work for others throughout the County. The wheelrights made all wagons, spinning wheels, reels, plow stocks, grain cradles, looms, etc., that were used on the homestead and other plantations. Every negro woman was provided with a spinning wheel, and on rainy or inclement days, the wool and cotton were spun for winter and summer clothing.

Two smiths at the homestead and one at each of the other plantations did all of the iron work.

In truth, everything used was raised or manufactured at the homestead, with the exception of iron, steel, trace chains, sythe blades, axes and hoes, blankets and hats, sugar, coffee, syrup and salt, which had to be bought.

At Mallorysville, 6 miles distant, was a tanyard owned by a Mr. Harmon (?). Under an arrangement between him and Col. Hill, the former furnished the yard and superintendence and Col. Hill furnished the tanner—one of his negroes who was experienced and efficient. Thus he secured the tanning of all of his hides and skins and his own shoemakers made all shoes and harness used.

Prior to the completion of the railroad to Washington cotton was marketed in Augusta, 75 miles distant. Four or five large six-mule wagons, loaded with cotton, in marketing season, on Monday mornings, would start for Augusta and the round trip made in six days, always returning Saturday afternoon loaded with merchandise for the store and plantation supplies.

For many years COL. L. M. HILL was the executor of some large estates and trustee for several wealthy minors. In consequence thereof Christmas-time was the occasion for assembling at the Homestead of a numerous body of both negroes and whites, the former to be hired out, and the latter—planters from far and near —either to hire negroes or to borrow money. The negroes would have their booths and dispense gingerbread (called ginger-cakes) and persimmon beer, as is now the practice with popcorn and lemonade on circus grounds. The caring for these negroes and the entertainment of these planters was no little undertaking. It is astonishing how many on occasions were entertained at this homestead.

During Associations at Station Church—a Baptist church one and one half miles distant—it was not unusual to entertain as many as eighty to ninety adults at a time. In 1867, the writer, on reaching the homestead, after attendance on Commencement of the University of Georgia, at Athens, found there, including the family, sixty-two adults, the majority for a few days' visit, the others to remain for weeks.

2. COL. L. M. HILL[5] (X, B, P, O.), 1804-1883, m. (I) Dec. 16, 1824, shortly after leaving college, his second cousin, NANCY HILL JOHNSON, b. July 11, 1808; d. Oct. 21, 1846, dau. of COL. WILLIAM AND NANCY (HILL) JOHNSON and gr. dau. of *Henry* (P. O.) 1730-1804, and SARAH (COTTEN) HILL, (See 6, IV, A. P. O., ante p. 36; m. (II) July 8, 1847, MARTHA STROTHER WELLBORN, b. March 16, 1816; d. Dec. 9, 1884, dau. of ABNER WELLBORN and his wife, MARTHA RENDER, dau. of Joshua Lewis Render, of Powhatan Co., Va., and his wife, Susannah Dickie. ABNER WELLBORN was the son of WILLIAM WELLBORN (a Rev'y soldier) and his wife, Hepzabah Stearns, dau. of Isaac Stearns and his wife, Rebecca Johnson, and gr. gr. dau. of Charles Stearns, of Waterbury, Mass., and his wife, Rebecca Gibson. WILLIAM WELLBORN was the gr. son of *Capt.* THOMAS WELLBORN, BURGESS from Accomac Co., Va., from May, 1699 to 1702.

ISSUE by 1ST MAR.: 1a.—William Wylie Hill[6], b. Mar. 31, 1826; d. Sept. 1, 1909 (q. v.); 2a.—John Meriwether Hill[6], b. Nov. 15, 1827; d. March 16, 1894 (q. v.); 3a.—Walton Pope Hill[6], b. April 4, 1830; d. May 7, 1898 (q. v.); 4a.—Abraham Chandler Hill[6], b. Oct. 23, 1831; d. April 18, 1867 (q. v.); 5a.—Burwell Pope Hill[6], b. Aug. 29, 1833; d. Dec. 12, 1886 (q. v.); 6a.—Ida May Hill[6], b. June 7, 1835; d. Aug. 4, 1919 (q. v.); 7a.—Duncan Chatfield Hill[6], b. May 8, 1837; d. March 3, 1908 (q. v.); 8a.—Thomas Webster Hill[6], b. June 17 (anniversary of battle of Bunker Hill), 1839; d. Jany. 18, 1899 (q. v.); 9a.—Henry Jordan Hill[6], b. March 24, 1842; d. Nov. 16, 1892 (q. v.); 10a.—James DuBose Hill[6], b.

Nov. 16, 1843; d. ......, 189.., (q. v.); LODOWICK JOHNSON HILL[6], b. Jany. 16, 1846 (q. v.).

ISSUE BY 2ND MAR.: 12a.—Abner Wellborn Hill[6], b. Feby. 22, 1849; d. Aug. 26, 1907 (q. v.); 13a.—Miles Wilkes Hill[6], b. March 26, 1851; d. June 7, 1851; 14a.—Edward Young Hill[6], b. Sept. 8, 1852 (q. v.).

1a. WILLIAM WYLIE HILL[6] (2, X, B, P, O), 1826-1909. Educated at home school and at Franklin College (U. of Ga.), graduated in 1849 with degree of A.B., was J. of P. in the Sixties, later served with the State troops in the Civil War (See Memoirs of Ga., Vol. 2, pp. 333-'4). Very early, in young manhood, learned "to do justly, to love mercy, and to walk humbly with his God", and his whole life was that of a sincere, devoted, cheerful and consistent Christian, an inspiration to good will and brotherly love, which commanded universal esteem and devoted friendships.

He m., 27 Nov., 1851, EMMA EUGENIA ANTHONY, b. 25 July, 1829; d. 20 Jany., 1892, dau. of Micajah and Mary Rembert (DuBose) Anthony, who was sister of James Rembert DuBose, Mrs. Julia A. (Robert) Toombs and Mrs. Louisa (DuBose) Bibb, wife of Dr. Joseph Wyatt Bibb. Issue: 1b.—Mary Rembert Hill[7], b. 27 Feby., 1853 (q. v.); 2b.—Ida Lou Hill[7], b. 16 Jany., 1855 (q. v.); 3b.—William Meriwether Hill[7], b. 11 July, 1856 (q. v.); 4b.—John DuBose Hill[7], b. 26 Oct., 1858; d. 16 March, 1898 (q. v.); 5b.—Martha Amelia Hill[7], b. 29 Aug., 1861; d. 14 Feby., 1915 (q. v.); 6b.—Dr. William Wylie Hill, Jr.[7], b. 3 Dec., 1863 (q. v.); 7b.—Emma Belle Hill[7], b. 3 April, 1868; m. 14 Dec., 1892, Anson King, —divorced; no issue.

1b. *Mary Rembert Hill*[7] (1a, 2, B. X. P. O), b. Feby. 27, 1853; m. Feby. 26, 1874, Boyce Ficklin, of Washington, Ga., b. Aug. 4, 1851,—for many years the Treasurer of the County, and both representative and Senator in the State Legislature. Issue: 1c.—Fielding Hill Ficklin[8], b. Nov. 30, 1874; m. June 19, 1901, Celeste Bounds, b. Nov. 7, 1877, dau. of Rev. Dr. Edward M. and Emmie (Barnett) Bounds; 2c.—Nannilou Ficklin[8], b. Aug. 12, 1876; m. Grier Martin, of the firm of F. J. Cooledge & Sons, of Atlanta,—several children; 3c.—Emmie Ficklin[8], b. July 11, 1878, single; 4c.—Fannie Julia Ficklin[8], b. March 25, 1880, single; 5c.—Boyce Ficklin, Jr.[8], b. July 23, 1883; m. June 28, 1911, Lucy Reese Dillard, b. Oct. 29, 1886, dau. of George and Sarah (Reese) Dillard and gr. gr. dau. of Judge William M. Reese, decd.

2b. *Ida Lou Hill*[7] (1a, 2, X, B. P. O), b. Jany. 16, 1855; m. June 21, 1875, Albert Augustus Barnett, b. July 5, 1845—for many years, and until his death, the Ordinary of Wilkes Co. Issue: 1c.—William Hill Barnett[8], b. Jany. 28, 1877; d. July 26, 1877; 2c.—Clara Beall Barnett[8], b. July 13, 1878 (q. v.); 3c.—William Meriwether Barnett[8], b. Nov. 30, 1880 (q. v.); 4c.—Emma Anthony Barnett[8], b. Feby. 10, 1884 (q. v.); 5c.—Albert Augustus Barnett, Jr.[8], b. July 14, 1886; d. May 11, 1888; 6c.—Graham DuBose Barnett[8], b. July 11, 1889; m. Dec. 6, 1917, Camilla Louise Pharr, b. Jany. 3, 1891, and had: 1d.—Aurelius Pharr Barnett[9], b. Jany. 15, 1920.

2c. Clara Beall Barnett[8] (2b, 1a, 2, X, B. P. O), b. July 13, 1878; m. Oct. 15, 1902, Addison Wingfield Simpson, M.D., b. Nov. 19, 1875, son of Col. W. W. Simpson, decd. Issue: 1d.—Albert Franklin Simpson[9], b. Sept. 15, 1904; 2d.—Addison Wingfield Simpson, Jr.[9], b. June 23, 1907; 3d.—Graham Temple Simpson[9], b. Oct. 9, 1909; 4d.—Eugenia Floyd Simpson[9], b. July 8, 1912; 5d.—Robert Barnett Simpson[9], b. Dec. 9, 1915; d. June 27, 1918.

3c. William Meriwether Barnett (2b, 1a, 2, X, B, P. O.), b. Nov. 30, 1880; m. Nov. 29, 1910, Leila Milton Irwin, b. July 6, 1879. Issue: 1d.—William Meriwether Barnett, Jr.[9], b. July 29, 1913; 2d.—Elizabeth Irwin Barnett[9], b. Aug. 11, 1916; d. Oct. 16, 1918.

4c. Emma Anthony Barnett[8] (2b, 1a. 2, X, B. P. O.), b. Feby. 10, 1884; m. Feby. 16, 1910, William Armstrong Slaton, b. Oct. 20, 1878. Issue: 1d.—Clara Barnett Slaton[9], b. Jany. 11, 1911; 2d.—Margaret Hill Slaton[9], b. Sept. 1, 1913; 3d.—William Armstrong Slaton, Jr.[9], b. July 28, 1916.

3b. WILLIAM MERIWETHER HILL[7] (1a, 2, X, B. P. O.), b. 11 July 1856; m. 19 Nov., 1884, SUSAN MONTGOMERY STOKES, b. 9 Sept., 1861, dau. of William Anthony and Margaret (Rhind) Stokes. Issue:

1c. Gardner Meriwether Hill[8], b. 5 Nov., 1885; d. 28 Nov., 1885; 2c.—Margaret Rhind Hill[8], b. 14 Oct., 1886 (q. v.); 3c.—Eugene DuBose Hill[8], b. 2 March, 1889; graduated at "Ga. Tech.", 1st Lieut. Signal Section, Officers' Reserve Corps of the U. S. A., A. E. F., April 19, 1913; m. Oct. 6, 1921, Lila Helen Robinson, dau. of Mr. and Mrs. Arthur Lee Robinson, of Louisville, Ky.; 4c.—Montgomery Stokes Hill[8], b. 1 Dec., 1890, graduate of "Ga. Tech.", Captain, Signal Section, O. R. C., of the U. S. A., A. E. F., 402 Telegraph Battalion, Nov. 2, 1917. He m. 2 Feby., 1921, Miss Grace Kinard Earle, dau. of Mrs. William Earle, of Columbia, S. C. She graduated at the Columbia High School and completed her education at Fairmont Seminary, Washington, D. C. Mr. Hill now holds an important position in the "Southern Enterprises, Inc."; 5c.—Marion Gardner Hill[8], b. 16 Oct., 1892; m. 10 Aug., 1918, John Augustus Richards, b. 24 Aug., 1890. Issue: 1d.—Marion Hill Richards[9], b. 16 Dec., 1919; 6c.—Susan Rembert Hill[8], b. 6 July, 1894, single; 7c.—Albert Barnett Hill[8], b. 12 Aug., 1896, member of famous "Golden Tornado" of Ga. Tech., 1917, and later 1st Lieut., Field Artillery, U. S. A., World War; 8c.—Julia Golden Hill[8], b. 22 March, 1899, single; 9c.—William Meriwether Hill, Jr., b. 5 Sept., 1901.

2c. Margaret Rhind Hill[8] (3b, 1a, 2, X, B. P. O.), b. 14 Oct., 1886; m. 26 Nov., 1913, Milton Wells Williams, b. 30 June, 1827. Issue: 1d.—Milton Wells Williams, Jr.[9], b. 3 Feby., 1915; 2d.—

Susan Montgomery Williams[9], b. 1 March, 1917; 3d.—Eugenia Hill Williams[9], b. 10 May, 1919.

4b. JOHN DUBOSE HILL[7] (1a, 2, X, B. P. O.), 1858-1898; m. (I) 2 Oct., 1882, NONA LEWIS, b. 2 Oct., 1859; d. 8 Jany., 1887; m. (II), 31 March, 1891, SOPHIE LEWIS, b. 9 Sept., 1855,—wives were sisters—of Greene Co., Ga., daus. of Miles W. and Mallie A. Lewis, and sisters of HENRY THOMAS LEWIS, 1847-1902, late Associate Justice of Supreme Court of Ga., and who, as spokesman of the Georgia delegation in the famous Chicago Convention of 1896, electrified the assembly by his speech placing WILLIAM JENNINGS BRYAN in nomination for the Presidency.

Issue by 1st mar.: 1c.—Mallie Sophia Hill[8], b. 31 July, 1883; m. 5 Sept., 1906, Willard M. Pope, son of Henry and Katherine Pope, of Fla. 2c.—Graham DuBose Hill[8], b. 4 Dec., 1885; d. 23 Nov., 1900.

Issue by 2nd mar.: 3c.—William Lewis Hill[8], b. 10 April, 1892; d. 18 July, 1917. 4c.—Nona Lewis Hill[8], b. 15 April, 1894; m. 28 April, 1920, Augustine Statham Quin; 5c.—Henry DuBose Hill[8], b. 7 Dec., 1896, unm.; served in Signal Corps, World War; 6c.—Emogene Hill[8], b. 24 Oct., 1898.

5b. Martha ("Mattie") Amelia Hill[7] (1a, 2, X, B. P. O.), 1861-1915, m. 7 March, 1883, Judge H. Graham Lewis, of Greene Co., son of Miles W. and Mallie A. Lewis, and brother of the wives of her bro. John DuBose Hill. Issue: 1c.—William Hill Lewis[8], M.D., of Siloam, Greene Co., Ga., b. 16 Dec., 1883; m. 22 Nov., 1912, Louise Kendrick, dau. of J. A. and Addie M. Kendrick; 2c.—Nona Belle Lewis[8], b. 4 July, 1886; d. 23 April, 1901.

6b. Dr. William Wylie Hill, Jr.[7], (1a, 2, X, B. P. O.), b. 3 Dec., 1863; m. 5 March, 1890, Kate Harper, of Wilkes Co., divorced. Issue: 1c.—Kathleen Hill[8], single.

2a. COL. JOHN MERIWETHER HILL[6] (2, X, B. P. O.), 1827-1894, educated at home school and at the U. of Ga.; had no aspiration for public office, preferring the peace and quietude of home life. He, however, served as Colonel of the 3rd Reg. Ga. State troops, Genl. P. J. Phillips' Brigade, under Major Gen. Gustavus W. Smith, in 1864 ("Avery's His. of the State of Ga.", pp. 284-'5), and there is on file in the Adjt. Genl's Office, at the State Capitol, a notification to him of his appointment as Brigadier General of the State Militia. His stature, bearing and commanding person, made him a notable figure in any assembly. He was esteemed, honored and beloved by all who knew him, of unsurpassed popularity in his community and section, and especially was he the friend of, and beloved by the poor, to whom his benefactions were widespread and boundless. He and his younger brother, Burwell Pope Hill, purchased and operated plantations in Dougherty Co., Ga., but sustaining heavy losses in negroes from malaria, sold out there and purchased plantations on White Oak Creek, in Coweta County, Ga.

HE m. (I), 16 Feby., 1851, Mary W. G. Greer, of Coweta Co., Ga., b. 7 March, 1834; d. 14 April, 1872. No issue; m. (II), 18 Dec. 1872, SUSAN CATHERINE CALHOUN, b. 6 June, 1848; d. 18 Oct., 1918, dau. of Dr. ANDREW B. CALHOUN, b. 17 March, 1809, in Abbeville Dist., S. C.; d. Aug., 1897, and his wife, SUSAN S. WELLBORN, b. 22 Aug., 1813, in Wilkes Co., Ga.; d. 18 Aug., 1857, dau. of Abner Wellborn and his wife, Martha Render.

Issue by 2nd mar.: 1b.—NANNIE SUE HILL[7], b. 1 July, 1874 (q. v.); 2b.—Calhoun Meriwether Hill[7], b. 2 Jany., 1877 (q. v.); 3b.—Wylie Pope Hill[7], b. Oct., 1879, d. 2 April, 1901, at Va. Polytechnic Institute, while a student, unm.

1b. NANNIE SUE HILL[7] (dau. of Col. John M.), m. 23 Nov., 1898, WALTER COLQUITT CARTER, formerly Clerk, U. S. District Court for the Northern Dist. of Ga., and now U. S. Commissioner in Atlanta, Ga., son of Samuel McDonald Carter (and his wife Emma Colquitt, dau. of Judge WALTER TERRY COLQUITT and his first wife, NANCY HILL LANE), son of Col. Frank Carter, d. 1861, and his wife, Miss Eliza McDonald, d. 1865, sister of *Hon. Charles James McDonald, Associate Justice* of the *State Supreme Court* and *Govr. of Ga.*, 1839 to 1843. Issue, an only son:

1c. Walter Colquitt Carter, Jr., b. 12 June, 1904, graduated from Boys' High School of Atlanta, in May, 1921, winning the Silver Trophy awarded by the Atlanta Journal for the best all-round student-excellence in scholarship, in which he was second, and all school activities. He was also the class orator at the graduating exercises. He was chosen for the honor by the joint action of the faculty and students.

2b. Calhoun Meriwether Hill[7], son of Col. John M., b. 2 Jany., 1877; m. 26 Oct., 1904, Ridy Logan Powell, dau. of Capt. Thos. W. Powell, decd. Issue: 1c.—Rebecca Catherine Hill[8], b. 31 July, 1905; 2c.—John Meriwether Hill, II[8], b. 30 Oct., 1906; d. 21 Aug., 1907; 3c.—Susan Calhoun Hill,[8] b. 25 Dec., 1907; 4c.—Sallie May Hill II[8], b. 1 Dec., 1911; 5c.—Thomas Powell Hill[8], b. 7 Nov., 1913; d. Aug., 1915; and 6c.—Nancy Carter Hill[8], b. 7 Nov., 1913, d. 12 Dec., 1913, twins.

EXCURSUS: *CALHOUN*

DR. ANDREW B. CALHOUN was the youngest son of Ezekiel Calhoun (and his wife Frances Hamilton, dau. of Maj. Andrew Hamilton), son of William Calhoun (and his wife Agnes Long), son of James Calhoun (and his wife Catherine Montgomery, dau. of Hugh Montgomery, of Scotland), the youngest of the three brothers, David, John and James, who emigrated from Donegal, Ireland, circa 1733, to make a new home in America. ("Notable Southern Families", pp. 48, 50, 51, by Zella Armstrong; Article from Atlanta Journal, Sept. 20, 1920, by James Barnwell Heyward).

Dr. Andrew B. Calhoun, 1809-1897, and his wife Susan S. Wellborn, 1813-1857, had issue:

1. Martha Frances Calhoun, b. 16 Feby., 1841; d. 2 Oct., 1885 (q. v.).
2. Ann Elizabeth Calhoun, b. 18 Nov., 1842; d. 13 July, 1907 (q. v.).
3. Abner W. Calhoun, b. 16 April, 1845; d. 21 Aug., 1910 (q. v.).
4. Susan Catherine Calhoun, b. 6 June, 1848; d. 18 Oct., 1918; m. 18 Dec., 1872, Col. John Meriwether Hill. (See a, p. 124.)
5. Andrew Ezekiel Calhoun, b. 9 May, 1851 (q. v.).
6. Ephraim Ramsey Calhoun, b. 29 Sept., 1854; d. 6 July, 1875, unm.

1. Martha Frances Calhoun, 1841-1885, m. 3 May, 1864, Dr. Kinsman C. Divine, d. in the 80's. Issue:
1a. Andrew Calhoun Divine, b. 12 Feby., 1865; d. 31 Jany., 1866.
2a. Kinsman Calhoun Divine, b. 29 Nov., 1866, d. s. p.
3a. Susan Elizabeth Divine, b. 23 Dec., 1868; d. 23 Oct., 1870.
4a. Frances Lydia Divine, b. 29 July, 1871; m. 14 July, 1893, Arnold Broyles, Clerk Sup'r Court, Atlanta, Ga. Issue: 1b.—Edwin Nash Broyles, b. 14 Sept., 1894; 2b.—Louize Phinizy Broyles, b. 25 Oct., 1896; m. 8 Dec., 1917, Thomas Barrett III, and has one child: 1c.—Frances Arnold Barrett, b. 14 Nov., 1918. 3b.—Frances Elizabeth Broyles, b. 22 Sept., 1898; m. 20 Nov., 1918, Julian Barrett and has one child: 1c.—Julian Barrett, Jr., b. 12 Jany., 1920. 4b.—Morris Arnold Broyles, b. 14 Aug., 1901; 5b.— Susan Calhoun Broyles, b. 21 Dec., 1909.

2. Ann Elizabeth Calhoun, 1842-1907, m. 18 Nov., 1868, Dr. William R. Caldwell, of Charleston, S. C. Issue:
1a. Anne Frézil Caldwell, b. 19 Aug., 1869; m. June, 1895, Michael Powell, of Newnan, Ga.
2a. Andrew Calhoun Caldwell, b. 1874, unm.

3. Dr. ABNER WELLBORN CALHOUN, 1845-1910, the eminent occulist, m. 20 Sept., 1877, MARY LOUSE PHINIZY, dau. of Ferdinand Phinizy (and Harriett Bowdre, his 1st wife), son of Jacob Phinizy and Matilda Stewart, his wife. Issue:
1a. Dr. FERDINAND PHINIZY CALHOUN, the occulist, b. 20 Sept. 1879 (q. v.).
2a. Susan Wellborn Calhoun, b. 17 April, 1881; m. June, 1903, Junius G. Oglesby, Jr. No issue.
3a. Andrew Calhoun, b. 25 April, 1881 (q. v.).
4a. Harriet Hays Calhoun, b. 14 Jany., 1882; m. 7 April, 1915, William Stewart Witham, Jr. Issue: 1b.—William Stewart Witham III, b. 7 Jany., 1916.

1a. Dr. *Ferdinand Phinizy Calhoun*, 1879-......, m. 30 June, 1909, Marion Peel, dau. of Col. William Lawson and Lucy (Cook) Peel, dau. of Genl. Philip Cook and his wife, Sarah G. Lumpkin, dau. of Henry Hopson Lumpkin, a bro. of Gov. Wilson Lumpkin. Issue: 1b.—Ferdinand Phinizy Calhoun, Jr., b. 29 Nov., 1910;

2b.—Lawson Peel Calhoun, b. 4 March, 1912; 3b.—Marion Peel Calhoun, b. 7 Sept., 1913.

3a. Andrew Calhoun, 1881—, m. 25 April, 1906, Mary Guy Trigg, of Chattanooga, Tenn. Issue: 1b.—James Trigg Calhoun, b. 19 Feby., 1907; Abner Wellborn Calhoun III, b. 26 Dec., 1909; 3b.—Louize Phinizy Calhoun II, b. 6 April, 1916; 4b.—Katherine Mae Calhoun, b. 19 Aug., 1918.

5. ANDREW EZEKIEL CALHOUN, 1851-....., *Judge of the Criminal Court of the City of Atlanta*, m. June, 1896, Carobel Heidt. Issue: 1a.—Abner Wellborn Calhoun II; 2a.—John Heidt Calhoun; 3a.—Andrew B. Calhoun II; 4a.—James Vreland Calhoun.

3a. WALTON POPE HILL[6] (2, X, B. P. O), 1830-1898, educated at home school and at Emory University; planted in Dougherty Co.; on account of malaria removed to Arkansas, where he served in the Trans-Miss. Dept. of the C. S. A.; after the war removed to Oglethorpe Co., Ga.; m. Feb. 14, 1855, *Ann Haseltine Hampton* (b. in 1833; d. Dec. 23, 1901), dau. of John M. and Ann J. Hampton, of Dougherty Co. No issue.

4a. Dr. ABRAHAM CHANDLER HILL[6] (2, X, B. P. O.), 1831-1867, educated at home school, at University of Ga. and Emory College; read medicine under Dr. A. B. Calhoun at Newnan, Ga.; attended medical college at Charleston, S. C., later Jefferson Medical College, at Philadelphia, Pa.; was a practicing physician in Dougherty Co., Ga., in partnership, at first, with Dr. Twitty at "Pinchum Slick", some 6 or 8 miles from Albany. The unhealthy condition, at the time, of that section, the paucity of doctors and the vast extent of territory he was called upon to serve, both day and night, overtaxed his strength and brought an end to his promising career. He m. (I) May 24, 1855, Rachel E. Hampton, b. Oct. 23, 1835; d. Nov. 8, 1863, dau. of John M. and Ann J. Hampton; m. (II) March 7, 1867, Ellen Harper, a sister of Mrs. Whitehead of Dougherty Co., d. March 24, 1867, and his death followed 25 days later. Issue by 1st, none by 2nd, mar.:

1b. LODOWICK MERIWETHER HILL II[7] (Jr.), b. March 10, 1856; d. Oct. 29, 1908 (q. v.) ; 2b.—Samuel Ashton Hill[7], b. June 26, 1859, d. July 30, 1863; 3b.—Willie May Hill[7], b. Sept. 4, 1863, d. June 9, 1866.

1b. LODOWICK MERIWETHER HILL II[7] (4a, 2, X, B. P. O.), 1855-1908, m. Jany. 2, 1884, ANNIE LEE HUDSON, of Greenville, S. C., b. Feby. 15, 1865, dau. of William Alexander and Rosaline (McCann) Hudson, and gr. dau. of Mathew T. and Ann Fleming (Collins) Hudson, dau. of Joseph, son of Thomas Collins, Sr. (See "J. H^m Coll", Vol. 1, pp. 228-235; "His'y of Spartanburg Parish, S. C.", by Landrum, p. 417). Issue:

1c.—IDA LEE HILL[8], b. March 2, 1886 (q. v.).

2c. ROSA MCCANN HILL[8], b. March 26, 1892; m. Nov. 14, 1916; William Roberts Strickland, of Valdosta, Ga. Issue: 1d.—Leona Roberts Strickland[9], b. May, 1920.

3c.   Chandler Hill⁸, b. Aug. 9, 1894; d. June 10, 1896.
4c.   Lois Tyler Hill, b. Aug. 5, 1900; d. Oct. 24, 1900.
1c.   IDA LEE HILL (1b, 4a, 2, X, B. P. O.), b. March 2, 1886; m. Oct. 1, 1913, Isaiah Tucker Irwin, Jr., atty.-at-law, son of Capt. Charles E. Irwin, decd., of Washington, Ga. Issue:
1d.   Ann Hill Irvin⁹, b. March 25, 1917; 2d.—Charles Edgar Irwin⁹, b. July 30, 1919; 3d.—Isaiah Tucker Irvin III⁹, b. 22 Dec., 1921.

5a.   BURWELL POPE HILL⁶ (2, X, B. P. O.), 1833-1886, was of perfect physical development,—agile, fleet and athletic, excelling in all games and sports. He was educated at home school and Emory College, settled as a planter in Dougherty Co., Ga.; on account of malaria removed to Newnan, Coweta Co., Ga.; served in Phillips' Legion, . . . Cavalry, C. S. A., and lost right arm in battle of Gettysburg; m. (I) Sept. 13, 1855, Mary Henley Taylor, b. March 22, 1832; d. June 24, 1861, dau. of Col. Clark Taylor, of Oglethorpe Co., Ga.; m. (II), May 7, 1884, Bessie Taylor, niece of 1st wife. Issue by 1st, none by 2nd, mar.: 1b.—Bessie May Hill⁷, b. Dec. 27, 1856; d. Nov. 1, 1857; 2b.—Lodowick Henry Hill⁷, called "Harry" Hill, b. April 19, 1858; d. Feb. 8, 1913, unm., in Jacksonville, Fla.; 3b.—Raymond Clingham Hill⁷, b. June 13, 1859; d. Oct. 27, 1864.

6a.   IDA MAY HILL⁶ (2, X, B. P. O.), 1835-1919, educated at Greenville, S. C., LaGrange and Washington, Ga., graduating at the latter in 1852 or '3, with first honor. The winter of 1858-'9, during the administration of Pres. Buchanan and Vice-Pres. Breckenridge, she passed with U. S. Senator and Mrs. Robert Toombs in Washington City. Being the only sister of 12 brothers, she received and enjoyed an unusual degree of homage, attention and love, which she reciprocated, in fullest measure, throughout life, by tender ministrations and devoted, helpful service. She survived all of her brothers save two—the youngest by each marriage. She m. Jan. 29, 1867, Dr. HENRY ROZIER CASEY, of Columbia Co., Ga. (his 2nd wife), b. Sept. 23, 1816; d. April 1, 1884. Issue, an only child:
1b.   Nandon Casey⁷, b. Aug. 4, 1872; d. Dec. 23, 1873.

DR. CASEY m. (I) in Dec., 1842, Caroline R. Harris, of Columbia Co., and of five or six children, the fruit of that marriage, only two are now (Nov., 1920) living, viz., Mrs. Sallie Berrien (Casey) Morgan and Mrs. Fannie (Casey) Meldrim, wife of Genl. Peter W. Meldrim, both of Savannah, Ga.

DR. CASEY was the son of Dr. John A. Casey and his wife, Sallie Berrien, dau. of John Berrien of Revolutionary fame, and sister of John McPherson Berrien. He was a delegate to the famous Charleston Convention, 1860; a delegate to the Secession Convention at Milledgeville, Jany., 1861. He was a member of the State Senate 1865-6, 1878-9; of the Constitutional Convention in 1877, and was Medical Director of Maj. Genl. Gustavus W. Smith's

Division of State troops in the Civil War (Avary's His. of the State of Ga., pp. 284-5, and other pages as in index).

7A. DUNCAN CHATFIELD HILL⁶ (2, X, B. P. O.), 1837-1908, educated at home school, at Furman University, Greenville, S. C.; settled as a planter in Ark., serving in the Trans-Miss. Dept. of the C. S. A., and after the war returned to Ga. by request of his father to take full charge of his planting interests. He represented Wilkes Co. in the legislature in 1898 and 1899. He m., Feby. 12, 1861, OPHELIA JORDAN HALLIDAY, b. Feby. 26, 1839; d. Aug. 30, 1898, dau. of Dick and Mary Ann (Hill) Halliday, dau. of Theophilus and Polly (Jordan) Hill (vide ante p. 92, 4a, 8, VII, B. P. O.). Issue:

1b.—Thomas Meriwether Hill⁷, b. Nov. 14, 1861; d. March 17, 1865.
2b. William Augustus Hill⁷, b. Oct. 8, 1863; d. March 12, 1865.
3b. Mary Amelia Hill⁷, b. April 15, 1867; d. Aug. 3, 1869.
4b. Nannie May Hill⁷, b. Nov. 6, 1869; d. Sept. 14, 1874.
5b. Mattie Ophelia Hill⁷, b. Dec. 27, 1872; d. Sept. 16, 1877.
6b. Duncan Chatfield Hill, Jr.⁷, b. Sept. 10, 1874; d. c. 1900, unm.
7b. LUCY JORDAN HILL⁷, b. Jan. 17, 1877 (q. v.).
8b. Clifford Halliday Hill⁷, b. July 3, 1879; m. March 4, 1914, Ella Amanda Godwin. Issue, one child: 1c.—Jane⁸, b. in Dec., 1919.

7b. LUCY JORDAN HILL (7a, 2, X, B. P. O.), b. Jany. 17, 1877; m. Sept. 12, 1900, AUGUSTUS POPE ANTHONY (1b, 2a, 8, IV, B. P. O.), see ante p. 89, son of CAPT. JAMES REMBERT and ABBIE (POPE) ANTHONY. He is the president of the "Bank of Jacksonville", Fla., and with his brothers, owns and operates a chain of high class stores at West Palm Beach and other places in Fla., and at Asheville, N. C. *He and his wife* are the *present owners* of the *old Hill homestead in Wilkes Co., Ga.* See frontispiece. Issue: 1c.—Hilda Ophelia Anthony⁸, b. July 16, 1901; 2c.—Roslyn Hill Anthony⁸, b. May 9, 1903; 3c.—Mary Chatfield Anthony⁸, b. July 9, 1906; 4c.—Henry Duncan Anthony⁸, b. May 11, 1908; 5c.—Lucy Hill Anthony⁸, b. April 7, 1912; 6c.—Augustus Pope Anthony, Jr.⁸, b. July 24, 1913.

8a. THOMAS WEBSTER HILL⁶ (2, X, B. P. O.), 1839-1899, a Hercules in sinew and of magnificent physique; was educated at home school, at Trenchard's Academy at Elberton, Ga., and later at Furman University, Greenville, S. C. Served with Phillips' Legion—Cavalry, Army of Va., C. S. A., under Generals Stuart, Hampton and Butler. He was conspicuous for daring and courage. On one occasion the Reg. Comdr., Col. Rich, presented him with a fine pistol in appreciation of his gallantry. Again after the war, Col. Hugh Buchanan, of Newnan, Ga., of the C. S. A., ex-Member of Congress and Judge of the Superior Court, at an entertainment given to a dau. of Mr. Hill, referred to him as a second Marshal Ney (Memoirs of Ga., Vol. 2, p. 333). He was offered promotion, but declined, saying that he preferred to fight shoulder to shoulder with his old comrades, to whom he was endeared by dangers faced and hardships endured together. He m. Jan. 20, 1869, *Mary Starke*, of Elbert Co., b. Nov. 5, 1847, d. March ..., 1921, dau. of S. C. Starke, b. in S. C., in 1818 (and his wife, Mary A. Brewer, b. 1824, dau. of Edmund H. and Lucy (Carter) Brewer), son of S. C. and Ann (Mickle) Starke, and gr. son of William Starke, native of S. C. Ann Mickle was dau. of John and Jane Mickle, of S. C. (Memoirs of Ga., Vol. 1, p. 636). Her sister, Sarah Starke, married U. S. Senator Benjamin R. Tillman, decd. Issue:

1b. Sallie May Hill[7], b. May 27, 1870; d. March 15, 1890.

2b. Amelia Starke Hill[7], b. Dec. 29, 1871; d. Aug. 30, 1873.

3b. Thomas Webster Hill, Jr.[7], b. July 6, 1873; m. Nov. 19, 1902, Mrs. Jennie (Sledge) Phillips, of LaGrange, Ga., b. Mar. 1, 1874. No issue.

4b. Samuel Meriwether Hill[7], b. Sept. 13, 1875. Unm.

5b. Mary Addie Hill[7], b. Dec. 5, 1877; m. June 11, 1907, Carroll Summerson, of New York City. No issue.

6b. Nancy Johnson Hill[7], b. March 1, 1880; m. (I) Dec., 1905, —divorced; m. (II) May 4, 1907, Louis Godshall, of N. Y. City. No issue.

7b. Irene Pope Hill[7], b. Aug. 29, 1881. Unm.

8b. Lodowick Wellborn Hill[7], b. Nov. 21, 1883; m. Feby. 16, 1910, Jessie Sledge, of LaGrange, Ga., b. March 24, 1887, sister of his elder brother's wife. Issue: 1c.—Mary Pauline Hill[8], b. April 21, 1911; 2c.—Dorothy Wellborn Hill[8], b. Aug. 27, 1913.

9b. Ruby Hill[7], b. Dec. 22, 1885; unm.

10b. Maude Barker Hill, b. March 1, 1888; d. Oct. 13, 1918; m. June 24, 1915, Robert Walter Willis, of Jacksonville, Fla.

9a. HENRY JORDAN HILL[6] (2, X, B. P. O.), 1842-1893, educated at home school and at Mercer University; had completed his Junior year when he joined Cutt's Battalion of Artillery, C. S. A., and served throughout the war, unscathed. His death was tragic—while overlooking the ginning of his cotton, his hand got caught in the saws and his arm was almost literally torn from the shoulder, and delay in arrival of the doctor occasioned such a loss of blood that he died within a few hours. He was a most successful and progressive planter, his plantation on Broad River one of the most highly improved and best equipped in the State. He represented his County in the State Legislature in 1886 and 1887. He m. Dec. 10, 1867, *Dempie J. Jones* (d. 30 Oct., 1920, aged 77 years) and had an only dau.:

1b. Fanida Hill[7], b. Mar. 12, 1870; m. (I) Ben A. Neal, divorced; m. (II) John T. Moore, of Atlanta, Ga. No issue.

10a. JAMES DUBOSE HILL[6] (2, X, B. P. O.), 1843-189—, was

educated at home school, 2 years in Okolona, Miss., later attended Male Academy at Newnan, Ga., and then Mercer University, but withdrew in his Sophomore year. When a lad, had his elbow badly crushed when caught between the band and driving wheel of a gin. The arm was restored without disfigurement but never strong, yet he entered the service in the Civil War as a courier on the staff of Genl. Robert Toombs. He m. (I) Nov. 17, 1868, *Rebecca Harvey Williams*, a dau. of George and Elizabeth (Allen) Williams. (See Annals of Athens, by A. L. Hull, pp. 477-8). (Mrs. Elizabeth (Allen) Williams' sister Susan B. Allen m. Y. L. G. Harris, of Athens, Ga.). George Williams was son of William and Rebecca (Harvey) Williams, of Hancock Co., Ga.

He m. (II), July 26, 1888, Jennie Hampton and died a month or so thereafter. Issue by 1st, none by 2nd, mar.:

    1b.   Lodowick Chandler Hill[7], b. Dec. 9, 1869; d. c. 1890, when c. 21 years of age.

    2b.   Harvey DuBose Hill[7], b. March 15, 1871, d. . . . . . (q. v.).

    3b.   Janie May Hill[7], b. March 7, 1873. (q. v.).

    4b.   Henry Casey Hill[7], b. Jany. 4, 1879. (q. v.).

    5b.   Edward Chatfield Hill[7], b. Dec. 17, 1880; m. 7 (or 14th) Aug., 1920), Miss Marion Bloodworth, sister of Mr. and Mrs. Frank D. Bloodworth and dau. of E. H. Bloodworth, decd., of Barnesville, Ga. He is an atty. at law and ex-Assistant Solicitor of the Criminal Court of Atlanta.

    2b.   Harvey DuBose Hill[7] (10a, 2, X, B. P. O.), 1871—, m. Georgia V. Halliday, dau. of Abraham Halliday and his wife, Miss Mitchell (Vide ante p. 92, 1b, 1a, 8, VII, B. P. O.). Issue: 1c.—Rebecca Hill[8], b. April 24, 1895; 2c.—Virginia Hill[8], b. March 19, 1899.

    3b.   JANIE MAY HILL[7] (10a, 2, X, B. P. O.), b. March 7, 1873; m. Aug. 2, 1892, JUDGE BENJAMIN HARVEY HILL (his 2nd wife), b. . . . . son of U. S. Senator Benjamin Harvey Hill, decd. (who was also Confederate States Senator) and his wife, Caroline E. Holt; formerly Solicitor Genl., Atlanta Criminal Court, ex-Chief Justice State Court of Appeals, and ex-Judge Superior Criminal Court of Atlanta. He resigned the former to accept the latter as affording more congenial and less arduous work, and served until Jan. 1, 1920, and is now again Associate Justice of the State Court of Appeals. Issue:

    1c.   Benjamin Hill III[8], b. July 12, 1893; d. May 25, 1896.

    2c.   Rebecca Harvey Hill[8], b. March 20, 1896; m. June 20, 1918, Lt. Edward McGruder Leath, U. S. A., of Birmingham, Ala.

    3c.   Benjamin Hill IV[8], b. Feby. 27, 1900.

    4c.   Charles D. Hill[8], b. Aug. 25, 1904; d. Aug. 29, 1908.

    4b.   Henry Casey Hill[7] (10a, 2, X, B, P. O.), b. Jany. 4, 187..; m. Feby. 20, 1903, Alice Halliday, younger sister of his elder brother's wife. Issue.

1c.—Gladys Halliday Hill[8], b. Dec. 1, 1903; 2c.—Lorene Hill[8], b. Sept. 27, 1905; 3c.—DuBose Hill[8], b. Oct. 1, 1909.

11a. LODOWICK JOHNSON HILL[6] (2, X, B. P. O.), 1846-..., was educated at home school, at Elberton Academy, John A. Trenchard, master; Newnan Male School—Daniel Walker, Principal; Mercer University, attaining Junior class; Georgia Military Institute, at Marietta (Mem. Ga. Pi Chap. Z. A. E.), attaining Senior class, when he entered the army; here he was the Senior and ranking Cadet Officer and made instructor of a class, composed of all commissioned and non-commissioned officers of the Institute, in Army Regulations, Artillery and Cavalry tactics and drill; University of Va., from Dec., 1865, to July, 1868,—one and half years in academic and one year in law department; belonged to Va. Omicron Chapter of Z. A. E. fraternity and commissioned by it to establish chapters in the Universities of Europe; the Royal Frederick William University of Berlin, Prussia, from fall of 1868 to spring of 1870; then for a short time attended lectures at the Sorbonne and College of France in Paris, but departure was hastened and necessitated by rupture of the "entente" between France and Prussia—here at this time were Benjamin H. Hill, Jr., of Athens (now Judge, of Atlanta, Ga.), Dr. Lou Orme, decd., of Atlanta, and Dr. King (Rex) Wylie, of Savannah, Ga. On his return to America, took a course, with his younger brother A. W. Hill, at Bryant, Stratton and Sadler's Commercial School, at Baltimore, receiving their diplomas at end of six weeks' attendance, when none were ever before graduated within less than three to six months after entrance. From Dec., 1870, to June, 1871, read law under Chief Justice Logan E. Bleckley, decd., whose office and home was then at northeast corner of Peachtree and Harris streets, Atlanta, Ga.

In May, 1864, entered the war as 1st Lieut. of Co. "A" and Adjt. of the Battalion of Georgia Cadets, of whom Maj. Genl. Henry C. Wayne (in his report as set forth in the official war records (Series 1, Vol. 53, Supplement pp. 32 to 37, inc., in Serial No. III, on p. 36), in commending Maj. Capers' military qualifications says:

"They have been brilliantly illustrated by the Corps of Cadets, whose gallantry, discipline and skill equal anything I have ever seen in any military service. I cannot speak too highly of these youths who go into a fight as cheerfully as they would enter a ball room and with the silence and steadiness of veterans". (See also "The House of Plant", by G. L. Dickerman, pp. 33-34). When at Milledgeville served as Adjutant of the Post; in Nov., 1864, at battle of Oconee bridge, was placed by Maj. Gen. Wayne in charge of Ordnance; at Augusta, about Jany. 1, 1865, was assigned to duty as Acting Asst. Inspector General on Staff of Brig. Genl. R. W. Carswell, Commander of the 1st Brigade of Ga. State troops.

In June, 1870, with *William Bird Berry*, organized the First National Bank of Newnan, Ga., Mr. Berry as President and Mr.

Hill as Cashier; on April 1, 1877, made Cashier of "The Atlanta Savings Bank of Ga.", successor of the Georgia Railroad & Banking Co. agency in Atlanta; in 1878 was made Vice-Pres. and Manager; in '79 converted it into The Gate City National Bank of Atlanta; in Oct., '80, was made its Pres., increased its capital by July, '81, to $250,000.00, and in 1893, because of a heavy robbery, or embezzlement, by its Asst. Cashier, Lewis M. Redwine, voluntarily liquidated it, paying within ninety days from the discovery of the embezzlement its depositors in full—about $800,-000 without receiving a dollar of outside aid, notwithstanding its loss and the financial panic which then prevailed throughout the United States.

In the '80's, for several years was president of The Furman Farm Improvement Co.—a fertilizer mfg. company; sold his interest and it became the Adair Bros. and McCarty Co., later Adair-McCarty Bros.; was also Pres. of the Ga. Security Investment Co. for two years, gave one year to the organization, securing subscriptions to its capital and making financial connections; in the second year placed $800,000 in loans on Ga. farm lands at a net profit to the Company of about $60,000. About the same time (the late 80's or early 90's) the Ga. Improvement Co. which had undertaken to build the Atlanta and Florida Railroad from Atlanta to Fort Valley—now owned and operated by the Southern R. R. under its own name—after having built a small section of between fifteen and twenty miles from Atlanta, found their cash and credit both exhausted. In their extremity they invited Mr. Hill to accept the presidency of the Co. He did so, and soon built the road to Fort Valley, about 100 miles, and turned it over free of all indebtedness to the Atlanta and Florida Railroad Co., of which the late Col. R. F. Maddox, Sr. (father of R. F. Maddox, Jr., of Atlanta) was the President. After 1893, he engaged in the Building and Loan, Insurance and Real Estate business, retiring in 1916 on account of ill health. (Vide "History of Atlanta", by Wallace P. Reid, Part 1, facing p. 284, pp. 424, 427-'8; Part 2, page 158-160; His. of Z. A. E. Society, by Wm. C. Levere,—Indexed). He was for many years a member of both the Capital City Club and of the Piedmont Driving Club, but resigned from both in the middle nineties for personal and family reasons.

A PEREMPTORY WRIT
Returnable First June Rules, A. D. 1921.
To the Right Honorable Lodowick Johnson Hill, Atlanta, Ga.:
The Law Writ.

The Rector and Visitors, the President, the Dean and Members of the Faculty of the Law School of the University of Virginia, to their Right Liege and Beloved Son Lodowick Johnson Hill of the good City of Atlanta, in the State of Georgia, health:

We command you that on the 31st day of May next, in the

year of our Lord, 1921, and of our Foundation the 102nd, you shall enter your appearance, in propria persona, et non per alium, at our Seat at Charlottesville, there to remain, couchant and levant, for the Three Days thence ensuing, and then and there to do and receive such things as may be commanded you.

And Especially: Then and there to assist, by your corporal presence and personal endeavors in the celebration of the CENTENNIAL ANNIVERSARY of the Founding of our University and Law School and in doing proper and bounden auncestral Homage as a liege Son and Subject;

And Further: To partake in such Masks and Madrigals, Plays, Tourneys, Jousts, Feats of Arms and Archery, Falconry, Wrestling, Bowls, Quoits, Quarter-staff and Single-stick; Feastings of Pasties, Comfits, Junkets, Cates, Stikes of Eels, Creels of Carp, Venison Pies, Boiled Capons, Pots of Honey, Horns of Sack, Cups of Wassail, and such other Diversions and Refections, spiritual and physical, as may then and there *lawfully* be provided by our heralds pursuivants and serving-men, to make merry our right leal Sons, and to do Honor to Our Centennial Anniversary aforesaid;

And Further: Then and there to meet and greet, with right good will, other homagers who have been summoned by Like Summons, and who will gather at our said Seat from the Seven Seas and all Remote Parts bordering thereon or adjacent thereto;

And This You Will Do and Perform, without Delay or Plea, and no other Essoin shall cast, than as followeth, and then only by two good Essoiners, videlicet; Essoin of De Ultra Mare; De Infirmitate Veniendi; De Esse in Peregrinatione; Per Servitium Reipublicae; Per Inundationem Viae; In Curia Instanter; De Expectando Filio (aut Filia) in Praesenti; in Custodia Legis; In Coelo.

And This You Will in No Wise Omit, Sub Poena De Contemptu Brevium, De Recreantisa, De Utlagatoque.

Done at Minor Hall, sealed with our Corporate Seal, and made sure by the sign-manuals following, on this the 4th day of April, Anno Domini 1921, and of our Founding the 102nd.

For the Corporation: John Stewart Bryan,
Rector.
University of Va. Seal 1919

For the Faculty at Large: Edwin A. Alderman,
President.

For the Faculty of Law: Wm. Minor Riley,
Dean.

11a. LODOWICK JOHNSON HILL[6] (2, X, B, P, O), b. 16 Jany., 1846; m. Sept. 28, 1871, MARY RUTH HENDERSON, of Covington, Ga., b. Jany. 12, 1849; d. May 21, 1918, dau. of *Brig. Genl.* ROBERT JOHNSON HENDERSON, C. S. A. (b. 12 Nov., 1822; m. 2 April, 1846; d. 3 Feby., 1891), member of House of Representatives from Newton Co. in 1859-60 (Vide "Men of Mark", Vol. 3, pp. 232-3, by W. J. Northen; "Georgia and Georgians", Vol. 6, p. 2787; Ga. L. M. & L., Vol. 2, pp. 912-914, by Knight), and his wife Laura Elizabeth Wood (b. May 2, 1829; d. Sept. 26, 1899), dau. of Cary Wood, b. Feby. 10, 1794; d. May 6, 1857, and his wife Mary Richardson Billups (b. Sept. 13, 1803; m. Oct. 16, 1823; d. May 20, 1874), dau. of William Billups (b. Sept. 4, 1763; m. Oct. 9, 1787; d. Jany. 19, 1817) and his wife, Mary Richardson, b. Nov. 10, 1763; d. Nov., 1803, dau. of Col. Richard Richardson, Jr., b. March 4, 1741; m. 1761; d. 1818 (and his wife Dorcas Nelson, b. 1741, d. 1834), son of Genl. Richard Richardson, Sr. (b. 1704; m. Oct. 11, 1736; d. 1781) and his wife Mary Cantey, d. 1767. Issue :

1b. Claudia May Hill[7], b. July 4, 1872; d. Aug. 7, 1873.

2b. ANNIE LAURA HILL[7], b. Aug. 16, 1875—single—member Ga. Society Colonial Dames of America, by right of Abraham Hill, Jr. (1730-1792), John Pope (1700-1745), Col. Barnabie McKennie, Sr. (1675-1739), Jeremiah Exum (c. 1660-1720), Col. Richard Richardson, Jr. (1741-1818), Genl. Richard Richardson, Sr. (1704-1781), Thomas Walton, Jr. (c. 1714-1759) and Thomas Walton, Sr. (c. 1690-1751); member of Daughters of American Revolution by right of Abraham Hill, Jr., Burwell Pope (1751-1800), Col. Richard Richardson, Jr., and Genl. Richard Richardson, Sr.; member "National Society Daughters of the American Colonists" and eligible to membership United Daughters of Confederacy by right of her father and both grandfathers.

3b. LODOWICK JOHNSON HILL, JR.[7], architect and civil engineer, graduate of Boys' High School, of Atlanta, June, 1895, was b. Dec. 12, 1877; m. (I) in 1896, SARAH JAMES WILLINGHAM, of Washington, Ga., d. in 1897, no issue; m. (II) Nov. 28, 1917, ANNA REBECCA (called "REBIE") HARWELL, dau. of W. D., deceased, and Anna (Dunlap) Harwell.

12a. ABNER WELLBORN HILL[6] (2, X, B, P, O), 1849-1907, educated at home school, the Rock College at Athens, Ga., which combined military and academic instruction; U. of Va.; U. of Ga., at Athens, where he took his B.L. degree, and Bryant, Stratton & Sadler's Commercial School, at Baltimore, Md. In 1871 entered cotton commission business—firm of Daniel and Hill—Augusta, Ga.; in 1873 made Cashier Bank of Washington, Ga.; Oct. 13, 1881, appointed Asst. Cashier and Jany. 1, 1884, Vice-Pres., Gate City Natl. Bank of Atlanta, Ga.; in 1893-4-5-6 was Deputy Sheriff of Fulton Co. He represented Wilkes Co. in the State Legislature in 1880 & 1881; m. (I) Dec. 20, 1871, SALLIE CATHERINE BUCHANAN, of Newnan, Ga., b. June 17, 1850; d. Feb. 14, 1877, dau. of Col. Hugh Buchanan, decd., Col. C. S. A., member of the State Senate in 1855-6-7-8, member of Congress, and Judge of Superior Court, Coweta Circuit, of Ga.; m. (II) Dec. 16, 1880, LUCY COBB ERWIN, of Atlanta, dau. of Frank Erwin and *Mary Willis Cobb*, (who m. (II) Dr. John M. Johnson), the dau. of Maj. Genl. Howell, Cobb,

1815-1868 (Speaker of the House of Representatives; Sec'y of the Treasury under Pres. Buchanan; Govr. of Ga., and Pres. of the Provisional Congress at Montgomery), and Mary Ann Lamar, his wife. Issue by 1st mar.:

1b. Katie May Hill[7], b. Oct. 6, 1872; d. Aug. 25, 1880.

2b. MARY RUTH HILL, b. July 11, 1873; m. Nov. 14, 1900, Lewis Hamilton Hill—no kin—of Newnan, Ga. Issue: 1c.—Lewis Hamilton Hill, Jr.[8], b. Aug. 25, 1901; 2c.—Wellborn Buchanan Hill[8], b. Jany. 21, 1904; 3c.—Robert Duke Hill[8], b. May 31, 1906; 4c.—Catherine Hill[8], b. Oct. 24, 1908.

3b. Hugh Lodowick Hill[7], Electrical Engineer, West Point, Ga., b. Jany. 5, 1877; m. Oct., 1900, Vivian Brown, of Coweta Co., Ga.

Issue by 2nd mar.:

4b. Wellborn Erwin Hill[7], b. Dec. 24, 1880; d. July 18, 1882.

5b. LAMAR HILL[7], atty. at law, Lt. Col., U. S. A., b. May 27, 1885; m. Dec. 11, 1919, ADELAIDE VAUDON SINGLETON, dau. of Mrs. Nellie Luther Singleton, of Atlanta, Ga. In 1921, practicing law in N. Y. City.

6b. ASHBY HILL[7], b. Jany. 12, 1888; m. 26 April, 1916, OLIVIA BOGACKI.

7b. ABNER WELLBORN HILL, JR.[7], Capt. Coast Artillery, World War, b. 12 May, 1890. Single.

8b. THOMAS COBB HILL[7], Lt. U. S. A., World War, b. 24 Dec., 1892; m. Oct. 7, 1918, Minnie L. Rodgers, of Macon, Ga., b. Feb. 18, 1894.

14a. EDWARD YOUNG HILL[6] (2, X, B, P, O), b. Sept. 8, 1852, educated at home school and at Emory College. In the 70's and 80's was book-keeper, then Cashier of the Bank of Washington, Ga. Later he employed his time in loaning his capital to farmers and business men of that section. He represented Wilkes Co. in the State Legislature in 1888-1889, 1892 and 1893-....; m. Nov. 28, 1877, CLAUDIA LAWSON HENDERSON, b. Aug. 15, 1853, of Covington, Ga., dau. of Genl. ROBERT JOHNSON HENDERSON, C. S. A., and his wife Laura Elizabeth Wood, and a sister of MARY RUTH HENDERSON, who married his elder bro. (See ante 11a, 2, X, B, P, O), member of Ga. Soc'y Colonial Dames of America and of Daughters of American Revolution by right of Col. Richard Richardson, Jr., and Genl. Richard Richardson, Sr. Issue:

1b. MARY WOOD HILL[7], b. Sept. 30, 1878; m. Nov. 26, 1902, HENRY CANTEY, b. May 4, 1874, of Columbia, S. C. Issue: 1c.—Harry Cantey, Jr.[8], b. Aug. 28, 1903; 2c.—Claudia Hill Cantey[8], b. Jany. 10, 1905; 3c.—Mary Hill Cantey[8], b. March 14, 1909; d. April 10, 1912; 4c.—Roderick Hill Cantey[8], b. Sept. 13, 1913; 5c.—Sarah Davis Cantey[8], b. Sept. 13, 1913 (twins).

2b. Edward Young Hill, Jr.[7], of N. O., b. Oct. 9, 1882, unm.

3b. Roderick Henri Hill[7], b. Dec. 9, 1885; d. Aug. 18, 1905, unm.

3. SARAH CHRISTIAN WALTON HILL[5] (Wylie[4], Abraham[3], Abraham[2], Henry[1]) 1807-1842, m. 26 Oct., 1824, Dr. John Jordan, of Wilkes Co., Ga., b. 24 April, 1793; d. 30 Sept., 1855, son of Fleming Jordan and his wife, Miss .... Moore. (See Excursus—Jordan). A John Jordan, of Wilkes Co., was a drawer in a lottery of 1827 (D. A. R. Vol. 16, p. 338; Certified by Saml. West, Book DDD, p. 124). Issue:

1a. Martha H. Jordan[6], b. 15 Sept., 1825; d. 11 Oct., 1826.

2a. BENJAMIN FLEMING JORDAN[6], b. 19 Aug., 1831; d. 4 Oct., 1896; was the representative from Wilkes Co. in 1878-'79; m. 3 March, 1860, MARTHA VICTORIA ANDERSON, b. 15 June, 1837; d. 29 May, 1891, dau. of Dr. WILLIAM QUARLES ANDERSON, of Wilkes Co., and his wife, Sophia Walker. Issue: 1b.—John Jordan[7], b. 8 Dec., 1860; d. 20 May, 1862; 2b.—NANNALINE JORDAN[7], b. 13 April, 1862, m. 31 Jany., 1888, FRANK WILLIS BARNETT, b. 7 Dec., 1848, son of Samuel Barnett and Elizabeth Stone, his wife; issue: 1c.—Frank Willis Barnett, Jr.[8], b. 23 March, 1890,—single; 3b.—Benjamin Fleming Jordan, Jr.[7], b. 8 Nov., 1863 (q. v.); 4b.—Infant daughter[7], b. 2 Aug., 1866, d. 2 Aug., 1866; 5b.—Sallie Lou Jordan[7], called "Lalla", b. 26 Aug., 1867, d. 25 Aug., 1894; 6b.—Norma Victoria Jordan[7], b. 24 May, 1870; 7b.—Katherine Leslie Jordan[7], b. 25 Feby., 1875, d. 25 Sept., 1921; m. 19 Nov., 1902, Charles Kettlewell Ober, b. 7 Sept., 1870; d. 17 July, 1913, son of John Ober, of Baltimore, Md., decd.; issue: 1c.—Frances Victoria Ober[8], b. 9 Sept., 1903; 8b.—Edward Bowen Jordan[7], b. 16 Jany., 1878.

3b. Benjamin Fleming Jordan, Jr.[7], son of Benjamin F. and Martha Victoria (Anderson) Jordan, b. 8 Nov., 1863; m. 20 Nov., 1890, Annie Belle Gilmore, b. 4 Dec., 1871, dau. of John Gilmore. Issue:

1c.—Laura Victoria Jordan[8], b. 18 Aug., 1891;
2c.—John Fleming Jordan[8], b. 20 July, 1896;
3c.—Fannie Nannaline Jordan[8], b. 5 July, 1898, and whose photograph was chosen from 22,000 submitted to the War Dept. in the World War, for a War Insurance poster, with the statement, "Your photograph selected as the one portraying the characteristics most likely to inspire our Soldiers and Sailors".

4. MARTHA POPE HILL[5] (Wylie[4], Abraham[3], Abraham[2], Henry[1]), 1810-1848, m. 19 Nov., 1829, JAMES REMBERT DUBOSE, his 1st wife, b. 15 Nov., 1807; d. 21 May, 1867, Rev. Joshua Glenn officiating. (See Excursus—DuBose). Issue:

1a. William Edwin DuBose[6], b. 30 Oct., 1830; d. 15 May, 1850; was drowned; unm.

2a. Mary Elizabeth DuBose[6], b. 31 Dec., 1832; d. 8 July, 1834.

3a. Wylie Hill DuBose[6], b. 2 Oct., 1834; d. 29 June, 1862, while serving in C. S. A., the 1st Confederate soldier from Wilkes Co. to be killed in action; m. 20 Oct., 1857, Lucy B. A. Willis, b. 28 Dec., 1836, her 1st husband, dau. of *Judge James Dabney Willis*, b. 21 Oct., 1793, by his 2nd wife, *Nancy Tate Anderson*, whom he

m. 17 Aug., 1824. (For issue, see ante p. 37; and Excursus—Willis).

4a. JAMES REMBERT DuBOSE, Jr.[5], b. 27 Jany., 1837; d. 29 Sept., 1906, aged 69 years. (q. v.).

5a. Robert Meriwether DuBose[6], b. 31 July, 1840; d. in young manhood, unm.

JAMES REMBERT DuBOSE, m. (II), 29 Nov., 1849, Elizabeth Adams Vance, b. in Charleston, S. C., 24 Feby., 1827; d. 31 July, 1868, at Washington, Ga., dau. of William Vance II and Susan Mary Dart, his wife, of Greenville, S. C., Rev. W. A. Gamewell officiating. Issue:

6a. Wylie Duncan DuBose[6]—originally named Perry Duncan DuBose—b. 15 Oct., 1850; d. 25 May, 1909; m. 6 Feby., 1873, Nannie Stewart Wylie. Issue:

1b. Ethel Vance DuBose[7], b. 29 June, 1875; m. Harry Sudlow, Aiken, S. C. Issue: 1c.—Harry[8]; 2c.—Nancy[8]; 3c.—Eleanor[8]; 4c.—Duncan DuBose[8].

2b. Susan DuBose[7], d. in inf.;

3b. Finley DuBose[7], d. in inf.;

4b. James Rembert DuBose III[7], m. Fannie Williams. Issue: 1c.—James Rembert IV[8]; 2c.—Russell DuBose[8];

5b. Mattie Pope DuBose[7], m. Robert Halliday. Issue: 1c.—Catherine Stewart[8], b. Sept., 1912; 2c.—Robert Halliday, Jr.[8], b. 15 Nov., 1920;

6b. Clarence Henry DuBose[7], m. . . . . . ;

7b. Nannette DuBose[7], m. Clarence Eugene Mouts, Aiken, S. C., 25 Oct., 1916. Issue: 1c.—Clarence Eugene Mouts, Jr.[8];

8b. Wylie Duncan DuBose[7], killed 30 June, 1920, in automobile accident at Buffalo, N. Y., when a young man.

7a. Susan Mary DuBose[6], b. 25 Sept., 1852; d. 30 Oct., 1914, unm.

8a. William Vance DuBose[6], b. 22 Feby., 1854; d. 16 Feby., 1914, aged 60 years, at Fitzgerald, Ga. (q. v.);

9a. Louisa Toombs DuBose[6], b. 1 April, 1853, d. 15 July, 1856;

10a. BETTIE LOU (originally named Louisa Toombs for the little sister who died) DuBOSE[6], b. 1 Jany., 1857; m. 22 Jany., 1879, HUGH PHARR QUIN, Rev. W. B. Pledger officiating, son of Dr. Langdon Cheves Quin and Frances Jane McLoughlin, b. 17 Nov., 1847—marriage solemnized at home of Mr. Robt. Shand Smith (her gr. mother's home), in Washington, Ga. (q. v.).

4a. JAMES REMBERT DuBOSE, JR.[5], was Capt. in 1st Ga. Regulars, C. S. A., m. 1 Oct., 1857, ELZIRA CAROLINE SPANN, of Hendersonville, N. C., b. 22 Dec., 1836; d. 18 Sept., 1909. Issue:

1b. Edwin Rembert DuBose[7], b. 29 Aug., 1858. (q. v.);

2b. Wylie Spann DuBose[7], b. 22 Sept., 1861; d. 22 Oct., 1869;

3b. James Vance DuBose[7], b. 13 June, 1868; d. 2 Oct., 1871.

1b. EDWARD REMBERT DuBOSE[7] (3a, 4, X, B, P, O), b. . . . . . ., of the firm of Chamberlin-Johnson-DuBose Co. of Atlanta, m. 7

Nov., 1883, ELLA INMAN, sis. of Samuel M., Hugh T. and John Inman, all decd. Issue:

    1c.   EMMA BELLE DuBose[s], b. 4 Nov., 1885, m. ......, Harry B. Chamberlain, decd. No issue;

    2c.   Caroline DuBose[s], b. 8 Feby., 1888, d. ......; m. Herbert Sage;

    3c.   Edward Rembert DuBose, Jr.[s], b. 1 Jany., 1890; d. 7 Aug., 1897;

    4c.   James Rembert DuBose IV[s], b. 4 June, 1892; m. 12 Nov., 1919, Louise Moultrie, of Rome, Ga., dau. of Mr. and Mrs. Elijah Jones Moultrie;

    5c.   Samuel Inman DuBose[s], b. 31 Oct., 1897; m. 25 Sept., 1920, Miss Emma Briggs, dau. of Mr. and Mrs. Mathew A. Briggs;

    6c.   Hugh Inman DuBose[s], b. 21 Oct., 1901. Single;

    7c.   Catherine Lea DuBose[s], b. 14 March, 1890.

    8a.   William Vance DuBose[6], 1854-1914, m. (I), 5 Dec., 1876, Jessie Boring, Washington, Ga., dau. of Rev. Jesse Boring, by whom he had four children: 1b.—Howard DuBose, d. aged 2 yrs.; 2b.—Harriet Elizabeth DuBose, m. John Sullivan, of Anderson, S. C.; 3b.—Vance DuBose, m. James M. Coleman, of Atlanta; 4b.—Jessie Duncan DuBose, m. Enoch C. Prather.

William Vance DuBose[6] m. (II) . . . a lady of Mystic, Ga., on A. B. & A. R. R., near Fitzgerald, and had by her one child.

    10a.   HUGH PHARR and BETTIE LOU (DuBOSE) QUIN[6] have:

    1b.   Hugh Wallace Quin[7], b. 10 Aug., 1880;

    2b.   Elizabeth James Quin[7], b. 5 Dec., 1881; m. 16 March, 1910, Daniel Gabriel Wayne III, of Charleston, S. C., and have: 1c.—Elizabeth[s]; 2c.—Loulie DuBose[s]; 3c.—Julia Gertrude[s]; 4c.—Daniel Gabriel Wayne IV[s].

    3b.   Jennie Wood Quin[7], b. 20 Feby., 1883; m. 22 April, 1902, Horace Herndon Murray, of Newnan, Ga. Issue: 1c.—Samuel DuBose Murray[s]; 2c.—Elizabeth Wallace Murray[s]; 3c.—Katherine Herndon Murray[s], d. in inf.; 4c.—Hugh Quin Murray[s]; 5c.—Dorothy Langdon Murray[s].

    4b.   Marion DuBose Quin[7], b. 11 Dec., 1884; d. 7 Aug., 1885;

    5b.   Langdon Cheves Quin[7], b. 12 Nov., 1886; m. 10 Jany., 1920, Eugenia Caldwell, of Chattanooga, Tenn. Issue: Langdon Caldwell Quin[s].

    6b.   ROBERT SMITH QUIN[7], b. 15 April, 1889; m. 7 Nov., 1917, THOMAS EGLESTON PERDUE, youngest dau. of John Albert and Marion (Graham) Perdue, of Atlanta, Ga. Issue: 1c.—*Tommie Perdue Quin*[s].

    7b.   Louis DuBose Quin[7], b. 24 March, 1892; m. 5 Oct., 1920, Olga von Oven Jatho, of Charleston, S. C., dau. of Geo. W. Jatho and his wife Arnolda von Oven.

    8b.   Nannie Duncan Quin[7], b. 5 Feby., 1894; m. 12 Sept., 1916, Austin Henry Moore, of Washington, Ga., and had: 1c.—Nan DuBose Moore, b. 7 June, 1917; 2c.—Cornelia Milton Moore, b. 11 Jany., 1920.

9b. Martha (Mattie) Vance Quin[7], b. 27 May, 1896; m. 12 June, 1920, Arthur E. Dunaway, of Memphis, Tenn.;

10b. Helen DuBose Quin[7], b. 12 Nov., 1898.

5. MARY ANN TABITHA HILL[5] (Wylie[4], Abraham[3], Abraham[2], Henry[1]), 1814-1868, m. 25 Feby., 1834, Col. Perry Emory Duncan, of Greenville, S. C., b. 26 May, 1800; d. 16 July, 1867, near Albany, Ga. Issue:

1a. Burwell Alexander Duncan[6], M. D., b. 26 March, 1835; d. in July, 1917, at Moorehouse, Mo. (q. v.);

2a. Robert Perry Duncan[6], b. Feby. 18, 1838; d. in the 90's in N. Y. City. (q. v.);

3a. Wylie Hill Duncan[6], b. April 25, 1840; d. Jany. 25, 1882, in Washington, Ga. Unm.;

4a. James Meriwether Duncan[6], b. June 3, 1842; d. March 21, 1873, in Ark. (q. v.);

5a. William Thomas Duncan[6], b. Jan. 19, 1844; d. Dec. 20, 1854;

6a. Martha Pope[6], called "Mattie", Duncan, b. March 7, 1846; d. . . . . (q. v.);

7a. Amelia Jordan Duncan[6], b. Aug. 6, 1848; d. Jan. 25, 1884. (q. v.);

8a. Edwin DuBose Duncan[6], b. April 29, 1850; d. . . . , near West Point, Miss., unm.;

9a. George Washington Duncan[6], b. Feby. 22, 1852, d. in 1911 at Colorado Springs. (q. v.);

10a. Mary Millicent Duncan[6], b. Dec. 27, 1853; d. Aug. 4, 1857;

11a. William Jordan[6], called "Popcorn", Duncan, b. Oct. 23, 1856; d. Sept. 20, 1867, at home of his aunt, Mrs. Wm. M. Jordan, in Wilkes Co., Ga.

1a. Dr. *Burwell Alexander Duncan*[6] (5, X, B, P, O),1835-1917, m. (I) Feby. 9, 1858, Celestia A Strong, dau. of Elisha Strong, of Columbus, Miss., and his wife, Ann Hill, dau. of Thomas (1780-1816) and Sallie (McGehee) Hill (see post XII, B, P, O); m. (II) Jany. 30, 1893, Mrs. Julia Watson Manning. Issue by 1st, none by 2nd, mar.:

1b. Annie Strong Duncan[7], d. Oct. 17, 1915; m. Nov. 27, 1900, Judge Thomas Grant Blackwell. Issue: 1c.—William Duncan Backwell[8]; 2c.—Virginia Blackwell[8];

2b. Perry Emory Duncan II[7], d. Feby., 1905; m. April 15, 1891, Mary Lee Smith. Issue, 2 daus. and 3 sons, all living in 1914 in Oxford, Miss.; 1c.—Lucy Duncan[8], the eldest dau., has the Chair of Latin in the High School at Grenada, Miss.

2a. *Robert Perry Duncan*[6] (5, X, B, P, O), 1838-189—, Major Staff of Genl. Hoke, C. S. A.; m. Feby. 6, 1872, Lucie J. Harris, dau. of Genl. Harris, of Columbus, Miss. Issue, 3 children; a dau. m. . . . . . . , ... Howe and lives at Yonkers, N. Y.

4a. JAMES MERIWETHER DUNCAN[6] (5, X, B, P, O), 1842-1873, m. MARTHA MALINDA, called "MATTIE", TALIAFERRO. (See ante p. 98, 7a, 5, IX, B, P, O).

6a. *Martha Pope (Mattie) Duncan*[6], (5, X, B, P. O), 1846-...., m. March 20, 1867, George C. Beall decd., of Albany, Ga. Issue: 1b.—Mamie Beall[7], m. Charles Robinson, of Social Circle, Ga., no issue—both decd.; 2b.—Martha Beall—single—living in N. Y. City.

7a. *Amelia Jordan Duncan*[6] (5, X, B, P, O), 1848-1894; m. Joseph H. Burk, decd. Issue: 1b.—Duncan Burk[7]; 2b.—Fannie May Burk[7]; 3b.—Annie Burk[7].

9a. *George Washington Duncan*[6] (5, X, B, P, O), 1852-1911; m. *Caroline Johnson*, of Macon, Ga. Issue: 1b.—George Washington Duncan, Jr.[7]; 2b.—Annie Tracy Duncan[7], m. Rodney S. Cohen, of Augusta, Ga.

6. AMELIA THOMAS HILL[5] (X, B, P, O), 1817-1882, m. (I) April 10, 1838, Dr. WILLIAM MOORE JORDAN (by W. P. Arnold, M. G.), b. Feby. 11, 1817; d. May 29, 1873; had several children, but all d. in inf.; m. (II) 10 Nov., 1877, Dr. GILBERT HINTON, called "Gill", WOOTTEN (by Wm. L. Wootten, L. D.), his 2nd wife. No issue.

From the middle of the 50's she was the owner and resided at her father's homestead. Some years before the Civil War she razed the original building and erected in its stead a magnificent Colonial mansion—probably the handsomest in the County—which, alas! within a year after its completion, was totally destroyed by fire. It was replaced by a cottage, which was added to from time to time, and, it was said of it, that it would accommodate all comers, however many there might be. She truly lived for others; was a zealous and intense Methodist, but tolerant of all denominations and creeds. The Methodist Church, and the ministers thereof, were objects of her especial care, and to them her benefactions were limited solely by her means. She provided for the education of many of their children and her home was to them a Mecca and a Refuge.

Dr. William Moore Jordan completed his medical education in London in the spring of 1836. (See Jordan).

OBITUARY
(For the Washington Gazette.)

Departed this life on the 9th of January, at the residence of her brother, Col. L. M. Hill, Mrs. Amelia T. Wootten, formerly Mrs. Dr. Wm. Jordan, Amelia T. Hill, aged 65. The deceased was the daughter of Wylie and Martha Hill. There were four brothers and four sisters, all of whom are in the "spirit land," except Col. L. M. Hill, who is the only survivor. Death selected here a bright and shining mark, and while taking a member from the "church militant on earth," He has added another angel to that galaxy of immortal spirits that cluster around the "great white throne."

The deceased was for many years, not merely a member of the "Methodist Episcopal church south," but she was eminently and sincerely a truly pious, christian woman. This was signally made manifest by a daily walk and a christian example running back for more than a quarter of a century. She was a woman of very decided convictions and noble impulses, truly loyal to her home, to kindred, to friends, and to her church. As a neighbor, there was no one more kind, no one more popular. The name of "Aunt Em" was as familiar to all this people as "household words," beloved and endeared to them, by her many acts of kindness and attention; often times coming as a friend in need a true friend indeed. Her charities which were many, were not published to the world. She gave for the good of others, and without a selfish motive prompting. Her mission on earth seemed to be to minister to the wants and wishes of others, and in the bestowal of her charities, her pure unselfish heart was thankful to her God that she was able to help. Upon her own person, or for her own personal comforts, she used but little of her means, preferring to be a helper to the afflicted. In her death this entire community has suffered a loss that is irreparable, and the vacant chair at "Independence," will tell of the absent one gone before. But our loss is her gain. It was the lot of the writer to be in the same house with the deceased for nearly the entire time of her illness, and I can bear testimony to the fact that all of her expressions as to death were to the effect that her "pathway through the dark valley and shadow of death," presented no obstacles to her, that she could "read her titles clear to mansions in the skies," that there was no sting to death and no victory in the grave over her, that she would soon be "at rest." And when at last the coffin came, and the body cold in death laid therein, I read on the metallic head plate of the casket, "at rest," my mind in an instant caught at these significant words, and I felt in my heart of hearts, that "it is not all of life to live, nor the whole of death to die." "Aunt Em, is at rest." H. R. C.

In Memoriam

Truly "death loves a shining mark" and scarcely could have selected a brighter, than when on Monday morning last, his poisoned dart was directed towards our loved friend and counselor, Mrs. Dr. Wootten. For the greater part of her life a resident of this county, she was widely known even beyond its limits for her exemplary piety and "alms deeds which she did." Her house was the preacher's home, and its doors were always open to the orphan's cry, the poor and the suffering. Every Friday was observed by her for thirty-odd years, as a day of fasting and prayer, and who can calculate the amount of good those seasons of devotion have done to her, and are still doing for those for whom she thus wrestled? Thoughts of them cluster as a halo around her memory, and though the vase is broken and shattered, the scent of the roses lingers there still.

Passionately fond of reading, she laid by a certain sum each year for the purchase of books, and showing with these as well as every other possession her spirit of love and charity to those less favored, she gave of them liberally to the extent of her means, and when unable to give they were freely lent to all who desired to profit by their perusal. Many times have they brought such pleasures and profit to our own home circle and will be sadly missed now that the loving heart which prompted the noble deeds lies cold in death.

Her life's motto was "trust in God and do the right" and come weal or woe, sure was she to "take it all to God in prayer." Every ill of her life she bore as a correction from a loving Father's hand, and though at times clouds would gather thick and fast about her path, never one murmur was heard from her lips. Her little ones were taken one by one in their infancy. Father, mother, brother and sisters, all passed away, and yet another and heavier trial awaited her. The almost idolized husband of her youth and middle age went down to the cold waters of death leaving her heart torn and bleeding, and her life well nigh desolate, yet still her faith never wavered, but rather its brightness grew "more and more unto the perfect day." Surely of such the world is not worthy. For quite a number of years, she and Col. L. M. Hill have been the only surviving members of a large family of children, and now even of those two; "the one has been taken and the other left." She died at his house, whither she had gone on a visit, when she was taken sick, and though surrounded with every attention that loving hearts could devise, nothing could stay the march of the fell destroyer.

Peace to her ashes, and may the companion of her old age, and others she has left behind, so live that they too "may die the death of the righteous, and may their last end, be like hers."

F.

7. COL. WYLIE POPE HILL[5] (X, B, P, O), 1820-1864, m. 27 Feby., 1845, Miss JANE JAMES AUSTIN, b. 30 June, 1824; d. 23 Jany., 1913, dau. of Dr. Thos. Collins and Mary Turner (James) Austin, of Greenville, S. C.. Dr. Austin was the son of Col. Wm. Austin, soldier of the Revolution, and his wife Jane Collins, dau. of Thos. Collins, Sr. (His. of Spartanburg Co., p. 416, by Landrum; Cy[a] of Ga., Vol. 2, pp. 274-5).

His homestead is situated eight miles northwest of Washington, on the south side of the Danielsville road. It is a large two-story frame building, with a wide veranda. It stands in a beautiful grove of forest trees, and save an addition of two or more rooms made in recent years looks just as it did when built. An unmarried dau. and two unmarried sons now occupy it. (Ga. L. M. & L., Vol. II, p. 1050). He was a man of fine mental endowments, sterling integrity and magnetic personality; was a large planter and possessed a splendid fortune; was respected, esteemed, honored and beloved by all who enjoyed his acquaintance; was an accomplished violinist and took great delight in accompanying his wife at the piano for the pleasure and entertainment of his family and visiting friends; was very fond of the chase and took great delight in his perfectly trained pack of redbone red-fox hounds, unequalled in training, in fleetness, wind and nose, and envied by all true lovers of the sport. Their voices were musical, and at the height of a chase, as thrilling to the hunters as the clarion notes of a bugle sounding a charge to an army. He, in June, 1863, assumed command of the 1st Ga. Militia Regt., Genl. Toombs' Brigade, and served till May, 1864, when he resigned on account of ill health. Thereafter, until his death, was a recruiting and supply agent for the Confederate Government, to whose cause he was intrinsically and insistently loyal.

Issue:

1a. Thomas Austin Hill[6], b. Feby., 1846; d. Nov., 1892 (q. v.);
2a. Sallie McGehee Hill[6], b. Nov., 1848; d. 1879 (q. v.);
3a. William Edwin Hill[6], b. Nov., 1850. Unm.;
4a. Burwell Meriwether Hill[6], b. July, 1852. Unm.;
5a. Dr. John James Hill[6], b. Nov., 1854; d. Nov., 1906 (q. v.);
6a. Mary Austin Hill[6], b. Aug., 1858 (q. v.);
7a. Martha Pope Hill[6], b. 1859; single;
8a. William McGehee Hill[6], b. 1861; d. 1862;
9a. Lina Amelia Hill[6], b. 1864 (q. v.);
10a. Wylie Pope Hill, Jr.[6], b. 1865; d. 1908, unm.

1a. *Thomas Austin Hill*[6] (Wylie Pope[5], Wylie[4]), 1846-1892, educated at the Ga. Military Institute, at Marietta, Ga., and at the U. of Ga. at Athens; settled near Pine Bluff, Ark.; m. Aug., 1886, Maggie McCord, niece of Joseph A. McCord, of Federal Reserve Bank of Atlanta, Ga., b. 15 May, 1867, and had an only child:

1b. Thomas Austin Hill, Jr.[7], b. 24 July, 1889; m. 6 Feby., 1908, Nina Martin, b. 1891, and had: 1c.—Thomas Austin Hill III[8], b. 6 Nov., 1909.

2a. *Sallie McGehee Hill*[6] (Wylie Pope[5], Wylie[4]), 1849-1879, m. in 1871, Benjamin Semmes Irwin, 1st wife, b. 1847; d. 1913, atty. at law, Washington, Ga., bro. of Capt. Charles E. Irwin, decd., educated at U. of Va., member of Z. A. E. fraternity. Issue:

1b. Paul Hill Irwin[7], of N. Y. City, b. June, 1876; m. in 1904, Burdene Bieckle, b. 1881.

Hon. Benjamin S. Irwin m. (II) Miss Brownie Brewer, dau. of Col. Willis Brewer, historian and statesman of Ala., and had dau. Mildred Irwin, m. 3 Dec., 1921, Garnett Andrews Green, atty. at law, of Washington, Ga.

5a. Dr. *John James Hill*[6] (Wylie Pope[5], Wylie[4]), 1854-1906, m. (I) in 1883, Willie Callaway, b. 1863; d. 1883, of Wilkes Co.; m. (II) in 1889, Mary Lou Pope, b. 1868, of Washington, Ga., dau.

of William A. Pope, decd., and had: 1b.—Effie Pope Hill[7], b. 1892; m. Edward Alsop, b. 1838, his 2nd wife, divorced. No issue.

6a. *Mary Austin Hill*[6] (Wylie Pope[5], Wylie[4]), 1858-...., m. in 1885, Edward A. Barnett, b. 1855, of Washington, Ga. Issue:

    1b. Austin Hill Barnett[7], b. 1886; m., 1917, Mamie Clair Chapman, b. 1893;

    2b. Elizabeth W. Barnett[7], b. 1888; m., 1910, Marion Pembroke Pope, b. 1876, of Washington, Ga.;

    3b. Marion Hill Barnett[7], b. 1891;

    4b. Edward Augustus Barnett[7], b. 1893;

    5b. Samuel Hill Barnett[7], b. 1897; d. 1918, in World War, 1st Lieut., U. S. A., A. E. F.

9a. *Lina Amelia Hill*[6] (Wylie Pope[5], Wylie[4]), 1864-...., m., 1884, Edward S. McCandless, b. 1853, of Atlanta, Ga., and had:

    1b. Lina McCandless[7], d. in inf.;

    2b. Edna Hill McCandless[7], b. 1887; m., 1912, Albert E. Thornton, Jr., b. 1885, of Atlanta, Ga.

8. ABRAHAM THOMAS WALTON HILL[5] (Wylie[4], Abraham[3]), 1822-1845, noted for his piety, was returning from a visit to his fiancée, Eliza Alexander, dau. of Col. Mitchell Alexander, who lived on the French Broad River, some 10 miles from Asheville, on road to Warm Springs, and was taken sick with bilious intermittent fever, and died at his uncle, Perry Emory Duncan's six miles from Greenville, S. C. He was attended in his illness by Thos. Collins Austin, and buried at his uncle's, but eleven years later his body was removed to the new cemetery at Greenville. His fiancée later married the Rev. J. S. Burnett, Methodist minister, his 1st wife, and they were the parents of Col. Wylie Burnett, decd., a prominent lawyer of Athens, Ga. The Rev. J. S. Burnett m. (II) Miss Sallie Spann, sister of Caroline Spann, who married Capt. James Rembert DuBose, Jr. (See 3a, 4, X, B. P. O).

XI.—MARY (POLLY) HILL[4] (Abraham[3], Abr.[2], Hy.[1]), b. c. 1777; d. 2 June, 1849; m., 20 March, 1794, Wylie Pope, b. c. 1762; d. 16 July, 1819, bro. of Burwell, 1751-1800, Willis, John and Henry Augustine Pope. Issue:

    1. Josiah Woods Pope[5], b. c. 1796; d. 1823. (q. v.);

    2. John Clark Pope[5], b. c. 1800. His estate administered by James Huling in 1832;

    3. Sally Mary Ann Pope[5], b. c. 1804. (q. v.);

    4. Wylie Hill Pope[5], b. c. 1708. (q. v.).

1. *Josiah Woods Pope*[5] (XI, B, P, O), c. 1796-1823, m., 14 Feb., 1818, Almeda Calloway, her 1st husband, and she, after his death, m. (II) Baker Lipscomb. (See Excursus—Lipscomb, p. 146). She was the sister of Clarissa Calloway, who m. Abraham Hill[4], 1778-1852, and of Eliza Calloway, who m. (I) Ben Wootten, m. (II) Wylie Maxwell, m. (III) James Arnold, and bro. of Willis Calloway, whose dau. Mitt m. Stokes Walton, and dau. of Joseph Calloway and his wife Nancy Ragan, dau. of Jonathan Ragan, Sr., decd., of

Oglethorpe Co. Joseph Calloway was the son of Job Calloway and his wife, Mary ...... Issue:

1a. WYLIE MIDDLETON POPE[6], b. c. 1820, m. (I) his first cousin, Almeda Wootten, d. April, 1870, dau. of Ben and Eliza (Calloway) Wootten; m. (II) Elizabeth Whitehead (Taylor) Wootten, dau. of Col. Clark Taylor and widow of Dr. William Henry Wootten, d. March, 1861, who was his first wife's brother. Issue by 1st, none by 2nd, mar., *22 children*, of whom only five attained their majority, viz.:

1b. Mary Pope[7], d. c. Dec., 1869, m. Capt. John Walton, his 1st wife, and left 4 children. He m. (II) Lizzille Wootten, 1st wife's 1st cousin, dau. of John Ben and Agnes (Wootten) Wootten; m. (III) Sarah (Aycock) Willis. No issue;

2b. John Henry Pope[7], decd., m. ...... Smith and had several children;

3b. Lou Pope[7], m. William Faver;

4b. Amelia, called "Lady Bird" Pope[7], m. James David Faver, bro. of William;

5b. Tom Pope[7], m. Julia Ficklin, dau. of William and Julia (Anthony) Ficklin, living, 1921, in Atlanta, Ga. No issue.

3. SALLIE MARY ANN POPE[5] (XI, B, P, O), b. c. 1804, m. James Huling, either bro. or uncle of the mother of U. S. Senr. Robt. Toombs, decd. Issue:

1a. Henry Huling[6], m. Mat. Anthony; 2a. Gus Huling[6], d. unm.; 3a. George Huling[6], d.; 4a. Martha Burns Huling[6], m. Tignall Moss. Issue: 1b.—Georgia Moss[7], m. (I) ......; m. (II) ......; 2b.—James Alexander Moss[7], b. 4 Jan., 1857, of Tignall, Ga., m., in 1887, Amica Walton, dau. of Jim Walton and Amica, or America, Moss, his wife. Issue:

1c. Janie Burns Moss[8]; 2c.—Livingston Wesley Moss[8]; 3c.—James Wyatt Moss[8]; 4c.—Jessie Amica Moss[8], who m. I. C. Fields, of Albany, Ga.

MR. MOSS is one of the leading citizens of Wilkes, is a director of a bank of Tignall, and president of one in Washington, Ga.

4. WYLIE HILL POPE[5] (XI, B, P, O), b. c. 1808, d. in 1868, in Wilkes Co. James Huling was appointed his guardian April 13, 1827; m. Ariana Twining, her 1st husband, dau. of Mrs. Sarah Twining, who was 2nd wife of Henry Jossey, Jr. Issue: two sons; one b. in 1836, one named Middleton Pope.

COL. WYLIE HILL POPE and wife separated. She with the two boys removed to Coweta, or Meriwether Co., Ga., and there she m. (II) a Mr. ...... Hill, a stage driver—no kin to the Hills, of Wilkes,—and her son Middleton Pope changed his name to Middleton Hill. No further record.

EXCURSUS: The ELIZA CALLOWAY named above under (1, XI,

B, P, O, p. 144) and her 1st husband, Ben Wootten, b. 1790; m. in 1820, had:
1. John Ben Wootten, b. 1821 (q. v.);
2. Dr. William Henry Wootten, b. c. 1823 (q. v.);
3. Almeda Wootten, b. c. 1825; d. April, 1870, who m. Wylie Middleton Pope[6], his 1st wife. (See 1a, XI, B, P, O,)—p. 145.

1. *John Ben Wootten*, b. 1821, m. *Agnes Wootten*, dau. of Thomas Wootten (son of Thomas and Tabitha (Pope) Wootten) and his wife, Milly Smith, and had:
   (1) Eliza Wootten, m. Rev. Capt. John Sanders Callaway, a Baptist minister, and had several children:
   (2) Lizzelle Wootten, m. Capt. John, Walton, 2nd wife—see p. 145;
   (3) Ben Wootten, Jr., d. unm.,—and an adopted son named Isaiah Binns.

2. Dr. *William Henry Wootten*, b. c. 1823; d. 1861, in Newnan, Ga., m. in 1845, Elizabeth Whitehead Taylor, 1st husband (See ante 1a, XI, B, P, O), and had:
   (1) Ella Pope Wootten, b. c. 1847; m. William O. Sandwick;
   (2) William Clark Wootten, b. c. 1849; m. Alice McLain;
   (3) James Lewis Wootten, b. 31 Dec., 1851; m. Harriett Huff;
   (4) Richard Henry Wootten, b. 29 May, 1853; d. Oct., 1909 (q. v.);
   (5) Rosa Clifton Wootten, b. 24 March, 1855; m. 18 Dec., 1879, J. M. Spratlin, of Lincolnton, Ga., and has a large family of children.

(4) *Richard Henry Wootten*, 1853-1909, m. 11 Dec., 1878, Georgia LeSueur and had:
1. Katherine D. Wootten, b. 15 March, 1880; m. Robert S. Lokey, and had:
   (1) Robert S. Lokey, Jr., b. 14 Feby., 1920;
2. Harold LeSueur Wootten, b. 10 Dec., 1881;
3. Lalette Wootten, b. 9 Dec., 1883; m. William G. Love, of Columbus, Ga. Issue: (1) William G. Love, Jr., b. 6 July, 1914; (2) Richard Wootten Love, b. 2 Oct., 1916.
4. Maida Wootten, b. 1 Nov., 1887; m. Carrol D. Colley. Issue: (1) Frank Harris Colley, b. 24 April, 1915; (2) Carrol Colley, Jr., b. 17 Feby., 1919.
5. Jerome Alexander Wootten, b. 8 Jany., 1890; d. 4 Oct., 1918;
6. Walter Douglas Wootten, b. 21 Dec., 1891;
7. Elizabeth Wootten, b. 8 July, 1894;
8. Roselyn Reid Wootten, b. Oct., 1898; m. Hobart Miller.

EXCURSUS: *LIPSCOMB*

Baker Lipscomb, of Wilkes Co., Ga., b. 19 Dec., 1797; m. Almeda (Calloway) Pope, wid. of Josiah Woods Pope. Issue:
1. Lucinda Ann Lipscomb, b. 28 Jany., 1826, m. (I) 31 Oct.,

1849, Abram Marshall Hill; m. (II) Hilliary Talbert. (See p. 27);
  2. *Willis Webster Lipscomb*, b. 25 May, 1828;
  3. *Joseph Calloway Lipscomb*, b. 31 March, 1830;
  4. Mary Elizabeth Lipscomb, b. 10 July, 1833; m. Dr. Henry Willis Hill, 1st wife, son of Abram and Clarissa (Calloway) Hill;
  5. Martha Clarissa Lipscomb, b. 9 Oct., 1835;
  6. Sarah Louise Lipscomb, b. 26 Dec., 1837;
  7. *Almeda* Jane Lipscomb, b. 19 June, 1840, and
  8. George Willis Lipscomb, b. 19 June, 1840, twins;
  9. Elmira Rebecca Lipscomb, b. 28 Nov., 1842;
  10. Emma Eugenia Lipscomb, b. 26 July, 1846.

XII. THOMAS HILL^4 (Abraham^3, Abr.^{2}, Hy.^{1}), 1780-1816, m. 28 June, 1799, Sallie McGehee, 1st husband, b. 11 July, 1784; d. after 1852, dau. of Micajah and Ann (Scott) McGehee. She m. (II) Dionysius Oliver, whose 1st wife was Lucinda McGhee, younger sister of Sallie McGehee Hill. This 2nd marriage was after Jany., 1822, but exact date not learned. "*Sallie* the second dau. of *Micajah McGehee* was the prettiest woman on the frontiers of Ga., according to frontier taste. Her eyes were large, liquidly bright, with long, dark eye-lashes, shading them so as to add to their fascination. Her features were regular, and her cheeks rosy. Her person was straight and all the roundings of her limbs and chest beautifully perfect. She had just begun to run all the young men crazy who saw her, when she and Tom Hill fancied each other and married. After the death of Tom Hill, she m. her bro.-in-law, Dionysius Oliver. They moved West, whither all her children by her first marriage are gone. She had none by her last." ("Georgian", pp. 172-'3, by Geo. R. Gilmer). (See Excursus: McGehee).

Issue:
  1. Amelia Walton Hill^5, b. 12 Aug., 1800; d. . . . . (q. v.);
  2. Middleton Milledge Meade Hill^5, b. 12 May, 1802; d. 1849. (q. v.);
  3. Nancy (Ann) Scott Hill^5, b. 17 Aug., 1804; d. 8 Feby., 1878. (q. v.);
  4. Aliza Winfrey Hill^5, b. 22 May, 1806; d. 11 Aug., 1807;
  5. Lucinda McGehee Hill, b. 5 Jany., 1808; d. 9 May, 1811;
  6. Sarah Milton Hill^5, b. 3 Jany., 1810; d. 9 Dec., 1848. (q. v.);
  7. Mary (Polly) Christian Hill^5, b. 20 March, 1812; d. 10 June, 1835. (q. v.);
  8. Thomas Baytop Jefferson Hill^5, b. 27 Jany., 1814; d. 6 May, 1873. (q. v.);
  9. Abraham Wylie Hill^5, b. 10 Feby., 1816; d. 29 Dec., 1884. (q .v.).

1. *Amelia Walton Hill*^{5} (dau. of Thos. and Sallie (McGehee) Hill), m. (I) 29 Oct., 1818, James Alford Hill^5 her 1st cousin, b. 2 Dec., 1797; d. 28 Feby., 1831. (For issue, see ante 2. IX, B, P, O,, p. ...); m. (II) William (Billy) Gresham, bro. of Thos. and Ben Gresham, who lived and died in Lexington, Ga. No issue.

2. *Middleton Milledge Meade Hill*[5] (Thos.[4], Abraham[3], Abraham[2], Henry[1]), 1802-1849, went from Marion Co., Ala., to Bastrop Co., Texas, where his sister, Mrs. John McGehee, was then living, and finally, with his younger brothers, Thomas Baytop Jefferson[5] and Abraham Wylie Hill[5], purchased the headright of Gen. Edward Burleson on Colorado River, 12 miles from Bastrop City. The same year, owing to the disturbed condition in Texas, he returned to Ala.—the brothers remaining in Tex. In 1838 he went again to Tex., carrying his family and located on his purchase. He carried 2 wagons, a hack, 3 teams, 7 field hands and a number of young negroes. He immediately began to erect log houses, the floors made of split and hewed puncheons, and in a few years had 200 acres of his land in cultivation, and combined stock raising with farming. In 1841 he erected a cotton gin and mill—the 3rd in Bastrop County—operated by horse power, to which was brought cotton from all parts of the State, and people from many miles distant brought their grain to the mill.

2. *Middleton Milledge Meade Hill*[5] m. (1), 5 Aug., 1824, Olley Amelia Forster, d. 6 Nov., 1824; m. (II), 16 Oct., 1825, Julia F. Walker, d. in 1869. Issue by 2nd mar., 8 children, 5 boys and 3 girls:

1a. Sarah Hill[6], b. 1830; d. 19 April, 1920, aged 90 years; m. Ouilla J. Nichols and had 8 children, 6 boys and 2 girls: James[7], Middleton[7], Thomas[7], Robert[7], George[7], Han[7], Scottie[7] and Pinkie[7];

2a. Dr. Robert E. Hill[6], d. unm. He served in the 8th Texas Regt., C. S. A.;

3a. Thos. Abram Wylie Hill[6], b. in Marion Co., Ala., 24 July, 1834; d. in Smithville, Tex., in Feby., 1921. (q. v.);

4a. John Walker Forster Hill[6], b. in Marion Co., Ala., in 1837. (q. v.);

5a. James H. Hill[6] m. Lou Sanders and had, it is said, 7 children, names not given;

6a. Martha Elizabeth Hill[6], b. 1839 in Tex.; m. Thos. Jefferson Brooks and had: Robert A. Brooks[7], atty. at law, Bastrop, Tex.; Eula Lee Brooks[7]; Thos. Jefferson Brooks, Jr.[7], decd.;

7a. Mary Scott Hill[6], m. James Duncan Williams, decd., resides in Austin, Tex.; Issue: 1b.—Julia Williams[7]; 2b.—Mary Williams[7], m. . . . . Goldman, of Austin, Tex.;

8a. Middleton Hill, Jr.[6], d. s. p.

3a. THOMAS A. W. HILL[6] (Middleton[5], Thos.[4], Abraham[3]), 1834-1921, attended the common schools and two sessions at Bastrop College. At age of 18 was manager of Mrs. Olliver's farm, and at outbreak of the Civil War was engaged in same occupation for his uncle, Thos. B. J. Hill. In 1862 he joined Co. D, 8th Tex., or Terry Rangers, Army of Tenn. Was engaged in 1st and 2nd battles of Murfreesborough, Perryville, Chickamauga, and numerous others; was paroled at Lexington, when the U. S. furnished him with transportation for only a part of the way home, where he arrived June 1st, 1865; he remained at the old homestead from 1870 to 1889, when he removed to his own farm of 2100 acres in the Colorado River valley, the same being his portion of the farm. (His. of Tex., p. 700).

He m., in 1856, Miss Sarah E. Scates, of Fayette Co., Tex., d. 1 June, 1891, dau. of J. B. and Theodocia (Smith) Scates, pioneer settlers of the State. Mr. Scates was one of the signers of the Declaration of Independence of the State of Tex.; was twice married, by his 1st wife 2 chn.—Sarah E., wife of Mr. Hill, and J. R. Scates; by 2nd mar., had 3 children.

Thos. A. W.[6] and Sarah E. (Scates) Hill had 12 children, 10 of whom grew to years of maturity, viz.: 1.—Middleton[7]; 2.—Belle[7], m. R. A. Rutherford; 3.—Anna[7] and 4.—Austin[7], twins—former now decd., was wife of F. Hargrove; 5.—Fannie[7] (or Tommie), wife of Pierce Lowry; 6.—Sarah T.[7], wife of Dave Robinson; 7.—Julia[7]; 8.—Robert[7] and 9.—Mattie[7]—twins—Mattie decd.; 10.—Duckie[7](?).

Mrs. Hill was a member of the Methodist Church, and *Mr. Hill* affiliates with A. F. & A. M. J. Nixon Lodge No. 241 and Bastrop Chap. No. 95.

4a. *John W. F. Hill*[6], b. 1737, son of Middleton[5] and Julia F. (Walker) Hill, is a member of the mercantile firm of Yeager and Hill, Smithville, Tex. He received his education in the town of Bastrop and for 2 years before the opening of the Civil War was a clerk. In 1858 went to Mexico, purchased a drove of horses and sold them in Tex. In 1861 joined Co. D, Terry's Rangers—8th Tex. Cavalry, Army of Tenn., participated in battles of Shiloh, Perryville, Murfreesborough—in last named engagement was captured, taken to Camp Douglas 31 Dec., 1862, exchanged at City Point, Va., 7 April, 1863; rejoined his command at McMinnsville, Tenn., and took part in battles of Chickamauga, Resaca, Kennesaw, New Hope, Atlanta, Bentonville, and many minor engagements. He had during the struggle several horses killed under him, clothes riddled but never wounded. He entered as a private, but was made a noncom. officer.

In 1866 he established a saw-milling industry on Colorado River, in which he continued 2 years, when he purchased a farm on the River of about 2300 acres, near where he was reared and remained on it until 1875. In '75 took up his residence in City of Dallas, but remained there only a short time. From fall of 1875 to 1888 engaged in mercantile business at Alum Creek and later, in same year, came to his present location. The firm of Yeager and Hill has been in existence since 1875.

In 1868 he m. Miss Mariah Yeager (or Yerger), d. 29 Dec., 1875, dau. of John C. and Mariah (Kinkle) Yeager, and had a son Yeager Hill[7], who became a member also of the firm of Yeager & Hill, of Smithville, married and reared a large family, and died in June, 1921. Mrs. Mariah (Yeager) Hill was a member of the

Methodist Episcopal Church, South, and Mr. John W. Hill affiliates with the A. F. and A. M., J. Nixon Lodge No. 380. (Tex. His.—Bio., p. 715).

3. *Nancy (Ann) Scott Hill*[5] (Thos.[4], Abraham[3], Abraham[2], Henry[1]), 1804-1878, m., 18 Sept., 1821, Genl. Elisha Strong, b. in Va., son of Charles Strong (b. Hanover Co., Va., 18 Jany., 1763; d. 15 Oct., 1848, in Oglethorpe Co., Ga.) and his wife Sarah Thompson (d. 1849, over 80 years old—"White's Statistics", p. 611); came to Lexington, Ga., a merchant, in 1800; d. 21 Nov., 1879. He was in the wars of 1812 and 1836; was Q. M. Sergt. on Major William Alexander's staff, Ga. Militia, from 5 Nov., 1813, to 6 Jany., 1814, when he was promoted to 2nd Lieut. in Capt. Wm. Ford's Rifle Co., Floyd's Division, from which he was discharged 7 March, 1814, having served 123 days. Lt. Strong commanded the Co. the major portion of the time, Capt. Wm. Ford being sick.

He enlisted at Fort Hawkins—now Macon, Ga.,—was at the battle of Calabee Swamp. Residence at time of enlistment, Lexington, Ga. Date of application for pension, 6 Jany., 1874—claim allowed. Residence at time of application, Aberdeen, Monroe Co., Miss., age then 81 years. His Claim No. 29492, his Certificate No. 21310, Lt. and Acting Capt., War 1812. He organized the first Co. from his County in 1861, which was a part of the 11th Miss. Regt. Issue:

1a. Martin Luther, called "Doc", Strong[6]. (q. v.);

2a. Elisha Strong, Jr.[6], m. Rebecca Harris, of Columbus, Miss.;

3a. Celestia A. Strong[6], m. Feby., 1858, Dr. Burwell Alexander Duncan, 1835-1917, his 1st wife, of Greenville, S. C. (See ante 1a, 5, X, B. P. O., p. 139);

4a. Sallie Strong[6], d. y.; 5a. Charles Strong[6], killed at Gettysburg, C. S. A.; 6a. Augustus Strong[6], d. unm.; 7a. Thomas H. C. Strong[6], served in C. S. A., participated in 22 engagements, promoted on battlefield for gallantry; m. his cousin, Susie Strong, dau. of Charles Strong, Jr., of Newton Co., Ga., son of Charles Strong, Sr., 1763-1848, and his wife, Sarah Thompson. Charles Strong, Jr., served during 1781 in Va., in Rev'y War under Capt. Edward Smith and . . . . Miller, Col. Fleming and Gen. Nelson. (War and Pension Records, U. S. Govt., Ga. Pension Rolls, p. 53).

8a. Pope Strong[6], d. unm.;

9a. *Georgia*[6], called *"Little* GEORGE", *Strong*, b. 31 May, 1842; d. 6 June, 1901; m. 25 March, 1869, Dr. Richard L. Sykes, b. 28 Jany., 1840, in Columbus, Miss.; d. 6 May, 1912. Issue, an only daughter:

1b. ANNIE HILL SYKES[7], b. 1 Feby., 1870; m. 4 Dec., 1890, *Charles Frank Rice*, of Atlanta, Ga., b. 12 Feby., 1868. Issue: 1c.—Annie Sykes Rice[8], b. 8 Dec., 1892; 2c.—Mary Rice[8], b. 27 April, 1895; 3c.—*Georgia Strong Rice*[8], b. 19 May, 1898; m. 26 June, 1920, Dudley Stafford Golding, of Wichita Falls, Tex.

1a. *Martin Luther*, called *"Doc"*, *Strong*, son of Genl. Elisha and *Nancy (Ann) Scott (Hill) Strong*, d. 13 Aug., 1877, in Aberdeen, Miss., was a Major in the Western Army, C. S. A.; m. 14 Oct., 1852, Georgia Anna America Hill, b. 4 May, 1830, dau. of Blanton Meade, 1802-1857, and Elizabeth Ann, 1810-1894, Hill. Issue:

    1b. Anna Hill Strong[7], b. 30 Oct., 1854; m. 22 Feby., 1876, Henry Clopton;

    2b. Blanton Hill Strong[7], b. 6 March, 1857;

    3b. Abraham Hill Strong[7], b. 28 June, 1859; d. 30 July, 1859;

  6. *Sarah Milton Hill*[5] (XII, B, P, O), 1810-1848, m. (I) 4 March, 1829, John Gilmer McGehee, b. 20 March, 1804, in Carroll Co., Ga., d. 10 Sept., 1838; m. (II), Sept., 1845, Rev. Josiah W. Whipple, of Tex., a Methodist minister. (Vide "E. S. of Ala.", p. 521, III). Issue:

    1a. John McGehee[6]; 2a.—Tom McGehee[6]; 3a.—Henry McGehee[6]; 4a.—Edward McGehee[6]; 5a.—Elizabeth McGehee[6], d. in 1836.

  7. *Mary (Polly) Christian Hill*[5] (XII, B, P, O), 1812-1835, m. 4 Dec., 1828, Thomas H. Parks, of Newton Co., Ga., and had an only son: 1a.—John Ira Parks[6], b. 15 Nov., 1830. N. R.

  8. THOMAS BAYTOP JEFFERSON HILL[5] (XII, B, P, O), 1814-1873, moved to Tex. in 1835 with his brothers M. M. and Abraham Wylie; m. ...... 1840, SARAH LUCINDA SCOTT OLIVER, his *cousin* and *step-sister*, dau. of *Dionysius* and *Lucinda (McGehee) Oliver* —was living in 1896. (Vide "E. S. of Ala.", pp. 526-'7 and '9. Issue:

    1a. THOMAS ANDERSON HILL[6], of Weimar, Tex., b. c. 1842. (q. v.);

    2a. *Dionysius Oliver*[6], called *"Cap"*, *Hill*, of Smithville, Tex., b. Oct., 1843; d. 30 Jany., 1905. (q. v.).

    1a. THOMAS ANDERSON HILL[6] (8, XII, B, P, O), b. circa 1842, banker in Weimar, Tex., graduated at the Ga. Military Institute at Marietta, Ga., in 1861. In the same year joined the 3rd Bat. under Maj. Capers, of Ga.(?) as Lieut.; for a time assigned for duty on Gen. Stevenson's staff, then transferred to the 42nd Ga. Infantry as Capt. of Co. "I", was sent to Vicksburg, captured and paroled. Returning to Tex., remained until the exchange, after which was assigned to duty as Asst. Genl. Inspector of Cavalry under Gen. Gano, and was stationed principally in the Indian Nation. During summer of 1864 was sent back to his Co. in the 42nd Ga., rejoining the command at Dalton, Ga., was wounded in the battle of Resaca, but after a brief space returned to his Co. He was captured in the battle of Peachtree Creek and confined at Johnson's Island until the close of hostilities. The Colonel of the 42nd—Gen. Robt. J. Henderson—said of him, "Capt. Hill was a brave, most efficient and always dependable officer".

    In summer of 1866 began merchandising at LaGrange, Tex. From 1870 to '73 followed farming in Fayette Co.; was engaged in business at Columbus, until the Southern Pacific built its railway to Weimar, then merchandised there until 1885(?), when he entered the banking business. ("His. of Tex.", pp. 675-'6-'7). He m., 28 Nov., 1865, Sarah Louisa McGehee, b. 30 July, 1844; d. 12 Oct., 1916, dau. of Thomas Gilmer and Minerva (Hunt) McGehee. Issue:

    1b. Tye Yates Hill[7], of Hattiesburg, Miss., b. 29 Sept., 1867. (q. v.);

    2b. Cap C. Hill[7], b. 11 Sept., 1869; d. 9 May, 1909. (q. v.);

    3b. Thomas William Hill[7], b. 11 Sept., 1871. Unm.;

    4b. Scott Pearl Hill[7], b. 2 Feby., 1874. (q. v.);

    5b. Lula May Hill[7], b. 3 May, 1876; m. 6 Dec., 1899, George McCormick. No issue;

    6b. Eddie McGehee Hill[7] (dau.), b. 5 Nov., 1879; m. 27 Nov., 1911, Dr. C. H. Ratliff;

    7b. George Woods Hill[7], b. 12 Feby., 1882; d. 16 Aug., 1885;

    8b. Itasca Louisa Hill[7], b. 15 June, 1884. Unm.

    1b. TYE YATES HILL[7] (son of Thos. A. Hill), b. 29 Sept., 1867; m. 16 Jany., 1890, Lula Cole. Issue:

    1c. Scott Shelby Hill[8], b. 28 Oct., 1890; m. 25 July, 1917, Angeline Michael and had: 1d.—Yates Michael Hill[9], b. 18 May, 1918; 2c.—Mary Louisa Hill[8], b. 18 Oct., 1892; d. 2 Oct., 1899; 3c.—Cora Itasca Hill[8], b. 8 April, 1895.

    2b. CAP C. HILL[7] (son of Thos. A.), 1869-1909, m. 11 Jany., 1891, Annie Grace. Issue:

    1c.—Grace Hill[8], b. 27 Dec., 1893; m. 22 July, 1914, Hamilton W. Worrell, Surgeon of Heavy Artillery, A. E. F., killed 3 Oct., 1917, in collision of ships at sea, while en route to France;

    2c. Horace Bismark Hill[8], b. 19 April, 1896.

    4b. SCOTT PEARL HILL[7] (dau. of Thos. A.), b. 2 Feby., 1874; m. (I) 23 Dec., 1897, Eugene Sparks, of Waco, Tex.; m. (II) 12 Oct., 1910, Wayman Kindred. Issue, 1st mar.: 1c.—Thomas Eugene Sparks[8], b. 14 Oct., 1898.

    2a. DIONYSIUS OLIVER, called "CAP", HILL[6] (8, XII, B, P, O), 1843-1905, was educated at Bastrop, Tex. In Oct., 1861, joined as a private Co. "D" of 8th Tex. Cavalry, known as Terry's Rangers, Army of Tenn., under Albert Sidney Johnston. He participated in battles of Shiloh, Murfreesborough, Chicamauga, the battles from Resaca to Atlanta, from latter city to Savannah, then to Columbia, S. C., then to Bentonville, N. C. Was paroled at Charlotte April, 1865. Was never wounded. He rode his own horse from Charlotte to Oglethorpe Co., Ga., from which place to Central Ga. the U. S. Gov't furnished transportation, but from there to Tex. had to pay his way; arrived in Bastrop Co. Nov. 18, 1865. At the time of the surrender had but $5.00 in greenbacks. He engaged in agricultural pursuits, owned considerable land. In 1871 erected a beautiful home in Smithville, where he henceforth resided. (His. of Tex., pp. 675-'6-'7). He m., 25 Dec., 1866, Miss Nannie Aldridge, a native of Tenn. and dau. of John and Eliza (Hickerson) Aldridge, who came to Tex. in 1852. Mr. Aldridge engaged in farming and stock raising near Bastrop and was the first to introduce Durham cattle in the county. He d. 1862 and his wife in 1869. Issue, 3 children: 1b.—Susie Blanton Hill⁷, m. G. W. Jones, Jr.; 2b.—Walton Aldridge Hill⁷, and 3b.—Thos. Oliver Hill⁷.

Mr. Hill was a member of F. and A. M., J. Nixon Lodge No. 421 and of Bastrop Chap. No. 95.

The war records of these Texas Hills are taken mainly from a work entitled "Lone Star State", a series of Texas County histories.

9. ABRAHAM WYLIE HILL⁵ (XII, B, P, O), 1816-1884, was born in Oglethorpe County, Georgia, removed to Texas and settled in Hill Prairie, Bastrop County, in 1835; was in the battle of San Jacinto under General Sam Houston; m. 10 Jan'y, 1837, Evaline E. Hubbard, b. 29 April, 1818; died 1st June, 1893, dau. of Hon. Robt. Hubbard, b. c. 1789; d. 1846, aged 57 yrs., who was Capt. of Militia in Oglethorpe Co., Ga., from 16th Aug., 1821, to 8 June, 1824 ("Roster of Militia Officers" Adjutant General's Office), representative in Legislature in 1831-2, '34, '35,—list for 1833 not found (Roster of General Assembly of Georgia) (and his wife Nancy Waters), son of *John Hubbard*, a Revolutionary Soldier and his wife, Elizabeth, nee, it is said, Sanford (Bounty Certificates on file in office of Compiler of Records, State Capitol; Land Book G. G. G., page 110; Stub Entries to Indents for Rev'y Claims, Book L-N, p. 322, by Salley). Issue:

1a.—Mary Parks Hill⁶, b. 10 March, 1838. (q. v.) ;

2a.—Sarah McGehee Hill⁶, b. 22 Sept., 1839. (q. v.) ;

3a.—Robert Theus Hill⁶, b. 19 Nov.. 1841; d. 17 Dec., 1895. (q. v.) ;

4a.—Augustus M. Hill⁶, b. 26 Jan'y, 1846. (q. v.) ;

Two other children died before maturity.

1a. MARY PARKS HILL⁶ (XII, B, P, O), b. 10 March, 1838, graduated at Ga. Female College, Madison, Ga.; m. in 1856 Dr. John J. Watson, of S. C. Issue:

1b.—Eva Satira Watson⁷, b. 6 Aug., 1857; d. 15 July, 1917; m. Major Presley M. Woodall, dec'd, no issue;

2b.—Leroy Watson⁷, m. in 1894 Irie . . . . , and had: 1c., Robt. Lee Watson⁸, b. 1896, living, 1920, in Arizona or California;

3b.—Robt. Alfred Watson, b. 6 Dec., 1861; m. Vallie Owens. They live, 1920, at Hill's Prairie, Bastrop Co., had several children, all died.

2a. SARAH MCGEHEE HILL⁶ (9, XII, B, P, O), 1839-19—, m. in 1859, Wm. C. Powell, decd., and had:

1b.—Sarah Eva Powell⁷, m. Wm. A. McCord. No issue, they live. 1920, in Bastrop Co.

3a. ROBERT THEUS HILL⁶ (9, XII, B, P, O), 1841-1895, served

in Co. D of 8th Texas Reg., C. S. A., m. 11 Oct., 1865, Lucinda P. Caldwell, b. 20 Dec., 1843, in the Republic of Texas. Issue:

1b.—Augustus Hill[7], b. 3 Jan'y, 1867; d. in inf.;

2b.—Charles Watson Hill[7], b. 14 March, 1869. (q. v.);

3b.—Mary Caldwell Hill[7], b. 21 Oct., 1870; d. 28 March, 1873;

4b. ANNIE LOU HILL[7], b. 1 Nov., 1873; m., 28 Feb'y, 1893, Charles Trousdale Snyder, and had:

1c.—Wesley Hill Snyder[8], b. 14 Feb'y, 1894, Aviator U. S. A., World War; m. 19 Dec., 1921, Ruth Tarkington, dau. of Mr. and Mrs. Wm. B. Tarkington, of Laurinburg, N. C.

5b. John Caldwell Hill[7], b. 17 Dec., 1875; died 28 Oct., 1912. (q. v.).

6b.—Walter Hubbard Hill[7], b. 7 Jan'y, 1880; m. 20 April, 1901, Gertrude North. Issue:

1c.—Lucie Hill[8], b. 22 March, 1902;

2c.—Walter North Hill[8], b. 3 Sept., 1904;

3c.—Katherine Hill[8], b. 17 Dec., 1906;

4c.—Robt. Theus Hill II[8], b. 23 Oct., 1911;

5c.—Wm. Hill[8], b. 11th Sept., 1916.

2b.—Charles Watson Hill[7] (3a, 9, XII, B. P. O.), b. 14 March, 1869; m. 20 May, 1891, Tinnie Burleson. Issue:

1c.—Robert Aaron Hill[8], b. 17 Nov., 1893, member of A. E. F. World War;

2c.—Richard Augustus Hill[8], b. 30 Oct., 1898, served in U. S. Navy, World War, was in U. S. S. Tenadores, which was wrecked 28 Dec., . . . , 10 miles off the coast of France;

3c.—Rufus Arthur Hill[8], b. 2 Jan'y, 1901; d. June, 1901.

3b.—John Caldwell Hill[7] (3a, 9, XII, B. P. O.), 1875-1912, m. 3 Oct., 1898, Gertrude Fischer. Issue:

1c.—Theus Bernard Hill[8], b. 18 Oct., 1899;

2c.—John Caldwell Hill, Jr.[8], b. 23 June, 1901;

3c.—Alvy Fisher Hill[8], b. 20th July, 1905.

4a. AUGUSTUS M. HILL[6], M.D. (9, XII, B, P, O), b. 26 Jan'y, 1846; m. 27 Oct., 1870, in DeSoto Parish, La., Lizzie Holmes, b. in Oglethorpe Co., Ga. Issue, 7 children, all d. y. save two, viz.:

1b.—Eva Temperance Hill[7], b. 24 Sept., 1871; m. (I) Charles LeSueur, d. Aug., 1911, and had:

1c.—Wylie Hill LeSueur[8], b. 26 Jan'y, 1906; m. (II) David Karling, no issue.

They live, 1920, at the old homestead of her grandfather, bought in 1835.

2b.—Benjamin Oglevie Hill[7], b. 15 Dec., 1883, a Methodist minister, graduated at South Western Methodist University, Georgetown, Tex.; missionary to Cuba since 1912, and since 1914 or '15 president of Pinson College at Camaguey; m. Ethel Star Ellis, dau. of Rev. Henry Jossey Ellis, a Methodist minister, of

Union Point, Ga., of late blind, and Chaplain of the Ga. State Senate (vide ante 3b, 2a, IV, A. P. O.). Issue:
  1c.—Hattie Carson Hill[8], b. 1913;
  2c.—Sarah Elizabeth Hill[8], b. 1915.

HILLS.

"A merited tribute to the grand family of Hills of Bastrop County. Following is a tribute to the Hills from the pen of General John M. Claiborne, as published in the Bastrop Advertiser, April 18th, 1888."

"By the Hills, I do not mean the hills of nature that are to the East, overlooking the old historic town, but those other Hills, formed also by nature and made noble. Sitting at my library desk this beautiful April evening and reflecting back upon the joys, sorrows, pleasures and pains of the past, in the long past, and thinking of the old people and my boyhood companions. I wondered if it were true that there was, as is said, a skeleton in every family. This family was the most remarkable that ever came under my immediate observation, and if they had a skeleton then the saying is indeed a truism. In '49 I first knew Middleton, A. Wylie and Thomas B. J., all of whom participated in the struggle against Mexico and the Indians, for the freedom of this, the grandest State in the confederation of States, and A. Wylie Hill was a conspicuous figure in the battle of San Jacinto. From these noble sires sprung a younger generation of as good, almost perfect men, as has ever been known for the number. Middleton Hill was the father of Dr. Robert, Thomas A. W. and John W. Hill; A. Wylie Hill was the father of Robt. T. and Dr. Gus Hill; Thomas B. J. was the father of Capt. Thomas Anderson and D. O. Hill. These men and myself were nearly companions from 1847 until after the war; we were all at school together for years and we were all in the same company, same regiment, in the late war, and I know them, have tried them where alone you can know the man, on the tented field, by the campfire, in the hour of battle, and though often weighed they nor either one of them was ever found wanting. All of them born in gilded halls and surrounded by the richest prosperity, drank from golden goblets surrounded by all that wealth could procure, but never forgot for a moment that they were of the people. I never knew a Hill to tell a falsehood nor swerve from a duty of a citizen. I never knew a family that were so all brave and chivalrous by nature. I never knew one of them to speak unkindly of his neighbor. Either of these men could at any day or hour have put down his gun and returned to the comforts of home under the law of the confederacy under the 20 negro source of exemption, yet it never entered the mind of either of them. After the war they returned to their home and from affluence reduced to very humble circumstances, yet there as everywhere else tried they were equal to the occasion and buckled on the armor of labor and proceeded to rebuild their lost fortunes and all are successful, some of them affluent. The old sires of these men have gone. They sleep with their fathers silently in the tomb. Of the old men my recollection is of the most pleasant. A wild, reckless, bad boy, their gentle chiding yet rings in my ears, planted deep in my memory. Grand old men, few are their equals, and as an entirety no family of boys ever reached greater perfection, as useful men and good citizens. Old Bastrop has produced many good men and many of them learned the lessons of wisdom from men like the Hills, A. W. Moore, John H. Jenkins and others. Bastrop County should cherish the memories of these grand men of the past age.   Madeline Place, April 9, '88."

C.—ISAAC HILL³ (Abraham², Henry¹), b. c. 1734, was the third of six children named in his father's will, dated April 18, 1760. The 1st and 2nd were born probably between 1730 and 1732—their father married prior to October, 1729—the fourth married 3 Sept., 1762, therefore born probably before 1741; the 5th and 6th were married daughters—one with a daughter who m. 6 Jan'y, 1772, probably born at least as early as 1756, and her mother as early as 1739. It is, therefore, quite evident that Isaac Hill was born in the 30's. But, despite long and diligent research, no record has been found, to my knowledge, of his marriage. An ISAAC HILL, in 1785, removed, as did ABRAHAM HILL³, 1732-1792, son of Abraham², 1697-1760, from N. C. to Wilkes Co., Ga., and later, ISAAC to what is now Clarke Co., Ga., where he died. In "Revolutionary Pension Rolls" in Newberry Library at Chicago, Vol. 5, p. 218— pages numbered in ink after publication—we find: "ISAAC HILL, private, N. C. Militia, d. Aug. 15, 1833, aged 71 yrs., in Clarke Co., Ga." If this record as to his age is correct, and doubtless it is, then he was born in 1762, two years after date of will of Abraham Hill² (O), 1697-1760. He could not, therefore, have been the son of ABRAHAM HILL². Nevertheless, I feel quite confident that if he was not the son, then he was the grandson of ABRAHAM² and son of ISAAC HILL³. This conviction is warranted by the well known claim of relationship to the Clarke Co. ISAAC HILL by the children and grandchildren of both ABRAHAM HILL³, 1732-1792, and HENRY HILL³, 1730-1804, the sons of ABRAHAM HILL² and brother of ISAAC HILL³.

I.—This ISAAC HILL, Jr.⁴ (Isaac³, Abraham², Henry¹), was, as shown above, a Rev'y Soldier in N. C., received soldier's grant in Lottery of 1827, and in his will directs disposition of land drawn for services as a Rev'y soldier, and his wife, while with him in the war received a gunshot wound which crippled her for life. (See D. A. R., Vol. 7, p. 113,—Record of Mrs. O. A. (Amulet Ball) Dunson, Vol. 16, p. 336).

Georgia   } Will of ISAAC HILL, 1829-1833.
Clarke Co.   }

In the name of God, Amen.

I, Isaac Hill, of the State and County aforesaid, being of sound and disposing mind and memory, do make this my last will and Testament, towit:

Item 1st. It is my will that all my just debts be paid.

Item 2nd. I have given to my son, Middleton Hill, a Tract of land containing One Hundred Sixty Acres, more or less, part of the tract whereon I now live as his share of my estate.

Item 3rd. I give to my son Isaac Hill's daughter, Almeda, Four Hundred Dollars to be kept in the hands of my executors until she marries or becomes of age, and to be put out at interest, but if she dies before she marries, or without lawful issue to revert to and become a part of my Estate and be divided equally among my children.

Item 4th. I give to my son, Roderick Hill, after the death of his mother all the balance of my Tract of land, whereon I now live as his share of my estate.

Item 5th. I give to my daughter Elenor Hopkins, One Dollar.

Item 6th. I give to my daughter Charlotte Burney One Dollar.

Item 7th. I give to my daughter Olivia Harvey One Dollar.

Item 8th. I give to my wife Nancy Hill during her life, the Tract of land whereon I now live together with all my negroes and every discription of property which I may die possessed of, and after her death to be equally divided among the following children and Grandchildren (towit):

Elizabeth Lane, Sallay Hill, Catherine Lowe, Nancy Beavers, the children of my daughter Charlotte Burney, and the children of my daughter Olivia Harvey.

Item 9. I have given my daughter Eudocia M. Anderson a negro girl named Sophia, which is to be her share of my estate.

Item 10th. Be it remembered that I have a tract of land in the County of Muscogee when drawn, which I drew as a *Revolutionary Soldier* and not intended to be included in the foregoing bequeaths.

It is my will that the said Tract of Land, be sold after my death, at the discretion of my Executors, and the proceeds divided among the following children and grandchildren, Elizabeth Lane, Sally Hill, Catherine Lowe, Nancy Beavers, Eudocia Anderson, the children of my daughter Elenor Hopkins, the children of my daughter Charlotte Burney, the children of my daughter Olivia Harvey, Middleton Hill and Roderick Hill.

I do hereby appoint my son Roderick Hill and John H. Lowe my Executors to this my last Will and Testament.

In witness whereof I have hereunto set my hand and seal the 9th day of November, 1829.

                                        Isaac Hill   (Seal)

Signed, sealed and acknowledged in the presence of
Jacob Callahan
John Jones
William X Sims
    his mark

Georgia
Clarke Co. } Personally appeared in open Court, William Sims, one of the subscribing witnesses to the foregoing Will, who on Oath says, that he saw Isaac Hill, the Testator, sign the foregoing Will and heard him acknowledge the same to be his last Will and Testament, that he was of sound and disposing mind and memory at the time of so doing, and that he saw Jacob Callahan and John Jones the other witnesses sign the same.

                                           his
                                  Wm. X Sims
                                      mark

Sworn to in open Court this 9th of Oct., 1833.

                                Joseph Ligon, C. C. O.

Approved and ordered recorded Oct. adjourned Term 1833, and recorded 9th Oct., 1833.

This is to certify that the above and foregoing is a true copy of Will and Probate of Isaac Hill as recorded in my office. (Will Book B, p. 121-122-123).

This May 19th, 1903, witness my hand and seal.

                                S. B. Wingfield, Ord'y
                                  Clarke County, Ga.

I.—ISAAC HILL, Jr.[4] (Isaac[3], Abraham[2], Henry[1]), 1762-1833, m. Nancy Crain, or Crane, who survived her husband,—and had:

  1. Middleton Hill[5], b. 27 March, 1793; d. 3 March, 1853. (q.v.);
  2. Isaac Hill, III[5],—dead in 1829. (q. v.);
  3. Roderick Hill[5], an executor of his father's will, d. unm. N. R.;
  4. Elinor Hill[5], m ...... Hopkins, had, 1829, children. N. R.;
  5. Charlotte Hill[5], m. .... Burney, had, 1829, children. N. R.;
  6. Olivia Hill[5], m. ...... Harvey, had, 1829, children. N. R.;
  7. Elizabeth Hill[5]. (q. v.);
  8. Sallie Hill[5], m. John H. Lowe, his 2nd wife, after 1829. N. R.;
  9. Catherine Hill[5], m. John H. Lowe, his 1st wife. N. R.;
 10. Nancy Hill[5], m. ...... Beavers. N. R.;
 11. Eudocia M. Hill[5], m. ...... Anderson. N. R.

  1. MIDDLETON HILL[5] (I, C. P. O.), 1793-1853, in 1838 was made one of the original trustees of the Summerville Academy. Summerville was that year made permanent county-seat and the Academy chartered (L. M. & L., Vol. 2). He m. 26 Oct., 1819, Sarah Hinton,

b. 14 Dec., 1803; d. 23 Dec., 1870, dau. of Jacob Hinton, d 18 Oct., 1835, and his wife Polly (Mary) Bradford. Issue:
    1a. James Henry Hill[6], b. 17 Aug., 1820, d. unm.;
    2a. Sarah Elizabeth Hill[6], b. 31 July, 1823;
    3a. Mary Crain Hill[6], b. 1 July, 1826;
    4a. Isaac Hinton Hill[6], b. 7 Feb'y, 1828, d. unm.;
    5a. Polly Bradford Hill[6], b. 1 April, 1830;
    6a. William Roderick Hill[6], called "Rhode", b. 15 June, 1832; d. ...... (q. v.);
    7a. Penina Catherine Hill[6], b. Aug. 15, 1834;
    8a. John Middleton Hill[6], b. 11 May, 1837; d. 1912; m. Anna Carroll. No issue. He was a Capt. in Wheeler's Cavalry, C. S. A.;
    9a. Eleanor Olivia Hill[6], b. 4 Feb'y, 1840;
    10a. Martha Ann Hill[6], b. 14 June, 1842; d. Aug. 31, 1920. (q. v.);
    11a. Isabella Virginia Hill[6], b. 24 June, 1845;
    12a. Lou Hill[6], b. ......, 1848.
    6a. WILLIAM RODERICK HILL[6] (Middleton[5], Isaac[4]), b. 15 June, 1832; m. ......, LAURA NANCE, b. ......, d. ......, and had:
    1b. HELEN FAIRLEE, called "BUDDIE" HILL[7], b. .....; m. ...., JOHN CARROLL PAYNE, attorney-at-law, Atlanta, Ga. Issue:
    1c. Laura Hill Payne[8], b. ......; m. ...... Alexander Wylie Smith, Jr., Capt. U. S. A., A. E. F.
    2c. Helen Payne[8], b. ......; m. ......, Chas. Hopkins, Jr., Capt. U. S. A., A. E. F.
    3c. John Carroll Payne, Jr.[8], b. ......; d. ....
    10a. MARTHA ANN HILL[6] (Middleton[5], Isaac[4]), 1842-1920; m., at home of her sister, Mrs. Smith, in Atlanta, Ga., in 1875, William H. Penn, d. Aug., 1920,—two weeks previous to death of his wife. They resided in a beautiful country home between Summerville and Trion, and were one of the wealthiest families in the Co. She was one of Chattooga's first school teachers, many prominent people of the Co. having received instruction from her. She left three daughters:
    1b. Mrs. Bettie Williams, of Atlanta, Ga.;
    2b. Mrs. O. A. Selman, of Summerville, Ga.;
    3b. Miss Mary Penn, of Summerville, Ga.
    2. ISAAC HILL, III[5] (Isaac[4], Isaac[3], Abraham[2], Henry[1]). His father, in his will, 1829, says: "I give to my son Isaac Hill's daughter, Almeda, etc.", and as he makes no bequest to Isaac, and no further mention of his name, he, no doubt, was dead. This Isaac was, I think, very probably the Sheriff of Walton County who was killed in a horse race, or he may have been the early settler of Jasper County, for whom the town of Hillsborough was named. ("His. Col. of Ga. Illustrated", p. 50, by White).
    He m. ......, and had: 1 dau., Almeda[6], a minor in 1829.
    7. ELIZABETH HILL[5] (Isaac[4], Isaac[3], Abraham[2], Henry[1]), b...., d....; m. c. 1806, Joseph Lane, Jr., b. 28 March, 1775; repre-

sented Morgan Co. in Legislature in 1811-'12-'13-'14-'15 and again in 1817; and was State Senator from Morgan Co. in 1819 (Ros. of Ga. Assbly), son of Jesse Lane, b. 3rd July, 1733; died 16 Dec., 1806, aged 73 yrs., a Justice of the Peace of Johnston Co., N. C., 10 Feb'y, 1764, and a Rev'y Soldier (C. R. N. C., Vol. 6, p. 1065; Vol. XIII, pp. 518, 527) and his wife Winnefred Aycock, b. 11 April, 1741; d. 1794. Jesse Lane was the son of Joseph Lane, b. 1710; d. ......, will 29 Nov., 1773; pr. Feb'y, 1774 (son of Joseph (and wife Julian), son of Thomas Lane, of Isle of Wight Co.) and his wife Patience McKinney, dau. of Col. Barnaby McKinnie, Sr., 1673-1740, and his wife Mary (Exum) Ricks, dau. of Judge Jeremiah Exum and his wife Ann Lawrence, dau. of John Lawrence. (See McKinnie and Exum.) Issue:

    1a.   Nancy Hill Lane^6, b. 23 Jan'y, 1808; d. in 1840. (q. v.);

    2a.   Eudocia Lane^6, m. Hampton Wootten Hill, b. 9 Mar., 1800, son of Miles and Tabitha (Pope) Hill. See ante (3, IX, B, P, O), p. 97;

    3a.   Elizabeth Lane^6, m. Frederick Ball, parents of Mrs. O. A. (Amulet Ball) Dunson, of LaGrange, Ga. (D. A. R., Vol. 7, p. 113).

    1a.   NANCY HILL LANE^6 (7, I. C. P. O.), 1808-1840, m. 23 Feb'y, 1823, Judge Walter Terry Colquitt, his 1st wife, jurist, orator, statesman and minister of the Gospel, b. Dec. 27, 1799, d. in 1855, 56 yrs. of age. He was Judge of the Superior Court, Member of Congress, U. S. Senator and General of Militia, and Colquitt County, created in 1856, was named for him. See (Colquitt.) Issue:

    1b.   Alfred Holt Colquitt^7, b. 2 April, 1824; d. 26 March, 1894. (q. v.);

    2b.   Peyton H. Colquitt^7. (q .v.); 3b. Emma Colquitt, d. in 1867. (q. v.); 4b. Elizabeth Colquitt^7, m. Hon. O. B. Ficklen, of Ill.—at the time—a representative in Congress.

    1b.   ALFRED HOLT COLQUITT^7 (1a. 7, I, C. P. O), 1824-1894, was Colonel, 6th Ga. Regt., then Brigadier, and later Major General, C. S. A.—the "Hero of Olustee, or Ocean Pond", fought 20 Feby., 1864; was U. S. Senator, Governor of Ga., and minister of the Gospel.

He m. (I), in 1848, Dorothy Tarver, dau. of *Genl. Hartwell Hill Tarver* (d. in 1852) and his 1st wife, Ann Wimberly, sister of Dr. Henry Wimberly, of Jeffersonville, Ga. (Memoirs of Ga., Vol. 2, p. 945). Gen. Tarver was b. in Brunswick Co., Va., and descended from a family of brothers—all of whom were in the Rev'y War—and 2 sisters. He m. (II) *Harriett Bunn*, dau. of Henry and Nancy Bunn, from N. C.

Henry Colquitt, son of Anthony and Christian Colquitt, and father of *Judge Walter Terry Colquitt*, m. *Nancy (Singleton) Holt*, and after his death she m. (II) the father of Genl. Hartwell Hill Tarver. Nancy Holt was dau. of Simon Holt and his wife, Sarah

Hines, dau. of James Hines, son of Thomas Hines. (L. M. & L. of Ga., by Knight).

Alfred Holt Colquitt[7] m. (II), *Mrs. Sarah Tarver*, dau. of Rev. Hugh Bunn, of Twiggs Co., and widow of Jno. Frederick Tarver, who was the brother of his first wife, Dorothy (Dolly) Tarver.

Issue, 1st mar.: 1c.—Ann Lane Colquitt[8], (q. v.); 2c.—John Frederick Colquitt[8], d.; 3c.—Elizabeth Hill Colquitt[8] (q. v.); 4c.—Harriett Bunn Colquitt[8], single; 5c.—Laura Warren Colquitt[8] (q. v.); 6c.—Dorothy Tarver Colquitt[8] (q. v.); 7c.—Walter Terry Colquitt[8] (q. v.).

1c. *Ann Lane Colquitt*[8] (Alfred[7], 1a, 7, I, C. P. O.), m. *Capt. Thomas Newell*. Issue:

1d. *Alfred Colquitt Newell*[9], m. Ellen Hillyer, dau. of *Judge George Hillyer*. Issue: 1e.—Ann Lane Newell[10]; 2e.—Ellen Newell[10].

2d. *Isaac Newell*[9], *Col., U. S. A*. Single; 3d. Frederick Tarver Newell[9]. Single; 4d. Thomas Newell, Jr.[9] Single; 5d. Mary Newell[9]. Single; 6d. Dorothy Newell[9], m. ...... Shultz; 7d. Elizabeth Colquitt Newell[9]. Single.

3c. *Elizabeth Hill Colquitt*[8] (Alfred[7], Nancy Hill Lane[6], Elizabeth Hill[5], &c.) m., in 1886 or '7, *Brig. Genl. William L. Marshall, Chief of the U. S. Engineering Corps, and of international fame*, d. in Aug., 1920, a *descendant of Chief Justice John Marshall*, of Va. Issue:

1d. Alfred Colquitt Marshall[9], d.; 2d. Maitland Marshall[9], m. Lieut. Commander J. H. Knapp, U. S. N., and had: 1e.—John Marshall Knapp[10]; 2e.—Elizabeth Marshall Knapp[10].

5c. *Laura Warren Colquitt*[8] (Alfred[7]) m. *George P. Howard*, of Atlanta, Ga. Issue:

1d. Alfred Colquitt Howard[9], m. Sarah Eubanks. Issue: 1e.—Alfred Colquitt Howard, Jr.[10]; 2d. George P. Howard, Jr.[9] Single.

6c. *Dorothy Tarver Colquitt*[8] (Alfred[7]) m., 2 June, 1896, *Preston S. Arkwright*, of Atlanta, Ga., b. 24 Feby., 1871, son of Thos. and Martha (Stanley) Arkwright, president of Ga. Rwy. & Power Co. (Ga. & Georgians, Vol. 4, p. 1746 (or 1946), by Knight). Issue:

1d. Dorothy Colquitt Arkwright[9], m. Glenville Giddings, of Atlanta, Ga.; 2d.—Preston Stanley Arkwright, Jr.[9]

7c. *Walter Terry Colquitt II*[8] (Alfred[7]), attorney-at-law, m. Julia Dunning. Issue: 1d.—Walter Terry Colquitt III[9]; 2d.—Julia Dunning Colquitt[9];

2b.—*Peyton H. Colquitt*[7] (Walter T.[6]) was Colonel of 46th Ga. Regt., C. S. A., killed in the battle of Chickamauga, in 1863, at head of his Regt. while gallantly leading charge; m. *Julia Hurt*, of Columbus, Ga., her 1st husband; no issue. She m. (II) *Col. Lee Jordan*, of Macon, Ga., his first wife, and *he* m. (II), *Miss Ila Dunlap*, of Macon, *who*, after his decease, m. (II) *Col. John Dozier Little*, of Atlanta, Ga. No issue.

3b. *Emma Colquitt*⁷ (*Walter T.*⁶) m., in 1850, *Samuel McDonald Carter*, b. in 1826, graduated at Oglethorpe College in 1846, his 1st wife, son of *Col. Farish Carter* (d. in 1861) and wife, *Miss Eliza McDonald*, d. in 1865, *sister* of *Hon. Charles James McDonald*, an *Associate Justice* of the *State Supreme Court*, and *Governor* of the State, 1839 to 1843.

Col. Farish Carter, b. in S. C., came to Baldwin Co., Ga., circa 1809 and for him the town of Cartersville was named. He was the son of Maj. Carter, Adjt. to Col. Clarke, who served in the patriot army during the Revolution and was killed in the battle of Augusta, Ga., in Sept., 1780.

Col. Farish and *Eliza (McDonald) Carter* had:
1. Samuel McDonald Carter; 2. Mary Carter, m. Jonathan Davis, of S. C.; 3. Catherine Carter, m. Dr. John H. Furman, of S. C.; 4. James Carter (Memoirs of Ga., Vol. 2, pp. 597-'8).

3b. *Col. Samuel McDonald* and *Emma*⁷ *(Colquitt) Carter* had five children:

1c. Farish Carter⁸, d. while at Norwood School in Va.; 2c. *Walter Colquitt Carter*⁸ (q. v.); 3c. *Mary Carter*⁸ m. *Judge Benjamin H. Hill, Jr.*, of Atlanta, his 1st wife; d. without issue. He m. (II) *Janie May Hill*. (See 3b, 10a, 2, X, B. P. O. p. 130); 4c. *Kate Carter*⁸, m. *Prof. Robert Emmett Mitchell*, decd., and had: 1d.—Robert Emmett Mitchell, Jr.⁹; 5c. Benjamin F. Carter⁸, m. Lillian Whitman, of Dalton, Ga., and had: 1d.—Mary Hill Carter⁹; 2d.—Emily Cornelia Carter⁹.

2c. WATER COLQUITT CARTER⁸ (3b, 1a, 7, I, C. P. O.) formerly Clerk, U. S. Dist. Court for the Northern Dist. of Ga., and now U. S. Commissioner, Atlanta, Ga., m. Nov. 23, 1898, *Nanny Sue Hill*⁷, dau. of *Col. John M.*⁶, and gr. dau. of *Col. Lodowick M. Hill*⁵. See p. 124, (1b, 2a, 2, X, B, P, O).

Col. Samuel McDonald Carter m. (II) *Sallie Jeter*, dau. of William Lamar Jeter, of Columbus, Ga., and gr. niece of *Mirabeau B. Lamar* and of *Hon. Walter Terry Colquitt*. Issue by 2nd marriage, 5 children:

6c. Emily Colquitt Carter⁸, m. Hal Divine, of Chattanooga, Tenn., and had: 1d.—Rebecca Lamar Divine⁹; 2d.—Blanche Divine⁹.

7c. Sallie Jeter Carter⁸, m. Samuel Barnett; 8c. Pauline Carter⁸, m. J. Campbell Maben; 9c. Samuel McDonald Carter, Jr.⁸; 10c. Eliza Colquitt Carter⁸, m. John Beckwith Horne.

EXCURSUS: *COLQUITT*.

Hon. Walter Terry Colquitt, 1799-1855, m. (II), in 1841, *Mrs. Alphia B. Fountelroy, neé Todd*, sister of the late H. W. Todd, of West Point, Ga., and *aunt* of *Dr. J. Scott Todd*, decd., of Atlanta, Ga. She lived only a few months. He m. (II), 11 Jany., 1842, Harriet Malinda Ross, dau. of Luke and Mary (Grimes) Ross, of Macon, Ga., her 1st husband, b. 21 Feby., 1823; (she m. (II) Dr.

Jesse Boring), d. 1889, at Anniston, Ala. Issue, 4 children, among them being:
 1. *Hugh Haralson Colquitt, Capt., C. S. A.*, on staff of Gen. A. H. Colquitt; m. Miss ...... Walton, who d. in 1920;
 2. Walter Wellborn Colquitt, m. Lilla Neyle Habersham, and had:
 (1) Lilla Neyle Colquitt; (2) Harriet Ross Colquitt; (3) William Neyle Colquitt; (4) Jos. Clay Habersham Colquitt; (5) Anna Habersham Colquitt; (6) Walter Wellborn Colquitt, Jr., (7) Maybelle Habersham Colquitt, d. (His. & Gen. of the Habersham Family, p. 25; "The House of Plant", p. 148).

In a Poll of Freeholders at an election of Burgesses in Essex Co., Va., on the 6th day of May, 1761, the names of John Colquitt and James Colquitt are given. (Essex Co. Deed Book 29, p. 1).

D. THEOPHILUS HILL[3] (Abraham[2], Henry[1]), b. pro. a. 1740; d. pro. a. 1825; m. 3 Sept., 1762, *Teresa Thomas*, in Edgecombe Co., N. C. (Ms. records of Edgecombe Co. marriage bonds in keeping of the Historical Society at State Capitol, Raleigh, N. C.). In the will of his father, dated 18 April, 1760, in Chowan Co., N. C., is the following clause:

"Item. I give and bequeath my son *Theophilus Hill* the land and plantation I bought of Daniel Pugh containing two hundred acres to him and his heirs forever, *also* a negro man called Densa, a negro boy called Peter, a negro boy called Charles, one feather bed and furniture, *one Silver cup, two silver spoons*, one large iron pott, Twenty-five pounds of the best Peuter, one small Iron Pott, one iron Grey mare *after my wife's marriage or death*, to him and his heirs forever. Also I *give him all my land at the point* to him and his heirs forever". The limitation "after my wife's marriage or death" seemingly applies only to the personality. But as both *he* and his brothers *Henry* and *Abraham* sold their realty in 1763, obviously with the view of removing from the Co., it is altogether probable that their mother died prior thereto. (See ante pp. 53-'54). By tradition he is represented as having removed first to San Domingo, and later, because of an insurrection of the negroes, to South Carolina. That he was very wealthy, owned a large number of slaves, all of which he lost. At a later period he with his family, excepting his son Lodowick, removed to the Spanish possessions, then called East Florida, and settled on the St. Johns River, where he resided till his death. Among the effects of his son Lodowick was found an old newspaper headed "St. John's River, East Fla., 1788". His wife, whether before or after his death not known—time not stated—revisited S. C., when, it is said, her grandchildren were charmed and greatly impressed by her personality. Her dignity, mien, conduct and conversation were indubitable evidences of high birth and of rearing in an environment of culture and refinement.

James R. Hill, of Fruit Hill, S. C., in a letter Feb. 19, 1896, wrote: "My father was named *Theophilus, gr. father Lodowick and gr. gr. father Theophilus.* I understood from my father that his gr. father was a planter on the Island of San Domingo and at the time of the insurrection of the negroes he got off and settled in the lower part of S. C., but he and all his family, but gr. father Lodowick moved to East Fla. [at that time all Fla. east of the Apalachicola River was called "East Fla."]. I find a paper headed St. John's River, East Fla., 1788. I think gr. Pa Lod was only son he had. *He had 4 daus.*—one m. Dewitt, another m. Bellama. I have forgotten about the others".

Dr. J. Walter Hill, of Edgefield, S. C., on 17 Feby., 1896, wrote: "My gr. gr. father was *Scotch-Irish*, came 1st to Va., later to S. C., and finally to East Fla. He was very wealthy .... lost his property, land & slaves. His son, gr. father Lodowick, returned to S. C."

Much information relating to the family was given the compiler about the same time by Dr. Lodowick T. Hill, of Abbeville, John B. Hill, Clk. of Ct., Edgefield, Benjamin R. Hill, of 96, S. C., and several others.

D. *Theophilus*[3] and *Teresa (Thomas) Hill* had: I—Lodowick Hill[4], b. in 1765; d. 27 July, 1822 (q. v.); II—A dau.[4]—name not known—m. ...... DeWitt; III—Ann Hill[4], b. 6. June, 1787, in St. Augustine; d. in 1849, in St. Augustine (q. v.); IV and V—Two daus.[4], N. R.

I. *Lodowick Hill*[4] (Theop.[3], Abr.[2], Hy.[1]), 1765-1822, "was a private in Capt. Isaac Ross' troop in the 2nd Regt. State Dragoons, commanded by Col. Charles Myddleton, commenced service May, 1781, time of service 10 months. Pay and bounty in negroes, one grown negro and ¼ small negro. Pay Roll dated April 18, 1872. See ("Documents relating to the history of S. C. during the Revolutionary War", p. 44, by Salley).

"Lodowick Hill Oct. 1, 1784, 97£ 7S. *Bounty* due him for service as Serjeant in Ross' Troop, Myddleton's Reg., Sumpter's Brigade from *1 April 1782* to date hereof.
Prin. 105£ 15. 0
Int.   7   8 0

("Stub Entries to Indents for Rev'y Claims Book L-N, p. 180-'1", by Salley).

His P. O. address in 1822 was "Richardson's Tavern", Edgefield Dist., S. C.—a letter to him, of that date, from his cousin Wylie Hill, of Wilkes Co., Ga., is in the possession of the compiler of these notes.

He m., in 1785, *Miss Susan Grigsby*, b. 1771 (who lived near Mt. Willing, S. C.), dau. of *Enoch Grigsby* and his wife, *Susan Butler*, sister of *Capt. James Butler*—one of the victims of Bill Cunningham and his "braves"—and aunt of *Genl. William Butler*, of the Rev'y War. (His. of Edgefield, S. C., p. 96, by Chapman).

AND ALLIED FAMILIES 165

They settled on Indian Creek, Edgefield, now Saluda Co., near old Red Bank Church.

Issue—record taken from family Bible of his son Theophilus⁵: 1.—Mary (Polly) Hill⁵, b. 3 Aug., 1786; m. ...... Payne; 2.—Teresa Hill⁵, b. 27 Dec., 1787; m. (I) ...... Lewis; m. (II) Capt. Bryant Dean and had: Col. A. B. Dean⁶ and Capt. Theophilus Dean⁶, who lived, in 1891, at Mount Enon, S. C.; 3.—*Theophilus Hill*⁵, b. 10 Feby., 1790; d. 5 Dec., 1852 (q. v.); 4.—James Hill⁵, b. 21 May, 1792, N. R.; 5.—Sarah Hill⁵, b. 18 Feby., 1796; m. .... Sanchez, moved to Fla.; 6.—*Henry Hampton Hill*⁵, b. 22 March, 1798; d. 11 Nov., 1857 (q. v.); 7.—Rhydon Hill⁵, b. 24 Feby., 1800; m. ......, moved to Miss.; had a son, practiced medicine in Macon, Miss., who was a Surgeon in the Civil War; 8.—Jonathan M. Hill⁵, b. 19 Nov., 1803; m. ...... (pro. Lucinda Bond, sis. of Martha Sarah Bond, d. 1847), had son James Hill⁶—father and son lived a good while with James Lodowick Hill, son of Hy. Hampton Hill, then moved to Ala., settling near Montgomery, and later to Tex., near Galveston, where both were killed in 1856 by Mexicans; 9.—William B. Hill⁵, b. 14 Nov., 1806, N. R.

3. *Theophilus Hill*⁵ (Lodowick⁴, Theop⁵.³, Abr.², Hy.¹), 1790-1852, m. 22 Jany., 1819, *Susanna Richardson*, b. 19 April, 1801; d. 2 Feby., 1859, *dau.* of *David Richardson*, of Richardsonville, Edgefield Co., and his wife, *Frances Williams*, and had: 1a.—Lodowick Hill⁶, b. 16 Oct., 1820; d. 3 July, 1873; m. Mary Griffin, no issue; 2a.—Rhydon Grigsby Hill⁶, b. 7 March, 1823; d. 1 May, 1866 (q. v.); 3a.—Henry Hill⁶, b. 30 Aug., 1825 (q. v.); 4a.—James Richardson Hill⁶, b. 24 Jany., 1828; d. 1896, unm.; 5a.—Martha Elizabeth Hill⁶, b. 17 Mch., 1830; d. ......; m. Thomas Maynard, moved to Ga., left chn.; 6a.—William Hill⁶, b. 4 Oct., 1832; m. Jennie King, and had: 1b.—William Hill⁷; 7a.—*John Walter Hill*⁶, b. 28 Oct., 1834; d. 13 March, 1902; m. (I) *Mattie (Martha) Wardlaw*; m. (II) *Susan Brunson*. He left no chn. but legally adopted his sis. Susan Frances Pearce's baby girl at her mother's death; 8a.—Susan Frances Hill⁶, b. 7 Jany., 1837; d. June, 1873 (q. v.); 9a.—Thomas Theophilus Hill⁶, b. 29 March, 1839; d. 27 June, 1862—killed at "the crater" at Petersburg, Va.; 10a.—Benjamin Hill⁶, m. Jennie Lipscomb, of Ninety Six, S. C., moved to Ga., where his wife and children are now, 1921, living.

2a. *Rhydon Grigsby Hill*⁶ (Theop.⁵, Lod.⁴, Theop.³, Hy.¹), 1823-1866, m. *Elizabeth Smyly*, b. 2 March, 1827; d. 6 Feby., 1877, dau. of *James Smyly* and his wife, *Grace Coates*, and had 3 chn.: 1b.—Henry Hill⁷, m. Maggie Tompkins, dau. of John Warren Tompkins and his wife, Elizabeth Eleanor Allen, and had 4 sons and a dau.: 1c.—Roger T. Hill⁸, m. Miss Sallie Dunovant; 2c.—Jack Tompkins Hill⁸, m. Addie ......, and had: 1d.—Harry Hill⁹; 2d.—Margaret Hill⁹; 3c.—Carl Hill⁸, unm.; 4c.—John Walter Hill II⁸, unm.; 5c.—Nellie Hill⁸, m. Osman Williams, no issue; 2b.—

Grace Hill[7], eldest dau. of Rhydon[6], d. at 16 unm.; 3b.—Ina Hill[7], d. in 1920, unm.

3a.—*Henry Hill*[6] (Theop.[5], Lodk.[4], Theop.[3], Abr.[2], Hy.[1]), b. 30 Aug., 1825; d. 1896, aged 70 years; m. ......, and had: 1b.—*Dr. Lodowick T. Hill*[7], of Abbeville, S. C.; 2b.—Tabor Hill, of Greenwood, S. C.; 3b.—Mrs. Susan Turner[7], of Greenwood, S. C.; 4b.—George Hill[7], of Ninety-Six, S. C.

8a. Susan Frances Hill[6], y[t] dau. of Theop[s] and *Susan R. Hill*, 1837-1873, m. *George W. Pearce*, of Bainbridge, Ga., b. 1824; d. 1873—both d. of yellow fever—and had 4 chn.: 1b.—*Thomas Robert Pearce*[7], b. 7 Aug., 1862; d. 11 June, 1897; m. *Mariana Long*, dau. of *Dr. Moses Long* and *Carrie Jones Long*, and had: 1c.—George Hill Pearce[8], b. 28 July, 1889, unm.; 2c.—Samuel Brady Pearce[8]—girl—b .25 April, 1891, single; 3c.—Thomas Robert Pearce, Jr.[8], b. 26 Sept., 1895, unm.; 2b.—*John Walter Pearce*[7], b. 1863; m. 1896, *Bettie Watson*, dau. of John C. and Bettie Watson, and had: 1c.—Myra Watson Pearce[8], b. 1897; 2c.—Walter Hill Pearce[8], b. 1899; d. aged 15 yrs.; 3c.—John C. Pearce[8], b. 1902; d. Nov., 1921; 3b.—George Pearce[7], b. 1868; m. 1897, Birdie Ream, d. 1910; issue: 1c.—Edith Pearce[8], b. 1898; 2c.—Carroll Pearce[8], b. 1900; 3c.—George W. Pearce, Jr.[8], b. . . . . ; 4b.—*Mattie Sue (Tweetee) Pearce*[7], only 3 mos. old when her parents d. in 1873, *was adopted by her uncle, Dr. J. Walter Hill* and his wife, *Martha Wardlaw*, and thereafter bore the name of *Tweetee Hill;* m. 28 Oct., 1896, Joseph H. Cantalon and had: 1c.—Walter H. Cantalon[8], b. 23 Aug., 1897, who m. 16 Nov., 1921, Annie Wilson, dau. of Lide Wilson and his wife, Alice Bailey.

2. *Henry Hampton Hill*[5] (Lodowick[4], Theops.[3]), 1778-1857, m. 19 July, 1817, *Martha Sarah (Bond - Daniel) Spann*, b. 13 March, 1794; d. 25 Oct., 1870, in her 77th year, at the home of her son Dr. Lovick Hill. She m. (I) *Jesse Daniel* and had 3 chn.: a.—John Daniel m. and had chn.; b.—Walter Daniel, d. unm.; c.—Rev. Thomas Sumter Daniel, of the M. E. Church, b. 3 Dec., 1814; d. 188—, unm.; *m. (II), Henry Spann* and had: d.—Henry Russell Spann, b. 2 Oct., 1818; d. 2 May, 1858; m. Ellen . . . . After the Civil War the widow and children moved from Edgefield, S. C. to La.

2. *Henry Hampton* and *Martha Sarah (Bond - Daniel, Spann) Hill* had: 1a.—Whitman Robinson Hill[6], b. 31 May, 1822; d. 10 Feby., 1849 (q. v.) ; 2a.—James Lodowick Hill[6], b. 18 Jany., 1824; d. 19 Jany., 1867 (q. v.) ; 3a.—Florella Pauline Hill[6], b. 12 Jany., 1826; d. 28 July, 1895 (q. v.) ; 4a.—Dr. William Mays Hill[6], b. 14 Sept., 1828; d. 26 Oct., 1866; m. Mary Crawford—no chn.; 5a.—Dr. Lovic Sanchez Hill[6], b. 30 May, 1833; d. ......, 1919 (?) (q. v.) ; 6a.—Susan Abigail Hill[6], b. 9 Aug., 1835; d. Saturday, Aug. 3, 1887, at her niece's, Flora Trammell, LaFayette, Chambers Co., Ala., never married. All of the above b. in Edgefield Dist., S. C.

AND ALLIED FAMILIES 167

1a. *Whitman Robinson Hill*[6] (Henry Hampton[5], Lodowick[1]), 1822-1849, m. 6 June, 1843, *Sarah Anne Verdelle*, of Elberton, Ga., b. 23 Nov., 1824; d. 29 Sept., 1906. Issue: 1b.—Sarah Florella Hill[7], b. 25 July, 1844; d. in inf.; 2b.—Martha Ellen Hill[7], b. 4 Jany., 1847; d. 1920; m., in 1882, Stephen H. Fortson, of Elbert Co., 2nd wife (Mems. of Ga., Vol. 1, p. 630) and had: 1c.—Stephen Tallulah Fortson[8], b. 1885; m. Dec., 1903, Sidney A. Hunt, and they had: 1d.—Stephen Fortson[9], b. 1906; 2d.—Sidney Fortson[9], b. 1914; 3b.—*Tallulah Whitman Hill*[7], b. 10 Jany., 1849; m. (I) Dr. Shiland, of Phila., Pa.; m. (II), 14 Dec., 1875, *George Thomas Fortson*, b. 1 Aug., 1850; d. 10 May, 1918, and had: 1c.—*Sarah Pauline Fortson*[8], b. 11 Aug., 1878; m. 20 Dec., 1911, *William Duncan Gray;* 2c.—Elizabeth Hanson Fortson[8], b. 29 Aug., 1880; m. 18 April, 1916, Zack Clark Hayes, Elberton, Ga., and had: 1d.—Tallulah Hanson Hayes[9], b. 23 Aug., 1917; 3c.—Whitman Hill Fortson[8], b. 17 June, 1882, address Box 1620, Charlotte, N. C.; 4c.—Lovick George Fortson[8], b. 21 Jany., 1884, address Healey Bldg., Atlanta, Ga.; 5c.—Ellie Juanita Fortson[8], b. 3 Oct., 1887.

MRS. SARAH ANNE (VERDELLE) HILL was a woman of charming personality, of genuine culture and highly educated; reared in a home of affluence, surrounded by luxury and enjoyed every advantage and opportunity of the ideal ante-bellum life of that period. She was a true standard-bearer of everything that constitutes noble womanhood. She joined the Methodist Episcopal Church, South, at the age of 16, lived a consistent life and died in the blessed assurance of salvation by faith in the merits of a crucified Redeemer. Her gr. father came to Ama. with Gen. LaFayette. (Extracts from tribute by J. N. Wall).

2a. *James Lodowick Hill*[6] (Henry Hampton[5], Lodowick[1]), 1824-1867, m. in 1842, *Eliza Holden*, d. 1873, or '4. Issue: 1b.—Martha Hughes[7], called Mattie, Hill, b. 1843; d. 12 May, 1898 (q. v.); 2b.—Mary Bones Hill[7], b. 1845; d. 3, or 5, Feby., 1903 (q. v.); 3b.—*John Bones Hill*[7], b. 4 Nov., 1847; d. 22 Feby., 1914 (q. v.); 4b.—John Holden Hill[7], b. 1849, unm.; 5b.—Maria Magrand Hill[7], b. 1851 (q. v.); 6b.—Henry Lodowick K. Hill[7], b. 1 April, 1853; d. Feby., 1916 (q. v.); 7b.—Hughes H. Hill[7], b. 1855; d. 14 Feby., 1901, (q. v.).

1b. *Martha Hughes (Mattie) Hill*[7] (Jas. Lodowick[6]), 1843-1898, m. Felix Lake, decd., and had: 1c.—George[8], m. ......; 2c.—Jane[8], decd., m. Dr. J. H. Carmichael; 3c.—Elizabeth[8], decd., m. Dr. J. H. Carmichael; 4c.—Henry[8], m. Miss Hammond; 5c.—Hughes[8]; 6c.—Martha[8], m. Daniel Strother.

2b. *Mary Bones Hill*[7] (James Lodowick[6]), 1845-1903, m. A. Baron Holmes, of Charleston, S. C., decd., and had: 1c.—James H.[8], m. Septimia Towner, Charleston, S. C.; 2c.—A. B. H., Jr[8], m. (I) Miss Campbell; m. (II), ..., Charleston, S. C.; 3c.—Eliza H.[8], m. J. E. Agnew, Columbia, S. C.; 4c.—Francis S. H.[8], m. ....,

Macon, Ga.; 5c.—George Lee H.[s], m. Elizabeth Falk, Charleston, S. C.; 6c.—Harleston H.[s], unm.; 7c.—Hal H.[s], decd.

3b. *John Bones Hill*[7] (James Lodowick[6]), 1847-1914, m., 22 Dec., 1870, *Sadie Johnson*, of Johnston, S. C. Issue: 1c.—Eliza H.[s], m. William Rudy; 2c.—Lou[s], decd., m. Ed Mims; 3c.—*Elizabeth* Hill[s], m. *John G. Mobley*[s], of Johnston, S. C.; 4c.—Henry Hughes[s], m. Martha Mims; 5c.—Daisy[s], m. Sam Nicholson; 6c.—Marion[s], decd, m. (I) L...... (?) Jones; m. (II) E. A. Childress; 7c.—Warren[s], decd.; 8c.—Maria F.[s], m. John Rainford.

5b. *Maria Magrand Hill*[7] (James Lodowick[6]), b. 1851, m. *James D. Fraser*, of Winnsboro, S. C. Atlanta newspaper notice: "*James D. Fraser*, aged 60 years, a gallant Confederate soldier, d. at 2 o'clock yesterday at a private sanatorium. He was for a number of years an employee of the So. Bell Telephone Co. and is survived by his wife and several children. During the Civil War Mr. Fraser, who rose to the rank of Lieut., served in the 1st So. Carolina Cavalry under Gen. Wade Hampton and was engaged in some of the most desperate conflicts of the war. . . . . His body will be taken today to his old home in Edgefield, S. C., for interment."

Issue: 1c.—Jane H. Fraser[s]; 2c.—*Margaret R. Fraser*[s], m. *Thomas B. Bennett*, of Charleston, S. C.; 3c.—Eliza H. Fraser[s], m. I. W. Hume; 4c.—Mary H. Fraser[s], d. in inf.; 5c.—Malcom Douglas Fraser[s], d. in inf.; 6c.—*Hesse Crawford Fraser*[s], m. *William Love Richardson* and lives at 224 Crew St., Atlanta, Ga.

6b. *Henry Lodowick K. Hill*[7] (James Lodowick[6]), 1853-1916, m. Rosa Law, decd., and had: 1c.—John B. Hill[s]; 2c.—Law Hill[s]; 3c.—Roberta Law Hill[s], m. ......, d. ......; 4c.—Rosa L. Hill[s]; Baron H. Hill[s].

7b. *Hughes H. Hill*[7] (James Lodowick[6]), 1855-1901, m. Roberta Law, and had: 1c.—James Hill[s]; 2c.—Hal Hill[s]; 3c.—Rosa Hill; 4c.—Fanny Wright Hill[s].

3a. *Florella Pauline Hill*[4] (Henry Hampton[5], Lodowick[4]), 1826-1895, m. 23 Dec., 1845, *Dr. John William Cooper*, b. Edgefield, S. C., 27 June, 1821; d. 4 Dec.,1905. He received degree of M.D. from S. C. Medical College, Charleston, S. C., in 1844. *Col. James (Duke) Williams*, of King's Mountain Rev'y fame, was his great uncle. He lived, during the Civil War, at Fredonia, Chambers Co., Ala. With the first call for volunteers he joined a Co. of the 14th Ala. Regt., but when official list of the Co. was being prepared, a committee was sent with the request that Dr. Cooper remain at home to be the attending physician for the aged parents, wives and children of the enlisted men. Throughout the war he was faithful to the trust imposed. Night and day, in sunshine and storm, he ministered to the sick, wounded, and needy families, both medicinally and materially. His loyalty to the Confederate cause was recognized by the State authorities". (Mrs. J. P. (Sue Cooper) Barrow).

Dr. J. Scott Todd, an eminent physician of Atlanta, Ga., on 22 Oct., 1909, in a Certificate made to the gr. children, said: "I was acquainted with and lived near *Dr. Jno. W. Cooper*, of Chambers Co., Ala. He was a man of great probity of character, beloved by his neighbors, faithful and loyal to the Confederate cause. . . . . The help which Dr. Cooper rendered to the wives and children of the Confed. soldiers was as necessary, and involved almost as much danger, fidelity and self-sacrifice as did that of being at the front".

Issue: 1b.—Mary Pauline Cooper[7], b. 30 Sept., 1846; d. 13 Oct., 1851; 2b.—James Astley Cooper[7], b. 3 Sept. 1848; d. 16 Sept., 1870, in Charlottesville, while a student at the University of Va. He was presented a testimonial by the Temperance Society of the University for being the most exemplary member of the student body; 3b.—Whitman Hill Cooper[7], b. 4 Aug., 1854; d. 4 Aug., 1855, and 4b.—Washington Williams Cooper[7] (twins), b. 4 Aug., 1854; d. 8 Sept., 1919, at his dau.'s, Mrs. G. C. Dixon, in Indianapolis, Ind. He attended Howard College, Marion, Ala., m. 20 Dec., 1883, Effie Eighmy, of Springboro, Penna.; engaged successfully in business in Shirley, Ind., and Brownsville, Tex. Issue: 1c.—Pauline Hill[8], b. in 1884, in Chambers Co., Ala.; m. George C. Dixon, of Indianapolis, Ind., and has son: 1d.—Bonn Dixon[9], b. 3 April, 1916; 2c.—Sylvia Cooper[8], d. in Springborough, Penna., 17 March, 1910, c. 12 yrs. of age; 5b.—*Adelaide Beatrice Cooper*[8], b. 11 June, 1851; d. 30 May, 1903, reared in Chambers Co., Ala., graduated from W. P. Female College, 1869; from Baltimore Female College, under Dr. Brooks, June, 1870; went to Staunton, Va., to perfect herself in German and French, and while at school there met Gen. R. E. Lee, when on a visit to the school, who learning she was from Ala., praised very highly the Ala. soldiers. She m., 15 Sept., 1880, Isaac Thomas Morgan, of Dudleville, Chambers Co., Ala., b. 10 Feby., 1835; d. Dec., 1904. On 16 July, 1861, he joined Co. B, 4th Ala. Regt., Blee's Brigade. C. S. A. Issue: 1c.—Charles Lewis Morgan[8], b. 11 Oct., 1881; d. May, 1883; 2c.—John Frank Morgan[8], b. 8 Oct., 1883; 3c.—Celestia Adelaide Morgan[8], b. 14 Feby., 1888; m. 10 Nov., 1915, Lewis Coleman Benson, b. 29 Oct., 1888, son of Dr. F. W. Benson; was a student in the Electrical Engineering Dept. of Ga. Tech. and finished his Junior year; lives in Jacksonville, Fla. They have one dau.: 1d.—Adelaide Benson[9], b. 9 May, 1917.

6b. *Sue C. Cooper*[7], b. Sunday, 15 April, 1860, in Chambers Co., Ala.; m. 23 Dec., 1879, by Rev. Dr. W. C. Bledsoe, *John Pliny Barrow*, b. in Chambers Co., Ala., 3 April, 1848; d. in Atlanta 31 Dec., 1915, interred in Pine Wood Cemetery, West Point, Ga. son of *John Thomas Barrow* (and his wife, *Vira Anderson Standifer*, of Jasper Co., Ga., b. 11 Jany., 1812; d. 17 Feby., 1892), son of *William Barrow* and his wife, *Rebecca Heath*. Issue: 1c.—Lewis A. Barrow[8], b. 8 Nov., 1880; m. 23 Dec., 1901, Miss Berchea York, of Rockmart, Ga. They have: 1d.—*Lewis Barrow, Jr.*[9], b. 11 Nov.

1902; 2d.—Lillian Barrow⁹, b. 21 Dec., 1904; 3d.—Ralph Barrow⁹, b. 7 Oct., 1907; 4d.—Frances Barrow⁹, b. 14 Jany., 1910; 5d.—Virginia Barrow⁹, b. 7 April, 1912; 2c.—*Grover Barrow*⁸, b. 1 July, 1884, joined U. S. Navy Aug. 20, 1901; 3c.—*Reuben Barrow*⁸, b. 17 Jany., 1889; d. in 1889; 4c.—*Azile Barrow*⁸, b. 4 Sept., 1893, entered Shorter College, Rome, Ga., in 1914, remained two years, then went to University of Chicago and received *the Ph.B. degree* in 1917; m. 22 Dec. 1917, *Harry Winkler*, only child of Frederick Winkler and his wife, Barbara Van Ruch, of New Phila., Ohio, b. in Omaha, Neb., 28 Jany., 1894; in 1917 joined Co. M 329th Inf. Regt., at Camp Sherman, O.; selected as one of three from this Co. to attend 3rd O. T. C.; on 1st June, 1918, commissioned 2nd Lieut.; Oct. 9, 1918, transferred to A. G. D. Dept., served Asst. Camp Adj., Camp Sevier, S. C., to time of his discharge, April 5, 1919. He *graduated* with *B.S. degree* from the University of Chicago in Sept., 1921, and was elected a member of the *National honorary Society, Phi-Beta-Kappa;* 5c.—FLORELLA HILL BARROW⁸, b. 16 March, 1897, *graduated* from the Girls' High School of Atlanta, and later from the *Atlanta Normal Training School.* She is now, 1922, *training teacher* in the Atlanta Normal Training School at Lee Street School; has figured prominently in Sunday School and Camp work, being a *Counsellor* for 2 years at Camp Dixie for Girls, Clayton, Ga.

7b. *Flora Lee Cooper*⁷ (Florella Pauline⁶, Henry Hampton⁵), b. 9 Feby., 1864; d. 24 May, 1917, in Atlanta, Ga.; m. 10 Nov., 1880, Dr.*William Oliver Trammell*, b. 25 April, 1857; d. 30 Jany., 1921, son of Dr. Frank Trammell, of Lafayette, Chambers Co., Ala., and his wife, Olive Melton. Dr. W. O. Trammell was the founder and proprietor of the Trammell Drug Store, in Atlanta, which since his death is conducted by his sons, Willard and Ralph. Issue: 1c.—John Cooper Trammell⁸, b. 21 Aug., 1881; m. (I), 20 May, 1902, Mamie Wise, d. 24 April, 1907, and had: 1d.—Charles Cooper Trammell⁹, b. 8 Feby., 1903; m. (II), 11 Sept., 1917, Elizabeth Stearns, b. 3 April, 1888, d. Sept., 1921; 2c.—Alwin Trammell⁸, b. 1882, d. 20 July, 1903; 3c.—William Ralph Trammell⁸, b. 12 Dec., 1885; 4c.—Willard Oliver Trammell⁸, b. 24 Dec., 1891, recd. training at Camp Wheeler in World War; m. 30 June, 1918, Thelma Bradley, b. 23 July, 1898; 5c.—Ollie Trammell⁸, b. 7 Sept., 1893; m. 24 May, 1911, Hartwell Lester Moseley, of Cuba and Mobile, Ala., a graduate with A.B. degree from Furman University, Greenville, S. C., and had: 1d.—Robert Lester Moseley⁹, b. in Cuba, 11 Jany., 1914; 2d.—Mary Olive Moseley⁹, b. in Cuba, 10 May, 1918; 3d.—William Ralph Moseley⁹, b. in Selma, Ala., 7 Aug., 1920; 6c.—Addie Melton Trammell⁸, b. 5 Nov., 1897, graduated from Woodberry School, of Atlanta; m. 9 May, 1919, Henry Eli Watkins, b. 22 Dec., 1895, received E.E. degree from Ga. Tech.; entered service 4 Sept., 1917, at the Receiving Ship, Norfolk, Va., then put on U. S. S. C. 191, and honorably discharged at N. O., 19 July, 1919. Issue: 1d.—*Annice Watkins*⁹, *b. 29 Jany., 1922.*

5a. Dr. *Lovick Sanchez Hill*[6] (Henry Hampton[5], Lodowick[4]), 1833-1919, was a Lieut. in Co. A, *22nd* (?) 4th So. Carolina Regt., C. S. A., and later Surgeon for same Regt.; m. (I), Sophie Hughes; m. (II), Kate Griffin. Issue by 1st, none by 2nd, mar.: 1b.—Kate Hill[7], m. Jim Mimms and had: 1c.—Mattie Mimms[8], m. . . . . Hill; 2c.—Lura Mimms[8], m. . . . . Day; 3c.—Sophie Mimms[8]; 4c.—Katharine Mimms[8]; 2b.—Mamie Hill[7], m. . . . . Green and had one son; 3b.—Whitman Hill[7]; 4b.—Robbie Hill[7]; 5b.—Hal Hill[7], unm.

III. ANN HILL[4] (Theop.[3], Abr.[2], Hy.[1]), 1787-1849, m. (I) *Samuel Williams*, of St. Augustine; m. (II) *Gen. Joseph M. Hernandez*, of Fla.

Issue by 1st mar., 4 children: 1.—William Henry Williams[5]; 2.—Eliza Williams[5] (q. v.); 3.—Samuel Hill Williams[5]; 4.—John Theophilus Williams[5].

Issue by 2nd mar., 6 children: 5.—Anita Hernandez[5], m. Kingsley B. Gibbs, of St. Augustine; 6.—Ellen T. Rufina Hernandez[5], m. A. H. Walker, of N. O., 1st wife; 7.—Maria Josepha Hernandez[5], m. A. H. Walker, of N. O., his 2nd wife—after death of her sister; 8.—John Gaspur Hernandez[5], never married; 9.—Martin Edward Hernandez[5], m. his cousin, Anita Hernandez, Matanzas, Cuba—their children all live in Cuba; 10.—*Dorothea Fredrica Ignicia Hernandez*[5], m. *Gen. W. S. Walker* and had:

1a.—*Anita Walker*[6], m. *E. L. Anderson*, of Ga.; 2a.—Marion Walker[6], d. in childhood; 3a.—*Lucia Duncan Walker*[6], m. *Henry C. Peeples*, of Atlanta, Ga., a prominent atty.-at-law; 4a.—Dora Hernandez Walker[6], m. J. Archer Smith, of Fla., 1st wife; 5a.—Louisa Hernandez Walker[6]. m. her bro.-in-law, widower, J. Archer Smith, 2nd wife; 6a.—William Stephens Walker[6], m. (I) Miss Geer, of Penn.; m. (II) Miss Owen, of Ga.

2. *Eliza Williams*[5] (Ann[4], Theop.[3], Abr.[2], Hy.[1]) m. (I) *Col. Bailey*, of West Fla.; m. (II), *Gen. Bellamy*, a large planter of West Fla. *Issue by 1st mar.*: 1a.—Jack Bailey[6]; 2a.—Eugenia Bailey[6], m. John Mays, of West Fla., d. circa 1919,—she still living, 1922; 3a.—Virginia Bailey[6], m. Ben Tucker of . . . . , and had several children.

Issue by 2nd mar.: 4a.—Sarah Bellamy[6], m. Col. Cartenay Smith, of S. C.; 5a.—Barton Bellamy[6]; 6a.—Josephine Bellamy[6], m. Dr. Epps, of Va.; 7a.—Victoria Bellamy[6], m. Mr. Pelot, of N. Y.

(Copy).

Atlanta, Ga., Mar. 7, 1868.

Dr. Lodowick Hill,
My Dear Sir

I take the liberty to address you on a subject of genealogy in which I hope you take some interest. My wife is a descendant of Theophilus Hill of Edgefield Dist. S. C. Her mother was Ann Hill, the daughter of Lodowick Hill, who was the son of Theophilus. A branch of the S. C. family emigrated to Georgia of which one of the representatives is Col. Lodowick Hill of Wilkes County. A branch emigrated to Florida of which my wife is a descendant. Miss Ann Hill of Florida married twice. Her second husband was Gen. J. M. Hernandez of whom my wife was the youngest daughter. I will be obliged to you for any information you may be pleased to give me of the history of the family, particularly as to the origin of Theophilus the original preogenitor. In order to identify myself I would state that I was the officer who during the late War commanded for two years the third Military District on the Coast of South Carolina with my Headquarters at Pocotaligo. I have made so many friends in South Carolina that I would be glad to establish this claim of my children to a South Carolina ancestry and particularly to that nest of game cocks Edgefield District.

(Signed) Very respectfully,
Yr. obt. Servt,
W. S. Walker.

Extracts from Article in Atlanta Constitution, June 8, 1899:
"Gen. W. S. Walker, d. 7 June, 1899, son of Judge Duncan Walker, of Miss., son of Judge Jonathan Walker, of Penn. He was reared by his uncle Robert J. Walker, Secretary of the Treasury under President Polk and later Governor of Kansas, during the stirring times when it was called "Bleeding Kansas". He graduated with first honors in his 17th year at Georgetown College, and later attended for a short time the Princeton law college, but health failing accepted an appointment on the coast survey, where he received two gold medals for saving lives from the sea. Was appointed Lieut. and served in the Mexican War. At Chapultepec won renown by being first to scale the enemy's breastworks, in which he was closely followed by his commanding officer, to whom he chivalrously yielded the honor to cut down the Mexican flag. He entered the Confederate service as Capt. of infantry, in 1862 commissioned as Colonel, and on 22 Oct. of that year, while in command at Pocotaligo defeated and routed a largely superior enemy force who were attempting to seize the Charleston and Savannah railroad. Eight days later, on 30 Oct., 1862, was promoted to brigadier general and for two years commanded the third Military Dist. on the coast of S. C. On 20 May, 1864, was wounded in the foot, a portion of which had to be amputated.

Gen. W. S. Walker m. Miss Dora Hernandez, the youngest dau. of Gen. Joseph M. Hernandez and his wife Ann (Hill) Hernandez, her 2nd husband, who was the dau. of Lodowick Hill, 1765-1822, of S. C., and his wife Susan Grigsby. Gen. Walker was survived by his wife and 4 children, viz.: Mrs. Henry C. Peeples, Mrs. E. L. Anderson, Mr. W. S. Walker, Jr., and Mrs. Archer Smith, of Madison, Fla. [Ann Hill was dau. of Theophilus and Teresa (Thomas) Hill and sister of Lodowick.]

E. SARAH HILL[3] (Abraham[2], Henry[1]) m. c. 1756, Jacob Hunter, of Chowan Co., N. C., son of Isaac Hunter. Her father, in his will,

18 April, 1760, *names her* and her daughter, *Leah Hunter*. Issue: I.—Isaac Hunter[1]; II.—*Leah Hunter*[4] (q. v.); III.—Elizabeth Hunter[4].

II. *Leah Hunter*[4] m. 6 Jany., 1772, *Seth Riddick* (N. C. H. & G. Reg., 1-2-242; 2-1-52 and 69).

"ISAAC HUNTER moved from Lancaster Co., Penn., to Chowan Co., N. C., c. 1720; his will dated 17 April, 1752; pr. at April Court, 1753, in which he names sons Elisha, Isaac, Daniel and *Jacob* Hunter—all of whom became prominent, large property holders, and leading citizens of the Co."

"*Jacob Hunter*, Gates Co., *will* Feby. 5, 1780; Nov. Ct. 1784. *Wife Sarah*, all my children, Isaac, *Leah Riddick* and Elizabeth, son-in-law *Seth Riddick* and son Isaac Hunter exrs. Test. John Hodges, Wm. Freeman, Abram Harrell". (N. C. H. & G. Reg. 2-1-52).

"LEAH RIDDICK, Gates Co., *will* Dec. 29, 1816; Feby. Ct. 1817. Bros. Dempsey Costen and Isaac Costen, Eliz. Gordon, Peggy and Henry Lassiter, James Lassiter, Isaac Costen exr. Test. James Costen, Eliz. Costen". (N. C. H. & G. Reg., 2-1-69).

An abstract of the will of James Costen appears in N. C. H. & G. Reg., 1-4-536.

JACOB HUNTER was a member of the Vestry of St. Paul parish, and on June 19, 1776, the vestrymen passed a resolution to maintain and support all the acts, resolutions, and regulations of the Continental and Provincial Congresses to the extent of their power and ability. (C. R. N. C., Vol. 10, p. 612).

Jacob Hunter and his nephew William Hunter, son of Elisha and Anne (Walton) Hunter, were appointed by the April Congress in 1776 a committee in the Edenton district to establish manufactories and to secure muskets and bayonets for the army. (C. R. N. C., Vol. 10, p. 539).

Jacob Hunter was appointed Major in the Army by the April Congress; was a *member of the Congress* of May 12, 1776, that framed and adopted the 1st Constitution of N. C. (C. R. N. C., Vol. 10, p. 914); was one of the Representatives from Chowan Co., in the *House* of *Burgesses* in 1777 and '78 (C. R. N. C., Vol. 12, pp. 265 and 655); and when *Gates* Co. was formed, in 1799, he was cut off in the new Co. and represented that Co. in the Senate in 1783. (S. R. N. C. Vol. 19, p. 129).

"The *Coat of Arms* of *Isaac Hunter* is stamped on the seal to his will, on which is a dragon, which in the military annals of those days indicated that he was educated, trained and armed as a soldier.

In England, we find John and William Hunter in the parish of East Kilbride in Lanarkshire. They were sons of John Hunter and wife Agnes, who were the parents of 10 children.

William Hunter was b. 23 May, 1718, became a celebrated physiologist and physician and the 1st great teacher of Anatomy in

England. In 1764 became the physician extraordinary to her Majesty, Queen Charlotte, and d. full of honors 30 March, 1783.

John Hunter, youngest of the 10 children of John and Agnes Hunter, also obtained great eminence as a physiologist and surgeon, and as a leading instructor in medicine. He was b. 13 Feby., 1728; m., July, 1771, Anne Horne, dau. of Robt. Horne, and d. in 1793. Among the close friends of Wm. and John Hunter were Sam[l] Sharpe and William Cullen, the latter being of the same family as the wife of Major Robert West, who moved from Eng[d] to Chowan Co., N. C. Mrs. West was Martha Cullen, of Dover, Eng[d]. Several of the sons of John and Agnes Hunter moved to Ama." ("The Winbornes of Old", by Benj. B. Winbornes).

ANTHONY.

From "William Candler's Ancestry and Progeny", by Ex-Gov. Allen D. Candler.

"JOSEPH ANTHONY was the 2nd son of Mark Anthony, the 'Genoese Italian', who came to Va. about the beginning of the 18th century and settled on the Upper James River in Bedford County, and established a grist mill and trading post of considerable importance, and about the same time married, but to whom it is not known. We have no recorded account of his early life, but a somewhat apocryphal tradition supported, however, by some well established facts, supplies its place. This tradition has come down thru all the numerous branches of the Anthony family and they are scattered throughout the U. S. from Rhole Island to Georgia, and from Savannah to the Rio Grande. It says the father of the 1st Mary Anthony was a merchant in Genoa, Italy, who emigrated to Holland and settled. When his son Mark grew up, he was sent back when seventeen years old, to school. Becoming tired of school and being of rather adventurous disposition, he ran away, and embarked on a trading vessel which was in a few days captured by Algerian Pirates, and he was sold into slavery in Algiers by his captives. Soon after he thus became a slave his master sent him and another slave in chains and under an overseer into the forest to cut wood. Driven to desperation by the cruelty of their merciless taskmaster, they, taking him unawares, knocked him in the head with an axe, and concealing themselves in the woods until night, they made their way under cover of darkness to the beach, where finding a small boat, they rowed to a British vessel lying at anchor in the bay and telling the story of their captivity and brutal treatment to the Captain, prevailed on him to take them on board. He concealed them in two hogsheads which were shipped as part of the cargo till they got well out to sea. Finally he landed them at a Virginia port, where the master of the vessel sold them to a farmer in New Kent County for three years to pay for their passage. This was about the year 1698. After he had served these three years with his master who had bought him from the sea

Captain, Mark Anthony, as already stated, settled on the Upper James River near the site of the present city of Lynchburg and soon afterward married, but to whom is not known".

In the Anthony Tree, owned by Mrs. Frances V. Swain, Anthony Place, Munice, Ind., it is stated: "Mark Anthony[1], b. 1665, m. Isabella Hart and had twelve sons and one daughter. Only two sons are known: Joseph m. Elizabeth Clark, and John m. Elizabeth Banks".

Another Anthony tree, as reported by Mr. I. P. Cooper, of Rome, Ga., says: "Mark Anthony was b. in Holland about 1650— wife's name not given—space for same is blank. Mark Anthony landed in Virginia 1698 and soon after m. Judith Penelope Moorman. They had ten children."

In William and Mary Quarterly, Vol. 9, pp. 328-330, we find: "*Joseph Anthony* b. in Henrico, afterwards Goochland, now Albemarle Co., Va., 2 May, 1713; m. 27 April, 1741, *Elizabeth Clark*, b. 15 Feby., 1720; d. 23 Nov., 1785—His will, Will Book No. 1, of Henry Co., Va., p. 120 et seq.

After his death, widow with most of her children removed to Ga. He was a Quaker, gives his estate to his widow and 14 surviving children—one son, Charles, having died unm. and without issue. The children were (8 daus. and 7 sons):

1. *Sarah Anthony*[3], b. 15 Aug., 1742; m. 6 Feby., 1762, Capt. Thos. Cooper, Sr., Member House of Burgesses, Capt. of Militia, Revy. period and represented his County in Va. Convention 1788.

2. Christopher Anthony[3] b. 24 March, 1744; d. in Cincinnati, Ohio, 28 Oct., 1815; m. (I) Judith Moorman; m. (II), 5 June, 1775, Mary Jordan, dau. of Samuel and Hannah (Bates) Jordan. She died in Cincinnati, O., 28 Oct., 1815. (q. v.).

3. *Elizabeth Anthony*[3], b. 10 March, 1746; m. in 1761, William Candler, b. 1738, of English parents, at Beffort, Ireland; removed to Ga. in 1762. In 1771 was deputy surveyor; in Revolution served under Col., afterwards Genl. Elijah Clarke in attack on Augusta, at King's Mountain and Blackstock Farms, and rose to rank of Colonel; was member of Ga. Legislature 1784-'5 and appointed to a Judgeship; d. in Columbia Co., Sept., 1789; was gr. gr. father of Gov. Allen D. Candler, Bishop Candler, et al.

4. Penelope Anthony[3], b. 26 July, 1748; m. James Johnson (or Johnston), d. a widow in Leesbury, Ohio, 26 July, 1822. Note: E. B. Anthony, of Griffin, says "this Johnson was the gr. gr. father of the Confederate Genl. Jos. E. Johnson"; 5. Joseph Anthony, Jr.[3], b. 28 March, 1750; m. his cousin, Elizabeth Clark, and moved to Ga. (q. v.); 6. James Anthony[3], b. 18 Dec., 1752; m. (E. B. Anthony says Nannie Tate), moved to Ga. and was the father of Dr Milton Anthony. Mrs. Florence A. Sawin also says that James' wife was Nancy Tate; 7. Mary Anthony[3], b. 17 Nov., 1754; m. Major Josiah Carter; 8. Charles Anthony[3], b. 26 March, 1757, d. as stated before; 9. Micajah Anthony[3], b. 23 Feby., 1759 (m.

Mary Rembert DuBose). (q. v.); 10. Agnes Anthony[3], b. 7 March, 1761; m. William Blakeley; 11. Rachel Anthony[3], b. 8 March, 1763 (m. ...... Ware, says E. B. Anthony; m. James Lane, says Mrs. Florence V. Swain); 12. Winifred Anthony[3], b. 8 April, 1765 [m. William Carter]; 13. Mark Anthony II[3], b. 8 Oct., 1767; m. Nancy Tate; 14. Bolling Anthony[3], b. 23 Aug., 1769 [m. ...... Stone]; 15. Judith Anthony[3], b. 23 Oct., 1771; m. William Green.

2. *Christopher Anthony*[3] (Joseph[2], Mark[1]) and his 1st wife, Judith Moorman, had: 1.—*Mary* A.[4], b. 1766, m. David Terrell; 2.—*Joseph* A.[4], m. Rhoda Moorman; 3.—Chas. A.[4], m. Elizabeth Harris; 4.—Elizabeth A.[4], m. William Ballard.

2. *Christopher Anthony*[3] (Joseph[2], Mark[1]) and his 2nd wife *Mary Jordan*, had: 5.—Christopher A[4], b. 1776, m. Mrs. Anne Couch; 6.—Samuel B. A.[4], b. 1779, m. Mary Irvine; 7.—Hannah B. A.[4], b. 1781, m. John Davis; 8.—Sarah A.[4], b. 1784, m. Henry Davis; 9.—Jordan A.[4], b. 1788, d. in Va.; 10.—Rachel A.[4], b. 1791, m. Lot Pugh, Cin., O.; 11.—Charlotte A.[4], b. 1793, m. Ephraim Morgan, Cin., O.; 12.—Penelope A.[4], b. 1795, d. unm.

2. *Joseph Anthony*[4] (Chrisr.[3], Joseph[2], Mark[1]) and his wife, *Rhoda Moorman*, had: 1.—*Samuel* A.[5], b. 1792, d. 1876—aged 84 years—the gr. father of Mrs. Florence V. Swain—, m. Narcissa Haines, one child; 2.—Thos. Clark A.[5], m. Judith Timberlake; 3.—Charles A.[5], m. (I) Elizabeth Evans, 7 children; m. (II) Mary Holsey, 5 children; 4.—Rhoda A.[5], m. Mr. Townsend; 5.—Clarke A.[5], d. in inf.; 6.—Jane A.[5], m. Thos. Hussey; 7.—Rachel A.[5], m. John Baker; 8.—Sarah A.[5], m. John Fletcher; 9.—Penelope A.[5], m. Geo. Allen; 10.—Christopher A.[5], m. (I) Polly Newby; m. (II) Louise Sparling; 11.—James A.[5], d. in inf.; 12.—Joseph A.[5], m. Margaret McCulloch; 13.—Elizabeth A.[5], m. Dr. Crew.

1. *Samuel Anthony*[5] (Joseph[4], Chris[r3], Joseph[2], Mark[1]), 1792-1876, and his wife, *Narcissa Haines*, had one child: 1.—Edwin Clarke A.[6], b. 1818; d. 1884; m. Rebecca Vannerman. Issue: 1.—Florence V. A.[7], b. 1850, m. ...... Swain, 6 children; 2.—Samuel P. A.[7], m. Bayless; 3.—Edwin Clarke A., Jr.[7], decd.; 4.—Ella A. A.[7], m. ...... Gamble, decd.; 5.—Charles H. A.[7], m. Mitchell; 6.—Adelia A.[7], m. Robinson, decd.

The above record, beginning with 2 Christopher Anthony[3] and his 1st wife, Judith Moorman, was copied by J. A. Leconte from tree of Mrs. Florence V. Swain.

5. *Joseph Anthony, Jr.*[3] (Joseph[2], Mark[1]), b. 28 March, 1750, and his wife, Elizabeth Clarke, had, among others, a son: 1. Micajah Anthony[4], who m. a Williams and had one dau. and 5 sons: 1.—Barbara Anthony[5], who m. Dr. Huff; 2.—Mathew Anthony[5]; 3.—Mark Anthony[5]; 4.—Joseph W. Anthony[5]; 5.—Thomas Anthony[5]; 6.—Micajah Anthony[5].

4. *Joseph W. Anthony*[5] m. a *Render*, a desc'dant of Christopher Anthony[3] (Joseph[2]) and had 10 children,—4 d. in childhood and 6, 3 daus. and 3 sons, lived to be grown: 1.—*Sally Anthony*[6] m. Dr.

Joseph Terrell—the parents of *ex-Gov. Joseph M. Terrell*; 2.—Agnes Anthony[6] m. a Strozier, of Greenville, Ga.; 3.—Lucile Anthony[6] never married; 4.—Judson Anthony[6] m. a King; 5.—Joseph Anthony[6] m. a Henry; 6.—*E. B. Anthony*[6] m. a *Wimbish*, and has 3 children living—2 sons and 1 dau.: 1.—Render Anthony[7]; 2.—a daughter; 3.—Edd Anthony[7]; 4.—eldest, Mary Anthony[7], d. in inf.; 5.—eldest son, Scott Anthony[7], a promising physician, d. in March, 1908.

The record of 5—Joseph Anthony[3] (Joseph[2], Mark[1]) and his wife, Elizabeth Clark, is taken from a letter by E. B. Anthony, of Griffin, Sept. 26, 1908, to his cousin, Mrs. Vera Anthony Christian, of Athens, Ga. He further says, "from Joseph and Elizabeth (Clarke) Anthony have descended no less than 15 prominent families in Va., among them the Cabells and the Johnsons, and 15 in Ga., among them are the Coopers, Candlers, Carters, Hamiltons, Branhams, Stovalls, Nisbetts, Terrells, Jordans and Tates. Six of their sons settled in Ga. Three immediatel before, and three immediately after the Revy. War".

5. *Christopher Jordan*[4] (Chris[r3], Joseph[2], Mark[1]), b. 1776; d. ....., a leading lawyer of Lynchburg, Va., about 1830, and wife, Mrs. Anne Couch, had among others, a dau.: 1.—Margaret Anthony[5], m. Dr. Clifford Cabell and among others had a dau.: 1.—*Mary W. Cabell*[6], who m. *J. Cabell Early*, a nephew of *Gen. Jubal A. Early*.

9. *Micajah Anthony*[3] (Joseph[2], Mark[1]) and his wife, *Mary Rembert DuBose*, had besides others: 1.—Willie Anthony[4], m. Zeb. Colley, of N. O., La., and had: 1.—Mamie Colley[5], d. 2 Nov., 1917, m. Ralph Sherwood; 2.—Eugene Colley[5]; 3.—*Fannie Colley*[5], m. *Thos. Jackson Barksdale*, of Washington, Ga.; 4.—Dr. Willie Colley[5]; 5.—Henry Colley[5]; 6.—Dempsey Colley[5]; 7.—Alline Colley[5].

Thomas Jackson Barksdale and wife, *Fannie Colley*[5], have: Alline Barksdale[6]; Elizabeth Barksdale[6], m. Rocheford Johnson; Willamette Barksdale[6]; Irene DuBose Barksdale[6].

2. *James Rembert Anthony*[4], m. *Abbie Davis Pope*—See Hill record, p. 88, for issue; 3. *Emma Eugenia Anthony*[4] m. *William Wylie Hill*—See Hill record, p. 121, for issue; 4. Bella Anthony[4] m. *William Stokes, father of Mrs. Susie (W. M.) Hill* by his 2nd wife; 5. Julia Toombs Anthony[4] m. William Ficklen and had: 1.—Marion Ficklen[5]; 2.—Georgia Ficklen[5], m. A. G. Shankle; 3.—Julia Ficklen[5], m. Tom Pope; 4.—Elizabeth Ficklen[5]; 5.—James Ficklen[5]; 6.—Claude Ficklen[5]; 7.—Burwell Ficklen II[5]; 6. *Edwin M. Anthony*[4], m. *Clara Julia Pope*, d. 9 June, 1903, dau. of *Henry Jefferson* and *Sarah (Toombs) Pope*, and had: Roberta[5], m. John Burdette; Mamie Lou[5], m. William Burdette; Pope[5]; Ernest[5]; Gabriel Toombs A.[5], m. *Janet Paddison*, of Fla.; John Vance[5]; Julia[5], m. *Wylie Hill DuBose II;* Jean[5]; Katherine[5], m. Kimbrell

(or Kimball) Aubrey Wilheit; Sarah[5], m. . . . . . ; Ouida[5], m. . . . . . ; Willie Belle Anthony[5].

Wylie Hill DuBose II and wife, *Julia Anthony[5]*, had: 1.—Lucy Willis DuBose[6] and 2. Julia Toombs DuBose[6], twins; Kimball Aubrey Wilheit and Katherine Anthony[5], his wife, had: 1.—Katherine Aubrey Wilheit.

14. *Bolling Anthony[3]* (Joseph[2], Mark[1]) in 1810 was a stockholder of the Wilkes Mfg. Co.—manufactured cotton and woolen goods ("Ga. L. M. & L"., p. 1040, by Knight; Clayton's Compendium, p. 667).

Dr. Milton Anthony, boyhood spent in Wilkes, became founder and Presdt. of the Georgia Medical College, Augusta, Ga. (Mems. of Ga., Vol. 2, pp. 148, 173).

BILLUPS.

George Billups[1], 1663-1674, 750 A., Kingston Parish; George Billups, 1683-1700-1706; Richard Billups, 1682; John Billups, 1685;

(Gloucester Land Grants from Vol. IX, Va. Co. Recs., at Richmond, Va., pp. 42-45-'6; Crozier's Va. Co. Recs., Vol. III, p. 16).

George Billups[1], 1663 (above) was probably the father of *Richard[2]*, 1682, *George[2]*, 1683-1716, and *John[2]*, 1685.

1. *Richard Billups[2]* (1682) will 1751, p. 27 Feby., 1752. Will mentioned by Crozier as lost (Va. Co. Recs., Vol. III, p. 16). "Pro. the will was burned with the Chancery papers deposited in the Court House at Williamsburg, Va. Fortunately Mr. Crozier had copied many of these wills before the fire—now some years ago. I also copied many of them". (Mrs. W. C. Stubbs, Aug., 1921). It is not known whom he married, but the following marriages in the *Kingston Parish Register* are doubtless those of his children or gr. children: Lucy Billups[3] m., 1747, Thomas Harden; Sarah Billups[3] m., 1756, Peter Wiatt; Mary Billups[3] m., 1766, Geo. Alex[r] Dudley; Thomas Billups[3] m., 1769, Mildred Lilly; Capt. John Billups[3] m., 1776, Eliza[h] Beverly Whiting.

2. *George Billups[2]*, 1683, 1706, has descendants still living in Mathews Co.—among them George and Humphrey Billups—of 1782 taxes.

3. *John Billups[2]*, 1685, Vestryman Kingston Par. 1692, pro. was father of: (1) *Joseph Billups[3]* and (2) *Robert Billups[3]*.

(1) *Joseph Billups*, Sr.[3], taxed for 573 A. in 1782, b. . . . . . ., d. bef. 1795—mentioned in a survey 1752—will in Gloucester 179. . (?). Issue: 1.—*Robert Billups[4]*; 2.—Christopher Billups[4]; 3.—Joseph Billups, Jr.[4], student Wm. & Mary 1757, Capt. Lunenbury Militia 1777; 816 and 731 A., Lunenbury, 1782-1792.

1. *Robert Billups[4]* m. 14 June, 1755, *Ann Ransone* and probably moved with his brothers, Christopher and Joseph, to Lunenburgh. Issue: 1.—Elizabeth Billups[5], b. 1757; 2.—*William Billups[5]*, b. 4 Sept., 1763; d. 19 Jany., 1817 (q.v.); 3.—*John Billups[5]* m. *Susan (Carleton) Cox*, d. 1819, widow of Bartley Cox and dau. of Thos.

Carleton, (q. v.) ; 4.—*Robert Billups*⁵, will Oct. 23, 1797; pr. 9 April, 1798, widow, Lucy; bro. *John Billups* exr.; children—none of age—*Robert, Virginia* and *Maria*. Both parents of these children died when they were quite young. Their uncle and gdn. removed with them to near Lexington, Oglethorpe Co., Ga.

This dau. Virginia Billups, called also Virginia *Beverly Billups*, m. Walton Harris, son of Walton and Rebecca (Louise) Harris (J. H. Coll., pp. 354 and 392).

Robert and John Billups in Mecklenburg Co. in 1792—Robert had 3 slaves and John had 23. John in 1797, for love and affection, makes deed for 2 slaves to his nephew Robert and nieces Virginia and Maria.

2. *William Billups*⁵, 1763-1817, son of Robert⁴ and Ann (Ransone) Billups, m. 9 Oct., 1787, *Mary Richardson*, b. 10 Nov., 1763; d. Nov., 1803, dau. of Col. *Richard Richardson, Jr.*, and his wife, *Dorcas Nelson*. (See Excursus: Richardson). Issue:

1.—Richard Richardson Billups⁶, b. 28 Nov., 1788; m., in 1820, in Sumter Dist., S. C., Elizabeth Evalina Humphries, b. 1801, and they had 11 children, one being: John A. Billups⁷, b. 25 March, 1831, m. 26 Dec., 1867, Helen Garrett, of Summerfield, Ala., dau. of Greenbury and Mary Garrett—both natives of Tenn; 2.—Ann Ransom Billups⁶, b. 5 May, 1790, m. William Cabell, of Va.; 3.—Letitia Billups⁶, b. 1 May, 1792, m. Gabriel Mathis; 4.—*Robert Billups*⁶, b. 10 Sept., 1793; d. 9 Sept., 1862; m., in Warrenton, Ga., 31 Jany., 1831, *Elizabeth Rebecca Beall*, b. 9 April, 1808; d. June, 1898; 5.—Dorcas Rebecca Billups⁶, b. 26 July, 1797; m. Alexʳ Tate, of S. C.; 6.—*John Billups*⁶, b. 19 Jany. (year illegible), d. after the Civil War; was living in Walton Co., Ga.; m. *Susan Millicent Beall, sis.* of *Elizabeth Rebecca* above, and had a son and 3 daus.; after his death family moved to Fla.; 7.—*Mary Richardson Billups*⁶, b. 13 Sept., 1803; d. 20 May, 1874; m. 16 Oct., 1823, in Walton Co., Ga. (Owen Stroud officiating) *Cary Wood*, b 10 Feby., 1794; d. 6 May, 1857. Issue:

(1) *Laura Elizabeth Wood*⁷, b. 2 May, 1829; d. 26 Sept., 1899; m. 2 April, 1846, *Genl. Robt. Johnson Henderson*, b. 12 Nov., 1822; d. 3 Feby., 1891 (See Excursus: Henderson). (2) Paulina Frances Wood⁷, b. 20 March, 1831, d. ......; m. 30 Oct., 1848, Col. John Thomas Henderson, b. circa 1826. (For issue, see Henderson). (3) Mary Jane Wood⁷, m. (I) Charles Young Stokes, no issue; m. (II) Osborn T. Rogers, and died May 9, 1920, 88 years old (b. 1832 or '33). Issue: 1.—Mrs. Louise Green, of Decatur, Ga.; 2.—Mrs. W. F. Haygood, of Arizona; 3.—Mrs. Sallie Chancellor, of Savannah, Ga.; 4.—Mrs. John B. Davis, of Covington, Ga.; 5.—B. C. Rogers, of Savannah, Ga.; 6.—Dr. Osborn Rogers, of St. Louis, Mo. (Not in order of births). (4) *Robert Richardson Wood*⁷, m. Jackie Bates and had *Robt. Richardson Wood, Jr.*⁸, of Atlanta, Ga., of firm of Geo. Muse & Co.; m. *Janie Boyd* and has son, *Robert R. Wood III*. (5) Cecelia Billups Wood⁷, d. 27 Dec., 1916,

of paralysis; m. William Henry Gaither and had: 1.—Janie Gaither[8], m. Egbert Heard, of Rome, Ga.; 2.—William H. Gaither, Jr.[8]; and 3.—Hub. Gaither[8]; both sons married and have children. 4. *Robert Billups[6]*, 1793-1862, son of *William* and *Mary (Richardson) Billups*, and his wife, *Elizabeth Rebecca Beall*, 1808-1898, had 9 children but reared only three: (1) Robert William Billups[7], served 4 years as Capt. of an Artillery Co. in the C. S. A., d. leaving wife and five children in Texas; (2) Vashti Ann Billups[7], m. L. G. Kennon, of Chapel Hill, Tex., served in C. S. A. She d. in 1887, leaving a dau. and a son living in Fort Worth, Texas; (3) *Salome Susan Billups*, m. 30 Nov., 1865, *I. A. Patton*, of Goliad, Tex., son of Dr. John Worth Patton, b. 1808; d. 1886, and his wife, Matilda Pickens, dau. and only child of David Pickens and his wife, Susan Byars, of Tenn., who enlisted in C. S. A., as 2nd Lieut., Co. B, Yeager's Battalion, which later formed part of the 1st Tex. Cavalry Regt. Issue, 8 children: 1.—Salome Beatrice Patton[8]; 2.—John William Patton[8], d. circa 1882, aged 12 years; 3.—Alex[r] Beall Patton[8]; 4.—Harry Patton[8], d. circa 1882, aged 6 years; 5.—Robert Billups Patton[8]; 6.—Betty Patton[8]; 7.—Ethel Patton[8], d. at 12 months of age; 8.—Aubrey Patton[8]. John William[8] and Harry Patton[8] died on same day of diphtheria; Ethel[8] died a few months thereafter with measles. 6. *Betty Patton[8]* m. *Walter Gunby Mitchell*, of Atlanta, Ga.

3. *John Billups[5]*, son of *Robert[4]* and *Ann (Ransone) Billups*, bought of *Richard Marable*, in 1792, 823 A. for 500 £ and 184 A. for 100 £, in Mecklenburg Co.; in 1791 was Com[r] of Revenue for Lunenburgh, and mem. of the Vestry of Cumberland parish in 1784.

3. *John Billups[5]* and wife *Susan (Carleton) Cox* had: (1) pro. *John Billups[6]*, m. Jane Abbott and had: a.—Joel Abbott Billups m. (I) Susan Harris and had Lula Billups, who m. Thos. B. Gresham; m. (II) Mrs. Victoria Smith; b.—Henry C. Billups m. Emma Conley and had: Julia Billups, m. Dr. Ed[d] Branham; c.—Jane Billups, m. Rich[d] D. B. Taylor, and had Susie Taylor m. Fred B. Lucas; d.—Anna Billups m. Wescom Hudgen and had 3 children; e.—Thos. C. Billups, d.; f.—C. William Billups, d.; g.—John Billups, d.

"A fine old gentleman was Col. John Billups, from a few miles below Athens, was a typical planter of the old regime, owned large, fertile plantation and many negroes. His boys had horses and negroes, his daughters all they desired. A man of influence, an ardent Whig, at different times in the Legislature, Speaker of the House and President of the Senate. Came from Clarke Co., 1836". This account of John Billups[6] is taken from the "Annals of Athens", by Mr. Hull. His parentage is not stated but the writer, without investigation, conjectures that he was the son of John[5] and Susan (Carleton-Cox) Billups.

(2) *Col. Thomas C. Billups[6]*, of Columbus, Miss., who married for his last wife, *Frances Saunders*, niece of Dudley Dunn, and

dau. of Turner and Frances (Dunn) Saunders, aunt of Mrs. W. C. Stubbs and her gr. father's favorite sister, and had: (a) *Genl. Saunders Billups*[7], named for Col. *James E. Saunders, gr. father* of Mrs. Stubbs, d. recently (1921) in Columbus, Miss., leaving 3 charming young married daughters.

2. *Christopher Billups*[4], son of Joseph Billups, Sr.[3], b. ....; d. 1789, in Lunenburgh Co. In 1773 was security to marriage of Mary Billups to William Cowan, in Lunenburgh Co.; in 1778 Lieut. Col. of Lunenburgh Militia; in 1782-1792, 810 A. in Lunenburgh Co.; Estate 1789. He m. Ruth ......, who m. (II), 1790, Col. Thos. Scott, his 2nd wife,—no issue, whose 1st wife was Catherine Tompkins, b. 1773; d. 1766.

In 1795, Christopher Pryor (same family as Genl. Roger Pryor), Clerk of Gloucester Co., sent copies of the wills of Joseph Billups, Sr., and Robert Billups to Col. Thos. Scott, of Prince Edward Co., who m. for his 2nd wife, Ruth, widow of Christopher Billups.

In 1790 Richard Billups was one of the Committee in Gloucester to settle the accounts of Sir John Peyton, Sheriff, decd. In 1782 (Glo. Co. Ld. Bk. in Richmond, Va.) Thos. Billups 375 A.; *Robt. Billups* 320 A.; Humphrey Billups 100 A.; George Billups 40 A. 1709—*Thomas Swepson* lived in Pettsworth Parish, Gloucester Co. 1760—*Richard Swepson* 1326 A. in Lunenburgh Co. 1787—Henry Carleton 467 A. in Lunenburgh Co. Officers of Militia for Gloucester Co., *1775:* John Billups, Sr., Capt.; Richard Billups, Capt., and John Billups, Jr., Lieut. (W. & M. Qly., Vol. 15, p. 124).

CLARK.

Extracts from "History of Albemarle Co., Va.", by Rev. Edgar Woods, made by J. A. Leconte:

P. 4.—A Grant, 1734, to Edwin Hickman, Joseph Smith, Thos. Graves, and *Jonathan Clark* for 3277 A. on N. side of *Rivanna*.

P. 5.—Genl *Geo. Rogers Clark* 1st saw the light in Albemarle Co. His *gr. father, Jonathan Clark,* of King and Queen, joined with Hickman, Graves and Smith in patenting more than 3000 A. on the N. si. of the Rivanna opposite the Free Bridge. In the division of this land the upper portion fell to *Clark*, and there *John Clark*, the son of Jonathan lived and *Geo. R. Clark* was born. The *wife of John Clark* and *mother of George* was *Ann Rogers*, sister of Giles, George and Byrd Rogers. The birth of George R. occurred in 1752 and when he was 5 years of age the father removed to Caroline. William Clark, associated with Meriwether Lewis in his exploring expedition across the Rocky Mountains, was brother of George, but was b. in Caroline, 1770.

P. 55.—After the Revolution—1786-'7—many *emigranted* to *Ga.* For *a time* it was *customary* to apply to the County Court for a Certificate of good character. Among those so *recommended* to *Ga.* were *James Marks,* one of the magistrates, Absolom Eades, William Sandridge, *Christopher Clark*, Bennett Henderson, William and Samuel Sorrow. Soon after *Col. John Marks*, while Sheriff of the Co., followed his brother to Georgia.

P. 165.—Christopher Clark was a large land owner in Louisa, and obtained grants within the present limits of Albemarle, in 1732. He was a Quaker and with his son Bolling was overseer of a Friends' Meeting House, which was situated on land he had entered near the Sugar Loaf Peak of the Southwest Mountain. He and Bolling also took out patents on Totier Creek. Numerous tracts in the Eastern part of the Co. were owned by the *Clark* family. *John Clark* in 1788 purchased from

Robt. Nelson of Yorktown more than 2000 A. on Mechunk, which was patented, in 1733, by Thos. Darsie, and which Clark sold the same year to James Quarles and Joseph Brand. As well as can be ascertained Christopher and his wife Penelope (Bolling) Clarke had 5 sons and 4 daus.: Edward, Bolling, Micajah, *John*, Christopher (Jr.), *Elizabeth, the wife of Joseph Anthony*, who entered 2040 A. in Biscuit Run Valley and moved to Bedford Co., and a number of whose descendants intermarried with the Cabells, Sarah the wife of Chas. Lynch, Rachel, the wife of Thos. Moorman, and the wife of Benjamin Johnson. The most of the family removed to Bedford, now Campbell Co. In 1754 Edward and *Bolling* were overseers of the Friends' South River Meeting House, located on Lynch's Branch of Blackwater Creek, 3 or 4 miles from Lynchburg. Micajah m. Judith, dau. of Robt. Adams and his children are believed to have been Micajah, Robt., Jacob and William. Robt. m. Susan, dau. of John Henderson, Sr., and followed his relatives to Bedford. His children were: Robt. 1st manufacturer of iron in Ky., James, Govr. of Ky. when he d. in 1838, and Bennett, the father and gr. father of the two John Bullock Clarks, who were both members of Congress from Mo. and both Generals in the Confederate Army. William was Deputy Sheriff for John Marks in 1786 and was empowered by the Legislature on account of his Chief's removal to sell lands delinquent for taxes. He was also a Magistrate for the Co. and d. in 1800. His sons were: Jacob, James and Micajah, and his wid. Elizabeth (Allen) Clark is remembered by many as the proprietor of Clarksville, an excellent house of entertainment near Keswick, recently the country seat of James B. Pace, of Richmond. James was a Magistrate, m. Margaret, dau. of Thos. W. Lewis, of Locust Grove, and in 1836 with most of the Lewis family emigrated to Mo. Micajah became a physician and for many years was a successful practitioner of Richmond.

P. 224.—*John Harvie* was a native of Stirlingshire, Scotland, and at the time Albemarle was organized was living at Belmont, near Keswick, a place he bought from Mathew Graves. He was the guardian of Mr. Jefferson, and one of the earliest efforts of the great statesman's pen was an inquiry addressed to Mr. Harvic respecting the method of his education. He d. in 1767. His wife was Martha Gaines and his children Richard, John, Daniel, who m. Sarah Taliaferro, William, who m. Judith Cosby, Martha, the wife of John Marks, Margaret, the wife of John Davenport, Elizabeth, the wife of *James Marks*, Janet, the wife of *Reuben Jordan*, Mary the wife of *David Meriwether*. Some of these families resided for a time in Amherst, but *all except John emigrated* to *Wilkes* Co., Ga., in the decade of 1780. P. 227.—Susan, dau. of John Henderson, who d. 1786, m. *John Clark*. Sarah Henderson, gr. dau. of John, dau. of John, Jr., and Frances, dau. of John Moore, m. *Micajah Clark*. P. 238.—Orlando Jones in 1774 bought 400 A. on the waters of Totier from *Joseph Anthony*. P. 239.—In 1762 James Jones bought 800 A. from *Joseph Anthony* at the N. Wt corner of Dudley's Mountain.

P. 246.—*John Key* (d. 1791) had 12 children of whom *William Bibb* Key m. *Mourning*, dau. of *Christopher Clark* and went to *Elbert Co.*, Ga.

P. 258.—*Chas. Lynch*, a native of Ireland, commenced entering land in Albemarle Co. in 1733 and in the next 17 years had obtained patents for 6500 A. in different sections, d. in 1753. His wife was *Sarah*, dau. of *Christopher* and *Penelope Clark*. She joined the Friends about the time of their removal to Lynch's Ferry on the James. Her children were: Charles, John, Christopher and Sarah, wife of *Micajah Terrell*. Charles was Clerk of South River Meeting. In spite of being a Quaker he became a Colonel in the Revolution. Was the originator of *Lynch Law*, which was named for him. (He m. *Sarah*, dau. of *Henry* and *Anna Chiles Terrell*).

P. 285-'6.—*Chas. Moorman* came from Isle of Wight, England, and in 1744 was living in Louisa, not far from the Green Spring. He was a leading Quaker and at that time he and his son Thomas were overseers of the Friends' Meeting House on Camp Creek in Louisa. As early as 1735 they were both patentees of land within the present bounds of Albemarle. . . . Chas. m. Mary, dau. of Abraham Venable, whose home was on Byrd Creek in Goochland, and his children were: Thomas, Chas., Robt. Achilles, James, *Judith*, the *wife* of *Christopher Anthony*. . . . Thos. *Moorman* m. (I) Rachel, dau. of *Christopher Clark;* m. (II) Elizabeth, dau. of Robt. and Mourning Adams. He d. 1787, leaving one son Robt., who d. in 1813, leaving a widow and a number of children.

P. 299.—James Quarles in 1778 bought from John Clark nearly 1300 A. on Mechunk.

Appendix, PP. 375 et seq. Justices: 1745, Charles Lynch; 1746, *John Anthony;* 1790 *William Clark;* 1816 *James Clark.* Sheriffs: 1749, Chas. Lynch; 1785, *John Marks;* 1787, *Geo. Gilmer;* 1801, Thos Wills, Jailor. Attorneys: 1745, John Harvie; 1798, Thos. Clark; 1800, Wm. Clark. Rep. in the House of Burgesses: 1748, Chas. Lynch; 1765, John Harvie; 1799, *Geo. Gilmer;* 1793, William Clark. Emigrants to N. C. . . . . ; *Emigrants to Ga.: James Marks, John Marks, Richd. Harvie; Daniel Harvie, John* and *Margaret (Harvie) Davenport, William* and *Judith (Cosby) Harvie, David* and *Mary (Harvie) Meriwether,* all to Wilkes Co., *William B.* and *Mourning (Clark) Key* to Elbert Co., Ga. Necrology: . . . 1753 Chas. Lynch; 1774, Micajah Clark; *1774 Joel Terrell; 1776 Reuben Terrell;* . . . ; 1787, Thos. Moorman.

(Signed) J. A. Leconte.
5/10/1909.

DU BOSE.

In "The Transactions of the Huguenot Society of South Carolina," No. 5, we find: "No. 66.—Pierre Couillandeau, né a la Tromblade, fils de Pre Couillandeau et de Marie Fougeraut." "No. 65.—Marie Fougeraut, veuve de Moyse Brigaud." "No. 72.—*Isaac DuBosc*, fils de Louis DuBosc et d' Anne DuBosc de Dieppe en Normandie. "*Suzanne DuBosc* sa femme, fille de Pierre Couillandeau et de Susanne Couillandeau, native de la Tramblade en Xaintonge."

The names of Isaac and Suzanne DuBosc, of Pierre Couillandeau, Suzanne Couillandeau and Marie Fougeraut, appear in the "Liste des Francois et Suisses Refugiez en Caroline qui souhaittent d'etre naturalizes Anglais" prepared in 1695-1696. They emigrated from France after the Revocation of the Edict of Nantes and settled on the Santee River in South Carolina in 1689 in company with other Huguenots.

The coat of arms belonging to this branch of the DuBose family is not known, but it is supposed to be one bearing the motto: "DuBosc mais non pas DuBosc;" in English, "From the Woods but not of the Woods."

It is highly probable that the DuBose and DuBois families are derived from the same stirps, and the coat of arms used by *Louis DuBois* (Louis the Walloon), who settled in New York, is described as follows:

"Arms: Argent, a lion rampant, armed and langued gules. "Crest: Between two tree stumps, vert, the lion of the shield. "Motto: Tiens Ta Foy (Keep Thy Faith). ("Ancestral Records and Portraits," Vol. 2, pages 635-6.)

"The name *DuBois* is one of the oldest in France and exists also in Flanders and England. Pere Anseline and Dufourney in their great work, 'Maison Royale de France,' speak of the family DuBois as 'the Grand Masters of the Forests of France.' . . . The prefix *de, de la,* or *du,* is universally admitted in France to be a badge of noble extraction. . . . "

Isaac and *Suzanne DuBose* had:

1.—John DuBose (q. v.); 2.—Stephen DuBose, m. Lydia . . . Their son John b. 13 June, 1738 (S. C. H. & G. Reg., Vol. 18, p. 128); 3.—Andrew DuBose; 4.—Peter DuBose, m. Madeline DuBose, daughter of Isaac DuBose and his wife, Madeline Rembert; 5.—Isaac DuBose, Jr., m. Madeline Rembert, daughter of André Rembert, the emigrant; 6.—Daniel DuBose, m. Anne Rembert, daughter of Pierre and Anne Rembert (Trans. His. So. of S. C. No. 14, pp. 21-25-26); 7.—Martha DuBose.

John DuBose, whose southwesternmost plantation on Santee is mentioned in 1734 in an act providing for the erection of Prince Frederick Parish out of the parish of Prince George Winyah ("S. C. H. & G. Mag.", Vol. 18, p. 90; "Old Cheraws," pp. 91-2) later removed to Lynch's River in the Darlington District of South Carolina in 1756. He was member of a militia company of volunteers of which his son, Elias, was captain in 1775. He married . . . . (name of wife unknown) and had: 1.—Martha DuBose, m. John Warren; 2.—Joseph DuBose, m. Mary Ann Mell; 3.—Mary DuBose, m. (I) . . . Sparrow; m. (II) . . . Clemmons; 4.—Rebecca DuBose, m. her counsin, Andrew DuBose, son of Peter DuBose; 5.—Elias DuBose (q. v.), and 6.—Daniel DuBose (twins), m. 11 Nov., 1776, Mrs. Frances

Simons (Reg. 15, p. 198); 7.—Isaac DuBose (m. his first cousin, Sarah DuBose, dau. of Peter), and 8.—Elizabeth DuBose (no record), twins.

On page 91 of "Old Cheraws" we find: "About this period (1756?) came a family, in numbers and influence, prominently connected with Darlington District from an early period. John DuBose was the first of the name who removed to this region. He was of Huguenot descent, and came from that settlement on Santee to Lynch's Creek. His sons were Isaac, Elias, Daniel and Joseph. These brothers lived in the same neighborhood, were men of property before the Revolution, and took an active part in that struggle." A foot-note says: "This settlement was on the east side of Lynch's Creek, at a point just above the crossing of the Wilmington & Manchester Railroad; a neighborhood in which a sanguinary struggle was carried on with the Tories, and in which the DuBoses took an active part."

"Daniel was a captain, and Isaac bore honorable office. Elias, the second son, was prominent for character and influence. He was a magistrate of note before and after the war. He married Lydia Cassels, of Sumpter, and reared a large family." A foot-note again says: "Jesse, Isaiah and John were sons of Elias." "A sister, Rebecca, married her cousin, Andrew DuBose (son of Peter), whose name will appear in a prominent connection in the history of the Revolution," and had Benjamin, Samuel and Joshua DuBose who lived on Lynche's Creek. "Another sister, Margaret, married William Dick."

Elias DuBose[3] (spelling is here changed from DuBosc) born 19 October, 1737; died 16 March, 1789; married 20 January, 1763, Lydia Cassels, of Sumter County, S. C. On 22 June, 1775, he was appointed by the Provincial Congress as a member of the "Committee of Observation" for the Parish of St. David. This committee was composed of the most prominent citizens and their duty was to report to the Congress developments of interest to the American cause. He was chosen captain of a volunteer independent company organized in 1775 in "St. David's Parish" under provision of an "Act and Resolve of the Provincial Congress to protect the people of this colony whose liberties and rights" were "threatened by the arbitrary hand of despotism," and placed at the direction and subject to the order of the Provincial Congress and the Council of Safety. (S. C. H. & G. Mag., Vol. 3, pp. 132-3.) He served both as a private and as a lieutenant in the Revolutionary Army; was a magistrate of note before and after the war. ("Old Cheraws," pp. 91-2, 407, 434; "Stub Entries to Indents for Revolutionary Claims—Book O-Q," p. 21, by A. S. Salley, Jr.) *Elias DuBose*, Lieutenant, Marion's Brigade (Year Book of Charleston for 1893 p. 229); *Elias DuBose* (S. C.) Lieutenant in Marion's Brigade in 1781 (Historical Register of the Officers of the Continental Army, Heitman, Revised Edition, 1914, p. 215). He was appointed a justice in the commission of the peace for the Cheraws District by the General Assembly, 30th March, 1776 (Journal of the General Assembly for March and April, 1776, printed 1906, p. 20). *Elias DuBose*, on 21 March 1785, was named by the joint committee of the House and Senate as one of the Justices of Darlington County ("Old Cheraws" p. 434).

"*Elias DuBose*, on Lynche's Creek, had many adventures with the Tories. On one occasion before the removal of the family to Virginia, he had returned from the camp on furlough. The Tories being apprised of his movements approached his house in the dead of night and demanded admittance. Well knowing their designs, Mr. DuBose presented himself, gun in hand, with a heroic wife by his side also armed, and refused them admittance, threatening to shoot the first man who made the attempt to enter, and adding that he would sell his life as dearly as possible. They then threatened to burn them, and made preparations to carry the threat into execution. In this desperate emergency, no alternative was left but a compromise; the dauntless Whig proposing to surrender on condition that they would not tie or confine him, but that he should be carried to old Mr. Wilson, a neighboring magistrate and friend of the King who resided on the opposite side of the creek, and by whose sentence he consented to abide. Supper was then provided for them. Upon arriving at Mr. Wilson's, and submitting the case to him, he said such a neighbor should not be injured, and told his friend DuBose to go at large; upon which he returned to his family the same night." ("Old Cheraws," p. 329). A foot-note here says: "*Elias DuBose* was a lieutenant in General Marion's famous brigade. Many of the most devoted Whigs removed their families with haste to North Carolina and Virginia, returning themselves to the conflict."

Elias and *Lydia (Cassels) DuBose* had: 1.—Elias DuBose, Jr., born 24 October, 1763, m. 1st, 6 April, 1786, Martha Law; m. 2nd, 11 December, 1798, Mrs. Elizabeth Scott; 2.—Margaret DuBose, born 18 December, 1765, m. 17 June, 1783, William Dick; 3.—Daniel DuBose, born 10 January, 1768, m. 1st, 3 October, 1793, Mrs. Jane Shackleford; m. 2nd, Mrs. Effie Way; m. 3rd, Mrs. Ann Kirvin; 4.—Benjamin DuBose, born 16 March, 1770; died in infancy; 5.—Ezekiel DuBose, born 13 July, 1772 (q. v.); 6.—Mary DuBose, born 10 June, 1774; m. 13 January, 1791, William Law, of Williamsburg, S. C., and had nine children; 7.—Jesse DuBose, father of Alfred Bishop Cassels DuBose and grandfather of General Dudley McIvor DuBose, born 22 April, 1776; m. 16 January, 1800, Miss Rebecca Wilds; 8.—Martha DuBose, born 30 March, 1778; m. 12 January, 1797, Thomas Gordon; 9.—Isaiah DuBose, born 27 November, 1781; m. 6 October, 1808, Gilly Hinton Benton; 10.—John DuBose, born 23 June, 1784; m. 29 June, 1809, Dorcas Wilson; 11.—Lydia DuBose, born 3 June, 1786; m. 9 May, 1809, Samuel Wilson.

(5) Ezekiel DuBose[4], born in Darlington District, South Carolina, 13 July, 1772; died 25 December, 1819, and buried below Lisbon, Lincoln County, Georgia, near Savannah River, below plantation of Dr. Benjamin J. DuBose. He was a physician and planter of considerable wealth and prominence. He was one of the earliest representatives in the South Carolina Legislature from Darlington County, being elected to this office in 1794 and serving continuously to 1799, both inclusive, ("Old Cheraws," pp. 456, 459). He married (1st) in Sumter County, S. C., 21 February, 1799, Mary Rembert (born 17 November, 1781; died 26 January, 1817), the Rev. I. Smith, officiating minister; married (2nd) 1 July, 1817, Margaret E. Glynn, native of Raleigh, N. C., (born 21 February, 1799). He removed to Wilkes Co., Ga., where all of his children were born.

Issue by first marriage: 1.—Mary Rembert DuBose, b. 31 January, 1800; died 31 December, 1859. (See Anthony, pp. 175-'6); 2.—Ezekiel Edwin DuBose, b. 4 January, 1803; d. . . . ; 3.—Louisa Matilda DuBose, b. 8 August, 1804; d. 25 October, 1821; m. **Dr. Joseph Wyatt Bibb**, 1788-1831, his first wife, son of William and Sally (Wyatt) Bibb, of Prince Edward County, Va., and brother to Governors William and Thomas Bibb, of Alabama; 4.—Elizabeth Harriet DuBose, b. 9 April, 1806; d. . . . ; 5.—James Rembert DuBose, b. 15 November, 1807; d. 21 May, 1867, at 7:15 A. M.; m. (1st) Martha Pope Hill, b. 29 July, 1810; d. 5 November, 1848; m. (2nd) 29 November, 1849, Elizabeth Adams Vance, b. 4 February, 1827; d. 31 July, 1868. For issue, see Hill record, page 136.; 6.—William Elias DuBose, b. 8 November, 1809; m. (?) Elizabeth Alston, daughter of William Hinton Alston and his wife, Elizabeth Rucker (Alstons and Allstons, p. 237). This author says: Wm. E. DuBose, of Enon, Ala. He may not have been William Elias DuBose. 7.—Samuel Cassels DuBose, b. 22 August, 1811; d. 25 July, 1812; 8.—Martha Julianna DuBose, b. 15 May, 1813; d. 4 September, 1883; m. in fall of 1830, General Robert Toombs, b. 2 July, 1810; d. 15 December, 1885, son of Robert (d. 1815) and Catherine (d. 1848) (Huling) Toombs (q. v.); 9.—Caleb Sidney DuBose, b. 30 November, 1815; d. . . . . .

Issue by Second Marriage: 10.—Anthony Glynn DuBose, b. 26 April, 1818; d. 19 November, 1819; 11.—Honoria Ariana DuBose, b. 19 September, 1819; d. 19 October, 1819.

(8) *General Robert* and *Martha Julianna (DuBose) Toombs* had: 1.—Sallie Toombs, m. General Dudley McIvor DuBose; 2.—Louisa Toombs, m. William Felix Alexander; 3.—Julian Toombs, son, d. y.

Gen. Dudley McIvor DuBose and wife, *Sallie Toombs* had:

1.—Robert Toombs DuBose, b. 14 February, 1859; m. Jennie Stovall and had: Mattie Wilson and Bolling, and two others, Dudley and Julian, who d. in inf.; 2.— Camille DuBose, d. 5 June, 1917, m. Henry Colley, of Washington, Ga., and had: Catherine, Henry, and Sarah Frances; 3.—Louisa Toombs DuBose, m. Dr. George T. DuBose, of Sparta, Ga., later of Washington, D. C.; 4.—Dudley DuBose, d. 5 February, 1910; m. . . . . .

Mary Rembert, wife of Dr. *Ezekiel DuBose*, was, no doubt, the daughter of

Col. James Rembert, of Rembert Hall (S. C.), who was guardian of Ann Gillman, an orphan, who married Rev. Isaac Smith (they named a son James Rembert Smith after her guardian). Rev. Isaac Smith officiated at the marriage of Ezekiel and Mary (Rembert) DuBose. *Colonel James Rembert* was one of the wealthiest and most prominent men of his section, and *Bishop Francis Asbury,* in the 1790's, was regularly entertained at his home when travelling through that portion of South Carolina. *Bishop Asbury* wrote of him (et al) as one among the most distinguished and noble of the aristocratic families and the equal in social position to any in the land. He was descended from *André* and *Anne Rembert,* de Pont en Royan en Daufiné, the Huguenot emigrants to South Carolina.

Note.—In preparing the DuBose record the author has received valuable assistance from Mr. Robt. S. Quin, of Atlanta, an intelligent, persistent and resourceful investigator.

EXUMS.

The Exums were in Va. as early as 1640. In the early records the name is variously spelled as Exam, Exom, Axom, Exwin, and Exum,—in one place copied as Ewen. In Norfolk Co., Va., we find in a court record, 30th Jany., 1646, that, "John Nansel came into this country with *Richard Exam* by indenture for three years". (Book B, p. 24). At the State Land Office in Richmond, in Vol. II, p. 244, we find: "Sir William Berkeley did grant unto Richard Axum and Thomas Godwin 550 acres situated on Rappahannock River, lying on the South side, beginning at a point called Troublesome Point running for length South Southeast 320 poles, and for breadth 273 poles nigh or by the main riverside, unto a marked post standing by the side of a brook called *Axum's Brook,* and beginning again for length South southwest 320 poles bounding the said quantity of land, being deeded to the said *Axum* and *Godwin* by and for the transportation of 11 persons. To have and to hold, etc. . . . *May 22, 1650.* The headrights were: Edward Fisher, Ann James, John Burdix, John Kohnan, Robert Koggen, George Kelman or Kelly, Anthony Hunt, Susan Newman, Sara Thomblin, Thomas Keaton,—one name illegible.

Another patent: "Sir William Berkeley given and granted *Richard Axum* and *Thomas Godwin* 1000 acres situated on the Rapp. River lying in a bay called Brecknock Bay on the south side, beginning at a marked red oak, standing on a point of land by the main river and by the side of a great marsh and running by length south 320 poles and for breadth 500 poles by or nigh the main river unto a marked . . . . on a point by the main riverside, again south by west 320 poles adjoining on and enclosed by the lands of John Landman, including the said quantity of land. The said land being due the said *Axum* and *Godwin* for the transpn., etc., etc. . . . May 22, 1650". The headrights being as follows: Richard Lowry, Ann Pagett, Mary Carpenter, John Giblin, Amos Hamilton, Christopher Knight (?), Ann Alderson, Morgan Thomas, *Richard Axum,* Richard Harron, *Wm. Cotten,* Robt. Stephens, *Thomas Godwin,* Sarah Thomlin, Richard Topham, Thomas Harlow, Robert Morse, Thos. Morse, Wm. Morse, John Michell". In Essex Co. (Richmond and Essex Cos. were formed from Rappahannock Co.) Deed Book No. 3, p. 523, we find: "To all Xtian people to whom these presents shall come, I Thos. Godwin send Greeting. Whereas Sir Wm. Berkeley, Knt., Govr and Capt. Genl. of Va., with the consent of the Counsell of State did give & grant a patent for 1000 acres of land Scituate lying & being on the South side of Rapp^k Rivr unto RICHARD EXUM decd. & me the s'd Thos. Godwin Bearing date the *22nd of May, 1650,* as by the pattent may appear. Now Know Ye that after the s'd Richd Exum deceased his widow in behalf of *his children the Orphants* to whom the s'd Exum did give his s'd part of the s'd Land, did with my consent make Choyce of the upper or Westward side of the s'd thousand acres of land, & I Chose the lower or Eastward side (it being to be equally divided between us). I do hereby assign & make over all my Right title & Interest of the s'd Lower or Eastward si. of the s'd l'd unto Robert Tomlyn, &c, &c. . . . this 28th, 7th, 1668.

(Signed) Thos. Godwin.

Wit: Joseph Ivory, James Webb.

In Essex Co., in a book called "Land Trials", 1711-1716, pp. 44 to 48, inc., is a reference to these two patents granted to Richard Exum and Thos. Godwin, on May 22, 1650.

It will be noted in the 550 A. patent that mention is made of *"Axum's Brook"*, clearly showing the Axoms, or Exums, were settled here prior to the date of these grants.

In Rapp[k] Records (at State Library) Vo. 1, pp. 146-'7, we find: 'That *Thomas Exum* (Exwin?) and *wife Ann*, on 1 Jany. 1660, for 6000 lbs. of tobacco, deeded to Capt. John Weir, all his right to certain land conveyed 10 Nov., 1656 to *Thos. Ewen (Exum)* and Thos. Wright by John Paine and his wife Margaret, and which they had acquired from Francis Hobbs; also fragment of a record, *1653* (?), by Walter Bunce, concerning a servant who is to serve *William Exum.* Wit.: Sayer and Budge (page of book uncertain).

John and Margaret Paine to Thos. Exum (?) and Thomas Wright, 10 Nov., 1656. (Rapp[k] Rec., Vol. 1, p. 146). Walter Bunce on 24 March, *1663*, conveys a servant to William Exum. Wit.: Sayer and Budge (Bridger?). Rapp[k] Rec., Vol. 1, p. 367. Thos. Duke, Jr., in *Jany., 1667*, gives power to *William Exum* to receive cattle which belonged to my wife Margaret. (Ib. Vol. II, p. 136).

At a Court holden in Isle of Wight Co., 23rd day of 9th Anno. 1693 (Mr. Jere Exum one of the Justices) Mr. William Exum was allowed .0300, for one wolfe killed in a pitt. (Book 1688-1704, p. 9). This may certify that there is due to Wm. Exum 450 Acres of land for importation of Wm. Exum, Jane his wife, Francis his son, Francis Sullivant, Abrahm Broloh, Ruth Hickman, Thomas Harloo, John Allison, Saml Brown, 9th 1693 (Isle of Wight Co. Book 1, p. 8).

Will.—In the Name of God, Amen. I *Will Exum* of ye Upper Parish of Isle of Wight County in ye Colony & Dominion of Virginia being aged and weak but of good & perfect mind & memory, laud & praise be Given to Almighty God for it doe make publish & declare this to be my last Will & Testament bend desirous to settle ye Estate which God in his mercy hath lent me in such sort y[t] after my decease it may be disposed of without suit or Controversy of or in ye law.

First & principally I commend my soul into ye hands of Almighty God my most merciful Creator, etc.

As touching my worldly estate I give & dispose thereof as followeth.

I give & bequeath unto my dau. Deborah Jones a Mare & filly, a Gold Ring formerly her Grandmother's.

I give & bequeath unto my loving Wife *Jane* Exum my plantation whereon I now live during her Natural life, and after y[e] decease of my said wife, I give & bequeath ye s'd plantation to my son W[m] Exum his heirs for Ever.

Item. I give and bequeath unto my son William Exum 200 Acres being part of my land at Blackwater to him & his heirs forever.

I give unto my son ffra. Exum my Plantation at Blackwater whereon he now lives, to him & his heirs forever.

I give & bequeath all my personal estate to my loving wife Jane whom I make my full & sole Executor of this my last Will & Testament. In witness whereof I have set my hand & seal this 3rd Day of *December* in the year of our Lord God 1700. (Signed) William Exum.

Wit.:
    Nathaniel Whitby } Proved 10th Oct. 1700/1
    Geo. Gurney } Chas. Chapman Clerk.

(Deed Book 1661-1719, p. 436; W. & M. Q., 7, p. 253)

Will of William Exum[3] (*William*[2], *Thos.*[1]), April 25, 1720; Rd *Aug. 22, 1720.* My son John Exum; my son Wm. Exum; my son Joseph Exum; my son Robert Exum. My two daughters Anne and Sarah Exum (unmarried). My beloved wife Susan, Executor.

Wit.: Thos. Atkinson } Wm. Exum.
    Francis Exum (a bro.) }
    William Crocker. }

(Great Book, p. 51; W. & M. Q. VII, p. 264.—The Quarterly omits name of son John, but it is in the will).

John Exum[4], of Isle of Wight Co. (son and heir of Wm. Exum, late of said

County, deceased, to Thomas Davis, of same Co., 150 acres, for 20 £. *Aug. 18 or 19th, 1720.*
Wit.: Wm. Allen   John Exum.
     Jno. Chapman   Rd Aug. 21, 1720.
(Great Book, p. 281 (or 382).

In Essex Co. "Land Trials", 1711-1716, pp. 44 to 48 is a record of sale 8 May, 1685, by *Jeremiah Exum* and *Thomas Exum—sons of Richard*—of the land they inherited, to Mrs. Gouldman. On 24 March, 1676/7 *Jeremiah and Thos. Exum* were witnesses to the will of *Thos. Godwin,* the *joint patentee,* in 1650, with their father, *Richard.*

I *Thomas Exum* of the Isle of Wight County for various valuable considerations to me in hand Paid before the sealing & delivery of these . . . by John Ison of the County of Nansemond whereof I acknowledge the receipt etc. do sell to the s'd John Ison a parcel of Land in the Parish (?) of Chuckatuck containing 179 Acres by Patent bearing date the 6th Day of Feby. 1667. The 29th Day of May 1678.
    Joseph Moody   Thomas Exum
    Tho. Godwyn   Sarah Exum
                                   Rec. June 10th, 1678.
(Isle of Wight Book 1662-1715, p. 378).

Thos. Exum, Edmund Godwin & John Pellington were witnesses on Dec. 19, 1688, to a conveyance by Henry Reeves, of Rappahannock, to *Thos. Godwin,* of Chuckatuck, of 450 A. in Isle of Wight Co., on so. si. Chuckatuck river commonly known as *Beaver Dam* near a Wolf's pitt near a swamp known as Indian Bog. Recorded 9 Jany., 1688/9 (Book 1688-1704,—page omitted in copy).

Thos. Exum was a Justice of the Peace in Isle of Wight Co. in 1692. (So. His Assn. Pubs., Vol. VI, p. 306).

Jeremiah Exum was a *Justice* in *Surry County* and on the bench at Court held 9 Jany., 1681-'2, (Mis. Rec. of Surry Co., Vol. 1, p. 362); witnessed the will of Michael Mackquenney in Isle of Wight Co., 15 April, 1686 (Book 2, p. 254); with Robert Lawrence on 23 Oct., 1689, gave in the property of *Thos. Cullen* to the appraisers of his estate. (Deed Book 1661-1719, p. 298); was *Justice* in Isle of Wight Co. in 1693 and 1694. At a Court holden in Isle of Wight Co. on the 23rd day of 9th Anno. 1693. Coll. Arthur Smith, Capt. Hen. A . . . . . , Mr. Thos. Giles, Mr. Henry Baker, Capt. John Goodrich, Mr. Anthony Holloday, Mr. *Jere Exum,* Mr. Jos. Benn.

Isle of Wight Co.   Dr. lb. Tobacco
To Wm. Exum one Wolfe killed in a pitt   .0300
To Mr. Thos. Joyner 2 ditto   600
    (Book 1688 to 1704, p. 9).

"At a Court holden for the Isle of Wight County, the tenth day of December, Anno 1694. Present Coll. Arthur Smith, Lt. Coll. Sam Bridger, Mr. *Jere Exum,* Mr. Thos. Giles, Mr. Geo. Moor, Capt. Jno. Goodrich, Capt. J. A. Benn. John Williams, Quaker, being convicted by his own confession of assembling and meeting with diverse persons in diverse places in this County contrary to the tenour of the first Act of Assembly made in 7ber 1663, He is therefore fined, and ordered to pay two hundred pounds of tobo. as ye sd law provides, with Costs als Ex".
                                             (W. & M. Q. XII, p. 259).
Isle of Wight Deed Book 1 (1688 to 1704), p. 169:

"Be it known unto all men by these presents that I Elizabeth Booth ye Wife of Richard Booth of ye Blackwater doe Constitute empower and ordain my loving friend Mr. *Jeremiah Exum* to be my true Lawfull Attorney to act for me and in my name   before ye Court of ye Isle of Wight a Deed of Sale made to Isaac Ricks. To be my real attorney this 23rd day of July 1695.
Witnesses to Richard Booth's deed: Elizabeth Booth."
    Henry Pope
    Joseph Mondofh (?).

Jeremiah Exum m. Ann, dau. of John Lawrence, whose will dated 2 Jany., 1696/7, is mentioned in various records but no copy of it is found, (Deed Book 1704-1715, p. 115), probably son of *Robert Lawrence* and wife Eliza.

Robert Lawrence, Aug. 7, 1642, 200 Acres on the Easternmost .... of Lawn's Creek, &c., adjoining the land of Mr. Harding and Widow Barnett (W. & M. Q. 7, p. 294).

Robert Lawrence Pattent for 200 Acres in the Easternmost side of Lawn's Creek in the County of the Isle of Wight being due the s'd Robert Lawrence by a former Pattent bearing date the 20th day of August 1642 for the transportation of 4 persons into this Colony. Given at James City Sept. 12, 1644.

Richard Kemp.

Said Pattent made over to Daniel Washburne by Robert Lawrence July 8th, 1652.

Test.: Robt. Sabine }   Robert Lawrence.
    James Pyland }   Recd. Aug. 9th, 1652.

(Oldest Book—Deeds & Wills, p. 35).

L. O., Richmond, Virginia. Book No. 1, page 793.

To all and whomsoever, Now know you that I the said Sir William Berkeley Knight doe with the consent of the Council of State accordingly give and grant unto Robert Lawrance his heires and assigns for ever one hundred acres of Marsh situate and being in L   Creek in the County of the Isle of Wight Northward by East two hundred Sixtie five pole Joyning upon the lands of the said Robert Lawrance and Mr. Tooks West North west seaventy pole to the Creek South half a point Westerly along the Creek and East South East forty five pole to the lands of the said *Robert Lawrance* the said one hundred Acres of Land being due unto the said *Lawrance* by and for the transportation of two people into this Colony whose names are in this record mentioned under this pattent to have and to hold etc. to bee held & c. yielding and paying rent unto our said Souveraign Lord the King his heirs and Successors for every fifty acres of land having by these presents given and granted yearly at the feast of St. Michaell the Archangel the fee rent of one shilling to his Majesty's use which payment is to be made seven years after the Date hereof and not before. Provided etc. Given etc. this ——— of August 1642.

James Long
Margaret Aldridge

See oldest Book Isle of Wight, Deeds and Wills page 35, this has an exact copy of this Land Grant, but shows that Robert Lawrence transferred it (the land) to Daniel Washburn July 8th 1652

Edward Ison (Signed) *Robert Lawrance, Eliza his wife*
John Blackwell

Land Grant Book No. 3, page 22.

To All &c, Whereas &c., Now know yee that I the said Richard Kemp, Esq. Doe with the consent of the Councill of State accordingly give and grant unto *Robert Lawrance* and Ellis Brown four hundred acres of land situate lying and being in the County of Lower Norfolk, and lying on the northward side of the Eastward branch of Elizabeth River and beginning at a marked red oake standing on poynt on the mayne branch side and running for length North by east three hundred and forty poles on the land of John Sidney unto a mked holly tree, standing in a poquoson and soe West seventeen hundred and eight poles unto a marked post, and soe South South West and three degrees and Westerly one hundred and twenty eight poles on the land of Richard Weste unto a marked white oake, and soe southerly West one hundred and twenty pole on ye land of Richard Weste unto a marked maple tree standing on a poynt on the eastward side of the mouth of a gutt, and soe East two hundred and four poles by or nigh the mayne branch side unto the first mentioned marked tree including the said quantity of land. The said four hundred acres of land being due unto him the said Robert Lawrence and Ellis Brown as followeth, vizt. three hundred acres part thereof by assignment of a pattent bearing date the 22 th of May 1637 from Thomas Sawyer unto the said Lawrance and Brown, and one hundred acres the residue thereof by and for the transport of two servants into the Colony whose names are in the records mentioned under this pattent; To have and to hold; To be held &c., Yielding and paying unto our Sovereign Lord the King his heirs and successors for every fifty acres of land herein by these presents given and granted yearly at the feast of St. Michael the

Arch Angel the fee rent of one Shilling to his Majesties use, which payment is to made as followeth vizt. for 300 acres part thereof after ye date of first grant of the 22th of May 1637, and for 100 acres the residue then seven years after the date of this pattent and not before. Dated the 20th of August 1644.

Be it known unto all men that I Robert Lawrence the younger have souled made over & delivered unto George Pearce Smith of the County of Nanzemon all my right & interest in 300 Acres of Land contayned in a patent of 600 Acres lying in the County of Nanzeman and granted unto me by Sir William Berkeley Knight Governor & Capt. General of Virginia the eighth & twentieth day of May in the year 1673 by Beaverdam Swamp.   Robert Lawrence.
Witness: Wm. Scott, Jr.   (Deed Book 1, p. 30).
Henry Plumpton.

Same page. Sold by George Pierce Smith to Hodges Council for a valuable consideration of tobacco. Nov. 20, 1674.

Isle of Wight Deed Book 1704-1715, page 115.

I, Matthew Whitfield and Priscilla my wife of Nanzemond County for 5000 lbs. tobacco paid by John Lawrance of Isle of Wight, Parish of Newport, do sell to him John Lawrance a tract or parcel of land situated or being in Isle of Wight County in Newport Parish afsd., being part of a Pattent granted to Mr. *John Lawrance* now deceased (*Father to ye aforesaid Priscilla*) for 531 Acres bearing date ye 5th day of June 1678 given by ye afsd. Mr. John Lawrance by his Last Will to *his daughter Elizabeth*, and given by ye aforesaid Elizabeth to *her Sister Priscilla* afsd. by Will, to say all ye land given by my father John Lawrance to his daughter Elizabeth, in ye pattent afsd. by his last Will bearing date ye *2nd day of January 1696* and given by ye Elizabeth's Last Will to ye afsd. Priscilla as by ye record of Nanzemond will appear.

In witness whereof we have set our hand this 9th day of ffeb. in ye year of our Lord God 1708.
Wit.: *Richard Exum*   Matthew Whitfield
James Hunter   Priscilla Whitfield
Rd in Isle of Wight ye 9th day of Feby. 1708.

Edenton, Book W, page 58. (North Carolina.) A Convaiance of Land from *Richard Exum* and Robert Larrance unto Colonel Thomas Pollock, Ordered to be Registered, January ye 2nd 1704, Chowan Precinct in ye Province of North Carolina. *Richard Exum* and ―――――.

To all Xtian People to whom these presents shall come.

Robert Larrance Junior of the Isle of Wight County in her Majesty's Colony and Dominion of Virginia sends Greetings in our Lord God Everlasting Know ye y , we Ricd. Exum and Robert Larrance Junior In pursuance of a Power of Attorney to us made from Robert Larrance Senior and Jane his wife and from Henry Sanders and Richd. Taylor all of ye Colony of Virginia deputing Authorizing and Impowering us to sell and convey and make over a Certain Tract of Land and plantation sittuate lying and being on ye West side of Chowan River In ye province and precinct aforesd. called and known by the name of Black Rock on ye west side of Chowan containing three hundred   under   on ye South side by a tract belonging   Thos. Pollock   *which was formerly Possessed by John Laurance* to have and to hold ye aforesaid   Plantation to ye aforesaid Colonel Thomas Pollock his Heires and assigns for Ever with all ye Housing Gardens Orchards timber and timber trees thereon Standing Living and Growing with all other ways and Easements Profits and Commodities and Heridaments thereunto belonging or in any ways appurtaining and will Warrant and Maintain ye same of all and all manner of Claim   , Intrust of any person or persons whatsoever claiming by from or by their order or procurement and ye said sale to warrant.

In every Article and clause (   ) as is above Exprest we bind us and either of us in the   Constituents our Heirs etc. in ye penall Sum of One Hundred pounds Sterling and also   ye same in he precinct Court of Chowan when thereunto reasonably required.

hereof we have hereunto set our hands and fixt our Seals this 22nd day ye fourth

year of ye Reign of our Sovereign Lady Ann Queen of England and Ireland in ye year of our Lord 1704.
In presence of RICHARD EXUM
Nathanil Chevin ROBERT LAWRANCE
———— Henderson.

JON THOMAS' DEED TO COLL. POLLOCK A. D. 1704.

Edenton North Carolina Book W, page 57 A Convaice of Land passed from Jon Thomas unto Colln Thos. Pollock, Order to be Regd January 21 Chowan Precinct In ye Province of North Carolina. To all Xtian people to whom these presents shall come Jon Thomas of ye County of Nancymound of her Majs Colony and Dominion of Virginia sends Greeting In our Lord God Everlasting, Know ye yt, I Jon Thomas having good right and lawful title to a certain part of a Tract of Land Situate lying and being on ye west side of Chowan River In ye Precinct afsd. taken up and surveyed by John Larrance deceased containing two hundred and eight Acres and one third.

Now, Know ye yt , I ye sd. Jon Thomas having good Right and Title of and to ye afsd. parcell of land *by Right of Mary my now wife daughter of ye afsd. Jon Larrance* and a valuable consideration to me in hand paid by Coll. Thos. Pollock of ye same precinct ye receipt whereof I do by these presents acknowledge and therewith fully satisfied Contented and paid; Sell, Alien make over and forever confirm unto ye aforesaid parcell of land lying and being in ye Precinct aforesd. being a part of the aforesaid Pattent to have   for Coll. Thos. Pollock his heirs and assigns for ever and all timber and   commodities to ye same belonging or in any way Warranting ye same to be free and Clear of all Incumbrances and Molestations whatsoever from any person or persons yt shall pretend title thereto and ye sd. Sale to warrant and maintain in every article and class as is above Exprest as also to acknowledge ye same in ye precinct Court of Chowan when thereunto reasonably required. I bind me my heirs Esrs. Adminrs. and Assigns In y Penall sum of twelve pound Sterling. In Witness whereof I have hereunto set my hand and fixt my Seal this 22nd day of November, In ye fourth year of ye Reign of our Sovereign Lady Ann Queen of England, Scotland etc. and in ye year of our Lord 1704.   JON THOMAS

Sealed and delivered in Presence of, ffrancis Parrott, Nathl Chevin, David Henderson.

Jeremiah Exum and wife Ann, of Isle of Wight Co., Va., to Francis Branch, conveyed by Thomas Luten, attorney, 138 acres at the mouth of Mattacomack Creek bounded on the South East by land of Nicholas Crisp and on the North West by land of Nathl Chevin, as may appear by an assignment of Dower from *Thomas Cullen,* of Dover; May 23, 1687. Power of Atty. dated Sept. 22, 1707. Deed dated Jany. 6, 1707-'8. Test.: Nathaniel Chevin (N. C. H. & G. R. 1-1-94; Book "W", Edinton).

Jeremiah Exum, himself, and his wife were Quakers. Note the *affirmation* by his wife as the Exx. of his will. They are recorded as being witnesses on divers occasions to Quaker marriages, and, besides, one of their daughters, Mary, m. 1st a Quaker, Jacob Ricks. (So. His. Ass. Pubs., Vol. VI, and Vol VII,—indexed).

Jeremiah Exum and Ann Lawrence, his wife, had: 1.—Richard Exum, d. unm.; 2.—Mary Exum, m. (1), 14 Oct., 1699, Jacob Ricks, son of Isaac Ricks and Kathren, his wife; m. (II) in 1703, Col. Barnabie McKennie, Sr.; 3.—Ann Exum, m. George Green, predeceased her parents, leaving no issue; 4.—Elizabeth Exum, d. unm.; 5.—Jane Exum, m. Richard Outland; 6.—Mourning Exum, m. William Scott; 7.—Christian Exum, m. George Norsworthy (2nd wife), Lt. Col., Commander-in-Chief in Nansemond Co., Va., 1699. (Va. Co. Rec. 2, p. 105); 8.—Sarah Exum, m. her cousin, Robert Lawrence, Jr.

(W. & M. Q., Vol. 27, No. 1—July 1918, pp. 57-'8, article by Mrs. Annie Noble Sims.)

George Green, Isle of Wight Co. Will pr. Jany. 9, 1707. Wife *Anne;* bro. John; bro-in-law Jeremy Proctor; bro. William Green and bro. John; *Father, Jere Exum,* and bro. *Richard Exum.* Mentions lands and mills. (W. & M. Q., Vol. VII, p. 254.)

Will Book No. 2, p. 21, Isle of Wight, Virginia.

In the name of the Father, Son and Holy Ghost, one God, World without end, Amen:

I Jeremiah Exum of ye Isle of Wight county, being in good and perfect mind and memory, thanks be Almighty God, and calling to remembrance ye uncertain state of this life, do make, ordain and declare this to be my last will and testament, in manner and form following, first: being penitent and sorry for my sins past, humbly desiring forgiveness of ye same, I give and commit my soul unto Almighty God, who gave it, and my body to be buried in decent manner according to ye discretion of my Excurtx hereafter named, as for my temporal estate and such goods and chattels as it hath pleased God to bestow upon me, I do order, give and dispose of in manner and form following:

First: I will that all such debts as I owe to any pson, whatsoever be well and truly payd within convenient time after my decease.

Item: I give to my daughter, Elizabeth, one negro girle called Patty, one feather bed, rugg, blankett and sheets.

Item: I give to my daughter, Mourning, one negro boy, called Harry, one feather bed, rugg, blankett and sheets.

Item: I give to my daughter, Christian, One negro girle, called Doll, one feather bed, rugg, blankett and sheets.

Item: I give to my sd. daughter, Christian, all that   of land which I formerly bought James Collins.

Item: I give to my granddaughter Catherine Scott, one negro boy called Skipper.

Item: I give to my couzin, Jane Exum, one cow and calf.

Item: I give to my loving wife, the plantation whereon I now live during her natural life and after her decease to be equally divided between my two daughters, Elizabeth and Mourning. I likewise give to my wife, one negro woman, called Bess, one negro girle called Sarah, one negro boy, called Jo, all ye sd three negroes to be at her own proper disposall. I Likewise give all ye rest of my negroes, which I have not already disposed of, to my wife, during her natural life, and all other my personal estate, but it is my will that after my wife's decease all those negroes which I have given her during her life, may be divided among my daughters, Sarah, Mary, Eliza, Jane, Mourning and Christian, it being ye full part of my estate which I give to my three daughters (viz) Sarah, Mary, and Jane, I having already given them their part, and lastly I do nominate, ordain and appoint my loving wife to be my whole and sole executrix of this my last Will and Testament.

In witness whereof I hereunto set my hand and fix my seal this third day of September one thousand seven hundred and twelve.

JEREMIAH EXUM (Seal)

Signed and sealed in the presence of John Gibbs, Thos. Godwin and Mary Godwin. At a court held for Isle of Wight county, the 28th day of March 1720, the last will of Jerh Exum was proved by the Exx who made the *solemn affirmation* and proved by the oaths of Thos. Godwin, and John Gibbs, witnesses and ord to be recd. Test, H. Lightfoot, C. Cur. A Copy, Teste; A. S. Johnson, Clerk.

Isle of Wight, Book 3, page 19.

I, Ann Exum of the Isle of Wight County in Virginia being at present sick and weak of Body but of perfect senses and memory Calling to mind the uncertainty of this life think fit to make this my last Will and Testament Committing my soul to God that gave it and my body to have a Christian burial in the earth at the discretion of my Exrs. hereinafter named. And as for the worldly goods and estate I give and bestow in manner and form as followeth:

I give unto my daughter Elizabeth my large Walnut table and a chest to wit, the big chest the two large pots and two pair of iron pot kettles that stand by it and my Great Bible and the red iron pots and all the blue wooden ware and material as pails, tubs   and spinning wheel of wood that belongs to the kitchen and all my sheep and the Eighth part of Corn that may be at that time, and my negro boy Called Joe I give her the use of him for the space of ten years if she lives so long.

I give to my Granddaughter Katharine Godwin a Gold ring.

I give to my grandson Jeremiah Lawrence the value of 30 shillings to be paid out of my estate.

I give to my grandson Exum Scott to the value of 30 shillings to be paid out of my estate.

I give to my grandson Richard Exum Outland my silver   of a small   .

Also I give unto my three grandsons before named to wit: Jeremiah Lawrance, Exum Scott, Richard Exum Outland my negro boy Joe equally between them after ten years service to my daughter Elizabeth or at her death if it is in less time.

I give to my Granddaughter Ann Murphy a bedtick or bolstertick a rug and a pair of shoes.

And all the remaining part of my Estate within Doors and without doors negroes stock and house furniture I give equally to be divided between my five Daughters to wit: Mary Mackinnie, Elizabeth Exum, Jane Outland, Mourning Scott and Christian Narsworthy and as to the part to my Daughter Sarah deceased her children equally and I appoint and ordain my son-in-law William Scott to be my only and sole Executor of this my last Will and Testament which I own and ratify renouncing all other Will formerly by me made to which I set my hand and fix my seal this 3d day of February 1726/7,

Witnesses: Signed ANN EXUM.

Edward Sikoo

James Sanson

Henry Sanders Jr.   Recorded March 27th, 1727.

Isle of Wight Book, 1704-1715, p. 248. October 16-1713.

I, Mary Thomas, widow of the Upper Nancemond County for 5100 lbs. tobacco grant enfeeneoff, etc. to John Lawrence Senior of the Lower Parish of Isle of Wight County a parcel of Land or plantation being in Isle of Wight County upon maine Blackwater one hundred Acres being part of a pattent of 530 Acres granted unto John Lawrence late of Nancymond County Deceased Pattent bearing date the 5th day of June 1678, the said parvel of land by the afsd. *John Lawrence Last Will* bequeathed to his said daughter Mary, and is divided by a line of trees from John Lawrence's land.

                                                                          MARY THOMAS

Wit.: William Wilkinson, Thomas Mandew (?), Giles Driver, Junior.

Recorded October 26th, 1713.

N. B.—Priscilla, Elizabeth, John, Jr., Mary Thomas, Ann Exum . . . . . Lawrence, ... Sanders, ... Taylor were children of John Lawrence.

(Will January 2, 1696.)

Isle of Wight, Virginia, Deed Book 1, p. 340. Book 1688-1704.

Know all people to whom these presents shall come Barnaby Mackquinny and Mary his wife send Greeting in our Lord God Everlasting Know ye that I the said Barnaby Mackquinny and Mary my wife of the County of the Isle of Wight for divers good causes and Considerations we hereunto moving but more especially for and in Consideration of a Certain sum of Tobacco to us in hand paid the receipt whereof we do hereby acknowledge have give granted bargained sold conveyed and confirmed and by these presents do sell etc. unto Richard Exum of the aforesaid County a parcel of land to say my Father Michael Mackquinny's Manor plantation beginning at the foot of his Spring Branch touching Henry Gay's line, at the Main Swamp, that is to say all the land given me by my Father's last Will and Testament, situate lying and being in the Isle of Wight, being part of an escheat Pattent granted to my Brother John Mackquinney deceased, bearing date the 20th of April 1694.

Wit.: James Webb, Jno. Council   Barnaby Mackinne

Recorded 9th 30th 1703 to *Captain* Richard Exum.   Mary Mackinne

MICHAEL MACKQUINNY GIVES BOND FOR TITLE. 12,000 lbs. tobacco.

"John Macquinney conveyed this land to Barnaby his Brother by an instrument of writing bearing date Jan. 13-1694 but before John could make a lawful conveyance of same he dyed.

But notwithstanding Barnaby Mackquinny had made a conveyance to Richard Exume, if the heirs of John Macquinny when they come to age of 21 years shall make a lawfull Conveyance of sd. land to the sd. Richard Exum the above obligation to be void, otherwise to remain in full force.

                                                                        Barnaby Macquinney.

George Norsworthy, Dec. 4, 1724, wife *Christian Norsworthy*, son George Norsworthy, dau. Elizabeth Norsworthy, one negro boy in lieu of what her *grandmother Elizabeth Bridger* left her in my hands. My dau. Christian Norsworthy, my dau. Illian Norsworthy. Exr.: my wife Christian and my Brother-in-law William Scott. Geo. Norsworthy Exec. Dec. 4th, 1724. George Norsworthy.
Witnesses: Tris Norsworthy, Peter Legg, William Denson. (Great Book, p. 173) William Denson. (Great Book, p. 173.)

Christian Norsworthy, Will, Nov. 8th, 1727; Rd Nov. 26, 1727. My son George Norsworthy two negroes, my dau. Christian Norsworthy negro woman and household furniture. To my dau.-in-law Elizabeth Norsworthy one silver salt cellar. To my dau.-in-law Martha Norsworthy one silver plate. To my cousin Christian Outland my old silver tumblers. To my cousin Elizabeth Scott my new silver tumblers. To my friend James Turner 8£. The rest of my estate to be divided between my son George Norsworthy & my daughter Christian Norsworthy. I leave the care of their schooling to my brother-in-law William Scott, in case my children die in their minority my estate to be divided between the children of my Brother-in-law William Scott & William Ouland (Outland). William Scott is Exr. Nov. 8th, 1727. Wit.: Edward Mason, George Lawrence.

Christian Norsworthy.

Rec. Nov. 26, 1727. (Will Book 3, p. 50).

Item 6th of Will of Isaac Ricks, 20th day 7th mo., called Sept., 1721, Rd April 24, 1724, reads as follows: "I give to my two gran Children *Isaac & Martha* the *children of my son Jacob Rickes, deceased*, each of them one shilling". (Great Book, p. 157).

Capt. Richard Exum on April 10, 1710, rec'd deed from Michael and Rose Macquinney to 450 A. that their gr. father Michael Mackquenney lived on. (Book 1704-1715, p. 148). On June 9th, 1710 rec'd deed from William & Jane Carver to 230 A., in Isle of Wight, inherited by Jane Carver from her father John Moore. (Book 1704-1715, p. 163). He sold the above last named tract to Frances Seagraves. Deed recorded March 26, 1711. (Book 1704-1715, p. 178). On Aug. 4, 1704, *Thos. & Elizabeth Reeves* convey to Richard Exum 200 A. along Terrapin Branch. (Bk. 1704-1715, p. 19). On March 9, 1707/8 Richard Exum sells this last named tract to Richard Lewis, of Isle of Wight. (Bk. 1704-1715, p. 83).

Great Book, p. 291, I. of W., Va. To All Christian people to whom these presents shall come. Sarah Lawrence, Mary Mackinne, Elizabeth Exum, Jane Outland, Mourning Scott, Christian Norsworthy and Catharine Scott being *co-heirs* to *Richard Exum*, late deceased of Nansemond County, Robert Lawrence and Sarah my wife, and Barnaby Mackinne and Mary my wife, Elizabeth Exum, William Outland and Jane my wife, and William Scott and Mourning my wife, and Catharine Scott send Greeting in our Lord God Everlasting know ye that we ye sd. Robert Lawrence and Sarah my wife and Barnaby Mackinne and Mary my wife, and Elizabeth Exum, William Outland and Jane my wife, William Scott and Mourning my wife and Catharine Scott for divers Good Causes and Considerations, but more especially for as much as we have made an Equal Division *of our Brother's Land* Lately deceased before sealing and Delivering of this Resept Whereof we do confess and acknowledge that hereby we have given granted bargained and do by these presents Make over unto George Narsworthy of ye County of Isle of Wight to him and his heirs Executors and Assigns for Ever a certain tract or parcell of Land Lying on ye head of Indian Creek in ye Western Branch of Nansemond County by estimation 200 Acres more or less being part of an Escheat pattent, formerly granted to John Mackinne for 450 Acres bearing date ye 20th of April 1694 ye 200 Acres of Land being formerly in ye possession of ye sd. Richard Exum and bounded as follows, Beginning on head of Indian Creek on ye line of Mr. Jeremiah Exum, touching Henry Gay's line. Deed made September 8th 1719.

(Signed) Robert Lawrence and Sarah Lawrence, Barnaby Mackinne and Mary Mackinne, Elizabeth Exum, William Outland and Jane Outland, Catharine Scott, William Scott and Mourning Scott.

Witnesses: John Dunkley, John Watts.

Recorded October 25th 1719. Lightfoot, Clerk of Court.

To all Xtian people to whome these presents shall come. I Elizabeth Exum

of Isle of Wight Co., Va., for & in consideration of the natural love & affection which I bear to my well beloved Cousin Jeremiah Lawrence of the County aforesaid, give him the said Jeremiah Lawrence a negro boy named Mingo. Feby. 4, 1736.
Wit. Wm. X Gay.   Elizabeth Exum.
Recorded June 27, 1737. (Book 5, p. 117).

After a careful analysis and consideration of the early Exum records which I have herein given—and they are very nearly all I have been able to obtain—I am of the opinion that Thomas Exum[1] with wife Ann was the first to emigrate to America. That he was the brother of Richard[1]; that Thos. had son William[2], who had wife Jane; that Richard had two children, viz.: Jeremiah[2] and Thos.[2], who had wife Sarah. Jeremiah[2], in will, makes a bequest to his cousin Jane Exum—in this instance could not have been niece—showing that William[2], husband of Jane, was the nephew of Richard[1], father of Jeremiah[2], and consequently that Richard and Thos.[1] were brothers. Richard[1] and William[2] are named among the headrights, so were not natives but immigrants. No record found showing when Thos.[1] came, but we find that Exums had a settlement in Rappahannock when the grants to Richard Exum and Thos. Godwin were made May 22, 1650.

EXCURSUS: *GRIGSBY*.

Enoch Grigsby, of Mt. Willing, S. C., and Susan Butler, his wife, besides their dau., Mrs. Lodowick Hill, had:

1.—Col. Rhydon Grigsby; 2.—A dau., who m. Capt. Jonathan Weaver; 3.—A dau., who m. Samuel Mays, of Big Saluda; 4.—Another dau. who m. Thomas Butler, a brother of Gen. William Butler.

Sarah Butler, sister of Susan (Butler) Grigsby, and aunt of Gen. William Butler, m. Jacob Smith, a man of great wealth (d. in 1805). They left a son, Luke Smith, and a dau. Sophia Smith, who m. Capt. James Bonham, whose youngest son was Bridgadier Genl. Milledge Bonham, who also became Govr. of S. C.

HENDERSON.

James Henderson, in 1672, lived on the north side of Pocomoke river, Somerset Co., Md. ("Allied Fams. of Delaware", p. 80, by Edwin Jaquell Sellers).

Among the "Names of those who fought against the King, at Preston, and were *banished to Md.*—sent over as King's rebels,, Aug. 20, 1716, in the ship "Friendship", of Belfast, was that of *Robert Henderson*". ("Side Lights of Md. His.", Vol. 1, p. 214).

Benjamin Henderson, Sr., Worcester Co., Md., Will Nov. 18, 1769; Filed May 22, 1772. In the name of God Amen I Benjamin Henderson Senr. of Worcester County in the province of Maryland being sick of body but of sound and perfect in Judgment Wit Memory and knowing the uncertainty of this Life I do hereby make this my last will and testament.

first I give my soul into the hands of my ever blessed Savior and redeemer the Lord Jesus Christ hopeing in and through his merits resurrection and assention pardon from all my sins and

Secondly I give my body to the earth there to be decently Buried and Entred therein and as for my personal estate I dispose of as followeth.

Item I give and bequeath to my well beloved wife Mary all my land called haphazard during her widowhood not to be disturbed, and after her disceice to my son Benjamin Henderson him and his heirs forever.

Item I give to my son Lemuel Henderson my negro man Named Harry after my deceice to him and his heirs forever and also my hand mill after my disceice and my wifes.

Item I give to my sone Lemuel four black walnut chairs.

Item I give to my grandson James Henderson my Chist.

Item I give to my grandson Lemuel Henderson my gun.

Item I give to my Daughter Mary Harsey my feather bed that I shall die on and furniture with it.

Item I give to my grandson Thomas Collins one large Chist and also one Ewe an Lamb and one young heifer.

Item I give to my daughters Leah Roday and Betty—one shilling a piece.

Item I give to my wife Mary all my movable estate not before mentioned and after her deceice as she shall see fitt to leave it. I leave constitute and appoint my wife and my son Lemuel Henderson to be the whole and sole Excr. of this my last will and testament utterly revoking and disannulling all other wills by me made Baring date before this as witness my hand and seal this 18th day of November Anno Dom. 1769.

his
Benjamin B. Henderson (Seal)
mark

Signed, sealed and delivered in the presence of Solomon Webb, John Blades, William Franklin.

Admitted to probate May 22, 1772. True Copy. Test. Edwd P. Davis, Reg. of Wills for Worcester County.

Isaac Purnell Henderson, b. 11 March, 1789, at Snow Hill, Md.; d. 7 Dec., 1864—was the first of the family in Ga. He was the son of Lemuel Henderson, of Somerset Co., Md., d. circa 1825—whose mother's christian name, it is said, was Edith. Tradition says Lemuel Henderson was a nephew of Peter Henderson, m. Susan Anne Henderson and had:

1.—Isaac Purnell Henderson (above) (q. v.); 2.—Milby Henderson; 3.—Hamby Henderson; 4.—Sarah Henderson.

WILL OF PURNELL HENDERSON.

22 Jany., 1801; filed 12 Feby., 1801.

In the name of God Amen. I Purnell Henderson of Worcester Co., State of Md., being in a low state of health and knowing uncertainty of death do pronounce this my last Will and Testament.

Item. I do give and bequeath unto my *son Isaac Henderson* two young Steares.

Item. I do give and bequeath unto my *daughter Nancy Henderson* one black cow two chect one pine table and all her mother's clothes and one wheel.

Item. I do give and bequeath unto my *son John Henderson* one bed and furniture and the low bedstead.

Item. I do give and bequeath unto my *son Thomas Henderson* two beds and furniture large one and small one and two pine bedsteads one pot and pot hooks and Dutch oven and Hooks and lids and the rest of my property to be equally divided my four children Isaac Henderson, Nancy Henderson, John Henderson and Thomas Henderson that is after my lawful debts is paid.

I also do leave my trusty friend *Ananias German* my executor and to do the best he can in seaing that my children is taken care of.

As witness my hand and seal this 22" day of January Eighteen hundred and one. 1801. (Signed) Purnell Henderson (Seal).

Witness: Isaac Richards, Nehemiah Truitt, Levin Dereckson.

True Copy—Test.: Edwd. P. Davis, Reg. of Wills, Worcester Co.

An *Isaac Purnell* d. intest. in 1798, leaving as nearest of kin John P. Marshall and John Purnell, Snow Hill, Somerset Co., Md.

In a D. A. R. Mag. we find this: "Query—7714 (B) Henderson. John Milba Henderson was wrecked off the Va. capes before the Revolution. He died in Dalton, Ga., leaving sons John Milba Henderson Jr. and Hampton Henderson, who m. Mary Graham. Hampton resided in Gibson County, Tenn. and in 1846 moved to Helena, Ark. Wanted genealogy of John Milba, Sr., name of wife and his record of Revolutionary service". Signed—M. A. L.

Mrs. Mary (Henderson) Carr, b. 1829, dau. of Isaac Purnell and Ruth (Shepherd Johnson) Henderson, and who d. only a few years ago, said: "My father had two brothers, Milby and Hamby, and we are nearly related to the prominent Senator (now dead) from Arkansas".

Isaac Purnell Henderson, 1789-1864, said he was often told of his grandmother putting ear to ground to hear the guns of the Revolution. His mother had a sister, or an aunt, named Argante, hence the name Ary in the Henderson family in Ga.; and the name *Isaac Purnell* was for some of his mother's kin. He represented Newton, Co., Ga., in the legislature in 1837. He m. (I), 2 April, 1814, *Sarah Bridges*, dau. of Solomon Bridges, in Oglethorpe Co., Ga., d. 13 May, 1821; m. (II), 9 Dec.,

1821 Ruth (Shepherd) Johnson, widow of Walton (?) Johnson and dau. of *Providence Prosperity* Shepherd and his wife, Ann Walker. (See Excursus Shepherd). Issue by 1st mar.: 1. Lemuel Henderson, b. 26 March, 1815; m., 5 March, 1844, in Alabama, Caroline Buchanan; 2. Susan Ann Henderson, b. 8 May, 1817; m., 8 Dec., 1832, John Harris, of Newton, Co., Ga.; 3. Arrah Henderson, b. 19 June, 1819; m. . . . . March, 1834, Fortune N. Chisholm, in Newton Co.; 4. Sarah Ann Henderson, b. 10 April, 1821; d. 15 Aug., 1843; m., 17 Oct., 1834, A. B. Higgs.

Issue by 2nd mar.: 5. *Robert Johnson Henderson*, b. 12 Nov., 1822; d. 3 Feby., 1891; m. 2 April, 1846, *Laura Elizabeth Wood*, b. 2 May, 1829; d. 26 Sept., 1899. (q. v.); 6. Frances Caroline Henderson, b. 16 Jany., 1825; m. 13 Oct., 1840, Rufus M. Tarver; 7. John Thomas Henderson, b. 18 Dec., 1826; d. . . . . ; m. 3 Oct., 1848, Paulina Frances Wood, b. 20 March, 1831, d. . . . . (q. v.); 8. Mary Elizabeth Henderson, b. 23 Feby., 1829; d. . . . . ; m. 22 Feby., 1849, Benjamin F. Carr; 9. Martha Walker Henderson, b. 12 Jany., 1833; d. . . . . ; m. 11 July, 1850, Augustus H. Lee, of Covington, Ga.

5. *Robert Johnson Henderson*, 1822-1891, *represented Newton Co.* in the State legislature in 1859 and '60; organized and was made *Colonel* of the 42nd Ga. Regt., C. S. A.; *wounded* at battle of *Resacca;* made *Brigadier General* and surrendered with his command after last battle of war in N. C.

Genl. Robt. Johnson and Laura Elizabeth (Wood) Henderson had: (1) Cary Wood Henderson, b. 20 Feby., 1847; d. 12 Dec., 1880; m. 3 Oct., 1871, Mary Semmes Clayton, dau. of Judge W. W. Clayton of Atlanta, Ga., and his wife, Caroline Semmes, and gr. dau. of Hon. Augustus Clayton and his wife, Julia Carnes. He served as Sergeant in Battalion of Ga. Cadets in C. S. War, was active and prominent in military circles after the war, and was Captain for some years of the Atlanta Cadets; (2) *Mary Ruth Henderson*, b. 12 Jany., 1849; d. 21 May, 1918; m. 28 Sept., 1871 *Lodowick Johnson Hill*, b. 16 Jany., 1846, son of *Col. Lodowick Meriwether Hill and his first wife, Nancy Hill Johnson.* (See Hill Record, p. 133); (3) John Francis Henderson, b. 25 April, 1850; d. 19 April, 1917; m. 22 Oct., 1872, Julia Usher, d. 9 June, 1917, aged 68 years. Issue: Florrie, m. A. S. Burney, of Rome, Ga.; Fannie, m. Hugh Wright, of Covington, Ga.; and Clifford Henderson, Asst. Cashier of the Lowry National Bank; (4) Isaac Purnell Henderson II, b. 5 Dec., 1851; d. 30 Nov., 1881; m. 25 Sept., 1877, Mary Harrison Dyer. Issue: 1.—Isaac Purnell Henderson, of Washington, D. C., m. Edna Whitaker—divorced; no issue; (5) *Claudia Lawson Henderson*, b. 15 Aug., 1853; m. 2 Nov., 1877, *Edward Young Hill*, b. 8 Sept., 1852, *brother of Lodowick Johnson Hill* (above). (See Hill Record, p. 135); (6) Robert Johnson Henderson, Jr., b. 14 Sept., 1856; d. 25 Nov., 1857; (7) Charles Young Henderson, b. 3 May, 1858; m. (I), 19 Dec., 1883, Clara Carr; m. (II), Annie L. Mattox, of Cuthbert, Ga. No issue; (8) Robert Clifford Henderson, b. 6 Aug., 1860; d. 24 Feby., 1882, unm.; (9) *William Henry Henderson*, of N. O., La., b. 12 April, 1866; m. (I), 18 Dec., 1886, Martha Whitaker, of Hogansville, Ga., d. 5 July, 1915, divorced, and had one son: Robert Johnson Henderson III, of Atlanta, Ga., m. Mrs. Mittie *Johnson*, widow with 2 children; m. (II), 17 March, 1912, Emma Hill McAlister. No issue.

7. John Thomas Henderson and wife, Paulina Frances Wood, had: (1) Laura Genevive, called "Laulie", Henderson, decd.; m. Daniel Hightower, decd., and had dau., Louise Hightower, who m. . . . . Boyd, of Wilkes Co., Ga., and two other children; (2) Cecilia Billups Henderson, m. Paul Sledge, of Augusta, Ga., d. 20 Aug., 1919, in his 73rd year. He was for many years the head official, at Augusta, of the old South Carolina railroad, the Clyde Steamship Co. Issue, dau. and six sons, among them: 1.—Pauline, who m. Steiner Dunbar, of Augusta; 2.—Paul Sledge, Jr., and 3.—John Sledge; (3) William Billups Henderson, m. . . . ., and has several children; (4) John Thomas Henderson, Jr., d. in early manhood, unm.

JORDAN.

Samuel Jordan[1] was among those who came in the Sea Venture with Governor Gates in 1608-9 ("Facts and Figures vs. Myths and Misrepresentations", pp. 5, 9, 10, by Mildred Lewis Rutherford); in 1619 patented land and founded a plantation called Jordan's Jorney, in the present Prince George Co.; was Burgess for Charles City at the session of 30 July, 1619 (Col. Va. Reg., p. 52); fortified his house, Beggar's Bush, during the Indian Massacre of March, 1622, "and lived in despight of the enemy", but d. in March, 1623. Is said to have had by his 1st wife: *Thomas²*, *Samuel²*, and Robert², all b. in Eng., and each of whom came to Va.

He m. (II) Cicely . . . ., who survived him and m. (II), Capt. William Farrar.

Thomas Jordan², b. in 1600, named in census of 1623 as a soldier under Sir George Yeardley; m. Lucy Corker, dau. of Capt. John Corker, of Surry, who represented Pashehay, Va., in assembly 1632. He was Burgess at sessions 16 Oct., 1629, 21 Feby., 1631-'2, and 4 Sept., 1632. (Col. Va. Reg., pp. 54, 56, 57; W. & M. Qly. 27, p. 122; Cradle of Republic, p. 255). Issue, probably others:

Thomas Jordan³—the Militant Quaker—b. 1634; d. 8 Oct., 1699;Burgess from Nansemond, 1696-'7 (Col. Va. Reg., p. 91); m. in 1659, Margaret Brasseuer, b. 7 July, 1642; d. 7 Oct. 1708; dau. of Robert. Brasseuer, bro. of John Brasseuer (Huguenot family). He lived at Chuckatuck, in Nansemond, became a Quaker in 1660 and from 1664 onward was several times arrested, imprisoned and fined. (W. & M. Qly. 27, p. 122; So. His. Assn. Pubs., Vol. 7, p. 211). Their sons were: 1. Thomas⁴, b. 6 Jany., 1660; m. 6 Oct., 1679, Elizabeth Burgh, dau. of Col. Wm. Burgh; 2. John⁴, b. 17 Jany., 1663; m. 9 Dec., 1688, Margaret Burgh, dau. of Col. Wm. Burgh; 3. James⁴, b. 23 Nov., 1666; m. 29 March, 1688, Elizabeth Ratliff, d. last of June, 1695, dau. of Richard Ratliff, of Isle of Wight; m. (II), July 14, 1701, Jane Roseter, of Elizabeth River. (So. His. Assn. Pubs., Vol. 6, pp. 227-'8-'9 and 312); 4. Robert⁴, b. 11 July, 1688; d. 1728; m. (I), 7 Dec., 1687, Christian Outland, d. 26 June, 1689, dau. of Thomas Taberer, of I. of Wight, and relict of William Outland, whom she m. 15 Sept., 1678; m. (II), 7 July, 1690, Mary, dau. of Edmund Belson, of Nansemond Co., by whom he had, besides others: Mary, b. 24 Dec., 1699, m. Thomas Pleasants, of Henrico Co. Her will, undated, proved in Goochland Co., 17 July, 1797; 5. Benjamin⁴, b. 18 July, 1674; 6. Mathew⁴, b. 1 Nov., 1676; m. (I), 6 July, 1699, Dorrity Bufkin, widow woman—both of Nansemond; m. (II), 17 March, 1702, Susanna Bresey, widow of William Bresey, of whose estate an inventory was made in 1701—he was very wealthy; 7. Samuel⁴, b. 16 Feby., 1679; d. bet. 1 Dec., 1760, and 26 Feby., 1761. (q. v.) ; 8. Joshua⁴, b. 30 June, 1681; 9. Richard Jordon⁴, son of Thos., of Chuckatuck, m. 22 June, 1706, Rebecca Ratcliff, dau. of Richd and Elizabeth Ratcliff (So. H. A. P's, Vol. 6, p. 412).

7. *Samuel Jordan⁴*, son of *Thos.³* and *Margaret (Brassueur) Jordan*, 1679-1761, m. 10 Dec., 1703, *Elizabeth Fleming*, dau. of *Col. John Fleming* and his wife, *Mary Bolling* (W. & M. Qly., Vol. 27, p. 44). Their sons were 1. *Samuel Jordan⁵*, of Union Hill, b. 1714; d. 2 July, 1789; m. (I), Ruth Meredith; m. (II), Judith Scott Ware (mar. bond Goochland Co., Va., 18 Feby., 1744); 2. William Jordan⁵, m. Mary . . . .; 3. *Rev. Mathew Jordan⁵* (pro. b. c. 1718); m. Julia Scott, "dau. of the widow Scott". He was Justice of the Court of Albemarle, 1748; d. in 1769. ("Cabells and their Kin", p. 49). Issue: (1) Mildred Jordan⁶, m. (I) Charles Irving (of the firm of Irving, Gault & Co., Richmond, Va.); m. (II), . . Rose; (2) Sarah Jordan⁶, m. Charles Rose; (3) William Jordan⁶, d. early; (4) John Jordan⁶, entered Rev'y War at 17; never married; (5) Benjamin Jordan⁶, connected with Irving, Gault & Co., large mercantile Co., of Richmond, Va.; (6) *Fleming Jordan⁶*, m. . . . . Moore, dau. of *John Moore* and *Martha Harvie*, his wife; gr. dau. of Col. John Harvie and his wife, Martha Gaines, and niece of Jeannette Harvie, who m. Reuben Jordan; (7) Mathew Jordan⁶; (8) Judith Jordan⁶; (9) Elizabeth Jordan⁶; (10) *Reuben Jordan⁶*, d. 1816, m. *Jeannette Harvie*, dau. of *Col. John Harvie*, Sr., and *Martha Gaines*, his wife: Issue, 4 sons and 3 daus.: 1. Reuben Jordan, Jr.⁷, m. (I) Nancy Johnson, dau. of Col. Nicholas Johnson; m. (II), Martha Williamson; 2. Fleming Jordan⁷, m. Ann Meriwether; 3. Mortimer Jordan⁷, m. (I) Lucy Gray; m. (II), Amy Walton; 4. Charles Scott Jordan⁷, m. (I) Rebekah Johnson, dau. of Col. Nicholas Johnson; m. (II), . . . Reid; 5. Martha Jordan⁷, m. Dr. . . . Bradley; 6. Margaret Jordan⁷, m. . . . ., (planter); 7. Elizabeth Jordan⁷, m. (I) James Jackson Gilmer; m. (II), Dr. George Meriwether; 8. Anne Jordan⁷ (?).

5. *Benjamin Jordan⁶* (son of Mathew⁵), m. *Elizabeth* . . . ., and, among others, had: (1) *Josiah Jordan⁷*, d. 1821; m. *Judie (Judith) Hill*, d. 20 June, 1794, dau. of *Abraham³* and *Christian (Walton) Hill*. (See Hills, p. 67).

6. *Fleming Jordan⁶*, son of Rev. Mathew⁵ and Julia (Scott) Jordan (or *should this be son of Samuel, 1679-1760-61, and Elizabeth (Fleming) Jordan?*), m. . . . .

Moore, dau. of John Moore and Martha Harvie, his wife, niece of Jeannette Harvie, who m. Reuben Jordan. Issue: 1. *Dr. John Jordan*[7], b. 24 April, 1793; d. Sept. 30, 1855; m. 26 Oct., 1824, Sarah Christian Walton (Mrs. Barnett has it Wootten) Hill, b. 5 Dec., 1807; d. 28 June, 1842, dau. of Wylie Hill and Martha Pope, his wife. (For issue, see Hills, p. 136); 2. Dr. Fleming Jordan, Jr.[7] (q. v.); 3. Dr. William Moore Jordan[7], b. 11 Feby., 1809; d. 29 May, 1873; m. 10 April, 1838, Amelia Thomas Hill, dau. of Wylie and Martha (Patsy) Pope Hill (see Hills, p. 140); 4. Mathew Jordan[7], merchant in Maysville, 1852; of Madison Co., Ala., in 1854. (q. v.); 5. Benjamin Jordan[7], d. first of all; 6. Edwin James Harvie Jordan[7] (q. v.); 7. Reuben Gaines Jordan[7], the 3rd to die in young manhood; 8. Martha Harvie Jordan[7] (q. v.); 9. Mary Jane Jordan[7], b. 27 May, 1798; d. 16 March, 1886 (q. v.); 10. Lucy Jordan[7]—the 2nd to die while young.

2. *Dr. Fleming Jordan, Jr.*[7] (Fleming[6], Mathew[5], Samuel[4]), d. 24 Dec., 1882; m. Lucy Jane . . . ., living in Madison Co., Ala., in 1854. Issue: (1) Mary Lewis Jordan[8] b. circa 1834; (2) Charles Edward Jordan[8], b. circa 1836; (3) Fleming Jordan III[8], b. circa 1838; (4) Martha Ann Jordan[8], b. circa 1840; (5) Sarah Jordan[8], b. circa 1842; (6) Lucy S. Jordan[8], b. circa 1844; (7) William Jordan[8], b. circa 1846 (pro. Little "Will" of Huntsville, Ala.); (8) Mezzie Jordan[8], b. circa 1848; (9) Reuben Jordan[8], b. circa 1850; (10) John S. Jordan[8], b. circa 1852; (11) Ellen King Jordan[8], b. circa . . . . .

4. *Mathew Jordan*[7] (Fleming[6], Mathew[5]), m. . . . . . Issue: (1) Dr. *William Fleming Jordan*[8], b. circa 1835; (2) James E. Jordan, b. circa 1837; (3) Martha C. Jordan, b. circa 1839; (4) Louisa Jordan, b. circa 1849 (?). Living in Madison Co., Ala., in 1854.

6. *Edwin James Harvie Jordan*[7] (Fleming[6]), m. Elizabeth D. Seale. Issue: (1) Martha E. Jordan[8], b. circa 1842; (2) Charles S. Jordan[8], b. circa 1845; (3) Margaret Jordan[8], b. circa 1847, d. 1856; (4) Benajah Jordan[8], b. circa 1849; (5) Mary Jane[8], b. circa 1852. Living in Lowndes Co. and Columbus, Miss., in 1854.

8. *Martha Harvie Jordan*[7] (Fleming[6]), m. (I) James McCartney, d. 1829. Issue: (1) James B. McCartney[8], d. 1844; (2) Fleming J. McCartney[8], b. Aug., 1829; d. 12 June, 1853 (Dr. Fleming Jordan appointed 3 Feby., 1834, Guardian of Fleming J. McCartney); m. (II), in 1833, George I. Weaver, d. 1840. Issue, one child, d. 1836; m. (III), in 1842, Mathew H. Bone.

9. *Mary Jane Jordan*[7] (Fleming[6]), m. *James Walker*, b. 13 May, 1799; d. 4 Nov., 1869, son of William and Genette Walker. Issue: (1) Martha Jane Walker[8]; (2) Lucy M. Walker[8], m. John Higginson; (3) *William Fleming Walker*[8], m. 7 July, 1853, *Sarah Ann Eliza Render Hill* (see Hills, p. 104); (4) Mary Eliza Walker[8], m. Willis Burnett; (5) Margaret R. Walker[8]; (6) Narcissa L. Walker[8], and (7) Sarah J. Walker[8] (twins), m. G. L. Bryan; (8) Louisa Ann Walker[8], m. Dr. H. P. Bone. The above family were living in Aberdeen, Monroe Co., and Okalona, Chickasaw Co., Miss., in 1854.

"*Capt. Samuel Jordan*[1] in 1619 patented at Jordan's Point, on James River, 450 A. bounded by Capt. Woodleif's land. At time of Massacre in 1622, Capt. Jordan gathered together his neighbors at "Beggar's Bush", "where he fortified and lived in despite of the enemy", called "Jordan's Jorney, or Beggar's Bush". He died next year—1623, and his widow, *Cecilly*, was courted by Capt. William Farrar, after the minister Rev. Greville Pooley had received, as he alleged, a promise of marriage. The affair brought before Council who issued proclamation prohibiting women in future from contracting themselves in marriage to two several men at the same time". ("Cradle of the Republic", p. 214). In the 1st General Assembly the plantations of Bermuda Hundred, Sherly Hundred and Charles City were represented by Samuel Sharpe and *Samuel Jordan* ("Cradle of the Republic", p. 215; Col. Va. Reg., p. 52).

George Jordan[2], son of *Samuel*[1] and his first wife, was Attorney General of Va. in 1670; Burgess from James City 1644, '47, for Surry 1658-'9, 1674-'5-'6 (Col. Va. Reg., pp. 63, 66, 74, 80); m. Alice Myles, d. 1650, dau. of John Myles, Gent. of Brounstone, near Hereford, Eng. (W. & M. Q. IV, 196, and V, p. 6; Col. Va. Reg., p. 25).

On "4 Mile Tree plantation", south side James River, where a tree marked Western boundarie of James City as Defined by Gov. Argall, in graveyard near the house is the tombstone of Alice Jordan, daughter of John Miles, of Brauton Herefordshire, and wife of *Col. George Jordan,* Atty. Genl. of Va. in 1670. She d. Jany. 7, 1650-1. There is only one older tombstone in Va.—that of Col. Wm. Perry at Westover, d. 1637, the inscription on which is entirely worn away". ("Cradle of the Republic", p. 207).

Samuel Jordan[5], of Union Hill, *son of Samuel*[4] and Elizabeth (Fleming) Jordan was Justice of the Court of Albemarle Co., Va., 1746-47. Col. *James Jordan*[5] settled in the Seven Islands on the south side of the James River in the present Co. of Buckingham, where he owned a considerable body of land. He also owned 5250 A. on Jordan Creek in Halifax Co., and 4699 A. in Albemarle. He was J. of the P. for Albemarle Co. 1746-'65; a Capt. in 1753; Sheriff in 1753-'55; presiding Justice of the Peace in the new Co. of Buckingham, 1761; was Burgess from Buckingham Co., 1765-'6-'7-'8-'9 (Col. Va. Reg., pp. 171, 174, 176), and although an old man at the beginning of the Revn., he served as Colonel of the Militia and as member of the Co. Committee after June, 1776; was State Commissioner of the State foundry for casting Cannon in Buckingham. In "Bristol Parish", by Slaughter, it is said: "The law required that the most able and discreet persons in the Parish should be chosen for Vestrymen, and we find that the burgesses and magistrates, and men prominent in social and civil affairs were Vestrymen during the whole Colonial period.

"In 1776 we can scarcely err in the presumption that the representatives of the Church and of the State, during the interval indicated above, were the same. The rpresentative names at that time were: Wood, Jordan, Poythress, Wynne, Hatcher, Cocke, Hamlin, Eppes, Bolling, Bland, Jones, Randolph, Kennon, Batt, Bath, Gilliam, Walker and Mumford". (By Mrs. R. H. Carter, State Historian, Birmingham, Ala., in Birmingham News, Oct. 20, 1906; and So. Col. Dames of Ga. No. 362 (Mrs. James Silas Wright).

"The *Jordans removed from Amherst Co., Va., about 1784,* and *settled on the Broad River in Wilkes Co., Ga.*

Genl. Mathews had served in Ga. during the War. He made preparations soon after for removing to a tract of land then and yet known as the Goosepond, a disputed title to which he had purchased for a very small consideration. He was well known in Augusta and Albemarle Cos., in Va. Influenced by his judgment, Francis Meriwether, Benjamin Taliaferro, and one or two others visited Georgia in 1784. They went to the neighborhood of the Goosepond, were pleased with the land and purchased. They and many of their friends and relations—the Harvies, Meriwethers, Taliaferros, Gilmers, Mathewses, Barnetts, Crawfords, Johnsons, Jordans, McGehees, Markses, Freemans, &c., &c., removed to Ga. with their families immediately afterwards. They formed a society of the greatest intimacy—mutual wants making the surest foundation for the interchange of mutual kindness". ("Georgians", by Gov. Geo. R. Gilmer).

HARVIE.

"John Harvie, b. at Garywomack, Scotland, in the Shire of Sterling, North Britain, removed from Scotland to Va.—settled in Albemarle Co. about 40 years before the Rev'y War; wife's maiden name was Gaines—her husband being dead she accompanied her children to Broad River, Ga., and d. in her 80th year. Had 9 children—4 sons and 5 daus. The 9 weighed about 2700 lbs.—the 4 brothers a little less than 1200 and the 5 sisters somewhat more than 1500. Daniel Harvey reached near 400 and exceeded other men as much in strength as in size; m. Sallie, sister of Benjamin Taliaferro; she was left a widow with 5 children—4 daus. and a son.

Genette Harvie (dau. of John) m. Reuben Jordan, one of the descendants of the *Indian Princess Pocahontas.* She *was the largest* of the Harvie sisters. Reuben Jordan m. (I) an old maid, who soon d., leaving one child.

Reuben and Genette (Harvie) Jordan's eldest dau., Martha, m. at 16, Dr. James Bradley, twice her age.

Reuben Jordan, their eldest son, m. (I) Nancy, eldest dau. of Col. Nicholas Johnson; m. (II) dau. of Col. Williamson and niece of Mrs. Gen. John Clarke.

Fleming Jordan, their 2nd son, m. Anna, eldest dau. of Thos. Meriwether. Margaret Jordan, their 2nd dau., was a cripple, but m. a husband below her in fortune and quality (his name not given), but they loved each other and they became rich; Betsy Jordan, 3rd dau., m. Dr. Geo. Meriwether; Mortimer Jordan, 3rd son,

m. dau. of Hezekiah Gray and niece of Gen. John Scott; Charles Jordan, 4th son, m. Rebekah, dau. of Col. Nicholas Johnson. Elizabeth Harvie (John), another of the nine, was very large—considerably over 300 lbs.—m. James Marks. He was a little, low man. weighed about 120lbs". (Gilmer's Georgians", pp. 139 and 149). See p. 182.

LANE.

"In 1543, William Parr, bro. to Thos. Lord Parr, and uncle to the Queen, was created Baron Parr, of Horton in the Co. of Northampton, by King Henry VIII. His dau. and co-heiress, Magdalen, m. Sir Ralph Lane, being gr. gr. mother to William Fielding, the 1st Earl of Denbebight". ("Extinct Peerages of Eng., p. 226, by Bolton).

"Sir Ralph Lane, founder of that 1st short-lived colony on Roanoke Isalnd in 1585; Govr of Va., Col. under Drake; d. in Ireland".

In "Facts and Figures vs. Myths and Misrepresentations", by Mrs. Rutherford, we find: "Does Dr. Hart know that *Joseph Lane*, of the colony, in 1618 (?), was a descendant of Sir Ralph Lane, a relative of Catherine Parr, the best of Henry VIII's numerous wives, and was sent by Sir Walter Raleigh in 1585 to found Roanoke, N. C.? His descendants have made history, etc."

In Hotten's lists of immigrants to Va., we find: "Henry Lane, aged 20, 1623, came to Charles City in the "Southampton"; Thomas Lane, aged 30, *1613*, in the "Treasurer" and Alice Lane, aged 24, 1620, in the "Bona Nova"—the latter *two* living at Elizabeth City in 1623".

In "Early Va. Immigrants", 1623-1666, pp. 197-'8, by George Cabell Greer, we find: "Lane, Thos., 1636, by Richard Cocke; Lane, Thos., 1637, by Capt. Adam Thoroughgood, Elizabeth City Co.; Lane, Thos., 1648, by Lewis Burwell, Gent. . . . . ; Lane, Thos., 1653, by Wm. Debrane".

In Northumberland Co., Va., Book R. B., p. 75, we find: "I Robert *Burrell* Churgeon for love and affection I bear my only son John Burrell, all my estate. I make my friend, *Mr. Thos. Lane* my true and lawful attorney, May 19, 1670.
(Signed) Robert Burrell."

Wit.: Daniel Lane, John Russell. In same book, p. 110: "I John Burrell, ye son of Robert Burrell having most haynously offended God and my Father first against God by sinning against his divine Majesty and against my Father in so . . . . do make a full Deed of Gift for all that my father hath to be conferred upon me and that through ye instigation of *Thomas Lane,* her (?) for bringing a full Deed to Hand, one half of my Father's whole estate.
(Signed) John Burrell."

"This County (Surry) presents his Excellency the following persons for horse and foot, as they are severally set down: Thomas Lane, Sr., for foot (p. 103); Joseph Lane, for foot (p. 102); Thomas Lane, Jr., for foot (p. 101). The foregoing in Va. Co. Rec., Vol. 2, pp. 101-103, under head Militia in Surry Co., in *1687*.

Joseph and Thomas, Jr., were the sons of Thomas Lane, Sr. Joseph Lane recd. grant to land on both sides of Linn's Branch, Johnston County, on May 23, 1702, from Earl Granville. (Johnston Co. Book E.1, p. 383).

Deed from *Joseph Lane* and *Julian*, his wife, of Isle of Wight Co., Sept. 4, 1710, to *Thomas Lane,* of Surry Co., 200 acres given me by *my father* in his last will and testament (Father *Thomas Lane patent 1682).* Signed—Joseph Lane
Sealed in red wax. Ielion X Lane
Wit.: *Thomas Hart, Mary Hart, Thomas Lane, Jr.* (Surry Co. Deed 5, p. 37). These witnesses, Thomas and Mary Hart, were the son-in-law and dau. of Richard and Elizabeth Washington—his will Nov. 9, 1724, Surry Co.

James Day in will, 1700, names mother, Mrs. Cropley and friend, *Thomas Lane*. *Mary Hill,* dau. of *Maj. Nicholas Hill,* m. (I) Thos. Bland (dead before 1676), and m. (II), Luke Cropley, of Isle of Wight. (W. & M. Qly., 7, pp. 251-'2, and note).

Mary Gladhill, of Isle of Wight, in will 30 Nov., 1712, only surviving Ex'x of my dec'd husband, James Day, speaks of large sums of money in hands of Margaret Perry and Thos. Lane, arising from sales in Eng., etc., etc., her dec'd husbands John Johnson and James Day. (W. & M. Q. 7, p. 256).

Thos. Lane of Bethwall Green, Parish of Stepney, County Middlesex, merchant, will 17 July, 1710; 10 Nov., 1710, names wife Mary, bro. Valentine Lane, nephews Valentine Lane and John Hooste Lane, nephew Thomas Lane, son of his bro. Jonathan Lane, &c., &c. He was partner of Micajah Perry, an eminent merchant of London. (W. & M. Qly. 18, pp. 104-'5).

Thos. Lane, on 18 Feby., 1720, sells lands in Lancaster Co. to Owen Kelly. *Patence* Lane, on 7 March, 1720, gives power of atty. to her Friend and father Richard Wood, of Lancaster. (Lancaster book 11, p. 185).

Deed 24 Aug., 1721, from Joseph Lane, of the County of Albemarle, in North Carolina, Chowan, to John Thomas of the Lower Parish of the Isle of Wight, 250 A. on the south side of Nottaway River, being part of a patent for 1400 A. Granted to Joseph Lane June 16, 1714, for 58 £ silver money. (Signed) Joseph Lane. Quillian (Julian) his wife, relinquishes dower. Rec. 25 Sept., 1721. (Great Book, p. 446).

In *1726, Henry Pope* of Va. sold his son John Pope 90 A. lying in the Precinct of Bertie and the deed was witnessed by *Joseph Lane, Jun.* and Wm. Birkhead. (Bertie book B, p. 107). "Bertie Precinct ye May Court, *1726*. The above Deed of Sale from Henry Pope to John Pope was in Open Court proved by ye oath of Joseph Lane one of the Evidences thereto which is Ordered to be Registered."

Benjamin Perry to *Thomas Lane* 140 acres N. E. Shore of Chowan River or Deep River; 140 A. adjoining land of James Farlow, Jany. 6, *1728*. Test.: Robert Hicks, Susanna Perry. (N. C. H. & G. Reg., 2-3-445).

Joseph Lane, Sr., Maj. Barnaby McKinnie, Capt. John Spann, Mr. Benjamin Hill, Mr. Richard Pace (et al.) appointed Vestrymen for the North West Parish of Bertie, in *1727*. (S. R. N. C., Vol. 25, p. 210).

Joseph Lane (et al.) 25 Feby., 1740, on list of jurymen for Bertie and Edgecombe Cos. (C. R. N. C., Vol. 4, p. 521).

Land granted to Benj. Hill, Patent, Dec. 16, 1735, conveyed by Hill, on April 1, 1743, to *Joseph Lane* (of this Joseph Lane hath conveyed two acres to his Majesty's Justices, whereon the Court House and Jail is now built). I the s'd *Joseph Lane* and *Patience* my *wife* for 200 £ convey to John Hardy, Gent., land in Edgecombe County. (Signed) Joseph X Lane
Patience X Lane,

Wit.: John Lane, Barnabas Lane, Nathl Cooper.
Note:—This is where the old C. H. stood. Present C. H. not on this site. (Halifax Co. book 3, p. 213).

Aug. 20, 1747. Sale of 2 acres of land to the Justices of Edgecombe Co., 10 shillings. From Joseph Lane, Planter, to William Cathcart, David Colhace, John Hardy, Joseph John Alston, James Spiers, Saml Williams, Thomas Kearney, Joseph Howell, John Haywood, William Kinchen, James Connor, William Taylor, *John Pope, John Lane,* William West, Aquilla Suggs, Esqs., Justices.
(Signed) Joseph X Lane.

Test.: Robert Forster, Clk of Ct. (Halifax Co. book 5, p. 159).

In 1748, Mr. Joseph Howell and Mr. Joseph Lane appointed Commissioners to finish running the boundary lines between parts of Edgecombe, Beaufort and Johnston Cos., already begun and carried on to the mouth of Cheek's Mill Creek in Beaufort on Tar river, etc., etc. (S. R. N. C., Vol. 23, p. 287).

On Dec. 12, 1748, *Benjamin Lane*, of Edgecombe Co., for a valuable consideration (not named) conveys to Thos. Pope, Planter, 240 A., part of patent granted Benj. Lane. (Signed) Benj. X Lane.

Wit. Wm. Bryant, *Joseph Lain* (Lane). (Halifax Co. Book 3, p. 311).

James Gary, on 10 March, 1749, gives Power of Atty. to friend *John Lane, Jr.,* Gent. (Halifax Book 3, p. 312).

At a Council held at New-Berne, *11 Oct., 1749*, Ordered that a New Commission of the Peace and Dedimus issue also constituting and appointing *John Pope, Joseph Lane* (et al.) Esqrs., Justices of the Peace for and within the Co. of Edgecombe. (C. R. N. C., Vol. 4, p. 966).

Deed of Gift, Feby. 19, 1755, by *Joseph Lane* to his grandchildren, *daughters of my son John Lane*, viz.: Ann Lane, Mary Lane and Patience Lane, *Daughter-in-law Mary Lane*. (Signed) Joseph X Lane.

Wit.: *Jos. Lane, James Lane*. (Halifax Book 2, p. 211).

Joseph Lane, Gent., of N. C., for 10 £, 230 A. to *Henry Pope*.
Wit.: Blake Baker, Saml Johnston. (Halifax Book 2, p. 49).
Date omitted in copy sent me.
Aug. 12, 1755, Whereas Col. Barnaby McKinnie, Decd., by his will . . . . .
Daughters Patience Lane and Mourning Pope . . . . . This deed is from *John Lane, heir at law to the above s'd Patience* Lane, Planter, to *Col. Joseph Lane* of the Co. of Edgecombe, 400 £. This land in Edgecombe and Northampton Cos.
          (Signed) John Lane (SEAL)
 Wit.: John Haywood, *Henry Pope*, Theo. Haywood. (Halifax Book 2, p. 319).
 Lane, Joseph, of the County and Parish of Edgecombe, in the Province of N. C., Will, ...
 Item. I give my Bro. William Lane the plantation whereon I do now live & all the land adjoining thereto I say to him his Heirs and Assigns for Ever; and also the land whereon William Grissum now lives, I give to the sd. Wm. Lane his Heirs & Assigns forever, I also give and bequeath to Wm. Lane Eighteen head of cattle on the Manner Plantation, also all my sows & Pigs on the Manner Plantation, and also all my Household Furniture Except such as shall be hereafter mentioned & also I give to my Bro. Wm. Lane the Five following negroes that is to say, Tom, Cate, King, Annaca, Mingo, I say Given to him his Heirs & Assigns forever.
 Item. I give my Negro Boy Ploughman to my Bro. Newit Lane, to him his Heirs & Assigns for ever, and also I Lend the labour of my Negroes Jack and Cleavy to my Father During his natural life and his Decease to return to my bro. Wm. Lane & his Heirs & Assigns forever.
 Item. I Give & bequeath to *Winifred Pope* my Negroe Girl Vilet on Condition that the s'd Winifred Pope Delivers a bond of Twenty pound that then the s'd wench shall belong to the sd. *Winefred Pope* her Heirs & Assigns forever.
 Item. I give & bequeath to my Sister Faith Bynum my negroe woman Daffiny to her & her Heirs forever, and my desire is that all my Hogs & Cattle besides what has been before mentioned to be sold to pay my Debts further more my will & Desire is that my Negroe Woman Affrica can be saved without being sold to pay Debts that then my Will & Desire is that my Sister Dreusiller Bryant Shall have the s'd wench her & her Heirs & Assigns forever.
 Item. I give & bequeath to my loving kinswoman Mary McKinnie the Bed & Furniture whereon I now lie to her & her Heirs & Assigns forever.
 I do hereby make null & void all other wills by me before made I do ordain this my last Will & Testament.
 I do also appoint *John Bradford* and *Henry Pope* hole & sole Exrs. of this my last Will & Testament.
 In Witness Whereof I have hereunto Set my hand & Seal this 6th day of Dec., 1757.   Jos. Lane (Seal)
                      his
 Test.: Benjamin Merryman, *Barrabas Lane,* David X Dickson.
                     mark
Edgecombe Co. SS. Nov. Court, 1758.
 The within will was in Open Court Exhibited on Oath by the Exrs. therein named and proved by the oaths of Benjamin Merryman and *Barnabas Lane*, and the s'd Exrs. at the same time Refusing to take upon them the Admton thereon, therefore Admon with the Will Annexed was granted (on Mocon) to William Lane *next eldest* Brother & Residuary Legatee to the sd. Decdt. & he having given Bond &c as the Law Directs, it is therefore upon Ordered to be Certify'd.
                 Test. Jos. Morfort, C. C.
 Dec. 12, 1758. The Executors of *Joseph Lane former Sheriff* of Edgecombe Co., was allowed £ 16 as his Salary for the years 1751 and 1752 he having fully accounted with Mr. Haywood former Treasurer and paid all the Taxes for those years, as also forty shillings for summoning a Court of Tryal of a Negroe for Fellony and executing s'd Negroe &c., as by account Lodged with your Committee. 18..0. 0. (C. R. N. C. Vol. 5, p. 982).
 Lane, Christian, Edgecombe Co., Oct. 5, 1747; May Ct., 1748. Son Abraham, daus. Mary and Sarah, Christian Hill. Exr. Abraham Hill. Test. Stephen Jackson, Sarah Hill. (N. C. H. & G. Reg. 1-3-333).

Joseph Lane, Gent. of *Johnston* Co. makes deed 21 April, 1762, to William Speight of same Co. to 310 A. fro 15 £ (Book B, No. 1, p. 203). See also same book, p. 228, Feby. 13, 1762.

Joseph Lane and *his wife Sarah* make deed in 1760, in *Johnston* Co. (Book A, p. 65).

Robert Rowan, of Bladen Co., Lodowick Tanner, of Johnston Co., Richd Grove, of Cumberland Co., and Richd Caswell, of Dobbs Co., are held and firmly bound unto *Joseph Lane*, John McCullers and David Holleman, Esqrs., and others their Brethren Justices of the Inferior Court of Pleas and Quarter Sessions for s'd Co. and their successors, &c., in the full and just sum of 1000 lbs. proc. money, 19 July, 1763. (C. R. N. C., Vol. 6, p. 993).

The *General Assembly* of N. C., on 10 Feby., *1764*, ordered that a *Commission* of the *Peace* and *Dedimus* issue for the Co. of Johnston and that William Bryan, Bennett Blackman and *Jesse Lane* be added thereto and that Isaac Bush be left out. (C. R. N. C., Vol. 6, p. 1065).

Lane, John, Jr., Halifax Co., N. C., will May 21, *1766*. Leaves entire estate to his father *John Lane*. (Halifax Co. Book 1, p. 204).

Jesse Lane, soldier in Co. commanded by Capt. Jonathan Kittrell. List of Granville Co. Militia, *1771* (S. R. N. C. 22, p. 166).

Lane, John, Halifax Co., *will* Feby. 13, *1774*; Jany., 1776, names son David Lane; gr. son David Lane; daus. Olive Joyner, Ann Everard, Keziah McKennie, Patience Joyner, *Mary Pittman, Mourning Lane* and *Julian Lane*.

(Signed) John Lane (SEAL)

Wit.: McKensie Howell, David Summer.

[His wife Mary predeceased him]. (Halifax Book 2, p. 32).

Lane, Joseph, Halifax Co., Will Nov. 29, *1773*; Feby., 1774. Names sons *Joseph, James, Jesse, Joel* and gr. son Henry Lane, of whom Joel was residuary legatee and sole Exr. ("House of Plant", by G. S. Dickerman). Note:—I don't understand why the name of *John*, his eldest son, was omitted in the will. He was alive at this date. His, Joseph's, wife Patience predeceased him.

Jesse Lane, private, enlisted 1 March, 1777, served 3 years, in Lt. Col. Harney's Co., 2nd N. C. Battalion, Commanded by Col. John Patton. [U. S. State Dept. Army Returns, Book 27, p. 34]. (C. R. N. C., Vol. 13, p. 518).

"Return of Soldiers of the 2nd N. C. Battalion Reinlisted during the War, agreeable to Resolve of Congress and Genl Orders.

Paramus, March 12, 1779.

Jesse Lane, expiration Former Enlistment 1 Mar., 1780. Bounty paid in Dollars *100*, To Officers for each Man *10*." (C. R. N. C., Vol. 13, p. 527).

Jesse Lane, private, Turner's Co., date of enlistment, 1 Mar., 1777. Period of Service, 3 years. (C. R. N. C., Vol. 13, p. 1101).

Col. Nicholas Long, D. Q. M. G., says: "I have forgot Wagon Makers, etc., here is James Faucett 12 months, John Kelly, James Ames and *Jesse Lane, Continentals*. I think you have a number of men in camp that would render the public much more service in manufacturing necessaries, arms, accoutrements, &c, than to be in the lines and the chief of their time in idleness". (C. R. N. C., Vol. 15, p. 478).

Aug. 23, 1781. Return of Col. Long of Artificers at Halifax. *Gun Stockers Jesse Lane* (et al.). (C. R. N. C., Vol. 15, p. 619).

"There is a certified copy of Jesse Lane's records, issued by R. D. W. Connor, Secretary of the N. C. Historical Division, dated April 2, 1917". (Rec. of L. B. Robeson).

Joseph Lane, b. c. 1705; m. Patience McKennie, dau. of Col. Barnaby McKennie, Sr., and his wife, Mary (Exum) Ricks, and their son, Jesse Lane, b. 3 July, 1733; d. 16 Dec., 1806, aged 73 years; m. in 1755, Winnefred Aweck (Aycock?), b. 11 April, 1741; d. 1794, and had 16 children: 1.—Charles Lane, b. 2 Oct., 1756; m. Elizh Mallory; 2.—Richard Lane, b. 9 Feby., 1759; m. Polly Flint, gr. father of Mrs. Bishop Haygood; 3.—Henry Lane, d. in inf., 1760; 4.—Caroline Lane, b. 26 May, 1761; d. 25 Dec., 1842; 5.—Rhoda Lane, b. 21 May, 1763; m. John Rakestraw; 6.—Patience Lane, b. 8 March, 1765; m. John Hart, son of Nancy; 7.—Jonathan Lane, b. 3 April, 1767; m. (I) Patience Rogers; m. (II) Polly Colley; 8.—John Lane, b. Xmas Day, 1769; m. Elizabeth Street; parent of Gov. . . . . Lane, of Oregon;

9.—Simon Lane, b. 10 Mar., 1771; m. Judith Humphrey; 10.—Rebecca Lane, b. 8 Mar., 1773; m. James Luckie; 11.—JOSEPH LANE, b. 28 March, 1775; m. Elizabeth Hill, dau. of *Isaac* and Nancy (Crain) Hill, and mother of Mrs. Walter Terry Colquitt, et al.; 12.—Mary Lane, and *13.*—Sarah Lane, twins; b. 18 Jany., 1777, m. brothers, Kirkpatrick, of Illinois; 14.—Winnefred Lane, b. 1780; d. 1872, m. J. P. Rogers—gr. parents of Mrs. Lula Kendall Rogers; 15.—Jesse Lane, b. 1782; m. Rhoda Jolley—parents of the late Mrs. Judge Ezzard, of Atlanta, Ga.; 16.—Elizabeth Lane, m. Wm. Montgomery, and moved to Miss. (Data from Mrs. Lula Kendall Rogers; J. H. Coll., Vol. 2, pp. 619 & 623).

"The three sons of *Joseph* and *Patience* (McKennie) *Lane*, Joseph, *Jesse* and Joel, removed early from Halifax Co. on Roanoke river to Wake Co. and became proprietors of large landed estate there. All 3 became earnest participants in the Revy. War. Joel in 1775—Member of the Provincial Congress at Hillsborough, in 1781 served in Genl. Assembly, which was held in his own house. A gr. son of one of these brothers was a distinguished soldier in the Mexican War, attained to the rank of Major General for his gallantry, and later was appointed by Prest. Polk, Gov. of Oregon, from which, on its admission to the Union as a State, he was sent as Senator to Washington. In 1860 nominated for the Vice-Presidency on ticket with John C. Breckenridge. One son, Lafayette Lane, was Congressman from Oregon 1874-'7, and another, John Lane, is a lawyer in Lewiston, Idaho. Another gr. son of one of these 3 bros. was Henry Smith Lane, of Ind., Gov. of the State in 1860, and soon elected to the U. S. Senate, in which he served till 1867". ("The House of Plant", by G. S. Dickerman).

Joseph Lane, Abraham Hill, Thos. Wooten (et al.) appointed *Justices* of the *Peace* for *Wake Co.*, 23 Dec., 1778, by the Congress in session at Halifax. (S. R. N. C., Vol. 23, p. 996). 9 Feby., 1781, Resolved, by N. C. Congress, that *Joseph Lane*, of Wake Co., have leave to resign the office of a Justice of the Peace for s'd Co. (S. R. N. C., Vol. 17, p. 769).

A catalogue of Person's Names born and baptized in this place called Black River Winyaw (S. C.) before the same was constituted into a distinct Parish.

1.—*Peter*, son of *John Lane* [d. bet. 23 Apl. and 26 Nov., 1739] and *Sarah* [d. 7 Apr., 1751, buried 8 Apl., 1751] *his wife*, was b. Nov. ye 5th, 1713; m. 24 Feby., 1736, *Sarah Johnston*; 2.—*Tabitha*, dau. of John Lane and Sarah, his wife, was b. 8br ye 1st, 1716; 3.—James, son of John Lane and Sarah, his wife, was b. 8br ye 19th, 1719; m. 3 Feby., 1757, Ursula Henning; 4.—Sarah, dau. of John Lane and Sarah, his wife, was b. Jany. ye 15th, 1722/23.

1.—*Lane, Peter*, son of *Peter Lane* and Sarah, his wife, was b. Dec. 16, bapd Mar. 12th, 1737; 2.—*Tabitha*, dau. of *Peter* Lane and Sarah, his wife, was b. Nov. 9th, 1740, bapd Dec. 14, 1740; 3.—Elizabeth, dau. of Peter Lane and Sarah, his wife, was b. Jany. 12th, 1744/5; bapd Jany. 24th, 1744/5; 4.—Hannah, dau. of Peter Lane and Sarah, his wife, was b. 27 Oct., 1752; bapd 8 July, 1753; 5.—Hester, dau. of Peter Lane and Sarah, his wife, was b. 16 Aug., 1747; 6.—Sarah, dau. of do, b. 14 April, 1750; 7.—Mary Lane, dau. of do, b. 3 Feby., 1755.

1.—*John Lane*, son of *James* Lane and *Ursula*, his wife, b. Oct. 29, 1757; bpd 12 Mar., 1758, by Revd John Fairweather; 2.—Sarah, dau. of *James* Lane and Ursula, his wife, b. Jany. 6th, 1759; bapd May 6th, 1759; 3.—Thomas, son of James Lane, and Ursula, his wife, b. June 21, 1764; bapd Oct. 9th; 4.—*Tabitha, dau.* of *James Lane* and *Ursula*, his wife, b. Aug. 3, 1766; bapd Dec. 14th.

Drury Lane, son of Christopher Lane and Mary, his wife, b. Sept. 15, 1751, bapd May ye 29th, 1753.

John Lane was a *Vestryman* of Prince George's Parish from 1729 until his death in 1739. Peter Lane elected Vestryman in 1739 to fill place of John Lane, decd.; was elected in 1759 Register and, in 1769, Clerk.

James Lane elected Vestryman in 1747 and 1757, and at an inquisition, 6 Dec., 1790, was foreman of the jury.

The above records are from the Register Book for the Parish Prince Frederick, Winyaw, A. D. 1713, Published by the National Society of the Colonial Dames of America. It seems altogether probable that *John Lane*, head of the S. C. Lanes, was a son of Thos. Lane[1], of Surry, and a bro. of Joseph[2] and Thomas Lane[2], et al.

LEWIS.

The first ancestor of this family who emigrated to Va. early in 1600, came from Wales, where their ancestors were people of importance for many generations. Thomas Marshall Green, in "Historic Families of Ky.", says of them: "They were Sheriffs, County Lieutenants, Justices and Members of Parliament from Brecknock, Pembroke, Glamorgan and other Counties of Wales, and recognized for their ability in many directions." According to the Welsh Genealogist, they were descendants of *"Gwathford,* the representative of Teon of the line of the Princess Brittain" . . . 16th in descent from Gwathford was Richard Gwynn, whose son *Lewis* was the ancestor of all the Welsh families of that name. (Pittman, Vol. I, p. 230).

"Col. Henry Dudley Teetor (Genealogist) is authority for the statement that all of the Welsh Lewises who came to Va. prior to 1750 were *of the same family*—descendants of *Gwathford* . . . ". (Pittman, Vol. 1, p. 103).

John Lewis, who emigrated to Va. 1640, was probably the son (or gr. son, through Robert Lewis, of Gloucester) of Robert Lewis, of Brecon, Wales, who was the son of *Sir Edward Lewis* of Van and Edgington, Wiltshire, who m. Ann, dau. of Earl of Talbot. ("Habersham Family", p. 67).

In the 2nd Charter of Virginia, every planter and adventurer was to be inserted by name in the patent erecting them into a Corporation and Body Politic, and it was signed and sealed by the King May 23, 1609—(7 James)—among the names appears::

Edward Lewis, Grocer (Genesis of the U. S., Vol. 1, p. 222); *"Edward Lewis,* grocer, 2 Sub.—; pd. £ 37, 10s. Sworn to the freedom in June 1593; still on the Grocer's books in 1620". (The figure *"2"* in above denotes that he was an incorporator of the *2nd* Charter). (Genesis of the U. S., Vol. 2, p. 938).

"Ipswich.—Note of names and ages of all the passengers who took Shipping in the Elizabeth, of Ipswich, Mr. Wm. Andrews, Mr., bound for New England the last of April, 1634.

Edward Lewis, aged 33; *Mary, his wife,* aged 32. (Hotten's Emigrants, p. 282).

Ipswich.—A note of all the names and ages of all those which did not take the oath of allegiance or supremacy, of Ipswich, Mr. Wm. Andrews, bound for New England, the last of April, 1634.

Ed. Lewis: John Lewis, aged 3 years. Thomas Lewis, aged 3 quarters. (Hottens's Emigrants, p. 183).

Edward Lewis imported, in 1653, by Mr. *John Lewis,* Gloucester Co., Va. ("Early Va. Immigrants", 1623-1666", p. 205 (or 349?), by George Cabell Greer).

Pittman, in Vol. 1, p. 231, says, *John Lewis,* of Gloucester (1640) m. in Eng., Elizabeth . . ., had 2 sons, *John* and *William.* "Early Va. Immigrants", by Greer, says, this John of Gloucester imported *Edward, John and William* in 1653. Now, if John and William were the sons of this John who emigrated and settled in Gloucester in 1640, it is reasonable to conclude that *Edward* was also a son of this John, though we find no record declaratory of the fact.

"Sept. 10, 1660. Ann Holman, dau. of *Thomas Holman,* decd., being lately married to *William Hill,* ordered that Capt. Ralph Langley, Guardian of the said *Ann* deliver such property, &c., &c., part being joint property of *Ann* and *Mary Lewis,* left by *Henry Jones,* decd. (their brother by ye mother's side)". (York Co. Recs. MS. Copy, State Library, Richmond, Va., p. 228 (new number).

Edward Lewis, planter, and *wife Mary,* of Rappahannock, sell on Nov. 14, 1666, to Giles Coles, 200 A. on Totuskey Creek, part of 498 A. patented by *Edward Lewis, June 1, 1663,* for 4000 lbs. of tobacco. (Essex Co. Deed Book 5, p. 84).

On Nov. 1, 1665, *Humphrey Booth* made a Deed of Gift (of cattle) to *Edward Lewis,* son of Edward of *Totuskey Creek.* Wit.: Saml. Griffin, Thos. Robinson. (Essex Co. Will Book 1, p. 46).

On May 6, 1668, *Thomas Robinson,* Rappak Co., made "Deed of Gift" to *Mary* (under 12 years), *dau.* of *Edward Lewis.* (*Unnumbered Vol.,* p. 174).

Edward Lewis of the Co. of Rappak, gives power of atty. to Quintillian Sherman to answer in the suit of Miles Hugill. March 5, 1666. Edward Lewis. Wit.: Johanna Freshwater, Thos. Brooke. (Book 3, p. 209).

David Thomas, Essex Co., in will *Aug. 27, 1670*, gives his *whole estate* to his friend *Edward Lewis*. Wit.: Wm. Davis, David Hudnall. (Essex Co. Will Book 1, p. 118).

1662. Thomas Robinson and *Edward Lewis* recd. grant of *1140 A*. beginning at a Long Point, extending east *into Totusky Creek, Rappak Co., 20 Feby., 1662*. (Vol. 5, p. 149, State Land Office, Richmond, Va.).

Thos. Robinson and *Edward Lewis* to *Samuel Man* and *William Landman*, Northumberland Co., Va., land North side Rappahannock, *on old* Totuskly Creek. [No. of acres not stated in copy]. Wit.: Linton and Barber. [Date not given me]. (Rappak Vol. 1, p. 386L).

Born, Elizabeth, dau. of *Edward* and *Mary Lewis*, Mch. 8, 1674; born, *Joanna*, dau. of *Edward* and *Mary Lewis, Sept. 8, 1676;* born, J.me, dau. of Edward and Mary Lewis, July 30, 1693; born, Lewis, son of Edward and Mary Lewis, Sept. 30, 1695. John Lewis, b. (date of birth not given); d. Feby. 26, 1715. (North Farnham Parish Reg., Farnham Parish, at Warsaw, Richmond Co., Va., p. 51).

Edward and *Mary Lewis had other children* as the records which follow show, but we have discovered no records of their births and deaths.

Joanna Lewis, dau. of *Edward* and *Mary Lewis*, m. *William Lynton* (Linton), his first wife. He m. (II), March 31, 1730, the widow Mary Freshwater, relict of Thos. Freshwater, dau. of Bryan Hodgson and his wife, Mary, who m. (II) Henry Hagar. By first mar. he had 4 daus., of whom *Mary Linton* was one.

1682. Indenture Jany. 3, 1682, between *Edward Lewis*, of the Parish of Farnham, in the Co. of Rappak, Planter, and *Mary his wife*, to Thomas George, of same Parish, for 21700 pounds merchantable tobacco, 298 A. on Totusky Creek, being part of 498 A. patented by s'd *Lewis* June 1, 1663. *Edward Lewis*.

Wit.: Arthur Spicer, Wm. Segar. Rec. Sept. 5, 1683 (Essex Co. Deed Book 7 (1682-1688)—not indexed).

1670. John Williams makes deed, Dec. 28, 1670, to *William Linton* and *George Harrison* to 450 A. in *Westmoreland Co.*, on the head of Yeocomoco River touching land of Vincent Cox, for 4250 lbs. tobacco and cash. John Williams.

Wit.: George Hutton, Henry Linton. Rec. Dec. 28, 1671. (Book 1, p. 400).

Whereas, his Majesty King Charles the 2nd, &c., and Whereas King James the 2nd &c., and Whereas the sd. Proprietors have thought fitt &c., to depute me Philip Ludwell Esq., etc., I do hereby convey unto *Thos. Lewis* and *Edward Lewis* of Rappak Co., a tract of land partly in sd. Co. of Rappak and part in Northumberland Co., in the Forest containing 528 A. as appears by the survey of Mr. Edwin Conway Feby. 18, 1690, Land on a Branch of Yocomoco River and touching land belonging to Mr. Thos. Robinson, thence w. (?) to the Main Swamp touching land of John Headley and N. Wt line of Freshwater, then touching Mr. Robt. Chamberlain's line then touching a Branch of the *Marshy Swamp* of Totusky. *June 13, 1691.*

(Book 2, p. 184). Philip Ludwell.

Thos. Lewis, of Richmond Co., assigns his interest in this land, June 3, 1696, to *John Lewis*, of Northumberland. Thos. Lewis' wife Mary relinquishes dower.

Whereas &c., and Whereas &c., and Whereas King James the Second . . . and the sd Proprietors have thought fitt, etc., to depute me Philip Ludwell, Esq., &c., I do make over and assign unto *Thos. Lewis, Wm. Morgan* and *Edward Lewis*, of Rappak Co., a certain parcell of land lying part in the afsd Co. of Rappak part supposed to be in Northumberland Co., containing 360 A. touching Thos. Freshwater's line, Zacharias Nichols land formerly belonging to Henry Corbin, Esq., and along another Parcell of proprietor's land surveyed for the sd *Thomas* and *Edward Lewis, Aug. 21, 1691.* Phil. Ludwell.

On same page: Know all men by these presents that I *William Morgan*, of the Co. of Rappak, do assign and make over to John Lewis and Edward Lewis, of the afsd Co. all my right, Title & Interest of the land within mentioned. Mch. 2, 1691/2. [No consideration named]. Wm. Morgan.

Wit.: Philip Hunnings, John Barbredge, Elias Yates, Jonathan Taylor.

1693-4. I *Edward Lewis* of the Co. of Richmond and *Mary my wife*, for 6250 lbs. of tobacco to me in hand paid, Feby. 13, 1693/4, sell to John Crolle of Nortd Co., 100 A. where I the sd *Edward Lewis* now dwelleth, bounded by the land of Wm. Hammock, Geo. Nicholls and Mathew Willcocke. The s'd land being part of a

tract of 200 A. that *Thos. Freshwater* of Rappak Co. sold, on Jany. 5, 1673, to *Robert Wood*, and he, the sd. *Robt. Wood*, by deed Aug. 21, 1678, conveyed to me the sd. *Edward Lewis*.
Edward Lewis
Mary Lewis

Wit. Peter Flint, Collumb. Flint, Wm. Parker.
Rec. June 6, 1694. (Book 2, p. 26).

Mary Lewis, wife of *Edward Lewis*, of the Co. of Richmond, constitutes EDWARD JONES her atty. and relinquishes dower.

1692. This deed indented April 11, 1692, between *Edward Lewis, Thos. Lewis* and *John Landman,* of the Co. of Rappak, of the one part and *Thos. Walker,* of the same Co., of the other part, *Witnesseth* that the parties of the first part in consideration of the sum of 3429 pounds of Tobb. in cashe to them in hand paid by Thos. Walker, sell 92½ A. lying and being *near* Totusky Creek in the s'd Co. of Rappak and bounding on the line of George Early and Wm. Smyth and adjoining the land of the sd. Thos. Walker whereon he now dwelleth. The sd. John Landman's part conteyning 16 A. of land which was taken into *Edward Lewis* and *Thos. Lewis'* part of the overplus within the old lines of *Thos. Robertson* and *Edward Lewis,* being the remainder of the *1140* A. entered.
Edward Lewis
Wit.: Jos. Delke, Lewis Richards.
John Lewis
John Landman

Rec. Aug. 13, 1692. (Richmond Co., Va., Deed Book No. 1, p. 14—old number).

Mary Lewis, wife of *Edward Lewis appoints* "my very good friend *John* Morgan" her atty. and relinquishes dower.
Mary Lewis.
Wit.: Thos. Lewis, Wm. Smith. Wm. Colston, Clk.

1704-5. To all Christian people to whom these presents shall come—Know ye that we *Simon Taylor* and *Elizabeth my wife, Thos. Jasper* and *Ann my wife, Christopher Bodham* and *Mary my wife,* of the one part, and *Joseph Duke* and *Wm. Lynton,* of the other party,—Witnesseth that the parties of the first part for the valuable consideration of 3000 pounds of tobacco to them in hand paid by the parties of the second part, convey their whole estate, right, title and interest to and in two Letters Patent att Westminister (?) the 8th of May in the one and twentieth year (1681) of the Reign of Our Sovereign Lord King Charles the 2nd [his accession May 29th, 1660], granted by Philip Ludwell, Esq., unto *Thos. Lewis, Wm. Morgan* and *Edward Lewis,* the one containing 360 A. of land lying part in Rappak and part supposed in Northumberland, the other granted unto *Thos. Lewis* and *Edward Lewis* of Rappak Co. for 528 A. in Rappak and part in Northumberland, *March 8, 1704-5.*
Symon Taylor
Anne Jasper
Wit.: John Cain, Eliza A. Dogan, Hen. Parry.
Eliza Taylor
Rec. 6th day of 9th Nov., 1706.
Thomas Jasper
Christopher Bodham
Mary Bodham

Note attached to record:—"The parties above named residing and being in Richmond Co., in Farnham Parish, *excepting William Lynton,* who lives in Westmoreland Co., in Nomany." (Richmond Co. Deed Book 3, p. 179).

1712. Partition of land between *Joseph Deeke* of the Parish of Farnham, Co. of Richmond and *Katherine his wife,* of the one part, and *William Lynton,* of the Parh of Copley and Co. of Westmoreland and *Johanna (Joanna) his wife,* of the other part, March 2, 1712. Witnesseth that *Joseph Deek* and *William Linton* hold joyntly in common and undivided in one Messuage 397 A. formerly Granted to *Thomas Lewis, William Morgan* and *Edward Lewis* by Patent dated the 21st day of Aug., 1691, land partly in Richmond and Northumbd Cos., which land the parties above mentioned [Deeke and Linton] bougt of Simon Taylor and Elizabeth his wife, Thos. Jasper and Anne his wife and Christopher Rodham and Mary his wife, *Co-heirs* of *John Lewis* the *sole heir* of *Edward Lewis,* as by a deed of Bargain and Sale Mch. 3, (1704-5), in the 3rd year of the Reign of our *Gracious Sovereign Lady Anne.*

And now to the end that a perpetual division shall be had and made between the parties afsd.—It is agreed that *William Linton* shall have that part or portion that Lyeth on the Southward side of the *Marshy Swamp* in Richmond Co., with 47 A.

more being the Reversion of Another Pattent joining to ye above premises, Joseph Deeks gets the part lying in *Northumd* on the *North side* of the *Marshy Swamp*.
(Signed) William Lynton
Wit.: *Edward Jones*, George Blenford, ... Bayley. Johanna Lynton
Rec. Mch. 4, 1712. (Richmond Co. Deed Book 6, p. 115). Joseph Deeks
Catherine Deeks

William Lynton, Will, Feby., 6, 1732; Mch. 26, 1734. (Westmoreland Co. Will Book 8, p. 200). In the name of God Amen. I *William Lynton* of ye *Parish of Cople* and *Co. of Westmoreland*, being very sick and weak of Body but of sound mind and memory thanks be to God for ye same and knowing the certainty of Death but ye uncertainty of ye time thereof do make constitute and appoint this to be my last Will and Testament in manner and form as follows.

IMP. I give and bequeath my soul into ye hands of Almighty God yt gave it me and my body to be decently Interred at ye discretion of my Exrs. hereinafter named and as touching such worldly goods as it hath pleased God to bestow upon me I give and bequeath as follows.

Item. I give Bequeath unto my loving *wife Mary* all and singular ye estate which I had with her in marriage to her and her heirs forever.

Item. I give unto my sons *Anthony* and *William* my land at Totosky in Richmond Co. my son William to have 80 A. joyning upon John Singer's land and ye Marshy Swamp to them and their heirs lawfully begotten in marriage, and in failure of such heirs I give and bequeath ye said parcel of Land to ye heirs at law. I give unto my sd sons one cow and calf each one feather bed and furniture each and one Iron pot each.

Item. I give and bequeath unto my daughter *Elizabeth Lewis* one negro girl named *Betty* and all her future increase to her and her heirs forever.

Item. I give unto my Counsin James Smith my Riding horse named Spark and bridle and saddle, one negro wh my negro Loll is now going with or the last which she had either of which the sd James Smith pleases to him and his heirs forever.

Item. All ye rest residue and remainder of my estate not heretofore by me given I give and bequeath unto my loving wife Mary for and during her natural life and after her decease I give ye plantation whereon I now live I give unto my son John and ye heirs of his body lawfully begotten in marriage, and in failure of such heirs I give and bequeath ye sd plantation unto ye next heir at law.

My will and desire is yt whereas I have given unto my loving *wife Mary* all and singular my estate not heretofore by me given for and during her natural life upon the condition yt she continue a widow, but in case my sd wife should marry then my will is that she have what the law allows her, but if not then as afsd., I give her all and singular my Estate for and during her natural life and after her decease I give what she leaves of my estate to my children Anthony, John, William, and *Elizabeth* equally to be divided between them and to their heirs forever.

Item. I appoint, constitute and ordain my loving wife and my Cousin James Smith the joynt Execrs. of this my last Will and Testament Revoking and disannulling all other Wills heretofore by me made allowing and confirming this to be my last Will and Testament Whereof I have hereunto set my hand and seal this 6th day of Feby., A. D. 1733. William Lynton.

Signed, sealed and published to be his last Will and Testament in the presence of John Bridger, Thos. Templeman, George Walker. Rec. Mch. 26, 1734. G. Turbeville, Clk. C. Ct.

1735. This Indenture April 22, 1735, between *Anthony Lynton*, of the Co. of Stafford and Parish of Overwharton of the one part, and Alexander Clark of the Co. of Richmond and Parish of North Farnham, of the other part, *Witnesseth* that the sd Anthony Linton for the sum of 40 £ doth sell to *Alexander Clark* a certain tract of land containing by estimation 100 A. in the Co. of Richmond and Parish of Farnham on the south side of the Swamp. Touching the sd Anthony Linton's plantation near his dwelling, touching John Alverson's and Singer's and William Penley's Pond and Henry Corbin's land, which sd land was *Pattented* by *Edward Lewis*, decd., and descended to his son *John Lewis*, decd., thence the sd 100 A. fell by *Heirship* unto *Johannah Lewis Sister* and Co-heir at Law to the sd *John Lewis*, which sd *Johannah Lewis marryed* to *my Father, namely William Lynton*, decd., which sd tract of 100 A., be the same more or less, descended to me the sd *Anthony Linton* by being the Next heir at Law as by the sd Deed Relation thereunto being had doth and may appear.   Anthony Linton.

Wit.: Henry Williams, John Linton, Richard Brown. Rec. May 9, ...
Mary wife of sd Anthony Linton relinquishes dower.   M. Beckwith, Cl. Ct.
(Deed Book O, p. 186).

Book 9, p. 84: Nov. 4, MDCCXXXIV (1734). Deed from *Mary Linton, widow*, formerly *Mary Freshwater* of the Parish of Copley and Co. of Westmoreland (which *sd Mary* was one of the daus. of *Bryan Hodgson* and Mary his wife). Deed from her to Marmaduke Beckwith of the *Parish of Lunenburg* and *Co. of Richmond*, 10 shillings, 200 A. in Lunenburg Parish, Richmond Co., Part of a Patent granted *Col. John Walker,* for 900 A. dated Sept. 27, MDC1XII (1657 or '62), which by several conveyances became the property of Bryan Hodgson and Mary his wife, which sd Mary after the death of sd Bryan Hodgson intermarried with one Henry Hagar and with the consent of Henry Hagar sd Mary made her Will (recorded in Richmond Co.) and gave sd land to be divided among her four daughters of which *Mary Linton* is one. This said Mary (Hodgson-Freshwater) Linton having intermarried with Thomas Freshwater they (Thos. and Mary by their deed Oct. 4, 1699, sold their part of sd land to Mrs. Ann Metcalf, widow, which sd Ann Metcalf afterwards intermarried with Mr. *Edward Barrow* and these last sold the land to Mr. John Metcalf, Sept. 4, 1717, and he the sd John Metcalf sold it to Marmaduke Beckwith. Now *Mary Linton* relinquished all rights to sd Marmaduke Beckwith.
                                                                    Mary Linton.

Wit.: Thos. Barber. (Book 9, p. 84).

Elizabeth Linton, dau. of *William Lynton* by his first wife Johanna Lewis, m. (I) *Hilliare Rousseau,* who d. June 30, 1720; m. (II) *Surles Lewis*—his will Jany. 10, 1736; 29 June, 1736.

1736. Will of *Surles Lewis,* Westmoreland Co., Va., *Will Book 8, (2) p. 399.* In the name of God, Amen. I Surles Lewis of Westmoreland Co., being sick and weak in body but of perfect sense and memory do make and ordain this to be my last will and testament.

Imps. I give and bequeath my soul into the hands of Almighty God my Heavenly Father nothing doubting but of his great mercy ye same to receive again my body I give to the earth, my mother, to be decently buryed by my Executors hereafter nomynated and appointed.

It is my desire that my funeral charges and all my lawful debts shall be paid and discharged out of my personal estate.

Itm. I ordain and appoint my loving friend Capt. Anthony Thornton to be my whole and sole executor of this my last will and testament revoking and disannulling all other wills by me made. As witness my hand and seal this 27th day of December, 1739 [error, should be 1736].

Itm. It is my desire that my loving wife enjoye the negroes that belong to me during her life and afterwards to be equally divided amongst my children, that is to sae Moses to my *eldest son Thomas,* Benjamin to my son *Surles*, and *negro Moll* to my *loving wife*, negro Aaron to my *son* John, negro Ann to my *son James.*

Im. I give to my daughter *Sarah Render* 15 hundred pounds of Tobbacco, further it is my desire that if negro Moll which I have given to my loving wife should have any more children that *Elizabeth Rousseau* should have the first born either son or daughter, and in case the first born should die then the next that she bringeth she shall have and the next child that Moll has I desire that my daughter *Sarah Render* may have and if that should die she may have the next.

As Witness my hand this *10th day of January* and sealed.
                                        (Signed) Surles Lewis.

Signed, sealed and delivered in the presence of William Perkins and Thomas Dixon.

At a Court held for the sd Co. the 29th day of *June, 1736.* This last Will and Testament of Surles Lewis, decd., was presented into Court by Elizabeth Lewis his relict at May Court last and then proved by the witnesses thereto and that Capt. Anthony Thornton the executor in the said will named not being at Court the same was lodged until he should signife whether he would accept of the execution thereof, and now at this Court the said Thornton having signified his refusal on motion of the sd *Elizabeth Lewis* relict of the sd decedent she was allowed to make oath thereto and the sd will is admitted to record upon her performing what is usual in such cases, certificate is granted to her for obtaining Letters of Administration thereupon with the sd will annexed in due form.

Recorded July 13th, *1736*. Test. G. Turbeville, C. Ct. W.

Book No. 1, Inventory of Surles Lewis' estate by Elizabeth Lewis, his relict—a large estate. Rd Aug. 31, and Sept. 13, 1736.

This *Elizabeth Rousseau,* dau. of Elizabeth Lewis by her 1st husband, Hilliare Rousseau, m. Benjamin Wootten, of Halifax Co., N. C.—his will June 26, 1764; Oct. Ct,. 1764. (Will Book 1, p. 151).

Manassas, Prince William Co., Deed Book E, p. 231. This Inenture made 25th day of Oct. in the 14th year of the reign of our Sovereign Lord King George the Second on the year of our Lord Christ 1740, between *Charles McClellan* of St. Paul's Parish in the Co. of Stafford, planter, of the one part and *Elizabeth Lewis* of the Parish of Washington in the Co. of Westmoreland, *widow* and *relict* of *Surles Lewis,* late of the sd Co. of Westmoreland, decd., of the other part. Whereas *William Hackney* (or Harkney) obtained a grant out of the office of the proprietors of the Northern Neck of Va. bearing date the 11th day of March, 1722-'3 for 247 A. on Brent Town Run in the *Co.* of *Stafford, now Prince William,* etc., ... Said land (lying on both sides of the Brent Town Run) and has since by sundry conveyances come to the sd *Charles McClelland* party to these presents; Now the sd *Charles McClelland* sells to sd *Elizabeth Lewis* all that parcel afsd, 247 A. in the Co. of *Prince William* (except one small parcel thereof formerly sold by one George Allen to James Macon or Mocon) being the land lately in the possession of the sd George Allen and whereon he lately dwelt, etc., ...

(Signed) Chas. McClelland.

Wit.: Valentine Peyton, Thos. Stribling, Benj. Grayser, Jno. Hamilton. Rec. April 27, 1741. 22£ 4s current money of Va. Marginal note says: "Touches Michael Dermont's Land 22£ 10shs."

Westmoreland Inventories and Accounts No. 2, p. 76: To all Christian people to whom these presents shall come. Know ye that I Elizabeth Lewis, widow of Westmoreland Co. and Washington Parish for Divers good causes and Considerations me hereunto moving but more Especially for the Goodwill I have to My Daughter *Eliza Wooten* and *her children* I do hereby these presents lend unto my above sd Daughter During her natural life one young negro woman named *Jenny* and her increase and after my sd Daughter's decease that the said Negro and Increase if any to be divided to the eldest children of the s'd Elizabeth's body to each one if as many negroes as children, if not the younger to go without, but my desire is that my *gr. dau. Elizabeth Wootten* may have if alive at that time her first choice of the sd negro or negroes if not the eldest but if there should be more negroes than children then I desire that my *gr. dau. Elizabeth* have all except to each of the above sd Children one. As Witness my hand and seal this . . . day of . . . . . 1747.

(Signed) Elizabeth Lewis.

Test.: *Original Wroe,* Jane Wroe.

Westmoreland, S. S. At a Court held for the sd County the 29th day of Nov., 1748, *Elizabeth Lewis* came into Court and Personally acknowledged this *Deed of Gift* of *a negro* to *Eliza Woten* and ordered to be recorded. Recd the 27th day of Jany., 1748-'9. George Lee, C. C. W.

Book *2, p. 77.* To All Christian People to Whom these Presents shall come. Know ye that I *Elizabeth Lewis* Widow of Westmoreland Co. and Washington Parish, for Divers good Causes and Considerations me hereunto moving but more Especially for the good Will I bear to my *Daughter-in-Law Sarah Render* and her children I do here by these Presents Lend after my decease unto my above sd Daughter-in-Law during her Natural Life one young negro named Frank and her Increase Excepting the husband of the sd Sarah or herself should offer to sell or lend the sd Negro or increase to any person or Persons whatsoever if it should so happen that any of the above Persons should Endeavor to make away with any of the above sd negroes then shall immediately return to my *Grandson-in-law Lewis Render* and his brothers and sisters to each of them one if there should be so many Negroes if not the younger to go without and in like manner if they should not endeavor to sell the sd slaves that at the decease of ye sd *Sarah Render* that *Lewis Render* have his first choice and if more negroes than Children that the sd Lewis Render to have all but to each of the sd *Sarah's* children one.

As Witness my hand and seal this . . . of . . . 174. . .

Words interlined before signing after my Decease and Seal.

(Signed)   Elizabeth Lewis.

Wit.: Original Wroe, Jane Wroe.

Westmoreland County at a Court held for the sd Co. the 29th day of *November, 1748, Elizabeth Lewis* Came into Court and personally acknowledged this *Deed of Gift* of a negro to *Sarah Render* and her Children. Ordered to be recorded. Recorded the 28th day of January, 1748/9. Test. George Lee, C. C. W.

Westmoreland Co. Va., Will Book No. 11, p. 288. In the Name of God, Amen. I *Elizabeth Lewis*, of Westmoreland Co., being sick and weak of body but of perfect sense and Memory do make and ordain this my last Will and Testament.

Item. I give and bequeath my soul into the hands of God that gave it hoping through his grace to Receive Redemption for my sins and my body to the earth to be decently buryed by my Execrs hereafter mentioned.

Item. My desire is that my funeral Charges and all my Lawful debts shall be paid out of my Personal Estate.

Item. I give to my son *John Lewis* negro Tom, negro *Moll* and her increase after the date of this Will. As likewise my Tract of Land lying in the Co. of *Prince William*.

Item. I give to my son-in-law *Surles* (?) or James Lewis a negro boy named Will.

Item. I give to the son of *Kathne* Garrott (?) *named John* one negro girl named Bell and in case he dies without heirs my desire is this negro and her increase *go to Benj. Woten and his heirs.*

Likewise I give to *Katherine Garrott* one Feather bed and furniture, my *mare bridle* and *saddle*, a cow and a calf and a chest.

I give to *Hilliare* [pro. William] *Rousseau* one negro named *Doublin*. I likewise give to *his young Brother James Rousseau* a Negro boy *Simon* and in case the children before mentioned should die without heirs, *Hilliare* [pro. William?] and *James*, my desire is that both or either of the negroes return to William Rousseau's children.

Item. My desire is that *my son William Rousseau* have the care of these children *William* and *James Rousseau* as likewise of their estate given by me.

Item. It is my desire that *John Lewis* have the third of my moveable estate.

I *ordain* and *appoint* my loving *son William Rousseau* my whole and sole Executor of this my last Will and Testament. As Witness my hand this 6th day of December, 1750.   Elizabeth Lewis.

Signed, sealed and delivered in the presence of John Starks, John Hillton, John Pickett. At a Court held for the sd County the 26th day of March, A. Dom. 1751. This last Will and Testament of Elizabeth Lewis, deceased, was presented into Court by *John Lewis* and proved by the Oaths of John Hilton and John Pickett two of the witnesses thereto, is admitted to Record and upon the motion of the said *John Lewis* and his performing all such things as the Law in such Cases Requires therefore letters of administration with the said Will annexed is in due form granted to the said JOHN. Test. George Lee, C. O. *Recorded the 18th day of April, 1751.*

Inventory and Accounts Book No. 2, p. 157 (Westmoreland Co.). *Appraisement* of Estate of Elizabeth Lewis Mch. 26, 1751, before Wm. Witt Tyler, one Maj. Justices. 1 Large Bible and Small books.

Circuit Ct. of Pr. Wm. Co., Va. Deed Book I, p. 170. This Indenture made this 9th Aug. in the 20th year of the reign of our Sovereign Lord George II by the grace of God of Great Britain France & Ireland King Defender of the Faith— and in the year of our Lord 1746 Between *Andrew Dalton* of the Parh of Hamilton in the Co. of Pr. Wm., Planter & *Catherine his wf.* of the one part & *James Lewis* of the same place, *planter,* of the other part. Whereas Michael Dermont late of the Parh & Co. afsd, decd., was his life time seized in Fee Simple of & in one part of l'd wh. was gr'td to him by the proprietor of the Northern Neck situate lying & being in the parh & Co. afsd on the E. si. of Town run fr. the white oak Cabbin branch to the long branch going up to Tobias Woods contain'g 250 A. more or less, & so being thereof seized by his last Will & Testament in writing bearing date 3rd Feby. 1730 devised the s'd l'd to his dau. Catherine (party to these presents) in Fee tail as in & by the sd will more fully is contained. And whereas the s'd Andrew Dalton & Catherine his wf. by virtue of the sd devise have entered into the premises with the appurtenances & being minded to sell the same & to bar the *Intail* have sued out a writ pursuant to an Act of Ass'bly in that case made & provided in the nature of an ad quod damnum to the Sheriff of the sd Co. of Pr. William directed whereby it was commanded that by the oath of good & lawful men of his Bailiwic he sh'd diligently enquire if it may be to the damage or prejudice of his Majesty or others if the sd Andrew Dalton & Catherine sh'd sell the sd tract of l'd with the appurtenances &c. To wh. writ the Sh'ff of the sd Co. answered that 12 good & lawful men of his Co. being sworn & charged upon their oaths did say that it will not be to the damage or prejudice of our Lord the King if the sd Andrew Dalton & Catherine his wf. sh'd sell the l'd & appurtenances in the sd writ mentioned but that it will be to the damage of the Issue of the sd. Catherine & those claiming remainder & reversion & further the sd jurors upon their Oath did say that the sd ld & appurtenances were then of the value of . . . pounds good & lawful money of Gr't Britain & is a separate parcel & not parcel of or contiguous to the other intailed lands in the possession & seizin of the sd Andrew Dalton & Catherine his wf. & the sd Andrew Dalton & Catherine his wf. by Indentur of bargain & sale for the consideration therein mentioned bargained & sold 119 A. p't of the p't of l'd to Wm. Rousseau of the parh & Co. afsd as by the sd Writ & return & Indenture of bargain & sale remaining of record in the Secy's office of this Colony doth & may appear & the sd Andrew Dalton & Catherine his wf. by Indenture bearing date the 8th of Aug. inst. for the consideration of the sum of 7 £ have sold & conveyed unto the sd Wm. Rousseau & his heirs twenty-five (25A) acres other part of the sd tract of l'd together with all houses, outhouses, yards & appurtenances thereto belonging.

Now this Indenture Witnesseth that the s'd Andrew Dalton & Catherine his wf. for & in consideration of the sum of 33 £ current money of Va. to them in hand paid by the sd *James Lewis* the receipt whereof they the sd Andrew Dalton & Catherine his wf. do & each of them doth hereby acknowledge & themselves to be therewith fully satisfied & thereof & of every part thereof do & each of them doth acquit exonerate & discharge the sd. *James Lewis* his heirs Executors & adms. & every of them by these presents.

They the sd Andrew Dalton & Catherine his wf. Have & each of them hath granted bargained & sold aliened enfeaffed & confirmed & by these presents Do & each of them Doth fully freely & absolutely grant bargain sell alien enfeoff & confirm unto the sd *James Lewis* his heirs & assigns forever All the remainder of the above mentioned tract of ld. with all & singular the appurtenances thereunto belonging contain'g by estimation 106 A. & the reversion & reversions, remainder & remainders thereof & all the Estate right title & interest of them the sd Andrew Dalton & Catherine his wf. or either of them of, in or to the sd gr'td premises or any p't thereof. To Have & to Hold the sd premises hereinbefore mentioned or intended to be hereby bargained & sold with their & every of their rights members & appurtenances unto the sd *James Lewis* his heirs & assigns to the only proper use & behoof of him the sd *James Lewis* his heirs & assigns forever. And the sd *Andrew Dalton* & Catherine his wf., their heirs Executors & Adms. the sd hereby granted premises with their appurtenances unto the sd *James Lewis* his heirs & assigns against the sd Andrew Dalton & Catherine his wf. their heirs & assigns & all other persons whatsoever shall & will warrant & forever defend by these presents. And the sd Andrew Galton for himself & Catherine his wf. & for his heirs, Exrs. & Adms. doth Covenant & grant to & with the sd. *James Lewis* his heirs & assigns that the sd *James Lewis* his heirs & assigns the premises with the appurtenances shall or lawfully may from time to time & at all times Peaceably hold possess & enjoy without the suit hindrance molestation disturbance of any person or persons whatsoever having or lawfully claiming any right or title therein & that the same shall forever remain free & clearly discharged of and from all former & other estates, rights titles dowers entails debts mortgages & other incumbrances whatsoever.

In Witness Whereof the parties first above named to these present Indentures have interchangeably set their hands & seals the day & year first above written.

Andrew Dalton (Seal)
her
Catherine O Dalton (Seal)
mark & Seal

Sealed & Delivered in the presence of Howson Kenser, Simon Cummings, William Rousseau. Rec. Aug. 25, 1746.

Manassas, Prince William Co. Deed Book "M", p. 141. This Indenture made the *24th* Nov. in the XXIV (?) year of the reign of our Sovereign **Lord King George II** and in the year of Our Lord *1750* Between *John Lewis* of the Co. of Caroline of the one part & *William Rousseau* of the Co. of *Prince William* of the other part.

Witnesseth that the sd *John Lewis* for & in consideration of the natural love & affection which he hath & beareth unto the sd *William Rousseau* & of the sum of 10 shs. to him in hand paid by the sd. *William Rousseau* the receipt whereof the sd. *John Lewis* doth hereby acknowledge hath granted bargained aliened enfeoffed & Confirmed & by these presents doth fully & absolutely grant bargain sell alien enfeoff & confirm unto the sd *William Rousseau* his heirs & assigns all that tract or parcel of land situate lying & being in the *Parish of Hamilton* & *Co.* of *Prince William* containing by estimation 106 A. together with all, etc. . . . . Which sd tract or parcel of land *Andrew Dalton* & *Catherine his wife* conveyed to *James Lewis* of the sd Co. of Prince William by Indenture bearing date the 9th day of Aug. 1746.

The sd *James Lewis* is since dead & hereby the sd tract of Land descends to the sd *John Lewis* party to these presents *as his brother's* heir at law.

(Signed) John Lewis.

Wit.: Simon Cummings, Champ Carver, William Mallow. Rec. Nov. 27, 1750. (Exd Nov. 24, 1750).

(See *Excursuss Wootten*).

EXCURSUS: *LUMPKIN*.

Land Grant Book 7, p. 121, Capitol, Richmond, Va.: "1682. Land grant to *Jacob Lumpkin*, 565 Acres in St. Stephens Parish in the county of New Kent, on the north side Mattapony River. For transportation of nine persons, April 20th, 1682." George Lumpkin received a land grant of 400 A. in Amelia Co., Va., "on the south side of the Appomattox River, Sept. 20, 1748." (Ld. Grt. Bk. 28, p. 406.)

"Adjoining Montopike was Newington, established very early in the history of the county by the Lumpkin Family." ("King and Queen," p. 75, by Bagby.) *Gov. Lumpkin's family, of Georgia, was from King and Queen Co., Va.* ("King and Queen Co.," p. 366, by Alfred Bagby, A.B., D.D.) *Col. Jacob Lumpkin*, prominent in the early wars of the colony, who d. 1708, is buried at Mattapony Church, erected, probably, as early as 1690, which is 4 miles above the Court House in King and Queen Co. A marble slab just outside the north door, covers his remains, with this inscription:

Jacob Lumpkin
Obit 14 die September, 1708, Aetatis 64
Dux Militum, Victor Hostium,
Morte Victus, Pax Adsit, Vives Requies,
Eterna Sepultis.

From manuscript volume entitled "Incidents in the Life of Wilson Lumpkin, Written and Compiled by Himself, 1852," now in the De Renne Library, Wormsloe, Ga., Gov. Lumpkin says, referring to this tomb: "Amongst the early settlers of Va., I find the name of Dr. Thomas Lumpkin who settled in King and Queen Co. in the Old Dominion in the sixteenth century. He brought with him from England a small marble tablet or tombstone to be placed on his grave and there it stood a few years ago unimpaired by time. I had a copy of the inscription taken from this stone, but it is now lost or mislaid and *I cannot be accurate as to the date.* From this individual as far as I have been able to ascertain have descended all the Lumpkins of the United States. Some of whom are now to be found in many of the states of our great and widely extended confederacy. My father was probably the great grandson of Dr. Thomas Lumpkin. My father in his youth on a visit to the sea coast of Va., visited the tomb of this, our first American ancestor," etc. The circumstances as to the tomb, the inscription, and Gov. Lumpkin's statement that he could not be accurate, suggest that the name of this early ancestor was, in reality, Jacob, and not Thomas Lumpkin; if otherwise, then Jacob was the son of this Thomas.

The Lumpkin family seems to have been quite distinguished in the county. A Henry Lumpkin was a member of the Committee of Safety in 1774, John a member of the 4th Va. Militia in War of 1812, a presiding justice between 1830 and '50, representative in Legislature in 1843, and sheriff in 1849. ("King & Queen Co.," pp. 57-'8, 384-'5-'7-'8.) *George Lumpkin*[1] and *his son, John*[2], were among the first settlers of Oglethorpe Co. In 1784, they settled on Long Creek in Wikles, now Oglethorpe Co. George was named as one of the petit and grand jurors of Wilkes in 1788. His wife was Mary Cody, dau. of James and Sarah (Womack) Cody, and they had four children: 1.—John[2]; 2.—Joseph[2]; 3.—Robert[2], d. unm.; 4.—Mary[2], m. John Wilson, a Scotchman, and remained in Va. 1. John Lumpkin[2], b. in Pittsylvania Co., Va., 14 Jan., 1783, blessed by nature with a fine commanding person, upwards of 6 feet high, perfectly erect in his carriage, naturally fluent in speech, polite, courteous and exceedingly popular in his deportment, and social intercourse with others. He was for many years an acting magistrate, or justice of the peace in Wilkes Co. After the creation of Oglethorpe Co., was for many years a judge of the Inferior court; member of the convention of 1798 which formed the present Constitution of Ga.; member of the Legislature which passed the rescinding Act of the Yazoo Fraud; was elected a Jeffersonian Elector of President and Vice-President; for many years clerk of the Superior Court of Oglethorpe. He was a trustee of Meson Academy, at Lexington, Ga.,—founded as the Academy of Oglethorpe Co., but on Nov. 27, 1807, became "Meson Academy"; member of the executive committee under whose oversight Mercer Institute—founded 1832-'33—now Mercer University, was established; with Thos. Duke and John King was a supervisor of the Land Grant Distribution, 1784-1800, in Oglethorpe Co. ("Removal of the Cherokee Indians from Ga., 1827-1838," by Wilson Lumpkin, Vol. 1, Chap. 1; "L. M. & L.," Vol. I, pp. 774, 820, by Knight; also Vol. II, p. 925.)

John Lumpkin[2] m. *Lucy Hopson*, dau. of Capt. Henry Hopson, of Rev'y Army (and his wife, Martha Neville, dau. of James Neville and his wife, Lucy Thomas), son of William Hopson and his wife, Susan Ragland, dau. of John Ragland and his wife, Ann Dudley, dau. of John (?) Dudley and his wife, Ursula Beverley, dau. of Robert Beverley and his wife, Ursula Byrd, dau. of Wm. Byrd, of Westover. Issue: 1.—Samuel[3]; 2.—Wilson[3]; 3.—John[3]; 4.—Hopson[3]; 5.—George[3]; 6.—William[3]; 7.—Joseph Henry[3].

Will of Samuel Lumpkin, Feb'y 10, 1847, Will Book D, p. 303, Lexington: "Beloved wife, Lucy Lumpkin, formerly Lucy Johnson, property which I received as a legacy in her name from the estate of her first husband, . . one dozen Windsor chairs, one set of mahogany dining tables, carriage and horses, silver spoons, two looking glasses, my Bible and Scot's Commentary. My wife, Lucy, to be Exr. of my will and Guardian of my three youngest chn., (viz) Calender, George and Lena. My sons, George, Joseph, Jack C. Lumpkin. My nine chn., Henry H., Martha A., Sarah P., Samuel J., Jack C., Joseph, Callender, George and Lena.

"Wit: JOSEPH LANDRUM (Signed) "SAM'L LUMPKIN
"WILLIAM BOOTH   "Rec'd Nov. 12, 1853.
"JOHN LANDRUM   "HENRY BRITAIN, Ordinary."

Samuel Lumpkin[3], m., 21 June, 1815, Mary Arnold (Marriage License Book, Lexington, Ga., p. 190, No. 1366) of Oglethorpe Co., and had among others: Joseph Henry Lumpkin[4], of Lexington, Ga., m. Sarah Elizabeth Johnson, dau. of James and Lucy (Deupree) Johnson, and had, among others: 1.—Lucy Lumpkin, m. Thomas (?) Olive, and had Hon. Samuel L. Olive, lawyer of Augusta, Ga., and president of the Ga. State Senate; 2.—*Samuel Lumpkin*[4], *late Associate Justice State*

Supreme Court, m. *Miss Kate Richardson,* dau. of Walker and Martha Elizabeth (Sanford) Richardson, of Russell Co., Ala., gr. dau. of William Norville and Susan (Watkins) Richardson, of Glennville, Ala., of Adolphus Mitchell and Sophia Maria (Walton) Sanford, of Glennville, Ala.

Since the death of her husband, *Mrs. Kate Lumpkin* has given her talents and services unstintedly and wholeheartedly to the public. Though retiring, unassuming and self effacing; shrinking from the spot light of publicity; by preeminent success as leader in every cause to which she applied her splendid abilities, has won for herself the esteem and admiration, not only of Atlantians, but of all Georgians. She has been tactful, resourceful, efficient and eminently successful in her every undertaking. On 22nd Dec., 1921, the Board of Directors of the Atlanta Chamber of Commerce, by a unanimous vote, awarded her a citation, engraved on parchment, for distinguished service to City, State, and Humanity at Large, an honor richly deserved and graciously bestowed.

2. *Wilson Lumpkin*[3], b. in Pittsylvania Co., Va., 14 Jan'y, 1783. "This extraordinary man *(Wilson Lumpkin)* was one of the dominant figures of his day in Georgia. . . He was member of Congress and United States Senator. Twice in succession, he filled the office of Governor; in 1823 commissioned by President Monroe to mark the boundary line between Ga. and Fla. . . . Under the Cherokee Treaty, 1835, appointed by Gen'l Jackson to act for the Government. Was for years president of the Board of Trustees of the U. of Ga." (Knight's Georgia.) In 1805, when 22 years old, almost unanimously elected to the State Legislature; served in that body till 1814. In 1814, elected to Congress, served one term; in 1820, to State Legislature; 1826, re-elected to Congress, served continuously till 1831; Governor of Georgia, 1831, and again, 1833. In 1837, elected to U. S. Senate and continued a member until 1841. "From his 16th to his 60th year (a term of 44 years) he was constantly in public life, filling almost every office in the gift of the people, and in all performing arduous, faithful and valuable service." He was a devout member of the Baptist church, and fulfilled his obligations of service there as faithfully as in secular affairs." "His long and honorable public service proves he never lost the confidence of his fellow citizens. It was no small thing to serve in Congress and Senate with such men as Calhoun, Webster, Clay, Forsyth, Pinckney and Randolph. There were giants in those days." The county of Lumpkin in Ga. named in his honor in 1832, also the town of Lumpkin in Stewart Co., Ga.

Wilson Lumpkin[3] (John[2], George[1]) m. (I) at age of 18, 26 Nov., 1800, *Elizabeth Walker,* age 14, dau. of *Rev. Sanders Walker,* a Baptist minister, and his wife, *Sarah Lamar,* widow Cinquefield; m. (II) 1 Jan'y, 1821, *Annis Hopkins,* b. 18 Feb'y, 1790, of Morgan Co. (pro.). *Issue by 1st mar.:* 1.—*Lucy Hopson Lumpkin*[4], b. 28 Feb'y, 1803; d. 24 Aug., 1888; m. 27 Nov., 1820, Middleton Pope[5], 1794-1850; 2.—Ann Lumpkin[4], m. Augustus Alden[1], 10 Jan'y, 1823; 3.—Pleiades Orion Lumpkin[4], m. in August, 1830, Margaret Wilkinson; 4.—Wilson Lumpkin, Jr.[4]; 5.—William Lumpkin[4]; 6.—Elizabeth Lumpkin, m. Wilson O. B. Whatley, 15 Dec., 1836. (For issue of 2, 3, and 6 see "Annals of Athens," p. 463, by A. L. Hull.)

Issue by 2nd mar.: 7.—Samuel Hopkins Lumpkin[4], b. in Morgan Co., 17 Oct., 1821; d. in Athens, Ga., 18 Feb'y, 1839, said to have had a brilliant mind; 8.—John Calhoun Lumpkin[4], m. 1870, in Polk Co., Susan Whitehead Rosseau (or Reauson), no issue; 9.—*Martha Lumpkin*[4], m. 18 Dec., 1878, *Thomas M. Compton.* "Marthasville," first name for city of Atlanta, was in her honor. She d. in Decatur, Ga., circa 1919. No issue.

3. John Lumpkin[3] (John[2], George[1]), better known as "Jack," b. 4 Oct., 1785; d. 1 Aug., 1839, m. 15 Dec., 1807, his cousin, Ann Ragland Lumpkin (or Hopson?) d. 13 March, 1871. He was a Baptist minister and lived at Antioch, Oglethorpe Co., Ga.

4. *Hopson Lumpkin*[3] (John[2], George[1]) m. *Miss Milner* and had, among others, dau., *Sarah G. Lumpkin*[4], d. 1860, *m. Gen'l Philip Cook,* and they were the parents of Mrs. William Lawson (Lucy) Peel, and of Gen. Philip Cook, Jr., dec'd.

6. William Lumpkin[3] (John[2], George[1]), m. 29 Jan'y, 1801, Elizabeth Ragan, dau. of Jonathan Ragan, Sr., of Oglethorpe Co. (Mar. Record Book, Oglethorpe Co., p. 129, No. 306.) He was high sheriff of Oglethorpe Co. and Lieut. in the Indian

Wars succeeding the Revolution. One descdt. is Mrs. Sam'l McKnight Green, Missouri School for the Blind, St. Louis, Mo.

7. *Joseph Henry Lumpkin*[3] (John[2], George[1]), the first Chief Justice of the Supreme Court of Ga., b. in Oglethorpe Co., 23 Dec., 1799. Graduated with high honor from Princeton; admitted to the bar in 1820; elected chief justice in 1845. ("White's His'l Col. of Ga.," pp. 395-'6.) He m. Callender Grieve, of Milledgeville, Ga. Children, order conjectural: 1.—Lucy Lumpkin[4], m. Dr. William Gerdine. (For issue see "Annals of Athens," p. 462, by Hull); 2.—Marion McHenry Lumpkin[4], m. Gen'l T. R. R. Cobb and had: (1) Lucy Cobb, d. in girlhood—"Lucy Cobb Institute," Athens, Ga., named in her memory; (2) Sallie Cobb., m. Capt. Harry Jackson, dec'd; (3) Callie Cobb, m. Augustus Hull; (4) Marian Cobb, m. Hoke Smith, ex-U. S. Senator; 3.—Callie Lumpkin[4], m. Porter King, from which union came, with others, *Hon. Porter King*, dec'd, former mayor of Atlanta, Ga., who m. Carrie Remson; 4.—Joseph Troup Lumpkin[4], m. Miss King; 5.—William Wilberforce Lumpkin[4], m. Louise King, dau. of Gen'l Porter King, of Ala., and had: (1) Edwin K. Lumpkin[5], a prominent lawyer of Athens, m. Mary Thomas; (2) *Joseph Henry Lumpkin II*[5], late Associate Justice of the State Supreme Court, d. unm.; 6.—Miller C. Lumpkin[4], N. R.; 7.—Edward P. Lumpkin[4], N. R.; 8.—Robert Lumpkin[4], d. unm.; 9.—James Lumpkin[4], d. unm.; 10.—Chas. M. Lumpkin[4]; 11.—Frank Lumpkin[4], m. Kate Wilcox and left a son, Frank G. Lumpkin, m. Annie L. Garrard, of Columbus, Ga., and a dau., name not given.

From the foregoing it will be seen that from this *Lumpkin family* came: a Governor of the State, two U. S. Senators, three State Supreme Court Justices—a fourth declined appointment,—one having been chief justice, three Superior Court Judges, one Congressman, a president of the State Senate, and a Mayor of the City of Atlanta, Ga. Truly it is a distinguished record, unsurpassed by that of any family in the state, an heritage rich in honors and fame which should prove an inspiration to their descendants.

Rev. George Lumpkin, Will, 26 Nov., 1857; rd 19 Jan'y, 1858. Will Book D, pp. 365 to 374. Wife Lucy; dau., Angelina Davis; son, John H.; deceased dau., *Matilda Milner*; dau. *Sarah G. Varner*; my son, George; dau. Martha E. Moore. Wit.:
(Signed) GEORGE LUMPKIN

DAVID C. BARROW }
JAMES JEWEL }
WILLIAM JEWEL, Jr. }
(Vide Record Ante p. 68)

(Note.—I remember going to Marietta when I was a little child to see my bro., James Barrow, who was a cadet at the Ga. Mil. Inst. under Col. Brumby, commandant. We staid with some cousins named Varner and Milner.—Mrs. E. B. S.)

Joseph Lumpkin[1], Will, March 25, 1803; rd 27 Jan'y, *1806* (Will Book A, p. 164). Son John Lumpkin; dau. Ann B. Bailey; gr. dau. Polly Lumpkin; son William Lumpkin; son Joseph Lumpkin; loving wife, *Ann* Lumpkin. Exrs.: Sons, Joseph and William Lumpkin. (Signed) JOSEPH LUMPKIN
Wit.: JOHN DUNN, HUMPHREY HENDRICKS, JAS. D. COLE.

[The above Joseph Lumpkin was a brother of George, and gr. uncle of Wilson Lumpkin.—L. J. H.]

William Lumpkin, Will, Feb'y 8, 1847; rd 10 July, 1847. (Will Book D, p. 219, Oglethorpe Co.) My *wife, Susannah Lumpkin* (vide below) 605 A where I now live; son, Pittman Lumpkin; dau. Mary Ann Wright; dau. Frances Bell; son Richard B. Lumpkin; son-in-law, Thomas I. Britain; John B. Hawkins [relationship not stated]; son, Joseph I. Lumpkin; *Elizabeth Lumpkin, widow and relict of my son, William*, dec'd. Children of my deceased children, Frances Bell and William Lumpkin. Exrs.: my two sons J. I. Lumpkin, J. B. H. Lumpkin.
(Signed) WILLIAM LUMPKIN
Wit.: WILLIAM EDWARDS, JOHN A. BELL.
HENRY BRTAIN, C. C. O.

In oldest marriage license book, Oglethorpe Co., p. 190, is recorded mar. license of William Lumpkin to *Susannah Edwards*, 6 June, 1815, No. 1363. *(Vide Will of Wm. Lumpkin above.)*

Note:—In the following, the language of the inscriptions, but not the forms—the usual ones,—are given:

McINTOSH, MAJ. GEN. LACHLAN—Upright Granite Monument. Date, 1806.

IN MEMORY OF MAJ. GEN. LACHLAN McINTOSH. March 17, 1725; Feb. 20, 1806. Erected by His Great Grandson, Frederick Hampden Winston.

Note:—The McIntoshes were ruined financially by the uprising in 1715. John Mohr McIntosh was only 15, but his uncle, Brig. Gen. William McIntosh, was one of the most prominent in that fracas, and even his nephew's property was confiscated. Lachlan, 2nd son of John Mohr Mackintosh, Chief of the Borlam branch of the House of Moy, and his wife, Marjory Fraser, daughter of Fraser of Garthmore; was born in Scotland and came with his father to Georgia when 10 years of age. These Mackintoshes descend from Shaw MacDuff, second son of Duncan, fifth (5th) earl of Fife, who died 1154. (See Casey's Craig Phadric 1811). The name is written McIntosh in Georgia. In the attack on St. Augustine, 1740, John Mohr McIntosh, who had been put in command, by General Oglethorpe, of the outpost of Darien, commanded a company of Highlanders, and at the battle of Fort Moosa, was wounded and taken prisoner, and held a prisoner in Spain for two years. General Oglethorpe took his sons, William and Lachlan into his own Regiment as Cadets, and records show they fought with the "Highlanders" in the battle of "Bloody Marsh", 1742. John Mohr McIntosh was a delegate to the first legislative Assembly in Georgia, 1751, from St. Andrew's parish. In January, 1775, a District Congress was held in St. Andrew's parish, endorsing "the resolutions of the Grand American Congress" and declaring they "never would be slaves". Lachlan McIntosh was one of the signers, as were his brothers, William and George. He married Sarah Threadcraft, left no descendants in the male line, his sons dying before him without issue. He had several daughters who married and left children. McIntosh County in Georgia was named for the McIntosh family, (1793). See ("National Portrait Gallery of Distinguished Americans"; "Life of Gen. Oglethorpe", Vol. 1, Ga. Histl. Pubs.; Ga. Col. Records; Family Records; White's Statistics).

McINTOSH, GEN. LACHLAN—White marble slab, flat on the ground.

THE FAMILY VAULT OF GEN. LACHLAN McINTOSH, OF THE REVOLUTIONARY ARMY.

Note:—Revolutionary Services: Delegate from St. Andrew's Parish to important Provincial Congress assembled in Savannah, July 4th, 1775. Colonel of first battalion of troops for defense of Georgia, organized January 6, 1776. One of the two Generals appointed from Georgia in the War of the Revolution by Continental Congress. Representative from Council of Safety in Georgia, with John Houston and Jonathan Bryan, "to confer with Gen. Charles Lee, by his request to plan operations against the Banditti in Florida". Transferred in 1779 for service in Virginia under Gen. Washington's immediate command, taking with him as Staff officers, "his son, Captain Lachlan McIntosh and his young friend, Captain John Berrien". Served first in advance of the Central Army, later in "command of Western Virginia and Pennsylvania, in which campaign he was eminently successful". "Fort McIntosh" in Pennsylvania named in his honor. He applied to be returned to Georgia, in 1779, to take part in the campaign against Savannah. His application approved by General Washington in a complimentary letter, was granted by Congress. Served as 2nd in command under Gen. Lincoln, in the siege of Savannah and the assault on Spring Hill redoubt, October, 1779. When Charleston surrendered to Gen. Clinton he was taken prisoner, was exchanged for Gen. O'Hara. After the Revolution lived in Savannah until his death. Was delegate to Continental Congress, 1784. Commissioner on boundary line between Georgia and South Carolina, and filled other offices of honor and trust. He was an original member of "The Society of the Cincinnati in Georgia" and for years its President. One of the founders of the Scottish "Society of St. Andrew's" and its first President, (1791). See ("Biographical Sketches of Delegates from Georgia to the Continental Congress" by C. C. Jones; and other Histories).

Charles Harris, a leading lawyer of Savannah, married 1798 Catherine McCauley McIntosh, daughter of General Lachlan McIntosh. See his will.

Nicholas S. Bayard, M. D., married Sarah Elizabeth, daughter of Charles and Catherine McIntosh Harris and grand daughter of General Lachlan McIntosh.

Date relating to the demolition of the Family Vault of GEN. LACHLAN McINTOSH, OF THE REVOLUTIONARY ARMY—White marble slab flat on the ground, formerly affixed to the front of the vault.

Note:—During the "War between the States" when General Sherman occupied Savannah, 1864, the Colonial Cemetery, then enclosed by a high brick wall, was used as a stable yard for army wagons and teams. Many of the vaults were broken into, among them that of General McIntosh, which was so badly injured it fell into ruins. Mr. Charles Spalding Wylly, a great-grand nephew of General McIntosh, writes under date, February 25th, 1920: "I perfectly remember the condition of the vault in 1868, the roof had broken in, and had fallen inwards carrying the coffins in the debris. Mr. Nicholas Bayard, of Rome, Georgia, who had married Sarah Harris, grand daughter of General Lachlan McIntosh, and Colonel Charles Spalding, met in Savannah, the two, with the approbation of John McQueen McIntosh, ordered Mr. Walker, a stone mason of Savannah, to fill the enclosure, remove the sides, place the stones that bore the epitaphs flat on the ground and place an iron rail, supported by six stone posts around the spot. Which was done by Mr. Walker in 1869. The bill of Mr. Walker was $83.00, and was paid, one-half by Mr. Bayard and one-half by Mr. Spalding; even now I believe I could find Mr. Walker's receipt for payment."

Letter signed: C. S. Wylly.

SPALDING, JAMES—SACRED TO THE MEMORY OF JAMES SPALDING, ESQR., WHO DEPARTED THIS LIFE IN THE 60 YEAR OF HIS AGE AT SAVANNAH, ON THE 10th NOV., 1794—White marble slab broken in two, flat on the ground, formerly affixed to North front of the Family Vault of Gen. Lachlan McIntosh.

Note:—James Spalding of the "Ashantilly" Spalding family, County Perth, Scotland, was born 1735. He was heir to the estate and Barony of Ashantilly. (See Reg. Sassines, County Perth, 1743). He came to Georgia 1760, his home called "Retreat" was on St. Simon's Island, Georgia; he held the original grant to the land. Bartram in his "Travels", 1774-5, tells of visiting him on St. Simon's and the fine hospitality he received. He also owned and at one time lived in Gen. Oglethorpe's house, where his son, Hon. Thomas Spalding, of Sapelo Island, was born (1774). He married Margery McIntosh, daughter of Major William McIntosh of the Continental line and Mary MacKay, his wife, 1772. (Watkins Digest.) Died in Savannah on his way to a meeting of the Legislature in Augusta, the then Capitol, and was interred in the vault of his wife's uncle, General McIntosh. (Family Records; Watkins Digest; "Life of Oglethorpe", Vol. 1, Ga. Hisl. So. Pubs.; "The Spalding Memorial".

The Spalding family were impoverished by participation in the various absortive Stuart uprisings prior to 1745. Thomas Spalding had taken an active part in these and thereby ruined himself financially. He, shortly after 1745, mortgaged certain portions of the Ashantilly estate and took service, as many other Stuart adherents did, in the Lowlands—the Dutch Republic—as Lieut. under Gen. Sir James Stuart, and of a winter's night in 1749 perished while crossing the Rhine with his corps. He had married c. 1734, in Edinburg, Scotland, Anna Lermouth, d. 17 Feby., 1780, who some 5 or 6 years after her husband's death, m. Murdock McLean—of the McLean family, of the Island of Mullah—Capt. in the 1st Reg. English Troops.

Thomas and *Anna (Lermouth) Spalding* left several children, but only one grew to manhood, viz., *James Spalding*, b. 1735; d. 1794; m. 5 Nov., 1772, Margery McIntosh, b. 1754; d. 30 March, 1818, and had one child: *Thomas Spalding*, b. 25 March, 1774; d. 4 Jany., 1854, who m. 5 Nov., 1795, Sarah Leake, b. 1778; d. 18 May. 1843, and had: *James Spalding*, b. 12 Dec., 1797; d. 24 Nov., 1820, without issue; Charles Harris Spalding, b. 17 Jany., 1808; d. s. p., 4 Feby., 1887; m. 7 March, 1839, Evelyn Kell; *Randolph Spalding*, b. 22 Dec., 1822; d. 25 Mch., 1862; m. 7 Dec., 1843, Mary Dorothea Bass and had: Sarah Elizabeth Spalding, b. 6 Sept., 1844; m. Archibald McKinley, no issue; *Thos. Bourke Spalding*, b. 23 Feby., 1851; d. 5 Sept., 1884; m. 3 Nov., 1874, *Ella Patience Barrow* and had: *Randolph Spalding*, b. 30 Sept., 1879, and Clara Lucy Spalding, b. 27 May, 1881; d. 3 Sept., 1881. (See ante, pp. 81-82).

LEAKE, RICHARD—Box tomb, brick sides, white marble top and corners.
SACRED TO THE MEMORY OF RICHARD LEAKE, ESQR., DIED IN SAVANNAH, GEORGIA, MARCH 25, 1802, IN HIS 55 YEAR.

Note:—Richard Leake of the English family of Leke or Leake of "Sutton-Scarsdale", Derbyshire, England, was born in Cork, Ireland. Was educated as a surgeon in the office of his uncle, Dr. John Leake of London, who founded a hospital at Westminster. He came to Georgia prior to 1785, became interested in the culture of sea-island or black seed cotton, then being introduced, commercially into Georgia. His early experiments are carefully noted in his "Plantation Book", beginning 1786, now in possession of his grandson of the 5th degree, Mr. Randolph Spalding of this city; these were successful, as he was at one time the largest exporter of cotton in the State. He was Judge of the Inferior Court of McIntosh County, appointed by Gov. James Jackson, 1800. He married Jean Martin, daughter of Clement Martin, Sr., of Jekyl Island, Georgia, who was member Royal Council of the Province of Georgia, 1754-1761. Their daughter, Sarah Leake, married Thomas Spalding of Sapelo Island, Georgia, in honor of whom Spalding County, in Georgia, was named, 1851. (Georgia Colonial Records; Smith's "Story of Georgia"; Family Records; White's Statistics). "The Ga. So. C. D. A. made a complete record of all the tombs in old Christ Church Cemetery, now Colonial Park, for publication at some future time".

McGEHEE.

Micajah McGehee, b. c. 1745; d. 31 July, 1811; m. c. 1769, Anne Scott, b. c. 1753; d. 23 Feby., 1816, dau. of Capt. James Scott[6] (b. c. 1725; d. after the Revn., in S. C.; m. c. 1750) and his wife, Frances Collier, of Pr. Edward Co., Va., b. c. 1731, dau. of John Collier, d. 1735, and his wife Nancy Eyres (or Eppes). ("Goode's Va. Cousins", p. 50C; "E. S. of Ala.", p. 443).

John Collier was Capt. of infantry in King and Queen Co., Va., 12 June, 1702 (Va. Coll. Militia, p. 97). He m. 3 times—1st, Miss Ballard, no issue; 2nd, Miss Gaines—one child, John Collier, Jr.; 3rd, Nancy Eyres (or Eppes), who bore him 8 children—of whom Frances was either youngest or next to youngest.

Micajah McGehee, 1745-1811, was the son of Edward McGehee, of Cumberland Co., Va. (will 4 April, 1770; pr. 26 Jany., 1771), and his wife Elizabeth DeJarnette, pro. dau. of John DeJarnette—progenitor of the family in Ama. ("Francis Morgan, an Early Va. Burgess, etc.", p. 83, by Mrs. Annie Noble Sims).

Edward McGehee was the son of Thomas Mack Gehee, the immigrant and his wife, Ann Baytop, dau. of Thos. Baytop, b. in County Kent, England, 1676,—will, 1727, published in "E. S. of Ala." (His. of 2 Va. Fams. transplanted from Co. Kent, Eng. to Va.).

Capt. James Scott, 1725-178—, was the son of Thomas Scott and his wife, Ann Baytop[5], dau. of Thos. Baytop III and his wife . . . . Alexander[4], dau. of Dr. David Alexander and his wife Ann Morgan[3], dau. of Francis Morgan[2], son of Capt. Francis Morgan[1].

Thomas Baytop III, b. 9 May, 1676, in County Kent, Eng., was son of Thomas Baytop, Jr. (and his wife, Hannah . . . .), son of Thomas Baytop[1] and his wife, ... Pell, of Kent Co., Eng.

Capt. *Francis* Morgan[1] had only one child, *Francis Morgan*[2], b. pro. in 1736, who left two daus.: Sarah Morgan, who m. Thos. Buckner; *Ann Morgan*, who m. Dr. *David Alexander*, of *Gloucester* Co., Va. ("Francis Morgan", &c, p. 21, by Mrs. Annie Noble Sims).

Francis Morgan, mem. H. of Burgesses from York Co., 1647, 1652-'3. ("Francis Morgan, &c", p. 1).

Capt. James Scott[6] was a Capt. in the Revy. Army in Va. and later in S. C. He removed from Prince Edward Co., Va., to Abbeville Dist., S. C., where he d. after the Revn. For Revy. services see: ("Goode's Va. Cousins", p. 50C; "Stub Entries to Indents for Revy. Claims", p. 307, by A. S. Salley; D. A. R. records of Mrs. Annie Noble Sims, Natl. No. 42392, and of Mrs. Tallulah Gackett Woods, Nat. No. 12473; "Francis Morgan, &c", p. 52).

For Revy. services of Micajah McGehee, see: Certificate by L. H. Bacon, Ordinary of Oglethorpe Co., made 29 March, 1915, as given in "Francis Morgan, an Early Va. Burgess, &c", p. 77.

MACQUINNEY (McKENNIE).

Michael Macquinney was the first of the name in Ama. of whom we have definite knowledge, and the earliest record relating to him is his will, which we find in I. of W. Co., Va., Deed Book 2, p. 254, as follows:

In the name of God Amen this 15th day of April in the year of our Lord, 1686 according to the computation of the Church of England, I Michael Mackquinney of the Western Branch within the County of the Isle of Wight planter being of perfect sense and memory praysed be God do, make and ordain this my last Will and Testament in manner and form following viz:

First, I bequeath my Soul into the hands of Almighty God my maker, hoping that I through the meritorious death and passion of Jesus Christ my only Savior and Redeemer receive free pardon and forgiveness of all my sins and as for my body to be buried in Christian Burial at the discretion of my Executrix hereafter nominated.

(1) Item. I give and bequeath unto my wife Elizabeth Mackquinney my plantation that I now live upon during her life and after her decease unto my young Son Barnaby Mackquinney. Running upon the South east of the Spring Branch belonging to my manor house to Cart path to the white oak lying by said path.

(2) Item. I give unto my eldest son John Mackquinney all the rest of my land upon the north west side of the forest spring branch, always provided that he the aforesaid John doth settle and seat upon it, otherwise to redound to his Mother my wife Elizabeth Macquinney and she to dispose of the land as she shall think fit notwithstanding anything to the contrary.

(3) Item. I give unto my Son Barnaby Mackquinney one feather bed.

(4) Item. I do hereby constitute and ordain my wife Elizabeth Mackquinney to be my whole and sole Executrix of all the whole rest of my whole estate both moveable and immoveable by this my last Will and testament, revoking all other wills and testaments whatsoever in witness whereof I have hereunto set my hand and Seal the day and year above written.

MICHAEL MACKQUINNEY (Seal).

Witnesses: Robert Cooper, Mary Donel, Jeremiah Exum, John Moore.

Proved in open court held for the Isle of Wight County August 9th, 1686 by the oath of Robert Cooper, Jeremiah Exum and John Moore to be the Will of Michael Mackquinney. John Pitt—C. O. C.

THE SECOND HUSBAND OF ELIZABETH MACKQUINNEY.

I. of W., Va., Deed B'k 1 (1688-1704), p. 339.

The Deposition of Thomas Reeves about 52 years or thereabouts showeth that ye depon't knoweth that Michael Mackquinney was possessed of a piece of land in his life tyme and by his last Will and Testament he gave his mannor plantation to his younger son Barnaby Mackquinney, but after his decease the land was found to escheat, and I havin the land in my Custody holding it by my wife Elizabeth's right and possession, her aforesaid Husband Michael Macqu:nney gave it to her for her life tyme, but there was agreement made between ye depon't and John Mackquinney that he should enter an escheat upon his Brother's land in his name, in behalf of his Brother Barnaby, Because ye sd. Barnaby Mackquinney *was not of age* and ye depon't hath paid ye full Composition for ye Escheat in Barnaby Mackquinney's behalf therefore ye deponent will certify upon oath in open court and further saith not. January 10th, 1801. (Signed) Thomas Reeves.

Chas. Chapman, Clerk Ct.

I. of W., Va., Deed B'k 1 (1688-1704), p. 340.

The deposition of Elizabeth Reeves aged about 60 years or thereabouts that ye deponent knoweth that my afore. husband Michael Mackquinney was possessed of a Pattent of Land and by his last Will and Testament he gave his manor plantation to his younger son Barnaby Mackquinney but after my husband's decease the land was found to be escheat wherefore my sonne John Mackquinney entered an Escheat upon his Brother Barnaby Mackquinney's land in his own name   because that the aforesaid Barnaby was not of age and thus far ye deponent knows that my husband Thomas Reeves hath paid a   in my son Barnaby's behalf, this your deponent is willing to testify upon oath in Open Court,   Further saith not. Sworn in open Court, December 9th, 1701.   Elizabeth Reeves.

I. of W.B'k 1704-1715, p. 19.

Thomas Reeves and Elizabeth his wife of the County of Isle of Wight for a certain sum of tobacco sell to Richard Exum of ye afsd. County 200 Acres of land in County mentioned, lying along main Blackwater part of a Pattent of 740 Acres granted to sd. Thomas Reeves October 24th, 1701.   THOMAS REEVES.
Dated August 4th, 1704.   ELIZABETH REEVES.
Wit.: Phillip Raphard, Barnaby Mackinne. Rd. October 9th, 1704.

I. of W. B'k, 1704-1715, p. 83.

Richard Exum sells this land to Richard Lewis of Isle of Wight, March 9th, 1707/8. Wit.: Joseph Bridger, Jr., Wm. Speis (?). Recorded by Captain Richard Exum 9th . . . . , 1707/8.   Chas. Chapman, Clerk.

Richmond, Va., L. O. B'k 9, p. 98.—To all and Whereas a certain tract of land lying in Nansemond Co. containing 450 Acres late in the possession of Michael MacKenny late of the said County, deceased, is lately found to escheat to his sacred Majesty from the said Michael McKenny as by an inquisition recorded in the Sheriff's under the hand and seal of Thos. Milner Escheat of the County and a jury sworn before him for the purpose dated the 15th day of August 1692 may appear for which said land John MacKenny of the said County hath made his composition to the said Letters Patent Know you therefore that I the said Sir Edmund Andros, Jr., his Majesty's Lord & Governor General of Va. doe give & grant unto John MacKenny ye said 450 Acres of land lying in Nansemond County aforesaid according to ye most ancient & lawful bounds thereof to have & to hold, etc. Dated Oct. 20, 1697.   (Signed) E. Andros.
E. Jennings, Deputy Secretary.

John MacKenney[2], the elder son, was b. c. 1668, d. 1708-'10, leaving a son Michael MacKenney[3], who with his wife Rose on April 10, 1710, executed a deed as follows: Michael Mackquinny in Isle of Wight County & Rose, his wife, to Richard Exum of Nanzimond County for "a certain sum of tobacco" sell to Richard Exum 200 Acres of land in Western Branch of Nanzimond in ye County of Isle of Wight that is to say ye land & plantation my Grandfather Michael Mackquinny, deceased, lived on being part of a Pattent of 450 Acres of land granted to my *Father* John Mackquinny & adjoining Mr. *Jeremiah Exum* on ye upper side & the land of John Gay on the lower, now in the possession of ye sd Richard Exum.
Wit.: Wm. Crumpler, Wm. Scott, Jr.   Michael Macquinny.
(Book 1704-1715, p. 140; Deed Book 2, p. 148).   Rose Mackquinny.

Michael Mackquinny and Rose, his wife, to Henry Gay 150 Acres, part of a patent granted to John Mackquinny, *decd.*, for 450 acres, Isle of Wight Co., April 20, 1694.   Michael X Mackquinny.
     Rose X Mackquinney.
Wit.: Richard Exum, Wm. Crumpler, Wm. Scott, Jr. (Book 2, p. 157).

John MacKenny suit against Peter Cartwright, 1708. (Norfolk Co. Book 8, p. 17).

Barnaby Macquenny, the younger son, was b. c. 1673; d. c. 1740 in Edgecombe Co., N. C. He rec'd a deed to land from his brother, John Macquenny, June 7, 1694.
I. of W., Va., Deed B'k 1, p. 340. Book 1688-1704.

Know all people to whom these presents shall come Barnaby Mackquinny and Mary his wife send Greeting in our Lord God Everlasting Know ye that I the said Barnaby Mackquinny and Mary my wife of the County of the Isle of Wight for divers good causes and Considerations we hereunto moving but more especially for and in Consideration of a Certain sum of Tobacco to us in hand paid the receipt whereof we do hereby acknowledge have given granted bargained sold conveyed and confirmed and by these presents do sell etc. unto Richard Exum of the aforesaid County a parcel of land to say my Father Michael Mackquinny's Manor plantation beginning at the foot of his Spring Branch touching Henry Gay's line, at the Main

Swamp, that is to say all the land given me by my Father's last Will and Testament, situate lying and being in the Isle of Wight, being part of an escheat Pattent granted to my Brother John Mackquinny deceased, bearing date the 20th of April, 1694.
Barnaby Mackinne.
Mary Mackinne.

Wit.: James Webb, Jno. Council. Recorded 9th 30th 1703. To *Captain* Richard Exum.

BARNABY MACKQUINNY GIVES BOND FOR TITLE. 12,000 lbs. tobacco. "John Macquinney conveyed this land to Barnaby his Brother by an instrument of writing bearing date Jan. 13-1694 but before John could make a lawful conveyance of same he dyed.

But notwithstanding Barnaby Mackquinny had made a conveyance to Richard Exum, if the heirs of John Macquinny when they come to age of 21 years shall make a lawfull Conveyance of sd. land to the sd. Richard Exum the above obligation to be void, otherwise to remain in full force.
Barnaby Macquinney.

Wit.: Henry Pitt, John Council. Chas. Chapman, C. C. C. (Deed B'k 1, p. 345.)

Barnaby McKinnie[2] m., pro. in Sept., 1703, Mary (Exum) Ricks, widow of Jacob Ricks, son of Isaac and Kathren Ricks, and dau. of Jeremiah Exum and his wife, Ann Lawrence, dau. of John Lawrence. (See Exums.)

"Jacob Rickesis, the son of Isaac Rickesis, and Mary Exum both of the County of the Isle of Wight propounded their marriage before a meeting of Men & Women friends at our Publick meeting house in Chuckatuck on the ninth day of the ninth Mo. 1699 last past and coming before the meeting the second time at our publick meeting house in Chuckatuck on the 14 day of the 10 mo 1699 were married.
Joseph Rickesis
Mary M. Exum.

Isaac Rickesis, Jno. Rickesis, Abraham Rickesis, James Denson, John Denson, Daniel Sanborn, *Rich'd Exum,* Thos. Page, ffrances Denson, Rich'd Rattcliff, Mary Lawrence, Joane Lawrence, Jno. Ratcliff, ffrances Bridle, Elizabeth Lawrence, Nathan Newby, Henry Wiggs, Sarah Sanbourne, Sarah Horning, Elizabeth Rattcliff." (Early Quaker Records in Va.; So. His. Assn. Pubs., Vol. 6, p. 309).

Jacob Ricks was a *witness* on *March 16, 1703,* to the marriage of his brother Abraham Ricks to Mary Bellson (So. His. Assn. Pubs., Vol. 6, p. 408) and an imperfect record of his death is as follows: *"Jacob Rickesis* son of Isaac and Kathren his wife d. (5 & 9 [both erased, or rather crossed out] of the 5 mo. . . [the year not given, but it was 1703]. (S. H. A. Pubs., Vol. 7, pp. 209-210). We have before shown that Barnaby McKinnie and his wife Mary executed a deed on 9th month, 30th day, 1703. Appraisement made of Estate of Jacob Ricks, Oct. 1704, by Jacob Darden and Henry Pope. (Book 2, p. 483).

A DIFFERENCE ADJUSTED.

"ffrom our mans meeting held at Chuckatuck on the 14th day 7 mo 1704 the Difference depending between Jeremiah Exum and Isaac Ricks, Sr., is finally ended upon this Provisor Isaac Ricks Junior and Robt. Ricks his brother hath each of them alike past their obligation for two thousand pounds of tobacco to the Widow namely Mary Ricks the widow of Jacob Ricks, decd., which is done in lieu of his children's part or portion of land or anything else which may be claimed after the decease of the said Isaac Ricks, Sr., and we are witnesses of the same whose names are heare Inserted. Nathan Newby, Jno. Porter, Benj. Small, Daniel Sanborn, Jno. Small, and Jno. Murdah. ffrom our mens meeting at our Meeting House at Chuckatuck in ye County of Nansemond Virginia held the 8 day of the first 1703/4." (So. His. Assn. Pubs., Vol. 6, p. 409).

Will of Isaac Ricks, "26th day of the 7th month Called September in the year 1721"; Rd April 24th, 1724. To my son Isaac Ricks land he now lives on; to my son Abraham Ricks; to my son Robert Ricks, land where my son John formerly lived; to my son James Ricks my Great Bible and land; to my daughter Jean Ricks [unm.].

Item 6th. "I give to my *two gran Children Isaac* & *Martha the children of*

my son Jacob Rickes, deceased, each of them one shilling". Exrs.: My son James and my daughter Jeane   Isaac Rickes.
Wit.: John Sellaway, Thomas Sikes, Wm. Denson, John Page, Wm. Wilkinson.
. . . . Lightfoot, Clerk Ct.

Barnaby McKinnie[2] was a very large land owner. Besides what he inherited and much that he acquired by purchase, he received grants in Isle of Wight Co. aggregating 5448 acres of land for the transportation of 109 persons as shown by the records in the office of the Register of the Land Office, Richmond, Va. (Book 9, p. 472; Book 10, pp. 130, 147, 201 and 222; W. & M. Q., Vol. XXVII, No. 1, . . . July, 1918—p. 59, footnotes).

He removed to Edgecombe Co., N. C., about 1721 or '2, and settled near Caledonia (then a part of Chowan, later of Bertie, then Edgecombe), and became one of the most prominent, wealthy and influential men of the old North State, with large land holdings in Bertie, Edgecombe, Northampton, and other Counties. He was appointed a Justice by the Lords Proprietors July, 1722. A general Court for the Province was held at the Court House in Edenton, July, 1722. Present, Chris. Gale, Esq., Chief Justice. A new Commission from ye Lords Proprietors appointing Jno. Palin, Robt. West, Jno. Worley, Edmund Gale, Adam Cockburn, Henry Clayton, Jno. Solley, John Cotton, Cullen Pollock, *Barnaby McKinnie*, Justices, was read. (N. C. H. & G. Reg., 2-1-149); Commissioner of the Peace, Bertie Precinct, April 19, 1724 (C. R. N. C., Vol. 2, p. 526), and Oct. 31, 1724 (Ibid, p. 570).

Edmund Gale, *Barnaby McKinnie*, Wm. Downing, Robt. Lloyd, John Alston, John White, Thos. Lovick and Richard Greaves were appointed *Justices* of the *General Court* for that part of the Province of N. C. which lies East of Cape Fear River [date not given, but in the '20s]. (N. C. H. & G. Reg. 2-2-298). *Barnaby McKinnie*, General Court Oyer and Terminer, Edenton, N. C., Mch. 29, 1726, Christopher Gale, Chief Justice; Commission of *Barnaby McKinnie* as *Associate Judge* of the General Court of N. C., 6 Oct. 1725/6; also Assistant Judge in 1727. (C. R. N. C., Vol. 2, p. 572; N. C. H. & G. Reg., Vol. 3, No. 2, pp. 284, 290); Commissioner of the Peace for Bertie, 14 April, 1726 (C. R. N. C., Vol. 2, p. 607); Justice of the Peace for this Government, 29 Dec., 1726 (N. C. H. & G. Reg., Vol. 3, No. 2, p. 236); Member of the *General Assembly* for Edgecombe, 15 July, 1735 (C. R. N. C., Vol. 4, p. 115). In running the boundary line between Va. and N. C., April 4, 1728, *Barnaby McKinnie* was named as on Roanoke division line of Isle of Wight Co. from Brunswick. The line of division is north to Meherrin River (C. R. N. C., Vol. 2, p. 809). This probably refers to lands owned by him.

Col. Barnaby McKennie, Sr.[2], and his wife, *Mary (Exum) Ricks* had 10 children, viz.: 1.—Barnaby McKennie, Jr.[3], m. Mary . . . . (of whom presently); 2.—William McKennie[3], d. 1739 (Halifax Co. Deed Book 1, p. 312); 3.—John McKennie[3], m. Mary . . . . ; his will 28 Feb. 1753. (N. C. H. & G. Reg. 1-3-344; Halifax Co. Deed Book 1, p. 167); her will 13 Oct., 1754; Nov. Ct. 1754 (N. C. H. & G. Reg. 1-3-345); 4.—Richard McKennie[3], m. Mary . . . . ; his will 10 Aug., 1751; Aug. Ct., 1755. No Issue. (Reg. 1-3-350; C. R. N. C., Vol. 6, p. 384); 5.—Robert McKennie[3] (Halifax Co. Deed Book No. 4, p. 445); 6.—Ann McKennie[3], m. William Murphy. His will, Edgecombe Co., 23 Jany., 1735-'6; May Ct., 1737. (q. v.); 7.—Mourning McKennie[3], b. c., 1704; m. c. 1721, John Pope, b. c. 1700; d. in 1745. (C. R. N. C., Vol. 6, pp. 384, 481; S. R. N. C., Vol. 25, p. 465). (*See also "Popes"*); 8.—Patience McKennie[3], m. in 1730, Joseph Lane, b. c. 1705. His will 29 Aug., 1773; Feby. Ct., 1774, Halifax Co. (See "Isaac Hill" and "Popes"); 9.—Christian McKennie[3], m. William Hurst; 10.—A daughter[3], name not known, m. John Brown. Order of births not known. *The various petitions* for docking the entail of lands devised by *Col. Barnaby McKennie*[2] give much information as to the daughters who m. Pope, Lane and Hurst.

Petition of John Lane, of the Province of S. C., son of Patience (McKennie) Lane, 7 May, 1760 (C. R. N. C., Vol. 6, pp. 383-'4, 481), also Petitions by *Barnaby McKennie* and *William Hurst* (C. R. N. C., Vol. 6, pp. 481-'2, 485, 745-'6-'7, 759; Vol. 5, pp. 1026, 1029, 1032, 1071-'2-'7; S. R. N. C., Vol. 25, p. 465; Book 7, p. 35—at Halifax—Rec. of Deeds & Mortgages).

On 28 March, 1722, Col. Barnaby McKennie makes deed of Gift to his *son-in-law Isaac Ricks,* of 100 A. land in "Caledony Woods" called Napkin Work, patented by Nathaniel Holley. Test. Barnaby McKennie, Jr., Richard Jackson (N. C. H. & G. Reg. 1-3-470). It was thought by Mr. J. R. B. Hathaway et al. that this Isaac Ricks had m. a dau. of Col. Barnaby McKennie. The fact is, however, that he was his step-son—son of wife by first marriage.

Barnaby McKennie, Jr., 7 Oct., *1736*; pr. Nov. Court *1736*. (Sec. of State's Office, Raleigh, N. C. Grant Book 4, Will 58). In the Name of God, Amen. I Barnaby McKennie, Junior, being very sick and weak of Body but in perfect mind & memory thanks be to God for the same and remembering the mortality of my Body do make this my last will and testament in manner following, viz:

First, I bequeath my soul unto the hands of God who gave it and my Body to be buried in a Decent manner and form following, viz:

Item. I give unto my Daughter Patience McKinnie my now dwelling plantation and all my land thereunto belonging as also one hundred acres of the land more or less given me by my Father's Will to her and the heirs of her body lawfully begotten and their heirs forever after her mother's decease and if provided my two daughters Decease without Issue then to *Barnaby Lane son of Joseph Lane* and his heirs.

Item. I give unto my Daughter Mary McKennie two hundred and fifty acres of land which I bought of John McKennie the place where Dennis Morgan now lives upon, I say unto my Daughter Mary and to the heirs of her Body lawfully begotten and their heirs forever and if provided my two daughters should decease without issue then to Barnaby MacKennie son of William MacKennie him, his heirs.

Item. I give unto my loving Wife Mary MacKinnie the use of five negroes and their increase (viz.) Patt, Doll, Lucy, Mingo and Jack During her Natural Life and Likewise to keep them in the service of the manor plantation and after her Decease to be equally divided between *my two* children.

Item. I also give unto my loving wife Mary all and singular my household stuff also one gray horse C. P. and six cows and calves and ten young cattle as also my fishing Creek Mare and the horse colt to my *Daughter Patience*.

I likewise give unto my wife two companies of hoggs using about home.

Item. I give unto *Joseph Lane* the plantation and stock where Francis Scott lives upon, two gangs of hoggs using in the Swan pons being thirty six.

Item. I give unto my Brother William MacKennie one hundred acres of Land joyning to him the said William MacKennie.

Item. I give unto *Barnaby Pope, son of John Pope*, one hundred and ten acres of Land adjoining to the said land I give unto William MacKennie.

Item. I give unto *John Pope* one sorel Mare filley branded with Major MacKennie's brand C. S. as also one young bay horse branded with my own brand Cut and Doct. I say unto John Pope.

Item. I give unto my brother Robert MacKennie two mares a blac one and a gray mare and a skewbald horse colt I say unto Robt. MacKennie.

Item. I give unto my Brother John McKennie the plantation where George rauloson now lives upon I say unto John McKennie.

Item. I give unto James Howell all that tract of land where old Stevens did live I say unto James Howell.

Item. I give unto Nathaniel Cooper a young black mare belonging to my Fishing Creek Mare I say unto Nathaniel Cooper.

Item. I give unto my *cousin John Lane* a little sorrel horse I say unto my *cousin John Lane*.

I likewise appoint my loving Wife and *Joseph Lane* Exrs. of this my last will and testament in testimony hereof I have hereunto set my hand and fixed my seal this seventeenth Day of October in the year of our Lord Christ one thousand seven hundred thirty six. Barnaby MacKinnie, Junior.
Nathanl Cooper, John Crowell, Walford. Edgecomb P. Nov. Court 1736.

The above written will was duly proved by the oaths of Nant Cooper, John Crowell and John Walford the subscribing evidences thereto and also Mary MacKinnie and *Joseph Lane* qualified themselves as Executors of the aforesaid will according to law. Test. *Thomas Kerney*, Clerk.

Will of *William Murphy*, of Edgecombe Co., N. C., 23 Jany., 1735-'6; May Court 1737. Daus.: Mary, Martha and Esther. *Kinsman William Hurst*, Joseph Bradshaw. *Wife; Ann*, Jno Edwards, and *Isaac Ricks*, Exrs. Test.: *John Pope*, William Godwin, John Strickland. (N. C. H. & G. Reg. 1-3-351).

Col. Barnaby McKinnie, Sr.'s, will is shown by the various petitions to dock the entail of lands cited heretofore, to have been dated 31 Aug. 1737. The deed following is of the nature of a codicil.

Codicil to Will—BARNABY McKINNIE.

Halifax Court House, N. C., Deed B'k 1, p. 312. 1739. To all persons to whom these presents shall come greeting whereas I, *Barnaby McKinnie* of Edgecombe County by my last Will and Testament bearing date the 30th day of August, did bequeath unto my son William McKinnie and the heirs of his body lawfully begotten and to their heirs forever a tract of land containing two hundred acres being the plantation whereon my son William then lived who having since departed this life therefor to prevent any objection that may be urged against the descent of the said land as by the bequest in my sd. will intended know ye that I, *Barnaby McKinnie* of Edgecombe County in the province of North Carolina Esqr. out of the natural love and affection which I have and do bear to my grandson Barnaby McKinnie son and heir at law of my son Wm. McKinnie dec'd. and for and in consideration of the sum of five shillings to me in hand paid do by these presents give grant alien enforce and confirm to the sd. Barnaby McKinnie and the heirs of his body lawfully begotten and to their heirs forever all that tract or parcel of land situate lying and being in the county afsd. containing two hundred acres being the plantation whereon the sd. Wm. McKinnie lived at the time of his death lying on the outward corner of Nathl. Holley's survey from thence running outward an equal distance upon both lines of that survey whereof this is a part until the sd. 200 acres be included. To have and to hold the sd. land and premises with its appurtenances unto the sd. Barnaby McKinnie his heirs as afsd. forever together with all right profits benefits improvements thereon or anywise belonging or appertaining, provided nevertheless that it is the true intent and meaning of these presents that if the sd. Barnaby McKinnie should die without issue lawfully begotten of his body as afsd. then the above land and premises to descend to my grand-daughter Mourning McKinnie, sister of the afsd. Barnaby to her heirs forever and in case of the want of such issue of the afsd. Mourning McKinnie then the above land and premises to descend to my daughter Patience Lane and the heirs of her body, lawfully begotten and their heirs forever. In witness whereof I have hereunto set my hand and seal this 3rd day of December Anno Dom. 1739. BARNABY McKINNIE (Seal) Signed, etc., in the presence of J. Edwards, Wm. Hurst. Proven in Court 1739.

February Court 1739. The above deed was proved in open court in due form of law by the oath of John Edwards one of the Subscribing evidences thereto and O. M. O. R. Test. J. Edwards C. Ct.

The above is the *last* recorded transaction by *Col. Barnaby McKennie* that I have been able to find. As by all accounts he died shortly after making his will, his death most probably occured in 1740.

McKennie, Richard, Edgecombe Co., will, Aug. 10, 1751; Aug. Ct. 1755. Brother Bobert, Barnaby, son of Brother John, wife Mary, Wm. Kinchen, Sr., and Wm. Kinchen, Jr. Attys. to advise my wife whom I appoint Exx. Test.: Wm. Kinchen, Wm. Baker, *Lemuel* Kinchen. (Reg. 1, p. 350).

McKennie, John, Edgecombe, will, 28 Feby., 1753. Son Barnaby, daus. Mary, Patience and Martha, *dau.-in-law Angelina Parish, child in esse, Wife Mary*, Connor Cumbo: Wife and Montfort Eulbach Exrs. I give and bequeath my loving wife . . . . the use of my grist mill on Great Quonkee two years next ensuing for pay for the giving each of my children before mentioned two years schooling. Test.: Montfort Eulbeck, *Wm. Gaddy*, Mary Eulbeck. (Reg. 1—345; Abstract of N. C. Wills, p. 233).

It will be noted John McKennie does not name in his will a son John.

McKennie, Mary, Edgecombe, will, 13 Oct., 1754; Nov. Ct., 1754. Imprimis.— I most humbly bequeath my Soul to God my Maker beseeching His most Gracious reception of it through the all sufficient merits and Mediations of my Most Compassionate Redeemer Jesus Christ, Who gave himself to be an atonement for my sins and is able to save to the uttermost all that come unto God by him, Seeing he ever liveth to make intercession for them, and Who, I trust will not reject me a returning penitent sinner, when I come to him for mercy; in this Hope and confidence I render up my soul with comfort humbly beseeching the Most Blessed and Glorious Trinity, One God most holy, most merciful and gracious to prepare me for the time of my dissolution and then to take me to himself unto that Place of Rest and incomparable Felicity which he has prepared for all that love and fear his holy name Amen Blessed be God. (The foregoing given as a specimen of the preambles to the wills of the period.) Dau. Angeliany *Pope, Sons John* and Barnaby McKinnie, daus. Mary, Patience and Martha. Barnaby Pope, Exr. Test.: David Crawley, Wm. Caddy, Robt. Belcher. (Abstract of N. C. Wills, p. 233; Reg. 1—345).

Indenture Tripartite: . . . Day of July, 1767, Between Nicholas Long and Mary, his wife, of the Co. of Halifax, N. C., of the first part, John Geddy and Patience, his wife, of the town of Halifax, of the second part and Joseph Montfort of the town of Halifax Guardian to Martha McKinney an infant under the age of 20 years of the third part. Whereas Barnaby McKennie the younger, brother to the above mentioned Mary, Patience and Martha, being seized in his Demesne as of fee tail 300 acres in Halifax adjoining Roanoke River which land descended to the said Barnaby McKennie as son and heir to John McKennie to whom the same was . . . . in the last Will and Testament of Col. Barnaby McKinnie, decd., after the death of his son Richard without issue, is dead without issue of his body whereby all and singular the said messuage land and premises descended and came unto the said Mary, Patience and Martha. This Indenture Witnesseth that Nicholas Long and Mary his Wife, John Geddy and Patience, his wife, and Joseph Montfort Guardian to the said Martha have agreed to make partition. Witnesses: Joel Lane, Richard Freear. July Court 1767. (Halifax Book 10, p. 28).

POPE.

In letter, 22 Apr. 1910, by Dr. Geo. L. Pope, Louisville, Ky., to Mr. James Martin, Phila., Pa., we find: "Yours of the 19th inst. duly received. Gen'l John Pope and another member of the family made a trip to England some ago. . . . . They had a copy of the coat of arms granted to *Sir Thomas Pope, guardian* and custodian of *Elizabeth,* afterwards *Queen Elizabeth.* The motto on it, "Mihi, Tibi", (meaning justice) "To me and to you"."

"The arms are: Two chevrons gules, a canton azure. Crest: A cubit arm erect, habited gules, cuffed argent, holding in the hand proper a pair of scales or. Motto: Mihi tibi.

The arms granted to *Sir Thomas, Elizabeth's guardian*: Party per pale or and azure, on a chevron between three gryphons' heads erased fleurs-de-lis, all counterchanged. Crest: Two gryphons erased." (From a newspaper article by Frances M. Smith—Eleanor Lexington").

"One of the *Privy Council* of Henry VI. Was *Thomas Pope* . . . . . The guardian of the Princess, afterward *Queen Elizabeth,* during her minority, was Sir Thomas Pope. He resided with her at Hatfield House, and there he was authorized by her to decline the King of Sweden's offer of marriage. Sir Thomas is better remembered for his endowment of Trinity College, where he is buried. We may take it that he was a wise man, if the legend engraved upon his tombstone was his life motto: "Whatever you wish untold to no man tell".

"Robert Pargiter, of Grylworth, in County of Northampton, Will, 4 Feby., 1557; pr. 31 Jany., 1558. My son *William* and *Anne My Wife* shall have my farm in Shattiswell in the County of Worcester, which I hold by indenture of *Sir Thomas Pope, Knight.*

Item.—I ordain and make *Lawrence Washington my son-in-law* to be the Supervisor of this my last Will and Testament and he to have for his labor and paines taken therein 40 shillings". (N. E. H. & G. Reg. 45, p. 62).

A century later we find the Pope and Washington families transplanted in Virginia, having the same family names, socially intimate and intermarrying.

"Fourteen (14) persons by name of *Pope* settled in Md. *between* the years *1634* and 1683. Francis Pope was the first to arrive and settled in Charles Co. (Will 1671). (N. E. H. & G. Reg. 44, p. 83).

"The first Maryland Assembly [held] 1635-'6, just 11 months after formation left no records. The second Assembly, to which *Nathaniel Pope* was summoned, was held in 1637, and *he was at County Court* Feby. 12, *1637*". (Md. His. So. Vol. 9, p. 13).

Nathaniel Pope was one of the 24 freemen of the "Grand Inquest" in Md. in 1637". (W. & M. Q., Vol. 4, p. 37). "On 26 Feby., 1639, Pope's Freehold surveyed —1000 A.—being one of the first 1000 land grants". (Side Lights on Md. His. , p. 287).

"On 11th April, 1643, an order was issued on divers good and sufficient causes that *Nathaniel Pope* and all his menial servants—nine in all—be exempted from all watches and wardings, from all attendance at meetings and trainings, or from being called or commanded out of or from his house to or upon any leavie, march or partie without or against his will or consent, Witnesses or deare brother etc." (Md. Arc. Vol. 3, p. 130).

"In 1646 *Nathaniel Pope* was an agent or overseer for Leonard Calvert when the Governor was preparing his expedition to regain his place, and was sent to the Kent Islanders as mediator after the Governor had regained possession of St. Mary's". (Md. His. So., Vol. 9, pp. 13, 102-'3).

"*Nathaniel Pope* demands 700 A. for transportation of himself, wife and five men servants before year 1648. He received warrants to lay out upon Potomac River". [Note.—No children named.] (Md. His. Mag., Vol. 8, p. 266). Settlers on both sides the Virginia and Maryland banks of the Potomac frequently crossed the river. (N. E. H. & G. Reg. 44, p. 83).

"At a Court held for the County of Northumberland, 25th Nov., 1652. Present: Col. John Mottrom, Mr. Thomas . . . ., Mr. John Frussell, Mr. Wm. Pressley, Mr. *Nathaniel Pope*, Mr. S. H. O. Baldredge, Mr. *Robert Broadhurst*, Mr. Sam Smith, Mr. Nichs Morris", etc. (Oldest Book, p. 5 (Order Book), Northumberland Co., Va.).

Nicholas Heywood and brother to *Mr. Pope*, July 25, 1652. (Northumberland Co. Book, 1653-1685, p. 12).

On Nov. 25, 1652, Nicholas Heywood, merchant, of London, Engd, wrote a long business letter, despatching it by messenger, to his approved, loving friend, *Nathaniel Pope*, Appomattocks, in Va., which he closes with: "*Y'r brother* hath sent you a lr [letter] by the young man named Sam Mothershed—*Yor father* is well also. . . . From . . . [mutilated] the 25 Nov. 1652". (Signed Nichs Heywood. (Va. Mag. of H. & B., Vol. 9, pp. 332-'3; W. & M. Q., XI, pp. 169-171).

On Sept. 6, 1654, *Nathaniel Pope* patented 1000 A. on South side Potomac River, Westmoreland Co. (Grant Book 3, p. 279); on April 24, 1656, 1550 A. (Grt. Bk. 4, p. 51); on Nov. 30, 1656, 1050 A. (Grt. Bk. 4, p. 63).

On March 11, 1655, *William Pope* patented 200 A. in Westmoreland Co. (Grt. Bk. 4, p. 31). The compiler thinks this is an error, as he can find no record of a grant of land in *Westmoreland Co.* to *William Pope*. But in "Genealogical Gleanings", Vol. 1, p. 403, by Henry F. Waters, it is so stated by Mr. R. A. Brock, a genealogist of recognized accuracy and reliability. In connection with these grants to *Nathaniel* and *William Pope*, he says: "*these grantees were probably brothers.*

"On 4 April, 1655. Commissioned for ye Co. of Westmoreland; also appointed by ye Governor and Council to be of ye Militia for ye sd. C.: *Lt. Col. Nathaniel Pope.*" ("Amn. Records and Portraits, Vol. 2, p. 438).

The first land grant to *Nathaniel Pope* was one year and nine and one-half months after date of Heywood's letter, and that to *William Pope*, as given by Mr. Brock, was six months and five days after the one to Nathaniel Pope and a little more than 2 years and three months after Heywood wrote.

On *Oct. 8, 1656*, *William Pope* received grant for 190 A. in *Nansemond* Co., adjoining *Capt. Thos. Godwin's* land, *Due s'd Pope* for the transportation of four persons, Obedience Perkins, *John Godwin*, Robert Beadle [the 4th headright not recorded]. (Grt. Book 4, p. 89).

WILLIAM POPE'S PATENT. Ld. Grt. Bk. 4, p. 406, Richmond, Va., A. D. 1662.

To all and whereas etc. Know ye that I the said Frances Moryson Esq. Governor etc. give and grant unto William Pope Two hundred Acres of Land, Situate lying, and being in the County of Nansemond. Beginning at a dead red Oak on a small branch side near the Miles end of Symon Symon's Land, and running near the Said Land north west ½ point Westerly 240 poles to marked Oak, then north east ½ point northerly 140 poles, then South East ½ Easterly 130 poles, then east 20 poles, then South East 34 poles, then south south-east 118 poles to Captain Thomas Goodwin's Land and so by the said Goodwyn's Land to the aforesaid small branch to the first station. The said Land being formerly granted unto the said William Pope by patent bearing date the 8th of October 1656 and now renewed in his Majestie's name, by Order of the Quarter Court, To have and to Hold etc. To be held and yielding and paying etc. provided etc. Dated the 30th of October 1662. (By referring to Grant of date mentioned in William Pope's Patent of October 30th 1662, See the following) *Book 4, page 31.*

(Note.—Land Grant Book 4, p. 31—above—is the reference given by Mr. R. A. Brock for the grant of 200 A. in Westmoreland County to William Pope, March 11, 1655).

1665. To all and, etc., Whereas, etc., now know ye that I the said Edward Diggs Esq. etc. give and grant unto Captain Thomas Godwin Two hundred Acres of Land situate and being in the County of Nansemond near the head of the North West branch of the said River beginning at a marked Pine at the mile end of Symon Symon's Land running for Length North East by East 200 poles to a marked red Oak and so for breadth North West by North 160 poles to a marked White Oak and so again for Length South West by West to a marked tree butting on the Land of Symon Symons and so South East by South 160 poles to the first mentioned marked tree.

The said Land being due unto the said Captain Thomas Godwin by and for the Transportation of Four persons into this Colony etc.

To Have and to hold etc. yielding and paying etc. which payment is to be made etc. dated the 11th day of March 1655. DOROTHY LOYD.

1662. On the margin is written in ink the following:

This Patent was assigned to William Pope by the said Godwin in whose name it is renewed the 30th October 1662 and granted by Col. Francis Moryson Esq. Governor etc. FRA FICKMAN, Clerk.

"On 30 Oct., 1662. To all and Whereas, etc. Know ye That I the sd Francis Morgan, Esq., Gov. &c, &c, &c, give and grant unto *William Pope* 200 A. of Land situate lying and being in the *County* of *Nansemond* Beginning at a dead red Oak on a small branch side near the Miles end of Symon Symon's Land and running near the sd Land Northwest ½ point Westerly 240 poles to marked Oak, then North East ½ point Northerly 140 poles, then Southeast ½ Easterly 130 poles, then East 20 poles, then South East 34 poles, then South south-east 34 poles, then South South East 118 poles to *Capt. Thos. Godwin's Land* and so far by the s'd *Godwin's* Land to the afsd small branch to the first Station. The sd Land being formerly granted unto the s'd *William Pope* by patent bearing date the *8th day of October 1656* and now renewed in his Majestie's name by Order of the Quarter Court. To have and to Hold &c. To be held and yielding and paying &c, provided &c. Dated the 30th Oct., 1662". (Grt. Bk. 4, p. 406).

On July 25, 1665, patent granted to *William Pope* for 950 A. in Isle of Wight Co., near Indian Swamp. (Grt. Bk. 5, p. 114).

William Pope of *Nanzemond Co.* for 4500 lbs. tobacco, 10 sh., sells to Thos. Price 200 A. in Isle of Wight near Indian Swamp touching Godfrey Hunt's land and Everitt's land, it being part of a Pattent of 950 A. granted to *my father William Pope late of Nanzemond County, deceased,* pattent dated ye 25th of July, 1665. Deed dated ffeb. 1st, 1706/7. *William Pope.*

Wit.: John Bullock, Bran Milner; Recorded Feby. 10, 1706/7. [In copy—1606/7—obviously error]. (Isle of Wight Book 1704-1715, p. 48).

There was a *Thomas Pope* in Isle of Wight Co., who, in his will, 27 Sept., 1684; p. 9 Jany., 1691, names sons, Robert, *William, John* and *Thomas* Pope. (Will Book No. 2, p. 208). And a *John Pope* of the parish of Dawlish in England, mariner, on the 22nd July, 1690, gave "Power of atty. to his respected brother *Richard Pope,* of the County of *Isle of Wight* in Virginia . . . . to recover out of the of whomsoever it may concern all such sum or sums of money accts. goods lands or other estate as now is—or may become due owing or payable to me the constituent by bill bond book account or other demands or by any other wais or means whatsoever . . . . etc." (Deed Book 1, p, 29, of Isle of Wight Co.; W. & M. Q., Vol. 7, p. 259).

This *Richard Pope* d. intestate, in Isle of Wight Co., in 1703-'4 (Book 2, pp. 483 and 508), and until very recently I had thought it certain that he was the son of Thos. & Johanna Pope, but I find that this son Richard, a mariner, was living in London, Eng., on 5th Dec., 1716, when he, with his mother, made a deed to the Cliffs to his brother Nathaniel. (Westmoreland Co., Book 6, p. 324).

"After 20 days sight of this my second Bill of Exchange, my 1st & third not being p'd pay or cause to be paid unto Mr. *Richard Pope, Sr.*, of the City of *Bristol*, Soapmaker, or his assigns the sum of 44£ 9 shs. 9 pence & is for soo much worth in goods Out of the Ship Stephen from me Jno. Scott (?) the use of the Ship Katharine. Make good payment & charge it to ye accompt of ye Servant.

George Berham (?)

To Mr. Robert Yates, Mcht. In Bristol. Recorded this 16th day of July, 1668". (Isle of Wight, Va., Book 1662-1715, p. 142).

It appears from the records given that *Col. Nathaniel Pope* was b. pro. about 1614, settled in Md. about 1635—or 1636—he then had no children; removed to Northumberland Co., Va., before 1652; patented lands in Westmoreland in 1654 or 1656; was appointed Lt. Col. of Militia in 1653; that his father and a brother were living in England in 1652. In contemplation of an immediate visit to England, made his will, 16 May, 1659, but dying very soon thereafter, the trip was not made & the will was probated 16 April, 1660.

William Pope was probably the brother of Nathaniel Pope—mentioned, but not named by Nichs Heywood in letter Nov. 25, 1652. He certainly patented lands in Nansemond County in 1656, 1662 and 1665, and according to Mr. Brock, in Westmoreland Co. in 1655 [as before stated this is probably an error]. He, as was the intention of Nathaniel Pope, revisited England in the 1690s, and died in Nanzemond Co. very soon after returning home. Reference to this visit and his death appears in the Nansemond Co. records. One who personally examined this record gave me this information but did not give me the book and page where found. William Pope is mentioned among the Friends at Nanzemond authorized by George Fox to establish regular Quarterly meetings there in 1673. (Quaker Records in Ms. in Safety Deposit at Baltimore).

After carefully examining these early records, I am persuaded that Nathaniel and William Pope were from the same English stirp, and that William, Richard, John and Thomas Pope were brothers, and probably the sons of Richard Pope, Sr., merchant and soap-maker, of Bristol in 1662. Of course, this is a conjecture; no records discovered actually connect them. Among the descendants of Nathaniel and William we find in almost every generation and in every branch of their families, the family names of William, Henry, Thomas, Richard, and John.

As *William Pope* was a Quaker, somewhat of his family record has been preserved by them. Many of the leading men, Col. Joseph Bridger, Maj. Thos. Taberer and Genl. Richard Bennett, Col. Thos. Bushrod, Col. Thos. Godwin, et al., sympathized with the Quakers, when they did not absolutely belong to them; and while the Quakers were sometimes fined for non-conformity, and for failure to notify the authorities of their intended meetings and assemblies, they had their own meeting houses and practically their own way. (W. & M. Qly., Vol. 7, p. 212, and see Quakers).

The "Southern History Association Publications, Vol. 6, p. 508, gives the following:

"*William Pope* and Marie his wife, their children's nattivitties recorded as followeth: William Pope[2] sonn of the aforesaid William and Mary was borne the 15th of the 8th month 1662; *Henry Pope*[2] *sonn* of the aforesaid *William* and *Mary* was borne the *last of the 11th Month 1663;* Alse Pope[2] daughter of the aforesaid William and Mary was borne . . . . of the 8th Month 1667; John Pope[2] sonn of the aforesaid William and Mary was borne 6th of the 8th Month 1670".

William Pope[1] is recorded as present at several Quaker marriages.

William Pope[2] was living in February 1706/7, as evidenced by his deed to Thomas Price, previously referred to. (I. of W. Book, 1704-1715, p. 48).

Will of John Pope[2], Feb. 1, 1748. In the name of God, Amen, this first day of

February in the year of Our Lord Christ one thousand seven hundred and forty-eight, I *John Pope*² of the Isle of Wight County in the Parish of Nottaway being in perfect health and of sound and Perfect Memory thanks be to Almighty God for it calling to mind the uncertainty of my life do make and ordain this to be my last Will and Testament in manner and form following, viz.:

first of all I Recommend my soul to Almighty God that gave it and my Body to be buried at the Discretion of my executor and for what worldly Goods it hath Pleased God to bestow on me after my Debts paid dispose of as followeth.

Item. I give and bequeath to my son *John Pope* one shilling current money of Virginia.

Item. I give and bequeath to my son *William Pope* and his heirs forever the plantation whereon he now lives with two hundred and thirty acres of Land belonging.

Item. I give and bequeath to my daughter Elizabeth Pope the use of the Plantation whereon I now live with one hundred acres of land thereunto belonging during her life or till she marry. I also give my said Daughter Elizabeth one Feather bed and the furniture belonging to it.

Item. I give to my daughter *Mary Darden* Two puter Dishes and two Basons.

Item. I give and bequeath to my *Grandson John Pope*, son of William Pope and his heirs forever the Plantation whereon I now live with one hundred acres of Land thereunto belonging after my Daughter Eliza Marrys or Deceases.

Item. I give and bequeath to my Daughter *Else* Mosley two puter Dishes and two puter basons.

Item. I give and bequeath to my Grandson *Henry Darden* one young Horse called his and one cow and calf and one Gun called his.

And all the rest of my Estate both real and personal I give and bequeath to be legally divided between my son *William Pope* and my Daughter Eliza Pope and my Daughter *Sarah Barnes* [wife of *Edward Barnes*, of N. C., who had dau. Elizabeth Barnes—See will of Elizh Pope].

I also *appoint* my son *William Pope* whole and sole Exor. of this my last Will and Testament and do utterly revoke and make void all former Wills and Testaments by me made.

In Witness Whereof I have hereunto set my hand and seal the day and year first above written.

his
John P. Pope.
Mark.

In presence of Isaac   his   Johnson, Nathan Pope, Howel Edmunds. Recorded July 14, 1751.   mark.   R. I. Kells, Clerk. (Southampton Co., Va,, Booke 1, p. 46).

Elizabeth Pope, Nottaway Parish, Isle of Wight Co., Will July 12, 1757. To *Cousin Rebecca Gatling,* Cousin Benjamin Pope, *Elizabeth Barnes, daughter of Edward Barnes in N. C., Andrew McMiall,* Cousin *Henry Darden,* cousin John Pope, son of Wm. Pope, Brother William Pope. (Signed) Elizabeth X Pope.

Wit.: *Ann X Faircloth,* George Gurley, Jr. (On 9 Jany., 1727, *Wm. Faircloth* left legacy to *Sarah Pope, wife* of *Henry Pope*). (Southampton Co. Book 1, p. 230).

Elizabeth Pope was dau. of John², will *Feby. 1, 1748.*

Jacob Darden and Henry Pope², in Oct., 1704, admᵈ Est. of Jacob Ricks. (Book 2, p. 483).

John Pope, Sr., of Isle of Wight Co., made deed 5 April, 1740, to Andrew McMiall, of same Co. (I. of W. Deed Book 5, p. 462).

Appraisement June 27, 1743, Estate of *William Pope,* of Isle of Wight. Administratrix: Patience Pope. Examined: Henry Thomas, Richard Blow. (Book 4, p. 499).

Alse Blake, in 1702, witness to marriage of Mathew Jordan to Susanna Bresy. ("S. H. A. Pubs.", Vol. 6, p. 313).

Jno. Blake, Shff. of Nansemond Co., Feby. 8, 1701. (Ibid, p. 411). [There is a note of reference to Chuckatuck 1st of 7mo 1664—Alse Pope was-b. in 1667]. This Alse Blake was very probably Alse Pope, dau. of William and Marie Pope, or Alse Pope may have been wife of John Hardy. (See his will).

There is record of a deed from Richard Washington, of Surry, to *Richard*

Brassoll, of Isle of Wight, 150 A., 20 £, Nov. 25, 1717. (I. of W. Grt. Book 2, p. 333). Richard Washington.
Wit.: Frank West, Wm. Washington. Elizh Washington.

The will of a John Williams, circa 1727, of record in Book 3, p. 393. Richard Brassol and John Williams were probably the *sons-in-law* of Henry Pope[2] (will 1728).

John Williams, on Dec. 28, 1670, sold to Wm. Linton and Geo. Harrison 450 A. on the head of Yeocomoco River in Westmoreland Co., for 4250 lbs. Tobac. and cash. (Book 1, p. 400).

Henry Pope[2] m. Sarah Watts, dau. of John Watts and his wife, Alice English, dau. of John English. In Isle of Wight Book 1661-1719, p. 386 is the will of John Watts, as follows: In the Name of God Amen. I John Watts being Sick and Weak of Body but in perfect memory, praised be God for it; doe make this my Last Will and Testament in manner as followeth:

I doe bequeath to my sonne John Watts six head of Cattell, it is named to be .... with my horse Button and my *Troopers arms* and a small brass pott and one Iron pott which is the biggest and one feather bed which is up Stairs and ye furniture thereunto belonging and the great Brass Kettle and six hammered plates and four pewter dishes and three Ewers which my Will is he shall put *his Brother* in Stock out of them. I doe give to my daughter *Sara Pope* my Little Table, and a warming pann, a little Brass Kettle, six Earthen plates and an Earthen porringer. And after my debts are paid I doe bequeath the rest of my Estate to be equally divided amongst my *three youngest Children*, only I give to my sonne John Watts .... two dozen pewter spoons. Witness my hand and seal this 20th of January, 1697/8. (Signed) John Watts.

Wit.: James Tullogh, Jane Benn, Hewey Bulls. I doe make and ordayne my sonne John Watts and my *sonne-in-law Henry Pope* be whole and sole Execrs. of this my Will. Witness my hand. John Watts.

Proved in Open Court held for ye Isle of Wight County ye 9th day of Feb. 1697/8 by the oaths of all the witnesses and ordered to be recorded.

Cha. Chapman, Cl. Ct.

Will of *John English*, of Isle of Wight County, Va. In the Name of God Amen: I *John English* being sick and weak but in perfect sense and memory, I make this my last will and testament, in the manner and form as followeth:

I will and bequeath my soul to God who gave it to me, and my body to the earth to be buried in a decent manner.

I will and bequeath to my loving daughter Frances Ilis all my pictures.

I will and bequeath to my loving daughter Elizabeth Church ten shillings to buy her a ring.

I will and bequeath to my loving *son-in-law, John Watts*, all my wearing apparel, both linen and woolen.

I will and bequeath unto my Grand son *John Ilis* the first fould that the maire bringeth.

I will and bequeath to my Grand son John Watts the next maire fould my maire bringeth.

I will and bequeath unto my *daughter Alice Watts* six yards of serge.

I will and bequeath unto my three daughters Mary English, and Sarah English, and Martha English all the rest of my Estate as follows: Maires, and horses, and cattle, goods and household stuff, to be equally divided in kind and it is my will and desire that my daughter Francis Ilis and my son-in-law John Watts, to be my overseers, of this my will preformed, and to make a eakell division between my three daughters of my estate, as witness my hand and Seal this 13th day of August, 1678. John English (Seal).

Signed sealed and delivered in the presence of us Daniel Miles and Thomas X Bell, (the mark of). Proved in Court held for the Isle of Wight County the 9th day of October, 1678, by the oathes of Daniel Miles and Thomas Bell and ordered to be recorded. Test.: John Broomfield, Clerk Court.

Will of *Richard Church*, Norfolk Co., Jany. 5, 1705; p. 15 Feby., 1705-'6, names wife *Elizabeth Church*. (Abstract of Norfolk Co. Wills, pp. 191-'2).

I. of W. Deed Bk, 1662-1715, p. 584. Be it known unto all men by these

Presents that I Henry Bosman of the County of Nansimond have freely and of my own good will Given, Granted and made over from me my Heires, Executors, Administrators or Assigns unto *Henry Pope* for the Term of Time of Ninety nine years about two hundred Acres of Land lying and being in the Lower Parish of Isle of Wight County and being part of a Pattent of 300 Acres of land granted unto Ambrose Bozman bearing date the 2nd of June in the year of our Lord 1673, which said Land was formerly granted unto William Smelly by Pattent bearing date the 5th of October, 1667, which said 200 Acres of Land is lying on the West side of a Branch called the Head of Queen's Creek and to begin at or upon the Main Branch next John Moors's so running up the said Branch to a small Branch that is next above Ambrose Bozman's little House and so up that Branch to the Head Line.

And the said Henry Bozman for himself his Heirs Executors, Administrators and Assigns Covenants and Agrees to and with the said Henry Pope his heirs Executors, Administrators and Assigns and to and with every of them that they shall from the Day of this Date for the term of Ninety nine years hereafter Have hold Occupy and possess and quietly enjoy the said 200 Acres of Land before Demised with all my right freely given and with all Rights and Proffith thereunder appertaining without Lett or Hindrance or Molestation of him the said **Henry** Bozman his Heires Executors Adm'rs or Assigns by their knowledge or Consent, without any manner of Condition or limitation of use or uses, Rent or Rents (the King only excepted) and for the better Confirmation of the before Demised Premises the said Henry Bozman doth Oblidge himself to Acknowledge this to be his free and voluntary Act & Deed in Open Court when thereunto required. Witness my hand & Seal this 8th of ffebruary 1685/6. HENRY BOZMAN.
Signed sealed and Delivered in the Presence of us, John Brown, William Oldis.

Acknowledged in Open Court held for the Isle of Wight County February the 9th, 1685, by Henry Bozman to be his Act and Deed and Ordered to be Recorded. Test.: John Pitt, Clerk Court.

This Deed is copied a second time in the records of the Isle of Wight when Henry Pope makes a Deed of sd. land to Richard Pope July 22nd, 1717, (see Great Book, page 105) in consideration of 6000 lbs. of tobacco.

Sarah Pope, wife of *Henry Pope*[2], *receives an unique legacy*:

William Faircloth, Isle of Wight, will 9th Jany., 1727; Rd 28 May, 1728, contains the following: Item.—I give and bequeath to *Sarah Pope wife* of *Henry Pope* the Grinding Tole from all the Corn she brings for her family's use to the Mills during her natural Life to have that liberty whenever the Mill shall grind.
Wit.: Joseph Cobb, Robt. Scott. (Will Book 3, p. 96). William Farecloth.

WILL OF HENRY POPE, A. D. 1728. Will Book 3, p. 127, I. of W., Va.:—I, *Henry Pope* being at present weak in body, but perfect in sense and right in mind, calling to mind that it is once appointed for all men to dye, think fit to make this my last Will and Testament wherein I give and bequeath my Lands and other Estate which it has pleased Almighty God to bestow upon me in this World in manner and form as followeth:

Item 1. I give unto my Son William Pope five shillings Current money he having had his part before.

Item 2. I give unto my Son Henry Pope five shillings Current money he having had his part before. Deed of Gift, December 3rd, 1717.

Item 3. I give unto my Son Richard Pope five shillings, he having had his part before. (Deed of Gift, July 22nd, 1717.)

Item 4. I give unto my Son Jacob Pope five shillings, he having had his part before.

Item 5. I give unto my Son *John Pope* five shillings, he having had his part before.

Item 6. I give unto my daughter, Mary Williams, One Cow and Calf, she having had her part before.

Item 7. I give unto my Daughter Jane Brassole one Cow and Calf, she having had her part before.

Item 8. I give unto my Son Joseph Pope my tract of Land upon Black Creek to him and his heirs forever. Likewise two cows and calves and one Young Heifer and one young mare of Two years old also two breeding sows and one year old Barrow also one old feather bed and covering belonging thereunto.

Item 9. I give unto my Daughter Morning Pope my Tract of Land lying upon Meherrin river on the North side unto her and her heirs forever, also three Cows and calves and one three year old heifer and one four year old steer. Also one young mare of four years old, also one Bed and furniture which she has in her possession already, also one black leather trunk also one Entry of Land adjoining thereunto the said plantation.

Item 10. I give unto my Son Thomas Pope my plantation on the south side of Murrattock river to him and his heirs forever. Also two cows and calves and two two year old Heifers, also one young mare of two years old. Also one sow and piggs. Also one small gun. Also one feather bed which I have at Rone Oak and a Sheet and Rugg.

Item 11. I give unto my Son Samuel Pope my part of a tract of Land which I suppose to bee three hundred acres to him and his heirs forever which is taken up between us in his name and to be made over to him that is in my Son *John Popes* name pattented. Also two cows and calves and Two Heifers. Also one young mare. It is also my Will that if either my three younger sons die without Heir that the others may have all his part.

Item 12. I give unto Mary Clother one Cow and Calf at her freedom from my wife.

Item 13. I also leave unto my Son *John Pope* my part of the stock of Cattle which is in his hands now provided he will pay his Tobacco that I am bound for and have in possession for my Cousin Edward and *John Pope* and if he shall refuse then to turn the cattle into my Estate.

Item 14. I give and bequeath unto my well beloved wife Sarah Pope all the rest of my estate both out Doors and in Doors to her behoof, and I appoint her and my son John Pope my whole and sole Executrix and Executor to this my last Will and Testament performed whereunto I have set my hand and fixed my seal this 28th day of May 1728. HENRY POPE.

Test.: Epinctus Griffin, John Denson, Junior, Marblin Cluse.. Recorded October 28th, 1728.

Whether the daughter *Morning Pope* named in Item 9 of this will was his *daughter* or *daughter-in-law* is an open question. His son Jacob Pope had wife named *Morning* Pope and his son John Pope's[3] wife was named Mourning Pope.

William Pope[3], of Isle of Wight, July 28, 1718, conveys 90 A. of land, patented by him March 22, 1715, ... more especially of tender love and good will I bear *unto my loving Brother Jacob Pope.* (Great Book, p. 185).

Jacob Pope and *Morning Pope,* his wife, on 19 Feby., 1721, sell this 90 A. of land to John Joyner. (Great Book, p. 482).

William[3], Jacob[3], John[3] and Thomas Pope[3] patented lands in 1723 & 1728, on south side of Morratuck river, and paid 12 June, 1735, Quit Rent in Edgecombe for Albemarle County from 29 Sept., 1729, to March, 1732. (Land Book 3, pp. 179, 153 and 232; S. R. N. C., Vol. 22, pp. 241, et seq., 425).

William Pope[3], of the Co. of *Nanzemond* and *Mary Haile* of the Co. afsd did Publish their marriage In our Publick Meeting house Before a meeting of Men and Women friends upon the 11th day of the first Mo. 1707 and Coming Before the meeting the second time att our afores'd Publick Meeting house in Chuckatuck upon the eight day of the 2 mo. 1708 they did publish their marriage the second time and were married in the Public Meetung house on the Western Branch on the eleventh day of the 2 mo. 1798. Wm. Pope.
Mary Pope.

Bro. Henry Pope, Jno. Porter, Jno. Askin, Robt. Ricks, Philip Alsbury, Kathren Ricks, Thos. Page, Wm. Powell, Rebecca Alsbury, *Sarah Pope,* Eliz. Powell. ("S. H. A. Pubs.", Vol. 6, p. 413).

William Pope's[3] *will,* Edgecombe Co., N. C., 15 Jany., 1749: Feby. Court, 1749. (N. C. H. & G. Reg. 1-3-369). *Richard Pope's*[3] *will,* Isle of Wight Co., 4 Sept., 1733; 26 Nov., 1733. (Will Book 3, p. 378). *Joseph Pope's*[3] *will,* Isle of Wight Co., 29 Jany. [or June],1748; 13 April, 1749. (Book 5, p. 177). *Henry Pope's*[3] *will,* Southampton Co., Va., 23 Octo. 1758; 14 Dec., 1763. (Will Book 1, p. 278). Samuel

AND ALLIED FAMILIES   235

Pope's[3] will, Craven Co., N. C., 5 Jany., 1758; 6 Jany. 1758. (N. C. H. & G. Reg. 1-3-365).
   John Pope[3], b. circa 1699; d. intestate, in Edgecombe Co., N. C., in 1745; m. *Mourning McKinnie*, d. bet. 1741 and 1755; daughter of *Col. Barnaby McKennie*, Sr., 1673-1740, and his wife *Mary (Exum) Ricks*, relict of Jacob Ricks, d. 1703, and daughter of *Judge Jeremiah Exum*, 1660-1720, and his wife, Ann Lawrence (See Exum and Mackquinney). *John Pope*[3] *Justice* of the Peace for and within Edgecombe precinct Chowan Co., May 16, 1732. (C. R. N. C., Vol. 3, p. 417); on 6 March, 1739, was appointed Commissioner of Peace with *Barnaby McKinnie*, Joseph Cotten, Thos. Kearney, et al. (C. R. N. C., Vol. 4, p. 346); was a Church Warden for Bertie Co. prior to 1740 (N. C. H. & G. Reg. 2-2-303); was added to list of jurymen for Bertie and Edgecombe Feby. 25, 1739-'40 (C. R. N. C., Vol. 4, p. 521); *member* of the *General Assembly* from Edgecombe 15 March, 1742, 22 July, 1743, 24 Feby., 1743-'4, 15 Nov., 1744, 9 April, 1745 (C. R. N. C., Vol. 4, pp. 651-'2, 723, 774). On 9 April, 1745, Mr. James Castellaw reported to the General Assembly (House of Burgesses) that *John Pope*[3] *one of the members from Edgecombe* was dead. Report was also made by William Wilson, member from Newberne, that Mr. John Pope, member from Edgecombe, is dead. (C. R. N. C., Vol. 4, p. 744).
   John Pope[3] is shown as applicant for warrants and grants in 1738, 1740, 1743, &c. (C. R. N. C., Vol. 4, pp. 329-'30, 440, '4, 711, 588, 626, 631, &c); and on 2 Nov., 1744, was admitted to prove rights for 6 whites and 20 blacks for himself, also rights for John Jones and John Langston. (C. R. N. C., Vol. 4, p. 705).
   Deed from HENRY POPE of I. of W. Co., Va., to his son JOHN POPE of Bertie Co., N. C. Bertie County, N. C., B'k B, p. 107. To all to whom these presents shall come I Henry Pope of Virginia sendeth Greeting. Know ye yt I ye sd. Henry Pope for and in Consideration of the sum of 20 £ Current money of this Province to me in hand well and Truely paid the Receipt whereof is hereby acknowledged from *John Pope my son* and ye sd John Pope his heirs Exrs. Admrs. forever discharged, have bargained and sold and by these presents do grant bargain Alienate Enfeoff release and Confirm unto ye sd. John Pope his heirs and assigns a parcel of Land lying and being in the Precinct of Bertie and containing by estimation 90 Acres more or less being part of a Pattent of Land Granted to George Smith for 580 Acres and by him sold to William Pope the whole 580 Acres and by him the said William Pope conveyance was made to Henry Pope his Father for 290 Acres of this afore mentioned 90 Acres Lying and being on the So. side of Morrattuck River beginning at a Cypress standing in ye Beaver Dam Swamp yn turning on the No. Et. side of ye Swamp on the line of ye aforesaid Pattent to a White Oak still by the Course of ye Pattent to ye afsd. Beaver Dam Swamp down ye Swamp to ye first station. To have and to Hold ye sd 90 Acres of Land, be it more or less with all ye profits appurtenances and privileges to him ye sd John Pope his heires and assigns to him and their proper use and behoof for ever. And I the sd. Henry Pope for me my heirs Exrs. admrs. to and with ye sd Jno. Pope his heirs and assigns to covenant yt ye above Granted premises are free and clear of all Incumbrances and ye same do warrant and defend to him said John Pope his heirs and Assigns forever. In Testimony whereof I ye sd Henry Pope herewith set my hand and seal this . . . . day of . . . ., 1726.   HENRY POPE.
   Signed sealed and delivered in ye presence of us. Joseph Lane, Jr., William Birkhead. Bertie Precinct ye May Court 1726.
   The above Deed of sale from Henry Pope to John Pope was in open Court proved by ye oath of Joseph Lane one of the Evidences thereunto which is ordered to be Registered.
   (This land was inherited by Henry Pope[4] (son of John[3]) and sold by him and his wife Tabitha Pope on 13 Sept., 1759, to John Branch. (Halifax Co. Deed Book, 7, p. 67.)
   WILLIAM POPE'S DEED TO HIS FATHER HENRY POPE. Bertie, N. C., Bk A, p. 162:—Know all men by these presents that I William Pope of ye Isle of Wight in Virginia doe by these presents from me my heirs, Exrs. Admrs. and assigns firmly by these presents & in Consideration whereof for half ye sum of money paid to George Smith that I William Pope do bargain sell and make over and deliver my right title and interest of ye half of ye pattent of land sold to me by George Smith

to Henry Pope my Father to him his heirs, Exrs. Admrs. and assigns for ever to have a good quiet lawful and peaceable Right and possession to 290 Acres of land or plantation in Chowan precinct & on ye south side of Morattuck River and on ye lower side of ye great swamp Joyning and beginning at a marked hickory in Thomas Goodwin's line so running along a line of marked trees to a   standing in a meadow on ye swamp side to a marked   standing in ye swamp side. From thence up ye middle of ye swamp to ye line so along ye line to ye Corner tree between   Craford and John Pope so along ye line to Thomas Goodwin's line to ye marked Hickory for 290 Acres of land more or less being part of a Pattent of land bought of George Smith bearing date ye 3rd Day of December 1720 Containing 580 Acres of land.

I ye sd William Pope do Covenant give grant Confirm acknowledge and make over all my right hereunto belonging in as large and lawfull and ample manner as I myself could expect to receive by ye aforesaid Conveyance to him ye aforesaid Henry Pope or either of them for ever which right or title I ye aforesaid William Pope do warrant to have harmless and defend from any person or persons whatsoever from me or by or under us or either of us in ye penalty of 60 £ Current money upon demand at any time to ye aforesaid Henry Pope or his order or his heires or either of them upon any lett or hindrances Incumbrances whatsoever in Witness my hand & seal this 15th day of August 1722.   WILLIAM POPE & a seal.

Signed sealed & delivered in ye presence of us: John Bryan, John Griffith, Thomas Boone.

Bertie Precinct ye August Court 1723 the above Deed of sale was acknowledged in open Court by ye Granter in due form of law and ordered to be Registered and is Registered.   John Sutton, Deputy Clerk.

"The Popes settled in the extreme edge of civilization in 1720, near Caledonia (then a part of Chowan, later of Bertie, then Edgecombe, and then Halifax Co."). Letter of J. R. B. Hathaway, 13 Feby., 1902, to Mr. L. J. Hill, of Atlanta, Ga.

Valentine Braswell and wife, Jean, to Barnaby McKinnie (Book "F", No. 1, p. 185, at Edenton), Power of Attorney to acknowledge Sale and relinquish dower to 200 acres land sold *John Pope*³, July 21, 1721, on Aherron Swamp, where *John Pope* now liveth. Test.: William Pope, Wm. Ledbetter. (N. C. H. & G. Reg. 1-3-470).

In *1729 John Pope* and *Mourning his wife* of Bertie Precinct sell to William Bennett 200 A. of land lying on the South side Moratuck River and on the North side of Elk Marsh Swamp patented by John Pope July 24, 1728. Bertie Precinct, Aug. Court 1729. (Book "C", p. 136).

On *19 Aug., 1741, John Pope,* of Edgecombe Co., N. C., sells to John Pope of N. C. (no doubt his son) 200 A. in County aforesaid lying on the North side of Fishing Creek, part of a patent granted the said John Pope 17th June, 1741, and *Mourning Pope the wife of John Pope* freely and willingly yielded up and surrendered up all right of Dower and power of third, &c, &c. Wit.: Henry Craffold (?), Jacob Pope. Edgecombe Co. Aug. Ct. 1741. (Halifax Co. Deed Bk. 1, p. 396.)

On *Aug. 18, 1741, John Pope*³ and *Mourning Pope his wife,* of Edgecombe Co., made deed to 200 A. on North side of Fishing Creek to Aaron Etheridge, of Va. (Halifax Co. Deed Bk. 1, p. 398.

John Bryan [Bryant] in will, 14th day of ye, 1734 says: "I do Leave and Bequeath to my well Beloved friend *John Pope* one hundred acres of land in A place on Cohukee Line below ye place where Robt. Wright now Liveth, Edgecombe Precinct, N. C., *14 Sept., 1734.* (Wills and Inv. of N. C. by Grimes, p. 96).

Craven Co., N. C. (Newbern) Deed Book 2, p. 382. Jany. 10th, 1734:—John Pope Gentleman, of Edgecombe Co., N. C., made deed to William Kinchen, 200 A. of land on the North side of the *Meuse* river at the head of Horse Creek (land granted John Pope by patent).   (Signed) John Pope.

Wit.: Nathl Cooper, *John Lane.* Proved Nov. 29th, 1744, before Ed. Moseley, Chief Justice and ordered Recorded.

DEED: John Pope to John Pope:—To all people to whom these presents shall come Greeting. Know all ye that I John Pope of Edgcomb County No. Carolina for and in consideration of the sum of five pounds lawful money of Virginia have bargained and sold and by these presents do bargain and sell unto John Pope of No. Carolina his heirs and assigns forever a certain piece or parcel of land lying in the

County afsd. on the North side of Fishing creek containing by estimation 200 acres be the same more or less, butted and bounded as follows. Beginning on the upper line Pope's Branch on the east side S. 80 E. along the line to the center of S. R. Oks and hickory then S. 209 . . . . to a redoak on the creek to the mouth of Pope Branch so up the Branch to the first station, being part of a patent granted to me John Pope and bearing date the 17th day of June 1741. To have and to hold the sd. bargained and demised premises with all the appurtenances thereunto belonging free from the day of the date hereof forever and I the sd. John Pope Doe me my heirs Exes Admrs. do promise grant and agree to and with the sd. John Pope his heirs and assigns to warrant and defend to them and their heirs the sd. demised premises forever, after the date of these presents and I Mourning Pope the wife of John Pope doth by these presents freely and willing yield up and surrender all my right of Dower and power of third of in and to the above demised premises unto him the sd. John Pope his Heirs and assigns. In witness whereof I have hereunto set my hand and seal this 19th day of Aug. in the year of Our Lord 1741.   John Pope (seal) Mourning Pope (seal).

Signed sealed and delivered in presence of us. Henry Craffold, Jacob Pope. Edgecomb County. Aug. Court 1741. The within deed of sale was in open Court in due form of law acked. and . . . . Test Rt. Forster C. C. T.

Record of Deeds No. 1, p. 396, Halifax Co., N. C. Office of the Register of Deeds.

On July 12, 1915, a friend wrote me as follows: "Sometime ago I had the pleasure of a conversation with the Rev. L. R. Christie, of Columbus, Ga., who was born and reared in Halifax Co., N. C., and knew the many Popes of that county. He told me a number of interesting things. The old *John Pope*[3] place is well known and now belongs to the State of N. C. as an experiment station, and is considered the finest farm in the State. It is down on the Roanoke River. The old homestead is still standing—built of whiteoak logs, weatherboarded on the outside and plastered on the inside."

John[3] and *Mourning (McKinnie) Pope* had issue: 1.—*Henry Pope*[4]; 2.—*John Pope*[4]; 3.—*Winnifred Pope*[4]; 4.—*Barnaby Pope*[4]; 5.—*Lewis Pope*[4]; 6.—*Jesse Pope*[4]. Order of births not known.

Col. Barnaby McKennie, Sr., in his last Will and Testament made Aug. 13, 1737, names his *daughter Mourning Pope*, as shown in the various petitions by John Lane, Barnaby McKinnie and William Hurst to dock the entail of lands under said will. (C. R. N. C., Vol. 5, pp. 1026-'29-'32; 1071-'2-'7—year 1758; Ib. Vol. 6, pp. 383-'4-'7, 481; S. R. N. C. 25, p. 465-'6—1761; Deed Books, Halifax Co., No. 2, p. 49, and No. 7, p. 35).

Henry Pope[4] (John[3], Henry[2], William[1]), was b. circa 1723, in Edgecombe Co.; d. in 1764, in Halifax Co.; m., circa 1748, Tabitha . . . . , maiden name not known. She m. (II), circa 1768, Col. Thomas Wootten, son of Benjamin and Elizabeth Rousseau Wootten, of Halifax Co., and d. in 1808 in Oglethorpe Co., Ga. (See Lewis and Wootten.)

Henry Pope[4] appears to have dealt largely in lands, and by inheritance and purchase to have owned a considerable acreage. (Halifax Co. Deed Books No. 7, pp. 34-'5-'8 and 67; No. 8, p. 178; No. 17, p. 348). His will, dated 2 Jany., 1764; p. April Court, 1764, is recorded in Will Book 1, p. 144, as follows: In the Name of God Amen. I Henry Pope being very Sick and Weak but in perfect senses Thanks be to God, remembering the Mortality of Man do make and constitute this my last Will and Testament in Manner and Form following, *first* I recommend my Soul to God who gave it me and my Body to the Earth to be buried in a christian like Manner at the Discretion of my Executors, hereafter mentioned and as for my worldly Estate that hath pleased God to bless me with I give and dispose of in Manner and form following viz.: *Item.* I give and bequeath to my loving wife Tabitha Pope one negroe named Joe and all my household Furniture and all my live stock and all my Debts due me upon consideration she pay all my just Debts and each of my sons yt shall be living when they come to age, one good feather Bed and furniture and three good cows and calfs, to each of them, or in the Lue thereof, fifteen pounds proc money to be paid to each of them and also I lend the Manor plantation to my Wife Tabitha during her Natural Life. *Item.* I give and bequeath to my *oldest Son Burrel pope,* one plantation lying on *Roanoke* containing two hundred and nine Acres yt Land which fell to me by *Heirship* from *Barnaby McKenney* and also one negroe Girl named Patt to Him his Heirs and assigns forever.

Item. I give and bequeath to my four younger sons Willis pope, John pope, Henry Austin pope and Wiley Pope all ye rest of my Lands and negroes yt I have not bequeathed before, to them and their Heirs and Assigns forever, to be equally *divided* to them by *John Bradford, Jesse pope* and *William Lane* or either two of them and I also appoint John Bradford, Jesse pope and my well beloved Wife Tabitha, whole and sole Exrs. of this my last Will and Testament and likewise appoint the same three persons whole and sole *Guardians, to all my children.* In Witness whereof I have hereunto set my Hand and Seal this 2nd Day of January in ye year of our Lord 1764. Henry Pope (Seal).

                                                                                                           her

Signed and sealed in the presence of William Thralkel, Patience X Bradford,
                                                                                                              mark
Sarah X Thralkel her mark. Halifax Apl Court 1764 . . . the . . . . This will was exhibited on Oath in open Court by the Exrs. and duly proved by ye Oath of William Thralkel a subscribing Witness thereto, whereupon ye Executors therein named came into Court and were duly qualified. Ordered the said Will to be recorded. Test.—Joseph Montford, C. Ct.

Joseph Lane, of Edgecombe, in will 6 Dec., 1757; p. Nov. Ct., 1758, names as his principal legatee his brother *William Lane* and as his Exrs.: *John Bradford* and *Henry Pope.* These Executors refused to qualify, whereupon the Court appointed William Lane. (Query—Could Tabitha Pope have been the aunt of William Lane, and nee Lane?)

Henry Pope⁴ to Blake Baker, Halifax Co., Book 7, p. 35. This Indenture made the . . . . day of in the year of our Lord 1759 Between Henry Pope of the Co. of Halifax and province of N. C. of the one part and Blake Baker of the Co. and province afs'd of the other part Witnesseth that whereas *Col. Barnaby McKennie* late of Edgecombe Co. and province afsd *Grand father* to the said *Henry Pope* being seized in the Demesne as of fee of and in all those messuage lands and tenements situate lying and being in Northampton and Halifax, formerly Edgecombe Co. on the South and North side of Morattock River Containing by estimation two thousand five hundred acres, by his last Will and Testament in writing devised to his son Richard McKinnie all his land on the North side of Morattock river beginning at a Sycamore on the river bank above the landing running a direct course to a white oak on hogberry Gut being the dividing line between him the said Barnaby McKinnie and Capt. Wm. Kitchen including the Mill and all other appurtenances and all the land in that survey also that tract of land and plantation where the said Barnaby McKinnie then lived bounded as followeth beginning at the upper end of the Cypress Gut on Morattock River at a place called the Old Mill dam thence by the windings of the said Gut to the Great ditch thence along the Ditch to the corner thereof at the road and thence by the courses of the Cypress Gut to where Wm. Brown's lower head line crosses the same and thence by Brown's head line to his corner near the head of the Miry Marsh thence by Brown's lower line to a Maple on Morrattock River as also two hundred acres of land purchased of Col. Wm. Maul adjoining Brown's lower line and all the remainder of the said Barnaby McKennie's land on the South side of Morrattock River not before devised that is (if) his son Richard should die without lawfull issue that his said plantation where he then lived and three hundred acres of land adjoining should descend to his son *John McKinnie,* and all other his lands devised as afores'd to his son Richard McKennie should descend to his two daughters *Patience Lane* and *Mourning Pope* and whereas the said Richard McKinnie is dead without lawful issue whereby the property of the afores'd lands (except the three hundred devised to the afores'd John McKinnie) is vested in and become the property of the said *Henry Pope* and *John Lane* the lawful heirs of the said *Patience Lane* and *Mourning Pope* and whereas Col. Jos. Lane purchased of the said John Lane by lawfull conveyance all his right share and part of the afores'd land devised as afores'd to the said *Patience Lane* and *Mourning Pope* whereby the property thereof was vested in the said Jos. Lane by virtue whereof the said *Henry Pope* and the said *Jos. Lane* by articles of agreement bearing date the ninth day of December in the year of our Lord one thousand seven hundred and fifty-five made a division of the lands afores'd devised as afores'd to the said Patience Lane and Mourning Pope that is to say . . . . (here follows a long description of the property, etc., which I omit.—L. J. H.). This deed—In witness whereof the afores'd *Henry Pope* and the said Blake Baker have interchangeably set their hands and seals the day and year first above written.

Henry Pope (Seal).
Blake Baker (Seal).

Sealed and delivered in presence of *John Pope*, Alexr Enseley. Halifax County, S. S. June Court, 1759. This deed of partition was in open Court duly acknowledged and on motion ordered to be registered. Test.: Jos. Montford, Cler. Cur.

JACKSON, NORTHAMPTON COUNTY, N. C. Bk. 3, p. 38:—This indenture made this nineteenth day of July in the thirty third year the reign of our Sovereign Lord George the second by the Grace of God of Great Brittian & Ireland King defender of the faith &c and in ye year of our Lord Christ one thousand seven hundred & fifty nine *between Henry Pope* and *Tabitha* his wife of the County of Halifax and province of North Carolina of the one part & *Blake Baker* of the County & Provence aforesaid of the other part, Whereas Barneby Mackinny late of the County of Edgecombe & province aforesaid deceased being in his life time & at the time of his death seized and possessed of a tract of land & mill situate lying & being in the County of Northampton in the province aforesaid containing by estimation four hundred acres more or less and by his last will and testament bearing date the thirteenth day of August in the year of our Lord one thousand seven hundred & thirty seven devised the same together with other lands to his son Richd Mc Kinne in fee-tail & for want of issue of him the sd Richard devised the said four hundred acres of land with other lands devised as aforesaid to his son Richard as aforesaid to his two daughters Patience Lane and Mourning Pope and whereas the said Richard is dead without lawful issue whereby the property of ye aforesaid four hundred acres with other lands devised as aforesaid were & is vested in the sd Patience Lane and Mourning Pope and the heirs of their bodies lawfully begotten for ever to be devised as by the sd will duly proven & recorded in the County of Edgecombe relation being thereunto had may more fully & at large appear & also whereas John Lane the right heir of sd Patience Lane by deed of conveyance sold & aliened his part or share of the sd lands devised as aforesaid to Col. Joseph Lane who also conveyed the same to Blake Baker by deed of conveyance by reason whereof the property was & is vested in the said Blake Baker by means whereof the said Henry Pope & ye sd Blake Baker made partition of the sd lands devised as aforesaid & the sd four hundred acres of land was allotted & layed off for ye sd Henry Pope for part of his share of the aforesaid lands as right heir to the aforesaid Mourning Pope relation being had to the several deeds and conveyances may more fully appear by virtue whereof the sd Henry Pope is seized & possessed of the aforesaid four hundred acres of land with appurtenances thereunto belonging in fee tail & whereas by an Inquisition taken before James Turner Esqr. Sheriff of the County of Northampton the tenth day of July in ye year of Our Lord one thousand seven hundred & fifty nine by virtue of a writ in ye nature of an ad Quod Damnum bearing date the 28th day of June in the year of our Lord one thousand seven hundred & fifty nine issued out of the Secretarys office & signed by the Honorable Richd Speight Esquire Secretary of the sd province to the said Sheriff directed pursuant to an act of Assembly in such case made and provided to Enquire by the oath of at least twelve good & lawful men of his Bailiwick of the value of the aforesaid four hundred acres of land and whether the same be parcel of or contigous to other intailed lands of the sd Henry Pope which Inquisition (to-wit) William Bennett, Green Hill, Thomas Williams, Benjamin Branch, John Williams, Harwood Jones, John Paul, Joseph Exum, Thos. Barret, Barnabe Thomas, Epphretitus Killbe, & William Moore being sworn &c and viewed the aforesaid four hundred acres of land did upon their oaths say that the aforesaid four hundred acres of land was of the value of forty pounds sterling money of Great Brittain & no more and that sd four hundred acres of land is not parcel of or contiguous to other intailed lands of the sd Henry Pope relation being had to the writ & Inquisition remaining the secretarys office of this province may more fully & at large appear. NOW, this indenture witnesseth that for and in consideration of the sum of forty pounds sterling money of Great Brittain to us the said Henry Pope and Tabitha his wife hand paid by the said Blake Baker before the sealing & delivery of these presents the receipt whereof we the sd Henry Pope & Tabitha his wife do freely acknowledge & thereof do release, acquit, and discharge the said Blake Baker his heirs and assigns forever that piece or parcel by these presents do bargain, grant, sell, alien, release & confirm unto the sd Blake Baker his heirs, Exrs & admrs & assigns forever that piece or parcel of land and premises by estimation containing four hundred acres be the same more or less herein before mentioned to be devised as aforesaid by the sd Barnabe Mackinne and devised as above said by the sd Blake Baker & Henry Pope situate lying & being in the County of Northampton aforesaid and all houses, woods & underwoods, trees, ways & waters, steams, watercourses, rents mill, milldams ponds & Ponds of water, profits, commodities and hereditaments, rents issues & appertaining whatsoever to ye sd piece or parcel of land and premises belonging or in anywise appertaining and the reversions, remainder remainders, rents, issues and profits thereof and also all the estate right title interest, use trust possession benefit property claim and demand whatsoever of them ye sd Henry Pope & Tabitha his wife of in and to the same and all deeds evidences and writings touching or in anywise concerning the sd premises. TO HAVE AND TO HOLD the sd piece or parcel of land herein before mentioned or intended to be herein or hereby granted bargained and sold with their and every of their appurtenances unto the sd Blake Baker his heirs and assigns for ever and the sd Henry Pope & Tabitha his wife for them their heirs exrs and admrs doth covenant promise & grant to & with the sd Blake Baker his heirs and assigns by these presents that the sd Henry Pope & Tabitha his wife hath not made done or committed or willingly suffered any act matter thing whereby or by reason or means whereof the sd piece or parcel of land & premises hereby bargained & sold or any part thereof are or may be impeached, charged or incumbered in title charges or otherwise howsoever and also the sd Henry Pope & Tabitha his wife and their heirs and all and every other person or persons having or lawfully claiming or to claim any estate interest of in and to the sd premises hereby bargained and sold or any part thereof by from or under him them or any of them, shall and will from time to time and at all times upon the reasonable request of and at the proper cost and charges in the law of the sd Blake Baker his heirs and assigns make and execute or cause & promise to be made & executed all such further & other lawful & reasonable act or acts, thing & things devises & conveyances & assurances in the law whatsoever for the further better more perfect & absolute conveying & assuring the said piece or parcel of land and premises hereby bargained & sold with their & every of their appurtenances unto the sd Blake Baker his heirs and assigns as by the sd Blake Baker his heirs and assigns shall be lawfully & reasonably advised required & lastly that the sd Henry Pope & Tabitha his wife the above granted premises and every part and parcel thereof unto ye sd Blake Baker, his heirs and assigns against the lawful title claim demand of all person or persons whatsoever shall and will warrant and for ever defend by these presents. In witness whereof ye sd Henry Pope & Tabitha his wife have hereunto set their hand and affixed their seals the day & year first above written.

Henry Pope (Seal).
Tabitha Pope (Seal).

Witnesses: James Edwards, James Holdness, John Gilcott.

Halifax Co., N. C., Book 7, p. 67:—Deed from *Henry Pope* and *Tabitha, his wife*, of the Parish of Edgecombe and County of Halifax, Sept. 13th, 1759, sold to John Branch land consisting of two tracts, one tract containing 100 acres was purchased of John Branch, Sr. & John Branch, Jr., ye other piece of land 90 acres "I am lawfully possessed of in my own proper right by inheritance. Consideration 94 £ 9 sh. Henry Pope.

Wit.: Wm. Branch, Wm. Gulledge   Tabitha Pope.

Henry Pope[4] (John[3], Henry[2], William[1]) and his wife, Tabitha had—as shown in his will: 1.—Burwell Pope[5]; 2.—Willis Pope[5]; 3.—John Pope[5]; 4.—Henry Augustine Pope[5]; 5.—Wylie Pope[5].

1. Burwell Pope[5] was b. in 1751; d. 9 Jany., 1800, in 49th year of his age; m.

8 Sept., 1772, in Halifax or Wake Co., N. C., Priscilla Wootten, b. 1756; d. 19 Jany., 1806, in her 50th year, dau. of Benjamin Wootten (will 26 June, 1764; Oct. Court, 1764,—Halifax Co. Will Book 1, p. 151) and his wife, Elizabeth Rousseau. (See *Lewis* and *Wootten*.)

Deed Bk. 13, p. 324. Halifax Court House, N. C. Copy. Province of North Carolina:—George the third by the Grace of God of Great Brittain France & Ireland King Defender of the Faith etc.—To the Sheriff of Halifax County Greeting. We command you that by the oath of good & lawful men of your County by whom the truth of the matter may be better known you diligently enquire if it may be to the Damage or prejudice of us or others if Burwell Pope should sell two hundred acres of land with the appurtenances lying & being in Halifax County aforesaid whereof he is seized as Tenant in fee tail under the will of Barnaby McKinnie Senr. and if it be to the damage or prejudice of us or others, then to what damage or prejudice of us & to what damage or prejudice of others and of what value the said land with the improvements thereon made now is in good & lawful money of Great Brittain and whether the same be parcel of or contiguous to other lands whereof the said Burwell Pope is seized as Tenant in Fee Tail; and that you send without delay the Inquisition thereof Distinctly & openly made, to us in our Secretary's office under your hand & seal and the hands & seals of those by whom you shall make such Inquisition together with this writ. Witness Josiah Martin our Captain General Governor & Commander in Chief in & over our said province at Newbern the 30th day of December in the 15th year of our reign Anno Dom. 1774. By Virtue of an act of Assembly made in the 22nd year of the reign of our late Sovereign Lord George the second King of Great Brittain etc. James Parrott, D-Secy.

Halifax County, S. S.: Inquisition taken on the lands of Burwell Pope, if it should be to the prejudice of our Sovereign Lord the King etc, or others if Burwell Pope should sell two hundred acres of land lying & being in Halifax County aforesaid whereof the said Burwell Pope is seized as Tenant in fee tail under the will of Barnaby McKinnie Senr. according to a limitation therein, before Wm. Branch Esq. Sheriff of Halifax County by virtue of the writ of our Sovereign Lord the King directed to the aforesaid Wm. Branch Sheriff as aforesaid according to act of Assembly Good & lawful men of the County aforesaid To Wit Wm. Watson James Faucett, Edward Moreland, Frances Moreland, Richard Barrett, Michael Aaron, Peter Aaron, Peter Brown, John Smith, John Gunter, Patrick Garland & John Phillips who say upon their oath aforesaid that the said lands in the said writ mentioned is of the value of fifty pounds, lawful money of Great Brittain & no more nor injurious to any other claimant nor contiguous to or parcel of any other entailed lands belonging to the aforesaid Burwell Pope nor of any damage to any other person whatsoever as they can be any ways informed In Witness whereof they have hereunto set their hands & seals the 30th day of December Anno Dom. 1774 and in the 15th year of our Reign: John Branch Shff.

Wm. Watson (SEAL).
James Faucett (SEAL).
(his)
Edward Moreland (SEAL).
(mark)
Francis Moreland (SEAL).
(his)
Richard Barrett (SEAL).
(mark)
Michael Aaron (SEAL).

Peter Aaron (SEAL).
John Smith (SEAL).
John Gunter (SEAL).
Patrick Garland (SEAL).
(his)
John Phillips (SEAL).
(mark)
Peter Brown (SEAL).

Deed Showing Burwell Pope's Ancestry. Copy:—Deed Book No. 13 Page 247, Halifax Court House North Carolina. This Indenture made on this twenty second day of February in the year of our Lord Christ one thousand seven hundred and seventy five Between Burwell Pope and Priscilla his wife of the County of Wake in the province of North Carolina of the one part and Nicholas Long of the County of Halifax and province aforesaid of the other part whereas Colo Barnaby McKinnie late of the County of Edgecombe and province of North Carolina aforesaid Deceased being in his life time and at the time of his death seized and possessed of a tract of land lying and being in the County of Halifax formerly Edgecombe did by his late will and testament in writing bearing date the thirteenth day of August in the year of Our Lord Christ one thousand seven hundred and seventy seven [This date evidently was *1737*, as that was the date of Col. Barnaby McKinnie's Will, and this deed was itself made in *1775*, it could not refer to anything in 1777, no doubt the mistake was made in copying from the original to the Deed Book] devise the same to his daughter Mourning in fee tail which his said Daughter Mourning Intermarried with John Pope and had issue by him to wit Henry Pope since which the said Henry Pope is dead and the said land has descended to Burwell Pope in fee tail as aforesaid according to the will of the said Barnaby McKinnie reference being had thereto may more fully and at large appear also whereas by an Inquisition taken before William Branch Sheriff of the County of Halifax the 30th day of December in the year of Christ 1774, by virtue of a writ in the nature of an Ad Quod Damnum bearing date the 30th day of December in the year of Christ 1774 Issued out of the Secretarys office and signed by James Parrott Deputy Secretary of the said province to the Sheriff of Halifax County directed pursuant to an act of Assembly of the Province in such case made & provided to enquire by the oaths of good & lawful men of the said County of Halifax whether it is to the prejudice of our sovereign Lord the King or others if Burwell Pope should sell two hundred acres of land whereof he is now seized in fee tail and also of the value of the said two hundred acres of land of the said Burwell Popes and whether the same be parcel of or contiguous to other entailed lands of the said Burwell Pope which Inquisition to wit Wm. Watson, James Faucett, Edward Moreland, Francis Moreland, Richard Baratt, Micharl Aaron, Peter Aaron, John Smith, John Gunter, Patrick Garland, John Phillips and Peter Brown which Inquisition etc being sworn and having viewed the land aforesaid did upon their oaths say that the said land was of the value of fifty pounds Sterling money of Great Brittain and no more and that it is not parcel of or contiguous to others entailed lands of the said Burwell Pope nor is it of prejudice to our sovereign Lord the King or others for the said Burwell Pope to sell the said two hundred acres of land reference being had to the writ and Inquisition aforesaid now remaining in the Secretarys office of this Province may more fully and at large appear Now this Indenture Witnesseth that the said Burwell Pope for and in Consideration of the sum of three hundred and eighty pounds proclamation money to him in hand paid by the said Nicholas Long the receipt whereof he doth hereby acknowledge the said Burwell Pope and Priscilla his wife have granted bargained and sold aliened and confirmed and by these presents doth grant bargain sell alien and confirm unto him the said Nicholas Long his heirs and assigns for ever certain piece tract or parcel of land situate lying and being in the County of Halifax and province aforesaid on the South side of Roanoke River and bounded as followeth to wit Beginning at the mouth of the Cypress Gut thence running up the said Gut to the place called the old Mill dam thence up the said Gut to the mouth of the great ditch thence along the ditch to the corner on the road and where the said ditch crosses the Cypress Gut thence along the said Ditch to Nicholas Long's line formerly Richard McKinnie's thence along the said line to the corner A white oak thence along the said Long's line as aforesaid to a Sycamore on the river bank thence up the river to the first Station containing by estimation two hundred acres as aforesaid be the same more or less together with all profits commodities advantages hereditiments and appurtinances whatsoever to the same belonging or in any wise appertain and the reversion and reversions remainder and remainders rents and services of the said premises and of every part and parcel thereof and all the estate right and title Interest claim and demand whatsoever of them the said Burwell Pope and Priscilla his wife of in and to the said two hundred acres of land and premises and every part thereof to have and to hold the same to the said Nicholas Long his heirs and assigns to the only proper use benefit and behoof of him the said Nicholas Long his heirs and assigns to the only proper use benefit and behoof of him the said Nicholas Long his heirs & assigns for ever and the said Burwell Pope for him and his heirs and every of them doth hereby covenant and grant to & with the said Nicholas Long his heirs and assigns that he the said Burwell Pope & his heirs shall & will warrant & forever defend the said two hundred acres of land and premises and every part thereof to the said Nicholas Long his heirs and assigns for ever In Witness whereof the said Burwell Pope & Priscilla his wife have hereunto set their hands and affixed

their seals the day and year first above written. Sealed and Delivered in presence of
Burwell Pope (SEAL).
Priscilla Pope (SEAL).

Halifax County, S. S. February Court 1775. Then the afore going deed was in opin Court duly acknowledged by Burwell Pope the party thereto and Priscilla Pope the feme in the said deed mentioned being first privately examined by Jas. Allen Esq. acknowledged she relinquished her right of dower freely and voluntarily and without compulsion whereupon said deed was ordered to be registered.

Test: Jas. Montfort C. C.

BURWELL POPE'S WILL.

"I, Burwell Pope of the County of Oglethorpe and State of Georgia being in perfect health and of a sound mind do make and ordain this my last Will and Testament in manner and form following, viz.:—

Item. I give unto my beloved wife Priscilla,—James, Francis and Patt, and all my live stock, all my household furniture and plantation tools except the desk, she paying all my just debts,—and to each of my children the several legacies hereafter mentioned, Also the use of my plantation whereon I now live, during her natural life.

Item. I give and bequeath to my son Robert two negroes Jack and Judah, five hundred and seventy-five acres of land in Jackson County, on the north fork of Oconee River whereon he now lives, one feather bed and furniture, two cows and calves, he paying to the estate eighteen thousand weight of Inspected tobacco or one thousand dollars at his option.

Item. I give and bequeath to my daughter Tabitha two negroes, Moses and David, one feather bed and furniture, two cows and calves, and two hundred and eighty seven and a half acres of land on Big Creek where Miles Hill now lives.

Item. I give and bequeath to my daughter Ann two negroes, Abram and Peter, one feather bed and furniture, two cows and calves and two hundred and eighty seven and a half acres of land on Big Creek whereon Noah Hill now lives.

Item. I give and bequeath to my daughter Martha two negroes Adam and Dick, one feather bed and furniture, two cows and calves, also one other negro named Lucy.

Item. I give and bequeath to my son Wilie two negroes Daniel and Samuel, one feather bed and furniture, two cows and calves, and two small tracts of land, one of one hundred and fourteen acres and the other of sixty acres, and all that part of the tracts I now live on on the south of the branch, running through the plantation, all joining together.

Item. I give and bequeath to my daughter Sarah three negroes, Ida, Ephriam, and Richard, one feather bed and furniture, and two cows and calves.

Item. I give and bequeath unto my son Burwell two negroes Edward and James (the younger) one feather bed and furniture, two cows and calves, and all the land, including the plantation where I now live, not already disposed, also one walnut desk. All the rest of my estate both real and personal after paying all my just debts to be equally divided between all my children so as to make each child's part as nearly equal as possible, by John Pope, Henry Pope, and Wilie Pope who are appointed my Administrators to this my last Will and Testament in witness whereof I have hereunto set my hand and seal this first day of November 1799.

BURWELL POPE.

Signed and sealed in presence of John Gresham, Senr., Richard Bailey.

A true Copy taken from the Original last Will and Testament of Burwell Pope, deceased. Certified by me this eighteenth day of June in the year of Our Lord 1800. Erors excepted.—W. B. Bailey, C. C. O. O. C. Recorded Lexington, Oglethorpe County, Georgia—Book A, page 91.

"Ordered that Thomas Wootten, James Freeman, Benjn Taylor, Jas. Thomas and Phillip Wray, Esq., be and they are hereby appointed appraisers of the Estate of Burwell Pope decd. June 17, 1800". (Oldest Marriage Book, Oglethorpe Co., Ga., Mixed Records, p. 52).

Burwell Pope[5], 1751-1800, was a Justice of the Peace and Member of the Inferior Court of Pleas and Quarter Sessions, of Wake Co., N. C., during the Revolution. (N. C. Booklet, Vol. 5, 1905, No. 1, pp. 3 to 14.—Article entitled "Genesis of Wake

Co.", by Marshall deLancey Haywood); member of the House of Commons of N. C. from Wake Co. in 1781-'2 (Wheeler's His. of N. C., part 2nd, pp. 421-'2; C. R. N. C., Vol. 16, p. 2). He was reimbursed for sums expended in the Revolution as follows: To Burwell Pope, Member at Wake, Cer. No. 42 for 3,400 £. Warrant and Grant for Currency (N. C. His. Commission, Vol. XI, p. 46, folio 1); To Burwell Pope [Wake Co., in pencil, after it], Cer. 701, 1067 £. (Ibid, Vol. XI, p. 42, folio 3). On page 29 of this Vol. is the following: "Comptroller's Office, Kinston. The U. S. of Am'a to the State of N. C.. For sundries allowed by a Committee of Claims as per Report dated May 3, 1779".

He was a member of the Georgia State Senate from Oglethorpe Co., Ga., 1794-5 and 1799; of the Ga. State Constitutional Convention in 1795 (John Lumpkin and Thos. Duke were the other two delegates from Oglethorpe Co.)—voted against the "Yazoo Fraud". A copy of his affidavit as to an attempted bribery, and the discomfiture of those concerned in it, was in the possession of the late ex-U. S. Senator and Judge Pope Barrow at the time of his death ("Story of Ga. and the Ga. People", pp. 173-179, by Dr. Geo. Gilmer Smith; J. H. Chap. Coll. Vol. I, p. 302). The Senators who voted against the Yazoo Fraud, Feby. 7, 1795, were: Mr. Milledge, Mr. Lanier, Mr. Morrison, Mr. Irvin, Mr. Blackburn, *Mr. Pope*, Mr. Mitchell, Mr. Wood. ("Story of Ga.", p. 173).

As a member of the Revolutionary Legislature Burwell Pope risked his life for his country and was a patriot. See (W. T. R. Saffell's Record of the Revolution; Roster in Office of the Secretary of State of North Carolina).

1784. In the Office of the Secretary of State, Atlanta, Georgia. "Grants of the Commissions of the Confiscated Estates, Book B. 3, To Musgrove, *Pope*, and others, 500 acres in Camden Co. for Oglethorpe Academy, Nov. 15th, 1784.

The following extracts from a rare book in the Library of United States Senator Pope Barrow of Savannah, Georgia, were furnished by his sister, Mrs. Bourke Spaulding.

They show that *Burwell Pope* repudiated with scorn an attempt to bribe him in connection with the "Yazoo Fraud". It is recorded that the guilty members of the Georgia Legislature burned the Records of that Legislature, "using a sun glass to draw the fire from Heaven to burn them, hoping thus to purify or destroy the evidences of their guilt".

It was for this reason that Burwell Pope and the few others who had voted *against* the "Yazoo Fraud" made the following affidavits to put their course on record. The name of this book is

"Georgia's Speculation Unveiled. In two numbers. By Abraham Bishop, Hartford. Printed by Elisha Babcock (copy-right secured) 1797".

Page 5 , "Passing of the granting Act in January, 1795, and of passing the rescinding Act. 1796".

Page 105, "But a certain portion of the fraud shall be presented, from the following affidavits on the Journals of the House".

January 16th, 1796. Sworn in the presence of the Committee of the House of Representatives before me. Thomas Lewis, J. P.

1796. Extract from affidavit (Page 107) of Clement Lanier, Representative (Second affidavit): "The deponent further sayeth that the shares offered him as aforesaid, were expressly designed to induce him, the deponent, to vote for the bill for disposing of the western territory". Signed, Clement Lanier.
Qualified as aforesaid.

Page 114, "Eleventh" (affidavit): *"Burwell Pope, Esq.*, one of the members of the last and present senate of this State, being duly sworn, saith that being a member of the senate, at the last session of the legislature, he lodged at Mr. Herberts, in Augusta, with Mr. Harrison Musgrove then a member of the house of representatives, from the same county; that one evening whilst the bill for disposal of the western territory was on its passage (1796), the said Musgrove told the deponent he had found out more than he ever knew before, that he had discovered there were two shares in Cummings company, reserved for himself, and for every member that would take them, but that he did not know he should take them. The deponent further saith, that at another time the said Musgrove said to the deponent, friend Pope, I am authorized to tell you, that you can have one hundred guineas for your part;

to which the deponent answered, *he had no part;*—that at another time the said Musgrove further told the deponent, he might get five hundred silver dollars.
Signed, Sworn to as before: *Burwell Pope.*

In the first "Digest of the Laws of Georgia", by Robert and George Watkins, published by Aitken, No. 22 Market Street, Phila., Penn., is a list of the subscribers. One of these was *Burwell Pope, Esq.*, 1800. (This list is in the back of said book.)

Burwell Pope of the *County of Wake, N. C.*, on *May 19, 1783*, made deed to Thomas Tulloch and Harrison Macon to 640 acres, in Wake Co., on both sides Phillips Branch, beginning at *Joseph Lane's* corner, granted said *Pope* by his Excellency Gov. Caswell April 1, 1780, for 400 £. Wit.: *Thomas Wootten, Wm. Wootten*. Rec. April 26, 1785. Jas. Hinton Reg. Registered in the Register's Office of Wake Co., Book "H", p. 302, July 26th, 1789.

Burwell Pope of *Wake Co., N. C.*, on *26th Sept., 1783*, sold to Wm. Ward of Franklin Co., N. C., *639* acres of land on White Oak Creek, at mouth of Reedy Branch, in Wake Co., granted said Pope by the State of N. C., Aug. 9, 1779, for 113 £ 6 s. 8 d. Wit.: Wm. Yeates, Christopher Babb. (Wake Co. Book "G", p. 307).

Burwell Pope of *Wilkes Co.*, Ga., on *8 Feby., 1785*, sold to *Joseph Lane, Jr., of Wake Co., N. C.*, 640 acres on Williams' Creek, granted Wm. Williams Jany. 4, 1761, & registered in *Orange* Co. Book 8, p. 28, for 250 £. Wit: Nat Jones, Jr., Wm. Brown. Reg. *Aug. 24, 1785.*

The 3 records above show that *Burwell Pope,* as late as *26 Sept. 1783,* was still a resident of *Wake Co.,* N. C., and that between that date and the 8th day of *Feby., 1785,* he removed to and became a citizen of *Wilkes Co., Ga.* He received various grants in Wilkes Co.—five during July, 1787, aggregating 1300 A. (Land Grant Book "OOO", pp. 86-'7, 106, 141, 144), and one on 10th Oct., 1784 (?) for 200 A.—the copy of this grant as given me is dated 1774, but I think it must be so dated by mistake. "Burwell Pope *from* . . . . , 200 acres North side Broad River beginning at Thos. Wootten's corner red oak in a piece of fenced ground. Reserved until next Court, Dartmouth, Oct. 10, 1774". (Records of Land Commissioners on file in Clerk's Office, Greensboro, Ga., p. 18). It is claimed that this record was "copied by Dr. J. L. LeConte, decd., from the Record of Court of Land Commissioners appointed by Gov. Wright to issue the ceded lands 1773-5; with instructions to the Commissioners given at Augusta, Nov. 19, 1773. Records on file with Clerk of Court, Greensboro, Ga."

The lands inherited by the four younger sons of *Henry Pope* of Halifax Co., N. C., were sold by them in 1778, 1783 and 1786, as shown by the following deeds.

Book 15, p. 282. This Indenture made this *9th day of April,* in the year of our Lord *1778* Between Willis Pope, John Pope, Henry Augustine Pope and Wylie Pope of *Wake Co.* to John Wootten of Halifax Co. of N. C., of the other part, Witnesseth for the consideration of 800 £ current money of N. C. to us in hand paid by the said John Wootten . . . . all that tract of land on the South side of Beech Swamp in the aforesaid Co. by estimation 724 acres more or less. (Signed) Willis Pope (Seal).
Wit.: J. Branch, Henry Bradford, Lydia Brookes.   John Pope (Seal).
Henry A. Pope (Seal).
Wilie Pope (Seal).

Nov. 1, 1783 Signed by *Henry Augustine Pope* in the presence of Jno. Bradford, Junr., *Richd Bradford Wootten.*

Signed by *Willis* [Wilie ?] *Pope* Oct. 7, 1783, in presence of Elizabeth Bradford, John Bradford, T. Bradford, Halifax Co. [I think this was Wilie instead of Willis.]

1st Nov. Term. Then this deed was in open Court duly proved by the oath of Jno. Branch a subscribing witness thereto and ordered to be registered. Registered accordingly.   Test.: Wm. Wootten, C. Ct.
Jno. Geddy, C. Ct.

Book 15, p. 147. Oct. 8, 1783. This Indenture made this date between *Willis Pope* and *Mary his wife,* John Pope, *Henry Augustine Pope* and *Clary his wife* and Wilie Pope of the *County of Wake* and *State* of *N. C.*, and John Bradford of the Co. of Halifax and State aforesaid of the other part . . . . for consideration of 50 £ sell 510 Acres, &c, &c. Wit.: John Bradford, Elizabeth Bradford. [Signatures omitted in copy sent this compiler.] Halifax Co., N. C., May Court, 1784. Jno. Geddy Prob. Reg.

Book 16, p. 242. Aug. 29, 1786. *Willis Pope* and *Mary his wife,* John Pope, *Henry Augustin Pope* and *Clary his wife* and Wilie Pope of the *County of Wilkes* and State of Georgia sell to William Paradise of Halifax Co., N. C., two hundred and fifty four (254) acres in Halifax Co. for the consideration of 133 £ six shillings and eight pence. Wit.: *Jesse Pope,* Jonathan Joyner. [Signatures omitted in copy sent the compiler]. Recorded Feby. Court, 1787. Wm. Wootten, Clk. Ct.

It will be seen from these deeds that *Willis* and *Henry Augustin Pope* in *1778* were *single;* that in *1783* both were married; that in *Oct., 1783,* all four brothers were *residents* of *Wake Co.,* N. C., and that in *Aug. 1786,* residents of *Wilkes Co.,* Ga.; also that in *1778 Henry A.* and *Wylie Pope were minors* and so had to acknowledge their signatures after they became of age to make the conveyance valid.

An act to grant monies for the purpose of building and repairing Court houses and gaols A. D. 1791, No. 452. Digest of Laws of Georgia, Pub. 1800, p. 433. Extract.—Sec. IV. And be it further enacted, That Larkin Cleveland, Thomas Arington, John Connor Senior, *Burwell Pope* and William Harden be, and they are hereby appointed Commissioners for building the court house and gaol for Franklin County. Edward Telfair, Governor. Dec. 15, 1791. N. Brownson, President, Senate. William Gibbons, Speaker of the House of Representatives.

This act is repealed by act of 1792, No. 478.

Priscilla Pope, widow, appears "upon the Register of Land Grants, for services rendered as a Soldier of the Revolutionary War, or *as heirs of such soldiers",* as having drawn 2 lots. "No. 376 *Priscilla Pope, Widow,* 2 draws". Drawing Feby. 3, 1804. Records in Ordinary's Office, at Lexington, Ga.

Book NN, 1795-1796, p. 177—Wilkes Co., Ga. Burwell Pope and Priscilla, his wife, of *Oglethorpe Co., Ga., Dec. 27, 1793,* to John McLeod of *Wilkes Co., Ga.,* 173 A. in Wilkes Co., on *Broad River,* for 60 £. Burwell Pope.
Wit.: Benj. Taliaferro, J. P., Joshua Glass. Priscilla Pope.

Deed Book C, p. 20.—Burwell Pope and Priscilla, his wife, Aug. 31, 1797, to John N. Anderson, all of *Oglethorpe Co., Ga.,* 200 A. on Beaverdam Creek of the South fork of Broad River, for 50 £. Burwell Pope.
Wit.: Robert Pope, *Lewis Pope.* Priscilla Pope.

Note.—This is one of the tracts rec'd in grant from the State on the 25th July, 1787, as recorded in L'd. G't Book OOO, p. 144.

Burwell[5] and Priscilla (Wootten) Pope had issue: 1.—Robert Pope[6], b. 26 Sept., 1775; d. 7 Oct., 1831, unm.; 2.—Tabitha Christian Pope[6], b. 11 Feby., 1778; d. 25 April, 1852; m. 26 Jany., 1795, *Miles Hill,* 1774-1844. (For issue, see IX, B, P. O., p. 94, Hill records); 3.—Ann Pope[6], b. 28 April, 1780; d. 6 Jany., 1805; m. 28 Sept., 1796, Noah Hill, c. 1771-1805. (For issue, see VIII, B. P. O., p. 92, Hill records); 4.—Martha, called "Patsy", Pope[6], b. 18 April, 1782; d. 15 July, 1753; m. 29 March, 1799, Wylie Hill, 1775-1844. (For issue, see X, B. P. O., p. 103, Hill records); 5.—Wylie Pope[6], b. 14 Dec., 1784; d. Oct., 1864, in his 80th year; m. 11 Feby., 1807, Sallie Davis. (q. v.); 6.—Sarah Pope[6], b. 24 Nov., 1787; d., will 2 Dec., 1850; 20 Jany., 1851; m. 10 Feby., 1806, Robert Holmes. (q. v.); 7.—Burwell Pope, Jr.[6] (Brig. Genl.), b. 7 Sept., 1790; d. 11 May, 1840; m. 12 Dec., 1815, Sarah Key Strong, b. 1796.

Wylie Pope[6] (son of Burwell and Priscilla (Wootten) Pope) and his wife, Sallie Davis removed in 1838 to Wetumpka, Ala., where she d. in 1844, and he in Asheville, Ala., in 1864, in his 80th year. They had 3 sons and 2 daus.: 1.—Robert Samuel Pope, Sr.[7], who was a gold miner and d. in 1866 in California, unm.; 2.—Burwell Thomas Pope[7], b. circa 1810; d. 8 May, 1868, in Gadsden, to which he removed from Asheville, Ala., in 1867. (q. v.); 3.—Wylie Hill Pope[7], b. in Oglethorpe Co., Ga., 25 July, 1816; d. in Columbiana, Ala., 28 Nov., 1874. (q. v.); 4.—Mary Pope[7], m. . . . . Mulden, moved to Wisconsin and d. there, leaving children; 5.—Sarah Pope[7], m. Judge Gibbs, moved to Ill. before Civil War and d. there. [Capt. A. F. Pope, of Oglethorpe, thought her name was Martha, instead of Mary, and that they moved to St. Louis, Mo.]

Burwell Thomas Pope[7], 1810-1868, son of Wylie and Sallie (Davis) Pope, resided in St. Clair Co., Ala., was a lawyer and Circuit Judge; elected to Congress in

1865 but refused the ironclad oath; was arrested for prohibiting negroes being called as jurors in his court. His death believed to have been due to disease caused by excitement over his arrest. When the Alabama legislature passed and presented resolutions expressing the State's gratitude, a section of land and a gold medal, to *Miss Emma Sansom, the patriot,* Hon. Burwell T. Pope delivered for her the address of acceptance. She, b. in Social Circle, Ga., in 1847, moved with her family to Cherokee Co., and acted as guide for Genl. Forrest when he pursued and captured, near Rome, Ga., the command of Genl. Streight. (Mems. of Ala. His1 & Biol., Vol. 1, p. 1018, Acts of Genl. Assbly. 1863, pp. 213, 214; Gulf States Mag., Vol. 2, pp. 366-'7-'8). He m. Johanna Lester, of English descent, d. 1876, in Gadsden. They had 8 children, only 3 living when above account was written: Benjamin F. Pope8, b. 9 March, 1840; Sarah M. E. Pope8, m. Richmond Hammond, of Attala, Ala.; Lula R. Pope8, of Birmingham, Ala.

Benjamin F. Pope8, son of Burwell T. and Johanna (Lester) Pope, removed to Gadsden in 1861, m., same year, Sarah E. Germany. Was Solicitor of the City Court. They had 10 children, of whom 7 were living at date of this account: 1.—William B. Pope9; 2.—James Wylie Pope9, was Prest. of Enterprise Lumber Co. in Atlanta, removed to Fla.; 3.—Jos. Walter Pope9, was Sec. & Treas. of Gress Lumber Co., of Atlanta; 4.—John O. Pope9, was a dental student; 5.—Ada O. Pope9; 6.—Louis Wyeth Pope99; 7.—Wesley M. Pope. (Meml Rec. of Ala. His1 & Biol, Vol. 1, p. 1118).

Richmond and *Sarah M. E. (Pope) Hammond* had: Miss Nina Hammond, of Attala, Ala.; John Hammond and Joseph Hammond, both of Gadsden, Ala.; Mrs. John C. Staton, of Atlanta, Ga. Mr. John C. Staton was b. in St. Clair Co., Ala., in 1866; d. in Atlanta, July 15, 1921. He, at time of his death, and for many years previous, was Asst. Postmaster at Atlanta. They have two sons: John C. and Albert Staton, both prominent in athletic activities at Ga. Tech. in 1920 and '21.

3. *Wylie Hill Pope7,* 1816-1874, son of Wylie and Sallie (Davis) Pope, was Capt. in 25th Ala. Regt., C. S. A.; m. 28 Nov., 1844, Caroline (Bowden) McHenry, d. circa 1884 in Asheville, Ala., widow of Dr. Thomas McHenry, in Shelby Co., Ala., and had 5 children, viz.: 1.—William Wylie Pope8, b. 28 Sept., 1845, in Shelby Co., Ala., served in 25th Ala. Regt., C. S. A.; 2.—Sarah Elizabeth Pope8, b. 25 Oct., 1847, in Shelby Co., Ala.; m. 2 Aug., 1866, in Columbiana, Ala., *Judge John Washington Inzer,* living, 1921, in Asheville, Ala., and have 3 children: (1) *Clara Inzer9,* m. *James P. Montgomery,* Asheville, Ala. (this record received from her 27 May, 1921); (2) Lila Inzer9, m. Watt T. Brown, of Birmingham, Ala.; (3) John Manley Inzer9, of Asheville, Ala.; 3.—Mary Nancy Caroline Pope8, b. 25 Aug., 1849, in Shelby Co., Ala.; d. in 1855, in Shelby Co.; 4.—Robert Samuel Pope, Jr., or II8, b. 1 Aug., 1852; m. circa 1876, Mary Magruder, of Tuskeegee, Ala. He, in 1921, living in Atlanta, Ga.; 5.—John Franklin Greene Pope8, b. 13 March, 1857, in Shelby Co.; d. 21 Sept., 1918, in Cabot, Arkansas.

6. *Sarah Pope6* (dau. or Burwell and Priscilla (Wootten) Pope), 1787-1850, m. 10 Feby., 1806, Robert Holmes. Her will (recorded in Oglethorpe Co. Will Book 2, p. 262) 2 Dec., 1850; 20 Jany., 1851. To John Holmes and William Holmes in trust slaves for my son Burwell Holmes and his children. To Wylie Pope, son of Col. Wylie Pope, formerly of Wilkes; Mary Jane Brown; Methodist Episcopal Church South for Missionary purposes; "I direct my Executors to apply fifteen dollars towards defraying the expense of building an enclosure around the graves of my Father and Mother and other relatives". My children Burwell Holmes, Priscilla Moore, Tabitha Fullilove, William Holmes, Robert Holmes, Wylie Holmes and John Holmes. William Holmes and John Holmes Executors.

(Sigued) Sarah Holmes.

Wit.: Benjn F. Hardeman, Thos. E. R. Harris, Mathew F. Jackson. Her children all lived in La. and Texas.

7. *Burwell Pope6,* son of Burwell and Priscilla (Wootten) Pope, 1790-1840, was a Lieut. in the War of 1812; engaged in Indian Wars between 1812 and 1836 in Ga.; was commissioned as Brigadier General, 2nd Brigade, 3rd Division of the Georgia Militia on 24th Nov., 1828 (Roster of Ga. Militia Officers, Adjt. Gel's Office) and rendered efficient service in the Indian Wars, 1835-'6. Commanded the Ga. troops that went to Fla. in 1836. His will in Clarke Co., Ga., 30 April, 1840; pr.

July, 1840, names wife Sarah Key Pope, dau. Julia Ann Tabitha Pope; sons, John Hardeman Pope, Alexander Franklin Pope, Benjamin Henry Pope and William Edwin Pope. Wit.: James R. Carlton, Jno. D. Moss and William L. Mitchell.

Genl. Burwell[6] and *Sallie Key (Strong) Pope* had, as shown by his family Bible in possession of his grandson John Burwell Pope[6], in Austin, Tex., the following children: 1.—Edwin Elisha Pope[7], b. 1820; 2.—Charles Burwell Pope[7], b. 1822; 3.—Julia Ann Tabitha Pope[7], b. 1825; 4.—John Hardeman Pope[7], b. 1827; 5.—Alexander Franklin Pope[7], b. 1829; 6.—Benjamin Henry Pope[7], b. 1830; 7.—William *Alonzo* Pope[7], b. 1833. The last is not named in will, but a *William Edwin Pope*[7] is.

In "Mississippi", Vol. II—L-Z—p. 454, we find: *Panola, Miss.*, established in 1758 on lands of B. H. Pope[7]. In "Ibid", Vol. III, pp. 652-3, is an article on *William E. Pope*[7], which says he was b. July 8, 1836; m., 1883, Miss Bertha Steiner, dau. of Solomon and Hannah Steiner, of Illinois. He lived at Pope, Panola Co., Miss.

3. *Julia Ann Tabitha Pope*[7] (dau. of Genl. Burwell[6]), m. 8 Nov., 1854, Marcellus Stanley, Capt. Troup Artillery, C. S. A., son of Thomas and Ellen (Ramsey) Stanley, and had: (1) Thomas P. Stanley[8], m. Margaret Morton; (2) Sallie Stanley[8], single.

4. *John Hardeman Pope*[7], b. 1827; m. (I) Miss Damarias C. Hubbard, b. 23 May, 1828 (dau. of Robert and Nancy (Waters) Hubbard, and gr. dau. of John Hubbard, Revy. Soldier, and his wife Elizabeth), who bore him an only child, which d. in inf.; m. (II), in 1855, *Mary Caldwell*, d. 1918, by whom he had: 1.—Lula Pope[8], d. 1918, m. John D. Templeton; 2.—Maidee Pope[8], d. July, 1919, unm.; 3.—Minnie Pope[8], m. . . . . Watson, and had: (1) Arthur Pope Watson[9], Capt. World War, A. E. F.; (2) Eva Watson[9], d. July, 1917, m. . . . . Woodall; 4.—*John Burwell Pope*[8], of Austin, Tex., m. *Ruth Jones;* issue: (1) Mary Ellen Pope[9]; (2) John Burwell Pope, Jr.[9], b. 1916.

5. Alexander Franklin Pope[7] (son of Genl. Burwell[6]) was 1st Lieut. in Troup Artillery, which left Athens April 24, 1861 ("Annals of Athens", p. 222, by Hull), Genl. Loring's Brigade in Western Va. in 1861, in Genl. Howell Cobb's Brigade spring of 1862 to 1st of May, was in command of 3 pieces of Artillery at Dam No. 1 on the Pen below Richmond, where only one Gun could be used against 16 P's of Artillery, afterwards during balance of the war was Capt. of Artillery under Genl. Howell Cobb, on his staff in Ga. and Fla. He represented Oglethorpe Co. in the legislature. He m., late in life, Miss Mary Ward, and d. without issue.

2. *Willis Pope*[5] (Henry[4], John[3], Henry[2], William[1]), b. circa 1754; d. 23 Dec., 1795; was appointed 2nd Lieut. on 27 April, 1776, by Provincial Congress of N. C., at Halifax. (Wheeler's His. of N. C., Vol. 1, p. 80). He m., in N. C., in the '70s, Mary . . . . , maiden name not known. On 9th April, 1778, Willis Pope, John Pope, Henry Augustine Pope and Wylie *Pope, of Wake Co.*, N. C., make conveyance of 724 A. on South side of Beech Swamp in Halifax Co. to John Wootten, of Halifax for 800 £. (Halifax Deed Book 15, p. 282). On 8th March, 1783, Willis *and Mary his wife*, John Pope, Henry Augustin Pope and *Clary*, *his wife*, and Wylie Pope, of the *County of Wake* and *State of N. C.*, convey to *John Bradford* of Halifax Co., 510 A. for 50 £. (Halifax Co. Deed Book 15, p. 147.) Bounty Surveys by Surveyor General. Willis Pope 300 A. Washington County, Ga., bounded North and West by vacant lands, East by John Kimbro, South by Wm. Duke Cut by branch of Shoulderbone creek. Survey 494. *July 20, 1784.* (Surveyor General Book "F", p. 249). (Georgia Roster of Rev. Soldiers—The LeConte List, p. 273.)

"*28 July, 1784.* Sanders Walker vs. John Kimbrough, *Willis Pope* [et al.]. The Board are of opinion that the caveat of Pltff ought to be dismissed and grants passed for the Defdts.—Washington Co. lands. (Rev. Rec. of Ga., by Candler, Vol. 2, pp. 690, 726, 736 and 766).

Willis Pope received a grant in 1788 for 300 A. in Washington Co., Ga. (Land Book PPP, p. 394); on 2 March, 1791, 550 A. in Wilkes Co., bounded on South East by Thornton's and Butler's lands, North East by Thurman's, North by Wootten's, West by Beddingfield's and South West by Aycock's land. (Land Book UUU, p. 376 (or 516?); on 9 April, 1793, 200 A. in Wilkes Co. (Ld. Book WWW, p. 24).

Willis Pope and S. Gorham recd. grant, in 1788, for 1000 A. in Franklin Co., Ga. (Ld. Bk. QQQ, p. 424).

On Dec. 16, 1788, Curtis Wellborn sells to Willis Pope, all of Wilkes Co., 500 A. lying on both sides Golden Grove, granted Curtis Wellborn 17 Aug., 1785, for 100 £.

Curtis Wellborn,
Mary X Wellborn.

Wit.: Elijah Corven, Frances X George. (Deed Book 1790-1792, p. 34).

July 23, 1796, Benjn Glover and Polly Glover, his wife, of the State of S. C., at Cambridge, to *Polly Pope and her children*, being the *heirs* of *Willis Pope*, DECD., 400 A. in Wilkes Co., Ga., for 150 £.

Benjamin Glover.
Polly Glover.

Wit.: Betsy Oilver, John Freeman, Holmes Freeman, J. P. Rec. Dec. 5, 1796. (Deed Book OO, p. 132).

These records of deeds and grants are here given in order to show conclusively that the five brothers: Burwell, Willis, John, Henry Augustine and Wylie Pope, were all living in Wake Co., N. C., as late as 1783, that no one of them settled in Wilkes Co., Ga., before 1784, and the first record showing definitely their citizenship in Wilkes County is dated Feby. 8, 1785—by Burwell Pope (Bk. 9, p. 38, at Raleigh, N. C.), save only the Washington Co. grant to Willis Pope in 1784.

Pope, Willis, of Wilkes Co., Ga., d. 23 Dec., 1795. John Pope was the admr. of the Estate. Mary Pope and John Pope gave bond in the sum of $10,000. Nathan Bradford, Security.

Appraisement of the estate of Willis Pope by Drury Stovall, James Bridges and W. Gunnells shows $2363.94¾ in slaves, live stock, household goods, farm utensils, etc. *Another* appraisement, *seemingly,* of household goods, notes and accounts by same appraisers, whole amount $3385. *No land appraised.* Notes against Henry Jossey, Jno. Kelsey, Benjamin Blake, Nathaniel Bradford, David Gunnells, and many others, one of the small notes being for $18.00 by Barnaby Pope. The above by Clerk in Ordinary's office at Washington, Ga.—reference to book and page not given me.

Inventories of Appraisement records show on *Jany. 15, 1798,* that *John Pope administrator* of *Willis Pope,* recorded a sale made *5 Jany., 1798,* of a "Part of the personal estate of Willis Pope", proceeds amounting to $709.40. (Signed) John Pope, Admr. of Willis Pope.

On Aug. 5, 1794, *Barnaby Pope,* of Hancock Co., Ga., deeded to *John Pope* 6 slaves, 2 horses, 14 head of cattle, 30 hogs and all his household furniture for 189 £ 11 sh. 7d. (Signed) Bar. Pope.

Wit.: Absalom Thurman, Thos. Wootten, J. P. (Wilkes Co. Deed Book NN, p. 160).

On March 10, 1802, John Pope gave administrator's bond for $1000.00 as admr. of *Penia Pope.* Securities—John Heard and James Cade. (Signed) John Pope.

Saml. L. Cade.
Jesse Heard.

Attest: David Terrell. Rec. Aug. 20, 1806. (Book YY, 1800-1819, p. 20.) (In body of bond it is James Cade, but it is signed—as recorded—Samuel L. Cade). Signed, sealed and acknowledged in open Court. David Terrell, Clk Ct. of Ordinary.

2. *Willis Pope*[5] (Henry[4], John[3], Henry[2], William[1]) and his wife Mary . . . . ., had several children. Among them were John Pope[6], probably Penia Pope, et al. Such records as have been examined fail to positively identify their children, but they seem certainly to establish the fact that John Pope[6], who m. Keddy Hill, dau. of Henry and Sarah (Cotten) Hill, was their son. For record see Hills (VIII, A, P. O., p. 86).

Administrators' Bonds from 1800 to 1819, p. 183, State of Georgia, Wilkes County. Know all men by these presents That we Thomas Wootten, William Johnson, John Walker, Anderson Riddle and Thomas Anderson, are held and firmly bound unto their Honors the Judges of the Court of Ordinary for said County and their successors in office in the just and full sum of *Twenty-five thousand* ($25,000.) Dollars, for the payment of which sum, to the said Judges and their successors, we bind ourselves, our heirs, executors and administrators, in the whole and for the whole sum, jointly and severally, firmly by these presents, sealed with our seals and dated this, *2nd day of May, 1818.* The condition of the above obligation is such that if the above bound, *Thomas Wootten* and *William Johnson Administrators* of the goods, chattels and credits of *John Pope, late of this County, Deceased,* do make a true and perfect Inventory of all and singular the goods, chattels and credits of said deceased, which have or shall come to the hands or possession of said *Thomas* and *William*, or into the hands or possession of any other person or persons for them, and the same so made, do exhibit into the said Court of Ordinary when they shall be thereunto required, and such Goods, Chattels and Credits do well and truly administer according to law and do make a just account of their acting and doing therein when they shall be thereunto required by the Court of Ordinary for said County and all the rest of the Goods, Chattels and Credits, which shall be found remaining upon the account of the said administration, the same being first allowed of by the said Court, shall deliver and pay to such person or persons, respectively, as are entitled to the same by law and if it shall hereafter appear that any last Will and Testament was made by the said deceased and the same be proved before the Court and the Executors obtain Certificate of the Probate thereof and the said *Thomas Wootten* and *William Johnson* do, in such cases, if required, render and deliver up the said Letters of Administration, then this obligation to be void.

Seal: (Signed) Thomas Wootten (Seal)
Wilkes County Wm. Johnson (Seal)
Court of John Walker (Seal)
Ordinary Anderson Riddle (Seal)
1800 Thos. Anderson (Seal).
Georgia. Signed, sealed, acknowledged, in Open Court. D. Terrell, Clk.

Record this *27th* of *April, 1818.*

Note.—The instrument executed *2 May, 1818 and recorded 27 April*, 1818, evidently an error in copying.

S. D. Fanning, Ordinary, in letter May 6, 1915, to Mrs. T. B. Raines, of Dawson, Ga., says: "While the records contain several petitions of the Admrs. in regard to this estate, there is no mention made of his heirs".

It will be noted that John Pope[5] (Henry[4], John[3]) was living *May 24, 1819*, when he signed as a witness the will of his brother Wylie Pope[5], a year after the decease of the above John Pope[6], son of Willis, and husband of Catharine, or Keddy (Hill) Pope.

On Oct. 8, 1793, John Thurmond sold to John Pope, both of Wilkes Co., 80 A. on Pistol Creek for 50 £. (Signed) John Thurmond.
Wit.: Absolum Thurmon, *Thomas Wootten, J. P.* Reg. Nov. 12, 1795.

3. John Pope[5] (Henry[4], John[3], Henry[2], William[1]), b. c. 1755, in Halifax Co., N. C.; d. between May 24, 1819 and Nov. 19, 1821; removed to Ga., where on 15 Nov., 1785, he rec'd four grants, aggregating 1100 acres in Wilkes Co., Ga. (Ld. Grant Book III, pp. 253, 257, 285 and 322). In 1810 he was a representative from Wilkes in the State Legislature (Journal of the House of Representatives); was Capt. in the Indian Wars succeeding the Revolution (Natl Society of D. A. R. 5th Report, 57th Congress, 2nd Session, Vol. 16, pp. 352-'3). He m. Elizabeth Smith, dau. of John and Elizabeth Smith. Issue: (1) Huldah Pope[6], m. 10 Jany., 1812, Henry Jossey, Jr., 1st wife, son of Henry Jossey, Sr., and his wife, Mary Hill, dau. of Henry and Sarah (Cotten) Hill. (For issue see Hills, 3, V, A, P. O., pp. 39, 47); (2) Keturah Pope[6], m. James Mathews, Jr., and had, among others: Elizabeth R. Mathews, who m. Augustus F. Griggs and had James Mathews Griggs, who m. Theodosia Stewart, dau. of Daniel R. Stewart and Nannie O. Pope, his wife, dau. of Wiley Mobley Pope and his 3rd wife, Martha Williams Bryan. Wiley Mobley Pope was the son of Jonathan Pope and Elizabeth Cooper, his wife; (3) Mary L. Pope[6], m. . . . . Henderson; (4) Wylie Pope[6], d. unm. in 1826. In Wilkes Co. Admrs.' Bonds Book ZZ, p. 112, we find: "Henry Jossey and Jonathan Davis sureties on bond of Henry Jossey admr. on estate of Wylie Pope, Jr. (son of John). (Signed) Henry Jossey, Jonathan Davis. Attest: John Dyson; (5) Martha Pope[6], m. Rev. Wm. A. Calloway and had, among others: Abbie Calloway[7], of Atlanta, Ga., single; Jesse Mercer Calloway[7], m., his 2nd wife, Nancy Victoria Hill, b. 8 June, 1838; d. 1920. For issue see Hills (2a, 4, II, A, P. O., p. 26); (6) Rowanna Pope[6]; (7) Louisa Pope[6]; (8) Augustine Burwell Pope[6], who is said to have married and removed, 1st to Lumpkin, Stewart Co., Ga., and to have had 2 sons, one of whom was Dr. John Pope, and a dau., who lived in Lumpkin. Augustine B. Pope later removed to Mo., where he died.

Will of John Pope[5] (Henry[4], John[3], Henry[2], William[1]): In the name of God, Amen. I John Pope of Wilkes Co. & State of Ga., being in sound sense and memory but calling to mind my state of mortality and the certainty of death do make and ordain this my last Will and Testament in the manner and form following, viz.:

Item 1st. My will is first that my burial be plain and neat, without pomp or parade and that Doctor's bills on my last illness be promptly paid and as soon as possible all my just debts.

Item 2nd. I lend to my beloved wife Elizabeth Pope the land and plantation whereon I now live together with five negroes, viz.: Will and his wife Lavina, Necus, Annie and Jerry, also two good work horses, two good cows and calves, two good feather beds and furniture with slats and cords, also fifty barrels of corn and one thousand weight of pork, with a suitable supply of Household and Kitchen furniture, and also as many plantation tools as will answer her purpose to carry on the farm, also twenty bushels of wheat with two good sows and pigs and eight one year old hogs during her natural life; at her death or if she should marry, Will and Lavina shall become the property of my daughter Loisa in the same manner as the property hereafter named for her, but not the increase of Lavina which may arrive before such death or marriage. My will also is that Loisa shall have her support out of my land and plantation during her mother's natural life, and be equally entitled with my other children in her mother's dower.

Item 3rd. I lend my daughter Huldah Jossey one negro girl named Rachel now in her possession valued at four hundred dollars, which girl and her increase is to be hers during her natural life and then to be equally divided among her children.

Item 4th. I lend my daughter Keturah Mathews one negro boy named Hutson now in her possession, valued at four hundred dollars, which boy is to be hers during her natural life and then to be equally divided among her children.

Item 5th. I lend my daughter Mary S. Henderson one negro girl named Easter now in her possession valued at four hundred dollars, which girl is to be hers during her natural life and then said Easter and her increase is to be equally divided among her children.

Item 6th. I will to my son *Wylie Pope* eleven hundred dollars to be laid out for him in negroes *when he becomes of age*.

Item 7th. I lend to my daughter Martha Pope my servant girl Mary, also I lend to my daughter Rowanna Pope my servant girl Sarah in the same manner and upon the same principles that Rachel is lent to my daughter Huldah Jossey.

Item 8th. If either of those negroes lent to my daughters (viz.) Huldah, Keturah, Mary, Martha and Rowanna should die before the division of my estate it shall be made good to them out of the said division, if they should die after the division and before the death of my wife Elizabeth, it shall be made good to them out of the dower, after the death of my wife Elizabeth.

Item 9th. I lend to my daughter *Louisa* Pope two negroes (viz.) Sam and Susan in addition to Will and Lavina above named, also one good hundred dollar horse, one good cow and calf, one good sow and pigs, one feather bed weighing forty weight well supplied with good furniture and a good bedstead, the above property to be so far under the controll of my Executors that if she should marry, and in their opinion her husband is likely to waste the same so as to bring her to want, they shall take it into possession and rent or hire a part or the whole and place the value received to her best interest. Should she die leaving no . . . . then the property to return to her brothers and sisters.

Item 10th. My will is that Martha Pope, Rowanna Pope my two youngest daughters be made equal to seven hundred in property, valuing a negro woman at four hundred dollars.

Item 11th. My further Will is that the whole of the minors property be kept together with wife until they shall marry or become of age, and that she shall board, school and clothe them for the use of the same and that each one shall receive his or her own part upon marrying or becoming of age.

Item 12th. My last desire is that all my estate not heretofore disposed of be equally divided between my several children (viz.) Huldah Jossey, Keturah Mathews, Augustine B. Pope, Mary L. Henderson, Martha Pope, Wylie Pope and Rowanna

Pope and at the death of my beloved wife Elizabeth, Loisa shall receive an equal part of the property loaned to my wife Elizabeth.

Item 13th. I constitute and appoint Henry Jossey, James Mathews and Augustine B. Pope my Executors. (Signed) John Pope.

Test.: Baker Lipscomb, Joice Davis, James Davis. Recorded in Book HH, Folio 71, Nov. 19, 1821.

Henry Augustine Pope[5] (Henry[4], John[3], Henry[2], William[1]), b. in Halifax Co., N. C., 6 Aug., 1760; d. in Oglethorpe Co., Ga., 9 Dec., 1807; m. (1) in Wake Co., N. C., between 9th April, 1778 and 8 Oct., 1783, Clara Hill, b. 9 Aug., 1763; d. 16 Nov., 1798, dau. of Abraham Hill[3] and Christian (Walton) Hill. For issue, see (Hills, IV, B, P, O, p. 68); m. (II), 27 May, 1799, Mary Davis, in Oglethorpe Co. Her will 11 Oct., 1837; pr. Sept., 1843.

On 12 July, 1787, he recd. a grant in Wilkes Co. for 450 A. bounded Northwardly by John Burk's land, South West by Phillips' land, South Eastwardly by Silas Monk's land, Northwesterly by vacant lands. (Ld. Grt. Book OOO, p. 122).

On 12 July, 1787, he received a grant of 600 A. in Franklin Co., bounded North by vacant land, East by Benj. Black's land, South by *Thos. Wootten's* and West by *Abraham Hill's* land. (Ld. Grt. Book OOO, p. 35).

In 1787 John and Henry Pope rec'd grant for 747½ A. in Franklin Co. (Ld. Grt. Book NNN. p. 249).

Henry Augustine Pope, Will, 10 Nov., 1807; 14 Jany., 1808. State of Georgia, Oglethorpe County.—In the name of God, Amen.

I Henry Augustin Pope, of the County of Oglethorpe and State of Georgia, being weak in body, but of sound mind and memory, do make and ordain this my last will and testament, in manner and form following:

Item. I give and bequeath to my beloved wife, Mary Pope, one negro wench, named Penney, also an equal part of household and kitchen furniture, plantation tools, live stock of all kinds, and she is to live on the plantation until Middleton Pope comes of age, or Sallie should marry, at which time the household and kitchen furniture is to be divided, and after the one takes their share the balance is to be put together again until a second division is necessary to be made as my wife is to live on the plantation, and keep her children's negroes and their part of the stock and household and kitchen furniture untill Middleton comes of age, as she has nothing to do with their parts (that is, Sallie and Middleton Pope).

Item. I give and bequeath to my daughter Sallie Pope two hundred acres of land, whereon John Speers now lives, it being the land that I purchased from George Hinton, also five negroes, namely, Bettie, Isaac, Booker, Martin and Eliza, and an equal part of the household and kitchen furniture, live stock of all kind and plantation tools, to be divided whenever she becomes of age, or shall marry, and then the balance put together until a second division is wanted.

Item. I give and bequeath to my son Middleton Pope five negroes, to-wit: Joseph, Aleck, Amy, Judy and Nathan, only Nathan is to work in the shop with Phil, but my Executor hereinafter named is to draw his part for Middleton, also an equal part of the household and kitchen furniture, live stock of all kind, and plantation tools. Also I give and bequeath to my three sons Middleton, Benjamin and Henry Jefferson Pope the following tracts of land, to-wit: Five hundred and twenty-five acres, including the plantation whereon I now live, five hundred and seventy-five acres, including the Mill Tract, One hundred and twenty-five acres I purchased from David Martin joining the Mill, One hundred and four acres I purchased from James Martin, joining that I had of David Martin, fifty acres I purchased from William Harris, joining the Mill Tract, and one hundred and forty-four or one hundred and forty-seven acres, which I purchased from William Martin, to be equally divided by my Executors when Middleton comes of age, observing of the rents of this land is to go to Middleton Pope. It is my desire that *Thomas Wootten* continue on the place whereon he now lives during pleasure, or until the child whose lot it is comes of age, the *said Wootten* is to have the land to the first cross fence going to the Mill and then on both sides of the road upwards.

Item. I give and bequeath to my daughter Clary Pope one tract of land containing three hundred acres, be the same more or less, known by the name of the Corner Land. I also give and bequeath to my daughter Clary Pope, Benjamin Pope

AND ALLIED FAMILIES 253

and Henry Jefferson Pope the following negroes: Ben, Phil, Caleb, Jack, Moses, Jacob, Dinah, Lucy, Ruth, Silva, Nancy, Harriette and Aly and Bromfield, only Bromfield is to have his choice to say which of the last mentioned children he will live with, to be equally divided among them, when Clary Pope comes of age or shall marry, likewise each of them an equal part of the household and kitchen furniture, live stock of all kind, and plantation tools to be equally divided as above mentioned.

I also constitute my beloved Benjamin Blanton, Benjamin Taylor, Miles Hill and Robert Pope my whole and sole executors of this my last will and testament, revoking all other wills or bequeaths. In witness whereof I have hereunto set my hand and affixed my seal the 10th day of November, 1807.

(Signed) Henry A. Pope (Seal).

Signed, sealed and acknowledged in the presence of us. *Tabitha Wooten, Charles Finch, Thomas Wooten.*

Georgia, Oglethorpe County, Court of Ordinary, January Term, 1808. Personally appeared in Court Charles Finch and *Thomas Wooten,* two of the witnesses to this will, and after being sworn saith that they saw the within named Henry Pope, deceased, sign, seal, publish and declare the within instrument of writing to be his last will and testament, and at the time of so doing he was of sound mind and memory to the best of their knowledge and belief. Mathew Rainey, C. C. O.

Recorded the 14th day of January, 1808. Mathew Rainey, C. C. O. (Book B, p. 10).

The will of Mary (Davis) Pope, of Oglethorpe Co., Ga., dated 11 Oct., 1837; pr. Sept., 1843, is of record at Athens, Ga. She wills some property to her son Henry Pope and her son-in-law Samuel Baldwin. Wit.: Blanton M. Hill, Wilie Pope and Francis Burke. The above incomplete data sent me by the Clerk of the Court merely to show that such a will was of record.

5. *Wylie Pope*[5] (Henry[4], John[3], Henry[2], William[1]), b. c. 1762; d. 16 July, 1819; m. 20 March, 1794, Mary Hill, dau. of Abraham and Christian (Walton) Hill. (For issue, see Hills, XI, B, P, O., p. 119).

Wylie Pope, Aug. 22, 1791, guardian of David Hays (Wilkes Co. Book GG, p. 312).

Sept. 26, 1791. By the Hon. George Walton, Esq., one of the Judges of Superior Court of the said State of Ga., Wilkes County, Chambers, Washington, Wilkes Co., *Aug. 26, 1791:*

Whereas Henry Aycock, Joel Aycock, Rebecca Aycock, Richard Aycock, and Winney Aycock, Sons and Daus. of *Richard Aycock,* late of said Co., deceased, Upon the Consent of all parties Concerned and upon Motion of Mr. Watkins, in their behalf hath applied to his Honor the Judge praying *Wiley Pope, Esq., may be appointed their Guardian.* Henry Mounger Pre. C. S. C. W. C.

Sept. 24, 1791. I Ica Atkins of Cumberland Co., State of N. C., appoint Mr. *Wylie Pope* of Wilkes Co., Ga., my attorney to recover what is due me from the estate of Richard Aycock deceased. (Signed) Ica Atkins.

Wit.: Nat Jones, Mathew Jones. (Book GG, p. 353).

Nov. 1, 1792. Samuel Rylie of Edgefield, S. C., sells to Wylie Pope, of Wilkes Co., Ga., 400 A. on a branch of Long Creek in Wilkes Co., Ga., for 200 £—land granted to said Saml Rylie April 8, 1785. (Signed) Sam'l Rily.

Wit.: Ephrom Rogers, Henry Aycock, *John Pope,* J. P. Reg. Nov. 4, 1794. (Book MM, 1794-1795, p. 274).

Jany. 16, 1794, Adam Wyley sells to Wylie Pope, both of Wilkes Co., Ga., 150 A. land on Newford Creek in Wilkes Co., for 100 £—land conveyed from Joseph Collins to Adam Wylie Jany. 11, 1792. (Signed) Adam Willie.

Wit.: James M. Taylor, Levi Gils. Recorded April 25, 1796. (Book NN, 1795-1796, p. 288).

April 13, 1794, Joseph Gray to Wylie Pope, both of Wilkes Co., Ga., 75 A. on Long Creek, in Wilkes Co., for 100 £. (Signed) Joseph Gray.

Wit.: Joel Aycock, *Thomas Wootten,* J. P. Reg. April 25, 1796. (Book NN, p. 290).

Will of *Wylie Pope,* of Wilkes Co., Ga., 24 May, 1819; pr. 6 Sept., 1819; Rd 16 Sept. 1819. In the Name of God, Amen. I *Wylie Pope,* of Wilkes County and State of Georgia, being of Sound and disposing mind and memory and calling into view that all men are appointed to die, do make ordain and publish this as my last Will and Testament, hereby nullify and Revoke all former Wills and Testaments heretofore made or published.

First. I Recommend my soul to God who gave it and my body to be decently buried at the discretion of my Executors hereafter to be appointed.

Secondly as touching the worldly estate Real and personal with which it has pleased God to bless me with, my will and desire is that after my just Debts are paid, that there shall be an equal division of all my estate that I may die possessed of between my dearly beloved wife *Polly Pope* and my children as herein named, Josiah Woods Pope, John Clark Pope, Sally Mary Ann Pope, Wylie Hill Pope to them and their heirs forever, share and share alike, the division to take place as soon as my son Josiah Woods Pope shall arrive at lawful age of twenty-one years, or in case he should depart this life before he should arrive at lawful age, the division to be made at his decease, and until he does come of age or should depart this life, the property to be conducted and managed as my Executors may think for the best and at their discretion.

Lastly. I hereby nominate constitute and appoint my worthy friends *Lemuel Wootten, Thomas Wootten, Wylie Hill* and *James Jordan* my sole Executors to this my last Will and Testament hereby revoking all former Wills and Testaments by me made. In witness whereof I hereunto set my hand and seal this 24th of May, 1819.   Wylie Pope (Seal).

In presence of Thos. D. McLaughlin, Richard Sale, Talton Sheets, *Jno. Pope.*

Memorandum by way of Codicil. My Will and desire is that my *wife Polly Pope* is to have her part of the landed property as named in the foregoing will where I now live as witness whereof I have set my hand and seal this 24th of May, 1819.   Wylie Pope (Seal).

Wit.: Thos. D. McLaughlin, Richard Sale, Talton Sheets, Jno. Pope.

Georgia, Wilkes County. Appeared in Open Court Thos. D. McLaughlin, Richard Sale, and Talton Sheets, the [three] of the subscribing witnesses to the above will, who being duly sworn say that they saw *Wylie Pope* sign seal and acknowledge the foregoing instrument as his last Will and Testament and that at the time of doing so he was of sound and disposing mind and memory, that they signed the same as witnesses thereto in the presence of the said Wylie Pope and at his request and in the presence of each other and that *John Pope* also signed the same as a witness in their presence and presence of the Testator.

Sworn to in open
Court this 16th day of
September, 1819.
John Dyson, C. C. O.

Thos. D. McLaughlin,
Richard Sale,
Talton Sheets.

Recorded the 16th day of September, 1819. John Dyson, C. C. O. (Will Book HH, Folio 5).

On March 3, 1823, Lemuel Wootten and Abraham Hill, as administrators estate of *Josiah W. Pope*, gave bond for $10,000. with Philip Orr and Henry Jossey as sureties. (Admr. Bond Book ZZ, p. 112).

April 24, 1826, Baker Lipscomb made Guardian to Wylie M. Pope orphan of Josiah W. Pope. (Book AAA, p. 122).

April 24, 1826, James Huling appointed Guardian to John C. *Pope, orphan of Wylie Pope*, bond $15,000., John T. McGehee, surety. Wit.: Hon. Thos Wootten. (Book AAA, p. 126).

April 13, 1827, James Huling appointed Guardian to *Wylie H. Pope*, orphan of *Wylie Pope;* bond $15,000., *Osborne Stone*, Surety. (Book AAA, p. 131).

May 5, 1832, James Huling admr. estate of *John C. Pope*, gives bond with *Robert A. Toombs*, Surety. (Book AAA, p. 249).

On *Jany. 2, 1826*, *Baker Lipscomb* gave bond in the sum of $2000. as Guardian of *Wylie M. Pope*, orphan of *Josiah W. Pope*, Richard J. Willis, security. Recorded 24 April, 1826.

2. John Pope[4] (John[3], Henry[2], William[1]) m. Sarah . . . . (Halifax Co. Deed Book 9, p. 197), though his identity is not established, in express terms, by documentary evidence, was, no doubt, he who recd. a deed to land in 1741 from John and Mourning (McKennie) Pope, Deed Book 1, p. 396; who was appointed Commissioner of the Peace for Edgecombe Co. on 27 June, 1746 (C. R. N. C., Vol. 4,

AND ALLIED FAMILIES   255

p. 813), Justice of the Peace for Edgecombe Co. on 11 Oct., 1749 (Ibid, p. 966), and Sheriff of Edgecombe Co. for the years 1753-'4-'5 (C. R. N. C., Vol. 6, p. 211). *Dec. 7, 1759, John Pope* allowed salary as former Sheriff of Edgecombe Co., for years 1753-'4-'5 (C. R. N. C., Vol. 6, p. 211). In 1758 an act was passed refunding money to John Pope, Gent., that was paid by him as the result of a suit which was brought against him as Sheriff for failing to collect a tax which had been illegally levied and which, by reason of such illegality, *he would not collect.* He was therefore fully vindicated. (S. R. N. C., Vol. 25, pp. 389, 390).

John Pope gives bond to the King for 500 £ *as Sheriff,* May 16, 1753, Commission dated March 28, 1753, from Mathew Rowan, Esq., President and Commander in Chief, for two years.   Signed by *John Pope,*
  Wit.: Edwd Underhill, *Jno. Bradford.*   Jas. Spiers,
Edgecombe May Ct. 1753.   Jos. Lane,
(Book 4, p. 736).   Luke Prior.

In the Name of God Amen I Winefred Pope of North Carolina Halifax County being very and weak of body but of perfect sound mind and memory thanks be to Almighty God for the same and knowing that it is appointed for all woman onste to die do make and ordain this my will and testament in manner and form following first of all I give my soul to almighty God that gave it me and my body to the Earth to be buried in a decent like manner at the discretion of my Exors hereafter mentioned and as to my worldly estate my will and desire is that it be disposde in manner and form following.

Item I give and bequeath to my loving *Brother Jesse Pope* my negro girl Velate my bed and furniture and my walnut chest to him and his heirs and assigns for ever Item I give and bequeath to my loving *Brother Lewis Pope* my negro man Peter and one small chest to him his heirs and assigns forever. Item, I give and bequeath to my loving *Cousin Mourning Pope* my riding saddle one pair of silver sleave buttons one pair of silver shoe buckles I chinch gown d one Counly cloth ditto two petticoats two aprons two shirts two handkerchief two pair of gloves two caps one pair of stays and on neckles Item I give and bequeath to *Tabitha Pope* one blue stripid counbey cloath Gound 1 Gold Ring Item I give and bequeath to *Mary Pope* one worsted gown and one black silk bonnet Item I give and bequeath to *Ann Pope* striped County cloth, goun and one allapain quilt. Item give and bequeath to my *cousin Willis* Pope twelve pound Prove. money to be paid out of the money in the hand of John Bradford and the remainder of the money in his hand I give to my friend John Bradford in considering what trouble and expense to him in my sickns Further I constitute and appoint my loving *Brother Henry Pope* executor of this my last will and testament revoking all other wills or testaments by me made or don and do acknowledge and declare this to be my last will and testament and no other In witness whereof I have set my hand and seal this seventh day of February 1762. Signed and delivered in presents of us   Winefred W. Pope (Seal).
Elizabeth / Lane, Jemini Simmas.
          mark

Halifax September Inferior Court of plea and quarter sessions 1762 this will was exhibited in open Court on oath by the executors and duly proved by the oath of Jemini Simmans one of the subscribing witness there to who on his oath did say he saw Elizabeth Lane the other subscribing witness sign the sd. will as a witness
Whereupon Henry Pope the exors in the sd. will named came into Court and was duly qualified according to law on motion ordered said be recorded. Test J. Montfort CC. Will Book No. 1, pages 85 and 86, Halifax County, North Carolina. Office of the Clerk of Superior Court.

In the above will *Tabitha* was the *wife* of Henry Pope, *Mary* was the *wife* of *Jesse Pope, Ann* was the first *wife* of *Lewis Pope,* and *Willis* Pope was the son of Henry and Tabitha Pope. Mourning, was probably, the dau. of her brother Barnaby Pope.

4. Barnaby Pope[4] (John[3], Henry[2], William[1]) and his father John Pope received legacies under the will of his Uncle, Barnaby McKennie, Jr., on 13 Oct., 1735-'6 (Grant Book 4, Will 58 Sec. of State's Office, Raleigh, N. C.); on 9 Nov., 1753, sold the 110 A. received from his uncle, Barnaby McKennie, Jr., to William Hurst, of Va., who m. his aunt, Christian McKennie (Book 4, pp. 598 and 938); on 18 Jany.,

1755, bought 100 A. from John Branch, Sr. and Jr., in Edgecombe (Book 2, p. 201); in 1757 bought 90 A. from Abraham and Sarah Hill, of Edgecombe (Deed Book 6, p. 224); in 1757 sold to his brother *Henry Pope* 91 A. which he had also inherited in Edgecombe Co. (Halifax Book 6, p. 325) and his personal belongings (Book 6, p. 321). He removed to District 96 of Edgefield Co., S. C., was a leading citizen and one of the leaders of the Regulators in 1764. In the Revy. War a Company raised on Mine Creek, in Edgefield Co., was commanded by *Capt. Solomon Pope*.

Barnaby Pope later removed to Hancock Co., Ga., and on 12 July, 1787, received a grant from the State of Ga. for 1150 A. in Franklin Co., Ga., bounded South by *said Pope's land*, West by David Thurman's land and on all other sides by vacant land. (Ld. Grt. Book OOO, p. 102).

On Aug. 5, 1794, he sold to John Pope, of Wilkes Co., 6 slaves, 2 horses, 14 head of cattle, 30 hogs, and all his household furniture for 189 £ 11 sh. 7d. (Book NN, p. 160). Wit.: Absolum Thurmon and Thos. Wootten, J. P.

An abstract of his will, 1795, in Hancock Co., names "Sons: *Henry Norman Pope*, Barnaby McKennie Pope, Daus.: Mary Pope, Mourning Curry, Lucy Curry, Martha Gibson, Jane Rucker, Exrs.: Thos. Mercer, Jesse McK. Pope". This is as it was given me by one of his descendants. It is not known whom he married, but as he names a son *Henry Norman Pope*, the following will is suggestive.

Will of Elizabeth (. . . . , Southard) Norman. Georgia, Wilkes Co. In the name of God, Amen. I Elizabeth Norman [relict of Jesse Norman] being weak of body, but of sound and disposing mind and memory, and conscious of the certainty of death and uncertainty of life, make this my last will and testament.

1st. I give and bequeath unto my *grandson Henry N. Pope*, the sum of three hundred and fifty dollars, to be paid to him by my Executors within the time prescribed by law. 2nd. I give and bequeath unto Richard B. Wootten who intermarried with *my granddaughter Martha Hinton*, the negro woman Tener, with her child Adaline and their increase on the following terms, that he shall pay to the above mentioned *Henry N. Pope* the said sum, or legacy of three hundred and fifty dollars. 3rd. The remaining balance of my effects both real and personal, I give and bequeath in the following manner, that is one-third to my *son-in-law John Hinton*, and one-third to my *son-in-law, James* Hinton, and the remaining third to the children of my deceased son (Law B?) Norman, to be equally divided between them. 4th. I nominate and appoint Richard B. Wootten and John Hinton Exrs. to this my last will & testament. In witness whereof I have hereunto set my hand & seal this 15 Jany., 1821.

Signed and sealed in the presence of   her
Wm. Saffold, Wm. S. Muse.   Elizabeth X Norman.
                               mark

5. *Lewis Pope*[4] (John[3], Henry[2], William[1]) m. (I) Ann . . . . ; m. (II) Jemima . . . . , before 1773. He removed to Oglethorpe Co., Ga. His will 20 Sept., 1803; recorded 14 Feby., 1805. (Will Book A, p. 146). *Wife Jemima Pope* to see that my two youngest children Zachariah and Patsy are educated; my dau. Polly Ridley Jordan; son Archelus Pope; dau. Rebecca Ogilvie; dau. Betsy [pro. Patsy] Pope; dau. Jemima Phillips; son Willis Pope [m. Nov. 23, 1810, Agnes Hobson, of Jackson Co.]; son Zachariah Pope. Among other things, wills each of his children a "horse creature" of the value of $100. Exx.: my wife *Jemima Pope;* Exrs.: my son *Archelus* Pope, and my *son-in-law George Phillips.* Wit.: Alexr Lester, Wm. Hatchett, Benj. Wilks.   (Signed) Lewis Pope.

Lewis Pope and *Jemima his wife*, of *Halifax Co., N. C.*, made deed Feby. 15, 1773, to Elizabeth Moncrief for 120 acres of land in Halifax on the South Side of *Burn Coat Swamp.* Consideration 33 £ 6 sh. 8d.   Lewis Pope,
Wit.: James Lock, Jr., Sampson Moncrief.   Jemima Pope.
Rec. Aug. Court, 1774. (Halifax Co., N. C., Book 13, p. 141).

Lewis Pope and Jemima his wife, of Halifax, made deed to Ladymon Shelton to 81 acres on South side of *Burn Coat* Swamp in Halifax Co., Feby. 5, 1773. Consideration 26 £ 13 sh. 4d. (Ibid Book, 13, p. 143).

The will of *his sister, Winnifred Pope*, Feby., 1762, shows that his wife at that time was *named Ann*.

On 13th Jany., 1764, *Lewis Pope* and Peter Tatum were the witnesses to a deed of Bethiah Hardy, wid. and relict of Hugh Hardy, decd., Saml. Hardy, John Bradford, Benajah Saxon, Exrs. of Hugh Hardy, to *Thomas Wootten* of Co. & Province afsd. for 192 A. of wood land on North side of Burncoat Swamp, sd land granted sd Hugh Hardy deed by Nath'l Bradford. (Halifax N. C. Deed Book 9, p. 290).

*Archelus Pope*5 m., 1794-'98, Nancy Eason, of Oglethorpe Co., Ga.; was a grand juror in Oglethorpe in 1794 (J. H. Chap. 3, p. —); Zachariah Pope a Commissioner of Clinton, Jones Co., 4 Dec., 1816. (L. M. & L., Vol. 2, p. 824). Willis Pope m., 23 Nov., 1810, Agnes Hobson, Jackson Co. (Mar. Rec. p. 311). Lewis Pope, Aug. 31, 1797, was a witness to a deed executed by Burwell Pope and his wife, Priscilla Pope. (Deed Book 6, p. 20).

6. *Jesse Pope*4 (John3, Henry2, William1) m. Mary . . . , some of her descendants claim her maiden name was Fort, but give no authority, save tradition.

On 16 Feby., 1786, Jesse Pope and his wife, Mary Pope, sold his land in Halifax Co., N. C., to John Branch for 200 pounds in Gold and Silver. Wit.: Wm. Branch, Jurratt, Wm. Wootten, Clerk Ct. (Book 16, p. 140).

On 29 Aug., 1786, he and Jonathan Joyner were the witnesses to the deed by Willis Pope and Mary, his wife, John Pope, Henry Augustine Pope and Clary, his wife, and Wylie Pope, of the Co. of Wilkes, State of Ga., to Wm. Paradise, of Halifax Co., N. C. We have before shown that he was named in the wills of his brother Henry Pope and of his sister Winnifred Pope in 1764 and 1762, respectively.

Jesse Pope came from North Carolina, settled in Hancock Co., Ga., about 7 miles North of Sparta, where he died in 1818. He does not appear to have rendered any Revolutionary service. An abstract of his will recorded at Sparta, as given by a descendant, shows: "Children as follows: Jesse McK. Pope, Cullen Pope [b. 1752; d. 1829], Henry Pope, Samuel Pope, John Pope, Allen Pope, Mary Denton, Anna Long, Sarah Trippe. Granddaughters, Mary Weaver and Frances Godwin". Jesse McK. Pope and Henry Pope were of the earliest settlers in Jones Co., the former having been on its first grand jury. ("Story of Ga. & the Ga. People", pp. 276-'7, by G. G. Smith). The descendants of this family are very numerous throughout Georgia, Alabama and other Southern States.

RANSONE.

*Peter Ransone*1, the first of the family in Virginia of whom we have any knowledge, is mentioned in York County Records in 1641; was Burgess from Elizabeth City County in 1652, and in same year patented 1100 A. in Gloucester—since 1790 Mathews County—and 340 A. was patented by one of the family in 1667, all in Kingston Parish on North River. (Peter and James Ransone and John Billups vestrymen in Kingston Par'h, Mathews Co., beginning in 1677.—Old Chs. & Fams., Vol. 1, p. 324). His will bears date 26 April, 1658, in which he names sons as follows—without their later titles: 1. Col. James Ransone2, "gent.," (q. v.). 2. Capt. George Ransone2, (q. v.). 3. William Ransone2, (q. v.).

1. James Ransone2, Gent., in 1670, deeded land in Gloucester Co. to Abraham Savoy (W. & M. Qtly. 6, 74); vestry Kingston Parish 1677; justice of Gloucester, 1680; member House of Burgesses, 1692-'3; Lt.-Col. of Militia, 1699 (Va. Co. Rec., Vol. 2, p. 106); in 1707 owned 400 of the 1100 A. patented by his father in 1652, and also a lot in Gloucester town (Miles Cary Survey); in 1698-1702-1714, justice in Gloucester with Ambrose Dudley, et al. (Va. Mag. of H. & B., Book 2, p. 129). His land in Mathews in 1704 joined Col. Ambrose Dudley's. In 1745, at the instance of George Ransone, the original grant of 1100 A. patented 2 Sept., 1652, was surveyed by John Trench. The plat shows 400 A. having Madame Ransone's house, left to Capt. James Ransone, Burgess, Gloucester Co., March 3, 1692-'3 (W. & M. Qtly., Vol. 5, p. 138). It is not yet known whom he married. She was probably a dau. of Capt. Ambrose Dudley, of Gloucester. He was doubtless father of the five sons here named: 1. Robert Ransone3 (q. v.); 2. George Ransone3 (q. v.); 3. Peter Ransone3 (q. v.); 4. James Ransone3 (q. v.); 5. *Richard Ransone*3 (q. v.).

1. Robert Ransone3 witnessed, 1694, deed from Mrs. Jane Metcalf to John Armistead of "pearl" (?) on Pionotank (?) River in Gloucester Co.; Capt. of Ship "Planter's Adventure" in 1678 (York Co. Rec'ds), and of the "Thomas and John," 1707 (York Co. Rec'ds). He may have married Miss Armistead. 2. George Ransone3, master of the Peaseley's Free School in Gloucester in 1724, was living in 1748. 3. Peter Ransone3 was in the vestry of Kingston Parish and living in 1745, and dead

before 1750. Name of wife unknown. Issue: Richard[4] (admr. of Peter the younger)—survey in Kingston Parish, 1753-'4, land joined Mrs. Armistead and Joseph Billups[4]; *Peter[4] the younger*, survey 1750. 4. James Ransone[3], will in Surry Co., pr. 1740, issue: (1) James Ransone[4]; (2) Gwatheney Ransone[4]; (3) Catherine Ransone[4]; (5) Elizabeth Ransone[4].

(1). James Ransone[4] in 1754 m. Letitia (Hayes?). (Instead of being son of James[3] as above, he may possibly have been son of George[3], master of Peaseley's Free School, 1724). Issue: 1. James[5], b. 28 June, 1755. 2. Ann[5], b. 1756. 3. Robert[5], b. 1758. 4. Sarah[5], b. 1760. 5. Letitia[5], b. 1762. 6. Lucy[5], b. 1764. He remained in Kingston Parish, Gloucester Co.

5. Richard Ransone[3], son of James[2], will Brunswick Co., 1748; m. before 1739, Frances, dau. of Capt. Robert Hicks, of Brunswick Co., will 1739. Issue: (1) James[4]; (2) Robert Hicks[4]; (3) Elizabeth[4]. This James Ransone[4] moved to Warren Co., N. C., m. 1763, Priscilla Jones, dau. of Edward and Abigail (Shugar) Jones, widow of Gideon Macon and mother of Nathaniel Macon, and by her had six children: William[5]; Abigal[5]; Hixie[5]; Betsy[5]; Drusella[5], m. (I) Frank Thornton; m. (II) Plummer Willis; Seymour[5] (Alstons & Allstons, p. 511). Another account says his son Richard Ransone[5] m. Seymour and had: Seymour Ransone[6] (gr. father of U. S. S. Math[w] Ransone), and Elizabeth Ransone[6], who m. William Plummer, son of Capt. William and Mary (Hayes) Plummer (Mrs. W. S. Stubbs, Aug., 1921; Wheeler's Rem's, p. 32). This Richard[3] (son of James[2]) remained in Gloucester and according to U. S. Census, 1783, had five in family in Ware Parish, one of whom no doubt was his wife.

Catherine Ransone m. 23 April, 1719, Joseph Hall, Gloucester Co., Va.

Augustine Ransone m. 18 April, 1753, *Catherine Hill*, Glo. Co., Va.

1750.—Richard Ransone, the younger (adm'r. of Peter) and George Ransone pl'ffs. vs. John Porrin, *Robt. Dudley*, and *Wm. Hayes* (Old Survey Book).

Armistead Ransone 118 A Cumberland Co., Va., 1757 (Cumb'd Ld. Bk.).

Ambrose Ransone, Cumberland Co., Va., Will 1761; pr. 1762. Children: Armistead, Robert, William, Henry, Lucy, Katherine and Jane.

Richard Ransone m. 21 March, 1771, Anne Whiting in Kingston Parish and had Mathew James Ransone, b. 1773. Ambrose and Richard were probably sons of Robert, captain of the "Thomas and John," 1707, who *may* have married Miss Armistead.

1783.—Living in Kingston Parish, 1783, were: Letitia Ransone, 1783, 5 whites, 12 blacks; Thomas Ransone, 1783, 5 whites, 6 blacks.

1791.—Thomas Ransone m. Margaret Groves in Kingston Parish and she was living there 1831.

1786.—Thos. Ransone, two slaves in Abingdon Parish and living in Abingdon Parish.

Thos. and Augustine Ransone, seamen U. S. Revy. Navy. Thos. Ransone, of Gloucester Co., Lt. in 2nd Va., Rev. Army, d. 1817. (Va. His. Mag. 1, p. 128).

1768.—Sale of Col. Bill Armistead's, dec'd., slaves, of New Kent, was conducted on *Mrs. Thomas Ransone's* plantation (Jamestown Book, 91; Va. Gazette, 1768).

1812.—Robt. Ransone and son, merchants in Gloucester Co., had a store account with *Geo. E. Dudley* and in 1821 John Ransone, as adm'r. of Robt. Ransone, obtained judgment on this account vs. Thos. Ransone as ex'r. of George E. Dudley. (W. & M. Q., X, 256).

1814.—Thos Ransone, ex'r. of will of Geo. E. Dudley, recorded in Middlesex Co., 9 May, 1814. *The Dudleys* had moved to Georgia.

1821.—John Ransone, 4th Sergeant, Capt. James Baytop's Gloucester Artillery company. *John Ransone m. Eliz., dau. of Isaac Singleton* and Rebecca Robins, dau. of Wm. Robins, of Glo. Co., Will 1784.

1786.—Richard Ransone, trustee of Charlestown, Berkeley Co. (Hemming, XII, 371).

1737.—James Ransone, Tobacco Inspector, Isle of Wight Co., *1737* (Va. Gazette 1737). Wm. Ransone, teacher in Augusta Co., Va. (Cheekley's Augusta Records).

Mathew Whitaker *Ranson* (Robert, Seymour), b. in Warren Co., N. C., Oct. 8,

1826 (Wheeler's Rem's, p. 32), m. Miss Exum, dau. of Joseph Exum, of Northampton Co., N. C. His mother was Priscilla Whitaker, descended from family of that name in Halifax Co.

2. Capt. George Ransone[2] (son of Peter[1]) will 1674; pr. 1675, was on a jury in Middlesex Co., 1673. Repatented, with his brother James[2], the 1100 A. above, in 1663, which was again surveyed in 1745, and of which a "George" then owned 350 A. (his nephew). He m. Margaret, widow of John Gore, and left only one child, a dau., Elizabeth Ransone, who was left 500 A. in her father's will, 1675. M. (I), 1691, Major Robt. Dudley, will 1701. Issue: Robert[4], George[4], Elizabeth[4] and Averilla Dudley[4]; m. (II), 1707, Robert Dudley, Jr. (cousin of Robt. above), will 1709; pr. 1710. Issue: Ransone Dudley[4]; m. (III), Thomas Elliott, d. 1716, issue: Margaret[4] and Elizabeth Elliott[4].

3. William Ransone[2] (son of Peter[1]) was apportioned 350 A. of the above 1100 A. in 1658, which by 1667 had 340 A. added (making 1440 A.). A survey of this tract was made in 1744 at the request of James and George Ransone. It is not known if he left issue, though the name William occurred later in Gloucester Co.

There was a survey in Ware Neck (north River side) Nov. 1, 1754, at the request of Mr. Richard Ransone, beginning at A, on North River and running thence to a corner of Benj. Boswell's land and contained 169 A., John Throckmorton, surveyor. (See W. & M. Qtly., X, pp. 142, 143, 264-'5, 266-'7; XIV, p. 129; XV, pp. 93-99, 123-'4; Survey Book at Gloucester C. H.; Va. Co. Rec'ds., Vol. IV, p. 77; Old Churches and Families, by Meade, Vol. I, p. 324).

Ann Ransone, Kingston Parish, Gloucester, now Mathews Co., m. 14 June, 1755, *Robert Billups*[4]. (W. & M. Qtly., X, pp. 266-'7; XV, p. 97).

It is highly probable, in fact *almost, if not quite certain,* that *Ann Ransone* was the dau. of either *Robert*[3], or *Peter* Ransone[3] (*both sons of Capt. James*[2], *son of Peter Ransone*[1]) as they remained in Kingston Parish of Mathews Co., while George Ransone[3] had a school in *Ware Parish* and James[3] and Richard Ransone[3] moved to Surry and Brunswick Counties. (For issue, see Excursus: Billups).

RICHARDSON.

General Richard Richardson was born in Virginia in 1704, was the son of Charles Richardson and his wife, Miss Burchell (?), became a surveyor, removed in 1725 to South Carolina, where he surveyed, got grants for, and settled on a large body of land, not taken up, extending from Tavern Creek to Jack's Creek, in what is now Clarendon County, bordering on the Swamp of the Sautee River. He died in St. Mark's Parish in September, 1780 or 1781. He was Captain in Vonderdusen's Regiment (Militia) 15 May, 1740; Member Commons House, Assembly, for Prince Frederick, 1754-1760, and Justice of the Peace, 1756; Colonel of Militia in 1757; Colonel, Craven Co. Regiment in Cherokee War, 1760 to 1761, and in the Revolutionary War, 1775; Member of Provincial Congress, 1775; made Brigadier General March 25, 1778. He was a man of high character and great influence, possessing the entire confidence of the people, and noted for his prudence, firmness, self-possession, engaging deportment and fine, commanding person; and in the absence of courts, was frequently chosen by the people of Craven County as judge and arbiter of their feuds, bickerings and dissensions, and so possessed an equity jurisdiction from the Sautee to the North Carolina boundary of the State, and they never left his hospitable home with an inclination to dispute his decisions. For his distinguished and efficient services in the Cherokee War of 1760-'61, he received a handsome silver service, as shown by the following: The South Carolina Gazette of the 25 Sept., 1762, informs us that "A very handsome service of plate was lately presented by the inhabitants of St. Mark's Parish to Col. Richard Richardson as a mark of their gratitude and esteem, and to show their sense of the many services he rendered to this Parish during the late unhappy Cherokee War, and to that Parish, in particular, on every occasion". He was in command of the Militia and Regulars in the famous "Snow Campaigns" against the Tories at Ninety Six, in the Winter of 1775. (C. R., N. C., Vol. 10, p. 340), where Col. Williamson was besieged by the Tory Insurgents, and quelled the revolt in December, 1775. For this service, the South Carolina Provincial Congress, on March 24, 1776, resolved to present their thanks to Col. Richardson "for the very important and signal services he has rendered to this country and to the common cause, by putting a stop to the late dangerous and alarming isurrection which the enemies of America had excited in the interior parts of the Colony". In 1775, Col. (later General) Richardson and Hon. Wm. H. Drayton were commissioned by the Committee of Safety to make progress through the back country to explain the causes of present dispute between England and the Colonies and to secure a general union of the people (Chronicles of St. Mark's Parh., p. 86). General Richard Richardson, with his son Richard (who became a Colonel) were on the Committee of his section of the country to decide what cases should be tried in the courts in the disturbed state of Society at the beginning of hostilities. (Ibid, p. 87). As a delegate to the first Provincial Congress, Jany. 11, 1775, assisted in framing the first Constitution of South Carolina, and was active in organizing the new administration in the first Constitutional Government established in the Revolution, Charleston, S. C., March 26, 1776, and was one of the Committee to carry into effect the Continental association. He assisted, with his command, in defeating Sir Peter Parker's fleet, June 28, 1776, and commanded the State Militia at Purrysburg, in December, 1778. The capitulation of Charleston, in 1780, by General Lincoln, made him a prisoner of war, and he was sent to St. Augustine; but soon, by reason of broken health, from the infirmities of age and a loathesome prison, was paroled and sent home. While a prisoner, he was offered by Lord Cornwallis titles and offices under the Crown, with the alternative of close confinement. He replied: "I have, from the very best convictions of my mind, embarked in a cause which I think righteous and just; I have knowingly and willingly staked my life, family and property, all, upon the issue; I am well prepared to suffer or triumph with it, and would rather die a thousand deaths than betray my country or deceive my friends". Being 76 years of age, the prison confinement proved fatal. He died very soon after reaching his home in Sumter district. Very shortly after his death his plantation was occupied by Col. Tarleton and his forces. Tarleton, with his own hand, applied the torch and burned the house; had Col. Richardson's body disinterred and left exposed until the entreaties of the family finally gained permission to reinter it. Whether this act was to make sure that he was dead, or to get possession of family plate suspected of being buried with the body, or from pure hellishness, is an open question. From General Richardson have descended five Governors of the State of South Carolina, viz.: His son, James Burchell Richardson; grandsons, Richard J. Manning and John Peter Richardson; great-grandsons, J. L. Manning and J. P. Richardson, Jr., a most creditable showing for his blood and character. (Lossing's Pictorial Field Book of Amern. Rev., Vol. 2, p. 444; Lamb's Bio. Dicty. of the U. S., Vol. VI, p. 472; Johnson's Traditions and Rems. of the Amn. Rev., pp. 158, 159, 160; Sims His. of S. C., Vol. IV., Chap. 3, p. 185, and Chap. IV, pp. 190, 192, 193, and Chap. V, p. 198; Drayton's Memoirs of Rev., Vol. II, Chap. 12, pp. 124 to 138; Ramsey's His. of the Rev., Vol. I, Chap. VII, Sec. 11, p. 146, and Vol. I, Chap. VII, Sec. 111, p. 149, and Sec. N1, p. 169; Internl. Cya., Vol. 12, p. 633; Amn. Cya., Vol. 14, p. 71; S. C. His. & G. Mag., Vol. XI, p. 225-6).

General Richard Richardson married (1), 11 Oct., 1736, Mary Cantey (Prince Frederick's Parh. Regr.), died 1767, daughter of William Cantey, of Craven County, who married before November, 1703, Arabella Oldys, daughter of Joseph Oldys, who was Deputy Secretary of the Province in 1688, and also Deputy Registrar. (S. C. His. Mag., Vol. 5, p. 227; Journal of Grand Council, 1671-1680, p. 13), but unknown whether she was the mother of his children or not.

William Cantey was the son of George and Martha Cantey He. Genl. Richard Richardson, married (II) Dorothy Sinkler.

Issue by first marriage, order of births not known to me: 1.—Col. Richard Richardson, Jr., born 4 March, 1741; baptized 17 June, 1742; died in 1818 (q. v.); 2.—Major Edward Richardson (Major in Revolutionary War), m. Rachel Heatley; 3.—A daughter, Susannah, married Capt. Lawrence Manning, of "Lighthorse Harry Lee's Legion"; 4.—A daughter, Rebecca, married John Singleton, 1752; 5.—Margaret m. Dr. Burgess; 6.—Martha, m. Col. William McDonald; 7.—Elizabeth Cantey, b. 1758.

Issue by 2nd marriage, 3 boys, eldest only 7 years old at time of Rev'y War: 6.—James Burchell Richardson; 7.—John Peter Richardson; 8.—Charles Richardson.

1. Col. Richard Richardson, Jr., 1741-1818. In Lyttleton's Campaign against the Cherokees, 1759-'60, he was a Lieutenant in Capt. Sammie Comley's Company; Captain of 1st and also Captain of 2nd Regiment of Riflemen in South Carolina, May, 1760 (Ramsey's His. of the Rev. in S. C., Vol. 1, p. 52); was in the Snow Campaign as Captain and second in command under his father in 1775. (Chronicles of St. Mark's Parish, p. 87). In 1776, like his father, he was one of the Committee to carry into effect the Continental Association and was commissioned Captain in the 2nd Regiment, under Colonel Sumter, and later became Major; was taken prisoner at Charleston and paroled; returning to service, joined General Marion, made Colonel, and at battle of Eutaw Springs commanded the right wing of Marion's Brigade; was a representative to the Jacksonburg Assembly of Jany., 1782, and a Member of the House of Representatives in March, 1783. (S. C. His. & Gen. Mag., Vol. XI, pp. 247-8, and footnotes; Rec. in office Hisl. Comn., Columbia, S. C.; Appn. Cya, Amn. Bio., Vol. V, p. 243; Lossing's Field Book of the Amn. Rev., Vol. 2, p. 444, and note; "Johnson's Traditions", pp. 158, 159 and 160; "Ramsey's His. of the Rev. in S. C.", Vol. I, p. 52, and Vol. 2, p. 93; "Lamb's Bio. Dicty. of the U. S.", Vol. VI, p. 472).

Col Richard Richardson, Jr., 1741-1818; married, in 1761, Dorcas Nelson, born 1741, died 1834; daughter of Captain John Nelson, of Nelson's Ferry, on the Sautee River, and . . . . . Brumson, his wife (Famous Women of the Rev., Vol. I, p. 88, or 263, by Mrs. C. F. Ellett). They had among others: Mary Richardson, born 10 November, 1763, died November, 1803, married 9 Oct., 1787, *William Billups*, born 4 September, 1763; died 19 Jany., 1817; son of Robert and Ann (Ransom) Billups. (For issue, see Excursus: Billups).

SHEPHERD.

Providence Prosperity Shepherd married *Ann Walker*, who d. in 1837 at age of 90 years (so born in 1747). They lived 18 miles from Wilmington, N. C., where Providence worked in the ship yard in which, it seems, he owned an interest. They moved first to Raleigh, N. C., and later, circa 1797, to the neighborhood of Athens, Ga., and Providence is buried at Beaver Dam Church. Their children were: 1. Susan Shepherd, m. ——, and had children before 1791; 2. Tom Shepherd, m. Miss Rainey; 3. Jack Shepherd, m. Miss Sanders; 4. Sarah Shepherd, m. —— Norris; 5. Mary Shepherd, m. —— Walace; 6. Elizabeth Shepherd, m. —— Nash; 7. RUTH SHEPHERD, b. 15 June, 1791; d. 22 Nov., 1872; m. (I) at Beaver Dam Church in Clarke Co., Ga., Walton (?) Johnson. Family tradition says his name was Robert Johnson and that for him she named her first son by her second marriage. M. (II) 9 Dec., 1821, in Jasper Co., Ga., ISAAC PURNELL HENDERSON, 1789-1864. (See Excursus: Henderson).

WALTON.

"The Waltons in England were noted people, scholarly and literary in taste, but not noted for energy and industry. In Lancashire, Eng., there are the townships "Walton-Le-Dale" and "Walton-on-the-Hill". Among the leading men of the family were Brian Walton and Isaac Walton. The former was Bishop Chester and author of the Great Polyglott Bible of London. He was b. in Yorkshire in 1600 and d. 29 Nov., 1661. He was noted for his great learning. Hallom, in his history of the literature of Europe, makes favorable reference to this gentleman.

Isaac Walton was b. in Stafford, Eng., in Aug., 1593, and was the son of Jervis Walton. He lived rather an humble and quiet life, but was noted for his writings and noble character". ("The Winborns of Old", pp. 34-'5, by B. B. Winborn).

"In Oct., 1659, Col. Walton, with other military commanders, adopting the views of Monk, occupied with regiments the important town of Portsmouth [Eng.] on Dec. 4; their object being to restore the old Long Parliament, called the Rump, which was forcibly dissolved by Cromwell April 29, 1653". (N. E. H. & G., Reg. Vol. 30, p. 74).

1621. *John Walton* in the "Elizabeth", *aged 28, 1621*, "Muster Roll of Settlers in Va., 1624, Alex. Mourning, his muster". ("Hotten's Immigrants", p. 257).

1633-35. The Rev. William Walton, of Seaton, Devonshire, Eng., came to America between 1632 and '35, and settled in Mass. The births of seven of his children, 1627 to 1644, are given in the Essex Court files at Salem, in Vol. 1, p. 69. (N. E. H. & G. Reg., Vol. 29, p. 66).

He was b. circa 1600; d. 1668 (N. Y. Town Topics, Oct. 21, 1915). Doubtless some of his descendants drifted to the West and South, but the writer has discovered no records connecting them directly with the Waltons of Md. and Virginia.

1653. In Westmoreland Co., Va., on Feby. 20, 1653, John Knott makes an assignment to John Walton, and on Aug. 21, 1654, John Walton assigns this patent to John Pymly. (Westmoreland Co., Va., Rec. Book. 1, p. 1).

1654. John Walton and John Bagnall received land grants in Westmoreland Co., Va., in 1654. (Westmoreland Co., Va., records, p. 89).

1673. Isaac Burge, Kent Co., Md., in will dated 9 Oct., 1673; pr. 2 May, 1674, devises 50 A. part of Ship Point to Mary Walton, dau. of John and Jane Walton, to Eliza Walton personalty and names John Walton as Exr., and residuary legatee. (Md. Cal. of Willis, Vol. 1, p. 80).

1673-'4. John Walton, in York Co., with son Richard, 1673-4, when Chris. Colley made will leaving cow and calf to the son Richard. (Gulf States Mag., Vol. 2, pp. 116-118).

1682. Robert Walton[1] emigrated from England in 1682 with Wm. Penn. His son Robert[2] of Prince Edward Co. Va., m. Frances . . . . . . Issue: 1.—Robert[3], b. 7 Jany., 1717-'18; 2.—Rebecca[3], b. 20 April, 1720; 3.—Joseph[3], b. 21 April, 1721-'2; 4.—George[3], b. 6 Feby., 1724-'5: 5.—Sherwood[3], b. 10 July, 1728.

1. *Robert Walton*[3], m. Sally Hughes, dau. of Jesse Hughes, a French Hugenot from France to Va., who lived on Hughes Creek, on James River, above Richmond, and Sally Tarlton, of English birth.

Issue: 1.—George[4], b. 1749; d. 1804; 2.—Sally[4]; 3.— Robert[4], m. . . . ., Miss Carter, of Va.; 4.—John[4]. This 1.—George Walton[4] was the signer of the Declaration of Independence from Georgia. He, with his brothers Robert and John, removed to Georgia before or during the Revolution and were active participants in the patriots' cause.

1. George Walton[4] was Colonel in Revy. War, wounded and taken prisoner; was Governor and elected 6 times to Congress; was Chief Justice and also Trustee of the U. of Ga. at time of his death at his country seat "Meadow Garden" near Augusta, Ga., in 1804. He m. Dorothy Camber, circa or a. 1775; dau. of an English nobleman. She d. at Pensacola, Fla., in Sept., 1832, at the home of her son George Walton, who held the office of Sec. of State under Genl. Jackson, when the latter was Govr. of the Territory of West Fla. She is buried in St. Michael's Churchyard, her tomb bearing the following inscription: "Died in Pensacola, Sept. 12, 1832, Mrs. Dorothy Walton, a native of the State of Ga., a Matron of the Revolution, Consort and Relict of George Walton, a signer of the Declaration of American Independence". (L. M. & L., pp. 101, 1004 of Vol. 1, by Knight; Harris Geanealogy, pp. 102-'3, by Gideon Dowse Harris; Reg. of St. Peters Parish of New Kent Co., Va.—indexed).

4. *John Walton*[4], bro. of the signer, and son of Robert and Sally (Hughes) Walton, m. Elizabeth Claiborne, was, with his bro. George, a member of the Provincial Congress at Savannah, Ga., 4 July, 1775. John Walton styled one of the famous quartette of Liberty, Noble Wimberly Jones, Archibald Bulloch and John Houston being the other three. (L. M. & L., Vol. 2, pp. 642-'3 & 638, by Knight). His will June 11, 1778; p. . . . , 1783. ("Amn. Monthly Mag.", 27, pp. 288-'9).

4. *George Walton*[3], son of Robert and Frances Walton, m. Martha Hughes, dau. of Jesse and Sally (Tarlton) Hughes. Issue: Mary, baptized 8br 23, 1711; 2.—Ann 7br ye 13, 1713; 3.—Jane . . . 1715; 4.—George[4], b. 19 May, 1726; d. *will in Brunswick Co., Va., dated July 7, 1764; rd Jany. 26, 1767; (m. Elizabeth Scott). "To son John, dau. Mary Ledbetter, wife Elizabeth Walton, one shilling to Adam Timms (or Simms), dau. Catherine Harris". [m. 1737, Nathan Harris], son Isaac Row Walton. (Book 3, p. 412; Harris Genealogy, pp. 14, 15, 16).

This 4.—George[4], last named, was double first cousin of George the Signer. Elizabeth Walton, the widow's will dated Feby. 12, 1771; rd 24 July, 1775—named her Timmins grandchn.. Isaac Row Walton's chn., and my three now surviving children John Walton, Mary Ledbetter and Catharine Harris. (Harris Genealogy, pp. 16, 17).

1702. Siges John, Richmond Co., Va. *Will*, 21 Aug., 1702; 2 June, 1703. To

Sam Walton; *John* and *Thomas Walton;* to my children; my wife to be Exx. Wit.: John Key, Sam¹ Walton, *John Walton* and Mary Powell. (Va. Co. Rec., Vol. 7, p. 58).

I have not seen the full text of this record, but it seems to me not improbable that the Thomas Walton above named may have been the Thomas of King & Queen Co., who d. in Chowan Co., in 1719.

1716. John Walton, Somerset Co., Md., Will May, 1716; Feby. 5, 1716-'17. Eldest son John, son William. Should either of s'd sons John or Wm. die without issue, their share to pass to survivor, not to sell until 3rd generation, except to each other. Eldest dau. Elizabeth, daus. Sarah, Rebecca and Mary and youngest dau. Hannah. Sons of age at 18 years., daus. at 16. Wife Exx. Test.: Richd Holland, John Holland, Wm. Walton. (Md. Cal. of Wills 4, p. 105-'6).

WALTONS OF I. OF W. CO., VA.

1678. John Walton is named as one of the witnesses to the marriage of John Munon to Elizabeth Ganal on 22nd day of ye 6 month in ye year 1678 in I. of W. Co. ("Early His. of the Quaker Society of Nansemond Co.", p. 98, in MS. in Clerk's office at Suffolk, Nansemond Co.).

1698. *John Walton* named as due Estate of Thos. Proud 668 lbs. of tobacco, July 15, 1698. As Thos. Proud was a teacher, this account was probably due as tuition for a son of John Walton. (W. & M. Qll., Vol. VII p. 250).

1705. John Walton, I. of W. Co., Va., *Will,* 16 Aug. 1705; Rd 9 Nov., 1705. (Book 1661-1719—No. 2, p. 471). To Judith Williams one feather bed, bolster, blankets and Rug, one cow with calf to be delivered the day of her marriage, and 1000 lbs. of tobacco. Likewise I give unto Eliza Watts 1000 lbs. of Tob. and a cow and calf to be delivered the day of her marriage. My land I give wholly to my son *Thomas Walton* after his mother's decease. My loving wife Mary. Wife Executrix. My desire is that Mr. *Henry Baker assist* her, to him 5 £ Sterling. If my son Thomas should chance to dye (which ye Lord forbid) then I leave my plantation to my Cousin Jno. Hill, of Stafford, in Lincolnshire. (Signed) John Walton.

Wit.: Wm. Clark, Senior, Wm. Clark, Junior, Susanna Jordan, Mary X Clark, Wm. Wilson. Recd Nov. 9, 1705.

Book 1704-1715, p. 189. *Power of Atty., 1711.* Know all men by these presents, that I *Thomas Walton,* of the Upper Parish of the County of the Isle of Wight, have assigned, ordained and made in my stead and place put by these presents and constitute my trusty and *well beloved Friends Mrs. Mary Walton,* Col. Henry Baker, and Capt. Nathaniel Ridley, all of the aforesaid Upper Parish in the afsd. County of the Isle of Wight, Joyntly and severally to be my true and lawful attorneys, or attorney, either in *my own capacity* or as I am *administrator* of *Kathine Walton my late deceased Wife* for me and in my name, etc., etc. . . . July 6, 1711.

Wit.: H. Lightfoot. (Signed) *Thomas Walton*

July 23, 1711. *Thomas Walton, Gent.,* came into Court and acknowledged the above Power of Atty. to be his and it is admitted to Record.

H. Lightfoot, Clk. Ct.

1717. Thomas Walton made *Sheriff* for Isle of Wight County for 1717. (Va. Mag. H. & B., Vol. 17, p. 154).

1722. Thomas Walton and William Kinchen Signed as Church Wardens June 25, 1722, in Church Matters of Nansemond County. Wit.: John Worden, William Moore (or Moss?), William Kinchen. (Isle of Wight Book 2, p. 474).

1724. "Vestry of the Upper Parish, *5 June, 1724.* Present, Mr. Alexander Forbes, William Bridges, *Thomas Walton,* James Day, Lawrence Baker, George Riddick, Mathew Wills, Reuben Proctor, Samuel Davis.

July ye 13, 1724. Mr. Alexander Forbes, Minister, Capt. James Day, Mr. *Thomas Walton,* Mr. Wm. Kinchen, Mr. Willm Crumple, Mr. Mathew Wills, Mr. Lawrence Baker, Mr. Samuel Davis, *Church Wardens".* (W. & M. Qly., VII, p. 268).

1730. John Brantley, in will Mch. 22, 1730, leaves a Gold Ring to his friend *Thomas Walton..* Wit.: *Thomas Walton, Elizabeth Walton (his wife).* (I. of W. Bk. 3, p. 248).

1738. Thomas Walton, of I. of W. Co., sells on Oct. 23, 1738, a water mill to

Arthur Smith, of Surrey Co., for 30 £. Wit.: Thomas Brewer, Thos. Applewhite. (Deed Book 5, p. 280).

1742. Appraisement of the Estate of Thomas Walton, *Gent.*, May 24, 1742. 353 £. Chas. Portlock, Admr. N. Bourden, John Goodrich, John Davis. [It does not say what these three did—were probably appraisers]. Estate included two flutes and one violin. (I. of W. Book 4, p. 411).

1754. Appraisement of the Estate of *Thomas Walton, July 4, 1754.* John Hyntman, Joel Thomas, George Wilson. (I. of W. Will Bk. 6, p. 105).

1741. *Catherine Walton* receives *Gift from Elizabeth Walton,* July 10, 1741. (I. of W. Book 6, 9, 97). [This Elizabeth pro. wife of Thos. Walton, whose estate was appraised in 1754. See above and 1730, John Brantley.]

We see from foregoing records that John Walton, of Isle of Wight, 1678 and 1705, with *wife Mary,* had an only son Thomas Walton and *friend Henry Baker.* In 1711 a Thomas Walton, Gent., with deceased wife Katherine, gives power of atty. to his trusty and well beloved *Friends Mrs. Mary Walton, Col. Henry Baker* and Capt. Nathaniel Ridley. Surely *Mrs. Mary Walton was not his mother* and he not the son of *John and Mary Walton.*

In 1717, Thomas Walton made Sheriff,—probably, and quite certainly, the Thomas, Gent., above, as Thos. son of John, was hardly old enough to fill said office. In 1722 & '24, Thos. Walton, probably the Thos., Gent., Vestryman and Church Warden. In 1730, Thos., with wife Elizabeth, probably son of John and Mary Walton. In 1742, appraisement of Estate of *Thos. Walton, Gent.,*—as no sons are named in this record, as given to me, he very probably had none, at least of age, at the time of his death. In 1754, we have another appraisement of the Estate of Thomas Walton. In this record, as furnished me, no sons are named. He was, probably, the son of John and Mary Walton.

Where, then, is to be found record of the migration of a *Thos. Walton* from I. of W. Co., Va., to Chowan Co., N. C.? There may be such, but the writer has not been made cognizant of it.

WALTONS OF CHOWAN CO. N. C. Office of Secretary of State of N. C.

Thomas Walton. In the Name of God, Amen. I Thomas Walton, of Chowan of ye Province of North Carolina, being of perfect health both of body and mind but considering ye great uncertainty of human life have made this my last Will and Testament, declaring this only to be my last will and testament, in manner and as followeth.

Imprimis. I do in all humility bequeath my soul unto Almighty God that gave it, and my body to ye grave decently to be Intered and in relation to my worldly Estate I give and bequeath in manner and form as followeth:

Item. I give and bequeath after my Death unto my beloved *wife Ann Walton* of King and Queen county in ye Parish of Tatsie in ye Province of Virginia one equal share of all debts and money that shall prove due to me in North Carolina aforesaid, with my seven children viz.: Three sons and four Daughters all living in ye sd Parish of Tatsie. That is to say I give unto ye sd Anne and bequeath unto my sd Children one eight part of all money whatsoever proven to be mine unto them and their heirs forever.

Item. I give and bequeath unto my beloved wife Anne aforesaid and my seven children all and every part of my estate both personall and reall including all moneys Bonds bills book Debts or Claims of what so ever that are or shall become due to me ye sd *Thomas Walton* all wch. aforesd I freely give and bequeath unto my beloved Wife and Children and their Heirs forever I as large and ample a manner to all intents and purposes as if they in actuall possession of all ye premises afforesd.

Lastly. I doe appoint my true friend *John Plowman* Executor of this my last will and testament *Impowering them* to Act jointly or severally as ocation requires for ye good and wellfare of my sd Wife and Children and to the Confirmation thereof have hereunto set my hand and seal this *8th day of May* Anno Domini *1719.*

Thomas Walton.

Sealed and Delivd in presence And: Cockburn, John White, Mary White. June ye 8: 1719. Proved before ye Governour. Letters granted June 21, 1719. Charles Eden Governor of Province.

1727. Wm. Jones, of Perquinon to Abraham Hill of Nansemond Co., Va., 640 A. in Bear Swamp, assignment of patent dated Nov. 27, 1727. Deed dated *Dec. 15 1727.* Test.: *Richard Bond, Thomas Walton,* Wm. Havield. (N. C. H. & G. Reg. 2-3-445).

1728. Wm. Jones to *Thomas Walton,* 50 A. adjg. Orlando Champion's land, *Dec. 16, 1728.* Test. Robt. Hicks. (N. C. H. & G. Reg. 2-3-444).

1731. *William Walton* to *Timothy Walton,* Tract of land bought of Judah Speight, Judah husband of Frances Speight, 7ber 18, 1731 Test. *Thomas Walton,* Aaron Blanchard. (N. C. H. & G. Reg. 3-1-131).

1734. Geo. Spivey, son of Abraham Spivey, to *Thomas Walton, Jr.,* 100 A. on Catharine Creek, North East side, *4 Dec. 1734.* Test.: Benj. Spivey, Wm. Trevathon. (N. C. H. & G. Reg. 1-1-108 and 3-1-128).

1737. William Walton, Guardian of Henry Bond. 1737. (N. C. H. & G Reg. 1-3-448).

1735. *Thomas Walton,* Chowan Co., N. C., paid arrears of Quit Rent on 600 A., account of the receipt of one-half of the arrears of His Majesty's Quit Rent for Albemarle Co. (viz.) from 29 Sept., 1729, to March, 1732, computed at the Difference of 7 for 1 pound sterling in the currency of this Province, *12 June, 1735.* (S. R. N. C., Vol. 22, p. 241 et seq. & p. 258).

1735. William Baird, of *Nansemond Co., Va.,* to *John Walton, Jr.,* 100 A. on Hemby's Branch; *July 9, 1735.* Test.: John Walters, Wm. Walters, Richard Taylor. (N. C. H. & G. Reg. 3-1-129).

1735. To all to whom these presents shall come I *Thomas Walton, Junr.,* of Chowan Precinct in the County of Albemarle and Province afsd, send Greeting, &c. Know ye yt I ye sd *Thos. Walton,* for and in consideration of my tender Love and affection I bear to *my Brother William Walton son of Wm. Walton of ye County and Precinct* in ye Province aforesd [Note.—No intimation of his being deceased.— L. J. H.] the receipt whereof is hereby acknowledged, have given unto my loving Brother Wm. Walton and his Heirs etc. a certain plantation lying in Chowan precinct afsd. containing 100 A. being part of patent granted to John Keaton, Junr., of the County of *Nansemond* Dated ye 28th Day of October, 1702, bounded as follows: On a Branch of Meherrin Swamp called *Stafford's* and joining Thos. Walton's line. *Nov. 9th, 1735.* *Thomas Walton.*

Witnesses: John Walton, Benjamin Spivey, Wm. Trevathan. Rec. Jany. 17, 1735. W. Smith, Clerk Ct. (Book W, p. 272, Edenton, N. C.; N. C. H. & G. Reg. 1-1-108 and 3-1-128).

The abstract of above as published in the N C H. & G. Reg. 1-1-108, reads as follows, viz.: "*Thomas Walton, Jr.,* to my bro. William Walton, *before the sealing* and *delivery* hereof *by Wm.* Walton, *son of William,* etc."

In "Winbornes of Old", the author, Mr. B. B. Winborne says: "*Thos. Walton, Jr.,* was son of William Walton who d. in 1732", but gives no reference to support the claim.

Why should Thomas Walton, Jr., say, "to my *brother William, son of William*"? Does it not show that this brother William *was his half brother*, son of his mother by a different father? Again, if Thomas was the son of William who died in 1732, would he not here, in 1735, have said, William son of William, DECEASED? Or if Thomas and William—the brothers—were both sons of William, decd., would he—Thomas—not have said, "I Thomas Walton, Jr., *son of William, decd., to my brother* William"? Again, in the abstract above, as we find it given in the N. C. H. & G. Reg. 1-1-108, what means the phrase, "before the sealing and delivery hereof BY William Walton, son of William"? The deed of Gift, the conveyance is by Thomas Walton, Jr. HE *executes, seals and delivers it.* What is sealed and delivered by William Walton? It can have but one meaning, viz., that an agreement of some kind was executed, or entered into, by William Walton, the son of William, before Thomas consummated by delivery his deed of Gift to his brother.

It is true that Thomas Walton. Sr., in his will does not mention *a son* Thomas, but wills are usually very incomplete documents. Testators do not always mention all their children; no list of one's children can be made from them with safety, and no will *proves* the *non-existence* of a child not named in it. The stereotyped phrase "sick and weak of body, but of sound and disposing mind and perfect memory", in wills, is a legal fiction and seldom expresses the real truth. It is not conceivable that one in extremis or seriously ill should retain and exercise the full power of his memory as when in health and be able to enumerate correctly and fully all his possessions and all of his relations.

John Hunter, Chowan, will Dec. 1, 1771, names Wife Ala, *son William, son John, dau. Mary.* (N. C. H. & G. Reg. 1-4-548). He omits name of his son Theophilus.

Alie Hunter, widow of John, Gates Co., will April 12, 1781; Aug. Ct., 1781, names sons, Wm., *Theophilus* and John, dau. Mary. (N. C. H. & G. Reg. 2-1-51-'2).

"John McKinnie, Edgecombe, will 28 Feby., *1753*, names son Barnaby, daus. Mary, Patience and Martha, dau. Angelina Parish, child in esse, wife Mary", etc. (Reg. 1-345). He does not name son *John.*

Mary McKinnie, widow of John, Edgecombe, will 13 Oct., *1754*, names dau. Angeliny Pope, *sons* JOHN and Barnaby, daus. Mary, Patience and Martha. Barnaby Pope, Exr., etc." *Here she names a son John*—omitted in will of her husband. ("Abstract of N. C. Wills", p. 233, by Grimes).

In like manner, Joseph Lane, will 1773, omits name of his son John.

The above 3 instances, at the moment, occur to me where testators omitted the name of a son in their wills. Furthermore, we know that "Junior" affixed to a name—in the absence of explanation, qualifying word or phrase—denotes *the namesake* of a father, and that *Senior* denotes the *father* of *a namesake,* and that they must be so construed save in exceptional or explained cases.

So, notwithstanding, Thos. Walton, Sr., in 1750, does not name in his will a son, Thomas, and despite the peculiar wording of the deed of Gift by Thos. Jr., in 1735, *I feel assured that Thomas Walton, Jr., was the son of Thomas Walton, Sr.*

1730. *Francis Rountree,* will Sept. 30, 1730; June 27, 1734. Sons, Francis, William, Jesse, Jethro, Moses and John. Wife; daus. Jane, Rebecca, Susanna, Sarah, Elizabeth and *Christian.* (Reg. 1-1-70).

1714. William Copeland and wife Christian to Peter Parker, our son-in-law and heirs of my dau. Grace, wife of said Parker, 200 A. on south side Sandy Run Swamp; July 17, 1714. (Reg. 1-1-104); 2-3-456).

1720. *William Copeland,* Chowan, Oct. 3, 1720. Sons, William, John, James and Charles; *daus. Christian* and *Sarah; Wife Christian* Exx. Test.: John Cordain, George Turnedge, Elizabeth Turnedge. (Reg. 1-2-189).

It seems highly probable that Thomas Walton, Jr., m., 1735 or '36, Sarah, dau. of Francis Rountree. (Will 1730-34, as above).

1736. I John Glover of the Precinct of Bertie, 350£ Bills of this Province, to *Thos. Walton, Jr.,* of Chowan, 278 A. adjoining land of Thom. Ward (or Ware), *March 24, 1736.*
                                                   John Glover
                                                   Mary X Glover.

Wit.: Caleb Stephen, Wm. Jersey (?). (Book D, p. 280).

1736. Thomas Walton, Jr., of Chowan, to Thos. Hansford, of Bertie, 270 A. land in Bertie which was lately conveyed to sd Walton by John Glover and Mary his wife, 400 £ current money of N. C., *Nov. 9, 1736.*
                                       Thomas Walton.
                             Sarah Walton, wife of Thomas Walton,
                             relinquishes dower.

Wit.: John Wynns, Thos. Creer. (Book E, p. 45).

1737. Thomas Walton, Junior, of Chowan Precinct, planter, sold, Oct. 28, 1737, 100 A. in Bertie, to Abraham Spivey, Cooper, 20£.   *Thomas Walton*
                                                      Sarah Walton

Wit.: James Baker, William Poynter. (Book E, p. 285).

1739-40. *Wm. Walton, Wm. Walton, JR., and Thomas Walton,* 25 Feby., 1739-40, placed on list of Jurymen for Chowan Co. (C. R. N. C., Vol. 4, pp. 516, 517).

1740. *Thomas Walton,* elected 27 Feby., 1740, as a Member of the General Assembly of N. C. for Chowan Co. (C. R. N. C., Vol. IV, pp. 493-'99, 506).

"Thomas Walton, Sr., was the author of the bill to build a jail and Courthouse for Chowan Co. and secured its passage while he was a member of the Colonial Assembly from Chowan in 1740." ("Winbornes of Old"; C. R. N. C., Vol. IV, p. 740(?).

1740. The Freemen of Chowan Co. did meet at the Court House *(Easter Mon-*

day, April 7, 1740) and chose Benj. Talbot as Clerk for taking the poll for Vestryman and there and then did elect and choose for Vestrymen the fol'g persons, to wit, viz.: John Bount, John Sumner, Demsey Sumner, Richard Parker, *Thomas Walton,* John Benbury, Jacob Butler, Wm. Skinner, *Isaac Hunter,* Wm. Speight, Edward Hare, Richard Bond. All met, except Richard Bond, at the Court House in Edenton and qualived by taking the public oath. Mr. Jacob Butler and Demsey Sumner elected Church Wardens for the ensuing year. (N. C. H. & G. Reg. 1-4-603).

1742. *Thomas Walton,* 1742, made out he has 4 whites in his family. (N. C. H. & G. Reg. 1-3-447).

1742. *William Walton* from the Commissioners of Edenton, March 25, 1742, Lots Nos. 45 and 46, new plan of the town. (N. C. H & G. Reg. 1-1-131).

1743. Thomas Walton 700 A., Chowan, 16 Nov., 1743. (C. R. N. C., Vol. IV, p. 642).

1744. At a Vestry held at Edenton, Feby. 25, *1744,* Present, Mr. Wm. Haskins, Mr. John Benbury, Mr. *William Walton,* Mr. *Isaac Hunter,* and Mr. John Wilkins *Church Wardens.*

Ordered that the Rev. Clement Hall be allowed 60 £ Proclamation money per annum for officiating two Sundays in three at Edenton and the next Sunday at one of the Chappels above, and to preach every Monday at *Thomas Walton Junior's* at *Katharine Creek* that he preaches at the Knotty Pine Chapel on the Sunday. (N. C. H. & G. Reg. 1-4-604).

1745. *Thomas Walton, Jr.* to *John Hinton,* son of James Hinton, 27 April, *1745,* 150 A. in the *Indian Neck* on Catharine Creek. Test.: James Willson, Davenport Gooding. (N. C. H. & G. Reg. 1-1-118).

1746. Thos. Rountree, Sr., of Chowan, *Will,* Dec. 1, 1746, July Ct., 1748. Sons *Chas.* and *Thos.;* gr. sons *Wm. Wallis* and Thos. Rountree (son of Thos. & Mary), Son-in-law Elias Stallings and wife Elizabeth, my dau., their chn. Jacob, Elias, John & Eliz.; *Wife Elizabeth,* Chas. and Thos. Rountree Exrs. Test.: *Thomas Walton,* John Freeman. (N. C. H. & G. Reg. 1-3-374).

1750. *Thomas Walton,* John Sumner, Dempsey Sumner and Richard Bond were appointed Justices of the Peace, July 10, 1750, for Chowan Co. (C. R. N. C., Vol. IV, p. 1046; N. C. H. & G. Reg. 2-2-296).

1750. Thos. *Wallis,* Chowan, *Will,* Oct. 20, 1750; Jany. Ct., 1750-1, Sons *Wm.,* Jonathan and John, daus. Elizh, *Judith,* Mary and Susannah, Wife Elizabeth. Test.: *Thos. Walton, Timothy Walton.* (N. C. H. & G. Reg. 1-4-505).

1750. "Thomas Walton, Sr., Chowan, Will, Nov. 12, 1750; July 5, 1751. Gr. son Thomas Walton, son William, daus. Sarah Perry, Susanna Walton, Elizabeth Trotman, Judith Rountree and Ann Hunter. Son William Exr. Test.: Wm. Walton, Hardy Hunter, *Timothy Walton.* (N. C. H. & G. Reg. 1-4-512)".

Susanna Walton m., 6 Sept., 1753, Amos Hinton (Reg. 1-2-239). Elizabeth Walton m. Edward Trotman (Reg. 2-1-30). Judith Walton m. Charles Rountree (Reg. 2-1-19). Ann Walton m. Elisha Hunter (Reg. 1-1-47; 2-2-263). In "Winhornes of Old", p. 24, by B. B. Winborne, the author says that the *wife of Thomas Walton, Sr., was named Sarah*—her maiden name not learned. [No reference given].

1751. Thomas Walton admr. of Daniel Colly, decd. 1751. (N. C. H. & G. Reg. 1-3-451). [This must be Thos. Walton, Jr., as Thos., Sr., d. 1750-'51].

1752. William Walton m. (date not given) *Rachel,* dau. of *Isaac Hunter.* (I. H.'s will April 17, 1752; W. W.'s will *Nov. 20, 1771; Reg. 1-1-47; 2-1-33; 2-2-263).*

1755. *Timothy Walton* took his seat in the Ass'bly of N. C., Sept. 26, 1755. Ass'bly begun and held at Newberne, 12 Dec., 1754, & cont'd by prorogations to 25 Sept., 1755, being 2nd Session of present Assbly. (C. R. N. C., Vol. V, pp. 520, 522); adjourned to 30 Sept., 1756. (Ibid, p. 658).

1756. Abraham Hill m. Katherine [ERROR, should be CHRISTIAN] Walton, Jany. 7, 1756. Surety, Thomas Walton. (N. C. H. & G. Reg. 1-2-239; 1-3-463; 2-2-310).

1757. Deed of Gift from *Thos. Walton* to his *son- in-law Abraham Hill, Jr.,* and *wife Christian* (MY DAUGHTER), Aug. 3, *1757.* Test. *Chas. Rountree,* Hardy Hunter, *Thos. Rountree.* (N. C. H. & G. Reg. 2-1-159; 2-3-473-'4).

1757. Thomas Walton, 19 May, 1757, took his seat as a member of the House (Colonial General Assembly) from Chowan Co.—Assembly held at Newberne. (C. R. N. C., Vol. V, pp. 847-868); 27 May, 1757, *"Allowance due and payable to*

Thomas Walton—and other Members of the Assembly—this 4th session held at Newberne". (Ibid Vol. V, p. 868). This would seem to indicate that Thos. Walton was a member of the Ass'bly prior to May 1757.

1758. *Thos. Walton* in General Assembly of N. C., Dec. 14, 1758. (C. R. N. C., Vol. V, pp. 1026-'29-'32, and 1071-'6-'7).

1758. Nathaniel Spivey's will, Chowan, 1758, is attested by Thos. Rountree, Elijah Spivey and *Richard Walton* (N. C. H. & G. Reg. 2-1-24).

1759. *Timothy Walton*, 16 May, 1759, accepted office of Inspector for Chowan Co., thereby vacating his seat in the House. (C. R. N. C., Vol. VI, p. 138).

1759. *Timothy Walton, Guardian of Robert Walton, orphan* of *John Walton*, 1759. (N. C. H. & G. Reg. 1-3-456).

1758. *Zilpha* Walton adm'd Estate of *deceased husband John* Walton [pro. circa 1758]. Date not given. (N. C. H. & G. Reg. 1-3-452).

1759. *Sarah Walton*, widow and guardian of *John* Walton, orphan of *Thomas Walton, deceased*, 1759. (N. C. H. & G. Reg. 1-3-456).

1761. *Sarah Walton*, widow, Chowan, will June 23, 1761, Son Richard, dau. Christian Hill, dau. Sarah, Sons, *Thomas*, William and John. Sons, *Thomas* and *John* Walton, Exrs. Test.: Kesiah Taylor, Richard Garrett. (N. C. H. & G. Reg. 2-1-33).

1762. *Mrs. Sarah Walton*, 1762 (Division of Estates). William and John Walton. (N. C. H. & G. Reg. 2-2-272).

1760. William and Timothy Walton, members of Vestry, Chowan Co., 10 April, 1760,—other members were Demsey Sumner, *Josiah Granberry*, Richard Bond, *Jacob Hunter, John Gordon*, Luke Sumner and *Jethro Benton*. (N. C. H. & G. Reg. 1-3-456).

1760. *William Walton*, Chowan, Will, Dec. 24, 1760. Sons Palatiah, Henry and Edmund, daus. Mary Walton, Martha (Mathew?) Hobbs, Judah Perry and *Sarah Blanchard*, dau. Elizabeth Walton; sons *Richard* and *Thomas*, son Henry and *Capt. Wm. Walton* Exrs. Test.: *Josiah Granberry*, John Hunter, Wm. Walton. (N. C. H. & G. Reg. 2-1-33).

1760. Rountree, Charles, Chowan, Will Oct. 7, 1760. *Eldest son Thomas, son* Charles, daus. *Christian* and Rachel, gr. sons Cador Hunter and Chas. Freeman, *Wife Judith* [dau. of *Thos. Walton, Sr.,* decd.], sons *Chas.* & *Thos. Exrs.* Test. James Sumner, *Thos. Rountree*, Amos Hobbs. (N. C. H. & G. Reg., 2-1-19).

1762. Absolom Alphin, Chowan, Will, Jany. 6, 1762. Friend *William Walton* Exr., Sarah Bendall my Estate. Test.: Aaron Blanchard, *Robert Walton, Timothy Walton*. (N. C. H. & G. Reg. 1-4-516).

1762. George Gordon, Chowan, Will Feby. 17, 1762. Son Josiah, bro. *John Gordon*, Plantation in Perquimons my father willed me, Wife Edith, my seven chn. Josiah, John, George, Priscilla, Susan, Elizabeth Gordon, and Sarah Hinton, Sons Josiah and John Exrs. Test.: *James Hinton, Timothy Walton*. (N. C. H. & G. Reg. 1-4-546-'7).

1762. Benjamin Blanchard, Chowan, will April 3, 1762. Son Uriah plantation in Duplin Co. whereon he now lives, son Robin land in Hertford Co., son Absolom, son Robert, daus. Christian Hinton and Judith Hinton, wife Sarah Blanchard [nee Hinton?—v. below], daus. Eliz. Bethune, Milicent and Absole, son Robert and *William Hinton, Sr.*, Exrs. Test.: James Blanchard, *Timothy Walton* (now Gates Co.). (N. C. H. & G. Reg., 1-4-524).

Sarah Blanchard was probably dau. of Wm. Walton, will 1760, above given.

1763. *William Walton*, 22 Jany., 1763, 341 A. on *Stafford's* Branch. (Bk. XI, p. 105; N. C. H. & G. Reg. 1-1-21). Thos. Walton, Jr., in 1735, made deed of Gift to his bro. Wm. Walton, of 100 A. on Stafford's Branch

1764. George Walton m., 1764, Miss Sarah Earles, Perquimons. (N. C. H. & G. Reg. 3-3-413).

1764. George Dawkins, Edenton, will Feby. 27, 1764; Mch. Term, 1764. Wife Elizabeth, bro. John Dawkins, sister Ruth Dawkins, Wife, *Samuel Swift* and Joseph Blount Exrs. Test.: Fred Blount, *John Walton, Thos. Blount*. (N. C. H. & G. Reg. 1-4-540).

1764. Micajah Blanchard, Chowan, Will, Oct. 2, 1764. Sons Wm., Micajah and Abner, Wife Elizabeth, daus. Mary, Elizabeth and *Christian* Blanchard. Wife and

Jacob Hinton Exrs. Test.: *Timothy Walton, Aaron Blanchard*. (N. C. H. & G. Reg. 1-4-525).

Aaron Blanchard, Sr., d. 1751—Zilpha, the widow, admd. Estate and was guardian of his chn., viz.: Rachel, Monica, Aaron and Moses. (Reg. 1-3-451).

1766. Samuel Benberry, Chowan, Will Oct. 23, 1766; April Ct., 1768. My Father, my Wife, my bros. and sisters. Thos. Benbury and *Timothy Walton*, Exrs. Test.: Chas. Benbury, Ruth Benbury, John Benbury. (N. C. H. & G. Reg. 1-4-518).

1767. Samuel Swift, John Benbury, *Timothy Walton, William Walton, Jacob Walton*, and Wm. Hinton met and took the oath, Repeated and subscribed the Test for Vestrymen on May 20, 1776 [obviously an error in date]. Elisha Hunter, Richd. Brownrig, Saml. Johnson and Jas. Sumner qualified. Saml. Swift and *Jacob Hunter* were elected Church Wardens. The Church was commenced about 1736 and used for first time about April 10, 1760, called "St. Paul's Church", at Edenton. (N. C. H. & G. Reg. 1-4-607-'8).

1770. Priscilla Walton, dau. of Wm. Hunter and sister of James Hunter (1770). (N. C. H. & G. Reg. 2-2-265).

1770. James Hunter (son of Wm.), 1770. Mother Sarah Hunter, bros. and sisters John Nicholas, Hardy, Job, Timothy, Charity and Sarah Hunter, *Priscilla Walton*. (N. C. H. & G. Reg. 2-2-265).

1770. *Timothy Walton*, Chowan, Dec. 18, 1770. Sons *Timothy*, and John Benbury Walton, dau. Selah, James Freeman, Wm. Walters (?) and Thos. Benbury Exrs. Test.: Saml Dickinson, Wm. Freeman, Jonathan Tryer, Wm. Benbury. (N. C. H. & G. Reg. 2-1-33).

1770. Division of Estates, Chowan (no date—pro. 1770). Timothy Walton (pro. 1770), Widow, John Benbury Walton, Timothy Walton, *Celia Freeman*, Mary and Elizabeth Walton. (N. C. H. & G. Reg. 2-2-272).

1770. *Mary Walton, Widow of Timothy Walton*, m. 2nd, Thos. Hunter, 1770. (N. C. H. & G. Reg. 2-2-272).

1771. Mrs. Mary Walton m. Thos. Hunter, 1771. Surs. John Green, Aurt Elberson. (N. C. H. & G. Reg. 1-2-242).

1771 William Walton, Chowan, Will Nov. 20, 1771. Sons Timothy, Wm. and John, daus. Sarah Walton, Rachel Garrett, Ann and Celia Walton, Sons Thos., *Isaac* and James, *Wife Rachel* [dau. of Isaac Hunter]. Sons Timothy and William Exrs. Test. Palatiah Walton, Chas. Rountree, James Freeman, John Agar. (N. C. H. & G. Reg. 2-1-33).

1772. Division of Estates. William Walton, 1772. Widow [Rachel], Timothy, Wm., John, Thos., Isaac and James Walton, Sarah Lassiter, Mary, Ann and Celia. N. C. H. & G. Reg., 2-2-272).

1771. Richard Walton, 1771. Widow, James, Ellinor and Creeta Walton. (Division of Estates). (N. C. H. & G. Reg. 2-2-272).

Wm. Walton, Will 1760, and Thos. Walton, d. 1759, both had a son Richard.

1771. John Hunter, Chowan, Dec. 1, 1771. Wife, Ala, son William will come of age in 1782, son John, dau. Mary, Wife and Capt. Abner Eason Exrs. Test.: *Thos. Walton, Sarah Walton*, Elisha Hunter. (N. C. H. & G. Reg. 1-4-548).

1781. Alee Hunter, Gates Co. April 12, 1781; Aug. Ct. 1781. Sons Wm., *Theophilus* and John, dau. Mary. *Thos. Walton* and son Wm. Hunter Exrs. Test.: *Sarah Walton*, Mary Hunter, Elisha Hunter. (N. C. H. & G. Reg. 2-1-51-'2).

1772. Mrs. Sarah Walton m. Frederick Lasseter, 12 March, 1772. Surs.: Elisha Hunter, Nat Jones. (N. C. H. & G. Reg. 1-2-242).

1772. Mrs. Monica Walton m. Simeon Stallings, 1772. Sur., Joseph Riddick. (Query: Was she born Monica Blanchard, dau. of Aaron, d. 1751?) (N. C. H. & G. Reg. 1-2-242).

1774. Mary Walton m. Jacob Eason, 1774. Sur.: Frederick Lasseter. (N. C. H. & G. Reg. 1-2-243).

1774. Elizabeth Walton was a member of the Edenton Tea Party, Oct. 25, 1774. (N. C. H. & G. Reg. 2-1-122).

1776. Palatiah Walton, Chowan, Nov. 6, 1776. Wife Priscilla Walton [dau. of William Hunter], daus. Millicent and *Christian Walton*, daus. Sarah and Silpha Spivey, bro. Thos. Walton and *Jacob Hunter* Exrs. Test.: William Walton, Moses

Blanchard, *Rachel Walton* [widow of Wm. Walton, decd. 1771]. (N. C. H. & G. Reg. 2-1-33).

1781. *William Walton, Capt. 7th Regt.*, 1 Aug., 1781; Cols. James Hogun, Nov. 26, 1776, Robert Mebane, Feby. 9, 1777. (N. C. H. & G. Reg. 1-3-422).

In the "Winbornes of Old", by Judge Benj. B: Winborne, we find: "William son of Thos. Walton, Sr., enlisted in the Cont¹ Army as Lieut. April 17, 1777, in Capt. Pointer's Co., of Chowan Co., 7th Regt. He was appointed to Capt. Aug. 1, 1781, and served in the Army until he was "deranged" Jany. 1, 1783. "Deranged" is a military term, meaning honorably discharged. (C. R. N. C., Vol. 16, pp. 71-1185)".

1779. Timothy Walton bro.-in-law and ex. and witness of will of Frederick Lasseter, Aug. 30, 1779. (N. C. H. & G. Reg. 2-3-345).

1789. Mary Walton, 15th 6th month, 1789, named as dau. of Robert Newby, Perquimons. (N. C. H. & G. Reg. 3-2-180).

1793. Ann Walton m., Aug. 12, 1793, Jesse Fletcher, of Perquimons, N. C. (N. C. H. & G. Reg. 3-3-421).

1798. John Walton, Chowan, Will, Dec. Term, 1798. Bro. Timothy Walton and son Thomas Exrs. My wife and children. Test. Richard Woodward. (N. C. H. & G. Reg. 2-1-34). *See below.*

1800. Leah Walton, widow of John Walton, Chowan. (Division of Estates), 1800. (N. C. H. & G. Reg. 2-2-272). *See above.*

1805. Leah Walton witnessed will of Richard Skinner, Chowan, Dec. 21, 1805. (N. C. H. & G. Reg. 2-1-26-'7).

1806. Monica Walton m., Feby. 4, 1806, in Chowan, Wm. Birum, Sur.: Nathan Ward (N. C. H. & G. Reg. 1-3-396).

1808. Timothy Walton m. Sarah Gregory, dau. of Henry and Rachel Gregory, who later (prior to 1808) m. Solomon Elliott.

Henry Gregory, 1808, *Timothy Walton* and *wife, Sarah*, Henry Gregory, decd., his part divided between Solomon Elliott and wife and their children Lemuel, Alfred and Solomon, *Timothy Walton and wife Sarah.* (N. C. H. & G. Reg. 2-2-212).

1811. John Walton, Chowan, m. Dec. 31, 1811, Delilah Spivey. Sur.: Wm. Fores. (N. C. H. & G. Reg. 1-3-400)

1811 William Walton, Chowan, m. Nancy Jackson, May 30, 1811. Sur.: Wm. Jackson. (N. C. H. & G. Reg. 1-3-400).

BERTIE CO.

1793. Timothy Walton Exr. of John Freeman, Bertie, 1793. (Reg. 2-3-334).

1794. Timothy Walton witd will of Joshua Freeman, Bertie, Aug. 24, 1794. (Ibid).

1795. Timothy Walton Exr. of James Holley, Bertie, Jany. 27, 1795. (Reg. 2-3-339).

1796. Timothy Walton and Wm. Laine witnesses to will of Jesse Garrett, Bertie, Oct. 13, 1796. (Reg. 2-3-336).

1797. Sela Walton witd will of Sarah Kittrell, Bertie, Feby. Term, 1797. Reg. 2-3-344).

JOHNSTON CO

1769. Wm. Baker deed to *Wm. Walton*, June 19, 1769,—both of Johnston Co., 200 A. East side of Panther Branch in Johnston Co. for 5£ and a negro boy.

Wm. X Baker.

Wit.: Thomas X Nounce, William X Uttly. (Book L, old No., p. 135; new 348).

1769. Deed from Robert Nutt to Abraham Hill, both of Johnston Co., 1 April, 1769, 100 A. on Walnut Creek in s'd Co., for 22 £ 10 shs. Robert Nutt.

Wit.: *Theophilus Hunter, Wm. Walton*, Joshua Suggs. (Book L, p. old No. 11; new, 184).

1767. *William Walton* m., Nov. 28, 1767, *Elizabeth Smith*, Johnston Co. Bond signed by Wm. Walton and David Smith. (Marriage Bond Bk., p. 6).

WILKES CO., GA.

1791. *Wm. Walton* of Wilkes Co., Ga., to *Thos. Walton, Sr.*, sells a negro slave named Paddy, aged about 18 years, for 62 £, also, for 40 £ and other sums, other slaves. June 4, 1791. Wm. Walton.

Wit.: *Thos. Walton*, Holman Freeman, J. P. Rec. Sept. 3, 1791. (Deed Book 1790-1792, p. 317).

On page 318, same book: Deed from same to same, May 22, 1791, to 450 A. in Wilkes, land granted 1790. (Reg. Sept. 3, 1791).

1784. *Thos. Walton* 400 A. in Wilkes Co., Ga., bounded Eastwardly by Perkins land, Northwardly by Elijah Clarke's land, Westwardly Grey's land, Southwardly lands unknown. 30 Sept., 1784. By Gov. John Houston. *Wm. Freeman* O. C. E. C. Headright. (Book EEE, p. 207, at State Capitol).

1791. William Walton, of Campbell Co., Va., April, 1791, subpoenaed as a witness in Court; did not appear and was fined. In April, 1792, made application to Gov. & Council for remission of fine on ground that he had been excused by def't by whom usbpoenaed & besides had shortly before Sept. 1791 *removed* to the State of Ga. ("Calendar Va. State Papers", 1790-92, Vol. V, p. 494).

The Walton record is a complex and baffling one by reason of the oft recurrence of identical single names without distinguishing appellations. I have given much that is apparently irrelevant that the reader may be able to compare and form his own judgment.

WELLBORN.

John Wellborn[1], the progenitor of the family in America, emigrated from Wales to Jamestown, Va., in the ill-fated *Sea Venture*, which was wrecked on the island of Bermuda, and hence did not reach Jamestown until May 24, 1610. He m. (wife unknown) and had issue: 1.—Rev. Drummond Wellborn[2]; 2.—Jonathan Wellborn[2]; 3.—John Wellborn[3], who m. (wife unknown). Their sons moved to Accomac Co., Va.

3. John Wellborn[2] m. (wife unknown) and had: (1) Thomas Wellborn[3], an only child, who was b. in Accomac Co. in 1640. In 1678 by royal authority was appointed justice of the peace. In 1692 was made high sheriff. In 1694 was captain of the King's Militia. "Capt. Thomas Welbourne duly elected and returned Burgess to serve in this Assembly for Accomack Co., May 3, 1699" and was continuously a member till June 23, 1702 (Journal of the H. of B's., of Va., for 1695-1702). He d. in 1702. He m. Arcadia Taft, dau. of Henry and Anne Taft, and had issue:

(1) Samuel Wellborn[4]; (2) Daniel Wellborn[4], who d. in 1748; (3) Judge Benjamin Wellborn, of N. C., who d. in 1717; (4) Francis Wellborn[4], the ancestor of the West Virginia family.

(1). Samuel Wellborn[4], b. in Accomac Co., Va., moved to N. C. in 1700. He m. Mary Chapley, and had: (1) William Wellborn[5]; (2) Thomas Wellborn[5], b. 1760 or '62; (3) James Wellborn[5].

(1). William Wellborn[5], b. in 1733 in N. C., m. Hepsibah Stearns, dau. of Isaac Stearns and his wife, Rebecca Johnson, and gr. gr. dau. of Charles Stearns (who immigrated to Waterbury, Mass., in 1730?) and his wife, Rebecca Gibson. He was a soldier in the Revolution, was at the siege of Yorktown and the surrender of Cornwallis in 1781. Issue: (1) Abner Wellborn[6]; (2) Elias Wellborn[6]; (3) Johnson Wellborn[6]; (4) Clara Wellborn[6]; (5) James Wellborn[6]; (6) William Wellborn[6]; (7) Chapley Wellborn[6]; (8) Samuel Wellborn[6]; (9) Isaac Wellborn[6]; (10) Mary Wellborn[6].

(1). Abner Wellborn[6] m. Martha Render, dau. of Joshua Lewis Render, of Powhattan Co., Va. (his will recorded in Wilkes Co., Ga., in Will Book G. G., 1818-1819) and his wife Susannah Dickie. He moved to Wilkes Co., Ga., and settled on a fine body of land on the main road, leading from the Cherokee Nation of Indians through Washington to Augusta. He acquired great wealth. Issue: (1) Susan S. Wellborn[7], 1813-1857, m. Dr. Andrew B. Calhoun, of Newnan, Ga.; (2) Martha Strother Wellborn[7], 1816-1884, m. Col. Lodowick Meriwether Hill (his 2nd wife), of Wilkes Co.; (3) Hephzibah Wellborn[7], m. William Granville Hill, of Coweta Co., Ga.; (4) Dr. Abner Render Wellborn[7], m. Georgia Ann Ray, dau. of Judge John Ray, of Newnan, Ga.; (5) Ann Wellborn[7], m. (1) . . . . Simmons, of Wilkes Co., m. (II) John Broomhead, of Atlanta, Ga. Not sure as to order of births of the above.

(2). Elias Wellborn[6], b. in 1759 in Randolph Co., N. C.; d. in Columbia Co., Ga., in 1836; placed on pension roll of Ga. in 1831 for service as private in the N. C. Militia (D. A. R. Lineage, Vol. 35, p. 190, Nat'l No. 34,535). Another account says, he was a Lieut. in the Rev'y War. He received a grant in the Lottery of 1827

(D. A. R., Vol. 16, p. 349). He m. Mary Marshall, dau. of the eminent divine, Abram Marshall, and had; (1) Ruby Wellborn[7], m. Dr. .... Davis; (2) Marshall H. Wellborn[7], m. (I) Miss .... Hill; m. (II) Miss F. Hardaway; (3) Steven Wellborn[7], d. unm.; (4) Lucy Wellborn[7], m. (I) George Lewis, m. (II) .... Morrow; (5) James Madison Wellborn[7], m. Louisa Amanda Cody and had Mrs. Mary Wellborn (Dr. James) Camack and Miss Louisa Derrille Wellborn, and possibly others; (6) Martha Wellborn[7], m. William Briscoe; (7) Selina H. Wellborn[7], m. Theophilus Hill, son of Theophilus and Polly (Jordan) Hill, and gr. son of Abraham and Christian (Walton) Hill; (8) Mary Wellborn[7], m. .... Fleming; (9) Abner Wellborn[7], m. Miss .... Heard; (10) Nancy Wellborn[7], m. Nathaniel Bailey.

(3). Johnson Wellborn[6] (son of William[5]) m. Sallie Render and one of his daus. m. Isaac Ramsay and they had eleven children but reared only four, one of whom was Phocian Ramsay, who m. Emma Hill, dau. of Theophilus Hill, of Monroe Co., Ga., and his wife Selina H. Wellborn.

(4). Clara Wellborn[6] (dau. of William[5]) m. Mr. .... Dennis.

(5). James Wellborn[6] (son of William[5]) family unknown.

Genl. James Wellborn, of Wilkes Co., N. C., m. the 6th dau. of Hugh Montgomery, of Rowan Co. (he was a member of Provincial Congress at Hillsborough, Aug. 2, 1775, and also member Committee of Safety, 1774-'6) and his eldest dau. m. Newton Cannon, Gov. of Tenn. Gen. James Wellborn was a member of the State Senate from Wilkes Co., N. C., from 1796 to 1829. (Rem's of N. C., by Wheeler, p. 396).

(6). William Wellborn[6] (son of William[5]) m. ....., and had a dau. who m. Col. John Cochran. (7). Chapley Wellborn[6] (son of William[5]) family unknown. (8). Col. Samuel Wellborn[6] (son of William[5]). In Watkins Digest, Capt. Samuel Wellborn is named as a subscriber. His will is of record in Wilkes Co., Ga., in Will Book 1819-1836. He m. ....., and had: (1) Kitty Wellborn[7], m. W. C. Jack; (2) John Wellborn[7], d. unm.; (3) Colonel Alfred Wellborn, of Meriwether Co., Ga., m. Elizabeth Terry Martin and had Emily Caroline Wellborn, who m. 6 Jan., 1818(?), Edmond Howart Martin, M. D., of Edgefield Dis., S. C. (Colonial Families of So. States of America, p. 370). (9). Isaac Wellborn[6] (son of William[5]); family unknown. (10). Mary Wellborn[6] (dau. of William[5]); family unknown.

(2). Thomas Wellborn[5] (son of Samuel[4]) b. in N. C. in 1760, m. (I) Sarah (Wellborn ?) Cloud (b. in N. C. c. 1761); m. (II) Mary Cook, and had: (1) Esther Wellborn[6], m. Jesse Bramlett; (2) Martha Wellborn[6], m. John Cowan; (3) John R. Wellborn[6], m. Martha King; (6) Lewis Thomas Wellborn[6], m. Roxana Bethune; (7) Sarah Cloud Wellborn[6], m. J. Tindall; (8) Judge Marshall Johnston Wellborn[6], d. unm.; (9) Parmalea Cook Wellborn[6], m. Col. James Clark, of Atlanta, Ga.

(3). James Wellborn[5] (son of Samuel[4]) m. ....., and had: (1) Samuel Wellborn[6]; (2) James Wellborn[6]; (3) Aaron Wellborn[6]; (4) William Wellborn[6]; (5) Caroline Wellborn[6]; (6) Joseph Wellborn[6].

William Oliver (of Surry Co., Va.) m. 1750 Frances, and had Rebecca Oliver, b. 1771, who m. William Wellborn and had son, Benjamin Wellborn, father of Mrs. Scruggs, of Marion, Ala. (E. S. of Ala., p. 410).

William Wellburn, H. D., Oct. 1780, 50 (List of Rev'y Soldiers, Va. State Library 2).

William Welborn (6VR) W. D. 130, 1. (Rept. State Librarian of Va., p. 318).

William Welbourne, Aud. Acct. XXXI, 260. (Rev. Sol. of Va., part II, Va. State Library).

Curtis Wellborn, of Wilkes Co., Ga., and his wife *Mary* on Dec. 16, 1788, made deed to *Willis Pope*, of Wilkes Co., to 500 A. on both sides Golden Grove, granted to Curtis Wellborn, Aug. 17, 1785, for 100£. (Signed) Curtis Welborn
                       Mary (X) Welborn

Wit.: Elijah Cowen, Frances (X) George. (Deed book 1790-1792, p. 34).

Capt. Curtis Wellborn named in Watkins Digest as a subscriber.

The genealogy, above given, of the Wellborn family, is, in the main, taken from an article published some years ago in one of the Atlanta papers, I think The Constitution, and it was based upon data obtained from Mrs. John O. Blackmar, of Columbus, Ga., nee Miss Susie Wellborn, who is owner of the family tree used.

While the writer has verified by public and other reliable records only a portion of this genealogy, he believes that it bears the stamp of truth and accuracy in its entirety, and with reasonable effort and research could be authoritatively established as a whole. In a letter from Mr. Alfred Wellborn, Nov. 11, 1919, he says: "After working on the record for more than a year, found that the history is substantially as given by Mrs. Blackmar."

WOOTTEN—WOTTON.

In "Facts and Figures vs. Myths and Misrepresentations—The True History of the Jamestown Colony", by Mildred Lewis Rutherford, on pages 4 and 5, we find:

"The London Company chose their own settlers, able men, picked men, who would enforce their ideas of government. . . . Men . . who pledged themselves to introduce popular reform in the new government from the very beginning of the settlement were chosen. They took with them Rev. Robert Hunt for their religious instructor, and *Dr. Thomas Wotton* for their *Surgeon*, and Alexander Whitaker came later for a missionary to the Indians, which shows that they were religious and cared for the welfare of their bodies as well as for the salvation of their souls". On page 22: "The descendants of Dr. Thomas Wotton, the Surgeon of the Jamestown Colony in 1607, have descendants living in Georgia today and still making history".

I think it possible that this accurate and distinguished historian is *for once* in error, judging from the following:

"Thomas Wotton of London, Barber Chirurgeon, Will 15, March, 1635; pr. 28 April, 1638. Being now bound forth in Sir Wm. Courtiane's Voyage in the good ship called the Planter of London,—*Hill, Master*, I have constituted John Cartwright, Citizen and Salter of London my attorney. If it shall please God to call me out of this life in or during my intended voyage I doe then give all my goods, wages, adventures, substance and estate whatsoever *to* my said loving friend John Cartwright this to stand for my last will and testament whereof I make said John Cartwright sole executor. Witnesses: Thos. Symonds, John James, Humphrey Tompkyns, Ralph Fryth. Scr.

Let. 38."

(Note by the Editor: *Possibly* the Testator was "*Master Thomas Wotton*", who came with the first settlers to Virginia in 1607 as *Surgeon General* and who was one of the expedition in May-June of that year, which ascended James River to the site of Richmond. Sir William Curtien's voyage was to the East Indies"). (Va. Mag. of H. & B., p. 25).

If the above surmise as to the identity of this Thomas Wotton be correct, and it seems highly probable, then this Pioneer Adventurer died leaving neither wife nor children, and so no descendants. It is quite likely, however, that our present day Woottens in America are from the same English stirp as he.

From the Papers of Miss Katharine Hinton Wootten (same being "abstracts and copies of orders, &c. in the name of WOOTTEN in the records of York County, Va., made for William Wootton, Baltimore, Md., May 17, 1906, by T. T. Heedgivs, County Clerk, York County, Virginia).

Abstracts and copies:

Susannah Davis & Elizabeth Brooks to THOMAS WOOTTEN. Deed of date March 16, 1679, 100 acres, consideration 5,000 pounds tobacco. York County records, deeds, &c. No. 1, page 626.

To all to whom these presents shall come, I, Henry Chicheley, Knight, His Majesty's Deputy, Governor of Virginia, send greeting in Lord God Everlasting.

Whereas His Majesty hath been graciously pleased by his Royal Letters Patent under the great seal of England, bearing date at Westminster the 10th day of October, in the eighth and twentieth year of his reign, amongst other things in the said Letters Patents contained to continue and confirme the ancient privileges and power of granting fifty acres of land for every person imported into this His colony of Virginia. Now know you that I, the said Sir Henry Chichely, Knight Deputy Governor, &c. do, with the consent of the Council of State, according give and grant unto THOMAS WOOTTEN and Henry Hayward, 1708 acres of land, lying in the oaken swamp in the new Poquoson (?) Parish, in York County. Beginning at two markt white oaks, being ye corner trees of a former divident of land belonging to the said WOOTTEN, and from thence running Northwest by West 160 feet. Southwest by South 200 feet. Southeast by East 126 feet. Northeast along the said WOOTTEN'S land 200 feet to the first specified place. The said land being due by and for the transportation of four persons into this Colony, whose names are mentioned in the records under this Patent. To have and to hold the said land with their due share of all mines and minerals therein contained with all rights and privileges of hunting, hawking, fishing, and fowling, with all woods, waters and rivers, with all profits, commodities and hereditiments whatsoever belonging to the said land, to them, the said THOMAS WOOTTEN and Henry Hayward, their heirs and assigns forever. In as ample manner to all intents and purposes, as hath been used and allowed since the first plantation, to be held of our Soveraigne Lord the King, his heirs and successors as of His Manor of East Greenwich, in free and (??) and not in captive, nor by Knight service, Yielding and paying unto the said Souveraigne Lord the King, his heirs and successors forever, fifty acres of land hereby granted at the Feast of St. Michael the Archangel, the fee rent of four shillings, which rent payment is to be made yearly from yeare to yeare, according to His Majesty's instructions of the 12th of September 1662. Provided that if the said THOMAS WOOTTEN or Henry Hayward, their heirs of assigns do not plant or seat, or cause to be planted or seated upon the said land within these three years next ensuing date thereof: That it shall and may be lawful for any adventurer or planter to make choice and seat thereon.

(COLONY SEAL). Given under my hand and the seal of ye Colony this 22nd day of Icber (?) 1682. HENRY CHICHELEY. Deeds &c No. 1, page 319.

THOMAS WOOTTEN hath judgment against Major John Scasbrooke, Sheriff, for thr non-appearance of John Rogers, being arrested for 1,100 pounds of tobacco and caske (?) unless he produce him to the next court. Oct. 26, 1675. Deeds No. 5, p. 129.

THOMAS WOOTTEN and James Forsith securities for Elizabeth Brooks. Feb. 20, 1679. Deeds No. 5, p. 183.

THOMAS WOOTTEN about 40 years of age, deposition &c. Feb. 24, 1691. Book No. 9, p. 100. THOMAS WOOTTEN judgment against James Bloxton for 1,000 pounds of tobacco. Aug. 2, 1694. Book 9, p. 276. THOMAS WOOTTEN appointed Hugh Owen his general attorney in all cases. Nov. 12, 1694. Book 10, p. 51. The suit depending to this court upon an imparlance (?) between Josias Ship and the County Esses and Elizabeth his wife, ye only daughter and heir or Thomas Brookes, late of the County of York, carpenter, decd' agt. THOMAS WOOTTEN of the County of York, Cooper in an action of trespass, wherein ye plantiff now failing to appear and prosecute ye same, he is no suited with costs Mr. . . . . Po: Weldon and Mr. Hugh Owen appearing attorneys for ye defendant. May 25, 1692. Book 10, p. 288. THOMAS WOOTTEN appearing on a summons to answer ye presentment of ye grand jury for absenting from ye church and confessing ye fact. is fined five shillings, or 50 pounds of tobacco, and is ordered to pay it to the church warden of YORK Parish for ye use of the said Parish next Levy, otherwise to receive on his bare back the number of ten lashes well laid on by ye sheriff. June 27, 1707. Book 13, page 73. THOMAS WOOTTEN and PRISCILLA, his wife, deed of gift date July 18, 1715, to THOMAS WOOTTEN, their son, 111 acres Chas. Parish, York County, Va. (NOTE—If the said Thomas Wootten leaves no heirs at his death, then said land to go to son *Benjamin WOOTTEN*. THOMAS WOOTTEN administrator for John Clark, Bond &c. Dec. 21, 1719. Bonds &c 15, p. 527. THOMAS WOOTTEN and ELIZABETH, his wife, deed of date March 16, 1734, to GILES RIDOUT, 12 acres for 4 pounds and 10 shillings. JOHN WOOTTEN to WM. NELSON deed of date Sept. 28, 1754, conveying one negro man slave named Jack, 26 years old, 8 draught oxen, all marked with a swallow cut in the right and under keel in the left *year* consideration 50 pounds, 17 shilli- - MONDAY and CUPID two negro boys belonging to *THOMAS WOOTTEN* brought into court and adjudged each to be 14 years old July 17, 1738. Deeds 18, p. 433. Ordered that JOHN WOOTTEN be and is hereby appointed sur⌐from 17, 1742. THOMAS WOOTTEN died, appraisement of his estate £ 215ₐᵣ, of Jan. 20, 1783. The last will of THOMAS WOOTTEN, dec'd, proved by the c used.

John Toomer, a witness thereto, Sept. 17, 1782. Orders, &c 4, page 306. (NOTE—The will is not on record).

On the motion PRISCILLA WOOTTEN it is ordered that she be excused from the payment of levies and taxes on her slave, Monday, it appearing to the court that he is aged and infirm. April 19, 1784. Orders &c No. 4, p. 475.

On the motion of WILLIS WOOTTEN, a witness from Warwick County for Henry Jordan against Robert Gibbons. It is ordered that the said Henry Jordan pay him one dollar and one cent for attending this court one day, and travelling six miles and returning. Dec. 19, 1806.

WOOTTENS OF ISLE OF WIGHT CO., VA.

1669. Will of Thomas Wootten. Exrs.: *Wife Sara* and *only son Richard Wootten*. My wife's son *Thomas Wood*. Should my son die without issue to my next kin of name in Northamptonshire at a town called Castor near unto Peterborough. Friends James Sampson and Richard Briggs overseers. March 15th, 1669.
Thomas Wootten.
Witness: Elizabeth Sampson. Proved 1670. (Book 1661-1719, p. 95).

1686. Will of *Richard Wootten*, 28 Sept. 1686. My *son Richard;* my *son Thomas;* my loving wife and three children; Wife, Exx. *Henry Baker overseer* to will.
Richard Wootten.
Wit.: Thos. Wood, George Groves. Rd. Mch. 1686/7. (Book 1661-1719, p. 265). *Name of 3rd child not given.*

Va. Quit Rent Rolls—Isle of Wight Co., 1704. Thomas Wootten, 936 Acres. (Va. Mag. of His. & Bio., No. 3, July, 1921, p. 341).

1705. Richard Wootten and Thomas Wootten of Isle of Wight Co., Aug. 9, 1705, to John Buttler "for a valuable consideration", sell that plantation and tract of land yt now ffra. floyd lives on it being yt Land s'd Father Richard Wootten bought of Nich. Cobb by Conveyance bearing date 21st day of October, 1681, being bounded as followeth:—touches James Maning's land, being part of a Pattent of 900 Acres of land Pattented to Nicholas Cobb.
Richard Wootten
Thomas Wootten
Ann Wootten—wife of Thomas, relinquishes dower.

Wit.: Geo. Green, John Leech, Madison Street. Rec. Aug. 9th, 1708. (Book 1704-1715, p. 22).

1708. Thomas Wootten of the Isle of Wight, makes deed Nov. 8, 1708, to Richard Wootten, of same County, "for a valuable consideration" to all the land and plantation now in possession of Thomas Wootten being 150 acres, part of a pattent to Thos. Man for 300 acres, in Isle of Wight County touches Blackwater Swamp or Chowan, which 150 acres is Prin. part of pattent assigned by Thomas Man to Wm. Butler Feby. 9th, 1697, and William Butler Aug. 9th, 1705, assigned the same to *Thomas Wootten* (and *Richard Wootten?*).
Thomas Wootten
Ann Wootten

Wit.: Robert Brook, William West, Wm. Hunter. Rec. Feby. 8th, 1709. (Book 1704-1715, p. 132).

1720. Will of Sarah Bulger, Isle of Wight, Jany. 4, 1720/21. My bro. Wm. Smith; my sister Parker; my bro. Nicholas Smith; to Mary Loothlin; my sister Martha Smith; my bro. Joseph Smith; to Annos Barnes; my Couzen Wm. Smith; *my Sister Wootten*, and after her death to *Joseph Wootten*. Sarah Bulger.
Wit.: Jas. Brown, Wm. Hawkins. Rec. Mch. 27, 1721. (Great Book, p. 71).

1730. Deed from Hardy *Council,* Isle of Wight, Va., Gent., to *Richard Wootten* and *Lucy his wife,* and *William Wootten* their *son,* 27 March, 1730. Whereas a Law Suit was depending in the Honorable the General Court Mch. 3, 1726, between the said Hardy *Council* and the said *Richard Wootten* touching a trespass said to be done by the said Council and a Jury by order of the sd. Court when the same day Impannelled and Sworn to Layout the Land Controversy when Richard Wootten should Chuse, afterwards the Jury was withdrawn and John Allen, Gent., in Company with the Consent of the sd Councill and Wootten did Survey lay out Mark 500 Acres for the said Wootten's part of the Land in Controversy, and since settled. And for and in consideration of the Love and affection the said Hardy

Councill beareth to *his Sister Lucy the wife* of the *said Richard Wootten*, but more especially *to their son William* Wootten, and for divers other good causes and considerations, the said Hardy Council doth sell, bargain, Enfeoff and Confirm unto the sd *Richard Wootten and Lucy for their lives* and then to the said William Wootten, their son, his heirs, admrs., and assigns one tract of land in Isle of Wight containing by estimation 500 Acres in Beaver Dam Swamp 200 acres given to the sd Lucy Wootten by her father's [Hodges Councill] last will and testament [April 10, 1699]. Hardy Councill.

Wit.: Barnaby Kearney, Chris Reynolds, John Pitt. Rec. Mch. 22, 1730. (Deed Book 4, p. 98).

1736. *Thomas Wootten,* of Newport Parish Isle of Wight, Jany. 12, 1736, to Wm. Whitley of the Precinct of Bertie of the Government of N. C., 200 Acres in Isle of Wight (This land I Thomas Wootten purchased of *John Griffin,* Jany. 12, 1730) For a valuable consideration. *Thos. Wootten*
Mary Wootten (wife)

Wit.: Henry Edwards, Robt. Edwards, W. X Edwards. (Book 5, p. 88).

1738. *Richard* Wootten, of the Lower Parish of Isle of Wight, makes deed, Nov. 24, 1738, to Robert Duck, of the same Parish and County, to 200 Acres in the Lower Parish of Isle of Wight, on Beaver Dam Swamp, touching other land of *Richard Wootten* and *William Wootten*, for 2 bbls merchantable Tar. Richard Wootten.

Witnesses: John Butler, George Lawrence, John Darden. Rec. Nov. 27, 1738. (Book 5, p. 298).

1744. William Wootten and by the consent of his wife *Ann*, of Isle of Wight Co., Nov. 21, 1744, to *James Councill* and James Bryant of said County for a consideration fully paid, to James Councill a parcell of land in Isle of Wight containing 100 Acres being part of a tract and Deed that Mr. Hardy Council Recorded to the sd *Wm. Wootten* after his Father's decease. Deed dated 22 March, 1730.
William Wootten
Ann Wootten

Wit.: Peter Councill, John Corbit. Rec. Feby. 25, 1744. (Book 7, p. 16).

William Wootten granted 300 Acres in *Northampton Co.,* N. C., at a Council on 16th March, 1743. (C. R. N. C. 6, Vol. 4, p. 627).

William Wootten, April 21, 1749, was a witness to the will of George Norwood, of Northampton Co. (N. C. H. & G. Reg. 1-3-357). On 6 Jany., 1755, *William Wootten, of Johnston Co.,* N. C., sells to James Turner, of Southampton Co., Va., for 10 £, 300 A.—patent to William Wootten, March 16, 1742/3.

Wit.: Theo Hunter, Robt. Butler, John Bradford. (Northampton Co. Book 2, p. 200). (Note: This is the land described above).

1766. Richard Wootten, Isle of Wight, Aug. 1, 1766, to Benjamin Darden, of same Co., 150 Acres in the maine run of Blackwater, 8 £. Richard Wootten.

Wit.: Hardy Darden, Benjamin Holland, John Darden. (Book 12, p. 43).

1789. William Wootten, Dec. 30, 1789, makes deed to John Barnes. (Book 6, p. 222).

1794. William Wootten and wife, in 1794, to Josiah Geraltny. (Book 17, p. 203).

Benjamin Wootten, of Isle of Wight Co., in 1790, makes a deed to the town of Smithfield, of same Co. (Deed Book 16, p. 225).

On 25 Nov., 1756, James Wootten of Johnston Co., N. C., sells to Thos. Fergreson, of Edgecombe Co., for £ 1, 2 shillings, 100 acres.

Wit.: Green Hill, Jim Somersoll. (Northampton Co. Book 2, p. 335).

WOOTENS OF JOHNSTON, ORANGE, HALIFAX AND WAKE COS.

1748. Richard Braswell, of Tar River in Edgecombe Co., on May 26, 1758, sells to *James Wootten*, of the Parish of St. Stephen, *Johnston* Co., planter, 147 A. on Buffalo Swamp in Johnston Co., for 40 £. Richard Braswell.

Wit.: Richard Kemp, *Jesse Wooton*. (Book A, p. 5).

1762. James Wooton, Johnston Co., State of N. C., July 17, 1762, sells to Drewry (or Demsey) Rodgers, of same Co., 147 A. on North side Buffalo Swamp, for 40 £ proclamation money. James Wooton.

Wit.: Jos. Thomas, Elisha Thomas. (Book 1, p. 292).

1775. *James Wootten*, of Johnston Co., Nov. 27, 1775, sells to Jesse Green, of Edgecombe Co., N. C., 200 A. west side Buffalo Swamp. James Wootten
Faith Wootten
Wit.: James Branen, John Green. (Book H-1, p. 260).

1761. *Benjamin Hardy* and *Mary his wife*, of Johnston Co., N. C., sell, Sept. 17, *1761*, to Benjamin Wootten, two lots of land, one containing 260 A. and the other 238 A., and the old Court House at *Enfield* (former County seat of Halifax) was on this land. John Hardy purchased one lot of it from *Nathaniel Bradford*, and said John Hardy conveyed same land to Benjamin Hardy by Deed of Gift, Sept. Court, 1760. 22 acres of it lay near Bear Marsh. Benjamin Hardy
Mary Hardy
Wit.: *Wm. Lane*, James Jones. (Halifax Book 7, p. 334).

1763. *William Branch* and *Elizabeth his wife*, of Halifax Co., on *April 20, 1763*, sell to Benjamin Wootten, of Halifax Co., 50 A. on south side *Burncoat Swamp*, "*including old prison and court house and Spring*", for 53 £. This was part of a patent granted *Joseph Lane*. (Signed) William Branch
Elizabeth Branch
Wit.: Randal Daniel, Joseph Renn. (Halifax Book 8, p. 268).

1764. "This Indenture made this *13th day of January, 1764*, between Bethiah Hardy, widow and relict of Hugh Hardy deceased, Samuel Hardy, John Bradford, Esq., Benajah Saxon, Executors of the last Will and Testament of Hugh Hardy, of the one part, and of *Thomas Wootten* of the Co. and Province aforesaid of the other part"—parties of the first part sell to party of second part 192 A. of wood land on the north side of Burncoat Swamp for 15 £ 16 shs. proc. money. Said land was granted said Hugh Hardy, decd., by Nathaniel Bradford.
Wit.: Peter Tatum, *Lewis Pope*. (Halifax, N. C., Deed Book 9, p. 290).

1764. Thomas Wootten of the Co. of Halifax, N. C., on Jany. 23, 1764, sells to John Bradford 192 A. on North side Burncoat Swamp for 20 £. Said land bought from the Executors of *John Hardy*. Wit.: Benjamin Saxon, *Benjamin Wootten*, William Wood. (Halifax Book 9, p. 272).

1767. *Thomas Wootten*, of *Orange Co.*, N. C., to *John Saxon*, of Halifax, Oct. 16, 1767. Whereas Samuel Hardy, decd., did in his life by Deed dated 1760 convey to Samuel Saxon, of Halifax, land on Beaver Dam and Burncoat Swamp, 346 A. being part of a tract granted Hugh Hardy, late of Halifax, decd., a sufficient title does not appear on record, therefore on request of Benjamin Hardy and in consideration of 20 £ by him the said Benjamin Hardy paid Thomas Wootten, I do grant enfeoff and confirm to John Saxon all the right, title, interest, property claim and demand whatsoever of him the said Thomas Wootten to the aforesaid property to the said John Saxon. Thomas Wootten
Wit.: *John Wootten*, John Bradford. (Halifax Book 10, p. 208. May Court, 1768).

1767. James Turbeville, of *Halifax* Co., to Thomas Wootten, of *same Co.*, sells *80 A.* that was granted Wm. Uttley by patent 1753 and came to James Turbeville "by right of inheritance", for 25 £. James Turbeville.
Wit.: Isaac Turbeville, *Burwell Pope*. Ruth (his wife).
Oct. Court, 1767. (Hal. Book 10, p. 158.)

1767. James Wootten, Johnston Co., surety on marriage bond of Mark Sims to Elizabeth Watson. Nov. 3, 1767. (Mar. Bond Book p. 7.)

1769. Elizabeth Cook, of *Johnston Co.*, on 20th Oct., 1769, sells to *Thomas Wootten*, of *Orange Co.*, *300 A. in Johnston Co.*, on both sides *Richland Creek*, a branch of Crabtree Creek, for 58 £. Wit.: James Martin, Wm. X Mahleny. (Book L, p. old No. 11, new 184.)

Thomas Wootten member of *Genl. Assembly* of N. C., at session held at Newberne, 15 Nov., *1777;* his seat was vacated by his acceptance of *Sheriff's Office* of Wake Co. (C. R. N. C., Vol. 12, p. 265) and on Dec. 5, 1777, his successor appeared and took his seat. (C. R. N. C., Vol. 12, p. 337).

Provincial Congress at Halifax, Dec. 23, 1778, appointed *Thomas Wootten, Abraham Hill,* et al., *Justices* of the *Peace* of Wake Co. (S. R. N. C., Vol. 23, p. 995, or '6?).

1770. Joseph Barber, Orange Co., on 24th day of July, 1770, sells to *Thomas*

Wootten, of *Johnston Co.*, for 200 £ Proc. money, one certain tract or parcel of land situate lying and being in the *Co. of Orange* on *Crabtree Creek* containing 451 A. granted to Charles Young (?) and by his Executors conveyed to Joseph Barber.
    Wit.: John Gregory, Charles Lewis.   Joseph Barber.
    Rd July Ct., 1770. Test. F. Nash, C. Ct.
    1771. *Thomas Wootten*, of Wake Co., N. C., was a *Justice of the Peace* and *member* of the *first Inferior Court of Pleas* and *Quarter Sessions* for Wake Co., on June 4, 1771. (The County was chartered May 22, 1771). He was *High Sheriff* of the Co. of Wake from June, 1777, till Sept., 1780; in 1781 he was *Colonel* and commanded the military forces of Wake County.
    "One Timothy Duck failed to appear when summoned for military duty in April, 1781. In accordance with a power which was given him by law, Colonel Wootten ordered the Sheriff to seize and sell Duck's plantation. With the proceeds of this sale, John Abernathie was hired as a substitute and the unfortunate Duck had to hunt for another nest". ("N. C. Booklet", Vol. V, July, 1905, No. 1, pp. 3 to 17— Genesis of Wake Co., by Marshall DeLancey Haywood).
    By an Act of the Assembly Appointing the *Sheriff* of each County to be *County Treasurer*, Thomas Wootten was appointed to that office, 19 Feby., 1778. (Wake Co. Book 1, p. 132).
    The land of Duck lay on north side of Neuse River and on both sides of Bush Head Creek, and was sold to *John Hinton, Sr.*, the highest bidder. (Wake Co. Book A, pp. 192-193).
    1764. Will of *Benjamin Wootten*, 26 June, 1764; pr. Oct. Ct., 1764. (Will Book 1, p. 151). In the Name of God Amen: I Benjamin Wootten of the *Co. of Halifax* and the province of N. C., being weak of body but of perfect mind and memory thanks be to God for the same and knowing that it is appointed for all men once to die do make and ordain this my last Will and Testament in manner and form following:
    First and principally I recommend my soul into the hands of Almighty God and my body to the Earth to be decently buried at the discretion of my Executors hereafter mentioned.
    Imprimis: I will that all my just debts and funeral charges be first paid and satisfied.
    Item. I give and bequeath to my granddaughter Elizabeth Long eighty pounds proclamation and one feather bed and furniture and one cow and calf, but in case my said granddaughter should die without issue then the legacies above mentioned be equally divided among all my children.
    Item. I lend to my loving wife *Elizabeth Wooten* during her natural life or widowhood all the remainder of my perishable estate and after her decease or day of marriage to be equally divided among all my children to-wit: *Thomas Wooten*, Elizabeth Wooten, *John Wooten*, Mary Wooten and *Priscilla Wootten*, and William Wootten.
    Item. I lend to my loving wife during her natural life or widowhood the use of the plantation whereon I now live with all the land adjoining thereto, and at her decease or day of marriage all *the land and plantation aforesaid be vested in my Executors*, hereafter named, the survivor or survivors of them, and *that they, or the survivors* of them as aforesaid *make sale* of the said land and plantation and the money arising thereby to be equally divided among all my children before mentioned.
    Item. I will that upon the marriage of my children before mentioned my wife should think fit to share any part of the perishable estate among them so married that part so shared be appraised by some disinterested person and the value thereof be deducted out of their parts after the decease of their Mother.
    I do hereby nominate and appoint *Thomas Wootten*, *William Lane* and *John Bradford* whole Executors of this my last will and testament revoking and disannulling all other wills by me heretofore made in testimony whereof I have hereunto put my hand fixed my seal the 26th day of June, A. D. 1764.
                                                      Benjamin Wooten.
    Signed, sealed and declared to be the last will and testament of the testator in presence of *Mathew Rabun*, William Moore, David Pulley. Halifax October Court.

This will now in Open Court duly proved by the oath of William Moore, a subscribing witness thereto and the Exrs. were duly qualified ordered and test. J. Montfort, C. C.

(Will Book 1, p. 151, Halifax Co., N. C. Office of Clerk Superior Court).

1768. *John Bradford*, Esq., *Wm. Lane* and *Thomas Wootten* Executors of the Will of Benjamin Wootten, sell to Matthew Jones, Sept. 12, 1768, *538 A. on South side Burncoat Swamp on Reedy* Branch being land granted *Benjamin Wootteen* by Benjamin Hardy. (Signed) John Bradford,
Wit.: Christopher Dudley, Wm. Moon, Allen Jones. Wm. Lane,
(Halifax Book 10, p. 203). Thomas Wootten.

In Halifax Co. Book 7, p. 135, is record of deeds of gift by John Hardy, of Halifax, to his 3 sons, Benjamin, Samuel, and Hugh Hardy, bearing date Dec. 21, 1759, and recorded Sept. Court, 1760.

Benjamin Wootten m. *Elizabeth Rousseau*, dau. of Hilliare Rousseau, and his wife, Elizabeth Lynton, dau. of William Lynton and his wife Joanna Lewis, dau. of Edward² and Mary Lewis. (See Lewis). Issue: *Thomas*, Elizabeth, John, Mary, *Priscilla* and *William Wootten*, who m. *Frances Bradford*, dau. of Col. John Bradford, of Halifax Co.

Benj. Hill m., Nov. 28, 1787, *Mary Wootten*, in Johnston Co. Surs: Benj. Hill, John Green. (Mar. Bond Book, p. 35). [Could hardly have been the above Mary].

Thomas Wootten m. twice; name of 1st wife not known; m. (II) Mrs. Tabitha Pope, circa 1768. (q. v.).

Elizabeth Wootten m. Roland Taylor, as shown by the following: "Benjamin Wootten from Roland Taylor. Whereas Elizabeth Lewis [after death of Hilliare Rousseau, her 1st husband, she m. Surles Lewis] of the Parish of Washington in the ounty of Westmoreland in the Colony of Virginia did by deed bearing date the . . day of . . . in the year of Our Lord 1748 lend to her daughter Elizabeth Wootten, wife of Benjamin Wootten during her natural life one negro woman named Jenny and after her decease that the said negro and increase to be divided among the children of the said Elizabeth's body, and whereas Roland Taylor intermarried with Elizabeth Wootten daughter of the said Elizabeth Wootten, now know ye that the said Roland Taylor do acknowledge to have received of Benj. Wootten satisfaction in full of my part of the above negro and increase and I the s'd Roland Taylor for myself, my heirs, executors, admrs. and assigns do acknowledge myself therewith to be fully satisfied, contented and paid and do for myself, my heirs, exectrs., quit claim s'd negro and increase thereof affix my hand and seal this *26th Day of June, 1764.* Roland Taylor.
Wit.: John Bradford, Wm. Lane. Halifax Court, Oct., 1767. Jos. Montfort, Clerk. (Halifax Book 10, p. 60).

"Account Current of the Estate of Roland Taylor, deceased, Sept. 5, 1780". Burwell Pope and Thomas Wootten mentioned. (Wake Co. Book 2 (B), p. 10).

Priscilla Wooten, dau. of Benj. and Elizabeth (Rousseau) Wootten, m. 8 Sept., 1772, Burwell Pope. (See Popes).

Thomas Wootten, son of Benj. and Elizabeth (Rousseau) Wootten, by first wife had two sons, Richard Bradford Wootten and Benjamin Wootten. He m. (II) circa 1768 or 1769, Mrs. Tabitha Pope, widow of Henry Pope, and the mother of Burwell Pope, who m. Priscilla Wootten, his sister. Issue by this 2nd marriage, four children, viz.: *Mary Ann* Wootten, b. 28 June, 1770; d. 18 March, 1838; m., in March, 1789, James Cade. (q. v.); *James Wootten*, b. 1775; d. 1822, aged 47 years; m. Polly Smith, d. 1826, dau. of Benajah Smith. (q. v.); *Thomas* Wootten, Jr., b. 1777 (or '8); d. 1848, aged 70 years; m. Milly Smith, dau. of Benajah Smith. (q. v.); Lemuel Wootten, b. 1780; d. . . . ; m. Nancy Smith, dau. of Benajah Smith. (q. v.).

These three brothers m. three sisters.

"This Indenture made May 19th, 1783, between *Thomas Wootten* and *Tabitha his wife, of the County of Wake and State of N. C."* They make deed to Thomas Tulloch and Harrison Macon to 595 Acres in Wake County on Crabtree Creek for 800 £. Said land granted Thomas Wootten by James Acock by deed bearing date May 5th, 1771. (Signed) Thomas Wootten.
Wit.: Burwell Pope, Wm. Wootten. Tabitha Wootten.
Reg. Feby. 25, 1788. Jas. Hinton, Reg.

The following are true and exact copies of papers on file in office of Dr. L. L. Knight, Compiler of State Records.

"State of Georgia } Personally appeared before Three of the Justices assigned to Wilkes County } keep the peace: Thomas Wootten, who being duly sworn, made oath that *he has removed into this State with the intention of becoming a citizen* and that he never had any land granted him in this State either under this government or the former and that he has at this *one* head *Right, a Wife, and six children and ten negroes.* Sworn to before . . . this *3rd day of April, 1784*

John Rutherford, J. P., Z. Lamar, A. J. P.x, Daniel Coleman, J. P.

x Note.—This A. J. P. stands for "Affidavit Justice of the Peace".

"State of Georgia. To the honorable the president and members of Council now siting in Augusta for the purpose of granting lands in the two new Counties of Franklin and Washington. The petition of *Thomas Wootten, a citizen of Wilkes* County and State aforesaid, Sheweth, That your petitioner is Intitled to 1000 acres of land on the head Rights of himself, wife, six children and ten negroes in family as appears by affidavit annexed for which he hath never had any land granted him in this State. May it therefore please your Honorable Board to Grant your petitioner 500 acres of land in Franklin County and 500 acres in the County of Washington on the Rights aforesaid and on his complying with the Terms mentioned in the late Land Act, and your petitioner will pray. Thomas Wootten.

State of Georgia. To the Honorable President and Members of the Council now siting in Augusta for the purpose of Granting Lands in the two new counties of Franklin and Washington. The petition of *Richard Bradford Wootten, a citizen of Wilkes* in the State aforesaid, Sheweth, That your Petitioner is Intitled to 250 Acres of Land on the head Right of *himself and one negroe* as appears by affidavit annexed for which he hath never had any lands Granted him in this State. May it therefore please your Honorable Board to Grant your Petitioner 250 acres of Land in the County of Washington on the right aforesaid and on his complying with the Terms mentioned in the Late Land Act, and your Petitioner will pray.
Richard Bradford Wootten.

State of Georgia, } Personally appeared before us Richard Bradford Wootten and Wilkes County. } being duly sworn that he has in this State himself and one in family and never had any land Granted him either under this Government or the former.

Sworn to before us the 3rd day of *April, 1784.*
Z. Lamar, A. J. P., Daniel Coleman, J. P., John Rutherford, J. P.

State of Georgia. To the honorable the president and members of Council now sitting in Augusta . . . . The petition of *Benjamin Wootten,* a citizen of Wilkes County in the State aforesaid, Sheweth, That your Petitioner is entitled to 250 acres of land on the head Rights of himself and one negroe as appears by affidavit annexed for which he has never had any land Granted him in this State. May it therefore please your Honorable Board to grant your Petitioner 250 Acres of Land in the County of Washington on the Right aforesaid and on his complying with the Terms mentioned in the late Land Act and your petitioner will pray.
Benjamin Wootten.

State of Georgia, } Personally appeared before us Benjamin Wootten and being Wilkes County. } duly sworn that he has in this State himself and one in family and never had any Land Granted him either under this Government or the former. Sworn before us this 3rd Day of April, 1784.
John Rutherford, J. P., Z. Lamar, A. J. P., Daniel Coleman, J. P.

From foregoing records, we see that Thomas Wootten, who m. Mrs. Tabitha Pope was as late as May 19, 1783, still a citizen of and resided in *Wake* Co., N. C., that on April 3rd, 1784, he makes application for land grant as being a citizen of *Wilkes Co., Ga.,* or rather, "*as having removed into this State with the intention of becoming a citizen*"—that he brought with him a wife, six children and ten negroes. The children I have shown were Richard Bradford, Benjamin—by his first wife,—Mary Ann, James, Thomas, and Lemuel Wooten, by his second wife.

"To Thomas Wootten, County of Wilkes. Four hundred and twenty (420) acres bounded North by William Parten's and Marshall's land, south by Benningfield's and *Pope's* land, east by Parten's land, and West by Benningfield's lands, 16 Sept., 1785". (Land Grant Book HHH, p. 516).

Thomas Wootten and *Tabitha, his wife,* of the County of *Wilkes,* and State of Georgia, make deed, Dec. 24, 1790, to Nathaniel Moss, of same Co., to *220* acres in Wilkes Co., on waters of Chicasaw Creek, part of *420 acres* granted Thomas Wootten by his Excellency Samuel Elbert, Sept. 16, 1785 [See grant above], for 60 £.
Wit.: John Thurman, John Taylor. (Signed) Thomas Wootten.
(Book H, p. 371, Washington, Wilkes Co., Ga.). Tabitha Wootten.

To Thomas Wootten, Three hundred acres in Wilkes Co., Ga., bounded on all sides by vacant lands, 16 Sept., 1785." (Ld. Grant Book HHH, p. 531).

To Thomas Wootten 800 acres in Franklin Co., bounded westerly by surveyed land, southwesterly by Moses Millar and vacant land, Southeasterly by Benj. Ashworth's, Thos. Walton's and Thomas Wootten's lands. 31 March, *1786*.
(Ld. Bk. III, p. 678). Gov. Edward Telfair,
G. Handley, C. C.

To Thomas Wootten 500 Acres in Franklin Co., bounded east by Thos. Walton's and Samuel Knox's land, northerly by John Partain's land, West by vacant, and south by Thomas Wootten's and unknown land. 22 April, 1786.
(Ld. Bk. III, p. 813). Gov. E. Telfair,
G. Handley, C. C.

1788. Thomas Wooten and *Tabitha, his wife,* of the Co. of *Wilkes,* State of Ga., June 12, 1788, to John Abernathy, for 50 £ 385 Acres of Land in Franklin Co. on North side Oconee River, joining lands of Nathaniel Bradford, *Benj. Ashworth, Thos. Walton,* Wm. Bailey and the s'd Thomas Wootten, being Part of a *tract* of *800* acres granted by the State aforesaid on *Big School Creek* and *Rocky* Creek, in the Co. of Franklin, on *March 31, 1786*. Grant signed by Edward Telfair, Gov. [See grant above]. Thomas Wootten.
Wit.: Holmes Freeman, J. P., Curtis Welborn. Tabitha Wootten.
Rec. May 16, 1798. (Oldest Deed Book of Jackson Co., p. 88).

Jany. 3, 1785. Grant by John Houston, Gov., to Thos. Wootten, 287½ acres County of Washington, bounded Northwardly by vacant land and on all other sides by Oconee River. (On Bounty).
Geo. Handley, Depty. Clerk. Comn . . . (Ld. Book FFF, p. 330).

To Thomas Wootten 287½ acres in Washington Co., bounded northerly by upper form of Rocky Creek, Southwesterly by Peter Perkin's land, easterly by John Perkin's and Daniel Young's land, Westerly by York's and Welden's lands. *Oct. 12, 1785*. (On Bounty). (Ld. Book HHH, p. 673).

Dr. Richard Bradford Wootten[3], son of Thos. Wootten[2], by his 1st wife, was b. in N. C., c. 1765; d. in Wilkes Co., Ga., in 1798; m. Lucretia Cade, 1st husband, b. c., 1770; sis. of James Cade and dau. of pro. Drury or Henry Cade. Issue: 1.—Richard Wootten[4], Gent., who was apptd. Ensign of the 337th Dist. Co. of the Militia, 30th Dec., 1812 ("Military Commissions", May 6th, 1812 to Sept. 16, 1815", p. 265, Adjt. Genl's office); d. 1850; m. Martha Hinton, d. in 1882, in Nashville, Tenn., dau. of John Hinton, b. c. 1772, in N. C., d. 22 Sept. 1845, in Walton Co., Ga., and his wife, Elizabeth Norman, dau. of Jesse and Elizabeth (Southard) Norman. Issue, among others: (1) Powhatan Bolling Wootten[5], who m. Catharine Lynch and had among others: Miss Katharine Hinton Wootten[6], at one time, Carnegie Librarian in Atlanta, Ga.; 2.—Martha Hart Hinton[4], m. William Saffold, son of Reuben Saffold, and had among others: W. C. Saffold, of Amite, La., b. 1822; d. 1904, aged 82 years; 3.—William Wootten[4], d. y.

Lucretia (Cade) Wootten m. (II) . . . Thurmond.

Mary Ann Wootten[3], 1770-1838, dau. of Thomas and Tabitha (Pope) Wootten, m. in March, 1789, James Cade, b. 1769; d. 1822. Issue: 1.—Guilford Cade[4], m. (I) Nancy Pope, dau. of John and Keddy (Hill) Pope, and had: (1) Ben A. Cade[5]; (2) Wylie Pope Cade[5]; (3) Guilford M. Cade,—all d. bef. 1898; m. (II) Jesse Turman, niece of William Trion, and had: (4) James C. Cade[5]; (5) John R. Cade[5]; (6) Thomas W. Cade[5]. The three last were reared by William and Amelia (Cade) Trion. The father, Guilford Cade[4], died when his son James C. Cade[5] was 4 years old, and Mrs. Jane (Turman) Cade died 6 years later.

2. Bedford Cade[4] lived at Mallorysville, Ga., and when he married his 5th wife, moved to La.
3. John Cade[4], d.; 4.—James Cade[4], d.; 5.—Robert Cade[4], m. . . . ., settled in Jasper County, Tex. He had a son, Charles Cade[5] who represented his County in the Texas legislature. These last three brothers were all dead long before 1898.
6. Amelia Cade[4], b. 1796; d. 1849; m. 1815, William Lewis Trion, d. 1851, and had: William McKenney Trion, b. 1829; d. 1862, who m. 1851, Mary Ann Glasgow, and they had: Mary Trion, b. 1859; m. 1878, G. T. McElderry, of Talladega, Ala.
7. Tabitha Cade[4], m. . . . Dent.
8. Mary Cade, b. 22 June, 1804; m. 6 Dec., 1821, Argyle Norman, and had: James Argyle Norman, b. 11 Oct., 1830; d. 19 March, 1862; m., 17 April, 1851, Julia Elizabeth Norman, b. 27 Sept., 1832; d. 27 June, 1872, and had: Sarah Louisa Norman, b. 13 April, 1853; m. 21 June, 1872, John Bascom Jobson. Mary Cade[4] said to have left 2 daus., who settled in Grimes Co., Texas.
9. Winnifred Cade[4], and 10.—Samuel Cade[4] are supposed to have been children of James and Mary Ann (Wootten) Cade.

James Wootten[3], 1775-1822, son of Thomas[2] and Tabitha (Pope) Wootten and his wife, Polly Smith, had: 1.—Betsy Maria Wootten[4], m. in 1818, William Sales; 2.—John F. Wootten[4], m. Ann Hinton; 3.—Tabby (Tabitha) Wootten[4], m. Jesse Hinton; 4.—James Wootten, Jr.[4], m. . . . Norman and d. in Texas; 5.—Francis Wootten[4], d. s. p.; 6.—W. Lemuel Wootten[4], m. Sophie Hinton, parents of S. A. Wootten, of Tignall, Ga., and of W. C. Saffold's wife; 7.—Dr. Gilbert H. Wootten[4], m. (I) Polly Wootten, dau. of Lemuel Wootten[3], his 1st cousin; m. (II) Mrs. Amelia Thomas (Hill) Jordan; 8.—Theodorick Wootten[4], d. s. p.; 9.—Joel Abbott Wootten[4], d. s. p.; was classmate of Genl. U. S. Grant, at West Point Mil. Academy; 10.—Mary Hill (called Polly) Wootten[4], b. in 1805; d. in 1832, 27 years old; m., in 1824, Fielding Lewis Hinton, b. in 1805, d. in 1832, 27 years old (wife and husband b. and d. in same years), son of James Hinton and gr. son of Dempsey Hinton. Issue: (1) Rev. James Wootten Hinton, b. 3 Jany., 1826; d. 1903; (2) Rev. Benajah Burke Hinton; (3) Eliza Hinton, m. Rev. Dr. Morgan Calloway.

Thomas Wootten[3], 1778-1848, son of Thos.[2] and Tabitha (Pope) Wootten, and wife Milly Smith, had 8 children: (1) Charles Wootten[4], d. in 1851 in the Cherokee section; m. . . . Bivins; (2) Henry Pope Wootten[4], m. . . . Hinton, and had: a.—Dr. James T. Wootten[5], d. in Jasper, Ala., s. p.; b.—Whitfield Wootten[5], m. Miss Shropshire, who after his death, m. Thos. A. Barksdale, an uncle of Mr. Dick Barksdale, of Washington, Ga.; c.—Jesse Wootten[5], a journalist, m. Miss Dent and d. c. 1877, in Newnan, Ga., leaving several children; (3) Thomas L. Wootten[4], m. . . . Hinton, and had among others: a.—Mrs. James C. Wright[5], of Mallorysville; b.—Mrs. Sarah Gore[5], of Summerville, Ga.; c.—Dempsey Wootten[5], decd., whose family live in North Ga.; (4) Polly Wootten[4], m. Jesse Calloway; (5) Martha Wootten[4], m. . . . Murphy; (6) Richard Willis Wootten[4], m. Eliza Heard, d. s. p. He was a brother-in-law of Genl. B. W. Heard; (7) Agnes Wootten[4], m. John Ben Wootten, a cousin, b. 1821, son of Benjamin Wootten, b. 1790, who, in 1820, m. Eliza Calloway, her 1st husband. Issue: a.—Eliza Calloway[5], m. Rev. John Sanders Calloway; b.—Lizzelle Wootten[5], m. Capt. John Walton, his 2nd wife; c.—Ben Wootten, Jr.[5]. d.

Benjamin and Eliza (Calloway) Wootten had: John Ben Wootten, b. 1821; Dr. William H. Wootten, m. in 1845, Elizabeth Whitehead Taylor, her 1st husband; and Almeda Wootten, who m. her 1st cousin, Wylie Middleton Pope, his 1st wife, and had 22 children, of whom only 5 attained their majorities.

Lemuel Wootten[3], b. 1780, son of Thos.[2] and Tabitha (Pope) Wootten, and his wife Nancy Smith had 8 children, among them: (1) Josiah Wootten[4], d. unm.; (2) Wylie Wootten[4], d. unm.; (3) Polly Wootten[4], m. Dr. Gilbert H. Wootten, her 1st cousin, his 1st wife, son of James and Polly (Smith) Wootten; (4) Patsey, called "Paty," Wootten[4], was blind and d. unm.; (5) . . . m. . . . Thurmond; (6) . . . m. . . . Calloway; (7) Dr. John Lem Wootten[4], practiced at Mallorysville, moved to Panola, Miss., and d. unm. in 1897.

Both Thomas Wootten[2] and his wife, Tabitha (Pope) Wootten, d. in Oglethorpe Co., Ga., it is thought, in 1808. The last mention of them in any record is in the will of Henry Augustine Pope, Nov. 10, 1807, and in the probate of the will in Jany., 1808.

The writer makes no pretense of completeness in the record of James[3], Thomas[3] and Lemuel[3] Wootten's families, but has given such data as obtained by him from various members of these families, with the belief that what is given will be aidful to those seeking more complete and definite details.

There was another Thomas Wootten who came from N. C. and settled in Wilkes Co. Ga., in *1773*. He was a Lieutenant in the Revy. War, often referred to as the Pioneer settler. It seems altogether probable that this Thomas, and Benjamin who d. in Halifax in 1764, and the James Wootten who, in 1758, was in St. Stephens Parish in Johnston, N. C., were brothers. No records yet discovered expressly declaring the fact, but the records considered together indicate it.

"Greensboro, Ga. Old Roll—Typewritten: "A careful transcript of the records of the Court of Land Commissioners appointed by his Ecellency, Sir James Wright, Royal Gov'r of the Province of Georgia, to issue the Ceeded Lands", later formed into Wilkes County. Said original records now being a part of the records of Greene Co., Ga.". (Signed) July A. D. 1910, *J. A. LaConte, p. 15,*—"Wrightsborough, *Dec. 7, 1773.* Thomas Wootten from N. C., a wife, 7 sons and one daughter, from 1 to 18 years old, and 8 slaves. 200 acres on north side of Broad River opposite the mouth of Long Creek, whereon there is a tree marked T. W. and a fence; and 300 acres on south side said River, adjoining Vann's old field. Reserve 9 months. 13:4:8". p. 21. —Dartmouth Fort. Jan—bruary 1775. Thos. Wootten desires to remove his entry of 200 acres which he resigns for 200 acres on Beaver Dam Creek on South fork of River Dart (?) adjoining lands of Hardy Saunders on the river side. Reserve 8 months. T. W. 20:0:0". Note.—A Hardy Saunders was one of the Justices of Wake Co., N. C., June 4, 1771.

"No. 261—Watkins Digest", p. 238. "An Act amending the Several acts for the better regulation of the Militia of this State.

VIII. And whereas numbers of persons are daily absenting themselves and leaving their fellow citizens to encounter the difficulties of the present crisis, Be it enacted by the authority aforesaid, That any person or persons, who shall produce a Certificate from the Commanding Officers of the District to which he belongs, to the legislature of this State (on the total expulsion of the enemy from it) of his having faithfully done his duty from the time of passing of this Act, shall be entitled to 250 Acres of good land which shall be exempt from taxes for the space of 10 years thereafter) *Provided* such person or persons *cannot be convicted of plundering or distressing the country."*

"No. 289, p. 294. Feby. 25, 1784. Officers, Soldiers, Refugees, &c, &c, who are entitled to land in this State or *Bounties* for their services &c . . . shall be entitled to have included in their grants an additional quantity of 15 acres to each hundred in full for and in lieu of any exemption from taxes; also provides for a land Court at Augusta for granting out lands, beginning the first Tuesday in April, 1784, for and during space of 3 months".

"p. 311—Feby. 22, 1785. No surveys of land due as bounties from this State shall be allowed, unless brought in and claimed within one year from and after the passing of this Act"

State of Georgia, } To the Honorable the president and the members of the Council
Wilkes County.   } now siting in Augusta for the purpose of Granting Lands in the two new Counties of Franklin and Washington. The Petition of *Lieutenant* Thomas Wootten a *citizen* of the State aforesaid, Sheweth, That your Petitioner is entitled to 250 Acres of Land, *as a Bounty,* for his services, pursuant to the *Certificate hereto annexed;* That your Petitioner is desirous of taking up the said Land in the County of Washington. May it therefore please your Honorable Board to Grant your Petitioner 250 Acres of Land in the County of Washington on the Right aforesaid, and on his complying with the Terms mentioned in the late Land Act; and your Petitioner will pray.   Thomas Wootten".

"State of Georgia. These are to certify that *Thomas Wootten was an inhabitant of this State prior to the reduction thereof by the British Arms,* and was a *Refugee* from the same, during which time he cheerfully did his duty as a soldier and Friend to the United States. Given under my hand this *2nd day of February, 1784.*

By his order. H. Freeman.   Elijah Clarke, Col."

"State of Georgia. This is to certify that *Lieut. Thomas Wootten* hath steadfastly done his duty, from the time of passing an Act at Augusta, to-wit, on the 20th day of Aug. *1781* until the total expulsion of the British from this State; and the said Lieutenant Thomas Wootten cannot to my knowledge or belief be convicted of plundering or distressing the country, and is therefore under the said Act entitled to a Bounty of 250 Acres of good land, free from taxes for 10 years. Given under my hand at Savannah, the 2nd day of February, 1784.

By his order, H. Freeman.   Elijah Clarke, Col."
Georgia—. . . (No. 828).

These are to certify that Thomas Wootten as a citizen is entitled to 250 acres of Land as a *Bounty* agreeable to an Act and Resolve of the General Assembly, passed at Augusta the 19 August, 1781, as per certificate of E. Clarke Col. Given under my Hand at Savannah the 25 day of March, in the year of our Lord 1784. Georgia—(No. 860).

These are to certify that *Lieutenant* Thomas Wootten a citizen is entitled to 250 acres of Land as a *Bounty* agreeable to an Act and Resolve of the General Assembly passed at Augusta the 20th August, 1781, as per certificate of E. Clarke Col. Given under my hand at Savannah the 25 Day of March in the year of our Lord 1784.   J. Houston.
Attest.: D. Rees, Secy".

"Jany. 25, 1785. Granted to Thomas Wootten 287½ acres, Co. of Washington, bounded on all sides by vacant lands. (On Bounty).   Sam Elbert Gov. &c.
(Ld. Bk FFF, p. 545).   G. Handley, Clk. Council."

Deed Book 1, p. 474. *Greene Co., Feb. 3, 1790.* James and Charity Wootten, admrs. of *Thomas Wootten, late of Wilkes Co., decd.,* conveys 287½ acres of lands in Greene, formerly Washinton County, granted s'd Thos. Wootten on Jany. 25, 1785. Wit. Leonard Fretwell, Rozanna Johnson.   James Wootten.
                                                       Charity Wootten.

James and Charity Wootten, on June 17, 1791, of Greene Co., Ga., mentioned as administrators of Thos. Wootten, decd., of Wilkes Co. (Deed Book of Greene Co., Ga.). James was pro. the son and Charity the widow of Thos. Wootten, decd.

The Augusta Chronicle, April 11, 1789,—files in Library of Congress—gives Thos. Wootten, Collector (of Taxes) Wilkes Co., Ga., paying returns to State Treasurer, Feby. 4, 1785, 1786. It speaks of Col. Thos. Wootten's district (tax?).

James Wootten granted 287½ acres in Washington Co., bounded on all sides by vacant land. *13 Dec., 1785.* (On Bounty). (Ld. Bk. III, p. 342).

Thos. Wootten[1], Isle of Wight, Will. Mch. 15, 1669, and wife, Sara, relict of . . . Wood, had an only son:

Richard Wootten[2] who m. . . ., name of wife not given, will 28 Sept., 1686, had: Richard Wootten[3]; Thomas Wootten[3], and another child, name not given (pro. Joseph). Richard Wootten[3] m. Lucy Council dau. of Hodges Council and his wife *Lucy Hardy* dau. of *John Hardy* and his wife, *Alice,*—his will Oct. 7, 1676. They had: William Wootten[4], who m. Ann . . . , maiden name not given.

A William Wootten patented 300 A. in Northampton Co., N. C., 16 March, 1743, and the above William Wootten[4] and wife Ann sold to James Council and James Bryant, all of Isle of Wight, 100 A. in sd. Co., on Nov. 21, 1744. Then a William Wootten, on April 21, 1749, was a witness to the will of George Norwood, of Northampton Co.

Thomas Wootten[3] m. (I) Ann . . . ; m. (II) *Mary* . . . . In 1705, Thos.[3] and *Ann Wootten* join Richard Wootten[3] in a sale of land. In 1708 Thos[3] and Ann *Wootten* sell land to Richard Wootten. On 12 Jany., 1736, *Thos. Wootten*[3] and *Mary his wife,* sell 200 A. in Isle of Wight to William Whitly, of Bertie Precinct, N. C.

A James Wootten of Johnston Co., N. C., on 26 May, 1756, buys land in sd. Co.

On 17 Sept., 1761, Benjamin Wootten buys two tracts, one 260 A., the other 238 A., from *Benjamin Hardy* and his wife Mary. The land located in Enfield, former County seat of Halifax Co.

Considering the foregoing in connection with numerous other transactions in Johnston, Orange and Halifax Cos., we are led inevitably to the conclusion that Benjamin Wootten who d. 1764, in Halifax Co., was the son of either Thomas[3] and Mary Wootten (or Ann, the 1st wife), or of William[4] and Ann Wootten.

To settle the matter positively will require the discovery of some new Court or Bible record.

Benjamin named sons Thos., John and William. This son Thomas named sons by his 1st wife, Richard Bradford and Benjamin, and children by his 2nd wife, the widow Tabitha Pope, *Mary Ann*—combining names of both wives of Thomas Wootten[3], James, Thomas and Lemuel.

QUAKERS.

The Quakers at an early date cast in their lot with the Colony of Virginia; and many were compelled to fly from the execution of the severe laws passed against their Sect, and found refuge in Carolina. They were of English descent, and at that time too few, in either State to exert a preponderating influence on the community at large. (Foote's Sketches of N. C., p. 78).

Three Articles of belief were necessary to constitute any body of persons a church: (1) That there is a God; (2) That God is to be publicly worshipped; (3) that it is lawful and the duty of every man to bear witness to the truth when called on by the proper authority and "that every church or profession shall in their terms of communion set down the eternal way whereby they witness a truth as in the presence of God". No man was permitted to be a freeman in Carolina or to have any estate or habitation in it that did not acknowledge a God, and that he was to be publicly worshipped. No person above 17 years of age could have any benefit or protection of law, nor hold any place of honor or profit who was not a member of some church or profession. Locke provided that any 7 persons agreeing in any religion should be constituted a "church or profession, to which they shall give some name, to distinguish it from others. "Southern Quakers and Slavery", p. 10, by Stephen B. Weeks; C. R. N. C., Vol. 1, pp. 187, 207, & Sec. 100).

While the Friends are *proverbial* for soundness of piety, frugality, and industry, they are signally defective in aggressive power, because they reject the active and demonstrative instrumentalities of propagating the Gospel. It is a church of *negative*, rather than positive institutions. (His. of Methodism in N. C., Vol. 1, p. 11, by W. L. Grissom).

There were no provisions in Va. for Quakers to celebrate the rites of matrimony after their peculiar fashion before the law of 1780. In this matter North Carolina was ahead of Virginia. But we have the clearest evidence that they had married in their own fashion from very earliest times. The Va. law of March, 1662, provided that *all marriages* should be by license or publication of banns and be performed by a minister, all others being *declared illegal*. The laws of 1696 and 1705 provided that marriages should be celebrated only in accordance with forms in the Book of Common Prayer. It was the same under the law of 1748. The laws of 1780 and 1784 legalized marriages which had been celebrated previous to this date by Dissenters and gave the *Quakers* authority to celebrate the rite after their own fashion. They had married after their own fashion but without consent of the Government and therefore illegally until the passage of this law. ("So. Quakers and Slavery", pp. 168-'9, by Stephen B. Weeks).

QUAKER MARRIAGES.

"As early as 1661 Friends had forced the English law to recognize the legality of their forms of marriage. The initial step was by the parties who declared in meeting their intentions. The Women's Meeting then appointed a committee to see if the woman was "clear" from other "marriage entanglements"; the men's meeting did the same, and when this was settled the parties were "left to their liberty to take each other", which was done by calling on the Congregation as witnesses: Friends, you are my witnesses that in the presence of you I take this my friend Elizabeth Nixon to be my wife, promising to be a loving and true husband to her, and to live in the good order of truth, so long as it shall please the Lord that we live together, or until death". They were always advised against marrying outside of their own communion, such being spoken of as "accomplishing disorderly marriages", "outgoing in marriage", etc. ("So. Qua. and Slavery", pp. 126-'7, by Stephen B. Weeks).

For want of men in Holy Orders, both the members of the Council and

Magistrates were empowered to marry all those who would not take each other's word. But for the ceremony of christening their children they leave that to chance. (Extract from Wm. Bird's Journal—"Old Churches & Fams.", p. 283, by Bishop Meade).

Richard Bennett (Gen.) the great man of the County was a Quaker and an ancestor of Genl. Robert E. Lee.

Edward Major and Thomas Dew were also Quakers, or in sympathy with them, as were also Col. Joseph Bridger, Major Thomas Taberer, Col. Thos. Bushrod, Col. Thos. and Edmond Godwin, Judge Jeremiah Exum, Dr. John Grove, Wm. Bressy, the Jordans, and many others of the most prominent and influential men of that section. The records show that in 1682 both Thomas and Edmund Godwin were members of the Chuckatuck meeting house. The Quakers increased rapidly and seem to have been unmolested, except those who like Thomas Jordan refused to pay their tithes, defied the Court and malinged the clergy. The Godwins seemed to have severed their connection with the Quakers, for after 1682 both were vestrymen of Chuckatuck Parish, and both filled the office of Sheriff.

While the Quakers were sometimes fined for nonconformity, they had their own meeting houses and practically their own way. ("His. of Nansemond", pp. 23, 25, 27; W. & M. Qly., 7, p. 212).

VESTRY BOOK OF NANSEMOND CO.

In the Ms. of Suffolk Parish and Upper Suffolk Parish, in the Clerk's office at Suffolk, we find on p. 1, some who were Quakers, now, July 15, 1749, Members of the Church of England. Vestrymen present: Thomas Godwin, Jonathan Godwin, Anthony Holladay, John King, James Cowlings, Thos. Godwin, William Wright, Nathaniel Wright, Edward Wright, James Turner, Thomas Jordan, John Buxton. On p. 3.—Thomas Godwin, Clerk of the Court. On p. 6.—Thomas Godwin, Vestryman, deceased, called on p. 6, *Col. Godwin.* (1749).

VASSALBOROUGH, ME.

Friends Records of Marriage Certificates . . having declared their Intentions of Taking Each Other in Marriage, before Several Monthly Meetings of the People Called Quakers in the Co. afs'd according to the good Order used among them; their Proceedings after due Enquiry and Deliberate Consideration thereof were allowed by the Said Meetings, they appearing Clear of all Others and having consent of Parents Concerned. Now these are to Certify all Whom it may Concern, that for the full accomplishing of their Said Intentions, this Twenty third Day of the Eighth Month in the Year of Our Lord 1787 [written], they the Said Zaccheus Bowerman and Permela Jones appeared at a public assbly of the afsd People & others, in their Meeting Place in Fairfield & he the sd Zaccheus Bowerman, Taking the Said Permela Jones by the hand, did openly declare as followeth: Friends I take this my Friend Permela Jones to be my wife, Promising Through Divine assistance to be unto her a Loving and Faithful Husband, Untill it shall Please the Lord by Death to Separate us. And the sd Permela Jones, did then & there in Like Manner Declare as followeth: Friends I Take this my Friend Zaccheus Bowerman to be my Husband Promising Through Divine assistance to be unto him a Loving & Faithful Wife, Untill it Shall Please the Lord to Separate us, or Words of the Like Import. And the said Zaccheus Bowerman & Permela Jones, as a further Confirmation thereof have hereunto Set their hands. She *after the Custom of Marriage,* Assuming the Name of her Husband.   Zaccheus Bowerman.
                                                                                    Permela Bowerman.

And we whose Names are hereunto subscribed, being Present with Others at the Consummation of this said Marriage as Witnesses thereunto Set our hands the Day & year above written. [The entire Congregation present sign their names individually as witnesses]. (N. E. H. & G. Reg., Vol. 68, p. 162-'3).

"After the restoration of King Charles II the Quakers had a strong following, especially in the Upper Parish. William Edmundson, a friend of George Fox visited the neighborhood in 1671 and met Genl. Richard Bennett, who he said received the truth and died in the same, leaving two friends his Executors. The able lawyer and preacher, Thomas Story, of Phila., came in 1699 and 1705 and held many "open and comfortable meetings", visiting many and widely separated localities in that section, and at Chuckatuck, where he met with his "ancient friend", Elizabeth Webb of Gloucestershire, England, and John Copeland, who at his request, showed him his mutilated right ear, being one of the first of those who had their ears cut by the Presbyterians, or Independants, of New England". (W. & M. Qly., Vol. 7, pp. 211-212).

Major Taberer left his estate to his grandson Joseph Copeland, probably a relative of John Copeland visited by Thomas Story. (W. & M. Qly., Vol. 7, p. 215).

ORDER AGAINST THE QUAKERS.

Att a Councill held at James City ffebruary 20th 1690: Present the Rt Honorble ffrancis Nicholson, Esqr their Majties Lieut. Governor Nathanll Bacon Esqr Secy Coll. William Bird Coll: Chrisr Wormeley Coll: Jno. Armistead. This board having been informed yt ye Inhabitants of Pennsylvania declare that if ye ffrench or Indians Come agt them, they will acquaint them they have no Quarrell with them nor will not fight whereby if either of those Enemies shall go thither, they will not only be supplied with provisions, but a place of retreat after Mischiefe done wh. may prove of Dangerous Consequence to ye peace & Safety of this & all other Majties Plantations in these parts, & it being Considered that ye *ffrequent meeting of Quakers in severall places of this Collony* of their own appointing without ever acquainting the Governor with ye same or doing what is required by an Act of Parliament made in the 1st year of ye Reigne of our Soveraigne Lord & Lady, William & Mary, by the Grace of God of England, Scotland, ffrance & Ireland &c., King & Queen, entitled an Act for Exempting their Majties protestant subjects dissenting from ye Church of England from ye penalties of Certain Lawes, not only by the Inhabitant of this Collony, but those of Md., Pennsylavnia & other places as really present, by means whereof the ffrench or Indians if possest of Pa. have fitt opportunity to do mischiefe, accordingly, ffor prevention whereof for ye ffuter & to the end of afsd Act of Parliament May bee put into effectual Execution, itt is ordered that after publication hereof (wh. all their Majties Justices of the Peace in the respective Cos. in this Colony are required to Cause to be done att ye next Court to bee held for their said Countyes) that none of ye persons usually *called Quakers doe prsume to meet* at any place whatsoever without first doeing & performing what by the Recited Act of Parliament is required & Comanded upon penalty of being prosecuted & suffering such paines & penalties as by the said Act are to be inflicted on those whoe (do) not comply therewith, & to ye end that the said Act may be duly pformed, all their Majties Subjects within this Collony especially Justices of ye Peace, Sheriffs & other Majties officers Whatsoever are hereby required & Comanded to take care that noe pson or psons whatsoever presume to doe or act anything Contrary to ye full intent & meaning thereof. And it is further ordered that if after ye said psons *called Quakers have pformed* what is required by ye aforesd Act of Parliament any Strangers from any other Government shall come among them they give an acct of every such person to ye next Justice of ye Peace whoe is hereby ordered to Cause said pson or psons to appear before him & tak his or their Examination under his or their hands to what place he or they belong whither going & when, & of all things else wh. may be for their Majties service, & forthwith returne ye same (if he see Cause) to ye Rt Honoble ffrancis Nicholson Esqr their Majties Lieut Governor that such further order may be had therein as shall be agreeable to Law. & itt is alsoe ordered that if any pson whatsoever shall receive by letter or hear any strange news wh. may tend to ye disturbance of ye peace of their Govmnt that they doe not presume to publish ye same but with ye 1st Conveniency repair to ye next Justice of ye Peace & acquaint him therewith, whoe is to act therein according to law. Copia Vera. Test. W. Edwards, Cl. Cur. March ye 24th 1690/1. Published then in York Court & ordered to be Recorded. Test. I. Sedgwick, D. Cl. Cur. (W. & M. Qly. Vol. 27, pp. 130-'1).

QUAKERS.

"There were several Baptist Ministers in the Province, but of their character I know nothing. People in these circumstances could not be so grossly ignorant, as they have been represented, and the *Quakers*, although they differ from most others in their view of the Ministry, have always advocated and maintained a high degree of English Education". (Wheeler's Rems., p. 256).

Extracts from the "Annals of Newberry, S. C.", by O'Neal-Chapman, p. 33.

"No beggar or pauper was ever known among Friends. They take care of all such. Their Meeting of Sufferings provides for them and all other wants".

They were a "Hard working, healthy, yet an honest, innocent and mirthful, though a staid people, make up altogether an interesting picture".

The only objection which I know to the practice of Friends, is that they do not generally sufficiently attend to the religious instruction of their children and the reading of the Scriptures. In this respect, I know, there are many, very many, illustrious exceptions, and I believe their rules require the Scriptures to be read, and their children to be religiously instructed. In other points, I think no religious community can present better claims for respect, and even the admiration of men." (See *also* "Annals of Newberry", p. 709).

"John Archdale, the Quaker Governor", is app'd 1694; his sagacious and prudent administration". (Wheeler's His. of N. C.; p. 32—1st Series). The wife of Wm. Hill, Esq., the present Sec. of State of N. C., is a descendant of Gov. Archdale, through his dau. Ann, who m. July 1688, Emmanuel Lowe, whose dau. Anne m. Mr. Pendleton, whose dau. Mary m. Denby Connor, the father of Mrs. Hill (p. 33).

SUPPLEMENT.

Family record of John Bones Hill, p. 168, is here corrected.

John Bones Hill and wife, Sadie Johnson, had: 1c.—Eliza Holden Hill, b. Jany. 3, 1875; m., Nov. 4, 1897, William Daniel Ready, d. July 7, 1919. Had chn.; 2c.—Lou Brunson Hill, b. April 7, 1876; m. July 28, 1893; d. Oct. 8, 1911; m. Ed Mims, and had 3 chn.; 3c.—Elizabeth Hollingsworth Hill, b. Jany. 2, 1881; m. June 29, 1910, John Griffin Mobley. No chn.; 4c.—Sadie Daisye Hill, b. April 27, 1883; m. Dec., 1904, Sam Bones Nicholson and had one child; 5c.—Marian Hill, b. Sept. 14, 1885; m. (I) June, 1902, Dr. William Luther Jones, d. July, 1911—2 boys; m. (II), Aug., 1913, Arthur Childress; 6c.—Henry Hughes Hill, b. Aug. 26, 1887; m. Dec., 1912, Mattie Mims—2 chn.; 7c.—William Warren Hill, b. Oct. 28, 1900; d. Dec. 4, 1917, was accidentally killed in camp. Was Sr. Gd. Sergeant at Camp Sevier, Camp Electrician; 8c.—Maria Fraser Hill, b. April 27, 1904; m. Oct. . . . . , Floyd Rainsford—2 chn.

FINIS.

ERRATA.

Chart 2.—Priscill*i* shd. be Priscill*a*.
P. 13.—10th l. Almight shd. be Almight*y*.
P. 18.—17th l. G*r*anberry shd. be G*r*eenberry.
P. 69.—8th l. Ludowick shd. be Lodowick.
P. 69.—13th l. Cincequefield shd. be Cin*q*uefield.
P. 75.—19th l. fr. bot. Troop shd. be Troup.
P. 79.—12th l. fr. bot. Troop shd. be Troup.
P. 89.—1st l. Holliday shd. be Halliday.
P. 89.—23rd l *Edenton* shd. be. *Eatonton*.
P. 91.—20th l. fr. bot. *Blank space* should be filled with *Mary*.
P. 96.—14th l. fr. bot. Insert Ref. *p. 147*.
P. 97.—3rd l. *2* in parenthesis shd. be *1*, and insert *p. 147*, bef. the parenthesis.
P. 97.—20th l. fr. bot. *Brow* shd. be *Brown*.
P. 98.—13th l. fr. bot. L*u*tcher shd. be L*e*tcher.
P. 99.—10th l. fr. bot. Insert in parenthesis after O. *p. 140*.
P. 101.—15th l. fr. bot. *pleased* shd be *di*spleased.
P. 108.—20th l. fr. bot. Albigen*es* shd. be Albigen*ce*.
P. 108.—14th l. fr. bot. Albigen*es* shd. be Albigen*ce*.
P. 108.—11th l. fr. bot. At end, after Theophilus[3], add *p. 163*.
P. 122.—2nd l. fr. bot. *1827* shd. be *1872*.
P. 125.—15th l. fr. bot. *Louse* shd. be *Louise*.
P. 126.—6th l. Louize shd. be Louise.
P. 127.—Lines 4, 5 and 6. Ir*w*in shd be Ir*v*in.
P. 135.—15th l. *1880* shd. be *1881*.
P. 135.—17th l. *V*audon shd. be *J*audon.
P. 135.—4th l. fr. bot. Davi*s* shd. be Davi*e*.
P. 137.—26th l. Mo*u*ts shd. be Mo*n*ts.
P. 137.—27th l. *Clarence Eugene Mouts, Jr.* shd be *Eugene DuBose Monts*.
P. 137.—11th l. fr. bot. McLoughlin shd. be McL*a*ughlin.
P. 137.—2nd l. fr. bot. *Edward* shd. be *Edwin*.
P. 138.—20th l. fr. bot. *1902* shd. be *1903*.
P. 143.—12th l. fr. bot. *Semmes* shd. be *Screven*, and Irwin shd. be Ir*v*in.
P. 143.—5th, 7th, 9th, 11th and 12th ls. fr. bot. Ir*w*in shd. be Ir*v*in.
P. 143.—8th l. fr. bot. *Bieckle* shd. be *Biechele*.
P. 145.—10th l. Lizz*i*lle shd. be L*i*zzelle.
P. 146.—11th and 12th ls. fr. bot. Carro*l* shd. be Carro*ll*.
P. 147.—2nd l. fr. bot. Insert *96* after p.
P. 152.—7th l. *Hattiesville, Miss.*, shd. be *Hallettsville, Texas*.
P. 160.—3rd l. fr. bot. *Parenthesis sign shd. be omitted*.
P. 163.—19th l. fr. bot. Personali*ty* shd. be personal*ty*.
P. 166.—8th l. yt shd. be ye.
P. 166.—Middle of page. *2* bef. Henry Hampton Hill—*twice*—shd. be *6*.
P. 175.—4th l. fr. bot. Sa*w*in shd. be S*w*ain.
P. 177.—17th l. immediate*l* shd. be immediate*ly*.
P. 179.—2nd l. fr. bot. Jan*i*e shd. be Jane.
P. 182.—29th l. fr. bot. *Marks* prob. shd. be *Moore*
P. 213.—6th l. fr. bot. *G*alton shd. be *D*alton.
P. 219.—24th l. Capito*l* shd. be Capita*l*.
P. 223.—25th l. *Joseph* shd. be *Jacob*.
P. 230.—18th l. or shd. be *and*.
P. 240.—11th l. *devised* shd. be *divided*.
P. 253.—29th l. *119* shd. be *144*.
P. 260.—19th l. Loathesome shd. be *Loathsome*.
P. 272.—30th l. *1813* (?) shd. be *1853*.
P. 274.—13th l. fr. bot. *Mark*) of parenthsis after Wootten).
P. 282.—17th l. fr. bot. Eliza *Calloway* shd. be *Wootten*.

INDEX

NOTE:—Numerals over names denote their generations and the letters in parentheses following are the initials of their fathers.

		PAGE
ANDREW,	Benjamin	89
"	Elizabeth	89
ANTHONY—	Family	174-178
"	Abbie Davis-Pope	88, 177
"	Adelia[7]	176
"	Agnes[3]	176
"	Agnes[6]	177
"	Augustus P.	88, 128
"	Augustus P., Jr.	88
"	Barbara[5]	176
"	Bella[4]	177
"	Bolling[3]	176, 178
"	Charles[3]	175 (2)
"	Charles[4]	176
"	Charles[5]	176
"	Charles H.[7]	176
"	Charlotte[4]	176
"	Christopher[3]	175-6 (3)
"	Christopher[4]	176
"	Christopher[5]	176
"	Christopher Jordan[4]	177
"	Clara Julia-Pope	177
"	Clarke[5]	176
"	Edd[7]	177
"	Edwin Clarke[6]	176
"	Edwin Clarke[7]	176
"	Edwin M.[4]	177
"	Elizabeth[3]	175
"	Elizabeth[4]	176
"	Elizabeth[5]	176
"	Elizabeth-Clarke	176
"	Ella A.[7]	176
"	Emile DuB.	88
"	Emma Eugenia[4]	177
"	Ernest[5]	177
"	E. B.	175 (2), 176, 177 (2)
"	Florence V[7]	176
"	Gabriel Toombs[5]	177
"	Hannah B.[4]	176
"	Harry Duncan	88
"	Harry Jefferson	88
"	Hilda	88
"	James[3]	175 (2)
"	James[5]	176
"	James Rembert[4]	88, 177
"	James Rembert, Jr.	88
"	Jane[5]	176
"	Janet-Paddison	177
"	Jean[5]	177
"	John Vance[5]	177
"	Jordan[4]	176
"	Joseph[2]	174-5

		PAGE
ANTHONY,	Joseph, Jr.[3]	175 (2), 177 (2)
"	Joseph[4]	176 (2)
"	Joseph[5]	176
"	Joseph[5]	177
"	Joseph W.[5]	176
"	Judith[3]	176
"	Judson[6]	177
"	Julia[5]	177
"	Julia Toombs	177
"	Katherine	177, 178
"	Leila Davis	88
"	Lucile[6]	177
"	Lucy Hill[8]	88
"	Lucy Jordan-Hill	88, 128
"	Mamie Lou[5]	177
"	Mark[1]	174 (2), 175 (4)
"	Mark II[3]	176
"	Mark[5]	176
"	Margaret[5]	177
"	Mary[3]	175
"	Mary[4]	176
"	Mary[7]	177
"	Mary Chatfield	88
"	Mary Rembert-DuBose	177
"	Mathew[5]	176
"	Micajah[3]	175, 177
"	Micajah[4]	176
"	Micajah[5]	176
"	Milton, Dr.,	175
"	Penelope[3]	175
"	Penelope[4]	176
"	Penelope[5]	176
"	Pope	177
"	Rachel[3]	176
"	Rachel[4]	176
"	Rachel[5]	176
"	Render[7]	177
"	Rhoda[5]	176
"	Roberta[5]	177
"	Roscoe Tate	88
"	Roslyn[8]	88
"	Sally[6]	176
"	Samuel[5]	176
"	Samuel B.[4]	176
"	Samuel P.[7]	176
"	Sarah[3]	175
"	Sarah[4]	176
"	Sarah[5]	176
"	Scott[7], Dr.	177
"	Thos.[5]	176
"	Thos. Clarke[5]	176
"	Willie[4]	177

INDEX

	PAGE
AVENT, Col. Thos.	28
BARKSDALE, Thos. A.	282
" Thos. J.	177
" Dick	282
BARNETT, Albert Augustus	121
" Albert Augustus, Jr.	121
" Aurelius Pharr	122
" Austin Hill	144
" Clara Beall	121
" Edward A.	144
" Edward A., Jr.	144
" Elizabeth W.	144
" Emma Anthony	121
" Graham DuBose	121
" Samuel Hill	144
" William Hill	121
" William Meriwether	121
BARROW, Alice Barker	77
" Alice Josephine-Hand	80
" Alma L.-Jones	76
" Benjn Hy[8]	86
" Benjn White[7]	75, 83
" Clara Elizabeth[7]	74 (2)
" Clara Elizabeth[8]	77, 80
" Cornelia Augusta-Jackson	76
" Craig[8]	77
" Davenport Jackson[8]	78
" David Crenshaw, Sr.	70 (3) 71, 72 (4), 73 (2), 74 (2)
" David Crenshaw, Jr.	70, 75, 83, 84 (2), 85 (3)
" David Crenshaw III[8]	77
" David Crenshaw IV[8]	80
" David Francis[8]	86
" Eleanor Priscilla[8]	86
" Elfrida-DeRenne	77
" Elizabeth Church[8]	76
" Ella Patience[7]	74-'5, 81-'2
" Ella Patience Crenshaw[8]	78
" Emily-Hand	80
" Emma M.-Huger	77
" Florella Hill	170
" Frances Barclay[8]	77
" Frances Ingle Childs	85
" Francis Cuthbert[8]	80
" Henry-Lucas	86
" Henry Walker[7]	75, 86
" James[3]	71 (3) 84
" James[7]	74, 78-'9
" James[8]	77, 80
" John Pliny & Family	169-170
" Jennie-Turner	80
" Joyce-Smith	81
" Lucy Hopson Lumpkin	77-'8
" Lucy Pope[7]	74, 81
" Marie-McDd	80
" Mary Augusta-Arnold	86
" Middleton Pope[7]	74-'5 (2), 76 (3), 80, 84
BARROW, Middleton Pope, Jr.[8]	76
" Patience-Crenshaw	71
" Precious Patience	87
" Sarah Church-Craig	76
" Sarah Pope	69, 70, 71, 74
" Sarah Pope[8]	78
" Sue C.-Cooper	168-9
" Susan Childs[8]	85
" Thomas[1]	71
" Thomas[2]	71
" Thomas Augustine[7]	74, 79, 80
" Thomas Augustine, Jr.[8]	80 (2)
BENNETT, Thos. B.	168
BILLUPS—Family	178-181
" Ann-Ransone	178
" Ann Ransom[6]	179
" Christopher[4]	178
" C. William	180
" Dorcas Richards[6]	179
" Elizabeth[5]	178
" Elizabeth Rebecca Beall	179 (2), 180
" George[1]	178 (2)
" George[2]	178 (2)
" George[3]	178
" Henry C.	180
" John[2]	178
" John[3], Capt.	178
" John[5]	178
" John[6]	179
" John[6]	180 (3)
" John A.[7]	179
" John R.[7]	179
" Joel Abbott[7]	180
" Joseph[2]	178
" Joseph[3]	178 (2)
" Joseph, Jr.[4]	178 (2)
" Lititia[6]	179
" Lucy[3]	178
" Lucy	179
" Maria[6]	179
" Mary[3]	178
" Mary Richardson	179
" Mary Richardson[6]	179
" Richard[2]	178, 181
" Richard Richardson[6]	179
" Robert[3]	178
" Robert[4]	179
" Robert[4]	178 (2)
" Robert[6]	179, 180
" Robert William[7]	180
" Salome Susan[7]	180
" Sarah[3]	178
" Saunders[7], Gen.	181
" Susan Millicent-Beall	179
" Thos.	178
" Thos. C.	180 (2)
" Vashti A.	180
" Virginia[6]	179 (2)

INDEX

BILLUPS, William[5] 178, 179
BLACK, Col. J. C. C. 48
BOUNDS, Celeste 121
BRIDGER, Col. Joseph 28
BUSSY, Thos. 25
CALDWELL, Eugenia 138
CALHOUN Family 124-6
CALLAWAY, Albert G. H. 26
" Andrew W. 26
" Clarrissa 19, 28
" Ella Pope Hill 26
" Geo. Wiley Hill . . . 26
" Hendley Varner, Dr. . . 51
" Isaac 20 (2)
" Isaac 51
" Jacob 20
" Jesse Mercer 26
" Jesse Mercer Hill . . . 26
" Job 19, 22
" Job, Jr. . . . . . 20-'1-'2
" Joseph . . . . . 20-'1-'2
" Joshua 20
" Julia W. Hill 26
" Mary . . . 19, 20 (2), 22
" Mary Anne 51
" Mary-Parks 21
" Martha Henrietta . . . 51
" Martha Pope 51
" Martha Elizh Hill . . . 26
" Nany 23
" Rebecca 23
" Sarah Frances Hill . . . 26
" Thos. Merrill Hill . . . 26
" Winney 23, 51
CANDLER, Allen D. 175
" William 175
CARTER, Walter Colquitt 124
CASEY, Dr. Hy. Rozier 127
CLARK—Family 181-3
" Chrisr 181 (2), 182
" Elizabeth 182
" Penelope-Bolling 182
COBB, John Addison 81
" Family 81
COLLEY, Alline 177
" Dempsey 177
" Eugene 177
" Fannie 177
" Henry 177
" Mamie 177
" Willie, Dr. 177
" Zeb. 177
COLLINS, Joseph 126
" Thomas, Sr. 126
COMPTON, Thos. M. 216
COOK, Philip, Genl. 216
COOPER, Dr. John Wm. 168-9
COTTEN, Sarah 17, 19
CROWE, Samuel James, M.D. 85
CUNNINGHAM, Drury 32

CUNNINGHAM, Elizabeth-Johnson . . 32
DILLARD, Lucy Reese 121
DODD, Howell E. 38
DREW, Lionel Edward 78
DUBOSE—Family . . . . 183-'6, 136-'9
" Anne 183
" Bettie Lou[6] . . . . . 137-'8
" Caroline[8] 138
" Dudley McIvor[9], Genl., 185 (2)
" Edwin Rembert[7] . . . 137 (2)
" Elias[3] . . . . . 183-'4 (10)-'5
" Eliza Caroline-Spann . . . 137
" Elizabeth Adams-Vance, 137, 185
" Emma Belle[8] 138
" Ethel Vance[7] 137
" Ezekiel[4], Dr. . . . . 185 (3)-'6
" Hugh Inman[8] 138
" Isaac[1] 183 (3)
" James Rembert[5] . 136-'7, 185
" James Rembert, Jr.[6], Capt.
                                137 (2)
" James Rembert III[7] . . . 137
" James Rembert IV[8] . . . 138
" Jessie Duncan[7] 138
" John[2] . . . . . . 183 (3)-'4
" Julia Anthony . . . . 177-'8
" Julia Toombs[6] 178
" Louisa Toombs[6] 137
" Lucy Willis[6] 178
" Lucy B. A.-Willis . . . 136
" Lydia-Cassels 185
" Margaret E.-Glynn . . . 185
" Martha Juliana[5] 185
" Martha Pope[7] 137
" Mary Elizabeth[6] 137
" Mary Rembert . . 185 (2), 186
" Mary Rembert[5] . . . 176, 185
" Nanette[7] 137
" Nannie Stewart-Wylie . . 137
" Robt. Meriwether[6] 137
" Russell[8] 137
" Samuel Inman[8] 138
" Susan[7] 137
" Susan Mary[6] 137
" Vance Duncan[7] 138
" William Vance[6] . . . . 137-'8
" Wylie Duncan[6] 137
" Wylie Duncan[7] 137
" Wylie Hill[6] 137
" Wylie Hill II . . . . 177-'8
DUNNAWAY, Arthur E. 139
EASTON, Mary 14
ELLIS, Myron 47, 49
EXUM—Family 186-195
" Anne-Lawrence, 188, 191 (2), 193
" Jane 187
" Jeremiah 187, 188 (7),
                     191 (4), 192 (3)
" Mary . . . 191, 192 (2), 193 (3)
" Richard 186 (9), 187

INDEX

	PAGE
EXUM, Thomas	187 (3)
" William	187 (8)
FICKLEN, Boyce	121
" Boyce, Jr.	121
" Burwell II	177
" Claude	177
" Elizabeth	177
" Emmie	121
" Fannie Julia	121
" Fielding Hill	121
" Georgia	177
" James	177
" Julia	177
" Marion	177
" Nannielou	121
FORTSON, Stephen H.	167
" Geo. Thos.	167
FRASER, James D.	168
GRAY, Wm. Duncan	167
GREGORY, Ann	28
" James	28
GRIGSBY, Enoch	164
" Susan-Butler	164
" Susan	164
HALL, Ann Temperance	28
" Director	28
" James Gatling, Dr.	28
" Spencer, Jr.	28
" Spencer, Sr.	28
HEARD, Anna	48
" Stephen D. & Family	48-'9
HENDERSON	195-197
" Gen. Robt. Johnson & Family	197
HILL, Abner Wellborn[6] (L.M.)	113-4, 134
" Abner Wellborn, Jr. (A.W.)	135
" Abner Wellborn[6] (W.G.)	27
" Abram[4] (Hy.)	18 (4), 19 (2), 31, 147
" Abram[6] (J.M.)	25
" Abram Chrisr[6] (A.G.)	26
" Abram Marshall[5] (Abr.[4])	27
" Abram Scott[5] (Abr.[4])	64
" Abraham-Inventor	3
" Abraham-Lord of Trade	3 (5)
" Abraham[2] (Hy.[1]), 5, 7 (2), 8 (4), 9 (11), 10 (7), 11 (5), 12 (6), 14 (3), 15 (9), 16 (2), 17, 156 (5)	
" Abraham[3] (Abr.[2]), 12, 13 (2), 16, 17, 52 (2), 53 (9), 55 (6), 56 (6), 57 (6), 58 (2), 59, 60, 62 (3), 63 (2), 134, 156 (2).	
" Abraham[4] (Abr.[3]), 55-'6-'7 (3), 63 (3), 60, 62, 64, 92	
" Abraham[5] ('Theop's[4])	90
" Abraham Chandler[6] (L.M.II)	120, 126
" Abraham T. W.[5] (Wylie[4]), 101 (3), 102-'3, 144	

	PAGE
HILL, Abraham Wylie[5] (Thos.[4])	147, 153, 155 (3)
" Ada[6] (J.M.)	25
" Adelaide Vaudon-Singleton	135
" Adeline[5] ('Theop's[4])	91
" Albert Barnett[8] (W.M.)	122
" Albert Gallatin[5] (Abr.)	24, 26
" Albert Gallatin, Jr.[6] (A.G.)	26
" Albert Meriwether[7] (A.F.)	105
" Alexr Franklin[5] (Noah)	92 (2)
" Alexr Franklin[6] (B.P.), 93, 104,105	
" Alexr Franklin, Jr.[7] (A.F.)	105
" Aliza Winfrey[5] (Thos.)	147
" Almeda[6] (Isaac[5])	157, 159
" Alonzo Alexr Franklin[6] (B.M.)	64, 65 (3)-
" Alvy Fisher[8] (J.C.)	154
" Amelia Starke[7] (T.W.)	129
" Amelia Thomas[5] (Wylie), 100, 103, 140 (2), 141-'2	
" Amelia Walton[5] (Thos.)	96, 147 (2)
" Ann[4] (Theop's[3])	164, 171 (2)
" Ann[5] (Miles)	94, 98
" Ann Pope (B.P.)	92
" Annie Atwood[7] (Dr. J. A.)	28
" Annie Laura[7] (L.J.)	134
" Annie Lou[7] (R.T.)	154
" Ashby[7] (A.W.)	135
" Augusta[6] (H.W.)	97 (2), 98
" Augustus[7] (R.T.)	154
" Augustus M.[6] "M. D." (A.W.), 154	
" Baron H.[8] (H.L.K.)	168
" Benjamin (Bertie Co.)	4
" Benjamin[5] ('Theop's[4], Abr.[3])	90
" Benjamin Harvey, Judge	130
" Benjamin Harvey III (B.H.), 130	
" Benjamin Harvey IV (B.H.), 130	
" Benjamin Oglevie (A.M.)	154
" Benjamin R.[6] (Theop.[5], Lod.[4]) 164-'5	
" Bessie May[7] (B.P.)	127
" Bettie[6] (Jas. A.)	96
" Blanton[6] (H.W.)	97
" Blanton Abraham (B.M.)	64
" Blanton Meade (Miles)	64-'5, 93-'4, 98, 151
" "Buddie"-Helen Fairlee (W.R.) 159	
" Burwell Meriwether[6] (W.P.), 143	
" Burwell Obadiah[7] (A.F)	105 (2)
" Burwell Pope[5] (Wylie)	56, 101 (2), 102, 103 (2), 142
" Burwell Pope[6] (Col. L. M.)	112, 113, (7), 120, 127
" Calhoun Meriwether[7] (Col. J. M.) 124 (2)	
" Cap. C.[7] (T.A.)	152 (2)

INDEX

HILL, Carl[8] (Hy.) 165
" Caroline[5] (John) 19
" Carolyn Eugenia[6] (A.G.) . . . 26
" Carrie 19
" Catharine[4]-"Keddy" (Hy.), 19, 50
" Catharine[8] (L.H.) 135
" Catharine-"Pipp" (A.F.), 105, 107
" Catharine[5] (Isaac, Jr.) 158
" Chandler[8] (L.M.H) 127
" Charles D.[8] (B.H.) 130
" Charles Watson[7] (R.T.) . 154 (2)
" Charlotte[5] (Isaac, Jr.) 158
" Christian-Walton . . 5, 8, 9, 60-'1
" Clara[4] (Abr.[3]) 63, 68
" Clara[6] (J.M.) 25
" Clarissa-Calloway 147
" Claudia Lawson-Henderson . . 135
" Claudia May[7] (L.J.) 134
" Clifford Halliday (D.C.) . . . 128
" Cora Itasca[8] (T.Y.) 152
" Cordelia Ann[6] (Jas. A.) . . . 96
" Daisy[8] (J.B.) 168
" Dionysius Oliver-"Cap" (T.R.J.) 151-2
" Dorothy Wellborn[8] (L.W.) . . 129
" DuBose[8] (Hy. C.) 131
" Duncan Chatfield[6] (Col. L. M.) 89, 92, 112 (2), 113, 114, 120, 128
" Duncan Chatfield, Jr.[7] 128
" Eddie McGehee[7]—dau. (T.A.) . 152
" Edward, Col. 2 (2)
" Edward Chatfield[7] (J. DuB.) . 130
" Edward Young[6] (Col. L. M.) . 135
" Edward Young, Jr.[7] 135
" Edwin[6] (Theop. J.) 91
" Effie Pope[7] (Dr. J. J.) . . . 144
" Eleanor Oliver[6] (Midn) . . . 159
" Eli [5] (Abr.) 24, 27
" Elinor[5] (Isaac, Jr.) 158
" Eliza-Holden 167
" Eliza[8] (J.B.) 168
" Eliza Pope[8] (H. W., Sr.) . . . 106
" Elizabeth[5] (Theop. Hy.), 18, 29, 30
" Elizabeth[7]-"B.B." (Dr. J. A.) . 29
" Elizabeth[5] (Theop., Abr.) . . 90
" Elizabeth[8] (J.B.) 168
" Elizabeth-Smyly 165
" Elizabeth-Andrew 90
" Elizabeth Andrew[6] (Hy. Ph.), 90
" Elizabeth Ann[5] (Abr.[4], Abr.[3]) 64-5, 98, 151
" Elizabeth Lane (Isaac, Jr.), 157 8-9
" Elizabeth McGehee[6] (B. M.) . 64
" Emily[6] (J.M.) 25
" Emma[6] (Theop. J.) 91
" Emma[6] (Abr. M.) 27
" Emma Belle[7] (W.W.) 121
" Emma Eugenia-Anthony . . . 121

HILL, Emogene[8] (J. DuB.) 123
" Ethel Star-Ellis 154
" Eudocia M.[5] (Isaac, Jr.) . . . 158
" Eugene DuBose[8] (W.M.) . . 122
" Eugenia Victoria[6] (Theop. J.) . 91
" Eva Temperance[7] (A.M.) . . 154
" Evaline E.-Hubbard 153
" Fanida[7] (H.J.) 129
" Fannie Wright[8] (H.H.) . . . 168
" Felixina Augusta[6] (B.M.), 64, 66
" Florella Pauline[6] (H.H.), 166, 168
" Frank[8] (B.O.) 105
" Frankie W.[7] (A.A.F.) 65
" Gardner Meriwether[8] (W.M.), 122
" Gazalena-Williams 65
" George[7] (Hy.) 166
" George T.[8] (B.O.) 105
" George Woods[7] (T.A.) . . . 152
" Georgia Anna America (B.M.) 64, 66, 151
" Gladys Halliday[8] (Hy. C.) . . 131
" Grace[7] (R.G.) 166
" Grace[8] (C.C.) 152
" Graham DuBose[8] (J. DuB) . . 123
" Green-Greenberry-Granberry[5] (Theop. Hy.) 29, 30
" Green, Sr. (Bute Co., N. C.) . 4
" Hal[7] (Dr. L. S.) 171
" Hal[9] (H.H.) 168
" Hampton Wootten[5] (Miles) . 93, 94, 97
" Harriet[5] (Theop., Hy.) . . 29, 30
" Harriet A.[5] (Theop., Abr.) . . 90, 91 (2)
" Harry[9] (J.T.) 165
" Harvey DuBose (J. DuB.), 130 (2)
" Hattie Carson[8] (B.O.) 155
" Helen Fairlie-"Buddie" (W. R.) 159
" Henry[1] . . . 1, 3 (4), 4 (5), 5, 6, 7 (8), 8 (2), 9, 11, 12, 13, 14 (2), 15 (7), 16 (13), 17
" Henry[3] (Abr.[2]) 16, 17 (3), 53 (2), 54 (8)
" Henry[4] (Hy.) 18, 19, 50
" Henry[4] (Abr.) . . 60 (2), 62 (3), 63 (2), 89 (2), 90 (3), 91
" Henry[6] (Theop. Lod.) . . . 165-'6
" Henry[7] (R.G.) 165
" Henry Casey[7] (J. DuB.) . 130 (2)
" Henry DuBose[8] (J. DuB.) . . 123
" Henry Hampton[5](Lodwk), 165 (2), 166
" Henry Hughes[8] (J.B.) 168
" Henry Jordan[6] (Col. L. M.) . 120, 129
" Henry Lodowick K.[7] (J.L.), 167-'8
" Henry Philbin[5] (Hy. Abr.) . 89, 90 (4)
" Henry Willis, M.D., & Family, 27-'8

INDEX

	PAGE
HILLS of Bastrop	155
HILL, Hiram Warner (A.F.)	105 (2)
" Hiram Warner, Jr.[8]	106
" Holsey[6] (Abr. S.)	64
" Horace Bismark[8] (C.C.)	152
" Hughes H.[7] (J.L.)	167-'8
" Hugh Lodowick[7] (A.W.)	135
" Ida[6] (J.M.)	25
" Ida Lee[8] (L.M.H)	126-'7
" Ida Lou[7] (W.W.)	121 (2)
" Ida May[6] (Col. L. M.)	120, 127
" Ina[7] (R.G.)	166
" Irene Pope[7] (T.W.)	129
" Isaac (K. & Q. Co., Va.)	2
" Isaac (Bertie Co., N. C.)	4
" Isaac[3] (Abr.)	13, 16, 156 (4)
" Isaac[4] (Isaac)	97, 156-'7 (3), 158 (2)
" Isaac[5] (Isaac[4])	157-'8-'9
" Isaac Hinton[6] (Midn)	159
" Isabella Virginia[6] (Midn)	159
" Itasca Louisa[7] (T.A.)	152
" Jack Tompkins[8] (Hy.)	165
" James[5] (Lodwk)	165
" James[6] (Jonathan)	165
" James Abram[6], Dr. (Dr.H.W.), 28
" James Alford[5] (Miles), 94, 96, 147
" James DuBose[6] (Col.L.M.), 120, 129
" James Gatling (Dr. J. A.)	28
" James Henry (John)	18, 19
" James Henry[6] (M.M.M.)	148
" James Henry[6] (Midn)	159
" James Lodowick[6] (H.H.), 165, 167
" James Richardson[6] (Theop.)	163, 165
" James Woodroof[7] (Dr. J. A.)	28
" Jane Warner[8] (B.O.)	105
" Jane Warner II[9] (H. W., Jr.), 105
" Janie May[7] (J. DuB.)	130 (2)
" John (Bertie Co.)	4
" John[4] (Hy.)	18, (3), 19
" John[4] (Abr.)	63
" John, Gent. (Nansemond)	3
" John Bones[7] (J.L.)	164, 167-'8 (See Supplement, 288)
" John Bones (H.L.K.)	168
" John DuBose[7] (W.W.)	121, 123
" John James, Dr. (W.P.)	143 (2)
" John Holden[7] (J.L.)	167-'8
" John Meriwether, Col.(Col.L.M.) 120, 123, 162
" John Meriwether, Jr.[8] (C.M.), 124
" John Middleton[5] (Abr.[4])	24
" John Middleton[6] (Midn)	159
" John Walter[6], Dr. (Theop.)	164, 165, 166
" John Walter II[8] (Hy.)	165
" Jonathan M.[5] (Lodwk)	165
" Josiah Woods[5] (Abr., Hy.), 24-'5

	PAGE
HILL, Juda-Judah	9, 10, 16
" Judie-Judith[4] (Abr.)	63, 67
" Judith,	7, 10, 11, 12, 14, 16
" Julia Golden[8] (W.M.)	122
" Kate[7] (Dr. L. S.)	171
" Katherine[8] (W. H.)	154
" Kathleen[8] (Dr. W. W.)	123
" Katie May[7] (A.W.)	135
" Lamar[7] (A.W.)	135
" Law[8] (H.L.K.)	168
" Lewis Hamilton	135
" Lewis Hamilton, Jr. (L.H.)	135
" Lina Amelia[6] (W.P.)	143-'4
" Lizzie[6] (W.G.)	127
" Lodowick[4] (Theop.[3])	34, 108, 164 (5), 171-'2
" Lodowick[6] (Theop.[5])	165
" Lodowick Chandler[7] (J. DuB.), 130
" Lodowick Henry[7]-"Harry"(B.P.) 113 (5), 127
" Lodowick Johnson[6] (Col. L. M.) 87, 120, 131-'2-'3
" Lodowick Johnson, Jr.[7] (L.J.), 134
" Lodowick Meriwether[5], Col.(Wylie) 36, 65 101, 102 (2), 103, 108, 109, 110, 111 (4), 112 (2), 113 (4), 114 (2), 115 (2), 117 (4), 118, 119, 120 (2), 140
" Lodowick Meriwether II[7](Dr.A.C.) 126 (2)
" Lodowick T.[7], Dr. (Hy.)	164, 166-'7, 171
" Lodowick Wellborn[7] (T.W.)	129
" Lolis Tyler[8] (L.M.H)	127
" Lou[6] (Midn)	159
" Lou[8] (J.B.)	168
" Lovie Sanchez[6] (H.H.)	166, 191
" Lucie[8] (W.H.)	154
" Lucinda Ann-Lipscomb	27
" Lucinda Malinda[6] (J.A.)	96-'7
" Lucinda McGehee[5] (Thos.)	147
" Lucinda P.-Caldwell	154
" Lucy Cobb-Erwin	134
" Lucy Jordan[7] (D.C.)	89, 128 (2)
" Lula May[7] (T.A.)	152
" Madison[6] (J.W.)	25
" Malinda[5] (Miles)	94 (2)
" Mallie Sophia[8] (J. DuB.)	123
" Mamie[7] (Dr. L. S.)	171
" Margaret[9] (Hy.)	165
" Margaret Rhind[8] (W.M.), 122 (2)
" Maria Magrand[7] (J.L.)	167-'8
" Marian[8] (J.B.)	168
" Marian Gardner[8] (W.M.)	122
" Martha[5] (Theop., Hy.)	29, 30
" Martha[5] (Theop., Abr.)	90
" Martha[6] (Theop. J.)	91
" Martha[7] (A.F.)	105-'6

INDEX

HILL, Martha[8] (B.O.) 105
" Martha Amelia[7] (W.W.), 121, 123
" Martha Ann[6] (Midn) . . . 159
" Martha Catherine[6]-"Kitty" (B.P.) 104, 107
" Martha Elizabeth[6] (M.M.M.), 148
" Martha Elizabeth[6] (Theop. Lod.) 165
" Martha Ellen[7] (W.R.) 167
" Martha Hughes[7]-"Mattie"(J.L.) 167 (2)
" Martha "Patsy"-Pope 103
" Martha Pope[5] (Wylie) . . 103, 136
" Martha Pope[6],"Mattie"(W.P.), 143
" Martha Pope-Johnson . . . 107
" Martha Sarah Bond-Spann . . 166
" Martha Strother-Wellborn . . 112
" Martha Wellborn[6] (A.G.) . . 26
" Mary 5 (4), 7
" Mary[4] (Hy.) 39
" Mary[4] (Abr.) . . . 62 (3), 63, 141
" Mary[5], "Polly" (Lod.) 165
" Mary[7] (A.F.) . . . . 105-'6
" Mary Addie[7] (T.W.) 129
" Mary Agnes[6] (A.G.) 26
" Mary Amelia[7] (D.C.) 128
" Mary Ann[5] (Theop., Abr.) . 91-'2
" Mary Anna[6] (Theop. J.) . . . 91
" Mary Ann Tabitha[5] (Wylie) 103, 139
" Mary Austin[6] (W.P.) . . . 143-'4
" Mary Bones[7] (J.L.) . . . 167 (2)
" Mary Caldwell[7] (R.T.) . . . 154
" Mary ("Polly") Christian[5] (Thos.) 147, 151
" Mary Crain[6] (Midn) 159
" Mary Lou-Pope 143
" Mary Louise[9] (T.Y.) 152
" Mary Parks[6] (A.W.) . . 153 (2)
" Mary Pauline[8] (L.W.) . . . 129
" Mary Rembert[7] (W.W.) . 121 (2)
" Mary Ruth[7] (A.W.) 135
" Mary Ruth-Henderson . . 133, 135
" Mary Scott[6] (M.M.M.) . . . 148
" Mary Wood[7] (E.Y.) 135
" Mattie[6] (W.G.) 27
" Mattie Ophelia[7] (D.C.) . . . 128
" Maude Barker[7] (T.W.) . . . 129
" Middleton[5] (Isaac) . . . 157-'8
" Middleton Milledge Meade[5] (Thos.) 147, 148 (2)
" Middleton Milledge Meade, Jr.[6], 148
" Middleton Pope (Wylie Pope), 145
" Miles[4] (Abr.) . . . 53, 60, 62 (3), 63, 92, 93 (4), 94 (3)
" Miles H.[6] (H.W.) . . . . . 97-'8
" Montgomery Stokes[8] (W.M.) . 122
" Nancy[4] (Hy.) 18, 19, 30
" Nancy[5] (Wylie) 103

HILL, Nancy[5] (Isaac, Jr.) 158
" Nancy Carter[8] (C.M.) 124
" Nancy Crain 97, 157
" Nancy Hill-Johnson (Nancy) 32, 120
" Nancy Johnson[7] (T.W.) . . . 129
" Nancy (Ann) Scott[5] (Thos.) 147, 150-'1
" Nancy Victoria[6] (A.G.) . . 26 (2)
" Nannie[6] (H.W.) 97
" Nannie May[7] (D.C.) 89
" Nannie Sue[7] (Col. J. M.) . 124 (2), 162
" Nellie[8] (Hy.) 165
" Noah[4] (Abr.) 53, 60 (2), 62 (5), 63, 92 (3)
" Obadiah Warner[8] (B.O.) . . 105
" Ophelia Jordan-Halliday, 89, 128
" Pauline[5] (Noah) . . . 92, (2), 93
" Penina Catherine[6] (Midn) . . 159
" Polly Bradford[6] (Midn) . . . 159
" Polly-Jordan 128
" Raymond Clingman[7] (B.P.) . 127
" Rebecca[8] (H. DuB.) 130
" Rebecca Catherine[8] (C.M.) . . 124
" Rebecca Harvey[8] (B.H.) . . . 130
" "Rebie"-Anna Rebecca Harwell, 134
" Rhydon[5] (Lod.) 165
" Rhydon Grigsby[6] (Theop.), 163 (2)
" Richard Augustus[8] (C.W.) . . 154
" Robbie[7] (Dr. L.S.) 171
" Robert Aaron[8] (C.W.) 154
" Robert Duke[8] (L.H.) 135
" Robert E.[6], Dr. (M.M.M.), 149 (2)
" Robert J.[7] (A.F.) 105
" Robert Theus.[6] (A.W.) . 153 (2)
" Robert Theus. II[8] (W.H.) . . 154
" Roberta Laws (H.L.K.) . 168 (2)
" Roderick[5] (Isaac, Jr.) . . 157 (3), 158
" Roderick Henri[7] (E.Y.) . . . 135
" Roger T.[8] (Hy.) 165
" Rosa[8] (H.H.) 168
" Rosa Laws (H.L.K.) 168
" Rosa McCann[8] (L.M.H) . . . 126
" Ruby[7] (T.W.) 129
" Rufus Arthur[8] (C.W.) 154
" Sadie-Johnson 168
(See Supplement)
" Sallay-Sallie[5] (Isaac, Jr.) . . 157-'8
" Sallie Catherine-Buchanan . . 134
" Sallie May[7] (T.W.) 129
" Sallie May II[8] (C.M.) 124
" Sallie-McGehee 96, 147
" Sallie McGehee[6] (W.P.) . 143 (2)
" Samuel Ashton[7] (Dr. A.C.) . . 126
" Samuel Meriwether[7] (T.W.) . 129
" Sarah[3] (Abr.) 14, 172
" Sarah[4] (Abr.[3]) 63, 89

INDEX

HILL, Sarah[5] (Lod.) 165
" Sarah[6] (M.M.M.) 148
" Sarah[7] (A.F.) 105, 106
" Sarah Ann[5] (Abr., Hy.) . . 24, 25
" Sarah Ann E. R.[6] (B.P.) . . 103-'4
" Sarah Ann-Verdelle 167
" Sarah Christian W.[5] (Wylie) 103, 136
" Sarah-Cotten 17, 18, 19
" Sarah Elizabeth[6] (Midn) . . . 159
" Sarah Elizabeth[8] (B.O.) . . . 155
" Sarah Florella[7] (W.R.) . 167 (2)
" Sarah Frances[6] (A.G.) 26
" Sarah McGhee[6] (A.W.) . . 153 (2)
" Sarah Milton[5] (Thos.) 147
" Scott Pearl[7] (T.A.) . . . 152 (2)
" Scott Shelby[8] (T.Y.) 152
" Susan Abigail[6] (H.H.) . . . 166
" Susan-Brunson 165
" Susan Calhoun[8] (C.M.) . . . 124
" Susan Catherine-Calhoun . . . 124
" Susan Frances[6] (Theop.) . 165 (2), 166
" Susan F.-Holsey 64
" Susan Rembert[8] (W.M.) . . . 122
" Susan Tabitha[6] (B.M.) . . 64 (2)
" Susan Turner[7] (Hy.) 166
" Susanna-Richardson . . . 165-'6
" Susie[6] (W.G.) 27
" Susie Blanton[7] (D.O.) . . . 153
" Susie-Stokes 122, 177
" Tabitha-Pope 93, 94 (3)
" Tabitha[6], "Pug" (H.W.) . . . 97
" Tabor[7] (Hy.) 166
" Tallulah Whitman[7] (W.R.) . . 167
" Teresa[5] (Lod.) 165
" Teresa-Thomas 164
" Theophilus[3] (Abr.) . . 13, 53 (2), 54 (3), 63 (2), 164 (2), 171
" Theophilus[4] (Hy.) 19
" Theophilus[4] (Abr.) . . . 60 (2), 63, 90, 91, 128
" Theophilus[5] (Lod.) . . . 164-'5-'6
" Theus Bernard[8] (J.C.) 154
" Thomas[4] (Abr.) . . 53, 60-1-2 (3), 63, 96, 147 (3)
" Thomas[6] (Jas. A.) 96
" Thomas Abraham Wylie[6] (M.M.M.) 148 (2)
" Thomas Anderson[6] (T.B.J.), 151 (2)
" Thomas Austin[6] (W.P.) . 143 (2)
" Thomas Austin, Jr.[7] (T.A.) . . 143
" Thomas Austin III[8] (T.A.,Jr.), 143
" Thomas Baytop Jefferson[5] (Thos.) 103, 147-'8, 151
" Thomas Cobb[7] (A.W.) 135
" Thomas Meriwether[7] (D.C.) . 128
" Thomas Powell[8] (C.M.) . . . 124
" Thomas Theophilus[6] (Theop.), 165

HILL, Thomas Walker Forster[6] (M.M.M.) 148
" Thomas Webster[6] (Col. L. M.), 120
" Thomas Webster, Jr.[7] (T.W.), 129
" Thomas William[7] (T.A.) . . . 152
" Tweetee 166
" Tye Yates[7] (T.A.) 152 (2)
" Virginia[8] (H. DuB.) 130
" Virginia[9] (H. W., Jr.) . . . 106
" Walter North[8] (W.H.) . . . 154
" Walter Aldredge[7] (D.O.) . . 153
" Walter Hubbard[7] (R.T.) . . 154
" Walton Pope[5] (Noah) . . 93, 102
" Walton Pope[6] (Col. L. M.) . . 112, 120, 126
" Warren[8] (J.B.) 168
" Wellborn Buchanan[8] (L.H.) . 135
" Wellborn Erwin[7] (A.W.) . . 135
" Whitman[7] (Dr. L. S.) . . 171 (2)
" Whitman Robinson[6] (H.H.), 166-'7
" William 16 (2)
" William[8] (W.H.) 154
" William[6] (Theop.) 165
" William, Jr.[7] (W., Theop.) . . 165
" William Augustus[7] (D.C.) . . 128
" William B.[5] (Lod.) 165
" William Edwin[6] (W.P.) . . . 143
" William Granville[5] (Abr., Hy.) 24, 26
" William Lewis[8] (J. DuB.) . . 123
" William Mays[6], Dr. (H.H.) . . 166
" William McGehee[6] (W.P.) . . 143
" William Meriwether[7] (W.W.) 121-'2
" William Meriwether, Jr.[8] (W.M.) 122
" William Pope[8] (B.O.) 105
" William Roderick[6] (Midn), 159 (3)
" William Wylie[6] (Col. L. M.), 113-'4, 120-'1
" William Wylie, Jr.[5], Dr. (W.W.) 121, 123
" Willie[6] (W.G.) 27
" Willie-Callaway 143
" Willie May[7] (Dr. A. C.) . . . 126
" Winnie[5] (Theop., Hy.) . . 29, 30
" Wylie[4] (Abr.) . . . . 34, 36, 53, 60-'1-'2 (2)-'3, 100 (7), 103 (2), 164
" Wylie Pope[5] (Wylie) . . . 101-'3, 102-'3, 142
" Wylie Pope, Jr.[6] (W.P.) . . . 143
" Wylie Pope III[7] (Col. J. M.), 124
" Yates Mildred[9] (T.Y.) 152
HINTON, Elizabeth 5
" James 16, 56
" John 5
" Judah 14
" William . . . 5, 9 (3), 14, 53-'4
HUDSON, Ann Fleming-Collins . . . 125

INDEX

	PAGE
HUDSON, Mathew T.	126
" Rosaline-McCann	126
" Wm. Alexander	126
HUNTER, Isaac	172, 173 (2)
" Jacob	172, 173 (4)
" Leah	14, 16, 173
" Sarah-Hill	14, 16, 172
JATHO, Olga Von Oven	138
JOHNSON, Catherine A.	32, 36, 38
" Elizabeth	35
" John Pope	32, 35, 38
" Martha Pope	32, 36
" Mary	35, 36
" Nancy	18, 33 (2), 34, 35 (2)
" Nancy Hill	32, 36
" Sarah	36
" Stephen	34
" Stephen W.	32, 36
" Susan M.	32, 35, 37
" William, Col.,	30-'1, 35 (2), 50
" William, Jr.	32, 35 (4), 36
JORDAN	197, 200
" Benjamin[6]	198 (2)
" Benjamin Fleming[6] (Dr. John) and Family	136
" Fleming[6]	136, 198
" John[7], Dr.	136, 199
" Josiah[7]	67, 198
" Margaret-Brassueur	198
" Mary Jane[7]	199
" Mathew[5], Rev.	198
" Reuben[6]	198
" Samuel[1]	197
" Samuel[4]	198
" Thomas[2]	198
" Thomas[3]	198
" William Moore[7], Dr.	140, 199
JOSSEY, Christiana ("Keddy"),	18, 39, 48
" Harriet	47 (2)
" Henry, Sr.	39, 47
" Henry, Jr.	18, 39, 47
" James	39
" John	47
" Kitty	47
" Mary	18 (2), 45
" Mary Elizabeth	47 (2)
" Sarah	39, 46, 47
KAROW, Gustav Ludwig	78
LANE	201-205
" Elizabeth-Hill	205
" Jesse[4]	204 (5)
" John[4]	202
" John, Jr.	204
" Joseph[2]	201 (2), 202 (2)
" Joseph, Jr.[3]	202 (10), 203 (2), 204 (3)
" Joseph[5]	205
" Julian	201-'2

	PAGE
LANE, Patience-McK.	202 (2), 203 (2), 204 (2)
" Thomas, Sr.[1]	201
" Thomas, Jr.	201-'2
LAWRENCE, Ann	191
" John	189-191
" Robert	189 (2), 190
LEAKE, Richard	220
LEWIS	206-214
" Edward	206 (3)
" Edward	206 (2)
" Edward, Sr.	206 (3), 207
" Edward, Jr.	206-'7
" Elizabeth	207, 211, 212
" Joanna	207 (2), 209, 210
" Mary	206, 207, 208 (2)
" Mary-Holman	206
" Surles	210 (4), 211
LINTON (Lynton), Elizh	210, 211
" Mary	210
" William	207 (3)
LIPSCOMB Family	146-'7
LONG, Dr. Moses	166
LUMPKIN	214-217
" Elizabeth-Ragan	23
" Elizabeth-Walker	216
" George[1]	215
" George, Rev.	68, 217
" Hopson[3]	216
" Jacob, Col.	214
" John[2]	215 (4)
" Joseph[2]	215
" Joseph Henry[3] & Family	217
" Kate-Richardson	216
" Lucy-Hopson	215
" Lucy Hopson[4]	216
" Martha[4]	216
" Mary-Cody	215
" Samuel[3] & Family	215
" Samuel[4]	216
" Sarah G.[4]	216
" Thomas, Dr.	215
" Wilson[3]	214, 215, 216
MARTIN, Grier	121
MATHIS, Atwood Hill	29
" Joel Kendall	29
McGEHEE, Micajah & Family	220-'1
" Nancy-Tate	25
" Samuel	25
McINTIRE, Frank Percival	77
" Lucy Hopson-Lumpkin	78
McINTOSH, John Mohr	218
" Maj. Gen. Lachlan	218-'9
" Margaret	83
" Major William	82 (2), 218
McKINLEY, Precious Patience-Barrow,	87
" William & Family	87
McKINNIE	221-227
" Col. Barnaby,	221-2-3-4, 226
" Col. Barnaby Family	224

INDEX

McKinnie, Barnaby, Jr. 225
" Elizabeth 221
" Michael (Mackquenney) 221-2
" Mourning 224, 226
" Patience 224, 226
Moore, Austin Henry 139
Mobley, John Griffin 168
Murray, Horace Herndon 138
Neville, John 87
Norman, Argyle 282
" James Argyle 282
" Elizh 282
" Sarah Louisa 282
" William 33, 35
Orr, W. Ben 27
Oslin, W. E. 26
Pearce, Geo. W. 166
Pitt, Col. Robt. 28
Poitevant, Mary E. Girault . . . 28
Pope 227-257
" Alexr Franklin . . . 246, 248 (2)
" Ann . . . . 255-'6
" Ann[6] 243, 246
" Augustine Burwell[6] 250
" Barnaby[4] . . . . 237, 255-'6
" Benjamin[6] 252
" Benjamin F.[8] 247
" Benjamin Hy. 248 (2)
" Burwell[5] . . . 240-1-2-3-4-5(5)-6
" Burwell[6] (Genl.) . . . 243, 247-'8
" Burwell T.[7] . . . . 246-'7
" Clary (Clara)-Hill . . 245-6, 252
" Clary[6] 252 (2)
" Damarias C.-Hubbard 248
" Elizabeth-Smith . . . . . 250-'1
" Henry[2] . . . . 230-'1-'2-'3-'4-'5-'6
" Henry Family . . . . . . 233-'4
" Henry[4], 237-'8-'9, 240, 245, 255, 257
" Henry Augustine[5] . . . 240, 245-'6, 252 (3)
" Henry Jefferson[6] 252
" Henry Norman 256 (4)
" Huldah[6] . . . . 250-'1
" James Wylie[9] 247
" Jemima 256 (3)
" Jesse[4] 237, 246, 255, 257 (2)
" Johanna-Lester 247
" John[2] 229, 230
" John[3] (Hy.) . . . . 235-'6-'7, 250
" John[4] . . . . 237; 254-'5
" John[5] . . . . . . 240, 245-'6, 250
" John[5] Family 250
" John[6] (Willis) 249, 250
" John Burwell[8] 248
" John Clarke[6] 254 (2)
" John Hardeman[7] 248
" John O.[9] 247
" Jonathan 250

Pope, Joseph Walter[9] 247
" Josiah Woods[6] 254
" Julia Ann Tabitha[7] 248
" Keturah[6] 250
" Lewis[4] 237, 246, 255 (2)
" Lewis Wyeth[9] 247
" Louisa[6] . . . . 250-'1
" Lula[8] 248
" Maidee[8] 248
" Marie 230
" Martha[6] (Burwell) . . . 243, 246
" Martha[6] (John) . . . 250-1 (2)
" Mary, ... 245-'6, 255
" Mary-Caldwell 248
" Mary-Davis 252 (2), 253
" Mary L.[6] . . . . 250-'1
" Mary (Polly)-Hill . . . 254 (2)
" Mary-Ward 248
" Middleton[6] . . . 68-'9-70, 252 (2)
" Minnie[8] 248
" Mourning-McK. 235-6-7-8
" Nathaniel (Col.) . . . . 227-'8, 230
" Priscilla-Wootten . . 241-2-3, 246
" Richard 229, 230
" Richard, Sr. 230
" Robert[6] 243, 246, 253
" Robert Samuel, Jr.[8] 247
" Robert Samuel, Sr.[7] 246
" Rowanna[6] 250 (2)
" Ruth-Jones 248
" Sallie[6] 252
" Sallie-Davis 246
" Sallie Mary Ann[6] 254
" Sarah 243, 247
" Sarah Eliza[6] 71 (2)
" Sarah Elizabeth[8] 247
" Sarah E.-Germany 247
" Sarah M. E.[8] 247 (2)
" Sarah Key-Strong . . . 246, 248
" Sarah-Watts . . . . . . 232-'3
" Tabitha 235, 237, 240, 255
" Tabitha[6] 243, 246
" Sir Thomas 227
" Thomas[2] 229, 230
" Wesley M.[9] 247
" Wilie[6] 243, 246
" Wiley Mobley 250
" William[1] . . . . . . 228-'9, 230
" William Family 230
" William B.[9] 247
" William Edwin 248 (2)
" William Wylie[8] 247
" Willis . . . 240, 245-'6, 248 (7), 249 (7), 250, 255
" Winnefred[4] . . . . 237, 255-'6-'7
" Wylie[6] . . . . 250-'1
" Wylie[5] 253 (8), 254
" Wylie Hill[7] . . . . . . 246-'7
" Wylie Hill[6] 254 (2)

INDEX

	PAGE
POPE, Wylie M.[7]	254 (2)
QUAKERS	285-8
QUIN Family	137-9
" Elizabeth James[7]	138
" Helen DuBose[7]	139
" Hugh Pharr	137-'8
" Hugh Wallace[7]	138
" Jennie Wood[1]	138
" Langdon Caldwell[8]	138
" Langdon Cheves[7]	138
" Louis DuBose[7]	138
" Marion DuBose[7]	138
" Martha ("Mattie") Vance[7]	139
" Nannie Duncan[7]	139
" Robt. Smith[7]	138, 186
" Thomas Eggleston-Perdue	138
" Tommie Perdue[8]	138
RAGAN, Jonathan	22, 24
" Nancy	19, 23
" Winney	23
RANSONE	257-9
" Ann	259, 261
REEVES, Abner (Judge) & Family	25-'6
" Elizabeth-McK.	221-'2
" Thomas	221-'2
RICHARDSON	259-261
" Dorcas-Nelson	261
" Mary-Cantey	260
" Mary	261
" Rich[d], Sr. (Gen.)	259, 260
" Rich[d], Sr. Family	260
" Rich[d], Jr. (Col.)	260-'1
" Rich[d], Jr. Family	261
" Wm. Love	168
RICKS, Isaac, Sr.	223-'4
" Isaac (Jacob)	223-'4
" Jacob	223
" Martha (Jacob)	223
" Mary-Exum	223
RIDDICK, Leah	173
" Seth	173
ROUSSEAU, Hilliare	210
" Elizabeth	210
SANSON, Emma	247
SHEPHERD	261
SLATON, John Marshall	108
" William F. & Family	107-'8
" William M.	108 (2)
SPALDING Family	81-'2, 219, 220
" Ann-Lermouth	82, 219
" Clara Lucy	83, 219
" Ella Patience-Barrow	82, 219, 244
" James[2]	82, 219
" Randolph[4] (Col., C. S. A.)	82, 219
" Randolph[6]	82, 219
" Thomas[1]	82, 219
" Thomas[3]	219
SPALDING, Thomas Bourke[5]	82, 219
SPRATLING, Henry	33, 35, 36
" Mary	32
STATON, Albert	247
" John C.	247
" John C., Jr.	247
STEWART, Nathl Bacon (Genl.)	81
STOVALL, T. J.	26
SUPPLEMENT	288
TALBERT, Hilliary	27
TERRELL, Joseph	175
" Joseph M.	177
THOMAS, Montgomery ("Doc")	27
TRAMMELL, Dr. Wm. Oliver	170
WALKER, James	199
" William Fleming, Dr.	199
WALTON	261-271
" Christian	267 (2), 268
" George[4] (Signer)	262 (2)
" (J of W. Co.)	263-'4
" (Chowan Co.)	264-270
" Sarah	266 (2), 268 (3)
" Thomas, Jr.	265 (7), 266 (6)-'7 (2), 268 (2)
" Thomas, Sr.	265-'6 (3) 267 (5)
" (Bertie Co.)	270
" (Johnston Co.)	270
" (Wilkes Co., Ga.)	270
WATTS, Albert (?)	39
" Alice-English	233
" John	232
" Sarah	232
WAYNE, Daniel Gabriel III	138
WEBSTER,	45-47
" Family	39-45
WELLBORN	271-273
" Abner[6]	271 (2)
" Hepzibah[7]	271
" Martha-Render	271
" Martha Strother[7]	271
" Susan S.[7]	271
" Susie[8] (Mrs. J. O. Blackmar)	272
" William[5]	271
WHITE, Harold H.	38
WILKINSON, Uriah Baylis	36
" John R.	36-'7
" Mell R.	37
WILLIAMS, L. Jewett (Rev.)	86
WILLIS Family	49-50
" Rich[d] J.	33, 35, 48
WOOD, Cary	179
" Ann Granberry	28
" Cecillia B.	179
" Elizabeth S.	28
" James	28
" Laura Elizabeth	179
" Mary Jane	179
" Paulina	179

	PAGE
Wood, Robt. Richardson, Jr.	179
" Sarah (Hill)	18
" William	28
Woodroof, James M.	28
" Sarah Elizh	28
Wootten	146, 273-285
" Dr. Thomas, Chirurgeon	273
" (York Co., Va.)	273-'5
" (I. of W. Co.)	275-'6
" Ann	275 (2), 284
" Ann	276, 284
" Lucy-Council	275-'6 (2)
" Mary	276, 284
" Richard[2]	275 (2), 284
" Richard[3]	275 (2), 276 (4)
" Mrs. Sarah-Wood	275
" Thomas[1]	275, 284
" Thomas[3]	275 (2), 276, 284
" William[4]	275-'6 (3), 284
" (Johnston, Orange, Halifax & Wake Cos.)	276-'9
" Benjamin[1]	277 (3), 278 (3), 279, 284 (2)
" Benjamin[3]	279, 280 (2)
" Benjamin Family	279

	PAGE
Wootten, Elizabeth-Rousseau	278
" Elizabeth[2]	278
" James[1]	276-'7
" James[3]	279
" James Family	282
" John[2]	278
" Katharine Hinton	273, 281
" Lemuel[3]	279
" Lemuel Famliy	282
" Mary[2]	278
" Mary Ann[3]	279, 281
" Priscilla	278-'9
" Richard[4], Gent.	281
" Richard Bradfork[3]	279, 280 (2)
" Tabitha-Pope	279, 280-'1 (4), 282
" Thomas[2]	279, 280 (4), 281 (7), 282
" Thomas Family	279
" Thomas[3]	279
" Thomas[3] Family	282
" Thomas (Lieut.)	283 (4), 284 (7)

www.ingramcontent.com/pod-product-compliance
Lightning Source LLC
Chambersburg PA
CBHW070847290526
45795CB00001B/22